COURAGE–SACRIFICE-DEVOTION

THE MEN AND WOMEN OF THE 'PUCKERED PENGUINS.' THE ICE PRIATES

THE HISTORY OF THE UNITED STATES NAVY' ANTARCTIC AIR SQUADRON VXE - SIX
A PROUD PIONEERING ANTARCTIC AIR UNIT.

BY NOEL GILLESPIE

A LIFE MEMBER OF THE OLD ANTARCTIC ASSOCIATION

ISBN 0-7414-2912-8

Published by:

INFINITY
PUBLISHING.COM

1094 New Dehaven Street, Suite 100
West Conshohocken, PA 19428-2713
Info@buybooksontheweb.com
www.buybooksontheweb.com
Toll-free (877) BUY BOOK
Local Phone (610) 941-9999
Fax (610) 941-9959

Printed in the United States of America
Printed on Recycled Paper
Published March 2006

DEDICATIONS

This book is dedicated to the proud American men and women who served their country in Antarctica as members of VX-6 and VXE-6 Squadron, which without their assistance in allowing me to relate their stories, writing this book would have been impossible.

This is their story; I was only the vehicle to put their story it into words and above all, dedicated to the fifty American personnel of Operation Deep Freeze who paid the ultimate price to advance the cause of science and Antarctic Exploration.

I am forever indebted to my late wife Shirley, for without her inspiration and encouragement I would never have undertaken this project, and finally to my wife Lois for her patience, forbearance and diligence in checking and bringing sanity, both to me and to the manuscript. With her faith and trust in the project, the history of the squadron and their stories can be told, allowing me to keep a promise I made to those old Antarctic Explorers that are no longer with us, that their story would be entrusted to history.

"Courage-Sacrifice–Devotion"

<u>COURAGE-SACRIFICE-DEVOTION.</u>

These words are imprinted on the Antarctic service medal. Perhaps they apply most, to all those who endured many months without husbands, fathers, or son or daughter. This book is also dedicated to them   YOUR FAMILIES.

<u>ACKNOWLEDGEMENTS</u>

Preparing the history of the squadron would have been impossible without the assistance and co-operation of many people, Staff of the United States Navy have been most helpful in providing access to information and photo files, the USAF, the Christchurch Press, Christchurch Star, Otago Daily Times, Southland Times. New York Air National Guard, Major Robert Bullock NYANG, Lockheed-Martin Aircraft, Boeing Airplane Co, Antarctic Journal, the Naval Aviation News, US Navy's 'All Hands' Tony Phillips, David Gilson, Martin Sponholz, the Old Antarctic Explorers Association, members of the VX-6/VXE-6 squadron, and in particular the OAEA Explorers Gazette, Rear Admiral George Dufek, Eddie Ward, Eddie Frankiewicz, James Waldron, Dave Riley, Frank and Mike Hudman, Dennis Brown, Paul Panehal, Bob O'Keefe, 'Buz' Dryfoose, 'Art' Herr, Brian Vorderstrasse, Stan Manning, Don Angier, Billy-Ace Baker, Bruce Raymond, Jim O'Connell, Frank Witty, Bob Nyden, Jim Eblen, Marc Swadener, Mike Subritzky, Frank 'Kaz' Kazukaitis, Jack Cummings, James O'Leary, David Weyer, Harold Butler, Edgar Potter, Bill Burch, Dennis Olson, Fred Holt, John Hoshko, Bob Owler, Fred Schneider, 'Lefty' Nordhill, Dave Crouse, Cal Lawson, Jim Kelly, Robert Epperly, Dave Hazard, Robert Woods, Larry Sharpe, Leslie Swadener-Culippert, Bruce Raymond, Dennis Brown, Joseph 'Apache Joe' Madrid, John Colson, and Whit Whitney to name but a few of those Old Antarctic Explorers.

A Memorial Plaque Honoring the Fifty
Americans Who Died in Antarctica
During Operation Deep Freeze, Paying the
Ultimate Price to Advance the Cause of Science.

**THIS PLAQUE WAS ERECTED AT THE INTERNATIONAL ANTARCTIC CENTRE
AT CHRISTCHURCH INTERNATIONAL AIRPORT IN 1999.**

"COURAGE-SACRIFICE- DEVOTION".

THE MEN AND WOMEN OF THE FAMOUS UNITED STATES NAVY IN ANTARCTICA WITH "OPERATION DEEP FREEZE."

INDEX:

The Author Noel Gillespie.
A New Zealand freelance aviation writer
and a life member of the Old Antarctic Explorers Association

INTRODUCTION:

DEEP FREEZE 1 & 2 1955-1957-
THE SQUADRON'S FIRST COMMANDING OFFICER
COMMANDER EDDIE M D'I WARD USN [RET].

Late August 1954 while attached to the Navy Bureau of Aeronautics, I was invited to attend a meeting in the Pentagon chaired by Captain George J Dufek. Also present were several interested Navy Bureau and officers. Captain Dufek began by announcing that the Third International Geophysical Year would take place commencing January 1957. Further, the Navy was charged with the responsibility of providing personnel, ships, planes, air and surface transportation and the construction of bases and landing strips, to support the scientific effort in the Antarctic. Our comments were requested.

Due to time constraints, I recommended we draw on planes within the Navy's inventory. These would include R5-D Skymasters, ski-equipped R4-D Dakotas, ski-equipped P2-V Neptune's, Grumman UF-1 Albatross tri-phibians and HO4S helicopters. For general utility purposes I proposed an off the shelf procurement of Canadian De Havilland, JA Noorduyn Norseman, or the larger UC Otter. Following the meeting and to my surprise and sheer delight, Captain Dufek invited me to join his staff as Air Operations Officer.

And so it was that quite by chance I was privileged to have been associated with the Deep Freeze programme from its conception. Shortly hereafter Captain Dufek was promoted to Rear Admiral with the title of Commander, US Navy Support Force Antarctica. During my tour on the Admiral's staff, I met many of the old legendary Arctic and Antarctic explorers. Most notable of these was the man whose name is synonymous with the Antarctic, Rear Admiral Richard E Byrd. The Admiral had volunteered to come out of retirement and serve as Officer in Charge of Antarctic Programmes.

The task faced by Admiral Dufek, was overwhelming as a task force, comprising ships, aircraft and men that would have to be organized, along with heavy equipment, bulldozers, tractors and building materials purchased. Heating oil, fuel, food and medical supplies stocked to support the summer residents and wintering over parties, and all this with a limited time to plan the operations, co-ordinate the Task Force Units and most importantly, execute the deployment on schedule. In my opinion, Admiral Dufek was totally responsible for the success of the Deep Freeze Programme.

My tour of duty on the Admiral's Task Force 43 Staff ended on January 17 1955. I reported to Air Development Squadron Six [VX-6] on January 17, 1955 becoming the first member and acting Commanding Officer of the Squadron. I was relieved by Commander Gordon Ebbe in April 1955 and assumed the duties of Operations Officer.

And just what was it like to have served in VX-6 during *Deep Freeze 1 & 2*, the Squadron whose legacy of Antarctic conquests would continue until decommissioned on March 31 1999. I will not attempt to go into details as they will be adequately covered by the author, Noel Gillespie in his magnificent VX-6 –VXE-6 *Deep Freeze* documentary. His courage is in undertaking and preserving their achievements in the annals of polar aviation and exploration. This story had to be told for future generations to fully appreciate the deeds of Air Development Squadron Six. From all Old Antarctic Explorers, I thank you.

Briefly, however, to quote the immortal words of Julius Caesar, *'Veni, Vidi Vici'*, we came, we saw, we conquered, culminating with Admiral Dufek's epic landing at the South Pole, on the morning of October 29, 1956.

During the initial two Antarctic deployments, tragedy, anguish, disappointments, triumphs, and good fortune, would all play in the never-ending battle to gain our objectives. Tempers flared, feelings were hurt, aggravated by the friction of harsh and confined living conditions. Squadron morale however, remained high. Good humour and laughs gradually replaced the tense and sombre moments of the early days. I can best sum up my Deep Freeze tour by saying I was deeply honoured to have served with such an outstanding group of dedicated and courageous men. At the completion of *Deep Freeze,* Squadron VX-6 was awarded the Navy's Unit Citation for meritorious service.

During *Deep Freeze 1*, two DeHavilland Otters crashed, both sustaining strike damage. Five planes crashed during *Deep Freeze 2*, all strike damage. Most serious of these was the P3 V that crashed at McMurdo Sound on October 18 1956, killing four of the eight-man crew. Heartbreaking as the P2-V crash was, considering the number of aircraft accidents, fatalities could have been considerably greater. Was this luck? - I don't think so.

On a beautiful fall day in September 1956, the Squadron held a full dress inspection, and resplendent in their dress blues, the crews lined up in front of their aircraft with the remainder of the squadron personnel flanking either side of the formation. While the officers and men stood with heads bowed, the Chaplain implored Devine Providence for guidance and protection from the perils that lay ahead. Following the Fleet's blessing I asked the Squadron Legal Officer what his thoughts were in the matter. He smiled, turned to me and quipped, 'All I can tell you Commander, is it's the most reasonable insurance you'll ever get.'

To that I say 'Amen'.

Commander Edward Ward US Navy [Ret]

JIM EBLEN

PAST-PRESIDENT - OLD ANTARCTIC EXPLORERS ASSOCIATION.

This is an extraordinary book about an extraordinary US Naval Air Squadron of Navy and Marine Corps personnel. The squadron was established in 1955 and was designated Air Development Squadron Six [VX-6]. In later years, the squadron was changed to VXE-6. Their mission was to provide air support for scientific research on the continent of Antarctica.

I would like to introduce myself and offer a bit of history of my time in the squadron. My name is Jim Eblen, President of the Old Antarctic Explorers Association, and I reported for duty in VX-6 in March of 1958. This proved to be the beginning of an adventure of which I have many pleasant memories. The squadron was based at Naval Air Station Quonset Point, Rhode Island, and consisted entirely of volunteer personnel. After reporting, the majority of the new personnel were assigned to duties according to their rating speciality, so for most of us, this involved both maintaining and crewing the many types of aircraft.

I was assigned to the flight crew of a P2V-7 Neptune but this proved to be a short lived assignment, as a jammed ski caused the aircraft to crash during a test flight after a factory overhaul. All of the crew survived the crash, however the aircraft was destroyed. This was my first flight as a crewmember in the squadron, and after this we trained for the upcoming deployment in Antarctica where I was assigned to winter over, and in September we boarded an aircraft and headed for the continent of Antarctica.

Our trip took us across the United States to Hawaii, Canton Island, Fiji and on to Christchurch, New Zealand. Our short stay in Christchurch proved to be the most enjoyable part of the trip. I was to spend many days in the southern city and during my seven years in the squadron and I can't say enough about the super hospitality of New Zealanders. The Christchurch folk opened their hearts and homes to us and I will always think of the city as my second home.

From New Zealand, I headed to McMurdo Sound, Antarctica. My first glimpse of the Antarctic continent was somewhat overwhelming, as it presented a hostile beauty that is difficult to describe. My next year was spent in the Antarctic as I wintered over that year and was assigned as crewmember on a DHC-3 DeHavilland Otter aircraft. Shortly thereafter, I was on a flight with a group of scientists, when the aircraft was damaged during landing on a rough surface, rendering it unsafe for flight, so we taxied the aircraft back to McMurdo, a distance of 20 miles. That was a trip to remember. After the winter I remained with VX-6 and attended C-130 school. The introducing of the ski equipped LC 130 Hercules opened up the entire Continent of Antarctic for scientific exploration, and I was to spend seven years as a flight engineer on these marvellous aircraft.

In 1999, the squadron was decommissioned. It was a sad day for all who had spent time in VX-6/VXE-6. A large contingent of former squadron members attended the decommissioning, which rekindled old friendships and many fond memories. All personnel who served in Antarctica are referred to as OAE's [Old Antarctic Explorers] and a group of OAE's decided that a means of getting together more often needed to be developed. With a lot of computer time and the Internet, the Old Antarctic Explorers Association [OAEA] was born. The Association is comprised of those personnel who have served in Antarctica or surrounding seas, and I was honoured to be elected the President of the OAEA. The association had its first reunion in Pensacola, Florida in late 2002 that was a huge success, with the OAE's attending from all over the world.

I know that everyone who reads this marvellous book by Noel Gillespie, himself a lifetime member of the Old Antarctic Explorers Association, will be able to visualize in their minds what it is like to fly on the frozen continent.

Enjoy Shipmates-
Jim Eblen

Past President OAEA.

AUTHOR'S PROLOGUE.

'Penguinmania is an incurable disease that can only be contracted on the southernmost continent. It can be contagious, but the purest strain causes one to walk with a waddle and emit strange squawky sounds. It intensifies with age. If you read this, you have it!'

As a part time freelance aviation writer based in Christchurch New Zealand, I am privileged to be able to cover the United States Navy's Deep Freeze air operations in Antarctica. In early 1999, I wrote an extensive historical history of VX-6 Squadron –1955-99, for a British historic aviation journal *"AIR Enthusiast'*.

At this point, the idea to write a book of the renowned Squadron's illustrious history in Antarctica was conceived and encouraged by my late wife Shirley, along with many old OAE's. The book had to be written of their exploits in Antarctica, and their story had to be told as a chronicle of their achievements on the frozen continent, their sadness, their joys, their lifetime friendships, and the links they cemented with Christchurch.

Like early aviators who had only their wits and reflexes to bring their aircraft down safely, as their planes were mere collages of wood, cloth and wire, difficult to control and so sensitive to air currents that even a moderate zephyr could knock them to the ground, while their engines were weak and unreliable, not dissimilar to those early VX-6 aviators, risking their lives, but unlike their early aviation pioneers, the Navy were not risking pride, fame and fortunes, their role was risking their lives to open up the frontier of science and Antarctic exploration.

While other books and publications have been written on *Operation Deep Freeze*, the part that the famous Air Development Squadron Six played in those 44 years, and the US Navy's role in Antarctica, I believe this is the first book written about the very men and women whos exploits could best be described as the last bastions of aviation exploration. They were the *Boy's Own* flying ace heroes, the Biggles of the 20th century, or the Baron von Richthofen's, or the American's Eddie Richenbacker of World War I *'Flying Circus'*.

These young intrepid aviators of VX-6, were continuing the *'Heritage of Kitty Hawk"* and their achievements are acknowledge with profound gratitude, for their exploits and heroism in the finest traditions of the United States Naval aviation.

Of these OAE's, many of whom I never met, yet after communicating with them over the past three years would consider them all, without exception, life time friends. I am indeed privileged to have known such a gathering of a bunch of talented and brave aviators who changed Antarctic aviation forever.

This is the story of their achievements flying with planes never manufactured to operate in such harsh climates, and their enormous contributions towards writing this book would otherwise have made it impossible. Their stories are spattered with humour, for humour was part of what life was on the ice. Their wit, using their tongue savagely at times or charmingly or seductively, was all part of life on the ice in their Jamesway huts. Laughter and seriousness, all happening at the same time, was one way of surviving the isolation and absent families. Beneath the banter, there was a pride in what their mates had achieved, and taking great pleasure in recounting these episodes at length, over a long cool beer.

Some paid the ultimate price to advance the cause of science and Antarctic exploration, others have passed away to walk with the angels and catch up with old mates. Men like Eddie Frankiewicz, whose assistance in the writing of this book was immeasurable, although, I never meet Eddie, who passed away on May 9 2003, but he sent me original copies of valued personal, precious material, press cuttings and photos. *'Just copy what you want and post it back in your own time'*, he said. That was this man's elephantine trust in me. Eddie embodies hundreds of other OAE's, all of whom I treat as personal friends with a colourful treasure trove of Antarctic aviation knowledge, who without hesitation searched their minds and memories for me, exchanging e-mails on a regular basis.

To all these proud American men and women who have served their country in Antarctic, I have dedicate this book

This is a story of *Courage-Sacrifice–Devotion,* which just happens to be the Squadron's Motto. To them Christchurch, New Zealand was their second home for 44 years. The camaraderie and overwhelming hospitality they received from the folk of Christchurch was two way, the day the squadron said farewell to the city in February 1999 after their decommissioning was indeed a sad day, but memories of their occupation will last in the hearts of New Zealanders for many years.

It would be impossible to acknowledge all those who have assisted in the writing of this book, at times I felt inadequate to undertake such a project. I have taken every possible care to check and recheck. This is their story, told by the OAE's themselves, although contributions have come from many sources, every endeavour has been made, recognizing the fact that some stories related could vary a little or be coloured from the actual fact due the intervening 50 years, but stories which illustrate their comradeship in what must have been the most taxing and remote peacetime military operation in history.

I am grateful to the United States Navy, the US Naval News and all private collections for permission to publish all the photos herein as well as other material. To acknowledge everyone who contributed would be a volume in itself.

Noel Gillespie
Christchurch. New Zealand.
November 2004
noel.design@xtra.co.nz

Postscript:
Any readers deployed in the Antarctic with *Operation Deep Freeze* and particular with United States Navy's Antarctic Development Squadron Six [VX-6 / VXE-6] between 1955 and 1999 who would like to join the Old Antarctic Explorers Association [OAEA] meet old comrades, share their and your experiences, please contact the Association at their National Headquarters at 4615 Balmoral Drive, Pensacola, Fl 32504- or the Association's Secretary Jim O'Connell penquin64@worldnet.att.net They would love to hear from you.

CHAPTER ONE.

PLANNING FOR OPERATION DEEP FREEZE.

Operation Highjump provided the
Platform for another Antarctic expedition.

When the sunset at the American Antarctic base at McMurdo Station on April 13th 1998, the curtain came down on the United States Navy role in Antarctic logistic support and exploration, after 44 years. It was the end of a century and a half of exploration and science during which the Antarctic had unprecedented influence on polar exploration and Antarctic development.

The United States can reflect back with pride to the US Navy polar expedition led by Lt Charles Wilkes from 1838-42 aboard the US Ship *Vincennes,* an exploration sanctioned with the President's signature and authorised by Congress in the 1836 Naval Appropriations Bill. It was a milestone in the annals of American science, often referred to as the Wilkes Exploration, gathering a wealth of botanical, zoological, geological and anthropological material.

Following Antarctic explorations by Sir Herbert Wilkins, Ernest Shackleton, Sir Robert Falcon Scott and others, the United States again went to the frozen continent, organised and led by Admiral Richard Byrd for the 1929-30 Antarctic Exploration, establishing base camp at the first Little America on the Ross Sea.

Richard Byrd born in Winchester, on October 25 1888, was the second son of an old illustrious and well to do Virginian family. A determined and restless youngster, he entered the US Navy during World War 1 where the young Byrd was ordered to the Bureau of Navigation, but after making his way out of a desk job, he learnt to fly under the wing of Naval aviator Walter Hinton, and was awarded his wings on April 17 1918 and designated Naval Aviator *#608.*

Byrd's first Antarctic exploration, is best known for his historic South Pole flight at 3.29pm on November 28 1929 in a Ford Trimotor *Floyd Bennett* [named after his friend and pilot] that proved beyond doubt, even with their limited range, that aircraft would be the primary tool for the continent's exploration.

Byrd experimented with every aviation technique known at the time, including aerial photography, airdropping mail and material, and delivering scientific field parties, all during his first expedition.

A number of firsts were accomplished during the second Byrd Antarctic Expedition in 1933, one of these being the first time that automotive transport proved to be more than a valuable asset and was the beginning of the mechanical age in the frozen continent, while his second expedition took mechanical and electrical resources to an unheard of level with a power driven generator providing Little America with electric power allowing the use of electric tools.

He also carried four aircraft, a Curtis Wright Cordore, Fairchild Pilgrim, Fokker biplane and a Fellett K4 single engine autogiro. His success in the use of aviation in Antarctica was quickly taken up by other nations, including two Norwegian whaling expeditions, both of which carried aircraft to locate whales and explore the icy continents.

It was while wintering over during the 1933-34 expedition that Byrd almost died from carbon monoxide fumes, resulting from a faulty stove and exhaust from the engine that powered his radio. He was hesitant to call for help; concerned that Antarctic's violent weather would endanger his rescuers.

Byrd along with his associates were making plans for his third expedition to the Antarctic and like his first two expeditions, this one was again to be privately funded. Although the US government was showing interest in a small expedition to Antarctica, proposed by Richard Black and Finn Ronnie [both members of Byrd's second Antarctic Expedition] it captured the attention of President Roosevelt, and when Byrd became aware of the governments position, he sought a meeting.

On January 3 1940 the *North Star* departed Wellington, New Zealand, for the Ross Sea, taking Admiral Byrd on his third Antarctic expedition, subsequently sailing into the Bay of Whales to established his West Base, but with international tensions on the uprise, it was considered by Washington wise to evacuate the two bases rather than relieve the present personnel with new men who would continue to occupy the bases. The *North Star* arrived back in Boston on May 5 1941

With the ending of hostilities of WW2, the United States Navy embarked on its first Antarctic Development Project in 1946-47 code named *Operation Highjump* with Admiral Richard Byrd again leading the expedition as Officer-in-Charge with Rear Admiral R H Cruzen, commanding 4,000 men of Task Force 68 to the frozen continent.

Aircraft were again high on the list of necessary transport equipment, notwithstanding the R4-D's difficulties in respect of handling cargo in and out of Antarctic, refuelling them by hand pumps, and the extensive preheating required getting the twin engine Douglas aircraft started. The command, when considering these difficulties, found they were inconsequential when comparing them against their dependable and proven record, being an aircraft whose capabilities had already established itself as aviation's workhorse.

By late autumn, Dutchman Willem Barebdsz and the Soviet Union whaling fleet were operating in Antarctic waters for the first time. The Dutch Antarctic whaling operations were conducted between Bouvet and the South Sandwich Islands.

In November the *New York Times* ran a story on a six nation race to the Antarctic for the reported uranium deposits, and that the British were leading the race by sending a secret expedition to occupy Byrd's 1938-40 East Base at Marguerite Bay on the Antarctic Peninsula.

Admiral Byrd released a press statement on November 12 1946 stating *'The purposes of the operation are primarily of a military nature; a major purpose of the expedition is to learn how the Navy's standards and everyday equipment will perform under every day conditions'.*

Now at wars end, the Navy, if it was to avoid being stripped of its aviation role needed Richard Byrd to persuade the Secretary of the Navy, James Forrestal and the Chief of Naval Operations Chester Nimitz to launch the largest expedition to Antarctica to date.

Byrd had another political ally apart from Admiral Ernest J King, who, between 1941 and 45 had travelled to the war fronts in Europe, Alaska and the North Pacific, it was his brother Senator Harry Flood Byrd, then head of the powerful family machine who ran the Virginia Democratic. It was said that Flood Byrd got what ever his brother wanted and Richard Byrd wanted to go back to Antarctica and had the top Navy brass convince Congress to back him and subsequently fund the expensive expedition.

One can only assume it was because the US Navy had not been in charge of an Antarctic expedition since that of Charles Wilke a hundred years earlier, that Admiral D.C. Ramsay signed his name too, thus creating the Naval operations that would establish the Antarctic Development Project, to carry out operations in the forthcoming summer of December 1946- March 1947 code-named *'Operation Highjump.'*

The instructions were as follows, for twelve ships and several thousand top men to make their way to the Antarctic rim.

[1] Train personnel and test material in the Frigid Zone.

[2] Consolidate and extend America's sovereignty over the largest practical area of the Antarctic continent.

[3] Determine the feasibility of establishing and maintaining bases in the Antarctic, and to investigate possible base sites.

[4] Develop techniques for establishing and maintaining air bases on the ice, with particular attention to the later applicability of such techniques that had operated in the interior of Greenland, where it was claimed, physical and climatic conditions resembled those of Antarctica.

[5] Amplify existing knowledge of hydrographic, geographic, geological, meteorological and electromagnetic conditions in the area.

In his book *Operation Deep Freeze,* Rear Admiral George Dufek wrote that *Operation Highjump 11* was cancelled for economic reasons, but during an interview later, he told this writer that it had been his understanding that President Truman directed the cancellation because of his anger at Senator Byrd's insistence on economy and that his first intimation of impending trouble was when ordered supplies were not moving forward to ports of embarkation.

Under the headline '*The Sinking of Task Force 66*' columnist Jack Lait writing in the *Broadway and Elsewhere,* attributes the abrupt action not to differences about the economy, but to the defeat of a Truman backed candidate for the Democratic nomination to the Governorship of Virginia, by a candidate supported by Sen. Byrd.

Much of the material, directives, correspondence and miscellaneous papers as to the premature cancellation of the *Operation Highjump* were classified confidential, though not for reasons of national security so much as to prevent disclosure of the operation while in its planning stage. It was intended for example, to downgrade the operation plan to unclassified, when a public release was made to inform the press of the intended expedition, but no such release was issued on the tentative operations plan and so other papers retained their original classification.

Washington was also aware of the war clouds hanging over the Republic of Korea, prior to the invasion into South Korea by 60,000 North Korean troops, spear-headed by 100 Russian built tanks, on June 25 1950, bringing the US into the war on the demand of the UN, when President Harry S Truman ordered Gen Douglas MacArthur to aid South Korea. US forces under the command of recently designated General MacArthur entered the Korean conflict on June 30 as part of the international police action.

Antarctic explorations for whatever reasons were placed on hold until after the cessation of military hostilities and the birth of *Operation Deep Freeze* and the formation of the now famous VX-6 air squadron were formed.

Operation Highjump II, an expedition that never took place, perhaps merits no footnote in the history of American exploration of Antarctica, so little impact did the aborted operation have that the famous *New York Times* scientist writer Walter Sullivan failed to make mention of it in his book '*Quest for a Continent'.*

At the time of the operation's abrupt and some would say mysterious cancellation, the Secretary of the Navy in a letter to Congressmen Paul Brown, stated '*that planning data compiled for Highjump II would be saved, for use in connection that there be further operations of this same nature.'*

In early August 1954 Rear Admiral George Dufek was at Whidbey Island walking slowly from his garden towards his house with a dispatch from the Navy he had just received. Taking his muddy shoes off at the entrance, he slipped into his comfortable sneakers and entered the living room where his wife Muriel was preparing dinner, '*I've just seen the messenger, what was it. Washington? Antarctica'?*

'*Yes',*

'It will probably be cancelled again like Operation No Jump', was Muriel's cynical reply.

'Not this one, the scientists want this, we probably will furnish the support, build bases, fly the planes'.

'When do you leave?'

'I must go the day after tomorrow' was her seafaring husband's reply.

'A navy career may sound very romantic and interesting but it's a little rugged on a family, we had two teenage daughters and two boys, George age six and David four and a half. We take the boys to odd places, wherever orders send us' George Dufek wrote in his book. *'But the separations are hard. During the Korean War, when I commanded the Aircraft Carrier Antietam, I was absent from my family for most of the year. One day David asked his mother, 'What is Daddy- a man or a ship?' and one night at dinner when I tried to correct George, he turned to his mother and said, 'Who is he? Do I have to do what he says?' As one newspaper correspondent put it. 'If he's a vague character, it's about time this skipper stayed home for awhile.'*

But we survived. Today the two boys masquerade in my Antarctic parka and boots, and we are now well acquainted, and they know I am not a ship.'

Returning to Washington Rear Admiral Dufek commenced planning for *Operation Deep Freeze I*, and one of his first acts was to retrieve the Highjump files from the Naval Centre's files, and immediately requested the assignment of officers and staff who had participated in earlier planning. Capt W. H Hawkes for example, who had previously flown in the Antarctic during *Highjump I*, was one of the officers recalled.

Washington didn't realise it at the time, but while *Highjump II*, was never carried out, it was indeed a link between *Highjump I* and *Operation Deep Freeze*. It is also interesting to note that it reflected the shift of emphasis on the part the United States from its previous preoccupation with territorial claims, which played a major part in Byrd's earlier Antarctic expeditions and *Operation Highjump I*, to one of training possibilities of Antarctic operations, scientific investigation, and international co-operational programmes.

After World War II, the United States Navy had embarked on its first Antarctica Development Project, which was given the nickname *Operation Highjump*. In his report, the commander, Rear Admiral Richard Cruzen stated that the real advantages had accrued to the United States and to the naval service from the operation, but that these advantages would be lost if they were not followed up. The Rear Admiral recommended that a definite programme of naval operations be carried out yearly in the Antarctic, and pointed out that even a small expedition employing a single icebreaker would be worthwhile. This *Antarctic Development Project* was mounted with two icebreakers, rather than the one suggested by Cruzen. Although no official nickname was assigned to this expedition, it was popularly referred to as *Operation Windmill*, and *Highjump II* was, therefore, the third of these projects, and its implementing directives were designated as *Antarctic Development Project 1949-50*.

When *Operation Deep Freeze* was conceived, unbeknown by the Washington planners, including Rear Admiral George J Dufek in August 1954, was that they were embarking the United States on an Antarctic expedition which would last well into the twenty first century, and the creation of what would be known by military and aviation historians alike, as an air squadron the likes of which would never be seen again, AIR DEVELOPMENT SQUADRON SIX –VX-6

CHAPTER TWO.

IN THE BEGINNING -THE BIRTH OF OPERATION DEEP FREEZE.

Rear Admiral George Dufek begins planning for
another deployment on the ice.

This is the story of the men and women of the United States Navy's Antarctic Development Squadron Six [VX-6] the men and women who for 44 years travelled to the bottom of the world to serve as airmen of *Operation Deep Freeze.*

It's their story; told by the *Puckered Penguins* in their own exceptional, yet intimate way. For the aviators, and those who supported them were exceptional men, serving their country far beyond the normal peacetime call of duty; men who downplayed the heroics of their Antarctic flying exploits, aviators who were as worn out as their aged aircraft. They were not prima donnas, immersed and obsessed with their own achievements, they were aviators who took up the challenge offered to them by just carrying out the task, no mater how unusual and harsh.

In the words of Commander James Waldon in his book *The Flight of the Puckered Penguins.* *'Our squadron's insignia shows a bedraggled and malting penguin with bloodshot eyes, holding a half consumed glass in one hand and a bottle of 'Old Mo' brandy in the other. A cigarette dangles from his mouth and he appears to be suffering from a severe hangover.'*

To the Task Force 43 staff officers, VX-6 and the entire Seabee battalion, it was a strictly volunteer tour of duty. When Alnav 8 put out the word that applications were invited for duty with the task force expedition, BuPers was flooded with requests, with about 4,000 for the fewer than 300 billets to be filled. Officers' detail desk too waded through many letters beginning with the words. *'It is requested that I be considered for assignment to duty.'* To be known as Volunteer Task Force TF-43, it had a complement of 1805, a third the size of the 1946 *High Jump 1* with its approximate 4,000 men and 13 ships.

Many of those early volunteers may not have been fully aware that Antarctica is a vast cold land, mysterious and strange, lying at the bottom of the world, forbidding, desolate, and above all, locked in thousands of miles of ice, behind almost impenetrable barriers, with a vast interior of ice shelves, perpendicular cliffs rising without a break for hundreds of feet, with glaciers fed by millions of tons of ice pouring down from the ice caps.

Violent seas encircle and pound the entire continent, the meeting place of the Pacific, Indian and Atlantic oceans. These oceans virtually freeze overnight, taking hold of any ships, and holding them in a vice like grip, crushing the steel hulls into tiny fragments. There is a protective shroud of pack ice surrounding the frozen continent, encapsulating it from the outside world, like a nourishing mother, but there is also another side:

'At the bottom of the planet lies an enchanted continent like a pale, sleeping princess, sinister and beautiful, she lies in her frozen slumber, her billowy white robes of snow weirdly luminous, with amethysts and emeralds of ice, her iridescent ice halos around the sun and moon, her horizons painted with pastel shades of pink, gold, green and blue. Such is Antarctica, luring land of ever-lasting mystery.'

Rear Admiral Richard Byrd; writing in the *National Geographic.*

Born in South Australia on October 31 1888, Sir Herbert Wilkins made the first ever flight in the Antarctic region, when he flew from Deception Island in the South Shetland Islands in a Lockheed Vega Monoplane, the *San Francisco*.

Summing up Antarctica's first exploratory flight in his diary, *'we had left at 8.30 in the morning, had covered 1300 miles- nearly a thousand of it over unknown territory and returned in time to cover the plane with a storm hood, go to the 'Hektoria,' bathe and dress and sit down for dinner at eight o'clock as usual, in the comfort of the ships wardroom."*

A year later, Rear Admiral Richard E Byrd made the first flight over the South Pole.

Antarctica remained largely unexplored before VX-6 squadron was formed on January 17 1955 at Naval Air Station [NAS] Patuxent River. Maryland. Before then, no aircraft had touched down on the frozen surface of the South Pole, but now the United States Navy was to entrust the squadron to spearhead intercontinental thrusts into Antarctica and earn for themselves a proud place in Antarctic and aviation history. In the opinion of Capt Hawke and other aviators assigned to the squadron, *'If the Douglas R4-D aircraft couldn't get you anywhere on the continent, then you shouldn't go.'* That airplane was, along with the squadron, soon to become a polar legend.

Both Dufek and the Navy drew on the extensive polar experience of Commander Eddie Ward, who had flown extensively in the Arctic. Returning from a squadron in the Pacific in 1945, he was ordered to the Office of Naval Research to carry out an airborne magnetometer survey of north Alaska from the Brooks Range to the Arctic Ocean and from the West coast of Alaska to the Canadian border. This survey was an aerial survey for Navy Petroleum Reserve Four [Pet-4] as during WW-2, the United States, fearful of an oil shortage, made preliminary land surveys in Alaska for potential oil deposits, followed by an aerial survey flown by Captain Ward. Known as Project *SPAM* [Special Alaskan Magnetic Survey]. Ward suggested that a BBY-5 amphibian equipped with a magnetometer in its tail and a recording station amid ships, be used with a five-man crew, including a navigator, pilot, co-pilot and two scientists. This project lasted from May to September 1946.

Commander Ward's Polar flying experience was further enhanced in January 1951, when he was assigned a ski-equipped R4-D, similar to those that operated in the first 15 years with Operation Deep Freeze, but was configured for oceanographic research, in a joint effort by the Navy and the Wood Hole Oceanographic Institute. His crew consisted of five enlisted men, pilot, co-pilot and again two scientists. During the winter season of 1951-52, they established eighteen successful oceanographic stations on the polar ice cap.

Eddie Ward's recollections of the polar project had a tinge of what was to follow in Antarctica, although at the time, unknown. *'I pranged, when my ski struck a hidden ice block while taking off from station eighteen, four hundred miles from the North Pole and eight hundred miles north of Point Barrow, Alaska, it was very close to the point of relative inaccessibility, but we were eventually picked up and returned to Point Barrow.'*

In the spring of 1954, while assigned to the Bureau of Aeronautics, Eddie Ward was in the process of hand carrying aircraft procurement orders to the various interested Bureau Departments. Working from his office on the Bureau's fourth floor, he had chanced upon the Office of Rear-Admiral Richard E Byrd and rather apprehensively knocked at the door and entered, to be greeted by a smiling secretary. He recalled that chain of events in his memoirs.

'What can I do for you Commander?'

'My name is Ward' I stammered.

'Glancing at the stack of papers under my arm, she said 'Just a minute, I'll see if the Admiral is busy,' and so saying, she stepped into the inner sanctum and a few moments later to bid me enter.'

'Coming face to face with my boyhood hero was a totally awesome experience! My anxiety lasted but a moment. The Admiral could not have been more cordial, and shaking my hand he offered me a seat by his desk.'

'Now what can I do for you?' he asked.

'Sir' I began, *'I'm very interested in cold weather operations. I've read every book you've written about your polar flights and your expeditions to the Antarctic.'*

He smiled, and for the next half hour we discussed his epic flight over the North Pole on May 9 1926, his Antarctic record setting flight to the South Pole on Thanksgiving Day, November 28 1929 and his most recent Expedition, Operation High Jump in 1947.'

Byrd had read of Commander Ward's 1951 and 52 expeditions code named *'Project Ski-Jump 1 and 2'*, flying a ski-equipped R4-D out of Point Barrow and his distinction of making the Navy's first landing on an unprepared surface of the Arctic ice cap.

'I finally got around to asking the all-important question. 'Sir', I began, 'will you be making another Antarctic expedition and if so,' I hastened to add, 'I would like to volunteer.'

'I sincerely appreciate your offer,' he replied. *'I'm sure you'd be a great asset to the Expedition,'* but added, *'I'm afraid it's out of the question, it takes a lot of money to support an expedition and as you know, military budgets have been cut, if there is a future Antarctic expedition, and hopefully there will be, I'll be sure to add your name to the list.'*

' I was elated and thanked the Admiral for his consideration and the enjoyable chat, we shook hands and I returned to my office.' Two weeks later, Commander Ward received a letter from the Secretary of the Navy to Senator Gordon, dated May 25 1954, which stated in part: While the Navy has a continuous interest in scientific projects and research in all parts of the world, there are at present no military requirements in the Antarctic that would justify the expenditure of funds personnel and equipment to support an expedition to that area.

Then out of the blue Commander Ward's boss, Captain Henry Dietrich approached him one hot humid afternoon in September. *'If you have nothing better to do'*, he told Ward, *'then come meet a Captain in the Pentagon named Dufek who is holding a meeting this afternoon, -something to do with cold weather aircraft configuration. It starts at 2-30 sharp'*. Ward reacted enthusiastically- *'Yes Sir I'll be there.'*

In August 1954, the initial Pentagon Staff, planning Operation Deep Freeze consisted of three officers, Captain Byrd, Eddie Ward and Yeomen, but by September it had grown to twenty officers, moving into the old Post Office Building, Washington DC. Before going any further, the sole purpose of *Operation Deep Freeze* was to support the 'International Geophysical Year', which was to begin on January 1 1957.

Back at the Old Post Office planning meeting, *'Gentlemen,'* Captain Dufek began, *'I have requested your presence to discuss the Navy's participation in the forthcoming IGY, it is a worldwide scientific effort due to begin in January 1957. The Navy has been assigned the task of providing aircraft, ships and personnel in support of the IGY in Antarctica. Initially this would consist of an aircraft Squadron, two maybe three AK transporters and two or three icebreakers. A Construction Battalion of Seabees would be assigned to build bases with all these installations being entirely self-sufficient, providing food services, medical care and all the necessities of life. Bear in mind time is precious-the Navy will deploy to the Antarctic in the fall of 1955!'* Commander Ward was on the initial planning for the Antarctic Mission, planing the establishment of the continent's bases, personnel, ship's, aircraft, and funding requirements as well as the overall logistic support required for such a massive mission for the United States first deployment in Antarctica 1955-56.

Pausing, and lighting another cigarette, Captain Dufek shuffled his notes. *'This afternoon I requested representatives from the Bureau of Aeronautics, the Bureau of ships and Bureau of Naval personnel, and the various Op Nav officers as I thought they would have a direct interest in the*

Expedition. Now that you know the mission, I would like your recommendations.' Looking around the room, he suggested they start with BuPers.

As the various officers responded, Commander Ward became curious about the man in the chair; who was this Captain Dufek and how did he enter the picture? Was he just another Captain treading water until retirement? One thing for sure, he seemed to be knowledgeable about cold weather operations, particularly in the Antarctic, and what about Admiral Byrd? After all, he was the prime mover when it came to Arctic and Antarctic operations. It would be unthinkable for this great man to be overlooked, yet, strangely enough; no mention of his name had been made.

Captain George Dufek was by now on his twilight tour and no stranger to cold weather operations, so when the first smoke signal rose, the Chief of Naval Operations had hinted at a possible joint Army, Navy and Air Force effort to support the upcoming International Geophysical Year.

When Washington faced another Antarctic expedition, the first choice was Admiral Byrd, whose name was synonymous with polar exploration, but the admiral was now old and a little frail, and it was obvious that he would be unable to cope with the rigorous demands of the cold Antarctic. The Navy's Old Boy's Club, not wishing to upset the famous polar explorer, provided him with an attractive office on Pennsylvania Avenue, with a staff and the nebulous title of Commander US Antarctic Programmes. While this may have appeared that the Admiral would exercise overall directions of the Antarctic expeditions, it could not have been further from the truth.

This left the Navy with the only other logical choice, Captain George Dufek who came highly recommended by Admiral Byrd. However, there was one obstacle, his impending retirement, and as naval regulations state quite categorically that any United States Naval Officer who is in retirement status cannot exercise any sea command and only by a special act of Congress can this be waved as was the case of Admiral Byrd earlier, so if this could be done, then the rest would be easy, as Captain Dufek could be given a tombstone promotion to Rear Admiral.

Under existing Naval regulations an officer who had earned a combat decoration equal to or higher than, a DFC [Distinguished Flying Cross], would be promoted to the next highest rank on retirement, a strictly honorary rank that did not increase his retirement pay.

The distinguished navy career of George E Dufek encompassed an extraordinary variety of naval assignments, including leadership, he was one of the few officers qualified to command aircraft, air bases, submarine, surface craft and task forces. His previous polar expeditions to both the Arctic and Antarctic, the latter with Operation High Jump, led the Navy to appoint him to lead Task Force 43.

Born in Rockford, Illinois on February 10 1903, Dufek graduated from Rockford High in 1922 to enter the Navel Academe and was commissioned an Ensign in 1925. As an Lt he volunteered for the Byrd Antarctic Expedition in 1939, and was the navigator aboard the *USS Bear*, the Flagship of the Navy's Antarctic Development Project.

When word reached Dufek of the Japanese attack on Pearl Harbour on December 7 1941, he requested overseas duty and was subsequently assigned as Special Naval Observer for Aviation in London. Dufek's participation in the invasion on North Africa was as Senior Naval Aviator for the Commander of Naval Forces in North African waters, assisting in planning the invasions of Sicily and Salerno, Italy and later the invasion of Southern France.

In September 1944, Dufek assumed command of the *USS Bogue*, which with six accompanying destroyers formed the basis of an Anti-Submarine Killer Group in the Atlantic. It was the aircraft aboard the *Bogue* and her escorting ships that sank the final German sub lost in WW11. After the war, he was assigned to *Task Force 68*, and sent to establish weather bases in the North Polar region, and it was while on this mission, that the Navy ordered him to help plan *Operation High Jump*.

That November he sailed with his 13 ship Task Force, under the command of directions of retired Rear Admiral Richard E Byrd, then a Captain. In 1948 he commanded *Task Force 80*- a cargo ship and two ice breakers in a resupply mission to existing weather stations and to establish a new one near the North Pole.

He commanded the carrier *USS Antietam* from January 1951 until May 1952, including 79 days of combat operations in Korea, during which time, over 5,700 combat missions were flown with the loss of only three in combat.

'*I believe it was late September 1954, when Captain Dufek received word of his promotion to Rear Admiral and Congressional authorization to command at sea*' recalled Commander Eddie Ward. '*Once frocked, Admiral Dufek made it quite clear that he would welcome the advice and recommendations from Admiral Byrd and his staff. He then let it be known to one and all that he was the Commander of Task Force 43 and would be taking orders from no one.*

At the outset, I would like to say that the Navy could not have selected a better man to lead the Deep Freeze Programme than Admiral George Dufek. He was a competent, forceful leader, a man of courage with an iron will to succeed. The task he faced was overwhelming. A Task Force, comprising ships, aircraft and men would have to be organised, heavy equipment, bulldozers, tractors and building materials to be purchased. The logistic support along to support this operation was awesome, and most important, the submission of funding requirements to support the programme. All this with limited time to plan the operation, coordinate the Task Force Units and most importantly execute the deployment on schedule. In my opinion, Admiral Dufek was totally responsible for the success of the Deep Freeze Programme.' Commander Ward said.

Modesty prevented the unpretentious Commander Eddie Ward from taking on board more than a certain degree of credit for the operation's success, being in on the planing from the beginning. Commander Ward's vast experience of polar exploration, cold weather procedure and entrepreneurial planning ability, plus his enthusiastic passion for Antarctica were advantageous to the Admiral and the Task Force.

United States Naval expeditions are notorious for commanders to surround themselves with old shipmates and friends, and Dufek was no exception. Once he received the green light, Washington was awash with conspiracy theorists as his old buddies began arriving at Task Force headquarters, now situated in the Pentagon, having outgrown the old Post Office Building. Some friends dated back to the 1947 Antarctic expedition, *Operation Highjump,* and some from earlier polar expeditions. However, these men had a wealth of polar exploration experience, but it was Admiral Byrd who could and would contribute most to the upcoming expedition. Due to the time he had spent on the Antarctic ice shelf at Little America made him the most knowledgeable of all. It was their collective expertise, which Dufek would call upon to guide the operations in Antarctica.

This old boy's club was to become apparent on October 26 1956, when the Admiral selected his crew of *Que Sera Sera* the squadron's R4-D # *12418* for the first ever flight to land at the South Pole. Commander Eddie Frankiewicz had the only ski equipped R4-D # *17274* with the specially coated Teflon covered skis.

Now it was well past 4 o'clock and all the various departments had submitted their recommendations, except for the Bureau of Aeronautics, Captain Dufek turned to Commander Ward, '*Are you the only one representing BuAer*' he asked.

'*Yes Sir, Commander Ward, Plans Coordination Division*'.

Appearing a little surprised, the Admiral turned to Ward and asked rather condescendingly '*Very well what are your recommendations. If we deploy to the Antarctic next fall, we have about a year to configure the Squadron aircraft for cold weather operations.*'

Commander Ward replied. '*In that case Sir, I strongly recommend we draw on the aircraft presently available. I know where I can locate some R4-D's and ten sets of skis. Any major repair facility can rig them, or the squadron's maintenance departments can do it. We could also draw on two ski- configured P2V's, Lockheed would have to rig the skis as the Navy has none of their assembly drawings.*'

When asked if he was sure of his facts, Ward answered in the affirmative,

'Please continue.' Captain George Dufek responded.

'We might also consider requesting a UF Albatross, they are a twin-engine amphibian built by Grumman, and the Air Force has a tri-phibian version, the SA-16. They use it for Air Sea Rescue. I have no idea of its performance, however with the versatility of land, sea and snow operations it might be worth looking into.'

'How many UF's do we have in the Navy inventory', the Captain asked.

'Thirty sir with a follow up order from Grumman for an additional twenty-one.'

'Well that's interesting' he replied.

'If you were thinking about small, ski equipped, support aircraft', Commander Ward continued, *'I would strongly recommend the American aircraft manufacturers such as Cessna, Piper and Beechcraft be eliminated. They have yet to build a ski-equipped aircraft that would come close to the DeHavilland. I've flown the JA-1 Noorduyn Norseman which I consider to be an outstanding aircraft. The larger DeHavilland version, either the Otter or the Beaver should prove ideal.'*

Lighting another cigarette, Dufek stood and thanked the officers for their attendance; adding that the meeting was educational, then smiling *'If there is no further business, this meeting stands adjourned'* and turning to Commander Ward, he requested him to remain. When the last officer closed the door, the two men sat facing each other in silence. Placing his half smoked cigar in the ashtray, he reached for a glass of water then asked Ward. *'How would you like to go to the Antarctic?'*

'It hit me so cold I was speechless, then regaining my composure, I tried to hide my excitement. 'Captain between you and me', I responded, *'I would give my right arm for the opportunity. But there is only one problem, my tour of duty at BuAer is only half over and I doubt very much if my boss will let me go.'*

'Who is your boss?' the Captain asked.

'Captain Henry Dietrich.'

'Don't worry; if you want to go as my Air Operations Officer, I'll see you get there. The first order of business will be to form a working staff. As you mentioned it is of the essence. Planning for a joint operation this size with all its complexities is a demanding task. Your job and the job of every officer on my staff will not be an easy one; that I can assure you. I can't promise you a flying job, but when the squadron is formed and designated, it will be up to the Squadron commanding officer to select the pilots. If you are willing to take that gamble I wont stand in your way. Any questions?'

'Yes Sir,' I replied, *'when can I expect my orders.'*

'Anytime.'

'I was still completely flustered as Captain Dufek stood up to leave. 'Sir, I greatly appreciate your consideration, and I'm honoured to be a member of your Staff, whatever the case, Squadron or Staff, I'll guarantee I'll pull my weight in the boat.'

We shook hands and I left the Pentagon, where the corridors of power were quiet and empty, I looked at my watch, it was almost five thirty. When my orders finally arrived, as I expected, a rather irate Captain Dietrich confronted me 'Are you out of your mind' he bellowed.

'No Sir,' I then smiled at him.

'Do you really want to go to that god-forsaken place?'

'Yes Sir, positive Sir.'

'He sighed, 'well then so be it,' and held out his hand. 'Good Luck.'

This was Cdr Ward's first experience in the big league of exploration; the small Arctic Operations in which he had participated had no big names, no press coverage, a limited budget and a cooperative friendly spirit that made for high morale. He was soon to find out this would not be the case in Operation Deep Freeze. Cronyism was rampant, the old guard from the Admiral Byrd Little America expeditions and Operation High Jump [1947] were close knit groups, where new ideas were resented, favouritism was obvious and divisiveness, be it every so subtle, was widespread.

This type of infighting among the world's great explorers is well documented eg. Dr Cook claims that it was he, and not Captain Peary who reached the North Pole first, causing a bitter confrontation. Did Admiral Byrd and his pilot Floyd Bennet fly over the North Pole as claimed? Rumours by his critics would suggest otherwise, but after extensive research by the polar experts assisted by members of the New York Explorers Club, both Admiral Peary and Admiral Byrd were credited with their respective claims.

'It was intensely interesting and should I have stayed on Admiral Dufek's Task Force 43 Staff, I would have seen the big picture unfold, so to speak' recalled Eddie Ward. *'As it turned out I requested duty with the Navy's Aircraft Squadron –VX-6. The Admiral was far from happy with my request however he said if I could get a replacement he'd have no objections. Cdr Penny Pendergast volunteered, thus freeing me to join the Squadron.'*

Just before Christmas 1954, Admiral Dufek and the staff Meteorological Officer, Commander John Mirabito attended an IGY meeting with other participating nations in Brussels, Belgium, and as Mirabito could speak six languages fluently, he acted as the Admiral's interpreter.

The IGY sponsored the conference, for the participants to get acquainted and encourage them to exchange data of mutual interest.

With the cold war still in full swing, the conferences last days were interesting. The leader of the Russian delegation approached Admiral Dufek, and motioned to a large chart of Antarctica, which covered one wall in the conference room, but as neither could speak the other's language and with no interpreters present, the conversation was carried out by sign language.

Eddie Ward recalls the meeting in his Memoirs.

'The Russian pointed to McMurdo and then to Little America and finally back to Admiral Dufek. He then proceeded to pound his fist on the geographic South Pole. Then to Admiral Dufek's astonishment, he stamped both feet loudly on the floor. There was no mistaking his intentions!'

Now, the surprising thing about this turn of events is that heretofore the Russians had shown no interest in a base at the Pole. It was well known they intended to build their permanent base, Mirnyy, somewhere in the vicinity of Queen Mary Coast. A second and far more difficult station to construct, "Vostok" had been planned seven hundred miles inland, between Mirnyy and the South Pole, close to the South Geomagnetic Pole. Although there were many more locations in the Antarctic that would be more desirable from a scientific viewpoint than South Pole Station, the propaganda value was priceless. The race for the Pole was on!'

By January 1954, everything was falling into place, with the Chief of Naval Operations approving the deployment of the Naval Construction Battalion, two Navy Icebreakers-the *USS Glacier*, *USS Edisto* and the *USCG Eastwind*, three military sea transport service ships-the *Greenville Victory*, *Wyandot*, *Aarneb* and the oil tanker *Nespelen* were all under the direct control of Admiral Dufek.

On Dufek's insistence, his old mate William 'Trigger' Hawkes was included, along with others with polar experience, to join the team. Some staff officers were intrigued with the appointment of Capt Hawkes as the Squadron's Commanding Officer, based on a Naval technicality. William Hawkes had elected to specialize in the field of aviation engineering. Once accepted as an engineering specialist, he was given an AEDO [Aviation Engineering Duty Only] designation. Reverting from line officer to AEDO effectively precluded him from command at sea of a ship or aircraft squadron. He could however, command a shore facility such as a maintenance activity or an Engineering Centre, this was in accordance with Navy Regulations.

Commander Ward wrote. *'The first time the Admiral had broached the subject to me, I had cautioned him about proposing Trigger Hawkes as the Squadron's CO, but he had reacted in a stubborn and hostile manner. From my observation this was now a matter of principle.*

A rather subdued group sat facing the Admiral, with the exception of Captain Ketchum, Deputy Commander Captain Thomas USCG Chief Of Staff and Lt.Cdr Don Kent, Supply Officer, USN, the rest of the Admiral's Staff had been admonished for their poor performance. I had learnt long ago that you don't offer excuses to superiors, let alone Admirals! Several times the Admiral had told me that Capt Hawkes would make all the decisions concerning the number of aircraft, squadron compliment and funding requirements. As they said in the Old Navy, 'If the Admiral said it's going to rain today, you put on your raincoat and boots and walk around all day in the sun!'

Fortunately Commander Ward had all the personnel, funding and aircraft requirements prepared for distribution to the various Navy Bureaus, only lacking the Admiral's signature. He also had the foresight to verbally recommend to CNO the Squadron be designated, Air Development Squadron Six [VX-6], and CNO had tentatively approved it pending receipt of an official request by the Task Force Commander.

Following a Staff meeting, which concluded with suggestions for the operation's code name, the Admiral, requested his Staff Officers to come up with a proposed name. First Commander Dustin Dusty, suggested '*Snowbird*', and then around the smoke filled room, each officer in turn responded '*Bear*', was one, another suggested '*Snow White*', but it soon became apparent the Admiral didn't think too kindly to their creativity. He sat back in his leather chair, lit another cigarette and motioned for quiet. '*What do you think of 'Deep Freeze*' he suggested in an off handed manner, to which all agreed, then he left the room.

The following morning, on the Admiral's strict instructions, Commander Ward flew to Johnsonville to touch base with Trigger Hawkes.

'He is expecting you, and will give you the names of key Squadron personnel he wants, this list will be given to the Bureau of Naval Personnel, for the rest of the Squadron, both officers and enlisted men, will be on a volunteer basis.' He instructed.

After meeting Hawkes on the flight line, the pair walked over to the Naval Air Development Centre,

'Trigger handed me a list of his nominations and for the most part they were old friends and shipmates from previous squadron tours. He selected a Marine, Lt Col. Hal Kulp as Executive Officer. This surprised me, as I did not know of any Navy Fleet Squadron with a Marine XO. Next came his Operations Officer, Cdr, Paul Bouer, this selection was even more unusual as Paul Bouer was not a designated Naval Aviator. For his Maintenance Officer, Hawkes requested a shipmate from Operation Deep Freeze, Cdr. Rudy Weigand, and finally for his Air Officer he selected Lt.Cdr Conrad 'Gus' Shinn. This was an outstanding selection, as I knew Gus well. He was a feisty little guy, and one of the most capable and experienced aviators in the Navy.' Ward wrote later.

'On my flight back to Anacostia in my twin Beechcraft, I couldn't help thinking that if Trigger struck out as CO and I was almost sure he would, the new Commanding Officer would be saddled with an odd assortment indeed!'

Two weeks later two letters arrived on Commander Ward's desk, one from the Chief of Navy Operations, authorizing the code name *Deep Freeze* for the overall Antarctic Operation, stipulating inasmuch as this was an ongoing programme The first year would be designated *Deep Freeze 1* the second year *Deep Freeze II,* and so on. A second letter from the Secretary of the Navy, approving the CNO recommendation that Naval Air Station, Patuxent River, MD, be designated the Squadron's Home Port.

A message to all Navy Ships and Stations seeking personnel for the operation, met with overwhelming success, it requested officer volunteers for the Squadron broken down according to rank and designator, enlisted by speciality and rank. It further requested doctors, dentists and chaplain volunteers, further, the message emphasized that for those who wintered in from February 1955 until the following October there would be no air or ship transportation in or out of Antarctica

'All in all, we received over five thousand volunteers, so our dilemma, was how to separate the wheat from the chaff, as there were only fifty three officers billets and two hundred and sixty enlisted

specialist positions to be filled. To compound the issue, the phone was ringing off the hook with volunteers calling to ensure their names were on the list, and of course they all requested preferential treatment.' recalled Eddie Ward.

As one can imagine the selection process was a very tedious and difficult job, so in order to expedite the process, the Bureau of Naval Personnel reviewed the enlisted jackets and selected those they determined to be the most qualified for the job. Commander Herbert Whitney, the Commanding Officer of the Naval Construction Battalion [Special] assisted the Board in selecting the Seabees.

Towards the end of January 1955, the officers considered most qualified had been selected and BuPers issued orders. Cdr Paul Bouer's selection for Operation Officer had been turned down; however, he was assigned instead to the Squadron as Navigation Officer. The position of Operations Officer remained open, pending the outcome of Trigger Hawke's status. If the Navy turned him down, Admiral Dufek had promised Commander Ward a flying job with VX-6, providing the Commander could come up with a relief.

A few days later a letter from the Chief Bureau of Naval Personal arrived saying that Cdr William Hawkes designation as AEDO had in fact disqualified him for command of the Squadron, should the Admiral so desire, however, Capt Hawkes could be assigned to the *Task Force 43* Staff. A short time later Bill Hawkes, now a Captain selectee, received his orders to *Task Force 43*.

'Minutes after the letter from BuPers arrived, I called a friend in BuAer, Cdr Bill Bates and inquired if he knew anyone who would like a job as Air Operations on Admiral Dufek's staff. He laughed 'I sure do' he replied. 'An old friend of mine just arrived in the puzzle place. He's anything but happy with Washington duty.' Who is he?' I asked.

'Commander Prendergast, his friends call him Penny. He works in the BuAer Maintenance Division.'

'That afternoon I carried Penny's letter to the Pentagon and submitted it to his detail officer in Op54, so now, if I hurried, I could get back to the old Post Office building before they secured. I'm sure the Admiral smelled one of the biggest rats in his life. For once it was I who held the trump card and there was no way the Admiral could wiggle out of it. I placed a call to Op 54 and handed him the phone.'

'Well', he said as he hung up, 'I guess that takes you off the hook', then with a change of heart he smiled, 'I know how you feel about flying,' he said, 'I'm sure Cdr Prendergast will work out just fine. The Operations slot is still open. Tomorrow, I'll request BuPers write up a set of orders assigning you to Air Development Squadron Six', he sat back in his chair. 'Now, what are we going to do about a Squadron Skipper? Anyone you can recommend.'

Yes Sir I replied eagerly. 'An old friend of mine; we served together at Point Barrow, Alaska, his name is Ebbe. Cdr Gordon K Ebbe.'

Commander Ward's initial responsibility as Acting CO was estimating the squadron's personnel compliment, funding requirements, berthing arrangements, hangar space and many other mundane chores. This required weekly trips to Washington DC to co-ordinate his effects with those of Task Force 43. As the squadron's compliments were composed of all volunteers, approximately three thousand, with many picked from previous Antarctic operations, notably Admiral Byrd's 1947 *Operation High Jump.*

Officers, like Commander James Waldron, who prior to going to the Antarctic in 1956, was, in his words, *'a third tier Administration Officer; in effect, I wrote letters from the Captain and Executive Officer, read mail and occupied some desk space and at the same time spent a lot of time flying, refreshing my familiarity with certain types of aircraft and learning something about types I had never piloted before, like the R4-D,'* in which he would, within a very short time, fly the famous Douglas *Gooney Bird* over the frozen continent.

A number of VX-6's pilots for *Deep Freeze I,* had had previous Polar experiences and Cdr Gordon K Ebbe, the Squadron's Commander was a veteran of the North Polar expedition *Ski-Jump One,* and he had also made a number of Air Force Ptarmigan [Weather] flights over the North Pole while Cdr. Edward Ward, VX-6's Operations officer flew *Ski-Jump* I & II. Administration officer Lt.Cdr.O Fuske had sailed to the privately funded Ronne Antarctic Research Expedition in 1946, where he was engaged in extensive aerial mapping operations. Commander Wiegand and Lt.Cdr.Gus Shinn, where both engaged together, with Captain William Hawke in *Operation Highjump I.*

To accomplish the mission ahead, the VX-6 was assigned specially equipped aircraft, painted bright colours for assisting in identification in the event of accidents. It had been necessary in the 1955 expedition, to take aircraft designed for that specific mission in the Temperate Zone that could be adapted with skis.

VX-6 was made up of a variety of aircraft, including two P-2V-2N's Neptune's, four UC-1 De Havilland Otter's, Douglas, two R4D-5's, two R5D-'s Douglas R5D's, two C-117 Skytrains, C-121 Lockheed Super Constellations along with seven HO4S-1 Sikorsky helicopters. One of the Otters was delivered from DeHaviland's Canadian factory, while the others were borrowed then later purchased from the Royal Canadian Air Force.

Earlier Navy Antarctic expeditions had determined the ability of ski-equipped aircraft to land and take-off from ice and snow; however, planners expressed serious reservations in deploying the R5D's and its ability to operate on the southern continent, as they were the only squadron aircraft not fitted with skis.

Cdr.Jim Waldron: *'VX-6 turned out to be a very 'mixed bag' as compared with other Naval Squadrons and I was to find that it takes much getting use to as the squadron was made up with pilots and flight crews from all parts of the Aviation Navy. My first assignment to an R4-D flight crew came as a surprise because I had applied for the Antarctic mission as a helicopter pilot, and I hadn't realized that I would be considered for anything else.*

I had never flown transport aircraft, so it seemed strange that I should have been relegated to being a co pilot in something as ancient as an R4-D. Looking back now, I can see my assignment to the R4-D gave me more career versatility, because for the rest of my flying career, I would not be limited to helicopters and single engine aircraft. At the time, however I was very upset knowing that I would have to assume the role of a green co-pilot of an R4-D for the good part of my Antarctic stay. I was scheduled to go to one of the most demanding of places on this good earth as a green transport co-pilot! It just didn't seem right at the time'.

The Squadron became known as *Antarctic-Devron Six.* After only days of flight familiarization, the R4-D's were fitted with a 200-gallon auxiliary tank flown out from the Naval Air Station at Patuxent River, Maryland, for Christchurch, New Zealand. More preparation was taken before *Deep Freeze II* commenced- with R4-D and UF-1 aircrews spending some time on the Greenland Ice Cap.

Flight training at NAS Quonset Point included flights to check out the JATO [Jet Assisted Take-Off] bottles. Eighteen JATO rocket bottles were loaded onto the racks of the aircraft, while the crew sat on the edge of the runways.

'Once they were loaded and armed electrically, we were cleared for take-off' wrote Jim Waldron, *'Eddie Frankiewicz the R4-D's commander was at the controls so he added take-off power on both engines and started rolling down the runway. Once the tail wheel lifted off the ground, Eddie pushed the JATO firing switch and suddenly we felt the magnificent thrust off those 18,000 extra thrusts pushing us forward. It was as though we were suddenly transported to a high-powered fighter aircraft. Eddie had to place the aircraft into a steep climb to keep from flying too fast, since this ancient aircraft was not built to fly at rocket speed.*

I think now, that I sensed how it must feel to be launched in a rocket ship to outer space. For a few seconds while the rockets were giving us their full thrust, it seems as though we had unlimited power available to us. The system worked perfectly and we knew from that moment that we would have the necessary power available on the ice when we needed it for those dangerous takeoffs. Before we returned to Quonset Point for our landing, we flew out to sea where we dropped the empty JATO rocket casings into deep water.'

Strenuous years of planning went into the expedition to mankind's last frontiers, the frozen wastelands of Antarctica, Task Force 43 was to provide a complete logistic support, that not only required Antarctic flying unparalleled in the world, but requiring the pilot's total adaptability, not so much as last 'gung-ho' but more likened to 'barnstorming' aviation, conquering the last extreme boundaries of aeronautical exploration.

This was the third time in the history of mankind that scientists of the world had collaborated in a simultaneous and detailed examination of the earth's physical environment. The first such effort was in 1882-83, called the *First International Polar Year* when magnetic, meteorological and aurora stations were established in the Arctic and a single station established at South Georgia on the Antarctic continent. The American expedition to support this International study was let by Lt. Greely, who in 1884 had been rescued by the *USS Bear,* which ironically was to take Rear Admiral George Dufek on his first Antarctic expedition in 1939.

The IGY in 1957-58 was to be by far the largest joint enterprise ever undertaken by world scientists with representatives from 40 countries

During the 1954 American summer, men from Detachment one, a mobile Construction Battalion unit at the Climatic Laboratory, Detroit Arsenal, in Detroit, Michigan, learnt special training involving cold weather tests to determine the erectability of a 20 x 40 foot Deep Freeze building, under conditions as similar as possible to what would be faced in Antarctica, but without snow or icy conditions there to contend with. Similar training to build prefabricated buildings was underway at Davisville, but under normal working conditions, where the emphasis was on the working efficiency of the crew, covering all the problems which could be anticipated when working in the extreme cold.

Earlier, members of the Detachment 'Bravo' of Mobile Construction Battalion began training for their wintering over in the Antarctic. Each of the 152 enlisted men and 19 officers were specially selected volunteers, chosen on the basis of their professional capabilities, maturity and physical fitness, and then underwent rigorous training programmes in preparation for the expedition, which included physical exercises, field marches, safety and survival lectures as well as special cold weather work training techniques.

Small groups of men undertook a six-week training duty in northern Greenland during the summer, as the Arctic is subject to similar conditions as the Antarctic. Travelling over a 220 mile trek through blizzards and over crevasses was all part of the rigorous training along with having to bed down in sleeping bags and survive on 'C' rations. The Seabees also assisted in the testing of cold weather equipment, which included a new electronics device used in conjunction with an M29C weasel to locate by electronic impulses, any hidden crevasses.

Other Seabees attended schools at the Caterpillar Tractor plant at Peoria, Illinois, while others travelled to the company's Canadian factory where the large cargo sheds were made.

When one volunteer was asked why he chose for Antarctic duties to spend upwards of 15 lonely months on one of the Navy's most hazardous assignments, the Seabee replied that he wanted to finish a year at college via self-study, and since the Antarctic would be full of evenings with nothing to do and no place to go, it would suit him fine.

During the 1955-56 missions, the object was to build the Little America Station and the Naval Air Facility at McMurdo Sound as these bases were to be used as staging areas for the assault on the South Pole during Deep Freeze 11 in the 1956-67 season, and to be able to transport supplies and equipment for the construction of the Byrd and Pole Stations.

Other proposed installations included Wilkins Station on the Knox Coast, the Ellsworth Station on the edge of the Weddell Sea and a base jointly maintained with New Zealand at Cape Hallett.

Up to 1957 the United States Government was to spend $US32 million in building bases for scientists in Antarctica, so it was up to the scientists under the leadership of the National Science Foundation to select the base locations, and the Navy's job to build them and provide logistic services.

The United States interest in the Antarctic proceeded IGY, but it was not until the winter of 1954, that the Americans had decided to move down to the continent more or less permanently. So in the winter of 1954-55 the *USS Atka* [AGB-3] surveyed the ice conditions of Antarctica and attempted to locate a favourable coastal site to establish a base station.

It was during this visit that the *USS Atka* was instructed to search the Bay of Whales for the missing R4-D's that had been left behind after the withdrawal of *Operation Highjump* and abandoned on the Ross Sea ice shelf. They had been discovered the previous year by the US Icebreakers *Edisto* and *Burton Island,* and on that occasion in late January 1948, after the snow had been cleared away, one of the R4D's engines were started but no attempt had been made to fly the *Gooney Bird.*

On April 1 1955, VX-6 started to look like a Naval Aviation Squadron, with all the aircraft except the DeHavilland Otters, and by then most of the squadron's personnel, officers and enlisted men had reported for duty. Commander Gordon Ebbe had relieved Commander Ward as acting Squadron's CO, while Ward had now reverted to Operations Officer billets with his good friend Commander Hank Jorda as his assistant.

The Overhaul and Repair Department [O&R] at Naval Air Station, Jacksonville was chosen as the Maintenance Activity responsible for the cold weather configuration of the R4-D's, the first of which R4-D # *12418 Que Sera Sera* also known as *Korora,* was flown by Cdr Ward to Jacksonville for induction into the O & R on June 28th.

The following day, the Squadron's latest acquisition, a brand new Grumman UF-1L Albatross was schedule to be picked up for the flight to Patuxent. This aircraft, a triphibian, which has the ability to land on land, sea and snow, has a ski configuration that is rather unique with its main ski extending midway along the keel to be extended or retracted, and with smaller skis mounted on the wing tip floats.

'As I climbed aboard I could not help but notice the 'new' smell of this beautifully appointed airplane' wrote Commander Ward. *'And then to my astonishment, Chief Aviation Pilot Moore said with a yawn, 'like to fly her back? I think you'll like the way she handles.' Like it I did, and upon returning to Home Port, I requested assignment to one of the UF's. This was granted and for the next few weeks I studied and analysed the Flight Operation Charts, Tables, Curves and Diagrams in the Pilots Handbook.'*

During July, Eddie Ward flew the aircraft for over fifty hours, experimenting with cruise control settings in order to determine the maximum range. This was a very complex procedure as the weight of the aircraft, outside air temperature, pressure altitude, fuel flow, manifold pressure and propeller pitch settings [Rpm's], all go into the computations. Many of these flights were made transporting the Admiral and his staff to various contractors' plants. Among those Cdr Ward visited was the DeHavilland plant in Toronto, the Caterpillar Factory in Peoria, Illinois and the Teflon ski manufacturers located in Saginaw, Michigan.

'By September' Commander Ward recalled. *'I had completed test flying the UF and was sure that my cruise control calculations were sound. What remained to be done however, was to fly a simulated flight from New Zealand to McMurdo Sound Antarctica, so for this simulation, we would fly from Patuxent to Bermuda to Jacksonville then back to Patuxent, a distance of 2,350 nautical miles or 2705 statute miles."*

That flight was made on the morning of September 17 1955 when the grossly overweight Albatross waddled down the taxiway toting four large JATO bottles slung around its hull.

Lt.Cdr Charlie Otti, was a mate of Commander Ward and his old shipmate from VX-2 days in Chincoteague and later the General Line School, Monterey and the Bureau of Aeronautics where he was his co-pilot.

'I had requested Charlie for the flight, as he was an outstanding maintenance officer and pilot. Born of Swiss parents, he was meticulous to a fault, so when Charlie pronounced an airplane airworthy, you could literally bet your life on it.

Charlie followed me up with the throttles, as this overburdened Albatross slowly gained momentum. As forty knots indicated, the first two JATO were lit off, although the combined boost of the four bottles was of short duration [about twenty seconds] the acceleration and take-off was nothing less than spectacular. We jettisoned the empty bottles over Chesapeake Bay and continued to climb, levelling off at six thousand feet. Consulting our cruise control charts, power settings were reduced to maximum cruise and we gingerly eyed all the engine instruments for the slightest signs of malfunction. The next five hours would be critical, but after that, we would have burned enough fuel for engine reliability.

To say that our initial progress was slow would be the understatement of the year. By the time we reached Bermuda, some seven hundred and fifty nautical miles distance, we passed the critical first phase of the flight. Air speed picked up, angle of attack decreased and the Albatross started flying like an airplane should, after rounding the pylon at Bermuda we set a course due west for Jacksonville. After reporting our position to the local airways controller, New York cleared the flight to Jacksonville'.

Twelve hours into the flight and in sight of the lights of Jacksonville the crew encountered a solid line of thunderstorms, with the landscape below outlined by intense lightning flashes, giving an eerie indication of the severe weather ahead.

'A band of storms was moving at thirty knots to the east, so it now became a race as to whether or not we could make an end-run around the advancing cold front' recalls Commander Ward.

With the crew approaching Charleston, Flight Service issued a severe weather warning for the city area, of hail and the possibility of tornadoes, severe turbulence and winds gusting to fifty knots, a chilling forecast at best but weather they would encounter in Antarctica within months.

'Soon the race was over. We had lost to an adversary I was about to challenge; but the rotating green and white beacon of the Charleston Air Force Base was a welcome sight. A mile out on the approach, the parallel lights outlining the actual runway were brilliant and inviting, much like a mystical railway track that would lead us home safely. The subdued blue glow of the taxiway markers and the ominous red gleam of the obstruction lights surrounding the field completed the picture. To me, there has always been something terribly fascinating and enchanting about an airport at night.'

The following morning the crew dipsticked the main fuel tank to compare the readings with the cockpit gauges, and they matched perfectly. A quick calculation proved conclusively that the fuel remaining was ample to reach Patuxent River, their projected destination, the flight from Patuxent River to Charleston via Bermuda and Jacksonville had covered 1,960 nautical miles, 2,250 statute, at an average ground speed of 150 knots.

Cdr Ward was now quite sure, barring unfavourable weather, that the UF could make the 2,230 nautical mile flight from Christchurch to McMurdo.

Orders were written, flight crews assigned and the Otters and helicopters were crated for surface transportation to Antarctica, while many of the aircrew personnel would be transported to both McMurdo and Little America by ship.

Due to the limited range of the R4-D's and UF's, Commander Ward recommended they proceed to Christchurch via Seattle, Adak Island in the Aleutians, Midway Island, Hawaii, Canton Island and Fiji, then on to Christchurch, New Zealand.

Finally a training mission of the Otter pilots was a number one priority, as the Otters were scheduled to be shipped out in the middle of October. The Otter was a versatile airplane, which could be rigged with wheels, floats or skis; its large flaps, when fully extended slowed the approach speed to 35-40 knots, thus permitting extremely short field landings. During tests, the flaps were lowered in 15-degree increments, setting the flaps in either the full up or down position without going through increments, caused the nose to pitch up or down violently.

This could result in a stall, or at low altitude a dive into the ground. Squadron doctrine specified the flaps would be raised in increments and trim tabs set accordingly. There was no trick to flying the little plane as it had all the characteristics of a docile old horse. It was however, extremely important that vertical trim tabs be set properly during landing and takeoffs.

Just after these checks were completed, the Squadron received a 'safety of flight' directive from the aircraft's manufacturers, pending DeHavilland's investigations following two fatal Otter crashes in Canada, advising the flap settings were limited to 30 degrees down. Further investigations of the accidents disclosed that a pin linking the flaps to the flap actuator, had broken in flight, thus causing the flaps to retract suddenly from their down position, resulting in an uncontrollable nose up attitude followed by a spin. All Otters were subsequently grounded until the defective pins had been replaced and a slight modification made to the flap assembly.

With the approach of D-Day- November 12 1955- the Air Development Squadron Six –VX-6 aircrews were scheduled to deploy to the Antarctic. Commander Eddie Ward had one more duty to perform, the welcome of an addition to the Ward family, with the big event taking place at Temple Hospital, Philadelphia on November 7, He had requested ten days leave to take his wife Marilyn and their four children back to Philadelphia. On the day of the big event, as the hours passed concern was being felt for both mother and baby daughter.

He was given the news, that his daughter was in an incubator and Marilyn was still feeling unwell from the effects of the anaesthesia, so on their family doctors advise, the commander remained stateside to care for his wife and the five children.

'I called Patuxent from Philadelphia, and the Captain's yeoman answered the phone. As I waited for Gordon, a thousand things went through my mind. In a few seconds, at my request, all that I had thought, dreamed and planned for the past year would vanish. I understood the gravity of the situation, as doctor Beecham had made it clear. I knew my CO Gordon Ebbe would understand, but would my fellow Squadron Officers? Using a wife as an excuse to artfully dodge a hazardous assignment was not unheard of.'

'Hello Ed, Gordon, what's on your mind?'

'Hi Skipper, I have some rather depressing news.'

And his reply was, *'I'll write you a set of orders designating you Officer in Charge of the Patuxent River Detachment, I'm sure the Admiral will have no objections.'*

On November 14- the United States Support Force Antarctica-Task Force '43 sailed from Norfolk and steamed into the deepening night to round Cape Henry and set a southerly course for Panama en route for New Zealand under the command of Rear Admiral George Dufek aboard the flagship *USS Arneb* [AKA-56].

Once the three icebreakers arrived in Antarctica, their first task was to be to explore the pack ice and to verify a landing site at Little America. They would put a 10-man reconnaissance party ashore to begin making a safe trail from Little America Station to the site of the proposed Byrd Station, the second base to be constructed in the first year in Marie Byrd Land through many miles of hard trail over that part of the Ross Sea Ice Shelf and the high Rockefeller Plateau.

At both Little America Station and at McMurdo Sound, the site survey parties would land, their job being to determine the base sites and to evaluate the ice and snow in preparation for where the VX-6 squadron aircraft were to make their landings on December 20 or shortly after. McMurdo Sound is across the entire width of the Ross Shelf from Little America and is bordered on the Victoria Land Coast side by a network of the Mackay and Ferrar glaciers.

From beginning to end, the squadron would be flying ice reconnaissance missions, and would be on high alert at all times to assist any surface party in distress in an air or snow rescue. As a safety measure, the wingtips and tails of each VX-6 plane had been painted a brilliant International Orange for high visibility in the vast white world, to where the aviators were heading.

Cdr B P Wiegand and Lt.Cdr Gus Shinn were both members of Operation High Jump together with Capt William Hawkes. Lt.Col H R Kolp, USMC, VX-6 executive officer, while not familiar with polar regions, did have extensive experience in cold weather air drops in operations in Korea that would prove more than useful to him in his task ahead, and as the lone Marine assigned to the squadron, he had left his old job at MCAS Cherry Point, then spent a month prior to leaving for Antarctica, on the Greenland Ice Cap with the squadron to become acquainted with cold weather.

The squadron had a three-fold mission during Phase One of *Operation Deep Freeze*, with its aircraft lending support to the building of two major bases at Little America and Byrd Station, and also the Air Facilities at McMurdo. In Phase Two, known as Deep Freeze Two, VX-6 planes would support construction of two other bases, and during that time, some 500 tons of material would be air dropped for the Seabees in the construction of a base at the South Pole itself, where three USAF C-124's would undertake the airdrop. The third task of the mission was aerial mapping with the squadron's aircraft flying over unexplored areas of Antarctica.

Beset by terrible storms and hindered by heavy sea, Lt. Charles Wilkes when he reached the continent on January 19 1840, sailed for 1500 miles along the icy barrier, sighting land and making soundings, he wrote. *'I gave it the name of Antarctic Continent.'*

Ulysses, perhaps the greatest of all explorers, has, through Tennyson, laid down rules by which all men of great courage move-

> *'We are not now that strength, which in the old days*
> *Moved earth and heaven; that which we are, we are,*
> *One equal temper of heroic hearts,*
> *Made weak by time and faith, but strong in will*
> *To strive, to seek, to find, and not to yield.'*

With these words ringing in their ears, the aircrews after saying their goodbyes to family and friends climbed aboard their aircraft and readied themselves to fly into the unknown, and aviation history.

The squadrons two P2-V's were piloted by Jack Torbert and Joe Entrikin, the two R4-D's piloted by Gus Shinn and Eddie Frankiewicz, while the Squadron's Executive Officer Hal Kolp and Hank Jorda piloted the R5-D's via the conventional route of Alameda California to Hawaii and then on to New Zealand. The two R4-D's, two P2-V's, two R5-D's and the two UF's, were ready to be picked up and go.

After checking into the officer's mess at the Wigram AFB, Christchurch [N.Z.] the squadron's officers stayed in the city for sixteen days waiting for the big jump to the ice. *'During our short stay, we were able to meet many New Zealanders and to witness their amazing and sincere hospitality'* wrote Cdr James Waldron *'In many ways this was the nicest part of the whole trip, as we found ourselves being stopped in the streets of Christchurch and offered the hospitality in their homes. Everyone wrote down our names and after a day or so we found ourselves deluged with phone calls from our newly acquired friends, offering us options on what we might do with that day's free time. In short, it was impossible to satisfy all the invitations that we received, and we had to disappoint a lot of lovely people every day.'*

One day, only a few hours after arriving in the city, James and Eddie met a local tobacconist while having their last hair cut before heading south, and to the surprise of the aviators, he offered them his automobile for a day trip into the mountains to Hanmer hot springs, so after packing a lunch from a local delicatessen they drove the fifty miles into the mountains to the spa pool resort.

'The waters smelled vile, and it was surprising to me that this beautiful country spot was not visited more frequently, for it seems to me to be one of the most beautiful places I had visited in my military experience. A tourist mecca, Christchurch the jewel of the country, deserves special mention, because it is a distinctive and unique town that appears to be an exact copy of an ancient English village, with a river winding its way through the heart of the city. Both sides of the river are planted with trees, gardens and lawns, where after work, a goodly part of the male workforce gather at local inns to quaff a few beers before heading home. There is good cheer in their voices as the workday unravels and strangers, such as us, were welcomed as friends, certainly not strangers.'

While in Christchurch, the squadron engaged in a number of local flights for the purpose of flight checking the aircraft and radio equipment, making sure everything was working satisfactory, so all was readied for the flight south to Antarctica.

On his arrival at the Wigram Air Force Base, near Christchurch, Commander Ebbe told a press conference that they had left their home base in Maryland on November 14 and had staged to New Zealand via San Francisco, Honolulu, Canton Island, Fiji and Whenuapai, while the Dakotas and Albatrosses had come via the Aleutians, Midway, Honolulu, Canton Island, Fiji and Whenuapai. Admittedly, the flight to the Antarctic would not be a piece of cake, but comprehensive safety organization had been established and he was not worried.

Christchurch City would be the Operations home away from home for the next 44 years until February 20 1998, when the Squadron was disestablished and handed the Antarctic operations over to the USAF New York Air National Guard 109th Air Wing.

During the first week of October the two R4-D's and one of the Neptune's had arrived safely at Wigram Aerodrome, with the rest of the activity at Lyttelton Harbour, Christchurch gathering momentum as the Navy ships were off loading supplies and spare parts for the Christchurch detachment, and taking on fuel and cargo for their long southern journey to Antarctica. Among the cargo being off-loaded were two HO4S-2 helicopters and the four crated DeHavilland Otters, that would eventually make their way south to McMurdo Sound by either USN Icebreakers, or flown south aboard US Air Force C-124 Globemasters. Initially the helicopters would be flown from the Gladstone pier at Lyttleton for a short flight around the harbour and to say 'thanks' to the local Christchurch folk, then head to Wigram for routine maintenance.

Unfortunately, VX-6 suffered their first loss in Christchurch before the squadron even arrived in Antarctica, when a Sikorsky HO4S-3 helicopter BuNo 138519 crashed into Port Lyttelton harbour just after being unloaded from the USNS Greenville Victory [TAK 237].

The pilot 'Judge' Lathrop [Lt Commander Lathrop] a US naval reserve was to take his helicopter up for a test flight. As the news of the port activities broke in the city, it brought hundreds of locals to the port to seek early vantage points to witness the birth of Operation Deep Freeze and as 200 people watched in awe, Lt. Commander Lathrop climbed into the helicopter, his last words being prophetic. 'If anybody is going to get bust I want to be going first, so I won't hurt the passengers'.

He revved the engines and rose a few feet from the deck of the pier where the noise could be heard all over the inner harbour. Residents on the other side of the hill ran into their streets and looked out of windows, but with a limited amount of room available for manoeuvring, Lathrop commenced to turn out towards the inner harbour when a thin wire cable, barely noticeable, caught the tail rotor and snapped it off. In an instant the helicopter went out of control rolling and pitching towards the horrified onlookers.

As the tail of the Sikorsky spun about hitting overhead wires, one of its main rotor blades flew off and knifed over the heads of onlookers to smash into some sheep pens more than 100 yards away. The copter rotated twice and began to fall into the harbour.

A high-ranking naval officer aboard the Task Force's Flagship *Arneb* on the other side of the harbour said, *'There's been a helicopter flop'.*

Had Commander Lathrop stayed still, he could have force landed his helo on the wharf's decking, however, had he done so, there would certainly have been loss of life for those standing close by, prompting the master of a nearby freighter, Captain L Duchowski who was standing on his bridge watching, comment to reporters,

'That young man acted with great presence of mind. On the fantail were several bottles of acetylene and below decks aviation and diesel. If he had gone into the ship and one of those bottles had been cut open-well you know what happens when acetylene gas hit air- poof, and that would sure have been something'.

For a few moments the crashed helicopter floated, then with hundreds watching, Commander Lathrop and airman Frank Hoops of Ohio, a machinist's mate, sank 30 feet to the bottom of the harbour For about 30 seconds the two were beneath the surface and all the horrified onlookers could see, were a few bubbles and an oil slick. A serviceman Donald Cassa of Ohio, from the *USS Greenville Victory*, who had been serving with Commander Lathrop's special detachment, dived overboard to rescue the two airmen who had been stunned from a blow on the back of their heads and were fouled in their shoulder harnesses and life jackets.

Had the pair not been wearing their heavy steel crash helmets, which had large deep dents at the left ear, they would certainly have been killed.

'If he'd been any less qualified, a dozen or more other people would be sliced to pieces. He did a hell of a fine job' said the squadron maintenance officer, Commander R Wiegan.

The pair escaped after a shaking and bruising and swallowing some salt water, and Commander Lathrop recalled to me later that evening, that the tail swung around and he lost control.

'The aircraft was rotating rapidly, and the only thing I tried to do was to get off the docks, so that those people-God, there must have been a couple of hundred, would not get hurt at all. It was a failure of the flight mechanism. The plane had been at sea for a month and had done no flying.'

He later recalled that after he released his safety belt, he attempted to escape through the side hatch. *'I was about to pull the CO2 bottles to inflate my life jacket, when I notice my shoulder harness had become fouled. For a moment I panicked then just as suddenly settled down to methodically locate the problem. I felt the helicopter hit the bottom some thirty feet down! A final effort and I was free. Gasping for air, I pulled both bottles and shot to the surface.'*

Commander Lathrop flew military transports during World War 11 in the Pacific, and afterwards held an executive position with Standard Oil Company in California before venturing into partnership with a wartime aviator friend, flying helicopters in a crop dusting scheme.

After being accredited to the Bar, Commander Lathrop was recalled to active duty on the outbreak of the Korean War. At the time he was a legal advisor on the staff of a Pacific Fleet.

The helicopter destined for use in the Antarctic was destroyed, and the $250,000 machine was taken by road to the RNZAF [Royal New Zealand Air Force] base. The loss of the machine was serious; it represented a third of the Squadron's rotary wing aircraft and was to have been used in Antarctica for ice reconnaissance and search and rescue work.

[Footnote] The helicopter had been stored above decks on the *USS Greenville* Victory, and had not flown since leaving the Panama a month before. As the ship had experienced heavy weather on its voyage to New Zealand, it was thought that the plane may have suffered from salt spray working it's way into the bearings.

CHAPTER THREE.

OFF INTO THE UNKNOWN- THE FROZEN CONTINENT BECKONS

The establishment of the United States Navy Air Development
Six air squadron, for the Antarctic Operations, sets sail for
New Zealand.

History was being made on this cool morning in Lyttelton, New Zealand. It was an historic conference with Rear Admiral George Dufek, the quintessential United States Naval man, making his third trip to Antarctica and officer in charge of the world's most ambitious polar expedition, the commencement of *Operation Deep Freeze,* the American's Antarctic Expedition.

A naval photographer moved about the fluorescent lit red carpeted lower deck to the smoke filled wardroom of Task Force 43's flagship, *USS Arneb,* taking photographs while leaning through the coffee servery, holding his battle worn camera in one hand, his flash in the other, while a tape deck machine recorded the whole briefing.

Thirty Officers sat relaxed with coffee, pipes, cigarettes and cigars, their quiet voices, their questions, their concerns their suggestions. Listening to their first big briefing for the flight to the frozen continent, they heard they were to fly from Harewood and Taieri airports to McMurdo, and this had never been attempted before.

Against this interplay of nasal drawl of the operational conversations, were the hum of the ship's engines, the air-conditioning, the sound of feet on the metal decks above and the drawl of a loud hailer on the docks.

The chief consideration before the Officers was to iron out all bugs of flight communication. They spoke of inexplicable fadeouts in radio communications, of homing beacons that had not homed at two miles out, and of a burnt out armature in a transmitter. Communications between the ships and aircraft had been disappointing.

Dufek insisted that nothing be left to chance and no detail overlooked.

'If necessary we will put all ships at sea today to stage a rehearsal with every aircraft able to fly, just to evaluate the efficiency of communications.'

A voice from the back of the room *'what if a radio fails them?'*

'Then the smallest details must be checked and rechecked' the commander told his officers. *'These communications have to work, as the safety of the flights depends on them.'*

To get rid of all the bugs, the acting commander of VX-6, Lt.Cdr H.R Kolp suggested that all operable aircraft should fly each day at 9am from Monday to Thursday during the next week when the ships would be at sea, and aircraft could try to raise them by radio and perfect their exploration communications systems.

'If they are successful getting in touch with all the ships as is our plan, we will be ready to go as soon as the weather is right.' Kolp said, with the Admiral agreeing.

Eight fixed wing aircraft were to leave New Zealand in two groups around Christmas, perhaps December 23 with JATO take-off from two airfields. It could be made earlier if good weather reports were received from Australia and New Zealand meteorological stations and merchant shipping scattered over several million square miles of the South Pacific Ocean, and from the seven US task force vessels stationed at intervals between New Zealand and Antarctica.

The Royal New Zealand Air Force ordered a Sunderland flying boat to stand by at Bluff, at the bottom of the South Island, from dawn to dusk from December 17 until released. The Sunderland's area of responsibility would be a radius of 750 square miles and the route taken by the planes would be over the stationed ships, which would act as giant homing beacons to guide them.

The long range Neptune's and Skymasters would fly from Harewood, while the shorter ranged R4-D's and Albatrosses would leave from Taieri outside the city of Dunedin. The crew were told that if headwinds were encountered, the R4-D's and UF's, all heavily loaded, would have to turn back to New Zealand or ditch enroute to Antarctica, a sobering thought at best.

The R4-D's left Christchurch on December 15, and included in their cargo were 24 JATO bottles, leaving some of the bottles at Taieri in the event that one or two of the planes got overheated and had to return to the field to take off again, as each bottle has 1000 lbs.of thrust, the equivalent of a 250 horse-powered engine and will rocket for 15 seconds.

The pilot of one of the Albatrosses, whose range was given as 2200- 2400 miles, would have just under 2000 miles to fly, but asked rather anxiously. *'If the Albatross has to go down, I'd like to be sure of refuelling from an ice breaker so we are able to take off again.'*

Admiral Dufek asked whether the point of no return should be the geographical point or if its position should be fixed by the pilot after taking note of their machine's performance and the weather encountered or expected.

Captain William M Hawkes, the squadron's air advisor replied

'The pilot.'

Capt Hawkes, an intrepid and famous polar aviator who was the first flier to take a R4-D off from the flight deck of the aircraft carrier *USS Philippine Sea*, during *Operation High Jump*, rose to his feet and spoke slowly.

'It does not matter if the ship is not in its exact position. If the weather is very reasonable the aircraft can leave without waiting. We do not think there is anything sacred about this, because people are probably not going to be where they think they will be, and we probably will not be where we hope to be. We have no prima donnas who want to wait for the sun to shine' Hawkes concluded, cigar nonchalantly hanging from the corner of his mouth.

The *New York Times* correspondent onboard the icebreaker *USS Glacier,* the advance ship of the United States Antarctic expedition which had left Lyttelton on December 10, reported it had crossed the Antarctic Circle five days later and was directly on the International dateline. He also reported that the ship was only a day's sailing from McMurdo Sound, the proposed landing site for the expedition's aircraft. A message was flashed to Admiral Dufek that the Task Force should take advantage of the breaking pack ice 200-300 miles from McMurdo Sound in the Ross Sea,

The Admiral made the snap decision to sail south, and ordered cancellation of all shore leave, and had all ships and crews be prepared to depart on the Friday.

For the crews, hundreds of 'dates', numerous social functions, including one to which over 2000 had been invited, civic engagements, site-seeing trips, pleasure excursions in the city and liberty leave, were cancelled. The Admiral himself was just about to leave his ship to spend a days fishing at Lake Coleridge, when he receive the report, so he did not take long to make his decision to sail south, ordering all ships ready to sail at 2pm.

Few departures of vessels from the Port of Lyttelton on December 16 could have been as stirring, as the sailing of the main surface group of the US Antarctic expedition, with the four ships sailing within hours of the snap decision.

The quick departure caught many naval crews unaware, with more than 20 men left behind in various parts of New Zealand, as the main fleet of the United States Navy put to sea, even though every effort was made to locate the 'missing' men when the expedition made its completely unexpected decision to sail from Lyttelton.

Police Stations were notified to look out for the American officers and ratings, while radio stations broadcast messages of the impending early departure, and army and navy personnel cruised the streets of Christchurch, while officers spent hours telephoning local folk known to the servicemen.

Two ratings visiting the West Coast of the South Island made a dash by taxi to reach the ship, telephoning to say they were on their way, and arriving just before the gangway was drawn up. A local publican phoned the ship to say he found a member of its crew, but the man was in an alcoholic stupor and refused to go to the vessel. The master of the freighter sent a guard up the hills overlooking the Port of Lyttelton and manhandled the rating, who was still protesting violently.

All the men who missed the ships either had to report to the Christchurch Police or Naval authorities, and were taken into custody by the Royal New Zealand Naval Reserves *Pegasus,* and kept in temporary charge at the shore establishment until a US Icebreaker expected to arrive in the Port of Lyttelton in a few weeks for loading additional oil, and to collect the mail, delivered those latecomers to Antarctica.

As the hour of departure drew near, enlisted men and officers pulled up alongside the ships in hurriedly hired taxis, or piled out of friend's cars while many a local Christchurch girl straightened the knot of a sailor's collar or gently fondle his cap, then stood quietly at the edge of the crowd about them. Amazingly the Antarctic expedition and the 1800 men picked had caught the imagination of the Christchurch people.

Before he left, Admiral Dufek told the story relating to a visit the previous Sunday, to the Chatham Islands, where an islander made him welcome with a bottle of rum. The islander had bitten the cap off the bottle and the Admiral said he was not going to let the local fishermen outsmart him, so he took a bottle of beer and bit the top off that too, but the islander won, as in his actions the admiral had lost a piece from one of his teeth.

Admiral Dufek stood on the flying bridge of the *USS Arneb* as it steamed out slowly from the inner harbour and turned to the open sea for three months of rigorous polar activity, as several thousand Christchurch onlookers cheered from the wharves.

As the flagship drew out, the deep tone hailer was turned up to a deafening amplification and boomed out across the port with the measured words of the speaker reverberating in the surrounding hills.

'The officer commanding Task Force 43, Rear Admiral George Dufek, gives the following message. - We thank you for the warmth of your welcome and the gracious manner in which you have opened your homeland to us. We have a warm spot in our hearts for you, a merry Christmas, and God bless each one of you'.

First away from Gladstone pier was the white painted Coast Guard icebreaker *USS Eastwind,* which cast off from its moorings alongside the freighter *USS Greenville Victory,* a few minutes after midday. Down the harbour near the heads, it hooked on to a gasoline barge, which it towed to McMurdo for the refuelling of the aircraft there.

The cargo ship *Wyandot* left amid the hooting sirens of the ships berthed nearby, and with crackers exploding all around, followed the cargo vessel *Doric.*

A long streamer was handed down aft to an onlooker and up floated a big white meteorological balloon painted with a brief message to the hundreds standing nearby. *'Sincere thanks to the people of New Zealand'.*

The New Zealand Prime Minister Mr. Sidney Holland in a message to Rear Admiral George Dufek wrote:

'We feel it an honour that New Zealanders are associated with your expedition and that we as a nation can co-operate with our American friends in such a notable venture. I am sure that your visit to New Zealand will have strengthened even further the ties which bind our two countries together,

and I can assure you that we are looking forward very much, to extending a welcome to you again on your return from the Antarctic'.

The Mayor of Dunedin Mr. L.M. Wright paid a sincere tribute to the 20 US Navy officers at a mayoral reception prior to the departure of the R4-D's and Albatrosses.

'We are welcoming a band of courageous men who are also representatives of a wonderful country.'

In reply the Commander of the Taieri base group. Lt.Commander Ben Sparks said that *'The aircraft did not normally take-off from grass fields with such a heavy load, but with the help of Jet Assisted take-off, the feat should be achieved, and God willing, we will reach their destination of 2035 miles away soon'.*

Others in the group from Dunedin were Lt. Commander Gus Shinn, a Dakota pilot who was to make Antarctic aviation history the following year.

Eddie Frankiewicz recalled the days before taking off from Taieri for Antarctica, *'Soon after arriving at Taieri, we had to familiarize ourselves with the essentials of the airfield that was a sod field but firm. Runway 03-21 was about 5000 feet long; the other was 4,000 feet. For use, only runway 21 was useable because the other had hills within three miles which would necessitate a steep turn with a grossly weighted aircraft.*

Hugh Skilling, the Chief Instructor of the Otago Aero Club, put on a superior aerobatics display flying a biplane Tiger Moth to welcome us, while Wing Commander J J O'Brien, gave us all the assistance and advice needed to operate on such a small airfield.

On the Wednesday before our proposed flight south, I flew to Invercargill with Hugh Skilling and a Wellington building contractor, Mr. Williamson, who was most interested in our plans for Antarctica. When we departed he gave us a large crate of live lobsters for that evening's dinner at the Officers mess at Taieri- a tremendously enjoyable culinary treat, Oh you wonderful Kiwis!

That night we had our press conference and weather briefing for the big flight next morning. Mr. Brown, the local meteorologist predicted unfavourable headwinds- how right he was.

The night we arrived at Taieri, we were welcomed by the RNZAF officers and their wives and had an excellent dinner at the Officer's Mess. The following day we received a civil reception by the Mayor of Dunedin, Leonard Wright, and on the Saturday evening we were invited to the Otago Flying Club's annual Christmas dinner.'

When the *Glacier* arrived at McMurdo on December 18, the amount of bay ice was disappointing in that it extended 5 miles north of Cape Byrd, so an airstrip was laid out on firm ice about 30 miles south of open water, and a tent city was hurriedly thrown up at Hut Point to accommodate the VX6 crews.

On December 19 the *Edisto* arrived at McMurdo and the *Glacier* ordered her plane guard station near Cape Adare, so before the day was out, everything was ready at the McMurdo terminus for the Squadron's fly in by December 20 with all vessels on station.

As the VX-6 aviators waited in both cities for their departure for Antarctica, their thoughts were on the first Antarctic summer. The temperature of the water, over which they would fly, would be about 28 degrees Fahrenheit; making it a chilly place to ditch an aircraft, where life expectancy would be short, even with exposure clothing.

It is impossible to describe the Antarctic flight conditions let alone a whiteout, to someone who has never seen or flown in one. Imagine how these aviators felt as they waited to leave New Zealand, knowing they could be flying in good conditions one minute, but then could suddenly find themselves without visual reference points the next.

A whiteout occurs when the light rays penetrate cloud cover then reflect off the snow and ice. This diffused light bounces back and forth until the horizon blends with sky and surface, but there is no surface, no skyline, no horizon definition, therefore the body system becomes confused and the pilot's ability to judge height and distance is lost.

People on the ground, if faced with this situation, will stumble and fall while aviators will fly their aircraft into the ground.

Another problem is that a radio altimeter can be off by as much as 60 feet over loosely packed snow; thereby the pilot can make mistakes involving hundreds of feet. Glaring sunrays reflected from undisturbed snow and ice can blind the pilot momentary, so he must take due caution least his flight ends up like so many, a crumpled monument in the wastelands of Antarctica. To the inexperienced Antarctic pilots, landing on the frozen continent may well appear deceptively simple but this could be his undoing.

The crews were told that smoke flares were the only safe method of determining wind over landmass, and that the pilot must always be prepared for an erratic wind shift.

Waiting at Christchurch for the historic flight south, were two R4D-6's, two [DC-4's] R5D's, two Neptune's [P2V-7], two Albatrosses [UF-1L] while all the ships of the task force were at sea. The US Icebreakers *Glacier* [GB-4] and the *Edisto* [WPB-1313] were steaming towards McMurdo Sounds. The US Naval cargo ships *Arneb* [AKA-56] *Wyandot,* [AKA-92 her hull number changed in 1969 to AK 283] the *Greenville Victory* [AK 237] and the tanker *Nespelen* [AKA-55] had left to precede to Ocean stations, while the Coast Guard *Eastwind* [WAGB-279] towed the YOG 34 with her load of fuel to McMudo.

Admiral George Dufek, was leading an armada of seven ships and 1850 men to establish an airfield and operational base at McMurdo Sound. With ship ocean stations starting from New Zealand, spaced every 250 miles along meridian 170-degree east, being the path guide for the aircraft leaving Christchurch for their historic flight south.

As the Flagship *Arneb* approached her ocean station on December 19, Dufek received word from Captain Ketchum that the ice runway at McMurdo was "*A-OK*" for receiving the aircraft. The helicopters and the Canadian UC-1 DeHavilland Otters were delivered to McMurdo, Little America, Little America V, and to Wilkes Station by ships across the Weddell Sea.

Captain Ketchum aboard the *USS Glacier* told the Admiral that they had broken through the Ross Sea pack ice and were standing by to escort the cargo ships to McMurdo Sound. The Admiral radioed Christchurch to advise that the squadron take the following day off, instructing all crews to '*make last minute adjustments and preparation, and write that last letters home, then get ready for your appointment with destiny. Good luck chaps, see you at McMurdo.*'

Dufek issued a three-word command '*Launch all aircraft*' which set in motion the final New Zealand stage of the United States *Operation Deep Freeze 1.*

December 20th 1955 was an historic day as at 4am the first to leave were the VX-6 Squadron's Neptune's P2V-2N *BuNo 122465*, followed by the four engine R5-D's Skymaster *BuNo 56505* and *BuNo 56528* leaving Wigram Air Force Base, NZ on the 2,100 non-stop, nautical mile flight to Little America, Antarctica. VX-6 Squadron's *Ice Pirates* or *Puckered Penguins* [as the crews were to become known] were ready, with VX-6 aircraft carrying side numbers XD- [X-ray Dog]

The night before departure was more than a little apprehensive for the aviators stationed at the RNZAF Station at Taieri. One airman in a broad accent and with the trace of a smile admitted that the impending flight would not be all beer and skittles once the point of no return had been passed at approximately 1,000 miles south of Taieri. '*Everything is in God's hands. If the weather should come up nasty down there, they would have to press on and pray that they could land. Maybe, we could even land on rough ice, certainly the undercarriage would be ripped off, but we should be able to walk away.*'

While out on the tarmac, in the glow of arc lamps, final mechanical checks were being made, while inside the Mess, there was a rather subdued air of apprehension. With one or two of the officers, it was understandably a case of final night nerves and who could blame them? Hands clenched firmly around their glasses, they walked from group to group in the room filled with cigar smoke, passing the odd word, but quite obviously preoccupied with the job ahead.

The officer's mess scene was almost reminiscent of the night before a major wartime bombing mission, as Navy aviators mingled with a few RNZAF officers on duty, quietly chatting.

One spoke of conditions way back in the states, another was worried about getting all his gear aboard the small aircraft. By 11pm they had all retired after writing final letters to their families, most telling of the warm hospitality accorded them during their brief stay in New Zealand. While two happier souls waited until 10pm to enjoy a quick cup of coffee and biscuit before going to bed, another was anxiously checking to ensure that the clock alarm would call him at 4am.

Cdr Eddie Frankiewicz and his co-pilot Lt.Cdr Harvey Speed had taken a R4-D up to Greenland in preparation for this journey south into the unknown, making a number of touch and go landings at 10,000 feet, while Cdr Eddie Ward, the squadron's acting CO for Deep Freeze, was to stay back home, thus handing command over to Cdr Gordon Ebbe, who had put the Albatross to the test in September with Lt Charlie Otti. But still there were worries.

It was just before 4am when the station sprang into life in a scene that suggested a wartime operational airfield, the VX-6 pilots and aircrew wakened from their last sleep in civilization for many months, washed and shaved and trooped in for an early breakfast and a 5.30 am briefing, before standing about on the tarmac smoking and chatting with small groups of friends they had made in the few days they had been on base.

Then came the important stage of the pre take off period, pilots and their navigators crowded into the small operation room for a minute briefing by Mr M Browne, a resident meteorological forecaster at Taieri, with charts compiled from information radioed from the Antarctic regions and other points between. It wasn't a particularly happy story he told the group. A light tail wind for the first stage of their journey south and then cross winds and finally on the all important final stage to McMurdo it was head winds.

The grim look on the pilots' faces showed that they appreciated in full, the implications of this information. Even under the most favourable conditions it could prove hazardous, as with headwinds tossed into the mix on the last leg it could more than likely be disastrous, but no one mentioned that. A final briefing on the route and then the navigators had to work out their intricate calculations for the fifteen plus, hour flight.

One Albatross pilot gave his maximum flying endurance as 15 hours, which would make his tanks completely dry, and estimated that he would cover the distance in 15 hours and 6 minutes. That extra six minutes naturally had him more than worried, given the head wind predictions, but he wasn't saying much. At the end of his journey he would somehow provide the answers to this problem.

One airman was wearing on his flying jacket a greenstone Maori tiki, which he proudly displayed to a fellow airman from another machine, saying it was his good luck charm. The reply was simple. *'My good luck charm is a case of champagne. I guess I'll be the first man to fly to the South Pole sitting on champagne.'*

All had donned their survival suits, made up of an under suit of insulated padded nylon and a top suit of rubberised silks. One pilot had only donned his undersuit.

Asked by a reporter *'Why?'* he replied

'Brother, if we don't clear those bloody trees', pointing to a belt of trees beyond the southern boundary of the airfield, *'then I don't want to be hampered by no survival suit when I'm getting out. I want to survive.'*

All the aircrews were in good spirits, but the underlying tenseness of the situation was easy to discern. These aviators, all volunteers, were about to make a perilous flight and they realized the dangers, so with last farewells not too drawn out, Lt Commander Ben Sparks strode from the operations rooms towards his machine calling to the other pilots on the tarmac. *'Okay fellers, let's go!'*

Now the aircraft with engines idling, lined up on the perimeter of the airfield, then at 6.45 am the Albatross, piloted by Lt Cdr. Ben Sparks, leader of the fleet's slow contingent, started up with billows of smoke from her engines. With his American drawl coming clearly over the radio, he called the control tower for permission to take off.

This given, the engine roared as Sparks opened the throttle and the huge aircraft moved slowly across the grass runway. Within seconds the four JATO lifted the machine into the air, a whining roar reverberating through the still morning, with flames pouring out from the aircraft for several seconds, followed by huge billows of white and black smoke.

The first takeoff was always a tense moment, as anything could have gone wrong, but nothing did, and two minutes later the first R4-D piloted by Lt. Commander Gus Shinn, taxied across the grass field and another aircraft was on her way to Antarctica. Another Dakota, piloted by Lt. Commander Frank Frankiewicz, who had a reputation of hauling her off the deck after a short run, lived up to his reputation that morning. Spectators gasped when they saw his R4-D become airborne without the use of JATO, but when it was obvious she still needed them at about 15 feet up, he fired to give him the required extra lift, and as the mauve flames shot out he was up up and away.

At 6.58am when Lt Commander R E Graham, the pilot of the last Albatross was due to take off, a message came through to the control tower from Lt Commander Ben Sparks reporting that at 3,500 ft, he was breaking through the cloud bank and was at that stage out over the sea. Graham took the longest runway of all the aircraft, but even then did not have to make use of it all, such was the excellence of the JATO thrust.

Flashing through many pilot's minds as their R4-D and 5's left New Zealand, creeping forward at about 200 feet per minute, must have had them wondering what was awaiting them in Antarctica. Getting the *Gooney Bird* off some unprepared ice in minus 85 degrees on remote locations with no runways, no boundary markers and no signals telling them where to land on ice surfaces that have been roughened by winds producing sastrugi, in the loneliest place in the world was mind boggling. Would the engines fail or would the skis freeze to the surface, would their landing gear survive the icy terrain?

As the take-offs had been routine the aircraft flew low the first few hundred miles to conserve fuel, until reaching the bottom of New Zealand, then they began to climb just before passing over the *Greenville Victory* at Station 'Able', halfway into the flight. The armada now encountered 20-knot headwinds, which caused them to consume fuel at an unacceptable rate, so it soon became evident that the Gooney Birds and Albatrosses were in serious trouble .To make the journey successfully, these aircraft needed to maintain an average ground speed of 115 knots, but with such head winds, the aircraft reported achieving only 105 knots.

In Christchurch it was pitch dark and still two hours to dawn, when the aircrews, after just two hours sleep, left their RNZAF's Wigram Station quarters, and after a midnight breakfast they drove through the gates of Christchurch Airport where 150 Christchurch folk, had gathered in the chilly overcast early morning, along the east side of the field to see the last preparations made for the flight, which would, for the first time directly link a temperate land with the Polar Regions.

The Neptune piloted by Lt. Commander Jack Torbert, after a false start, led the long-range aircraft off on their flight south at 4.59am, concern showing on the faces of the Navy officers watching, as Lt. Commander Torbert's P2V Neptune #*124466,* throttled back after taxing two thirds of the runway. He coasted down his taxing speed and requested from the control tower to return to the head of the runway for another attempt, which was granted.

A stream of blue smoke pouring from his port engine, drew Torbert's attention as the Neptune taxied back, however, after a further run-up on his brakes, he told the Tower he was ready to go. Just before take-off a defect had been located in the cabin's heating system, but once more the throttles were opened and the Neptune, loaded down to the last ounce with fuel and equipment, began to again pound heavily along the north-south runway, firing the JATO bottles, for this time the pilot was committed to take-off.

Quite abruptly, just beyond the point of its first throttling back, the vents on the lower set of bottles flamed, and like a fire spurting through dry tussock, the upper three vents flickered in turn as Jack Torbert selected his switches and set alight the complete bank of power. A brilliant and spectacular flame six feet long illuminated the Christchurch dawn sky like the 4th of July, searing back from the four parallel bars of scarlet as the jets came into full play.

The nose rose in the clear air above the roar of the twin piston engines, a vast billowing exhaust of white smoke poured out behind as the aircraft gathered speed with the jets still burning fiercely, and left the ground, climbing to 300 feet when the jets cut out with a burst of black smoke. The Neptune appeared to sink momentarily, and then it was steady on its flight to the packed ice at McMurdo.

Due to pressure by Admiral Dufek, Captain Trigger Hawkes joined Jack Torbert's crew as co-pilot in the P2-V. This move effectively cut the Squadron Commanding Officer Cdr Gordon Ebbe out of the pattern, and to make matters worse Cdr.Eddie Ward had to travel to McMurdo as a passenger aboard the *USS Glacier*. In a most subtle way, Admiral Dufek accomplished in the Antarctic what he had failed to do in Washington, and now his protégé Trigger Hawkes was the de facto VX-6 commander.

The second Neptune *# 142465* [Cdr Entrikin] was off the ground at Harewood at 5.14am and the two R5-D Skymasters *# 56505* and *# 56528* piloted by Cdr Jorda went at 8.15 am and 8.33am and a few minutes after taking off, the voice of Lt. Commander Jack Torbert crackled over the radiotelephone in the control tower with the message.

'I am on course for Antarctica.'

Lt Commander H R Kolp, captained the first Skymaster, *#56505* that with the assistance of six booster rockets took only 250 feet, shorter than the 4000 feet needed for the heavily loaded Neptunes, eighteen minutes later the second skymaster was airborne.

The pilot of one of the R4D-5 *BuNo 142460] Korora II* Lt. Gus Shinn got a radar check on the *Nespelen* at station 'Charlie', then he reported:

'STRONG HEADWINDS-DON'T THINK WE CAN MAKE IT TO MCMURDO.REQUEST PERMISSION TO CONTINUE AND IN EMERGENCY CRASH-LAND ON CAPE ADARE'.

Cape Adare is a headland of Victoria Land, 270 miles north of the ice landing strip at McMurdo. It is rough and rugged, surrounded by turbulent water and the ice of the Ross Sea, with no landing strip, not even a flat area of ice. The pilots had courageously proposed making an emergency landing here short of McMurdo, and while the Task Force Commander admired their determination, the expeditionary timetable was too tight to lose precious time, even days, in calculated search and rescue operations, and with strong headwinds and their gasoline dwindling at an alarming rate, it was obvious, though disappointing, that they would not make McMurdo.

Dufek refused to accept the high percentage of risk involved to the aircraft and their crews, so ordered them back. The R4-D5 and UC-1 pilots were far from happy, returning to Dunedin under protest a few meagre miles short of the point of no return. Had they continued, they would have ditched in the icy Antarctic water 250 miles short of McMurdo, to almost certain death. The aircraft had been airborne for just under fourteen hours by the time they touched back down in New Zealand.

So in the face of increasingly adverse winds, which threatened their safety, the four Albatrosses and R4-D's turned back, arriving at Taieri, and landing safely between 5.49 and 8.35 that evening as dusk was falling and a flare path was lit to guide the aircraft safely home.

The scene at Taieri as the two Albatrosses touched down was one of extreme contrast to that earlier in the day. The aircraft captain, Commander Graham payed a tribute to Mr M L Browne the resident forecaster at the airfield. *'You are the best forecaster we have known'.* Mr Browne who passed on official weather forecasts compiled from information radioed from the Antarctic region, had been asked at the final crew briefing at 5.30am that morning, for his personnel opinion, and had advised against attempting the long flight, but to wait further forecasts at least until noon.

Commander Spark told reporters that had they continued on to McMurdo, they would have fallen 200-300 miles short of their destination as the head winds did not assist them as expected, so Mr Browne's predictions were absolutely correct.

Lt Commander Graham said *'that as they turned back, the squadron's Grumman Albatross's were within range of the emergency landing strip at Cape Adare in the Ross Sea, while another crew member was heard to mumble, 'Yeah, emergency strip! There was no strip there, sure we would have landed, – crash-landed'.*

Still dressed in their spacemen like survival suits, Lt Commander Graham and his crew soon rid themselves of this cumbersome clothing when they arrived back at Taieri as the boys were *'too hot stuffed up in these suits'.*

At ten past eight, the first R4-D was sighted returning from its long trip, it roared in from the hills behind Taieri with all its navigation lights blinking making a low swoop over the airfield as its tired crew safely landed the aircraft.

Crews of both the Dakotas were fairly confident they could have made it to the ice, although one said that weather conditions ahead might not have been so good, as they approached McMurdo.

The two twin engine aircraft had reached 57 degrees south, about 850 miles south of New Zealand and were forced to retrace their course as they had just six hours fuel left when they landed back at Taieri on December 20. Orders to launch the aircraft in December from both Christchurch and Dunedin, was given in the face of adverse advice to the contrary by the New Zealand meteorological service. Due to the speed of a high-pressure ridge approaching the New Zealand Antarctica flight path from the west, the United States task force meteorological team aboard the Flagship *Arneb* sadly miscalculated them.

The strong head winds that the meteorological team aboard the flagship thought would have passed over the intended flight path by Tuesday, were slower to pass than expected. When weather arrangements for the flights were being worked out, it was decided to forward all information to the New Zealand meteorologists who would have the responsibility of advising on the day of each flight, but later the arrangements were altered and the Task Force decided that the *Arneb* would have the final say.

Later the Task Force expressed a message of congratulations for the work done by radio stations in New Zealand in assisting the expedition to the Antarctic.

'Please express my thanks to the much appreciated communications organization which has co-operated so outstandingly in assisting our communications network,' said Commander Charles Snay, United States Navy Staff communication officer for *Operation Deep Freeze.*

Back at Taieri *Operation Deep Freeze* and the crews of the four aircraft who had to abandon their long dangerous 14-hour flight to McMurdo were mighty glad to be back, but there was still the question as when to attempt a further bid to reach Antarctica.

The idea of getting the two Albatrosses to the ice were soon abandoned, while plans were made to fly the two R4-D's south in the second week in January. By January 4th the Navy had established a new emergency landing strip and fuel cache at Cape Adare, which would provide safety for the two Dakotas to reach the Antarctic on their attempt on January 24. Cape Adare is 400 miles from McMurdo and would reduce the maximum compulsory distance from New Zealand.

The Task Force planned the attempt to time with a voyage north to New Zealand by the Icebreaker *Glacier* and three other vessels, the icebreakers *Edisto* and *Eastwind* and the cargo assault ship *Greenville Victory* would also form a chain of homing beacons for guiding the aircraft south.

The R4-D's were urgently wanted for transport purposes in the Antarctic, so it was imperative to have the aircraft for the operation's success and to maintain the Task Force's programme.

The two Albatrosses were to remain on the ground in New Zealand unless they were required for rescue, so it was decided 'one way or another' to return the aircraft to Wigram to await further instructions, for it was certain they would not go to Antarctica, but would remain in New Zealand and go back to the States.

By January 23, it was increasingly unlikely the Dakotas would make another attempt to fly south, as it was assumed by the command that such a flight so late in the season would just tie up the ships. The same day the *New York Times* correspondent Bernard Kalb's despatch from Antarctica was that Admiral George Dufek advised that, due to the risk of the ice runway at McMurdo Sound breaking up, the planes on the ice would return to New Zealand, which subsequently spelt the end for the R4-D's getting to the ice for *Deep Freeze 1*.

The aircraft returned to Christchurch on January 24, bringing with them the spare JATO bottles, which were placed in the RNZAF's bomb store at Wigram. Both Lt. Commander Shinn and Frankiewicz flew the R4-D's back to their Maryland Base at Patuxent.

The first aircraft to land on the ice at McMurdo on December 20 was Lt. Commander Joseph Entrikin's Neptune *BuNo 122465*. He remarked as he stepped out onto the ice, *'It's the most miserable flight I ever made'*. *'Routine'* said Commander Henry Jorda, as he stepped out from his Skymaster *BuNo 56528*, with duffel bag in hand. *'We're the first in history to land aircraft on wheels in the Antarctic from land outside Antarctica. Pan American can now start their schedules to the Antarctic'*.

The surface snow on the airfield was two inches deep with patches up to five inches with very hard ice, so before landing, the crews were informed that the ice was more than seven feet thick, with a wind force of 20 knots to the east. The ice at the bay was smooth for miles with occasional six to twelve inch pressure ridges.

The plane crews had been led to expect austere living conditions on their arrival, and they weren't disappointed, as the crews unloaded their survival tents from the aircraft and pitched them on the ice, stacking blocks of ice around the bottom to keep the cold Antarctic wind out, while others lived in their aircraft until the surface ships arrived.

Unfortunately the epic flight evoked a few hard feelings. The two Neptune's were first to arrive, and both had plenty of fuel in reserve in spite of the severe icing encountered en-route and the thirty-knot headwinds, to find the weather conditions at McMurdo ideal.

This prompted Capt Hawkes to order Lt.Cdr Jack Torbert the plane commander, to fly a reconnaissance mission along the Royal Society Range, but on hearing that order, Lt.Cdr Joe Entrikin, the plane commander of the other P2V, after reporting his arrival to McMurdo, and receiving Hawke's order for him to fly a reconnaissance mission along the Ross Sea Ice Shelf, said that as far as he was concerned he had completed his bloody flight, and promptly landed.

This established Joe Entrikin and his crew in the record books as the first aircraft to land after flying non stop between New Zealand and Antarctica.

With the safe arrival of the four aircraft, the Task Force's ships left their ocean stations, returning to McMurdo, while an Otter and the HO4S-3's from the icebreakers were sent out to conduct ice reconnaissance and to locate a site for the Operation's base camp.

That night the pilots and crews were quartered aboard the Icebreaker *USS Edisto* and the following day they moved onto the Ross Sea at Hut Point, where they lived in tents for their duration, similar to the VX-6 aviator's experiences of Antarctica in 1947. Luckily they too had trained for the harsh conditions of the Antarctic, as on reaching the continent after the flight from New Zealand, the aviators had to survive in tents and huddle in their aircraft in -38 degrees to await the arrival of the ships.

An aviation fuel supply depot was built, and included in this were all the aviation stores, parts of which were some 6,500 barrels of fuel that had to be handled in the sub zero conditions, four barrels at a time. All cargo, including fuel when off-loaded from the supply ships was a double handling operation, with the icebreakers alternating taking loads from the AK's, then proceeding down the channel they had just broken through in the pack ice. They were then off loaded onto waiting sleds, which were pulled over the torturous flagged trail, across the bay ice to the camp, or supply dumps. These operations were continuos around the clock for over a month, before the last of the cargo was hauled to the supply dumps, which covered about 90 acres and contained some 10,000 pounds of stores.

During this time, the harsh Antarctic weather and the continuous operations had the personnel plagued by machinery breakdowns. Some equipment didn't last a day so subsequently all through the operations it caused a Herculean task for the garage mechanics. Known as the *Home for Broken Down Cats,* one of the first buildings to be constructed was in the charge of C M Slaton CMC. It was manned by mechanics, steelworkers, aerographers and air control men who were kept busy all during the Antarctic winter maintaining 35 pieces of huge equipment, from tractors and bulldozers to weasels and 20-ton sleds.

A few days later on December 22, while engaged in reconnaissance operations, the squadron Otter *BuNo 142424* crashed on take off near Cape Byrd, Ross Sea, when Lt [jg] Hoffman, a rather chubby yet good natured Dutchman from up state Pennsylvania, was assigned to fly ten passengers from McMurdo to a Navy ship on the edge of the ice, a distance of around six miles.

One of the passengers that day was Captain William Hawkes and as they were boarding the aircraft, Hawkes pulled rank and told Hoffman that he would do the flying, and so saying climbed into the left hand seat. Thinking he was qualified in this type of aircraft, Hoffman slid into the co-pilot seat, then just before takeoff, the Squadron Maintenance Officer, Commander George Oliver, a close friend of Hawkes came forward and crouched between the pilot and co-pilot, presumably for a better view of the area. As Hoffman took over the co-pilot duties and commenced to call the pre takeoff checklist, Hawkes replied in the affirmative and was cleared for take off. They started down the ice runway, but just after take off, the Otter's skis brushed the snow, making the aircraft hit the ground hard and flat, thus forcing both main ski struts into the fuselage.

It didn't take long for one and all to realize that something was very wrong, as the plane abruptly nosed up, gained about fifty feet altitude when the pilot, Commander Hawke called '*I can't hold it*', and just before it spun in, Hoffman cut the power. The plane dropped in a flat attitude hitting the ice with such force it was a total loss.

At 1500 hrs when the rescue aircraft Neptune, flown by Lt.Cdr John Torbert received word of the crash, he made immediate preparations to evacuate the crash survivors, even though he was low on fuel. All moveable gear was removed from the nose well and aft section of the P2V to make room for the injured, and they were then able to lift the injured men through a newly created entrance.

Some of the survivors were so badly injured that the only possible loading procedure to get them inside the Neptune bomber was to lift the stretchers into the station via the tunnel hatch, then go over the auxiliary power unit to the rear section of the P2V.

Another problem hampering the rescue operations was that the nearest medical facilities were aboard the icebreaker *Edisto* that was escorting ships through the pack ice into McMurdo Sounds. With no ships present, now having left their stations, the nearest ship *Edisto*, was already steaming north to assist and escort the Task Forces supply ships through the pack ice and was 300 miles to the north of McMurdo. After several attempts to contact the *Edisto* or radio Auckland for medical aid, Auckland finally answered the 'SOS', but could not read the voice transmission from McMurdo. Earlier attempts to call New Zealand failed due to atmospheric conditions which garbled radio transmission, but the communication problems were solved a short time later when Lt.Cdr Hank Jorda's R-5D, with less than 90 minutes fuel aboard, was ordered to take off and transmit the messages by CW. Climbing to 10,000ft Lt.Commander Jorda's radio operator got a Roger from Radio Auckland, who in turn relayed the message to Radio Honolulu where it was broadcast to the *Edisto* still pounding her way through the pack ice. Two hours after the message was sent from the R5-D, the *Edisto* had revised her course and was racing back to McMurdo Sound with medical assistance aboard.

Meanwhile back at the base tent camp at Hut Point, a blizzard had blown up with gale force winds, collapsing the tents around the injured, and for twenty minutes they were buried under snow. Their comrades set it right by placing a few stoves in the sick bay, where the injured servicemen were given morphine, and what good food was available. The remainder of the party lived in their tents with no heaters and subsisted on C rations until the *Edisto* returned. At that time most of the tents lacked stoves, and with the temperature always hovering around low freezing and food strictly rationed, to say life was miserable would be an understatement.

While there were no fatalities, one of the passengers Cdr George Oliver the squadron's engineering maintenance officer, suffered a fractured left knee cap and a fracture to his lower right leg. He was flown back to Christchurch on January 16, after the pilot was forced to return to the base for fuel, but finally made it on his second attempt, and Cdr. Oliver was flown back to Christchurch for specialist treatment, making this the first medical evacuation flight in Antarctic history.

In a letter to the commanding officer of VX-6 Commander Ebbe, Capt Hawkes reported that he had noticed something wrong with the controls on take-off. They felt 'spongy' and could not be moved forward of the neutral position. About 50 feet after take off, the Otter's skis brushed the snow and the airplane hit hard, forcing both main struts into the fuselage to such an extent that the aircraft was a strike [a strike occurs when an aircraft is sufficiently damage to be removed from the Navy inventory.]

Cdr.Gordon Ebbe ordered an immediate Accident Investigation. This was a very comprehensive inquiry consisting of photographs, sworn statements from witnesses and a meticulous examination of the aircraft engine and airframe, and last but not least, the qualifications of the pilot and co-pilot. Appointing Commander Eddie Ward as a senior member of the investigation team, the initial investigation disclosed that Lt Hoffman was qualified in all respects, while Captain William Hawkes was not. Clearly it was one hundred percent pilot error, and this led to a further disturbing revelation that there was some doubt as to Hawkes qualifications as a P2V co-pilot.

After due deliberation it was the unanimous opinion of the Board of Inquiry, that the cause of the accident was pilot error on the part of Captain Hawkes and Gordon Ebbe as the Squadron Commanding Officer concurred in the Board's findings, signed the report, and forwarded it to the Chief of Naval Operations. Relationships between both Admiral Dufek and Captain Hawkes, was less than cordial from that time on.

On December 23 Rear Admiral Dufek, took Capt Thomas and Cdr. Frazier with him to act as fleet ice pilots when he shifted his flagship from *Arneb* to *Glacier*.

As their friends and families settled down to Christchurch life at the bottom of the world, it was Christmas week with a difference, but unlike those back home, the men of VX-6 were in serious top gear, as these dedicated men faced many hard tasks in the cold, with limited time in which to achieved their objectives.

When the *USS Edisto* steamed into McMurdo Sound on December 20, carrying the advance party of *Task Force 43,* it was assigned to a mission most of us would never imagine. It was the first task of the Seabees and a detachment of VX-6 to build an Air Operation Facility at McMurdo Sound with a runway capable of accommodating the large cargo C-124 Globemasters of the United States Air Force, scheduled to arrive in October 1956.

As soon as the supply ships arrived they broke out the equipment, repaired that which was broke en route, and were thus working 24 hours a day, seven days a week. They were also to winter over in the Antarctic while accomplishing their assigned tasks. Hut Point at the lower tip of Ross Island was selected as the air facility site, with this location playing an important role in Antarctic exploration. It was here in 1902-04, that Capt Robert Scott's party erected their hut, still standing today in perfect condition, thus given its name 'Hut Point'. Here, MCB personnel set about their task of establishing a tent city around Scott's Hut and for the first time they experienced life in sub zero temperatures.

Almost as soon as they stepped ashore on Christmas Eve 1955, the men of MCB set about their task with urgency as October 1956 was their deadline for the completion of the McMurdo runway, but on Christmas Day 1955 that seemed a long way away. Day after day they toiled, and as the weeks began to tick away with disturbing rapidity, so the darkness was setting in, but the cold Antarctic winter didn't disrupt their mission, as their unmoveable deadline was to have a 6000 ft runway to handle a Globemaster by October 20.

Initially plans conceived in Washington called for a runway to be constructed of compacted snow, so experiments were carried out until mid July on snow compaction, but then a setback, as the results were not satisfactory for the giant Douglas C-124 cargo plane to operate on.

It was now back to the drawing board, so on July 20 plan B went into action to remove six feet of snow from the 6,000-foot strip of bay ice. This change meant a greater work effort and called for a twenty-four hour seven-day working week, with temperatures now at minus 65F and an equal wind chill factor for the wintering over party, including VX-6 members, to contend with. After what seemed like an unbelievable 100,000 man-hours, the strip was completed, with water flooding smoothing off the surface.

But just as the men were rejoicing in their success a massive Antarctic blizzard dumped five feet of snow on the runway, eradicating several weeks' work, in a few days. This left the Task Force command with no alternative but for the now exhausted men to begin to construct another air strip, and as if by some superhuman effort, a 5,000 foot strip was ready for the proposed October 20th fly-in for the squadron's R4-D's. Another 1000 feet was added by the end of October with only a few hours to spare before the Globemasters arrived to land on the only runway in Antarctic that handled wheeled landings.

In addition to those men working on the airstrip, there were many more who must be credited for the successful completion of the difficult task they accomplished as all the radio operators, aerologists, GCA men, the overworked chaplain, and in fact the entire group on the ice, worked at it. These men were faced with discomfort, boredom, loneliness and danger, but every one of the 93 naval personnel had, through his individual and team efforts, contributed to the future exploration of the continent.

In addition to this task, the men of the MCB working alongside VX-6 personnel, constructed the camps, packed material and equipment in readiness for the proposed South Pole landing for October 31 1956, while establishing the Beardmore Auxiliary Base, which was located midway between Williams Field and the Pole at the base of the Beardmore, the world's largest glacier. That base would serve as a refuelling site and air navigational air centre, and was run by Lt N Eichorn and his eight man crew until the Pole Station was operational.

Charles Bevilacqua, a 25-year old chief petty officer, along with a Seabee, went to the Antarctic as a volunteer chief builder and found himself within the Antarctic Circle on Christmas day 1955, after a very frightening trip through the stormy waters from the roaring 60's southwards. As they approached McMurdo, the ice was very bad, leaving their ship held up more than 60km from Hut Point, where the other Seabees were to construct their first building. Before McMurdo was initially established, the heavy ice had prevented the Task Force's shipping convoy from getting near the winter quadroons, prompting the need for a long and hazardous traverse.

While Captain Ketchem kept up the relenting pressure of pounding the bay ice with three icebreakers, nature reduced this distance daily, thus increasing the risk of a catastrophic accident. With the northern edge of the ice breaking up, the unloading continued with cargo ships manoeuvring around the ice floes, to return and moor at a new edge of the bay ice to resume unloading, while the Seabees continued their road and bridge construction.

Refuelling aircraft in Antarctica in the first year of *Deep Freeze* meant unexpected problems for the squadron aircrews. When the surface ships reached McMurdo on December 30 1955, they were moored at the edge of the sea ice, some fifty miles from Hut Point, the location of the first airfield. While the icebreakers began to open up a channel to the unloading site, the tanker, the source of aviation fuel for the long range flights, could not be discharged until the sea ice channel could be opened, so no 'fuel farm' was available for the squadron at first.

Before flying back to New Zealand, the crews of two P2V's and two R5D's, in eight days of flying, explored a sixth of the Antarctic continent, covering an area of more than a million square miles. Of the officers who returned from Antarctica just after Christmas, Lt Commander J W Entrikin was the most gaudily dressed when he strolled into the officers Mess at RNZAF Station, Wigram. He was dressed in new white snow-boots and drill trousers with a brilliant orange, white and brown patterned Fijian style shirt hanging outside his belt, a stark contrast to the previous week when less than 100 miles from his base on a reconnaissance flight, one of the motors on his twin engine Neptune patrol bomber began to falter.

'We were on our second flight over an 11,000 ft plateau, when the engine lost power and then cut out. We had to strip the aircraft and jettison everything moveable; our radar equipment, radio gear and all our personal belongings, that's when spare clothes went overboard, hence my dress today,' he told those gathered, with his usual modest description of the incident, making it sound almost everyday.

Commander Ebbe interjected *'What Joe hasn't told you, is that the single engine power performance of the Neptune's limit is about 8000 ft –that's about 5000 ft below ground level, in the area he was flying, and they were on a twelve hour flight and it took them five and a half hours to reach base again. It was truly an outstanding performance.'*

Then in his usual quiet unpretentious manner Entrikin went on to explain how he came to be dressed as he was, so unbecoming of an US Naval Officer in their host country's Officers mess.

'The pants I brought on the US Glacier, and the snow-boots I found hidden away in the back of the aircraft this morning before I left Antarctica – the previous crew must have overlooked them. The shirt I brought in Hawaii, but when I was passing through Fiji they told me it was one of their traditional patterns only to be worn on the most important occasions.'

The Americans who arrived back in Christchurch, told of how they celebrated Christmas Day in their R5-D Skymaster, parked on the lonely ice airstrip in McMurdo Sounds four miles from the nearest United States camp. Eighteen of them were gathered in the aircraft, and above the noise of the howling blizzard they heard a thumping on the fuselage. They went to answer the 'door' and wondered who the hell would be calling in this isolated part of the world in this bloody awful weather.

Standing in the driving wind and snow was the Commander of one of the Neptune's parked close by.

'In plane #505 there were 16 to 18 people and then Commander Torbert came out of the blizzard singing carols, it was bitterly cold, so I played some carols on my clarinet and then I read out of the bible the Gospel from the Catholic midnight Mass. That was our Christmas cheer and it was real Christmas weather too.

We had a good time down there', recalled the commander of the Skymaster Lt Colonel Hal Kolp relating the incident. *'If it had not been for your people [referring to the RNZAF] here, we would not have had much to eat, but instead we had milk, we had butter, we had meat-beef and very good beef- and we had bread that the Royal New Zealand Air Force had been so good to give us before we left. It was all thanks to these people here, and of course we had all the food we could scrounge on the ice.*

We didn't get to bed until 2 or 3 o'clock in the morning light, and at the time the sun at midnight was only a little lower than the sun at midday, so you never really knew what time it was, I guess it was almost noon when we started Christmas while we were stuck on that strip sitting and waiting for the supply ships to arrive to bring us some gas.'

However, he was quick to add, not all the weather was cold, '*One day, and one day only, there was a heatwave and the temperature soared to 56 degrees F and the ice started melting, I walked around in a pair of shorts and shoes, however most of the time it was 30-33 degrees.*'

By early January 1956, the situation was desperate. Summer was rapidly going by, and 93 Seabees were supposed to stay the winter and nothing had been built to house them. Heavy tractors and sleds were lowered over the side of the *USS Wyandot* and they began hauling building supplies miles over very treacherous and deteriorating ice.

Despite warnings regarding the pending hazards of the operation, it was soon realized by the Task Force Command what a tough job it was going to be in selecting McMurdo as the site. It had everything required- a large area of land supporting base, an ice lake, which melted in the summer to supply fresh water, and a winter harbour adjacent to it for mooring the YOG's. This area when frozen in during the winter would be the operations fuel station and a large expanse of firm ice in the Ross Sea for air facilities. They had to take the risks; it was a military operation, after all.

However the edge of the bay ice in McMurdo Sound was over 40 miles north of Hut Point, so the Seabee battalion also had to construct bridges to span the crevasses.

Friday the 6 January 1956 couldn't have started worse for the Task Force, when a small advance group of Seabees was hauling cargo from the *USS Wyandot* about four miles northeast of Cape Evans. '*We had passed over many small ice cracks, when we came upon a very large crack with open water, too large to cross with our heavy loaded tractor and shed.*' Bevilacqua recalled.

The following day, in freezing conditions, the group built a timber bridge and pushed it across the treacherous crack. One of the Seabees, driver Third Class Richard Williams, known to his mates as 'Willy' and Charles Bevilacqua took the monster thirty-ton D-8 tractor and drove over the bridge without a sled to test the structure first.

'*Petty Officer Williams was the driver, while I was lookout and guide. We had crossed the bridge successfully, then about 15 metres beyond, the D-8 broke through the weak ice without any warning what-so-ever, pulling Willy and me under the ice.*

Somehow I managed to claw my way through the broken ice to the surface and immediately began pushing the broken ice aside, looking for Willy but I could not find him. I was pulled out of the frozen water and removed my heavy outer clothing and boots and jumper.'

When the D-8 was half way across the bridge, the construction party notice the ice beginning to sag, and shouted and waved for Williams to go back. He evidently failed to hear them for he kept on coming and on the far side the ice gave way and swallowed both the tractor and Williams, and even though the doors of the cab were open, Williams was unable to extricate himself, and the tractor carried him to the bottom of McMurdo Sound, a depth of over six hundred feet.

Clawing the ice with his frozen hands, Bevilacqua pushed more ice aside, making a hole while trying desperately to find his mate and pull him to safety, but try as he may his efforts were to no avail, and he was pulled from the water. Going into shock and hypothermia, he was placed into another D-8 with the cabin heater full on in an endeavour to revive the brave Seabee. Willy's body was never recovered. [Williams was born in Oppenheim, New York on August 30 1933.]

Admiral Dufek wrote in his book *Operation Deep Freeze*. '*A feeling of gloom pervaded the hatch parties, unloading gangs and tractor operators, as Williams had been well liked and respected by his shipmates. He was sorely missed. Silently the men continued their tasks of unloading.*

The distance had been reduced to thirty miles from the cargo ships unloading area to Hut Point but this was still too great a distance and took too long for tractor trains to make a turn around. Captain Ketchum had the 'Glacier' cut a lane in the ice, which other icebreakers were unable to do, and in just thirty hours cutting, had a lane to within seven miles of Hut Point.'

This was to be the new loading bay for the tractor trains, enabling them to speed up their turnaround time, hence cargo which had begun to pile up, could be moved more steadily, reducing the number of times the cargo was handled. The icebreakers picked up their cargo from alongside the cargo vessels in the open waters of the Ross Sea, then forced their way back through the ice choked lanes to the new unloading facilities where it was transferred to sleds, then the tractors moved it seven miles to Hut Point, where it was off-loaded to storage dumps.

'Willy was our first loss, on Deep Freeze 1 so Williams Field or Willy Field was named in his memory. We were to lose six more before we left for home in February 1957.'

'Eventually the icebreakers broke in closer to Hut Point and then we began, with much hardship, to build the first building at McMurdo, working throughout the winter improving the station and preparing to go to the South Pole the following year.' Charles Bevilacqua concluded.

McMurdo's chaplain Lt. Condit suggested the base be named after Williams, knowing his work mates and friends would like to have it that way. Dufek before departing for home, at the conclusion of *Deep Freeze 1* sent a message to the Task Force and Naval Department requesting permission to designate it as Williams Air Operation Facilities, McMurdo Sound. Antarctica.

A memorial was erected in his memory,
CR3 RICHARD T .WILLIAMS
US NAVY- SEABEES.
OUR LADY OF THE SNOW SHRINE.
This shrine is dedicated to Construction Drive First Class
Richard Thomas Williams United States Navy Seabees.

From a ship 30 miles out from Hut Point, Petty Officer Williams was bringing in supplies for Seabees to commence the initial construction of McMurdo Sounds during Operation Deep Freeze.
On 6 January 1956 he lost his life when a DC-8 tractor he was operating broke through the bay ice 4 miles NNW of Cape Royds
and plunged 350 fathoms to the bottom of McMurdo Sound.
His body was never recovered.
Petty Office Williams was a member of the US Naval Mobile Construction Battalion_[Special], Task Force 43.
Byrd Antarctic Expedition V, under the command of Rear Admiral Richard Byrd and Rear Admiral George J Dufek US Navy.
Petty Officer Williams gave his life in the logistical support of scientific exploration of Antarctica.

The designer/ builder of the shrine, was Seabees Chaplain Father John, Lt CHC, US Navy, originally dedicated this shrine in January 1957, and on January 6 1996, the CEC/Seabees Historical Foundation re-dedicated the shrine with a bronze tablet to Petty Officer Williams and all the other heroic colleagues of all nations who had given their lives in order to help us better understand Antarctica and the world in which we live.

Chief Petty Charles Bevilacque, who now lives in Meredith New Hampshire, returned to McMurdo from the South Pole in early January 1957, in time for the dedication of the shrine built of volcanic stones and with a statue of the Virgin Mary for his old mate Willy.

The monument has been repaired and restored more than once, the most recent being in 1995-96 when the statue was refurbished and repainted by the Carmelite nuns in Christchurch. For many years the statue had faced McMurdo Station, but after the rededication she was moved around to face north out of the Station towards Williams Field, where Williams lost his life.

During the dedication on January 6 1996, David Grisez a close friend of Williams played 'Taps' during the dedication.

By early January 1956, the Command were planning to make a second attempt to fly the R4-D's to the ice, as they were a vital part in the operation's logistic and statistic planning. Later in the month the Task Force would station three ships to provide a sea and radio safety chain and the emergency landing strip would then be ready at Cape Adare, some 400 miles short of their destination, McMurdo Sound. The Albatrosses that were held back in New Zealand back in December would be on standby to give rescue cover for the Douglas aircraft whos flight was planned for between January 23 and 26. Lt Commander Ben Sparks told a Christchurch news conference that it was hoped to pick a better day than the last time.

The two R4-D's with Lt Commander Eddie Frankiewicz and Lt Commander Gus Shinn, departed Christchurch for Dunedin on January 23. Shinn said that the flight would follow similar lines as the aborted one earlier, with each using the full complement of four JATO take off bottles. The distance between the ships would be about 350 miles, where the most southern ship, an icebreaker, would be stationed off Cape Adare. When the aircraft left Taieri, they would have about 800 miles to fly over open seas before they passed over the first ship.

The flight was timed to coincide with the voyage north of the icebreaker *Glacier* and the other vessels, the icebreaker *Edisto* and *Eastwind* and the cargo assault ship *Greenville Victory*, who would form a chain of homing beacons for guiding Frankiewicz and Shinn to McMurdo, but on January 23, the flight south was cancelled and the four aircraft and crews were flown back to Wigram.

Commander Ebbe ordered Lt.Cdr Torbert to fly out to the *Nespelen* and take on board enough fuel to bring the R5-D's up to 1600 gallons each. Torbert encounter rough ice on landing, tearing the polyethylene coating from the skis as he taxied to a point some hundred yards from the tankers stern and took on 2000 gallons of aviation fuel. His take off from the ice, with his metal skis bouncing over the rough surface, gave a 12-G accelerometer reading.

The transfer of fuel took up so much time from the *Neptune* to the Skymaster that the squadron commander decided to land all planes alongside the tanker for refuelling. After that, the tanker was moved and moored to the opposite side of the channel to take advantage of the somewhat smoother sea ice.

More than 200,000 gallons of avgas had to be transferred from the oil tanker *Nespelen* to permanent fuel tanks near Hut Point, and this could only be accomplished through a fuel line. Laying this three and a half mile line from the tanker to the fuel tanks over rough ice and snow and in freezing conditions, was done by a party of Marines specially trained in hose handling, who had been sent down from Camp Lejeune. These men working with the MCB, battled constant freeze-ups in the line but still they laid the 3 inch pipe with its several pumping stations, and had it completed for the fuel transfer by the time the remaining cargo had been unloaded.

During the first phase of *Deep Freeze*, two US Navy YOG's containing 500,000 gallons of aviation gasoline had been towed to Antarctica and was anchored almost in the exact location in the Ross Sea, to where Captain Scott's flagship lay beset in the ice for two years- 50 years previously.

Moored by dead men to the adjacent hilltops, the fuel tankers were soon frozen fast to the ice, and Capt Harold Fisher, who commanded one of the moored ships and was responsible for their safety, maintained a constant watch over them during their long winter in Antarctica, ably assisted by Harold Lundy. MM1.

These vessels were the lifeblood of the Squadron and the whole Operation, and were at the mercy of the Antarctic weather as the ice shifted and the pressure ridges formed. These ships, just as the wood constructed ships of Capt Scott's did, listed and strained at their anchors and the bow and stern lines along with the anchor chains, frequently had to be lengthened to relieve the strain from the tons of crushing ice moving against the ships. These lines and chains often snapped like cotton thread, but the YOG's survival in the Antarctic winter is credited to the 3500 hours of close watch over them, which wasn't without its difficulties in the extremely cold weather with dangerous adjustment to the chains and lines done in total darkness, resulting at times with serious injuries.

With the *Glacier* being the last ship to leave Antarctic in March, Williams AIROPF men realised the isolation facing them, but Officer-in-Charge Lt.Cdr W.Canham and his McMurdites settled down to their routine tasks connected with the construction of the air facilities to occupy them through the Antarctic winter. Every man at the base regardless of rank or rating was given full time employment and much more.

Several flights were carried out to familiarize the squadron's pilots to adapt themselves to the runway conditions, and the R5-D pilots soon discovered that taking off from the ice required a special skill and unorthodox methods. The skymaster required 1100 feet to take off, and lacking the usual runway markers, the squadron pilots had to take a walk to measure off 1500 feet and mark the way as they went, keeping a close watch for holes, cracks, snow drifts, seals, and the occasional penguin on the ice, plus other unstable impediments which would be a hazard. Any deficiencies would be marked with red flags placed at 1100 feet intervals down the runway, a task that had to be repeated daily.

With gross takeoff weights in excess of 72,000 pounds, the R5-D pilots fired a pair of JATO bottles at 50 knots, so to increase their speed upwards of 60 knots allowing them to lift the nose wheel, gaining proper nose attitude that attained the aircraft to reach 70 knots. Then the second and third pair of rockets would be fired at three-second intervals, allowing the plane to take off at 95 knots.

With the summer season only a little more than three months away, chores for the squadron's maintenance crews varied, such as hand rolling barrels of oil from the outside and caching them in the tunnels, at time a distance of 100 yards, stacking them four high to a total of over 900. But it was the maintenance of the squadron's aircraft, which created the greatest difficulty, where no facilities were available for aircraft repair and at best, but the maintenance crews rolled with the punches and the aircraft were returned to service in record time. Sometimes this meant using a 37 ton tractor to hoist a new engine into a R4-D, or it meant flying a Neptune engine to the South Pole for installation after first flying in with a disassembled cherry picker to handle the task at hand.

The Squadron began their major exploration of the Antarctic continent in January 1956 and before the season ended, nine long-range flights were made. For the first time man was exposed to many areas of the Antarctic never before seen, coping with sudden storms, whiteouts, and unseen mountaintops hidden by cloud and plaguing these flights.

The first exploratory flight took off from McMurdo on January 4 1956, when Lt.Col H.Kolp, USMC and his crew climbed into their R5-D *#56505* on a cool Wednesday morning, their destination Wilkes Land on a course due west, but 'Hal' Kolp encountered whiteout conditions at 1350-17 E. In unexplored regions such as the commander was flying over, there was a danger of crashing into the mountainside, so Kolp prudently revised course and returned to Longitude 1450 E, where visibility was normal, and not wishing to return to base empty handed he flew down that meridian to the South Pole.

While over the Pole he descended to 500 feet for a closer look where the areas appeared to be quite flat with gentle elongated snowdrifts, inferring the snow to be soft and rather powdery, with a low order of density. On his return flight over the polar plateau south of 800 South Longitude was found to be decidedly flat and featureless.

The second long range flight was made the following day, with Lt.Cdr Henry Jorda in an R5-D *# 56528,* this time the flight was into the unexplored heart of Wilkes Land to 80 degree South 90 degree East and returned on the 82nd parallel to Barne Inlet [a glacier valley on the west side of the Ross Ice Shelf], thence on to McMurdo.

Two mountain ranges were discovered on Jorda's flight. The first one was estimated to be thirty miles wide with numerous peaks towering between 7,000 and 10,000 feet, the second was estimated to be 60 miles wide as it thrust jagged peaks aloft upwards of 10,000 feet, but apart from these, the rest of the landscape lacked any form of relief.

On the same day, Capt Hawkes and Lt.Cdr Torbert flew out of McMurdo aboard a P2-V # *124466* and winged their way across the unknown to Vincennes Bay on the Knox Coast, and then westwards for 50 miles before turning back to McMurdo, a flight distance of 2,600 miles. Apart from the mountains immediately west of McMurdo, the landscape was entirely a featureless icecap along the Bay, which sloped gently to the sea but was scored with crevasses.

Capt.Hawkes reported that is was interesting to note that when they approached McMurdo, Mt Erebus with its plume of volcanic smoke could be seen 200 miles away. This 13,000-foot peak enhances the value of McMurdo Sound for operation of aircraft since it was an excellent landmark and an indicator of upper air-currents as well.

A near tragedy occurred on January 6, during the 4th long-range exploratory mission as the *USS Wyandot* controlled the flight.

Joe Entrikin in a P2-V Neptune, which should have earned official recognition but was never mentioned at the time, made the most spectacular flight of all during the Squadron's first deployment on the ice. Later, and by chance, the *'Naval Aviation News'*, who, each month awards the 'Old Pro' title to a Navy pilot who had distinguished himself demonstrating extraordinary flying ability in the prevention of an aircraft accident, heard about Joe's flight and awarded the VX-6 aviator the title.

It appeared that as they neared the end of their outward-bound leg, and nearing the Queen Mary Coast on January 6, his starboard engine lost power. A mayday distress call followed, and in order to reach home, they would have to cross a 12,000-foot ice plateau, which is an Antarctic aviator's worst nightmare.

As they neared the end, Joe noticed a malfunction in the starboard engine as the cylinder head temperature was rising and the oil pressure falling making the situation critical. The VX-6 aviator knew that he would never make it back to McMurdo on one engine and yet, if he did shut the bad engine down, it would either catch fire, explode, or freeze up. Joe radioed his position to McMurdo, declaring an in flight emergency, then notified the crew that he was going to keep the plane in the air as long as possible, because, as Joe put it, *'It's a long walk home'*. Fortunately for the pilot, the Antarctic ceiling and visibility were unlimited during the entire flight.

The first thing they did was to throw out of the aircraft everything not absolutely essential for survival. Even so, Joe knew that he could not maintain altitude above terrain level on one engine, so he decided the only course of action was to gain as much altitude as possible on both engines, then, when the head temperature and oil pressure gauges on the failing engine reached the redline, he would feather it and start a slow decent down to 10,000 feet, and on reaching 10,000 feet, he would re-start that engine, climb back up, and repeat the process.

It must be remembered that in order to make this operation work, he would have to exceed the engine limitations on the good engine, as the longer he could stretch out the distance before re-starting the bad one, the better chance he had of getting home. For five hours Joe literally hopped, skipped and jumped his way back home, as courageously he fought for every foot of altitude, clawed for every mile and as his co-pilot described later, *'Joe just wants the plane to fly'*.

Approaching the Farrar Glacier, around a hundred miles west of McMurdo, the starboard engine let out a final gasp where he feathered it for the last time. Coming down the Glacier, the elevation gradually dropped from 7,000 feet to sea level. Pulling all the power he could get out of his working engine, Joe slipped down the glacier and landed safely back home at McMurdo- a truly magnificent piece of aviation.

When the distress alarm was flashed to McMurdo Sound, a R5-D and a Neptune were hastily flown out to the tanker *Nespelen*, fuelled up and took off to escort the crippled plane to McMurdo, to watch Lt. Joe Entrikin land his single engine plane with only 150 gallons of avgas left in the Neptune's tanks.

On January 7, the squadron undertook its fifth long range flight when Lt Colonel Hal Kolp piloted his R5-D #56505, flying directly to Latitude 71 degree-00'S then to 69 degree S, 130 degree, from this point he headed north until he reached the coast of Wilkes Land. Only the coastal mountains broke the monotony of the featureless icecap during Kolp's 2,350-mile flight, plus a ship painted bright red that was observed to be standing westwards along the barrier, but radio contact couldn't be established with the vessel which was later proven to be the Danish *Kista Dan,* under charter to the Australian Antarctic expedition.

The following day Cdr.Gordon Ebbe, the squadron's commanding officer, made a flight in # 56258 with Rear Admiral Byrd aboard. Their flight plan included a flight over the geographical centre of Antarctica to return via the South Pole and Beardmore Glacier. They reported that the icecap averaged 10-11 thousand feet elevation and was completely devoid of features, and the South Polar surface appeared to be hard with low drifts.

The command's decision to use Hut Point as a site for Air Op Facility posed another major problem for both Dufek and the Squadron's command as the ice was already showing signs of deterioration, and as the *Glacier* tracked to Hut Point it could slice through the airstrip, so it was decided to break a channel no further than the one which had already been carved, until after the wheeled aircraft could be evacuated. Following Rear Admiral Dufek's shift from his flag ship *Arneb* at Little America to *Glacier* via a short flight aboard a P2-V- # 124466, Rear Admiral Richard Byrd also shifted his flag as O-I-C, US Antarctic Programmes to *Wyandot* on the same day, as construction began for the Air Op Facility at Hut Point.

However, because of the rapidly deteriorating condition of the ice at McMurdo Sound, the Task Force Commander decided to terminate the squadron's long range reconnaissance operation to an earlier date, and he accordingly scheduled exploratory flights as a finale to the long-range air operations for the season, having these flights penetrate previously unexplored regions.

The first was with Lt Col Hal Kolp on the flight deck of #56505, making a 14 hour 7 minute flight, which took him to the Pole of Inaccessibility returning by the South Geographical Pole. This was the first time the former Pole had ever been viewed by man. However, its vastness held nothing exotic, only featureless plateau whose altitude was 11,500 feet. After leaving the South Pole, the plane encountered a complete whiteout, which forced Kolp to complete the mission on instruments.

The Pole of Inaccessibility is the geometrical centre of the continent, but it would be ten years before the squadron could land a plane on its surface, when on December 13 1965, the then Squadron Commander Cdr 'Moe' Morris would touch down in a C-1340 Hercules # *148318*- aptly named *City Of Christchurch.*

The last two flights would be made by Cdr Ebbe and Lt. Cdr Jorda in a fourteen hour flight from the heart of Antarctica at 81 degree-00'S, 62 degree-00'E- in P2-V # *124466*, and again this region was found to be a featureless ice plateau. Later Cdr. Hawkes and Lt.Cdr Jack Torbert flew to the Weddell Sea via the South Pole in a record-making 19-hour flight, with the return trip made over the Leverett Glacier, discovering four new mountains ranges and several detached peaks.

Answering a question, Squadron Commander Ebbe told reporters that no souveniring had been done from any of the Scott or Shackleton huts, saying that the Task Force Commander Rear Admiral Dufek had set a prohibition for his men not to go near the historic huts and remove items. *'The Scott huts at Hut Point and Cape Evans and Shackleton's at Cape Royds were considered shrines, we left them as they were, out of bounds. Snow had drifted in through the eaves to Scott's Hut at Hut Point, where the squadron's aircraft were based and we did think we could excavate it, but it had turned to ice, and we didn't get around to it.'*

Dr Trevor Hatherton, one of the three New Zealand observers with the operation, had at first expressed a note of anxiety and deep concern over the possibility of indiscriminate souvenir hunting by the American Navy personnel at the historic huts which are some twenty miles apart. Reportedly several navy helicopter pilots from the *Edisto* and *Glacier* had visited the half-century-old huts, had said memorial prayers and then flown back with several mementos of their heroes. One Navy pilot remarked that he had visited the Hut on Hut Point and had to crawl in under a wall of snow to reach the door and enter it.

'The inside looked as though the men had just left it a few minutes ago and might come back at any moment.

In general the aviators and ground crews, after having set up their camp, made a small community of tents on the rocky front yard of Scott's famous hut to house the 25 naval aviators who had landed on the frozen McMurdo Sound on the Tuesday night after their historic 2550 non stop flight from New Zealand. They were forced to live in tents for some weeks until the task force ships returned with materials to start erecting a more substantial station' relates one aviator.

'After spending a week in tents, we quickly remembered how both early explorers had died in an effort to conquer the most hostile continent on earth, and their 'huts' had to be protected.'

Adm. Dufek wrote: *'In one month's time these Navy and Marine Corps fliers had opened the airways to the earth's last unknown continent. Operating under adverse conditions and suffering hardships, they lifted the veil from a million square miles of unknown territory. They were modest and uncomplaining; but theirs is the glory for having gazed upon a large portion of God's earth never before seen by men.'*

On January 18 1956, two Skymasters and two Neptune's took off from McMurdo Sound on an uneventful eleven-hour flight to the Wigram Air Force Station, Christchurch. With only one ship on station duty, the squadron's senior pilot Lt Commander Ben Sparks flew his Albatross from Wigram to Dunedin to stand by as air-sea rescue in case of an emergency, while the other Albatross remained in Christchurch.

Their arrival back in New Zealand was a quiet one when the first planes arrived at Wigram. The bearded crew clambered down from their aircraft, some dressed in their full survival kit, some in snow boots and denims, while three sported brilliant red wind jackets, and shortly after their eleven-hour flight from the ice, the crews quickly dispersed to their quarters to bathe slowly and shave. Commander Torbert, after throwing off his heavy survival gear replaced it with a cool flapping Hawaiian shirt, and tucked into a welcoming meal in the Officers Mess.

Within hours of touching down in his Skymaster, Lt Commander Jorda was airborne again, this time in a R4-D piloted by Lt K Enney, heading for Auckland to be reunited with his wife Jeune, a New Zealand girl, and their three daughters, Shelly aged 10, Beverley seven and one year old Carole, who had flown out from the US to be reunited before he left again for the Antarctic. His wife did not expect to see him on his return, as the family were due to leave about ten days before the squadron was due back at Wigram, so the early return of the aircraft made the reunion in New Zealand nicely possible.

With the long-range exploration flight completed for the season, the daylight hours were becoming limited and the cracks to the ice runway widening. The squadron's mechanics were set the task of overhauling aircraft for their return to Christchurch and home. The *USS Eastwind* sailed northwards to take up her position as station ship for the squadron's flight to New Zealand. This time the *Eastwind* was the only 'station ship' for the fly-out compared to the six for the fly-in to McMurdo the previous December, as now the flight for the VX-6 aviators had become routine.

A brief 1956 radio announcement stated, *'On January 13, members of the US Antarctic expedition penetrated a land extent of 2,300 miles 'beyond' the Pole, the flight was made by Rear Admiral Dufek's Navy Air Unit.'*

On his return to the United States from his Antarctic expedition on March 13 1956, Admiral Byrd remarked, *'The present expedition has opened up a vast new land'*. Before his death in 1957,

Admiral Byrd called the land beyond the South Pole, 'that enchanted continent in the sky, a land of everlasting mystery.'

As January ebbed, Byrd grew anxious to leave Antarctica, after all the Americans had achieved their main objects for *Deep Freeze I,* and as Byrd pointed out there was no longer a need to linger. This personal view of a man on his fourth Antarctic expedition was in sharp contrast to that of Rear Admiral Dufek and that which he had exhibited in *Operation HighJump.* Admiral Byrd was just tired, and as Dr Paul Siple wrote in his book *'90 Degrees South'*, 'when it came time to depart in 1947, a striking sunset had turned the sky into a Kodachrome world. Even as the last call had been shouted, Byrd had kept his eyes fixed on the iridescent sky,' - 'but I don't want to go yet Paul', he had said, shaking his head.' But now with his failing health, times had changed.

'So on February 3, Byrd and I pulled out of McMurdo Sound and headed for home. For Byrd it was his last departure from the Antarctic. His wisdom had been responsible for bringing about the great new era of Antarctic activity. Others would carry on his work of exploration, making even greater use of scientific and mechanical tools of the modern world. None could live long enough to hope to make a greater contribution than he had.'

'Moose Remington came to me about three pm. on March 12 [1957] his face was clouded and his eyes avoided mine. 'What is it?' I asked.'

'I just heard the news over the Armed Forces Radio he said softly, that Admiral Byrd died today in Boston.'

His passing was the greatest loss to Antarctic exploration and an even greater loss to polar aviation, as his contribution was immeasurable, his earlier exploits and his vision were the momentous part that aviation would play in polar exploration. Richard Byrd was the elite cadre of aerial explorations who made the first flights of discovery in the Arctic along with pioneering polar aviators such as Hubert Wilkins, Ronald Amunsden and Lincoln Ellsworth. These men, the grandfathers of polar aviation and the surrogate fathers of the famous VX-6 squadron, where the aeronautical frontiersmen who in a single leap of man's imagination, took their satisfaction, not of blazing trails for commercial routes, but for the heady thrill of discovery and taking the flying machine to places where man had never walked.

They all served their apprenticeships in the Arctic, yet it was the unknown Antarctic continent so forbidding, that it was as late as the 1920's, before anything was known about it. Even over hundreds of years, venturesome whalers in search of the migrating leviathans dared not to penetrate the pack ice, so had only charted the fringes of Antarctica.

Families and friends greeted the returning Neptune and R4-D's crews at their Patuxent River base in early February. Lt.Cdr Entrikin flying the same P2-V in which he and his crew narrowly escaped going down in, was detained for some days at Hills Air Force Base, Ogden, Utah with mechanical troubles. The first aircraft to arrive home was Lt.Cdr Torbert's plane, the now famous *'Amen'* that made history when it became the first plane to fly over both poles; it was also the first heavy aircraft to have skis fitted. His crew included the Antarctic aviation veteran Capt William Hawkes.

His arrival was followed four days later by the two R4-D's that didn't make the ice. Lt.Cdr Frankie Frankiewicz and his crew, Plane Captain J. Crisp, and Radioman AT2 Jack Covalt, aboard *Charlene* arrived home on Tuesday January 31, after the long flight from Christchurch.

Two days later in bad weather, friends and families with their 'Welcome Home' sign had to wait as Lt.Cdr Gus Shinn piloting the other R4-D-8 *Que Sera Sera* had been held up after a stopover at Lincoln, Nebraska.

With Operation *Deep Freeze 1* completed the Navy left 73 men at Little America, and 93 at McMurdo Station with the materials for the two stations to be used on the polar cap the next season.

The men wintering over began the task of building the stations before the ships were able to force their way through the ice, and head for New Zealand.

Twenty-four hours after the aircraft had taken off for Christchurch, New Zealand, the barometer dropped through the floor, the wind shifted to the south, and whitecaps appeared in the open waters heralding an Antarctic storm so the tractor train operations were suspended, equipment secured, and the personnel base dug themselves in, as the Antarctic storm blew up as only an Antarctic storm can. Winds of up to 35mph blew across the Sound, the ice airfield which had supported heavy aircraft before, was now open sea, taking the new ice edge 'wharf' to only 11 miles from Hut Point.
As the storm subsided, the *Glacier* escorted the Task Force's ships into McMurdo Sounds.

With operations settling into a monotonous routine of unloading and base construction and preparing for the cold winter sunless months ahead, news was passed onto the Task Force at McMurdo that the fuel storage complex was nearing completion at Little America. The *Nespelen* which was escorted by the *USS Edisto* to Kainan Bay to discharge fuel for the base, had to then stand by and wait until the storage tanks were completed, perhaps one of the hardest duties of the Task Force's ships to encounter.

In the meantime work was progressing on the four mile of hose being laid down from the unloading area to the storage tanks at Hut Point, as Admiral Dufek put it. *'It was like a long black snake sleeping on a white carpet.'* With the improvement in the weather, temperatures at -20 degrees F and little wind, the season's operations would be completed without further problems and the curtain came down *on Operation Deep Freeze I.*

In March 1956, VX-6 after having completed its first deployment mission to the Antarctic had their squadron's home base transferred from Patuxent River, to Naval Air Station, Quonset Point Rhode Island, with Capt. Douglas Cordiner, former Task Force operation officer, assuming command. During the wintering over, all hands, regardless of rank, pitched in performing various maintenance tasks. Prior to the beginning of the first fly-in from Christchurch, all aircraft had to be dug out and de-wintered and readied for flight.

Then came the operations first SOS, at 9.50am on February 4 1956, when the ships of the task force and Little America Station reported they had received a distress signal from a plane down on the continent.

In the Antarctic trouble comes when least expected, and a message received at the McMurdo command post was that an Otter was an hour overdue and its last transmission had been heard three hours previously, and as it was mandatory to report the plane's position every 30 minutes, this caused concern. With communications notoriously bad in Antarctica, the lack of communications could mean a radio failure, but the overall fear is that the aircraft had possibly met disaster, and that had to be considered.

With the passing of time, hope was that the plane had encountered bad weather and made an emergency landing deciding to sit it out. It could also have been an engine failure causing a forced landing, or the plane had flown into a dreaded Antarctic 'whiteout' and crashed on the ice. One officer grimly suggested that it may have flown off course and crashed into the Rockefeller Mountains.

Search and rescue operations went into action, with Commander Jacob Bursey and his men ordered to retrace their tracks towards Little America. Warrant Officer Victor Young and seven men started from Little America over the tractor trail to meet up with Commander Jacob Bursey, and over the next two days, two attempts were made to fly an Otter from McMurdo, but on both occasion, it was forced back due to bad weather.

The signal received was identified as that of a Gibson-Girl, a hand-cranked emergency radio set, which could be operated by raising the antenna with a balloon or kite or by inserting a whip antenna, although this didn't have the range of the kite.

The last transmission was heard at 9.00 pm on February 4 at Little America, after twelve hours of periodic distress signals. What concerned the task force was the fact that a key arrangement for all aircrew sending distress messages was to use Morse code, but none came through. They feared the worst, could the pilot be dead, leaving Admiral Dufek worried as to why the signals had ceased. Were there poor atmospheric conditions in the crash area, or had the balloon blown away in an Antarctic storm, or more fearful, had the men simply given up?

Writing in his book "*Operation Deep Freeze*" Dufek wrote.

'*Shortly after midnight of the second day the two trail parties met 250 miles east of Little America. There had been no sign of the lost plane or its party of seven men.*

Sorely needed was the long-range aircraft that had departed from McMurdo for New Zealand and onto the United States. The temperature had fallen to below zero, so a new study if the ice at McMurdo was made to determine whether it was suitable again to support the aircraft. It was not. The ice further south, near Hut Point, was covered with three feet of snow on top of a hard sastrugi melt and rough ice.

The Eastwind ploughing its way towards Little America with an Otter and a helicopter was informed by dispatch from Little America that all the bay ice had gone out. It was not possible to unload the Otter onto the Barrier. This was bad news, but there must be some way to unload that plane.'

Captain Cordiner was placed in charged of the search and rescue operation, after the *Eastwind* moored alongside the Barrier, and shortly after, the damaged Otter was repaired and took off for a four hour reconnaissance in the Rockefeller Mountains, returning with a negative result.

Later the communication messenger came in to the task force headquarters with a message from Trigger Hawkes in Washington.

PROPOSED FLIGHT P2-V WITH LCDR J.H. TORBERT FROM PATUXENT RIVER, MARYLAND, TO LITTLE AMERICA, ANTARCTICA, VIA SOUTH AMERICA, TO ASSIST IN SEARCH.

'*Good old Trigger! What a flight! But how could I refuse? The Otter had been missing for four days and at Little America all that we had available were one Otter and two helicopters. If anything should happen to them on the search flights, the situation would be hopeless. One Otter was still in McMurdo weathering in. The R5-D's could not be flown in from New Zealand because the ice at the former airfield had broken up.*'

Wrote Rear Admiral Dufek: '*If anyone could do it Torbert could. Hawkes and Torbert had made flights from New Zealand to Antarctica and return, for the first time in history. They had made the two unequalled round-trips from McMurdo Sounds across the Antarctic continent to Knox Coast and the Weddell Sea. They had reconnoitred and photographed the trail party route for Bursey. I radioed Trigger: APPROVED.*'

Rear Admiral Dufek ordered the Officer in Charge of VX-6 Detachment Patuxent River, Commander Eddie Ward, to dispatch a rescue aircraft from the States, as there were no long range aircraft with search and rescue capabilities, and there was no ice runway at Little America to accommodate a landing.

Another Otter flying from Little America finally located the Antarctic crash site, and the helicopter was sent to recover the survivors, who had abandoned the wreck and had walked 40 of the 110 miles back to base.

Two hours later Rear Admiral George Dufek was on the bridge of the *Eastwind* when Commander Paul Frazier came up to him and said, '*I believe this is what you are waitng for Admiral*', handing him two messages from Captain Cordiner,

The first said. *PLANE FOUND BY LT DON SULLIVAN IN OTTER AT LATITUDE 77 DEGREE 32 SOUTH, LONGITUDE 154 DEGREE 10 WEST.PLANE UNABLE LAND, RETURNING BASE.PERSONNEL BELIEVED WELL. WILL PRECEDE RESCUE USING HELOS AND TRAIL PARTY.* The second reported: *ALL HANDS SAFE.WALKED AWAY FROM PLANE.FOUND BT LCRD LARSON IN HELP NOW WITH PARTY.*

This news was flashed about the task force, lifting the men's spirits and morale, for the first time in days they joked even hummed a song as they wrestled with cargo in sub zero temperatures.

On February 2 Lt. Streich had landed his Otter at the most advanced point of the trail party about 380 miles from Little America as his orders were to evacuate Lt.Commander Bursey of the US Coast Guard and his party to the proposed site of the Byrd Base, so he decided to do this in two flights. When airborne he sent a departure report and a weather report, which was received and acknowledged at Little America at 5-15am, then he ran into bad weather which got progressively worse, so he sent out a blind report at regular intervals but without getting any response.

Now flying on full throttle, nothing could be seen of the ground below and he dared not attempt a power stalled landing as the wings and propellers were icing up.

At this point, the commander elected to climb out on instruments and hopefully break out on top, so they climbed to 7000 ft and levelled off unable to break out into the clear. For two hours they continued on course but the windows were heavily icing up leaving visibility at zero. Unable to maintain altitude they slowly started down with their estimated position, placing them in the vicinity of the Edsel Ford range, an area surrounded by jagged mountain peaks, so their only option was to ride the plane down to a crash landing and hope for the best.

Around 7am, Streich shouted to his crew, 'We're going to hit the bloody ground'. Unable to see out, the crew felt and heard the aircraft make contact with the surface, but miraculously, they had landed on the down slope of the mountain, allowing the crew to suffer only superficial injuries.

After sliding several hundreds of feet, the Otter finished up on its nose with its propellers bent, the engine out of alignment, and the landing gear forced up into the cabin. The crew stepped out into freezing rain and snow and offered a prayed for their good fortune.

They turned to survival by constructing a shelter, for with the Otter's wings and fuselage in tact, they were able to dig a hole in the snow under the wing and surround it with snow blocks as a windbreak. Not able to operate the plane's radio, they turned to the Gibson Girl, and for hours after the crash it was hard work cranking out the messages for help.

Having only three days supply of food, it had to be rationed, so on even days each man got an ounce and a half of pemmican, a vitamin pill and a candy bar, while the crew took it in turns to look and listen for a rescue plane.

George Moss and Ed Edwards, a former lumberjack, and by far the biggest man in the party, started dragging a sled with 200 lbs. of equipment, and headed out. Commander Streich and Chief Machinist's Mate John Floyd on the skis broke the trail ahead while Lt. Commander Glen Lathrop, Chester Sevens and Roland Lovesick brought up the rear.

On the third day, the party struggled through an Antarctic blizzard, but they still planned to make ten miles a day, and the weather, except for the blizzard, was reasonably good.

After the fourth day, the sky was bright blue and a meeting of the survivors to review their plight was made, leaving a few to feel they could survive longer if they had stayed where they were. The uphill trail led over rough terrain and heavily crevassed areas, with the party advancing for only a hundred yards, then having to stop for a few minutes and continue on their journey. It was thought that fifteen miles had been covered on the first day, however, a series of observations disclosed their advancement had been only seven miles.

As the men plodded on into the fifth day after the crash morale was still high, with each man attempting to outdo the other, but by the sixth day, travelling was a little easier and had them still on course. Moss had taken the compass from the Otter, but by now the men were showing signs of fatigue, cold and hunger with each losing weight by the mile, having had advanced 14 miles that day.

The worst part of the trek was the snow underfoot; at times they sunk up to their knees, and most of the time, the temperature was down to 20 degrees below zero

As the camp broke at 8am on the seventh day, and the men now lethargic, they resumed their slow climb uphill and at 1.00 pm Streich who was leading the troop started waving his arms. *'Three men on skis up ahead'* he cried.

With that George Moss arrived, dragging his sled, *'that's a mirage'* he said, as he drew level with the rest of the group, peering into the continuous whiteness, and the survivors slugged onwards till about six in the afternoon when one of the trail breakers ahead, started waving his ski poles in the air and again shouted to the rest of party. More than a little sceptical, the rear party stopped to look around, using the break to give them a chance to rest on their ski poles, when they heard and saw it too; a beautiful bright red helicopter hovering above.

Lt Commander Don Sullivan, the pilot of the searching aircraft was flying at 4500 feet in poor weather when he sighted the crashed Otter. He then directed a squadron helicopter piloted by Lt.Commander S C Larson with Dr Edward Ehrlich aboard, to the crash site, but when he landed, there were no signs of the survivors, so Don Sullivan surmised they had attempted to walk out, and shortly afterwards he located the group some 45 miles from the crash site, suffering from exhaustion, exposure and hunger. They were extremely fortunate to have been found.

George Dufek again. *'What a joyful meeting! The survivors, with tears in their eyes, hugged and danced with their rescuers, through a jumble of words everyone was laughing and crying. Dr Ehrlich passed out chocolate candy, which was wolfed down by the men, and a shot of bandy to each uplifted their spirits more and opened a new flood of conversation.*

Then Lt. Daniel J Sliwinski arrived in his Otter, circled the group, and came in for a smooth landing. Lathrop and Floyd took off in the helicopter, while the rest followed in the Otter. Landing at Little America, the survivors were greeted by cheers from their comrades. They got everything they had been wishing for during the past seven days- those hot showers were working, the steaks were ready, and, when the excitement had died down, there was blessed sleep.'

A message came in from Captain Cordiner at Little America *'ALL OTTER SURVIVORS SAFE AND WELL AT LITTLE AMERICA.DO YOU HAVE ANY INFORMATION ON P2V AIRCRAFT THAT CRASHED IN SOUTH AMERICA.'*

'I glanced up at the clock and notice it was three o'clock in the morning It was February 10- 1956- my birthday. I sent this dispatch to Little America: P2V FOUND AND CREW RESCUED.ALL SAFE. NO INJURIES. THE TWO RESCUES MAKES THE BEST BIRTHDAY PRESENT I EVER HAD.

I have never been a deeply religious man in observing the rituals of the church, but I believe in God and his infinite wisdom. There have been so many times in my life that all my experiences and the resources at my command have been futile, I could not control the weather, and I could not control the ice and winds. There have been times when my companions have been lost and there was nothing I could do about it, nothing but wait for the weather to change. At these times, I would go to my cabin and kneel before my bunk and pray as my mother taught me to do-for help and guidance, and it has always worked.'

A senior officer Lt.Commander Glen H Lathrop, and another member of the party, Construction Driver First-class Roland Levesque recalled their grim seven days of surviving, to this writer after their return to New Zealand aboard the US Navy's Supply ship *Wyandot*.

'The first three days when we stayed near the crash site, the Gibson girl radio was working and after 36 hours the weather had cleared. From then on we were on short rations - some oatmeal concentrated food tables to be dissolved in water, a little candy, a few dried prunes, some biscuits and a piece of margarine, I set the rations at six oz per man for 14 days, we would eat one meal a day on rising up.

By the end of the third day, I decided to leave the plane and walk overland back to base 110 miles away. Under the circumstances it was the thing to do, and nothing will convince me that if the weather had stayed good and they found the aircraft, they would follow our tracks and find us.

We started to walk back, with five sleeping bags, a primus stove, several gallons of kerosene, four blankets, two tents, a parachute which we used as a ground sheet, an ice axe, a shovel and an extra pair of socks apiece. The gear was loaded on a main sledge hauled by the two biggest men in the party 'Big' Ed Edwards and George Moss- both Navy construction men over 6 foot 4 inches. Others relieved them on the sledge, but Moss and Edwards were the only two to have pulled it for any length of time.

After leaving the aircraft, we descended about 500 feet, and then climbed for 100 feet onto the plateau. On the third day, we struggled through a real Antarctic blizzard. We had planned to make 10 miles a day by keeping this up for 12 hours or until we could go no further. The weather except for the blizzard was fairly good and on the fourth day we were rescued -it was bloody fine.'

Cdr. Eddie Ward: It was 5am on a rather cool overcast Friday morning, February 3 1956, when, the Officer-in-Charge of the VX-6's Patuxent River Detachment was woken from a deep sleep by consistent knocking at his door, it was a grim looking Petty Officer holding a cable in his hand. Fearing the worst, the Commander read the 'operational immediate' message from the wintering over Naval Detachment party at Little America stating that one of the Squadron's Otters flying out of Little America in support of the trail parties with seven men had vanished in the vicinity of Edward 7th Peninsula. In his memoirs he wrote, '*Unfortunately I did no have copies of the Naval Messages, these quotes are from my memory and I believe almost identical to the originals.'*

NAVAL; MESSAGE OPERATIONAL IMMEDIATE 03 1002 ZULU FEB
FROM; COMMANDING OFFICE VX-6 USS GLACIER.
TO OFFICE IN CHARGE VX-6 DETACTMENT NAS PATUXENT RIVER
INFO. CHIEF OF NAVAL OPERATIONS COMNAVAIRLANT, UC-1 DEHAVILLAND OTTER BUNO 17224 WITH SEVEN MAN CREW MISSING AND PRESUMED DOWN X SEARCH IN PROGRESS X OFFICER IN CHARGE VX-6 DETACTMENT PATUXENT STANDBY TO RENDER ASSISTANCE X.

Eddie rushed back to his room to tell his wife Marilyn the tragic news while he was dressing, and their children slept. Eddie kissed Marilyn and headed for the squadron's operation room to confer with his senior staff and a welcome mug of coffee.

This tragic event could not have happened at a more inopportune time, there were no VX-6 aircraft remaining in the Antarctic with long range search and rescue capability, the two ski-equipped R5-D's were ruled out as they are not ski equipped and there were no ice runways at Little America to accommodate them. Gordon Ebbe, the squadron's skipper was still aboard the icebreaker on the way home with the Admiral.

NAVAL; OPERATIONAL MESSAGE 04 1623 ZULU FEB.
FROM; OFFICER IN CHARGE VX-6
INFO: COMMANDER TASK FORCE 43 CHIEF OF NAVAL OPERATIONS.
   COMMANDING OFFICER NAVAL DETACTMENT LITTLE AMERICA
    COMMANDER CARIBEAN SEA FRONTIER
   STATE DEPARTMENT WASHDC ALL CONCERN EMBASSIES
   REQ APPROVAL LAUNCH P2V BUNO 122466 LITTLE AMERICA VIA RAMEY AFB PUERTO RICO, MANAUS BRAZIL, ASUNCION PARAGUAY, BUENOS AIRES ARGENTINA, TERRA DEL FUEGO DIRECT TO LITTLE AMERICA X ETD PATUXENT P7 1200 ZULU X PILOT TORBERT X BACK UP R-4D BUNO 17274 PILOT WARD X NEW ZEALAND VIA ADAK ALASKA MIDWAY ISLAND FIJI ISLANDS, CHRISTCHURCH X STATE DEPT REQ APPROVAL DIPOMATIC CLEARANCE AIR SPACE COUNTRIES EN-ROUTE X.

The following day, another message from Cdr Gordon Ebbe aboard the *USS Glacier*:

NAVAL: MESSAGE IMMEDIATE 05 ZULU FEB
FROM: COMMANDING OFFICER VX-6 USS GLACIER.
TO OFFICER IN CHARGE VX-6 DETACTMENT NAS PATUXENT RIVER
INFO   COMMANDER TASK FORCE 43.
*   CHIEF OF NAVAL OPERATIONS.*
*   COMMANDING OFFICER NAVAL ATTRACTMENT LITTLE AMERICA.*
*   COMMANDER CARIBBEAN SEA FRONTER.*
*   STATE DEPARTMENT WASHINGTON DC*
REF YOUR 04 1623 ZULU X LAUNCH P2V BUNO 122266 IN ACCORDANCE PROPOSED
FLIGHT PLAN X R4-D BUNO 172274 REMAIN STANDBY PATUXANCE X STATE DEPT X
REQUEST DIPOMATIC CLEARANCE EARLIEST DUE URGENCY OF MISSION X
COMTASKFORCE 43 CONCURS X

As the squadron's Air Operations Officer of VX-6 Detachment back at the squadron's base at Patuxent River, Cdr Eddie Ward had only three aircraft capable of operating out of Little America, so an aircraft would have to be dispatched from the US. At best the mission would be anything but normal, while the P2V Neptune # *122466* was ski-equipped and had a fuel range of 4,000 miles emergency gear and skis, it would still make the rescue operation barely marginal.

The intended flight path from Venezuela to Terra Del Fuego Argentina was to be over many miles of dense jungle, and also against the mission was the lack of airstrips and radio navigation aids. Being that they were, few and far between, would make the pilot have second thoughts of ditching at any stage, with the numerous stagnated lakes and muddy rivers that teemed with flesh eating Piranhas!

Commander Ward had received diplomatic clearance from all Embassy's concerned, even from countries not involved, such as Columbia, Venezuela, Bolivia, Uruguay, Peru and Chile, all approving an over flight if required and assistance if necessary.

By eight am the following morning, February 5, the Neptune crew were briefed by Ward on the rescue mission, emphasizing the hazardous aspects of the flight ahead of them, but to a man they had volunteered *'I've often reflected on that day so long ago now, and how proud I was of them,'* wrote Eddie Ward in his memoirs, *'With complete disregard for their own personal safety these courageous officers and men chose to lay their life on the line to go to the aid of their less fortunate shipmates. A more fitting example of Christian ideals and principles I would find difficult to come by.'*

Lt.Cdr Jack Torbert, Plane Commander of # *22466*, together with his co-pilot Lt.Cdr Charlie Otti, eagerly accepted the challenge. Lt Tom Winkler requested to go as Navigator and Capt Ray Hudman USMC, an outstanding officer and qualified paramedic signed on in the event of casualties. The entire P2V flight crew volunteered to a man - Chief William Lyons, Plane Captain, AD-1 Frank Snider, 2nd Mechanic, ATC Paul Beyers radioman and an enlisted Marine Navigator, Staff Sergeant Robert Spann, who would act as Lt Walker's assistant.

On the morning of February 7 1956, the crew of # *22466* were about to set out on the most bizarre flight in the annals of Air Development Six. In the gloom of the early evening, the 'Home Port' seemed to reflect the gloom and a certain apprehension as Commander Ward walked to the plane with Jack and Charlie who stood under its wing to avoid the driving rain. The idling engines made conversation difficult *'I wished them Godspeed as they boarded and taxied out to the far end of the duty runway. Suddenly the two big engines came to life, the plane thundered down the runway, and I watched until its lights disappeared into the murk of a hostile night'*, recalled Commander Ward.

Their first stop was at the Marine Corps Air Station at Cherry Point, North Carolina to pick up Sgt Spann, and from there they flew direct to Ramey AFB, Puerto Rico for refuelling. The arrival and departure message from Ramey AFB was as per schedule. What Jack Torbert hadn't mentioned to Ward, was that they had planned to 'cannonball' straight through to Terra Del Fuego Argentina with a minimum of crew rest, then if receiving favourable weather on for the long perilous flight to Little America, some 2,400 nautical miles away.

Charlie Otti, his old shipmate of Squadron VX-2 days, told the following tale of this jungle odyssey to Commander Ward.

'Not long after departing Ramey AFB, former enlisted Aviation Machinist Mate First Class Charlie Otti sensed that all was not well on the flight deck, Charlie knew engines inside out. Commissioned during the War, he'd specialized as a Maintenance Officer, so his sixth sense detected a slight surge in the starboard engine. He thought about recommending that they return to Ramey, but all the gauges appeared normal, so they continued on, cruising at 12,000 feet flying in and out of rainsqualls and thunderstorms, the P2V crossed the north coast of Venezuela and took up a course for Manaus, Brazil.

At cruise altitude they skimmed above the cloud layer and circumvented towards black cumulous cloud. At 5.15pm, they arrived in the vicinity of Ciudad Boliviar. Venezuela, but minutes later the starboard engine backfired violently and lost power. Charlie pulled the mixture control back to lean, reduced power and hit the feathered button. The big three bladed propeller came to a stop. Jack then increased power on the port engine, reversed their course, and headed for Pierco Airport Trinidad, British West Indies. He called Pierco Tower, reported an engine out and notified them he was making an emergency landing.

For the next thirty minutes they encountered severe turbulence, hail and drenching driving rain, so upon reaching 2,000 feet they levelled off. Forty minutes after contacting Pierco Tower, and at 1800 feet, Jack experienced an aviator's worst nightmare; the port engine, without warning, went dead cold! He grabbed the microphone and broadcast a 'Mayday' on VHF/UHF followed by a position report. They were 64 miles south east of Pierco Airport and 16 miles from a small emergency landing strip at Perdernales. Venezuela.

Now they were flying a glider, while all hands were ordered to ditching stations, Jack pushed the nose down, and as heavy rain beat against the cockpit window, they plunged towards the unknown.

At 300 feet they broke out of the overcast, but with visibility down to about half a mile all they could see was jungle. Suddenly, off the port bow, Charlie saw a clearing. They veered to the left, and at the last moment Charlie helped Jack heave back on the yoke, slamming into a swamp and bouncing along they hit a tree, sheering off the port engine. Careening to the left the hull broke up into three sections slowing them down abruptly. The fuel tanks had ruptured on impact, engulfing the plane in ankle deep, high-octane fuel. Deadly fumes saturated the area, but miraculously no explosion or fire occurred.'

Although never verified, Commander Ward suspected the fuel Jack Torbert and Charlie Otti had taken on at Ramey Air Force Base in Puerto Rico was contaminated. First, the odds of two engines failing within an hour would seem highly suspicious. *'As I recall, a message was sent to Ramey AFB informing them of the possibility of contaminated fuel in their refuelling trucks or storage units. No reply, to my knowledge, was ever received.*

All hands scrambled out of the wreckage and hurriedly checked each other for injuries, and by the greatest good fortune all had survived without so much as a scratch. Wading ankle deep in high-octane gasoline, they searched the wreckage for survival gear and rations, which for the most part were contaminated, although a canister of drinking water was found useable.

Ironically their survival gear consisted of parkas, thermal boots, blankets, tents and insulated sleeping bags all practically useless in the tropics and as night approached, the rain continued to fall, and then a new adversary arrived, swarms of huge bloodthirsty mosquitoes. They jury-rigged mosquito nets from parachutes which at best were of little help and soaking wet, leaving them harassed by mosquitos and bugs, and awed by the shrieks and whistles of jungle night creatures, to settle down to a fitful night.

At daybreak, clear skies and a deep red sunrise greeted them, and for the first time they were able to survey their surroundings. The clearing was roughly a half-mile long and a quarter mile wide, while around the perimeter the foreboding jungle loomed tall and impenetrable.

Then the sweetest sound they ever heard echoed in the distance from an aircraft engine, faint at first, and then becoming ever louder. Afraid to fire rockets because of the fire hazard, they broke out signalling mirrors, waving them and shouting as they watched the rescue plane circle overhead, dropping ice and rations, and then signalling that a rescue helicopter was on the way.'

Suddenly, Charlie Otti noticed a lone tree about fifty yards from the wreckage; it was tall and almost barren of limbs and leaves, and armed with only the pair of salvaged binoculars, he decided to wade over, climb up, and have a look around. The crew shouted encouragement as Charlie struggled in the knee-deep muck, and after a great deal of effort he arrived at the tree, climbed to the top and waved.

'What do you see?' Jack called out as Charlie perched precariously on a limb.

'Nothing but jungle' shouted Charlie.

A minute later however, as he scanned the perimeter, he saw a sight he'd never forget. Eight of the most ferocious looking individuals imaginable emerged from the jungle, hair down to their shoulders and wielding huge machetes, were setting a course for the wreckage and the unsuspecting crew. Charlie not wishing to reveal his position tried to signal his shipmates by whistling but unfortunately this alerted the natives who changed course, making a beeline for Charlie's tree.

Now that he'd been sighted and fearing not only for his own safety, but the safety of the crew, he sung out load and clear: *'Standby to repel boarders!'*

The crew heard him, but not being able to see the advancing group did nothing. In the meantime, the natives in single file arrived at the tree, and peering up waved their machetes motioning for Charlie to come down. *'I've never seen such a wild looking bunch, and frankly I was scared to death, not only did they look loathsome, but their feet were about twice as wide as normal and I really thought we would all be killed.'*

The radioman was the first one to see Charlie's perilous predicament. *'Mr Torbert, Mr Torbert sir, come quick they got Mr Otti treed!'*

'What are you talking about?' Jack replied irritably as he crawled out of the wreckage and for a minute didn't know whether to laugh or pray. As Jack said later, *'It was the damnedest sight I ever saw, there was Charlie on top of a tree surrounded by eight ugly brutes waving machetes. I ordered the crew to break out the carbines and ammunition, but what they came up with were two totally useless carbines, their barrels bent like pretzels, so there was nothing we could do but watch Charlie and hope for the best.'*

After about five minutes with no signs of hostility from the group, Charlie started down the tree. He noticed the one giving the orders was an old man, so maybe he was the man to deal with. Reaching the ground, Charlie held up his right hand in a gesture of friendship and to Charlie's astonishment, the old man did likewise. As it turned out the Indian Tribe were inhabitants of the jungle, being father and seven sons and appeared only too willing to help.

At Charlie's request, done in pantomime, the group began to help, and in no time hacked out a landing strip for the helicopter. This gracious act however, was not entirely altruistic, as for their efforts they expected the salvage rights to the P2-V, which as it turned out was precisely what they got. The little Bell helicopter circled several times before landing, but instead of landing on the prepared site, the pilot elected to set down on the port wing, a short distance from the wreckage. The pilot motioned for Charlie and Sgt Spann, both nearby, to climb aboard and as Charlie hesitated and motioned for the crew to come forward, Jack Torbert shook his head and waved him on.

Charlie and Sgt Spann waded through the muck and climbed board, amused at the miniature twosome about to lift their combined three hundred and sixty-pound anatomies out of the jungle. Seated three abreast the pilot lifted off and after climbing above the surrounding jungle he attempted to go forward. '*It was then that we experienced the most hair raising adventure of the whole ordeal!'* Grossly overloaded and nose heavy, the little copter headed straight down for the jungle roof!

'*Lean back, lean way back!'* the pilot screamed, as he fought to gain altitude, so Charlie and Spann leaned back until their legs and backs arched, and it was then begrudgingly, that the nose came up. The twenty-minute flight to an airstrip on the Venezuela coastline was a series of climbs and descents with very slow progress, but all three men knew that if they crashed, the jungle would swallow them up without trace.

During one critical gyration Charlie suggested it might be advisable to ditch but then countered by saying the rivers and streams were teeming with piranhas. Their only hope was to make it to the coastline and make it they did- barely.

Later that morning a much larger helicopter was pressed into service and brought out the remainder of the crew, and by mid afternoon all hands had arrived at the Macquarie Beach Naval Air Station, Trinidad. This was one of the British bases leased to the United States during World War 11, and quite by coincidence their misfortune had been timed perfectly, and for the next three days they would enjoy a Trinidad 'Carnival'.

In the aftermath of the Squadron's jungle crash, on the morning of February 8 Commander Eddie Ward took off from NAS Patuxent in his R-5-D # *17274*, destination Ramey AFB, where they would refuel before heading for Trinidad. No word as yet from the missing aircraft and the way things were, it seemed that fifteen members of VX-6 were missing, and with each passing moment, hope for their survival faded. While Eddie Ward's mission was to bring the P2V's survivors home, inwardly, he felt despaired of ever seeing his old mates again.

'*As mile after mile of azure blue water and puffy white clouds passed under my wing, I could not help but dwell on the families of our missing shipmates. The anguish they were going through not knowing if their loved ones were alive or dead was heartbreaking.*

Then suddenly I was taken from the depths of despair to the pinnacle of elation, when my radioman received two messages within minutes with the first reporting the crew were safe and had been evacuated from the jungle floor, and the second, that the missing Otter had been found in the Antarctic and all had survived!

'*It was difficult to hold back the tears,'* Eddie Ward recalled later. '*There would be rejoicing and celebrating throughout the far-flung reaches of the Squadron and Task Force 43.But most of the jubilation and thanks given, would take place in the homes of the wife's and families, whose loved ones had been miraculously spared.'*

For one family, the Hudman's, their thanksgiving would be short lived, for one of the survivors Marine Captain Ray Hudman, was to become one of the Operation's first fatalities a few months later, when his Neptune was to crash on landing at McMurdo during the fly in of *Operation Deep Freeze II* on October 18.

'*As we crossed the Venezuela coast, we soon picked up the jungle clearing, where the twisted broken fuselage of the P2-V lay. I could only dwell on this inconceivable set of circumstances. Four years earlier, March 31 1952, I crashed attempting to take-off from the Arctic ice cap.*

My plane, R4-D BuNo 12417, was damaged beyond repair, and it was Jack Coley, flying a P2-V # 122466, who rescued us and brought us back to Point Barrow, Alaska, and now I was in a R4-D circling above that same ill fated Neptune #122466, sprawled below ignominiously in a steaming jungle clearing. It was now my turn to bring my P2-V crew safely home.'

As opposed to the P2-V crash, the Otter's forced landing could have been avoided. According to Cdr Ward it was a combination of pilot error and poor judgement on the part of the Plane Captain Lt Paul Streich together with the treacherous Antarctic weather also being a contributing factor. While Cdr Ward did not have the official Aircraft Accident Report, he provided facts and circumstances contributing to the accident.

'The Otter being small and versatile was ideal for assisting the tracked vehicles transporting trail parties working out of Little America. Trucked vehicles would take the scientists and their equipment to points of geological or seismic interests, and to minimize the risk of becoming lost or disoriented, red flags were placed at mile intervals along the trail, and as the trails ranged further and further away from Little America, the Otter proved a more expeditious way of transporting the scientists and their equipment and delivering food and fuel.

Squadron doctrine specifically states that under no circumstances should trail party flights be undertaken during instrument conditions. The pilots should keep the trail flags in sight at all times, so with no radio aids to navigation, unreliable charts of the area, and the capricious weather, prudence alone should have dictated compliance.

The Otter left Little America with seven men aboard, and with Lt Streich at the controls, they were bound for an outpost about 400 miles down trail in the vicinity of the Rockefeller Plateau. The flight arrived safely and prepared to pick up LCdr Jack Bursey and his trail party for the return flight to Little America, as this was to be the last trail party flight of the season. To stay within weight limitations, Lt Streich divided the trail party into two groups, taking half of them back to Little America and then returning to pick up the rest.

When airborne Lt. Streich sent a departure report to Little America, and while continuing on they flew into snow flurries, and icy conditions, reducing visibility. At this point, the Plane Commander elected to climb out on instruments and hopefully breakout on top. They climbed to 7,000 feet and levelled off unable to break out in the clear, then for two hours they continued on course with the ice building up steadily. To make matters worse, the windows were iced up, making outside visibility nil. Unable to maintain altitude they slowly started down, and their estimated position placed them in the vicinity of the Edsel Ford ranges, an area surrounded by jagged mountain peaks. Their only option now was to ride the plane down to a crash landing and hope for the best.

Now unable to see out, they felt and heard the aircraft make contact with the snow-covered ground, and miraculously, they landed on the down slope of a mountain. They were well off course, having landed in the Alexandria Mountain Range on Prince Edward VII Peninsula-some 180 miles from Little America.

The Otter had been damaged beyond repair, abandoned and struck from the squadron's records. They were extremely fortunate to have been found, as only under the direst of circumstances should an aircraft be abandoned after a crash. If the plane is intact as this one was, it provides excellent shelter, and additionally a downed aircraft presents a highly visible target for the search and rescue aircraft to spot. In this case, the virtue of patience would have far outweighed the alternatives' concluded Cdr. Ward.

On February 27 tractor train operations in support of the construction of Byrd Station were commenced with CWO Victor Young USN, in charge. It had been planned to establish caches of fuel between Little America and the proposed station site in Marie Byrd Land in order to provide for full payloads during the construction phase once the Navy arrived back for the summer season of *Deep Freeze II* in October or November 1956. But because of the bad weather, progress was slow, in fact painfully slow, and a week after commencing work, the party ran into a heavily crevassed area 110 miles east of Little America.

This area had been crossed and recrossed by lighter vehicles without the least suspicion of crevasses, and it was only by a hint of movement in the snow under a heavy D-8 tractor, and careful investigation that four crevasses were found to stretch directly across the trail.

Mr Young decided to fill in these crevasses and any others encountered, in order to make a safe trail, but before filling could be commenced, he carefully probed and blasted any snow suspected of spanning a crevasse. The two D-8's were engaged in the operation of filling a large crevasse on the section of the trail which had been crossed and recrossed after probing and blasting when the D-8 driven by Max Kiel CDI-USN [Fat Max to his mates] was backing, preparatory to dozing ahead, when suddenly and without warning, the snow beneath his tractor gave way.

The tractor plunged backwards and was swallowed up by a 100-foot 'V' shaped crevasse, with the cab of his tractor smashed by the impact with the narrowing ice walls, and Kiel was instantly crushed.

It was impossible to recover Kiel's body but Chaplain Peter Bol USN still conducted a service at the gravesite. It was now clear to Cdr.Whitney that further operations were futile with the season so far advanced, and crevasses appeared to be everywhere and could not be detected by ordinary means. The unhappy death of Max Kiel and that of Richard Williams earlier in the season cast a demoralizing gloom not only over the tractor train crew, but the whole of the naval personnel on the ice.

In his cabin aboard his flag ship *Glacier*, Admiral George Dufek had time to reflect and review the first season's Antarctic operations. While only four months in duration, it didn't come without a high price achieving Task Force-43's objectives. Several ships were expected to be damaged when operating in the polar region, and planning for such an operation, one had to be aggressive to work in such elevations and extreme sub zero conditions.

Breaking a thirty six mile channel through heavy pack ice, caused the ice breaker *Edisto* to lose a propeller, while the *Eastwind* broke a propeller shaft, and the oil tanker *Nespelen* was crushed between two ice flows, cutting a gash in her side, with the subsequent loss of 140,000 galls of avgas.

The *Glacier* ran aground in uncharted waters while breaking ice along the 'beach' to moor the YOG's, and the cargo ship *Greenville Victory, Wyanot* and *Arneb,* all received superficial ice damage while attempting to land a survey party at Cape Adare, with the landing craft overturning in rough seas and being lost, but luckily Capt Thomas and his crew were saved.

Six of the Squadron's aircraft were stricken from the operation's list, suffering damage beyond repair. An Otter lost in the Rockefeller Mountains, a Neptune in the Orinoco area of Venezuela when en-route to join the search, and could not be salvaged, although the parts from the Otter which crashed at McMurdo and a helicopter that was lost in New Zealand during training exercises, could. Another plane and helicopter suffered a surface accident in Antarctica. Two navy personnel-Richard Williams and Max Kiel gave their lives in the construction of the bases for the IGY and Cdr Oliver was the only squadron member to sustain serious injuries.

On top of all this, the two R4-D's that were to play a significant and pro-active role in *Deep Freeze I* couldn't make the trip and were eventually sent back to the US, thus abbreviating the Task Force's Antarctic programme.

The damage to the Task Force ships was estimated at $US300, 000 and several hundred thousand dollars on aircraft that required replacing. [1956 costing]

Admiral Dufek paid a tribute to the personnel of VX-6, writing that they could be extremely proud of their achievements. The long-range aircraft had opened the Antarctic airways, and they had sighted approximately a million square miles of previously unknown territory, which for the first time gave a comprehensive picture of the Antarctic continent. *'The bases at Little America and McMurdo Sound were established and self-supporting. Equipment for the construction of Byrd and the South Pole bases were now stored in supply dumps adjacent to these camps, so they had laid the foundation well, for the IGY 1957-58.'*

CHAPTER FOUR

'ALL HANDS ON DECK'
THE SQUADRON FLIES SOUTH AGAIN FOR DEEP FREEZE II.

*Operation Deep Freeze 11-the US Navy's second
Season in Antarctica in preparation for the International
Geophysical Year –IGY.*

By late April 1956, the Squadron's personnel had completed their first deployment in Antarctica, and with the exception of the wintering over party, had returned to their Home Port at Patuxent River Naval Air Station with the warm smell of spring in the air, leaving behind seventy-two personnel at Little America and ninety-two at McMurdo, who waited for the long Antarctic winter nights to begin, from April 22 and ending August 22.

'With the wind howling to blizzard force, and temperatures dropping to 78F below zero there were still many days of good weather with temperatures rising to a balmy 12 below, and on clear 'days' the stars stood out so brilliantly, you felt you could pluck them from the sky, while the aurora australis lit up the heavens in a blaze of glory from horizon to horizon, sweeping in grandeur across the sky, in a soft veil of moving lights that were mostly white, but with tinges of blue, red and green along the edges, merging into the outer darkness.' Wrote Admiral Dufek in his book *'Operation Deep Freeze'.*

The Admiral was painting a picture of life in Antarctica, for those squadron personnel left behind in their tight camp life that now seems a little primitive compared with Antarctica today. In 1956 the men were comfortable with ventilators bringing in fresh air, escape hatches in the roof providing an exit in case of fire, a diesel engine driving generators for electricity for the bases, supplying light, heating, cooking and water power.

Even with the isolation of an Antarctic camp, the basic surrounding was of a hotel without the frills, causing the various barracks to display signs such as 'Suite Sixteen', 'Beverly Hilton' and the 'New Wellington' [after a Christchurch Hotel]. Life in Antarctica for those VX-6 personnel was to always depend on each other, and the best cure for boredom from this isolation and being 12,000 miles from their loved ones, was as Cdr Whitney at Little America and Lt Cdr Canham at McMurdo knew, a routine schedule and hard work, broken with regular celebrations like Christmas and New Year and the 4th of July.

The Squadron Commanding Officer Gordon Ebbe along with the Executive Officer Lt Colonel Hal Kulp USMC would soon be leaving and although the new Squadron Commander had not been appointed, word had it that it was to be Captain Douglas Cordiner, who at the time was assigned to Admiral Dufek's *Task Force 43* staff. Gordon Ebbe had met him while embarked on the *USS Glacier* en-route to McMurdo the previous December, when commencing *Deep Freeze I,* and their working relationship had been less than satisfactory. From Gordon Ebbe's observation; he was moody, sullen and somewhat sarcastic. Born a son of a career Army Colonel, he had been raised as an Army 'brat', and true to Army military tradition of the times, he applied for, and was appointed to the United States Navy Academy, graduating with the class of 1935, and spent his first two years at sea aboard the USS Battleship *Arizona.*

It was not until 1942 that he went from the *'Black Shoe Navy'* into aviation as a lighter air pilot, flying Blimps convoying Merchant ships in the North Atlantic Ocean during World War 11.

After the war, the Navy instructed all lighter than air pilots, to train as normal aviators, and accordingly in 1947 he entered Pensacola, receiving his pilot's designation in May the following year. Like all his 'helium head' contemporaries, he was quite senior in rank, but however woefully limited in heavier than air flight and experience.

The designated name of VX-6 for the squadron is compiled from the letters V indicating 'heavier than air' aircraft, while the X distinguishes it from aircraft engaged on operational duties. Their target was the preparation for the *Deep Freeze II* summer season and the eventual arrival of the first C-124 Globemasters in October for the first polar landing on October 31.

From the time the Squadron arrived at NAS Patuxent in January 1955, the Squadron had been persona non grata for reasons not really understood by many senior officers. It had been on the recommendation of Admiral Dufek by Commander Ward, that the Naval Air Station [NAS] be designated 'Home Port' for the squadron, due to the relatively short distance between Patuxent and Washington DC for the anticipated frequency of meetings during the Squadron's formative period.

'Although this proved to be true, the attitude of the Patuxent River Station from the commanding Officer down was negative. They seemed to be of the opinion we were thrust upon them without the formality of an official request. In any event, on May 27 1956, the 'Home Port' of VX-6 was officially changed from Patuxent River to Quonset Point Naval Station, Rhode Island' recalled Eddie Ward.

This permanent move to Rhode Island had ramifications for the families of the Squadron's personnel, who had to be relocated twice within a year, being a far greater uproot for the school age children who had only just settled into their schooling, thus causing anxiety for parents in search of adequate housing.

Hank Jorda and Eddie Ward loaded up a R5-D with enlisted personnel and flew up to Quonset to look for housing, and fortunately the Navy had just constructed a housing complex at Hoskins Park, located on Narragansett Bay that was ideal for all the Squadron, officers and enlisted men. In contrast to the treatment the Squadron had received at Patuxent River, the Air Station personnel at Quonset Point couldn't have been more hospitable and co-operative, and they were assigned generous office space in one of the old seaplane hangers with the Station Supply Department provided outstanding services from the time they first arrived.

In mid June Rear Admiral Dufek deputy commander of the United States Antarctic Expedition and Captain Gerald 'Jack' Ketchum flew into Christchurch by USAF Globemaster for advanced planning discussions for *Deep Freeze II* which would begin eight weeks earlier than the previous season, and with a larger force. A ten-ship force with a destroyer escort operating between New Zealand and Antarctica was first thought to be too large to operate from the Port of Lyttelton, so the possibility of using Auckland and Dunedin was considered.

The destroyer *Brough* commanded by Lt Cdr W F Duhon would be requited at Lyttelton in early October to get on station between New Zealand and McMurdo for the schedule fly-in by XV-6 Squadron on October 20 with the Globemaster transporters of the USAF and the Navy's most powerful icebreaker required at the edge of the pack ice a day earlier, while other US ships would stage through New Zealand in early December. It was the first of the giant Douglas Transporters to land at Christchurch International Airport.

With Captain Ketchum it was Lt.Cdr Donald Kent, the USN's logistic officer, who told reporters that he had reserved 40,000 cubic feet of space in the ships for material. The USS icebreakers would carry one helicopter each, with the exception of the *Glacier*, which would carry two, to be used for spotting passages through the heavy pack ice. The one year old 8775 ton *Glacier*, the most up-to-date icebreaker, would lead the force, along with *Atka* who had called at Wellington and Dunedin eighteen months previously, while on an Antarctic reconnaissance. The Coast Guard icebreaker *Staten Island [96500 tons]* and the *North Wind,* who was the same class as the *Edisto,* had not been in New Zealand waters before.

Captain Kent travelled to Wellington for talks with Sir Edmund Hillary and the Ross Sea committee concerning New Zealand's requirements, as the US Navy would transport their material to Antarctica. Capt Kent then returned to Christchurch to begin a search for office space for the advance party due at Harewood in late July.

The destroyer escort was to be the 21 knot *Brough,* an Edsell class vessel of 1850 tons and one of the Navy's Atlantic fleet, its task, to act as a station ship between Christchurch and Dunedin airports, and McMurdo, for the fly-in.

While in the USAF discussions were held for the resetting up of a temporary maintenance base for their Globemasters at Harewood, for when the squadron of eight C-124's would arrive in October and bring with them 120 tons of spare engines, spare parts and repair equipment and be housed in huge tents set up on the edge of the runway. While some planes were flying from an ice strip at McMurdo to the South Pole, others would be taking part in a shuttle service between Christchurch and McMurdo.

The first cargo totting Globemaster arrived in early September bringing an advance USAF party of Administrative officers, maintenance men, cooks, bakers and other specialist men of the 18th Air Force, to be based at the RNZAF camp at Weedons, N.Z. Originally the 80 ton transporter at that time, was the largest plane of that type in the world and was due in Christchurch on August 23, where she remained to be joined later by her seven sister ships. Group Captain F.R. Dix, the officer commanding the RNZAF, spent three weeks in the United States inspecting the USAF's Strategic Air Command HQ at Offut Base in Omaha.

Following the Change of Command ceremony at Patuxent on June 26 1956, the new Squadron Commander, Captain Cordiner had elected to remain in Washington DC with his wife Kay, conducting the essential Squadron business from his offices at *Task Force 43* HQ, with the newly appointed Squadron's Executive Officer, Commander Eddie Ward, who was also Officer in Charge.

Captain Douglas Cordiner, who had been the Admiral's senior operations officer the previous year in *Deep Freeze I* was the son of an army officer, who had grown up in the military service. A tall blond man deliberate in his movements and thoughts, an able planner, organizer and leader with a dry wit, set Douglas Cordiner above his peers.

On Monday June 25 1956, Commander Ward received a call from Captain Cordiner to make reservations for him in the BOQ [Bachelor Officer Quarters], requesting a plane be sent to Anacostia to pick him up, so firing up an old UF-1 Albatross, Commander Ward headed south.

'Once airborne on the return trip, I was invited up into the cockpit, and there is nothing that breaks the ice faster than a cockpit conversation' wrote Commander Ward in his memoirs, *'For the better part of two hours we discussed everything from Squadron business to the whims of the 'powers that be' on the Task Force Staff. This was the start of an outstanding working relationship. I admired and respected Doug Cordiner and we became very close friends during Deep Freeze 11.'*

Now qualified as a R5-D Plane Commander, and with the deployment for the Antarctic only a few weeks away, Commander Ward was scheduled to fly the Admiral to Hawaii, and he and Hank Jorda had the task of making final crew and aircraft assignments, with nine aircraft in all, excluding the Otters and Helicopter. Shortly before deployment, Ward received a call from the Captain, *' Ed, I know you are in a hurry'* he said handing him a letter, *'but it's from the sky Pilot.'*

'I glanced at it; it was from the Base Chaplain's Office. The gist of it was that inasmuch as we were embarking on a dangerous mission, it might be a good idea to conduct a Fleet blessing. It struck me as rather amusing as the only Fleet blessings I'd ever witnessed were fishing fleets.'

On August 20 1956 the Admiral received a message in Washington from Commander Whitney *'Today is a significant milestone in the lives of all of us in the Antarctic. The American flag is again raised over Little America V and the Air Operation Facility to herald the sun's rising and mark the end of the Antarctic winter night.'*

'It was a significant day for us here at home too,' wrote Admiral Dufek *'It meant we would soon be on our way back to the ice-covered continent at the bottom of the world.'*

So on a beautiful New England September afternoon, all hands turned to, and fell in for the Captain's inspection. The flight crews lined up in front of their aircraft with the remainder of the squadron personnel flanking either side of the formation. Captain Cordiner went through the ranks of an obviously proud squadron resplendent in their dress blues, and following the personnel inspection, two navy chaplains conducted the blessing, imploring Divine guidance and protection from the perils that lay ahead. It was a very moving and a stimulating experience for all hands.

The objectives of *Deep Freeze II* were to be comprehensive, hazardous and resolute, with the first and highest priority to be the establishment of a permanent base at the South Pole, in preparation for the IGY, scheduled to commence on January 1 1957. The initial specifications called for accommodation to support a twenty-four-man crew, built to consist of connecting rooms providing a lounge, library, galley, mess hall, meteorology station three bunkrooms, storerooms, and a compact dental and medical dispensary, with heating systems designed to maintain a constant inside temperature of 62 degrees F.

To insure a constant flow of communications during the long winter nights, a radio tower would be erected adjacent to the main building, while the outlying sheds would house the seismograph and a myriad of meteorological instruments. An oil-fired generator with a backup system would supply the necessary electrical power, as the camp would be totally isolated from the outside world from the end of February to the following October, making it essential that one years supply of food, fuel, medicines and spare parts be on hand.

Of lesser priority were five other auxiliary stations, planned to be operated and occupied by IGY scientist at Byrd Station, seven hundred miles east of Little America in Marie Byrd Land, Wilkes Station, fourteen hundred miles west of McMurdo Sound on the Budd Coast near the Windmill Island, Cape Hallett Station, four hundred miles to the north of McMurdo at the foot of the Admiralty Range and Ellsworth Station, some eighteen miles diametrically opposite McMurdo Station on the Fitchner Ice Shelf.

In addition, a small supporting Station to be known as Beardmore Base was to be established on the ice lake near the foot of the Beardmore Glacier. This would act as an emergency landing site and refuelling station for the Douglas R4-D's returning from the South Pole.

The second obstacle to overcome, directly involved the aviators of VX-6, and the performance of the Squadron's ski equipped aircraft. At temperatures of thirty-degrees below zero F and colder, skis tended to stick to the snow rather than slide, and to compound this problem, at altitudes of 10,000 feet, an engine's performance is moderately reduced and hampered by the weight.

The following gross weight comparisons best illustrate the point. The maximum allowable gross weight for a commercial DC-3, the equivalent of the Navy R4-D was 25,500 pounds, the Navy and Air Force authorized a gross weight up to 29.000 pounds for their R4-D's and C-47'd. VX-6 was proposing to fly the R4-D's approaching a gross weight of 37,500 pounds! Accounting for the additional weight were the skis, fuel, survival gear, passengers and JATO bottles.

The South Pole Station is perched on top of a wind swept, desolate and thoroughly inhospitable ice plateau at an elevation of ten thousand feet, where temperatures were estimated to drop as low as 100 degrees below zero F during the bleak winter months. Actually –105 F was recorded in the first year, making these brutal temperatures a major concern for Paul Siple, who was destined to be the first Pole Camp Commander.

Deep Freeze II would be a big year for Task Force 43 and their roughest mission, with twelve ships and 3,400 men, to support the US National Committee for the IGY creating a sizeable undertaking. In September, talks were being held as to selecting Invercargill, New Zealand's most southern city, in preference to Taieri, Dunedin, as a take off point for the squadron's R4-D's, but no decision would be made until Admiral Dufek arrived in the country in October. Releasing the information in Christchurch on September 10, Captain John Cadwalader, the commander of the advanced echelon of *Task Force 43*, told the *Christchurch Press* that during this season four Douglas Dakotas would also be involved.

In the meantime the R4-D's would arrive at Taieri on October 15, the date pencilled in for their departure for the Antarctic, although Capt Cadwalader didn't give any reason why Invercargill airport was being considered, except to say it was a more southern position, and should it be possible for the R4-D's to leave from the city's airport with the assistance of JATO, it would be more advantageous, by giving the twin engine aircraft more than half an hour extra flying time, which was an important consideration in view of the 2,200 mile flight ahead for the pilots.

After many months of preparation D Day had arrived, and on Thursday September 13 1956 in Washington, Rear Admiral Dufek turned over the four ships of his command to their destination in the pack ice of the Weddell and Ross Seas and off the Knox coast to commence *Operation Deep Freeze II.*

'Early the following morning I went to give my sons a hug and say goodbye. George, the sleepyhead only murmured 'Good-bye Daddy, you going to the office?' But young David was full of questions, and as I drove away I saw him at the window waving to me. I blinked away the moisture from my eyes. It would be spring when I saw them both again,' wrote the Admiral in his book *'Operation Deep Freeze.'*

A Navy man grows accustomed to saying good-bye, but it's always hard. Yet I was leaving in the company of men whose ability I respected and whose friendship I valued. We were returning together to get on with the job we believed to be important to Antarctica, a land that was not a stranger. This year presented for the Navy, the most difficult task of the expedition, and because it was difficult, its completion would be all the more rewarding.'

The Naval planes were now stripped of their photographic installation and fitted with extra fuel tanks, which on tests, had indicated they would make it there this time. One of the most comforting results of the tests and training was reported by Capt Cordiner to his boss, being that his R4-D's landings and take offs on the Greenland icecaps in August at an elevation of 40,000 feet, were the same approximate elevation as at the South Pole, and all had been more than successful.

Under the command of General Chester McCarty, the 18th Air Force would provide the eight C-124 Globemasters that were on their way to Christchurch after extensive training in polar air drops, and under the command of Colonel Horace A Crosswell commander of the 63rd Troop Carrier Group.

Weeks earlier word had been received at Donaldson AFB from Greenville's 18th Air Force base, working in close association with Task Force 43 and it's Commander of VX-6 Cdr Gordon Ebbe, *'In preparation for the IGY of 1957, the United States plans to construct the first permanent scientific station at the South Pole. The Navy will do the building, and the USAF's job is to deliver and airdrop everything –500 tons of building materials, fuel, food and scientific supplies.'*

Next came the clincher from Major General Chester McCarty, the 18th Air Force's commander, when he made Cassity, Aerial delivery operations officer for Operation Deep Freeze. *'No problem, I had thought at the time. But now it's obvious this operation would be no picnic. Still, all my life I have tackled the impossible.'*

Capt Cassity [retired from the USAF as Major], joined the Air Force when just out of High School, and was told he would never get into pilot training without a college degree. *'I failed at the first try, but applied again, earned my wings in the upper ten percent of my class, and by 21, I was flying combat- then there was the Yugoslavia mission.*

My orders had me in a small grassy field behind enemy lines, the purpose: to rescue a group of displaced persons who would face almost certain death, if caught by the Nazi. But instead of the expected twenty, forty desperate souls waited. We simply didn't have room for more than twenty, yet I couldn't leave even one behind, so I flew them to safety, even though our overloaded little plane brushed treetops coming out.'

Reasoning that if the Navy needs a D-2 Cat to prepare the building site at the South Pole, then that he could do after returning to Donaldson to set out the assignment. At the time, the Air Force's giant jumbo military transport was the Douglas C-114 Globemaster, the only aircraft with the necessary range and cargo space to accomplish the Antarctica mission- trouble is that until then, nothing as heavy as a D-2 had ever been dropped from a C-124, in fact, the plane's manufactures had not designed it to make large airdrops.

While it could hold a Greyhound bus, the vehicles were roll in roll out from on the ground, so new rules had to be written, but time was running out, as the first flight to the Antarctic would depart from Christchurch in early October.   .

Gathering the top NCOs of the 1st Aerial Port Squadron, Capt Cassity began a series of brainstorming sessions to ascertain how best to achieve the impossible. '*Chaps here's what we have to do, first and foremost is the matter of an adequate platform on which to mount the D-2 tractor for air dropping. There exists a 6,000 pound load bearing platform, but designed for rear extraction, and we need downward ejection, for over twice that limit.'*

After extensive good American know-how, the airman came up with a set of drawings to construct an H-frame adapter which would fit the elevator uplocks of the C-124, then had it manufactured, figuring that such a drop would require a parachute at each corner of the platform for the giant six-ton Caterpillar. Test drops were arrainged in the snow covered Leadville, Colorado, and '*as I watched from the ground, my men dropped six tons of sand and water filled barrels, but inadvertently draped the large silk parachutes over high tension wires- knocking out power over the Hoover Dam area.'* recalled Capt Cassity,

The second attempt fared even worse, when just after take-off the C-124's main landing gear hit a snow bank, plummeting the Globemaster back to earth, and fortunately no one was injured, but the crew had to wait for another Globemaster to be dispatched from Donaldson to take them home.

Those vital observations provided answers as to what they could encounter in the Antarctic. In high winds the parachute disconnect system could drag the dropped equipment across inaccessible expanses of ice, or if the chutes detached prematurely, the vital equipment would disappear into deep snow.

The 'think tank' designed two quick release devices and had them manufactured for a D-2 Caterpillar as an electrically actuated explosive charge when coming in contact with the surface, so after months of modifications and testing, the team flew back to Quonset Point for a do or die test drop of the real thing.

On the day of the drop, the 18th Air Force Commander called a staff meeting at which he held two memos in his hand. '*Gentlemen, I hold in my right hand, this message from the Douglas Airplane Company, 'without extensive and costly modifications to the aircraft, a D-2 Caterpillar tractor CANNOT BE DROPPED FROM A C-124.' Yet,'* the General continued, '*in my left hand I hold a strike report, 'this afternoon at Quonset Point, NAS, Capt Oscar T Cassity successfully airdropped a D2-Caterpillar tractor from his C-124.'*

With mission go, the us Air Force could now deliver everything necessary for Operation Deep Freeze, while there would be further unanswered questions and obstacles, the biggest challenge by far was the hostile Antarctic environment, with the coldest, windiest, and highest elevations in the world, which could detrimentally effect the equipment. However, a few weeks later, after gaining praise and getting the green light from Admiral Dufek, Capt Cassity and his crews headed to the bottom of the world via Hawaii, Fiji Islands and their home base, Christchurch, New Zealand.

George Dufek wrote. *'A small supporting air base would be established on the ice near the foot of the Beardmore Glacier, some 400 miles from McMurdo.*

A Navy ski-equipped R4-D [accompanied in the air by a C-124, loaded with survival gear attached to parachutes] would make the landing on the polar plateau. If it flipped over, or the snow was too soft for take off, the C-124 would drop its equipment, including a weasel, fuel and sleds, for as the aviators said, if there was a choice they would prefer to drive mechanical equipment rather than to follow behind dogs.

With this mechanical train, a downed crew could search the area for a more suitable landing field. If the situation should prove hopeless, they would head for Beardmore, and McMurdo could follow their progress. The scientific station would then have to be established in a more suitable area closest to the Pole. Once this was ready, it is possible that a small weather station could be placed at the pole, aided by a small tractor train from the air base.

But we pinned all our hopes and plans on our belief that we could operate ski-equipped aircraft on the south polar plateau, though these planes were too small to carry the bulk of the equipment needed. If the snowfields were unusable, C-124's could then drop their load of twelve to fifteen tons of cargo.

The men would assemble the equipment as they did a year ago at McMurdo. An accurate geographic fix would be obtained from the ground, and then this part would be moved as necessary to the exact geographical position of the South Pole.'

All the planing that could be done was done - now it was up to the squadron's fearless magnificent men in their Flying Machines' and their intrepid crews, to bring that meticulous and fastidious planning to a successful conclusion.

At the end of August, Rear Admiral Dufek inspected Captain Cordiner's squadron at Quonset, Rhode Island. *'I was pleased with what I saw. I liked the looks of the young pilots- eager and ready to go, and there were enough seasoned aviators experienced in polar flights, to strike a conservative balance, as they would keep the youngest out of trouble. The crewmen were capable and experienced, the equipment in fine shape, and a review of the records of training, showed that a great deal had been done.'* he later wrote in his book *'Operation Deep Freeze.'*

On September 17 1956, the wheels of R5-D *BuNo 56505* lifted off the Quonset Point runway and would not return until March 22 1957- During that six month deployment, there were triumphs and good fortune.

In the first week of October, the fleet arrived safely at Wigram airdrome, Christchurch, New Zealand. The Admiral's first task on arrival at Christchurch was to meet the US Ambassador Robert C Hendrickson along with other government and military officials and New Zealand's IGY leaders and Sir Edmund Hillary, to confer about the two countries plans for the coming Antarctica season, and its ambitious programme.

After a twelve hour flight from Nandi in Fiji, the first of the Douglas R4-D's arrived at the RNZAF Station at Wigram on October 1 1956, to kick off *Operation Deep Freeze 11*, which would bring both tragedy and write aviation history, before the month's end.

For two weeks the aviators and aircrews of VX-6 Squadron spent preparing both themselves and their aircraft for the first fly-in of the season, and during their numerous flights checked the radio equipment and honed their flying skills, as they spent hundreds of hours in the skies over Christchurch, going on until everything worked to their total satisfaction. Sadly an incident was to have a tragic impact on the season's operations once the squadron arrived in Antarctica when the Neptune bomber *Boopsie* was to crash on the Ross Sea Ice Shelf a few days later, killing four crewmembers.

The Skymaster transporters went on a number of local training flights to test their operational skills of the newly formed parachute teams by flying around Christchurch, as each of the parachutists jumped from the Skymaster and landed on the Wigram airfield's grassy area.

The last to jump was Marine Captain Rayburn Hudman, but unfortunately his parachute opened only slightly, snagging on the transporter's horizontal stabilizer, necessitating the R5-D to fly in circles around the airfield for half an hour before Hudman was able to wrest his chute free and make a routine landing. While he sustained no injuries, it was as if it were a divine warning of the tragedy that was to unfold within seventeen hours.

Lt. Walker Harris the squadron's flight surgeon was one of eight passengers aboard the R5-D with the Admiral, which had departed the previous day, piloted by Commander Harry Jorda with co-pilot Lt. Commander Jack Donovan. Included in the team was Captain Rayburn Hudman, the lone parachutist attached to VX-6, from the elite group of specially trained paramedics, established in 1956.

Captain Hudman who had formed the 13-man unit the previous year in Antarctica, was on that fateful Neptune flight, which crash landed in the Venezuela Jungle in February. Today hundreds of OAE's owe their lives to this young Marine, who was stationed at Saunderstown, Rhode Island, when he was picked by Rear Admiral Richard Byrd to make the trip to Antarctica the previous year.

What Captain Hudman left to his predecessors was a skilled unit, experienced in Antarctic rescue, having later established themselves as a vital part of *Operation Deep Freeze*. The unit set a number of records, including Air Force Technical Sergeant, Richard J Patton becoming the first man to parachute at the South Pole, on November 25 1956, and PR1 Harry Gorick of the VXE-6 Para rescue team, setting an altitude record in Antarctica, when he landed at McMurdo after free falling for two minutes from 20,500 feet, on January 12 1972, just one day after Dick Spaulding jumped from 12,500 feet. These events not only demonstrated the unit's ability to perform under extreme Antarctic conditions, but also were a fitting tribute to the Marine Captain Rayburn Hudman.

His distinguished Marine military career would be truncated before he was able to implement his Antarctic mission, for he was to die on the continent, 10,000 miles from home. Fate took another bitter twist in the Marines life just hours before departing from Christchurch, due to a last minute shuffle of crew and passengers originally scheduled to fly south with the Admiral aboard the Skymaster, when he gave up his seat to Lt. Walker Harris USN, and was assigned instead to fly with Lt. Commander Dave Carey aboard the ill-fated P2-V Neptune.

Before Capt 'Trigger' Hawkes departed for the Antarctic he attended a meeting with the New Zealand Ross Sea Committee regarding progress on their proposed Scott Base at the foot of the Ferrar Glacier. Hawkes told the committee's secretary Mr A S Helm, that the exact site of the camp would need to be known to the wintering over party before they could make a survey and report on ground conditions. An immediate reconnaissance had not been possible until now, because the squadron's only Antarctic based helicopter had been grounded due to peeling on its rotor blades, making it unwise to send it out on such a flight, so a replacement helicopter was being flown down by Globemaster.

The main concern for the Ross Sea Committee was the depth of the permanent ice on the proposed site, for if the ice was too close to the surface, the radio and IGY aerials would be difficult to set up and liable to be blown down in the first gale, as were the American's aerials last summer.

Cpt.Hawkes explained that the Task Force men were particularly busy just now and he thought it would be some time before they had a serviceable helicopter and a crew available to carry out the job for the New Zealanders.

At Harewood airport, Commander John Marabito the Task Force meteorological officer, laid out two charts in the mess room remarking that *'This looks as good as it gets - conditions are static with a ridge of high pressure extending all the way to McMurdo, but with low cloud, so you will not see much of the sea.'*

Addressing Commander Henry Jorda, who would fly the Skymaster southwards ahead of the main fleet, Cdr. Mirabito continued *'At the surface the winds are nor-westerly, and increasing in force about 1000 miles out. If you find you are getting westerlies of 40-45 knots at 8,000 feet, then drop down and you will catch the nor-westerlies. The conditions are almost exactly the same as last year, though we are flying down much earlier than last year. There is a negative wind component and the clouds are thinning out.'*

After a short informal discussion and a few questions from Cdr.Jorda, and his co-pilot Lt.Cdr. Jack Donovan, the briefing broke up, and looking at his watch Jorda suggested to Jack Donovan, *'Let's have tea and toast, then we'll leave for Harewood just after four.'*

At noon on Wednesday October 17 Lt Dave Carey, the commander of the fatal Neptune was invited to join Cdr John Mirabito and Commander Ward for lunch. Following the meal they felt the weather conditions between New Zealand and the Antarctic were sketchy at best, but with three reporting stations, the Auckland Islands, McMurdo, and the US Destroyer escort located mid way along the flight path, forecasters were in agreement, although weather at McMurdo at the approximate arrival time would be marginal due to blizzard conditions.

Commander Mirabito was of a different opinion, as the genial VX-6 Staff Meteorologist had forecast 'hot and dusty' all the way with a tailwind thrown in for good measure and recommended the flight launch go on schedule. This likeable, friendly meteorologist was eternally optimistic, always smiling and bubbling over with enthusiasm. *'I really believe John never wanted to worry or disappoint the pilots with an ominous weather forecast'* wrote Commander Ward, for it was Admiral Dufek who had hand picked him for the job, so it was natural that the Admiral accepted John's forecast as gospel truth.

Harewood operations had provided the squadron with a telephone conference call to Captain Cordiner, who was flying as Gus Shinn's co-pilot in the lead R4-D aircraft from Dunedin. The Skipper and Commander Ward balanced the pros and cons of John Mirabito's forecast against that of the forecasters at Harewood and McMurdo, and as was his prerogative, the Squadron Commander would have the final word, but he was undecided.

'What do you think Number One' Commander Ward asked.

'Lets invite John to come along; it might change his mind. Frankly I think we're between a rock and a hard place. You know how eager the Admiral is to get underway.'

'I agree Ed' he said, *'we'll launch on schedule. Good luck.'*

'Thanks Skipper,' Ward replied, *'See you in McMurdo.'*

The crews for the flight south to commence Deep Freeze II were:
R5-D #56505- Cdr Eddie Ward, LCdr Hank Hanson, Lt Bob Anderson and Lt Dick Swadener, R5-D #56528 Cdr Hank Jorda, Lt.Cdr Jack Donovan, Lt.Cdr Harold Todd and S/Sgt Huff USMC. R4-D # 17274 Lt.Cdr Eddie Frankiewicz, Lt Jim Waldron and ENS Creech, R4-D #17276, Lt.Cdr Conrad Shinn, Capt Douglas Cordiner CO. S/Sgt Arrants USMC, R4-D #12418 Lt Harvey Speed, Lt Allen and ENS Hanson, R4-D #17163 Lt.Cdr Roy Curtis Lt Ray Hall, ENS Smallwood, P2-V # 122465 Lt Dave Carey, ENS MacApline, S/Sgt Spann, Capt Ray Hudman, P2-V-7 Lt.Cdr Charlie Otti, Lt Al Raithel, ENS Schick and T/s.Sgt Silberman, P2V-7 # 140438 Lt.Cdr Jack Torbert.

More than an hour before the expected 6pm take-off the crew arrived in their khaki flight suits, flying boots and an informal collection of headgear from Commander Jorda's uniform cap with a 'scrambled egg' on its peak, to a fishing hat worn by one of the aircrew.

Shortly afterwards the boss, Rear Admiral Dufek drove up with his aide Commander Donald Kent, both men in their blue dress uniforms, and after photographs they climbed up the narrow metal ladder to the aircraft door. The party included newspaper correspondents and television crews and as the doors swung in Mr. Bill Hartigan, the National Broadcasting Company cameraman who had won the lucky draw on Monday evening, was the only correspondent who would make the flight.

On October 15 1956 Cdr.Jorda got the thumbs up from the leader of the ground crew, so at exactly 6 pm, the Skymaster aircraft started to roll down the runway, the six JATO bottles beneath her wings were fired and with a thundering roar, she lifted into the air right on schedule for an almost 14 hour flight to Antarctica from Christchurch.

The lone Skymaster climbed into the early evening sky above Harewood airport, and apart from heavy icing four hours into the flight, the flight was normal, arriving at 7.15 pm. On the surface at least, it was little more than a routine flight, but still the most dangerous flight in the world, as it departed with eight men aboard, with little more fuss or bother than that of a departure of the *QANTAS* commercial DC-6 that had left for Sydney a few hours before. [The R5-D is the military version of the Douglas DC-6].

A USAF Globemaster *'The State of Carolina'* arrived off McMurdo 47 hours before the full naval squadron were scheduled to touch down on the ice. The C-124 commander Captain Henry Embree gave half hourly weather reports on wind direction and velocity, cloud cover, and other factors, which were radioed, back to another Globemaster on the ground at Harewood.

On its return to Christchurch, one of the pilots Captain Gaylord said that after flying about 100 miles south of the *USS Brough*, they had experienced some surface icing. *'When we first made contact with the weather ship, it was being battered by heavy seas, so we flew in close to the ship shortly after 2.30 pm but it was obscured by heavy cloud.'*

The Globemaster turned back to Christchurch at 3.10pm after travelling half way to McMurdo, touching down at 6.30 pm after more than twelve hours in the air.

New Zealand signallers at Addington Barracks, Christchurch, were maintaining around the clock radio contact to the US Antarctic expedition's McMurdo base with weather reports for the Navy fly-ins.

Cdr Mirabito was on continuous duty from 4am, except for a small break in the afternoon, checking weather reports from five separate sources. He received weather reports from McMurdo Station, Little America, from the *USS Brough,* thus keeping informed of conditions on the flight path. The *USS Glacier* reported from the edge of the pack ice and the New Zealand Met service at Harewood observatory gave him a general picture of conditions as received from all operational Antarctic bases, including the French, Russian and Australian bases and as far west as Mawson on the Mac Robertson Coast.

Weather for the October 17 fly-in was marginal. The day previously, a total whiteout virtually isolated McMurdo from the outside world, with communications all but cut off.

Before departure from Wigram for their southern take-off point Taieri, the R4-D crews said their sad farewells to their newly adopted Christchurch friends, *'We were agreeably surprised to receive telegrams sent to us in Taieri from our friends in Christchurch, wishing us well on our long flight to the Antarctic. One family even had a case of bottled beer delivered to our aircraft, which was intended as a reminder of the good times we had had in New Zealand. Unfortunately, the beer froze in the bottles on the long flight to the ice and after we had landed at McMurdo there was only a case of cracked glass and frozen beer to greet us',* recalled James Waldron, who was the co-pilot to Eddie Frankerwicz aboard the R4-D # *17274 Charlene,* who's name and story is told by Eddie:

'We were en route to Christchurch for Operation Deep Freeze 1, and as we approached Hawaii, we lost the power in the starboard engine of my R4-D aircraft and made an uneventful landing. An engine change was required, and while on the ground I was contacted by a ham radio operator who asked if he could patch me up by telephone with this young sick girl Charlene from Michigan, to cheer her up. Obviously I said 'of course darling.'

She was so surprised to be talking to a pilot on the way to the Antarctic and I'm such a sentimental fool that at night I still have tears in my eyes. When I suggested that I would get her name 'Charlene' painted on both sides of the aircraft, she was ecstatic, and I was in tears.'

Lt.Cdr.Eddie Frankiewicz and his crew corresponded with the little girl, sending her photographs of the plane and its crewmembers. Her silent courage inspired the crew while in the Antarctic.

More about Frankiewicz: after graduating from the Bay Path Institute co-educational college in Springfield, Massachusetts, Frankiewicz found employment in a Connecticut chemical factory, where he learnt about the American Legion in Stratford who were sponsoring a Civilian Pilot Training Programme, so Eddie entered with 200 other students. The object was to be instructed in navigation, aeronautics, aerodynamics, airframe, and radio, and to prepare the students for their written exams, being sponsored by the FAA at the time. Most of the students were engineers from the Sikorsky Aircraft Plant at Bridgeport [Stratford] Airport.

The top ten students were given flight scholarships, which gave them their private pilot licenses, and Eddie Frankiewicz was one of the ten.

'So that's how I became interested in aviation, and then followed the next course, called the secondary course which we flew in bi-planes-twin cockpits, goggles, helmets and the scarf around the neck- and we did aerobatics.' Eddie said.

That was 1940, and then the third course that the government sponsored and in that CPT programme was a cross-country. That was in a Stinson Reliant, a beautiful aircraft, and we flew all over New England on a cross-country navigational course; the fourth and final course was the flight instructors course, and at the completion of it, we were checked, and were given commercial pilot's ratings by FAA.

Now we not only had a private pilot's license, but a flight instructors rating and a commercial rating. At that time we found out that Pan American Airways were interested in accumulating pilots for the African Division they intended opening - Pan American Africa Limited and we were hired as pilots.

In early January 1942, all four of us went to Miami, and through the Pan American pilot training programme, we were sent to Africa to be stationed at Accra on the British Gold Coast. We flew up and down the west coast of Africa, across the continent and to Anglo-Egyptian Sudan and onto Egypt, Arabia, Iraq, and Iran and India. It was a glorious experience for us youngsters. It was now late 1942, and when our forces invaded Northwest Africa it became too dangerous for us to fly because of German activities, so I resigned from Pan Am, and joined the US Navy.

As I wanted to be a fighter pilot, and the Navy told us, 'yes we do need pilots already trained', but then told us ' If you want to become a fighter pilot, we've got to send you through extensive training, but we desperately need transport pilots and you already are a transport pilot'. So we joined the Navy on that basis and became early members of the Navy Transport Squadron VR-1, the first air transport squadron, as a very young Lieutenant junior grade. I was flying four engine aircraft across the North Atlantic and that's where I got my first real experience on cold weather flying, because those North Atlantic storms were pretty vicious.

I also got my first experience of icing and lots of snow.' Eddie told me. *'One thing that we used to do when a senator or Admiral came up into the cockpit on night flights and it was snowing, was to use a powerful hand held Aldis light in the darkened cockpit to check on the amount of snow falling or ice build up on the windshield and the leading edge of the wing. We would place the Aldis light against the windshield or side cockpit window and press the 'on' switch. The light reflected by the snow accentuated by the speed of the aircraft was a startling sight, scaring the dickens out of the uninitiated.'*

Eddie told me that throughout all of World War 11, they never had an accident in a four engine aircraft across the North Atlantic. *'After flying DC-4'S and DC-3's I got indoctrinated into cold weather flying in VR-1 and throughout the war we got plenty of icing and snowstorms, and instrument flying. I was stationed at Hutchison, Kansas in the Advanced Training Command on PB4Y2's, a four engine Convair patrol aircraft because I had just come back from the Korean War with VP-28, flying the same type of aircraft. So it was a pretty easy tour for me, when I heard about VX-6 Squadron wanting pilots, I flew to Washington to be interviewed by Lt Commander Pendergraff, who I believe was one of Eddie Ward's assistants.*

It was 1955 and we landed at Anacostia on the outskirts of Washington DC in a mild blizzard, but then the blizzard intensified while I was being interview by Pendergraff and he asked what were my intentions about going back in it, and I said 'it's a blizzard you know, there's nothing new about those, and we're ready to go back' and so I think I made an impression upon him as I was indoctrinated into VX-6- getting my orders very shortly thereafter, and reported to Navy Air Training Centre at Pautuxent River, Marylands.'

Four R4-D-5's with larger cabin [600-gallon] fuel tanks installed to increase their range, flew from Taieri to Christchurch and watched by several thousand, departed at 6pm, with *BuNo 17274 XD/4* commander Eddie Frankiewicz the first to take off. "Gus Shinn and the Squadron's Commander Capt. Cordiner took off next in *BuNo 17246*, followed by Lt. Harvey Speed *BuNo 12418* and Lt. Roy Curtis in *BuNo 17276* bringing up the rear.

The squadron's commanding officer, Capt Douglas Cordiner, told a press conference that with a forecasted headwind of 17 knots, and even against this wind, the Dunedin based machines would have enough endurance to reach McMurdo but too little safety margin would be left.

Recalling the take-off and subsequent flight to the Antarctic, Commander James Edger Waldron wrote in his book *'Flight of the Puckered Penguins.'*

'There was no runaway at Taieri, just a grass field for our take off. All four R4-D's taxied to the edge of this grass to wait takeoffs at ten minute intervals. I watched the first aircraft lumber into the air, with all eighteen JATO rockets firing. It looked impressive and I waited with great anticipation until our turn. The ten-minute wait seemed much longer than it really was and when it was our turn, Eddie advanced both engine throttles. When both engines came up to full power he released the brakes and slowly we started to roll. The grass field tended to slow the aircraft, so takeoff was even more sluggish than the takeoff that had been on a paved runway at NAS Alameda, California

.About midway across the field, when the trees ahead seemed to be getting ever so close, Eddie fired all the JATO's even though the tail wheel had not yet came off the ground. With this magnificent push from rockets we gained flying speed and climbed ahead only just missing the trees by several feet. When the JATO's quit firing and we were left with only two engines turning, it seemed as though we had almost stopped going forward. The coastal hills a few miles away appeared to be too high to surmount for a while since we were barely climbing, but after a few additional miles they passed below us and in crossing the coastline all we had ahead if us was level ocean all the way to the Antarctic.

Eddie kept a modest amount of climb power on the engines and we slowly crept upwards at about 200 feet per minute, until we reached 10,000 feet of altitude. Using more power than that, would have consumed fuel needed at the end of the flight and would reduce our chances of making it successfully all the way.

As we climbed in altitude it was nice knowing we were observed on the ground back in Taieri as we made our takeoff. If we had been told on the radio, I believe we would have been a lot more apprehensive about out flight south. Shortly after we left the field, we received a message from one of our aircraft still awaiting takeoff asking us if we had any in-flight difficulties. Feeling that everything was normal with our aircraft, we radioed back that things were proceeding smoothly and gave no serious thought concerning the call.

What happened was that Eddie fired the JATO rocket before the tail wheel had come off the ground and the searing rocket blast set the tail wheel on fire! Since the fire was behind us and out of slight, we didn't know it was there. We trailed black smoke for a long time until the tail wheel burnt itself out, doing no further damage. Our forward speed fortunately blew the flames behind the airplane, so none of the aircraft metal parts were singed or burnt.

Had such a fire occurred further forward on the aircraft, we could have turned into a magnificent fireball since we were so heavily loaded with fuel. Another situation which could have been catastrophic, would have occurred if we had lost an engine after leaving the ground, in such a case we would have started dumping fuel to lighten our load and the gas pipes ran next to the tail wheel. The burning tail wheel would have lit off those hundreds of gallons of gasoline trailing out of the dump pipe and our aircraft would then have become a burning torch.'

CHAPTER FIVE

SOUTH AND ONWARDS WITH COMMANDER EDDIE WARD – THEN THE SQUADRON'S FIRST FATAL - 'BOOPSIE' CRASHES ON LANDING KILLING FOUR.

*The first fatal accident in Antarctica- a Lockheed
Neptune PV-2 converted bomber 'Boopsie' crashes
on October 20 1956.*

At ten past six, Lt.Cdr Hank Hanson and Commander Eddie Ward settled down in the cockpit of their aircraft *R5-D # 56504* and commenced their pre-takeoff check list, when suddenly a red light on the control panel came on indicating the cargo door was open, so Cdr.Ward called the plane Commander Captain John Weir on the interphone. *'What the hell is the problem?'*

'We have another passenger coming aboard sir. He said he has the Admiral's permission' Captain Weir replied.

What follows is the first hand personal account of the Skymaster's historic flight to Antarctica as recanted in his memoirs written in 1998. To give readers an insight as to the flying conditions from New Zealand to Antarctic in the early days of Deep Freeze 11, October 18 1956,

'Proceeding aft through the main cabin, I was incensed. Who was this Johnny Come Lately forcing his way aboard? As I arrived at the open cargo doors, the stranger spoke up. 'Yes sir', he said, 'I apologize for being late, here are my credentials.'

For the first time I took notice of his size. He towered above John Weir, and according to his ID card, his name was Don Guy, a correspondent from Associated Press and the letter he presented was signed by the Admiral authorizing him passage to the Antarctic by either ship or plane.

I glanced at my watch. 'Mr Guy,' I said, 'I haven't got time to give you all the reasons, but the answer is no.'

The big man looked crestfallen. 'Sir', he pleaded, 'I wish you'd reconsider.'

It was nearing take-off time and the last thing I wanted to do was haggle with Don Guy, even though there were only ten of us aboard, and one more would make little difference.

'Ok' I said. 'Come aboard. I'll call the Tower and list you on the manifest.'

'Thank you Sir', the big man said.

As I turned to leave John Weir spoke up. 'Here', he said, handing him a May West [life jacket], 'See if you can squeeze into that.'

Back in the cockpit I turned to Hank Hanson, 'Start number one.'

Hank engaged the starter. The three bladed propellers began to turn. Number three, belching white smoke fired off then settled down. In sequence came number one, two, three and four. I signalled the ground crew to pull the chocks. Cleared to taxi, the overloaded Skymaster grossing 78,000 pounds waddled down the ramp for runway 'Two Seven.'

FIRST HOUR

Hank followed me up on the throttle and at sixty knots the first two JATO bottles were fired, with the last two seconds later. In a climbing bank to the right, trailing two plumes of billowing white smoke, we took up a course due south. JATO bottles jettison, throttles and props reduced to climb setting, propellers synchronized, we began the long climb up to twelve hundred feet.

Well off on the starboard side lay the verdant valleys and foothills to the white slopes of the spectacular New Zealand Southern Alps. It was late spring in New Zealand and the lovely island was liberally ablaze with blossoming flowers and plants. During my short stay of three weeks in the South Island, I had enjoyed every minute of it. The New Zealanders had opened their hearts and homes to us and we in turn had tried to repay their kindness, but they would have none of it. They loved the Yanks, and for us Yankees going to the South Pole, they loved us all the more.

Watching the South Island silhouetted against the setting sun, I marvelled at their tranquillity, their easygoing lifestyle and friendly provincial ways. Then as if to say farewell, this delightful view faded into the soft glow and shadows of the coming night.

It took forty minutes to climb out to the assigned altitude and now level, I scanned the instrument panel for the slightest sign of a malfunction. Temperatures and pressure were normal. The number four engine fuel flow metre however, was reading a shade high. Weir came forward after his visual inspection and reported all was well. Relaxed, I engaged the automatic pilot and settled back with a cigarette and a freshly brewed cup of John's coffee. This flight, I thought would be a piece of cake'.

SECOND HOUR

Wedged up in the astrodome, a bubble shaped blister just aft of the cockpit, Lt.Dick Swadener, navigator par excellence, shouted celestial observations to his assistant Sgt Stribing, USMC. Stribing would record the time and observation and the names and elevation of the celestial bodies, observed. From this data, through a series of computations, a 'three star fix' was plotted. From this the ground speed, drift and earthly position of the aircraft are established.

Wispy clouds began to form between the plane and the glow of a brilliant moon lending a touch of beauty to the lonely night. Gradually, the stars, shining like diamonds dimmed then went out. A slight buffeting and moments later rime ice formed on the wings, and in short order the cockpit windshield and the astrodome took on the appearance of an igloo. It was beginning to look like a 'long winter night'.

THIRD HOUR.

I left the cockpit and strolled aft. John Weir was in the crew compartment recording data from the fuel flow sight gauge meter, 'How do they look John? I asked.

John looked up and frowned. 'Not so good Sir.' he replied. 'The cabin gauge is reading lots higher than the fuel gauge in the cockpit, It's still too early to tell, but I'll check the fuel remaining at the 'point of no return'. That should tell the story.'

I continued aft to the main cabin that was warm and comfortable, but unlike the airline DC-4 version, the amenities in the military equivalent of the DC-4 were totally lacking. The best we had to offer were two reclining seats, so the others would have to be content with canvas benches along both sides of the fuselage. The big man and a sailor were reposing in the chairs, the other were asleep on the benches.

'Everything okay back there?' I asked.

'Yes,' replied the big man. He yawned. 'What time will get to McMurdo?'

'That depends.' I said, 'If the winds and the weather co operate, we estimate a twelve hour thirty minute flight. That puts us in about seven o'clock tomorrow morning.'

The big man squirmed around in his chair, 'that long.' he replied wryly. 'Well that leaves me plenty of time to interview you and some of the crew. Damn!' he cried out as ice particles slammed against the hull. 'What's that?'

FOURTH HOUR

Returning to the cockpit I stopped to chat with Dick Swadener and Master Sgt Stribing. They were seated in the navigation compartment looking bored to death. Dick pointed up to the astrodome. 'It's been frozen solid for two hours,' he said bitterly, 'Here's our dead reckoning position but it's an educated guess at best.'

'Assuming the fuel problem continues,' I asked, 'what do you recommend?'

Dick thought for a moment then grinned, 'Well, if the predicted tail wind holds up like John said it would and if the fuel problem doesn't get any worse and if the ice doesn't slow us down, we just might be okay.'

FIFTH HOUR

Hank Hanson and I sat in the cockpit discussing the fuel situation. The flight would be critical enough without the added aggravation of severe icing and a fuel shortage. Weir came up to the cockpit to report the latest readings from the cabin fuel flow gauges. 'Number four is burning a lot more fuel than I thought' he said apologetically.

'Any idea what's causing it?' I asked.

'No sir, only a guess till we tear the engine down.' He scratched his head, 'A fuel leak is always a possibility but I don't think so. I believe it's a carburettor malfunction. Somehow it's stuck in automatic rich.' then as an afterthought asked. 'What do you think we should do about it?'

'Well John' I hedged, 'There's not much we can do about it. Mr Swadener thinks we'll be okay if the tail wind holds. I'll let you know when we get to the point of no return. We should be there in an hour and a half.' As I spoke, a volley of ice particles from the two inboard propellers slammed against the hull. I reached up behind my head and turned up the rheostat on the propeller de-icers.

'Let's break out the Aldis lamp,' I ordered, 'we'll take a look at the wings.'

John snapped on the high intensity spotlight, and leaning over my shoulder he shone it along the leading edge of the wing. The rime ice had given way to a build up of clear ice and it was building fast. The wing boot de-icers were on but having little effect so I disengaged the automatic pilot, and added a little nose up trim. For the next ten minutes I watched as the air speed gradually backed down from 170 to a steady 145 knots.

SIXTH HOUR.

The outside air temperature read minus 15 degrees centigrade. At last we were getting out of the temperature range that produces the most severe ice build-up. Weir rigged a hose extension to the cabin heating system, then set about clearing the ice from the astrodome and cockpit windows. We were still on solid instruments and had been for four long hours.

Another annoyance set in; glazed ice. It formed from the vapour of our breath and produced a glazed coating of ice in the inside of the cockpit windows, reformed practically as fast as it was cleared, making a visual inspection of the wings and the engines difficult.

John came forward and handed me a fresh cup of coffee. 'How's Riley doing.' I asked.

'He shook his head, Not too good. Do you want me to send him up?'

'Yes, if he's not busy.'

The radioman came forward and handed me his log. For the first two hours he'd had excellent communications with the R4-D's, with all four of them coming through loud and clear on voice frequency, and the same held true when he switched to cw [code]. He then raised the P2V, and as he and Miller, the P2-V radioman were buddies, they had quite a long conversation. It was during this contact that communication faded out and then vanished. From time to time he was unable to get through on any frequency, including the New Zealand emergency frequencies.

'It's like we're out of touch with the rest of the world.' Riley sighed. 'I've tried everything. Trailing antenna, guard channel, high frequency, low frequency, you name it sir.'

'Thanks Riley. Try transmitting in the blind every ten minutes. When you make contact, let me know.'

As Riley went aft, Dick Swadener came forward and handed me a 'Howgozit' chart. This was a graphic presentation of the distance travelled verus fuel used and the fuel and distance remaining. If our estimated ground speed was accurate we would reach the 'point of no return' six hours and twenty minutes into the flight. A further projection put us at McMurdo with an hour and thirty minutes fuel in reserve.

SEVENTH HOUR.

According to Dick's dead reckoning we were well past the 'point of no return'. I felt greatly relieved as we were now better than halfway there. But there was another side of the coin. We'd been in and out of severe icing, which had reduced our ground speed, but by how much was anybody's guess. The number four engines were still burning an excessive amount of fuel, but most disturbing was that for over five hours Dick had been unable to take celestial sights and plot an accurate position.

My foremost concern however, was not our predicament, but the fate of the four R4-D's and their gallant crews. At their overloaded gross weight, severe icing was critical, so an emergency to jettison their fuel would be a long process. This made single engine performance so much wishful thinking until within sight of the great white continent.

Weir had just finished removing the glazed ice from the cockpit windshield when suddenly the sky lit up around us. Great tongues of fire sweep across the heavens, undulating throughout the far reaches of the firmament. This awesome phenomenon would erupt in iridescent colour, retreat, flicker as if to go out, then burst forth again in a display of absolute beauty.

I watched for some moments in silence. Never in the Arctic had I seen such a volatile sight. This was the awesome Aurora Australis! It continued its rendition for another twenty minutes before the final curtain came down, and as spectacular as it was, this was the culprit that caused the communication black out.

EIGHTH HOUR,

Dick Swadener came forward, sitting in the jump seat and placed a chart on the panel.

'Commander,' he said sombrely, 'Stribing and I have just gotten an accurate plot and we're running short of fuel but good.' he paused and lit a cigarette. 'Thirty-seven minutes ago and we're passed the point of no return, exactly an hour and twenty-eight minutes behind schedule. According to the latest plot and 'howgozet' we have five hours and fifty minutes to go. That puts us at McMurdo Sound with dry tanks! Riley can't get through to either Little America or McMurdo, and we don't have any idea of the winds aloft. One thing for sure, based on the information available, it's doubtful if we'll make it.'

'As bad as that Dick.'

'Yes sir, as bad as that.'

'Okay, keep a running plot of our position. Let me know if it changes either way. And while I'm thinking about it, send Weir up.'

John came lumbering up smiling as usual. He was a good old country boy from Arkansas with a decided accent to match. Nothing ever seemed to bother John. 'Yes sir, you want to see me?'

'Yes John' I replied, 'Has Mr Swadener briefed you on the fuel situation?'

He nodded and grinned,

'Let's turn the heaters off in the main cabin, to save some fuel. It won't be much but every little bit counts. Bring the passengers up to the crew compartment. It'll be crowded, but at least they'll be warm. Tell the passengers why we're doing it and not to worry about it, it's just a precaution.'

'I'll give you a hand,' Hank called out as he eased out of the co-pilot seat. 'And while I'm back there, I'll check on Riley, see if he's had any luck.'

NINETH HOUR.

The coffee, black as regulation shoes, and a cigarette, were a welcome respite. Now I could spend a few minutes contemplating the options. Hopefully we'd make it to McMurdo. But what if we couldn't? – It would be foolish to fly to dry tanks, become a glider and make an uncontrolled crash landing in the drink or ice cap. Granted, this was not the most desirable option, but I'd made many landings on the Arctic ice cap and felt confident about the outcome. An ice landing it would be- provided we had an ice field below us.

Deep in thought I gazed out of the cockpit window into the black, treacherous void beyond. Preoccupied as I was, I failed to notice another in the cockpit.

'Commander I order you to turn back.'

Startled, I looked over my shoulder, it was Don Guy. 'I know why you turned the heat off.'

His head and body seemed to crowd me out of the cockpit. His eyes were glazed and he repeated the order in a raspy belligerent tone, while our eyes were less than a foot apart.

'Sure we're short of fuel,' I replied, 'and as far as turning back- forget it.'

His mouth opened as if to say something, but nothing came out, and he didn't budge an inch, just glowered.

I was getting uneasy. From his crouched position he had me pinned against the seat. The situation was explosive, and then he spoke.

'If you won't turn back to New Zealand I order you to ditch alongside the guard ship.'

That did it. 'Get this straight' I said trying to control my rage. 'The only one who gives orders on this plane is me.'

He stared straight ahead.

'Now I'm giving you an order, Mr Guy. Get to hell out of here.'

He hesitated a moment then turned and left.

I called Weir on the intercom and briefed him on what had occurred. 'If he tries to get back in the cockpit', I said. 'Deck him. I don't care how you do it, just do it.- deck the bugger.

'Gladly Sir', John replied.

TENTH HOUR.

The hands on the cockpit clock seemed to take forever, moving from one hour to the next. The fuel state was still critical, and we had not been able to communicate with the R4-D's or anybody else for that matter. Our predicted tail wind was a thing of the past. It was now 16.35 ZULU [Greenwich Mean Time] and we had been airborne for over ten hours. In four hours the crisis would be over. Now we were so near and yet so far away.

'Commander', it was Dick Swadener speaking softy so as not to be heard by the big man standing a scant four feet behind him. 'Mr Guy wants to speak to you.' 'Okay send him up'.

I looked over my shoulder. Directly behind Don Guy stood John Weir wielding a fire extinguisher, his eyes firmly glued on the back of the big man. 'Sure Dick' I replied, trying not to laugh, 'Send him up. Lets see what he has to say.'

Once more Don Guy crouched beside me, only this time looking a bit more composed and contrite 'Commander', he blurted out, 'Two years ago I was on an oil rig in the Gulf during a hurricane. I thought I was scared to death then, but please believe me I've never been so terrified as I am now.'

He'd hardly gotten the words out of his month, when the number four engine backfired so violently it kicked the throttle back on the throttle quadrant. The right side of the plane lit up. We were on fire.

'Secure number four' I called out to Hank. As he scrambled back into the cockpit, I eased back on the mixture control as Hank pressed the red feathering button. As the blades came to a stop I reached for the red handle marked 4. About to release the CO_2, when the flames trailing back to the tail suddenly subsided, and the fire warning light flickered and went out. A visual check by both Hank and John Weir confirmed the fire was out.

Hurriedly Hank and I reviewed the cruise control tables. Under normal conditions, proceeding on three engines presented no problem. In our case however, with reduced air speed and increased fuel consumption due to higher power settings, we'd never make it to McMurdo.

There was only one option. We could attempt to restart number four, which defied every safety procedure in the book, and yet, if it worked, we just might make it all the way to McMurdo.

'Let's give number four a whirl,' I called out to Hank. 'If she lights off again, we still have the CO_2.'

Hank reached over and hit the feathering button; the big blades began to turn, so I eased on some throttle, moved the mixture control slowly from lean to rich and waited. The engine caught, and gradually power was added to the cruise setting. It began to balk, power was reduced and the engine settled down, and after John Weir made a visual check, he smiled and gave me the thumbs up.

ELEVENTH HOUR

'Some good news and some bad news,' Dick Swadener announced. 'Riley is in contact with McMurdo. He's given them our ETA.'

'So what's the bad news Dick?'

'McMurdo is reporting ceiling obscured, visibility zero in blizzard conditions and it's not expecting to let up.'

'Any word from the other aircraft?'

'No sir.'

'Any change in our air speed?'

Dick shook his head. 'No sir, our last fix put us right on course. I'm still estimating McMurdo at 20.22 ZULU. Anyway as I figure it, we'll be down to the fumes.' He reached over and set the cockpit radar remote scope on the 100 miles scale, 'In twenty minutes you should be able to pick up Cape Adair.'

Well, it could be worse, I thought, but not much. Looking up ahead I saw a glimmer of light on the horizon, the first hint of a welcome sunrise. We were emerging from the bleakness of a night filled with anxiety and dread. Now a new day had arrived, although nothing had changed, at least we'd survived the night.

I thought back to past flights filled with uncertainty and fear. Every pilot has been down that dreaded road. When the god of fate turns against you, troubles never came in small doses. It seemed like one misfortune beget another and yet another. Sudden emergencies that resolve themselves in seconds are one thing, prolonged emergencies, quite another. The hapless feeling of being trapped for hours on end in a losing battle with the elements never varied, anxiety, spirit, the will to overcome adversity, the primordial instinct to survive.

TWELFTH HOUR

A bleak sunrise gave way to a subdued grey morning sky. Ahead and slightly off to starboard, Cape Adair came into view. Beyond the Cape, Mt Sabine, rising thirteen thousand feet, stood like a sentinel guarding the entrance to this awesome land, From Cape Adair the coastline paralleled our course to McMurdo Sound, 400 miles to the south.

From our 10,000 foot flight level, the panorama of the Antarctic unfolded with every mile, behind the towering mountains of the Admiralty Range, lay the enchanting wilderness of Victoria Land, a six thousand foot plateau of snow covered ice. It stretched eastwards as far as the eye could see with the overflow from this mammoth ice field creating spiralling blue glaciers that edged relentlessly down to the open sea.

In stark contrast, the weather to the south and west of our course was deteriorating rapidly. A broken ceiling had given way to solid grey overcast. Snow showers had sprung up along the way and a glance down below at the surface of the Ross Sea, confirmed my suspicions as the pronounced wind streaks and foamy white caps spelled gale force winds. Although still far from the solid ice field, I could see large pieces of jagged pack ice bobbing up and down between the waves. It was not very conducive to an emergency ditching.

Far off our port, I happened to catch sight of the big red tail. It was the P2V. How reassuring it was to have company and I was anxious to talk to the Plane Commander Lt Dave Carey and compare notes. I made repeated calls on voice and Riley tried to get through on code, but nothing worked. Cruising slightly faster, Dave gradually pulled ahead, and then vanished in a snow squall. Minutes later the curtain came down and we were back on the gauges

THIRTEENTH HOUR

The navigator arrived in the cockpit with an armful of charts. He spread one out on the console. 'Here's our present position' Dick said, his voice anything but optimistic, 'at 19.34 ZULU we'll be one hundred and fifty miles out. From that point, take up a grid heading of 185 [note Grid navigation is used in Polar Regions due to a rapid convergence of Longitude lines]. That will put us on a direct course for McMurdo. This should take us well clear of Cape Byrd, but only a mile at most from Cape Royds, and from Cape Royds, its twenty miles to the ice runway' Dick paused. 'Hank tells me you're not going to make a Ground Control Approach [GCA].'

'That's right, it will take too long, so I'm requesting a straight in.'

'What will be our approach altitude?' Dick asked.

'Right down on the deck, why?'

Dick screwed up his face. 'Well sir.' He began, 'there are a couple of small islands just to the left of our path, and they're seven miles north of the runway. Take a look.'

The two small dots on the charts, hardly noticeable, were identified as Tent and Inaccessible Islands. The elevation was 100 feet plus or minus.

'One hundred feet plus or minus' I mused 'is that the best they can tell us?'

'Afraid so' Dick replied.

One hundred miles out of McMurdo, I disengaged the autopilot and eased back on the throttle. We started down. It felt good to be on the home stretch. The altimeter was unwinding at 200 feet per minute, and occasionally we'd break out between cloud layers. Snow was falling intermittently and the outside temperature read minus 35 degrees centigrade. Most of the ice picked up en-route was gone and the fuel gauges now became the focus of my attention, as slowly but surely, they were lining up with the big letter 'E''

'Let's even up the tanks,' I called out to Hank.

He leant over and switched on the fuel selector valves to cross feed, 'You've got it all now' he called back.

Dick called on the intercom, 'At 19.52 we were fifty miles out. The sight gauges back here show about forty minutes fuel remaining. The heading looks good, and I'm estimating twenty minutes to McMurdo.'

'Thanks Dick, send the passengers and crew to their ditching stations. Be sure to tell them it's just a precaution.'

Switching to McMurdo GCA frequency, I was relieved to hear they'd made contact with the P2V, he was at 12,000 feet, estimating the Station at 19.52. ZULU. So time now became the critical factor, and the sooner they worked him a round pattern the better. I was to imitate a call to McMurdo when they called me.

'Navy 56505 McMurdo Tower. How do you read?'

'Navy 505, reading you loud and clear. Request your present altitude and ETA McMurdo.'

'We're out of 4,000 at five three, descending to approach altitude. Estimating the runway at 20.12 ZULU, I'm declaring an emergency due to a low fuel state. Request a straight in to runway ONE NINE.'

'Roger Navy 505. Copy okay. Understood-emergency due to low fuel state. Continue your descent and advise when out of 2,000 feet. For your information the latest observation McMurdo, visibility one tenth mile, ceiling indefinite in blowing snow.'

'Copy okay, McMurdo, request the progress of the P2V.'

'Standby 505.'

Lt, Jim Bergstrom, a very capable officer, was in charged of a portable GCA installation at McMurdo. It lacked the precision gear of a larger unit being limited to directional and centreline heading but had no glide slope information.

'Navy 505 Tower, Navy 465 is on base leg at 2000 feet descending.'

'Roger McMurdo.' I looked over at Hank. By his expression, I knew we both had the same thought in mind. If all went well we'd have ample separation, if not, both of us might be in the approach pattern together!

'McMurdo, Navy 505, out of 2,000 at one five nine. Continuing let down to 500 feet.'

'Roger 505, you're cleared to continue approach and cleared for a straight in to runway ONE NINE.'

'Pilot from navigator.'

'Go ahead Dick.'

'Commander, we're right on course. According to radar we're coming up abeam of Cape Royds. That figures with our plot. In twelve minutes you'll be on the ice.'

'Thanks Dick.'

I looked at the remote scope. It showed Cape Royds coming up on our port beam. As I looked out of the window, between snow and showers I could dimly make out Cape Royds. I switched back to GCA frequency. The P2V was turning final as I continued to monitor the approach.

'Navy 465 McMurdo GCA, you are now on final approach. Do not acknowledge any further instructions. Your heading ONE NINE FIVE. Continue your descent to 200 feet. Check gear down and locked. Flaps set. McMurdo reporting one-tenth mile visibility in blowing snow ceiling indefinite, wind twenty-five knots gusting to thirty five from two three zero grid. You will have a crosswind from right to left. Continue your turn to TWO ZERO ZERO correcting nicely to centreline, on course, one mile from runway. Continue descent at pilot's discretion. Drifting slightly to leave off centreline. Continue right to TWO ZERO FIVE. You are now one half mile out. Drifting slightly to leave off course. Over threshold. Touchdown!'

I looked over to Hank and smiled, Dave was on the ice. Seconds later a terse transmission from P2-V. 'McMurdo, GCA 465 missed approach! I'm turning right for a low visibility approach.'

The low visibility approach procedure, consisted of a climbing right turn to the downwind heading. Two minutes on the downwind leg then a 180 degree turn back to the inbound heading. It would take Dave about six minutes to complete his approach. With this latest development, I could not risk continuing my approach,

'McMurdo Tower, 505, I'm taking a wave off. Advise me when P2V is on the deck.'

'Will do 505. McMurdo'

Level at 500 feet, I held the outboard course for three minutes then made a 350-degree turn to the left. Descending to 300 feet, I rolled out on the outboard course.

The Automatic Direction Finder [ADF] needle was wandering five to fifteen degrees to the left course and figuring the crosswind component, this looked about right. I called the Tower, 'McMurdo. Inland on final. Is P2-V clear of the active?'

'505 McMurdo stand by one.'

The silence seemed an eternity.

'505 McMurdo. You are cleared to continue your approach and clear to land.'

Now inbound at 200 feet I called over to Hank, 'When you see the runways tap my arm. Gear down, fifteen degree flaps.'

There was a tremor as the gear jolted down and locked in place.

'Three in the green' Hank called out.

According to the radio altimeter we were at 100 feet and still on solid instruments, I eased down to 50. The ADF needle was holding steady at ten degrees of course. Seconds passed. The ADF needles wavered then swung around one eighty degrees.

'There it is'. Hank cried out as he struck my arm.

'Full flaps.'

'You've got 'em.' Hank called out.

I glanced up from the instrument panel. All I could see was the ice directly below so easing back on the throttles we started down the last few feet. Here the sky seemed to blend with the ice, then gradually the runway materialized, a light grey in contrast with the huge mounds of white ploughed *snow along both sides. The wheels touched down at 20-26 ZULU 08-26 local time. Our elapsed flight time was thirteen hours and fifty minutes.*

I rolled to a stop having no idea where the taxiway might be, or how much runway lay ahead. I'd wait until the 'follow me' vehicle arrived.

While waiting I happened to glance out of the window, something that resembled the tail of a plane was off to the left of the runway. I rubbed the glaze ice from the window and to my surprise it was a big red tail!

'Hey Hank,' I called out. 'Looks like Dave landed in the boondocks!' I looked again and there was the tail all right, but where was the rest of the aircraft? The thought of Dave crashing was inconceivable, I could only hope they all survived.

Minutes later a tracked vehicle pulled up ahead of us and a man leaned out and waved. We fell in behind as he led the way to the parking area. Line crewmen with lighted wands picked us up and turned us into the wind. Across wind, the signal to cut engines was the most beautiful sight I ever saw. Never before or since had I been so thankful that a flight was over.

All this time *Deep Freeze* Headquarters in Christchurch were aware of the weather at McMurdo where a whiteout had virtually isolated McMurdo, with the six VX-6 Squadron's aircraft all reaching the airstrip together. Communications between the Antarctic and New Zealand were all but cut off, although one of the few signals to reach Christchurch on the 18th was *'visibility zero, total washout, blizzard has covered runway walking area. Do not send any aircraft until further word.'*

So that evening the USAF's Globemaster's departure was postponed indefinitely but by late evening on the day of the fly-in, the task force advanced headquarters had received no official confirmation that the aircraft had arrived safely, *'however, if a plane was lost or overdue we would have heard about it fast'* a navy spokesmen told the waiting media at Christchurch airport.

Just as the squadron's fleet had passed the Point of Safe Return, the weather at McMurdo deteriorated resulting from a severe snowstorm, and a low ceiling level, but nothing could be done, as Cdr Hank Jorda and Lt Commander Dave Canham, the commander of the wintering over party at McMurdo stood with Admiral Dufek at the ground control station and watched as the plane come down through the overcast to the left of the runway. The ceiling level was just 300 feet, and with extremely poor visibility, the radio operator, fearing the worst, told the pilot that he would bring him over the runway for a low pass then for a landing. Those on the ground suddenly caught a glimpse of Carey's Neptune slightly to the left of the runway, and at this point he reported to ground control that he could now see and would bring the plane in on his own. Lt Carey was making the first ever Antarctic ground controlled approach [GCA]

Making a right turn on his downwind leg, the right wing dropped and the Neptune nosed down. Realizing he was out of control, those on the ground were horrified and helpless as they watched, unable to believe what was unfolding before them. With the landing gear down, he banked to the right [there were hills in close vicinity to the left] and the Neptune fell on its nose, and as its right wing struck the ice it cartwheeled to the left and disintegrated.

A grief stricken Admiral Dufek watched the tragedy unfold from the ice *'with a sickening feeling, I realised he [Carey] was out of control and would crash. The operator yelled 'pull up', but it was useless. Horrified and helpless, I stood by and heard the grinding of metal on the ice as the right wing struck, and the crash squad fought its way through the snowbank to the plane. Just as the rescue crew began work in the tangled wreckage of the Neptune, the weather closed in to zero visibility, with blurring snow.*

I could hear the fourth plane overhead circling for an approach, and standing on the drift snow at the edge of the runway, I watch the plane flash pass me, but visibility was so poor I could not see the body of the plane. I never cared much for the expression 'coming in on a wing and a prayer' but that was all I could think of, as the pilot and the GCA operator guided the plane towards the runway making a perfect landing.

Grimly each plane crew learnt of the tragedy to Neptune and her crew. Medical Officer LT J Harris, who had flown south with me, the base medical officer Lt Taylor, their corpsmen, the chaplain and volunteers, worked endless hours with the injured.'

When rescuers reached the tangled wreckage of Neptune # *122465* they found Carey and ADI Charles Miller, the radioman, were killed instantly. Capt. Raymond Hudman, USMC, the leader of the Para rescue team, died a few hours later, but miraculously, Petty Officer Clifford Allsup was thrown clear on impact with nothing more than minor head and chest injuries.

As the VX-6 pilots flew south, Lt.Cdr.Gus Shinn [BuNo *17246*] reported that he had lost control of his gyro-stabilizer compass, the most important navigational equipment for Antarctic flying since the magnetic compass became unusable as the fleet approached the magnetic pole, and they had to rely on a special gyrocompass for direction. Should this instrument cease to function properly, there was nothing left to give the pilot the information as to how he should steer his aircraft. With no stars, the pilot would have wandered aimlessly until his fuel was gone.

Just ahead of Shinn, was Lt. Harvey Speed the commander of another R4-D-5 BuNo *12418 Que Sera Sera* [later to make aviation history in the Antarctic], who heroically revised his aircraft and flew northwards until he picked up the disabled R4-D on his radar. The two aircraft joined up in the dark and Speed did the navigating for both R4-D's all the way to McMurdo. In doing this Speed jeopardized his own aircraft somewhat, since he had used up fuel he needed to reach McMurdo. Had there been navigational errors or if the weather was bad on his arrival, necessitating several instrument approaches to the ice runway, this lack of fuel would have spelled disaster.

After passing the 'point of no return' Cdr. Eddie Ward's R5-D *BuNo 56505* number 4 engines backfired violently and momentarily flamed up *'We proceeded at reduced power for the rest of the flight, when we arrived at McMurdo I was down to a 30 minute reserve',* he later told me. Both groups of aircraft were two hours behind schedule- the R5-D's and P2-V landed at 8.30am after almost 14 hours in the air, while the last R4-D-5 BuNo 17246 arrived at 11.15am, 17 hours out of Taieri.

James Waldron again, *'As we approached the Antarctic Continent sometime in the early morning hours we slowly became aware of a change in the light in the sky. At first it was a light grayness on the horizon, which grew brighter in degrees until we could make out the mountains covered with snow that ringed the continent. It was an unusual sight since the greyness turned first to a golden pink and then to bright white, so bright, that we were forced to put on our dark glasses or suffer snow blindness.*

I had seen a few snow covered mountains from the air before but bits and pieces of rock always showed through the snow covering. Here in the Antarctic there was little rock showing through the snow, instead the mountains appeared like giant scoops of vanilla ice cream. All the mountains were over 12,000 feet high and they fell steeply into the frozen sea with no discernible beach. Since the continent was just emerging from an intense winter period, the ocean below us was frozen solid, leaving no open water in sight.

We had been told that there was a very small Navy unit located at Cape Adair, near where we first intercepted the continental coastline. Should one of our aircraft have to make a forced landing near this camp there would have been other humans around to assist us but there was no fuel or repair facilities to get our aircraft back in the air again. Should this have become necessary we would have lost days or weeks in repairing the aircraft and this would have jeopardized the summer expedition operations. Fortunately all our R4-D's had sufficient fuel on board as we passed Cape Adair, so a forced landing did not become a necessity.

As the four sluggish R4-D's slowly plodded their way southwards to McMurdo, there was another of our squadron aircraft making the flight with significantly better airspeed. Lt. Dave Carey's

P2-V Neptune aircraft [a converted bomber] that took off from Wigram Field hours after we did and with the advantages of about 90 mph, he was scheduled to reach the ice runway at the Naval Air Facilities McMurdo, well before us. If he had tried to contact any if us by radio when he passed enroute, I never heard his call.

From Cape Adair we flew along the coast of the Antarctic continent, which ran north and south for hundreds of miles all the way to McMurdo, our final destination. As we drew closer to McMurdo the visibility became worse close to the surface, but at our altitude we could see ahead quite well. On our right was the magnificent row of mountains, which encircled the continent, and ahead and to our left were Mount Erebus and Mount Terror, both heavily covered with snow. Mount Erebus had a spire of smoke from its peak because it is still an active volcano, while Mount Terror, once a volcano, is now dormant.

When we were within radio voice range of the airfield at McMurdo, we called the portable tower, just recently placed on the sea ice, and next to the scrapped runway. We were greeted by a friendly voice, which assured us that they had our aircraft on radar and that we would be given a Ground Controlled Approach for a landing. This type of radar used by the tower gave such specific information about our location from the runway, that the operator in the tower could direct our heading and descent so as to bring us to the very end of the runway, and all we would have to do is to level the aircraft and place the skis on the ice surface.

As we approached the runway and got closer to the surface, the reduction in visibility became more apparent to us in the cockpit, and when the tower told us we were over the end of the runway we were still unable to see any outline of it. Eddie got a glimpse of the runway after we had flown halfway down its length, but since there wasn't enough room left to land, we added engine power, choosing to make another approach with the guidance of the tower radar operator's instructions, until we were at the end of the runway again. This second time our speed was slower and Eddie was able to get us lined up for a landing. The ice wasn't at all smooth but it felt comforting to be at last on the surface after all those hours in the air.

As we taxied from the ice runway to the parking area, I noted in the distance, the tail of a P2V aircraft sitting at a crazy angle and almost upside down. For a moment I couldn't surmise what I was looking at. My mind was weary from the long hours in the air and it refused to accept the reality that this was the tail of a P2V that had overflown us during the long flight southwards, and it's crew had come to a violent end there on the sea ice. I communicated this to Eddie, as he taxied the aircraft to our parking spot, and I can still hear his repeated curses as he realized that some dreadful thing had happened on the ice in front of us.

Back to Eddie Ward, again, who was later appointed to conduct the official investigation. Eddie climbed down from his R5-D to be greeted by the carnage, and the loss of his shipmates who only a few hours earlier, had been enjoying each other's company in Christchurch.

I recognized two of the parka-clad figures standing by the side of the plane as Admiral Dufek and Operations Officer Cdr Hank Jorda. Admiral Dufek looked up, grasped his two mitten covered hands together and raised them above his head.

As I climbed down the cargo door ladder, Hank Jorda came walking up. 'I guess you know about the P2-V, happened just before you landed.'

'I know, I saw the tail off the runway. Are the crew okay.?'

He shook his head, *'afraid not. Dave Carey and two others were killed, we don't know about the others.'*

A wave of nausea hit me, 'any idea how it happened?'

'Apparently he was making a tight right turn at low altitude, we couldn't see it but we heard him go in,' he paused and puffed on his pipe. 'Ed,' he remarked, 'Pull your parka hood up, it's twenty five below.'

The Admiral, Hank Jorda, Hank Hanson, Jack Donavon and myself, boarded the sledge for the mile ride to Camp. It was bitterly cold and there was no let up in the weather. Hank Jorda told me the Base was in contact with the R4-D's, and I was greatly relieved, as they were plodding along estimating McMurdo in an hour and a half.

The library adjacent to the sickbay had been converted to a makeshift operation room. The storeroom behind, transformed into a morgue where minutes earlier a grim faced rescue crew had gently placed the bodies of Lt. Dave Carey, and Petty Officers Miller and Marze.

The Admiral, Hank Jorda and I went directly to the library to check on the survivors. As we walked in Dr Taylor the base Physician, and the Squadron's Flight Surgeon, Lt Bucky Harris were preparing for emergency surgery. Dr Taylor turned and looked at us over his shoulder.

'We're doing everything we can Admiral,' he said. 'So far we have five survivors. Ensign MacAlpine is unconscious as well as Sgt Spann; Allsup was thrown clear of the plane and appears to be okay. Lewis is in a stable condition, but Captain Ray Hudman is unconscious, he's haemorrhaging badly, and we're poorly equipped to deal with this.'

I watched in disbelief. It was a nightmare unfolding. The stench of gore, disinfectant and alcohol permeated the room. Two corpsmen placed Ray Hudman on the library table, his breathing was laboured- more like gasps. The doctors worked quickly in a desperate effort to save Ray's life, and we watched silently as Ray's breathing faltered, regained and then suddenly stopped.

Hank and I followed the Admiral as he trudged out of the library door. It felt good to be out in the cold air, but we walked along in silence, there was nothing left to say. At the VIP quarters we excused ourselves and Hank and I proceeded to Operations.

Inside an Aerologist was plotting isobars on a large weather map. He summoned the Duty Officer Lt. Jorgy Jorgenson. Jorgy was an old friend of mine from Point Barrow, Alaska, and he was an outstanding weather guesser, having called the shots right for me many times, and after a few minutes reminiscing, he pointed to the weather map, 'There's a clearing tread' he said, 'By the time the R4-D's arrive, most of the snow will have moved off to the east,' and the R4-D's landed an hour later without incident, for the weather was exactly as Jorgy had predicted.

The last aircraft roared down the rugged ice runway with only seconds to spare in the interval between snows qualls. Lt.Cdr. Roy Curtis reported compass trouble, causing him to make a landfall 350 miles west of their planned course to Cape Adare, which marks the West End of the Ross Sea.

Later Commander Ward again:

I knew then that the P2-V had crashed and feared the worst for my friends.

So my first impression of the Antarctic was, as Captain Scott said. 'God, what an awful place this is!' The following day however, with visibility at over a hundred miles, I gazed to the Admiralty Range in the distance. That view and my subsequent flights deep into the interior of the Antarctic changed my impressions dramatically. I can truly say that I have never seen such magnificence. Words cannot adequately describe it. The Alaskan scenery is somewhat of a miniature version of the Antarctic which has beautiful mountain ranges, glaciers, rivers, lakes and streams.'

Lt. Commander David Canham Jr., USAF from Selfridge Air Force Base, standing with his boss, witnessed the disaster from the Ground Control Approach [GVA] shack.

'They transferred from GCA to visual approach. There must have been a lapse of two or three seconds when they lost orientation. The plane banked sharp right and dropped and dived into the ice.'

A feeling of gloom pervaded the camp as the men went silently about their duties- the tragedy and the weather had deeply affected the squadron's spirits, and to make matters worse and adding to the Station's depression, a sudden Antarctic blizzard set in, making outwork difficult, and keeping men indoors, so a message was sent to Christchurch to ground the Globemaster flights until the weather had cleared and the snowdrifts could be removed from the runway.

The lost crew members:

Pilot: Lt. David W Carey USNR aged 32, seated in the pilot seat; instant death from transaction of the body at the level of the diaphragm.

Observer Marine Captain Hudman had been strapped in the radar operator's seat and died later. Had he been sitting in his normal seat, without doubt he would have survived; he died after eight hours, from internal bleeding and shock.

Co-Pilot ENS Kenneth D MacAlpine USNR Naval Aviator age 24 in co-pilot seat, injuries, unconscious 3 days, brain contusion, deep penetrating wound to right buttock, fracture right clavicle and right elbow, partial collapse of right lung with hemothorax.

Plane Captain Marion O Marion Marze ADI USN on Flight Deck, instant death, fractured skull and brain damage.

First Radioman, Charles S Miller AT1 USN in radioman seat, instant death from fractured skull and brain damage.

Second Mate Clifford C Allsup. AD2 Navigator's compartment, injuries, and minor contusions.

Second Radioman Richard E Lewis. Radar compartment AD2 USN .Injuries, fractured upper right leg and left shoulder.

Navigator Sgt.Robert C Spann.USMC on Flight Deck. Injuries indefinitely unconscious, fractured skull, brain contusion, and subdued haematoma.

The popular saying that life must go on is doubly true in the Antarctic, because the weather and the remoteness from civilization makes it imperative that everyone participates actively towards the survival of the group. The after shock of David Carey's P2-V Neptune crash had taken an enormous toll on the emotions of all who had just flown in from New Zealand, and after a few hours of sleeping off the effects of the cold flight south, found work had to continue next day, none more so than for Commander James Waldron, who had been appointed the Squadron's Administrative Officer.

He had the task of making a squadron's report, and one task he would rather have avoided was the positive identification of the personal effects of the crash victims, which were inventoried and prepared for shipment to their next-of-kin.

When the accident occurred, those on the scene at the time sent messages to the States, giving the names of the deceased and the injured, as well as brief details of the crash. Subsequently the families of the deceased were notified and representatives of the squadron in Rhodes Island gave condolences. In the case of the enlisted crewmen who had been killed, an unexpected reaction came from his family, because of the time difference of New Zealand being nineteen hours ahead of the America's west coast.

When the representative of VX-6 arrived to report the death, he was told that their son had called the family before he took off from Christchurch in the afternoon of 16th, and not realising, that because of the time difference being a factor, they reasoned their son was still alive at McMurdo. *While we realized that this was the cause of the discrepancy in their reasoning, I still told the Executive Officer that I should take steps to positively identify the deceased airman and the advise our Rhode island squadron office my feelings.*

I went first to the enlisted quarters at McMurdo Station and located a man who had known the deceased man and sadly asked him if he was willing to identify the remains of the airman, he said he was prepared to assist and the two of us proceeded to the tent, which had become our temporary morgue. The four corpses had been placed in zipper bags and since the air in the tent was well below freezing, the bodies were frozen solid. I unzipped the bag of the deceased in question and asked the enlisted man if he could identify the body, which he acknowledged that he did. After identification was completed I sent a message to squadron HQ, verifying that the airman had indeed died', Commander Waldron said.

After the fatal crash, the Squadron's Commander Office D L Cordiner ordered an informal board of investigation and appointed Lt. Commander Eddie J Frankiewicz USN, Commander Eddie Ward Lt. Joseph Harris, the base's physician [M C] USNR Dr.Taylor.

The scope of the investigation conducted included the securing of a detailed account of the events as they occurred and the obtaining of written statements.

Within hours of the fatal crash, Commander Hank Jorda assisted Commander Ward in the initial phase of the accident investigation, a tracked vehicle took the pair to the end of runway ONE NINE ZERO, where the wreckage lay one hundred yards beyond and to the left. Pacing off distances, they identified and marked parts of the aircraft, then compared notes.

From the point of impact the wreckage was strewn 159 yards, but by now snow had almost covered smaller pieces of the Neptune. The starboard wing panel and fuselage however, were clearly visible, followed by an engine standing straight up into the snow, beyond this was the red tail section showing very little damage and clearly displaying the plane's name 'Boopsie' named after Lt Dave Carey's youngest son aged only two months.

Crossing the runway threshold, it appeared that Carey was off to the left, he may have been able to swerve back and land safely, however, according to Commander Ward, this was highly problematical, and his decision to take a wave off and make a low visibility approach was certainly valid. Due to terrain obstructions on the left, he entered a steep right hand turn, and in doing so lost altitude, and with a wingtip impacting with the ice, the P2-V cart -wheeled and was totally destroyed.

Commander Ward said that while the accident happened in daylight hours, visibility was extremely limited due a blizzard and a whiteout condition. Ward wrote that yet another item had to be considered, as in a safety bulletin by Lockheed, it advised the ski configured P2-V with the skis in a down position had a tendency for the nose to drop while making a steep banked turn. The Plane Commander should have been well aware of this, but being under stress, this too may have contributed to the accident.

'As I surveyed what remained of this once beautiful machine, for a few moments I became lost in time. My thoughts strayed back to the Naval Air Station Patuxent River, Maryland, and the date February 7th 1952. On this day three unique aircraft, an R4-D and two P2-V's were parked on the flight line. Ski equipped, they were about to embark on a mission code-named 'Ski-Jump 2". While photographers snapped pictures, reporters jotted down the objectives of the polar mission, and then amid a rousing farewell, the three planes took off for Point Barrow, Alaska. Their mission was to land and establish oceanographic stations on the vast Arctic ice cap.

A month later, this little armada suffered its first causality, my R4-D BuNo 12417 crashed taking off 400 miles from the North Pole. Its remains were destined to drift in an endless odyssey on the polar ice, eventually plunging to the bottom of the Arctic. On February 7 1956 P2-V BuNo 122466 the aircraft which crashed in the jungle of Venezuela, while on a mission to rescue an Otter Crew in the Antarctic, piece by piece it was dissected by Indians and carried away from the floor of the steamy jungle swamp.

Now on October 27 1956, the last of a once proud VX-6 fleet lay in ruins. Resting in the solitude of the frozen Antarctic wilderness, P2-V BuNo 122465 Boopsie would soon be forgotten and vanish under a gentle blanket of snow and ice.'

As soon as the weather broke, plane Captain John Weir and his crew tore down the number four engines of Commander Ward's R5-D Marilyn # 56505 [named after his wife] and a close inspection revealed a carburettor malfunction as suspected and a valve had to be changed. Changing an engine on the Antarctic is quite a challenge due to the intense cold; wrenches have a tendency to freeze in the mechanic's hands, sometime snapping in two. Oil congeals like thick molasses, while frostbite could disable a man within minutes.

To overcome the ever present bitting cold and discomfort, the squadron rigged parachutes around the engine and then blew hot air inside, thus enabling the mechanics and air crews to work with some degree of comfort.

Two days after the fatal crash, and with the weather at McMurdo only marginally improved it allowed the first USA's C-124 C Globemaster to leave Christchurch. As *Miss North Carolina* of the 18th Air Force left to airlift an injured airman back to New Zealand, the Douglas transporter was under the command of Col. Horace Crosswell, the USAF Group Commander.

By October 25, after the worst weather on record at McMurdo, which almost cut the station off from the outside world, there wasn't a bunk to spare, with 40 men sleeping in the chapel and in tents. Major General Chester McCarty, commander of the 18th USAF intended taking a party of five Colonels to McMurdo on the Thursday when he departed in his Globemaster, but Rear Admiral Dufek said he had accommodation for just one of the senior officers and 'pulled rank' on the other disgruntled Colonels leaving them behind in Christchurch to return to their hotel and wait.

Major Chester E McCarty was born in 1905 in Pendleton, Ore, being active in the Oregon National Guard for many years, advancing from Infantry private to battery commander of Artillery, holding all enlisted ranks through to master sergeant. His reserve commissioned status dates from 1926.

During World War II, McCarty served as squadron commander and operations officer at Morrison Field, Florida and at Borinquen Field, Puerto Rico. He was staff officer with the North Africa Wing of the Air Transport Command and later, commander of a chain of air bases in the Middle East. On his return to the United States in 1945, he commanded the brass hat transport group at Washington National Airport.

Recalled to active duty, General McCarty resumed practice as head of a Portland law firm and became active in the Air Force as commander of the 305th Air Division and later of the 403d Troop Carrier Wing and flew combat missions in Korea. In 1952 when the 403rd Wing was deployed to the Far East, General McCarty assumed command of the 315th Air Division [Combat Cargo] in Japan and directed the Korean Airlift. In 1953 and 1954 the General commanded US Air Force airlift operations in support of the French in Indo-China, including support for the massive airdrops to Dien Bien Phu.

Returning to the United States in 1954, General McCarty became commander of Tactical Command's Eighteenth Air Force Donaldson AFB, South Carolina, flying C-124 Globemaster airlift missions which built the Dewline in the Arctic , making more than 700 landings on frozen lakes and bays from Alaska to Baffinland and directed TAC airlift operations throughout the world with a fleet of C-124's C-130's and C-123's.

General McCarty was a command pilot with more than 12,000 flying hours, including 469 hours of combat time. He had flown almost every type of USAF aircraft including the supersonic F-100 and F-104 jet fighters.

General Chester McCarty died on April 5 1999.

Last season, during *Deep Freeze I*, the McMurdo Sound base was used as an air facility and most officers and personnel of the expedition lived aboard ships. This season more than 60 men had already flown south from Christchurch, adding considerable strain on the facilities at the base camp built by the 90 member wintering party.

Several of the first Globemaster flights had taken prefabricated huts to McMurdo and they were being erected as soon as they were unloaded. The USS Icebreaker *Glacier* was still trying to break a passage through the pack ice to McMurdo, and the ship's Captain Cdr Bernard Lauff reported that she was lying to some 800 miles from McMurdo amid uncentrated hummocky and pressured ice about 7 ft thick. She had proceeded slowly and with difficulty until the visibility dropped, and would wait until the weather lifted enough to send out scout helicopters to locate a usable lead or open water.

This was Antarctic October 1956.

Two days after the tragic crash, the huge Globemasters of the 18th Air Force began their flights to McMurdo with cargo and priority passengers. This gigantic airlift operation brought the first planes of this size to Antarctica, the first being commanded by Colonel Crosswell, departing from Christchurch at 5.20pm on October 20, and arriving at McMurdo, twelve hours and twenty three minutes after taking-off from Christchurch, carrying a six ton payload including a VX-6 Otter. The second Globemaster departed at dawn the following morning.

The first Globemaster was quickly turned around to fly the three survivors back to Christchurch, arriving late on Sunday evening. The C-124's Commander, Colonel Horace Crosswell said that all four men were *'very sick'*, and arrangements to fly out the bodies of the four crew members and Captain Hudman, would be made after the next-of-kin had advised the Navy of their wishes.

Within15 minutes of the Globemaster's arrival at Wigram AFB at 9.45am on the morning of December 22, two RNZAF ambulances with a motorcycle escort, sped from Christchurch Airport to Christchurch Public Hospital with the three survivors from the Neptune crash

The evacuation of the injured was only one of the many tasks for which the C-124 was built, serving such missions during the Korean War.

Flight Lt. S M Cameron, doctor at the RNZAF station at Wigram, saw the three US airmen, Richard Lewis, C.C Allsup and Sergeant R S Spann. With them was a fourth man, a walking patient, who was one of the wintering parties, who had been injured at McMurdo.

Ensign MacAlpine, the fourth survivor was still at McMurdo, too seriously injured to return on the flight, but was brought back to Christchurch late on Monday evening with the USAF Medical Officer Capt William Driscoll, the same time that AT2 Richard Lewis regained consciousness in Christchurch Hospital, *'he appeared to be very groggy from pain killing drugs which had been administered, but his eyes were open and he was beginning to mumble unintelligible greetings'*, a Navy spokesman told the waiting media.

The Neptune was a total write-off, but Col Crosswell said there were some parts of the airplane, which might be used as spare parts 'I only saw it as I circled above it this morning', he said when pressed re the state of the airstrip, by the media at Harewood. Of the runway, he said that the general condition was good, although a little bumpy, but that was to be expected when one considers it sits on fourteen feet of ice, but the Navy blokes had done a Herculean job over the cold Antarctic winter to get it in any condition at all for landings and takeoffs.

A few days later the United States Ambassador to New Zealand [Mr R C Hendrickson] visited the crash survivors in hospital. The Ambassador was in the city to inspect the Air Force's Globemaster squadron and to have talks with Task Force command and VX-6 Officers. After lunching with Major General McCarty at their Weedon base, Mr Hendrickson paid a visit to Ensign MacApline and Aviation Technician Lewis.

'It was a great consolation to me to find the boys recovering nicely, I wanted to assure them that they would receive every aid and comfort possible from the Navy and Christchurch folk. Both men were quite cheerful and hopes were that they would be fully recovered soon.'

Many messages had been received in his office, which confirmed to him the tremendous bonds of friendship between our two countries, and in particular the City of Christchurch.

Within hours of the crash, the Squadron's Commander Officer Douglas Cordiner, in accordance with his verbal instructions, formed a formal board of investigation inquiring into the crash, to be set up on October 19 1956 or as soon after as practical. The senior squadron's aviator Lt.Cdr Eddie Frankiewicz and the Navy's Medical Officer Lt Joseph Harris were appointed to provide the convening authority with their opinion as to the cause of the crash and whether or not the crash occurred within the line of duty of those concerned.

However, the inquiry board met on November 2 1956, as an earlier convening was prevented by the requirements for the high priority flights to air lift from Williams Field Air.Op and Little

America V in order to establish the Beardmore Base in readiness for the initial South Pole Landing planned for October 31.

By October 21, all six Globemasters were ferrying cargo and passengers south. This operation began late on Saturday afternoon when six C-124's rumbled down the runway loaded with priority stores, equipment and personnel to be carried to the Antarctic. An initial six turn around flights would be made by the squadron to lift navy men and material, before moving their own staff to support their major objectives for the South Pole air drops.

Given the fact that the USAF first flew the prototype Globemaster in 1949 and entered it into service in May 1955 before they were familiar with polar flying, had them encounter a number of mishaps in the first few months of *Deep Freeze II.*

These flights could not become routine until a suitable airfield was located on the ice, or an aircraft was capable of a round trip for when the Antarctic airstrips were closed. As it was, many Globemaster flights were turned back to New Zealand when the weather was not suitable, and as it happened, every C-124 who landed at McMurdo within this period after their fly in from Christchurch, knocked out their nose wheel.

The third Globemaster to arrive *The State of Washington, # 52-0982*, carrying an additional Otter for VX-6, arrived at 9.30pm landing nose wheel first, buckling the nose wheel strut as it skidded along on its nose doors down the ice runway. When the propeller pitch was reversed, the huge transporters skidded to a sudden halt causing three of its propellers to strike the ice.

Capt MacMurray grimly held the huge aircraft on course on the narrow airstrip bordered by high piles of shovelled snow, in a landing that an Air Force spokesman described as '*one of the best I have ever seen'.* USAF's Captain Gaylord Knapp who eye witnessed the landing from McMurdo Sound said it a beautiful landing '*but I was as mad as hell when I ran out of film.'*

When it arrived back in Christchurch for the second time, it carried a souvenir- a two foot long piece of its No 3 propeller, bent in into the shape of a 'dog kennel'-'*we lost a bit of paint work*' Capt MacMurray said ruefully.

'*Ever since this difficult landing, bulldozers at McMurdo airstrip have been trying to grind down the hard ridges which had wiped off his nose wheel. We are having more success, but the ice was still bloody hard and rough in patches, chiefly at the end of the runway, so a heavily loaded plane has to be handled very carefully.'*

Four tractors worked rapidly in the fading midnight sun to remove the C-124 from the runway so the next C-124 could land, by pulling the plane off to a parking area where the squadron personnel struggled to prop up the plane's nose so the Otter ski plane could be unloaded and put into urgent operation.

A sixteen-man repair team was sent from the US Air Force Material Command and the Douglas Aircraft Company, to Christchurch, with two C-124C's full of parts and repair equipment.

The damaged aircraft on the isolated continent posed new problems for the US Air Force, while the team of Douglas engineers from Long Beach, and military engineers and personnel were being assembled in the US, the first message they received from the ice was that they would only have between eight to nine weeks to carry out the necessary repairs to have the 80 ton aircraft in the air again before the sea ice would break up, trapping the aircraft in for the Antarctic winter.

This meant a change of plans by the 'think tank', and the recovery was brought forward, meaning that any idea they may have had of physically surveying the damaged C-124 was not possible. Obtaining the spare parts also posed a major problem, while the Air Force had none available, the plane's manufacturer Douglas Aircraft Company could not provide them in the now restricted time frame. The idea of cannibalising a C-124 undergoing overhaul maintenance in San Bernardino California, allowed Douglas to come to the rescue with the necessary parts taken from a C-124A static test Globemaster, but by the time the team of sixteen specialists arrived at Christchurch International Airport ready for the final stage to of their operation, more problems had arisen at McMurdo.

It was now a race against time and the pending Antarctic weather, so a two-shift system was implemented in a round the clock repair operation. The work was completed by December 12, when # *52 0983* was flown back to Christchurch with its nose wheel locked in place. Work continued on *#52-00982* at the Ice Aircraft Repair Shop, after which it too was flown back to the RNZAF Station Wigram who had made their workshop facilities available, thus enabling one Globemaster to be completely repaired there while the other returned to the States, also with its nose gear down.

In 1956 the giant 80 ton Douglas Globemaster, huge by New Zealand standards, had Christchurch locals looking in awe, as eight C-124C's of the 52nd Troop Carriers Squadron [TCS], were parked at the airport waiting to carry material for construction of the South Pole Station.

The giant transport aircraft were 130 feet long 48 feet high with a wingspan of 174 feet. They had Clamshell nose doors to access the cargo hold, which was 77 feet long 12 feet 3 inches high and 13 feet wide and had two adjustable hydraulically operated loading ramps, built inside the nose. The four Pratt & Whitney R-4360-63A Wasp Major air cooled piston engines powered the C-124C's- which at that time were the largest reciprocating aircraft manufactured in the United States, with each giving 3,800 bhp .

Even so, the Globemaster was not pressurised but with a gross weight of 84 tonne was able to carry a 19 tonne payload over a distance of 2,000 miles. Used for airdropping, as was their major task in the Antarctic, the plane was fitted with an electrically operated platform located in the centre of the cargo floor, but when not in use, the platform formed part of the floor and the cargo could be airdropped or jettisoned through this hatch, by operating two external hydraulically operated doors in the underside of the plane. The two overhead travelling cranes could then be raised and lowered to move the cargo around the giant hold.

As a troop transport, a hinged upper deck could be folded down to allow the C-124C to carry 200 troops fully equipped for combat, or when required, rigged out as a flying ambulance with 127 stretchers cases.

During its Antarctic operations it carried a crew of seven- pilot, co-pilot, navigator, flight engineer, scanner/mechanic, radio operator and a loadmaster.

C-124C's were limited to landing and take-off from the ice runways at McMurdo, so their flights had to be carefully planned for the good weather, as there was no other place for these immense birds to land except at McMurdo.

During a normal season, the C-124's had to drop 3,000 barrels of the diesel fuel required at the South Pole, 1,400 drums of aviation fuel required by VX-6 Squadron at Byrd together with 600 drums of diesel fuel for the station's personnel. When the Douglas C-124's first flights commenced in Antarctica, it was necessary for an alternative airfield to be constructed.

Many early flights were forced to return to Christchurch when the weather closed in, so a new runway was established and named Kiel Field in memory of driver Max R Kiel, or 'Fat Max.'

With the USAF hastily assembling their repair teams for their first Globemaster casualty, VX-6 personnel were making final preparations for the first landing on the South Pole in a few weeks. Planners called for the landing of personnel at the site before the Air Force's airdrop operations could begin.

The Venerable R4-D which was to become the workhorse over the next decade or more, was about to be tested in Antarctic operational flying. Before they had left home port, they had sat idle on the tarmac at NAS Quonset Point for days while the squadron's maintenance crews made minor adjustments to the engines as well as checking the airframes and flight controls for possible discrepancies, for the models selected for their Antarctic flight mission were a conglomeration of many add-ons to the original DC-3 commercial transport. A new style radar was installed into its nose, making it a foot or so longer, and later proving invaluable in assisting flight crews locating objects in the snow that otherwise may well have been missed.

There were skis on both main wheels and the tail wheel, with the main wheels able be raised and lowered depending on whether a wheeled or snow landing was to be made. Once the squadron arrived in Antarctica, the tail wheel was removed to reduce weight. Two 400 gallon fuel tanks and one 200 gall tank was installed to the R4-D's interior, with a discharge system that allowed fuel to be discharged rapidly if the pilot was faced with an emergency landing while heavily loaded. This quick fuel dump would also be used to transfer diesel fuel to rubberised fuel bladders at remote landing sites, for use by automotive vehicles, so the squadron's R4-D's often carried diesel fuel for the tractor parties between Little America and Marie Byrd Station, and once the hose was connected between the aircraft and the rubberised fuel tanks, several hundred of gallons of fuel could be transferred in a matter of minutes.

Commander Waldron recalled that one of the commanders flying the large four engine transports was an electronic enthusiast, and at his own expense he installed a complete high fidelity sound system throughout his assigned aircraft, allowing him to play recorded music to his crew and passengers as they passed the time away while winging their 10,000 miles flight across the Pacific to New Zealand, and later across the Antarctic.

'Its no wonder the journalist and news photographers wanting to cover Deep Freeze 11 operations, scrambled amongst themselves for a seat on the R5-D's [the Skymasters] across the continent. Could it be that sitting in a warm and comfortable seat, listening to hi-fi music and feasting on kitchen cooked meals, was the draw card showing their appreciation while learning from the air how rugged the Antarctic wastes really were. I have no recall of any of these pseudo-explorers requesting to fly with us in our venerable but icy R4-D's. That might have been taking 'roughing it' a little too far, I suspect.'

During *Deep Freeze II*, the R4-D's were also used to bring dynamite to the Advance Tractor Parties, delivering much more than they could have carried themselves, bearing in mind that a fully loaded tractor train party could only move at four miles an hour. The squadron delivered the dynamite and diesel fuel to various staging areas along the trail marked by the Advance party, leaving enough fuel to take them to the next fuel stop. James Waldron's recollection of these flights:

'Red flags on bamboo poles had been placed along the trail to mark the way for the tractor train once it started out from Little America. Sometimes we could see these tiny flags while flying low over the trail, but at other times, when our in-flight visibility was obscured by blowing wind or haze we had to rely on our radar to pick up the fuel tanks and occasional metal drums which had been spaced alongside the trail every ten miles.

Whenever we arrived at one of the pre-placed fuel tanks we would land and then taxi over the snow so as to get close enough for our enlisted crewmembers to hook up a hose between our aircraft tanks and the rubberised tanks on the ice. After a time or two our crew became quite proficient at transferring the fuel, so we had to spend only a short while on the surface before taking off for the flight back to Little America. On some days we made several of these flights, because the success of the Trail Party depended heavily on our getting the fuel cached along the trail.'

James Waldron's pilot Eddie Frankiewicz remembers well the landing at these fuel dumps. *'Sometimes during whiteouts it became very hazardous being unable to locate the tractor train by radar, we would make a descent until the skis hit the snow, but not knowing where the snow was made the operation difficult. That one was the first and my only opportunity ever to make a zero –zero landing and a zero-zero take off, and some of that sistroid was rough. Douglas sure made a strong airplane, when we'd land on that sastrugi, which is wind carved little ridges of snow anywhere from four to eight inches high on a slope. If you landed right onto one, it was really-really rough and I remember many times on landing-the instrument panel would jiggle up and down so you could not read it and your earphones would fall off your head as would your sunglasses, and your teeth would make a rapid clicking sound shaking them almost out, It's a wonder the airplane didn't fall apart.'*

Approaching the Pole Station for the first time in the early days of the operation, sent blood rushing through the aircrew's veins, with all the five-crew members scanning ahead to locate the lone building. At times the R4-D was almost on top of the station before it was seen through a recent snowstorm, with snow covering the small building that housed the people, living there.

'Eddie found the wind line and he landed our aircraft as close to the assembled group on the ground as was possible, since our actual ground speed was higher than it would have been at sea level, we hit hard on landing, but no damage to the aircraft was incurred. It was minus 35 degree F on the surface, and we planned to off load the aircraft in record time as any lingering on the surface at that temperature was to invite trouble as bits and pieces of the aircraft froze up, and we did not want to be stranded on the Pole, as did another aircraft the following year.

It took many days before sufficient aircraft heaters could be flown to the Pole to get the frozen aircraft back in the air. Eddie and I took turns in the cockpit keeping the engines turning because if allowed to stop they would shortly freeze up. When my turn came to leave the cockpit I went outside just to say that I had stood on the South Pole. It was so miserably cold, that any pleasure I might have derived at being in so remote a spot was quickly diminished, I soon lost my built-up body heat and started to suffer real pain as the super cold air attacked my face and hands. No one had to beg me to get back into the cockpit.'

Looking out of the cockpit window, they could see a large circle of empty oil drums with a flag pole with the American Flag standing at the geographic South Pole, and the oil barrels laid out indicating the slight wobble that the earth has as it turned on its axis. Once the cargo was discharged the aircrew prepared for take-off, hooking up the eighteen JATO bottles so the flight crew could fire them when required. Eddie applied full power and the R4-D started its takeoff into the wind.

'I had thought that Eddie had learnt his lesson back in McMurdo and would be more than willing to use the JATO to get us airborne, but I was wrong thinking he could get us off the ground with engine power alone. He started a take-off that seemed endless, the surface was hard and rough and it seems we went about three miles while being constantly jarred and thrown about. Eddie was still trying to evaluate the Teflon skis but he was battering the aircraft unmercifully and every moment we continued this way along the ground took us further away from the Pole Station and the personnel who could have helped us should we have crashed. The crew chief, who was not buckled into a seat, was holding on to the airframe with all his strength, not wanting to get thrown free and injure himself.'

Finally sensing he was not going to make it on airpower alone, he hit the JATO switch, and the R4-D was quickly airborne, but not before he exasperated his whole crew. Looking back at the surface they had just left, was a dense smoke trail from the fired rockets.

It was after moments like these that Jim Waldron would seek out the tranquillity of the Antarctic's peacefulness to reflect back to the day on September 11 1956 when he departed Quonset Point for Antarctica. It was just sunrise *'I will always remember the brave, but so sad, smile I received from my wife as we said our goodbyes, she had been a constant encouragement to me as I prepared for my icy adventure, but I sensed a weakening of her resolve as the time to leave approached, she had planned on staying with her sister in the Atlanta area, after I had left for the ice, so at least she would have someone with whom to share her lonely days with, once I departed. As the time to depart grew closer, I believe the long months ahead, coupled with the imminent dangers, started taking its toll on her emotions, as we said our last goodbyes.'*

It would be late 1958 before he would next see Merle and their children again.

While the *Gooney Bird* was on the Pole's surface, their radio man had picked up a message from Headquarters, ordering them to fly to Beardmore to pick up a passenger before returning to

McMurdo, then fly onto Little America for more cargo and passengers, then return to McMurdo, adding four hours of flying to this mission, plus two extra hours to be added on the surface time at Little America, while the aircraft was refuelled. Six hours added to the fifteen-hour mission.

'On reaching Little America we discovered the entire station mess celebrating Christmas Eve with all hands partying, but Eddie and Jim and their aircrew where off again, after being forced to refuel the plane themselves, because the majority of the ground crew were 'two sheets to the wind'. When we finally arrived back at McMurdo, we found the Christmas merriment still a factor even though it was well after midnight, and though we felt sorry for having missed this party, we were happy to be back where we could once again sleep in our own beds. My bed felt wonderful, I was dead tired and I desperately wanted to fall to sleep but the stay awake pills I had taken at the Pole and the buckets of coffee I drank along the way, were still coursing through my veins. Every time I closed my eyes they seemed to pop open of their own accord even though I tried my hardest to keep them shut. Several hours of twisting and turning went by before sleep finally came. When I did drop off I fell into a state of total oblivion and it was twelve hours later before I was able to push myself up from the sheets.'

Many stories and heroic verse have been told about Lt.Commander Harvey Speed, his exploits on the ice are almost legendary, almost as legendary as the famous Donald Douglas airplane he flew. He towered above most men, and was the embodiment of a true American homespun hero, a pleasant, modest and unassuming personality, and of all the old OAE's, Speed and James Waldron, had both reported to Air Development Squadron Six at the same time and both men came to the squadron from the Training Command in Pensacola, seeking high Antarctic adventure and both had volunteered to winter over in the Antarctic *'because they were tired of instructing fledging aviators.'*

There's something irresistible about aviators like Harvey Speed, his wit and charm enthusing knowledgeably about something he's passionate about; his turn of phase was priceless, and he was driven by desire to fly in Antarctica. Lt Commander Harvey Speed was something special

In the words of James Waldron *'He possessed a true sense of human nature of what was humorous and just what type of stories his all-male audience would appreciate that always guaranteed him popularity on the ice. He supplied us with a constant string of funny sayings and he could always apply these sayings to the exploits of the day. He was always a stabilizing influence among the officers and enlisted men of the squadron. His character and personal presence led others to place total trust in any order he might give.*

He was modest about his flying exploits and would not seek the approval and interest of the newspaper and television reporters, as many of the other squadron aviator's had. He wore clothing on the ice that gave him the appearance of being a country boy, in order to escape the attention of the reporters with cameras and note pads. When he was cornered into telling someone about his latest flying experience, he minimized the importance of it instead of embellishing the story, as one would expect.'

His store of folksy sayings and funny stories made him a favourite among his fellow officers and the enlisted men as well. During a 'bull session', he would keep everyone highly amused with down-to-earth sayings and homespun stories, and it was the habit to encourage him in hope of making what might have been a dull event into a lively time for all.

Commander Eddie Ward had final summing up of the Squadron's second deployment season in Antarctica. *'I thought back to that beautiful fall day in September 1956, the day the Fleet was blessed. While the Officers and men stood by their aircraft with heads bowed, the Chaplain implored Divine Providence for guidance and protection from the perils that lay ahead, and perils there were. During Deep Freeze 11, VX-6 lost five aircraft; all were strike damaged, two helicopters, one Otter and two P2V's. Tragic as the P2-V crash was at McMurdo Sound, total fatalities could have been in the thirties, rather than four.'* The prophetic quip of Lt.Cdr Glen 'Judge' Lathrop had come true. Yes Providence had spared us from many of the perils that lay ahead, Amen.

But another peril that lurked was not a blessed one, for by following simple military thinking, the bases waste sat 'out of site, out of mind' in a semi-frozen state, and the area was dubbed by all as Honey Bucket Lane. I will let James Waldron tell the story recalling the day he got stuck in Honey Bucket lane while going to meet one of his former helicopter students.

'The feature of the base was that a tidal crack was where the sea met the land upon which McMurdo was located. As the daily tides made the sea ice rise and fall there was often an opening in the sea's surface a foot or so wide leading to open water about eight feet down. If you were walking to cross this crack in the surface, you had to be very careful so as not to fall into the water below.'

With this explanation in place, James proceeded with his story of his foolish moments on a wonderful, clear and warm Antarctic day after his mid day meal in the Mess.

'As I walked down one of McMurdo's two streets I heard the sound of an approaching helicopter, and as it flew overhead I noted it to be a small Bell helicopter which are carried on the icebreaker ships. One of the ships was reported to be breaking up sea a few miles from McMurdo Station so the cargo ships could discharge their cargo at a reasonable distance from McMurdo Station.

As the ship's helicopter flew low and slow over the street I was walking on I instantly recognized the pilot as one of my former helicopter students. He recognized me at the same time, and I motioned for him to land on the sea ice so that I could go down there to greet him. It was here that I abandoned my usual caution and raced down the hill towards where the helicopter landed. Since I did not want to make a former student wait too long for me to reach him I ran in a straight line to his helicopter, but halfway down the hill I found the surface I was running on suddenly become soft. In looking down at my feet I discovered that I had entered Honey Bucket Lane and from my knees down to my trousers and shoes were coated with a considerable amount of the camp's offal. Needless to say, I was a mess and very aromatic.

At this point I revised my course and once clear of Honey Bucket Lane I selected another route to the open sea ice. As I approached the waiting helicopter on the run, I completely forgot the need to take caution in crossing the tidal crack. Suddenly I fell into the open crack and disappeared from sight of my friends on the hill. They instantly thought that I had fallen into the open seawater, and all rushed down the hill to try to save me from drowning. Since I was running quite fast when I fell into the gaping crack, my momentum caused my shoes to become imbedded into the softened sea ice's vertical wall and it stopped my falling into the open water. I threw my arms upwards and I used my hands to grasp the surface ice so as to keep from falling further into the open crack. I then started to dig my shoes higher and higher into the softened sea ice and I was soon free of the crack and safely back on the surface.

As I stood up on the ice I did not consider how dangerous my fall had been, at the time, and with the help of my friends, I came to see how dangerous my actions had been. I resolved that for the foreseeable future I would take much greater precautions when moving on land about the continent.'

Once free from the crack, the R4-D aviator, went onto the helicopter and spent a few delightful moments with his former student, who related how he had instructed his crewman to hop out and rush to his instructors aid, however, by the time he arrived, Waldron had emerged from the ice cold Ross sea. While he never met with them again, he often wondered what they had thought of his careless act.

'I retraced my steps to the top of the hill with considerably greater caution than when I came down. I took a lot of kidding from my friends and when they refused my entry into the Bachelor Officers Quarters, I was forced to go to the washerteria building where I stripped down and did some unpleasant washing of shoes and clothing. Don't believe that I was allowed to get over this goof easily. It was a matter of great embarrassment to me for a long time.'

During the early years of Antarctic air operations, one of the loneliest sites anyone could have imagined were the new facilities at Beardmore Station at the foot of the Liv Glacier about 80 miles east of the Beardmore Glacier. The station was planned as a base for the proposed landing on the South Pole in October 1956.

'*Somewhere back in the States someone who anticipated the need for a toilet facility at this remote site, took out his carpentering tools and hammered a wooden frame with its usual half moon over the door. This outhouse*', wrote Commander James Waldron, '*was prefabricated so that it was easily snapped together once we had it delivered to the camp. It was built like any outhouse might be, with one exception; inside it was so narrow that your knees stuck outside the door and it couldn't be closed. If there was any wind, and there usually was, you managed to conclude your business in short order. Still, with the view of a mountain rising upwards of 10,000 feet just out side the outhouse, it was nothing short of magnificent.*'

CHAPTER SIX

ONWARDS TO THE SOUTH POLE.

*The historic landing at the South Pole- Dufek and seven other
Americans become the first to step on to the Polar Plateau since
Captain Robert Falcon Scott.*

A feeling of gloom prevailed at the camp as men went silently about their duties, this feeling of helplessness coupled with the blizzard which had set in over McMurdo only added to the depression.

With the tragic crash of the Neptune now behind the squadron, work had to return to normality at McMurdo, and preparations for the Polar Landing on October 20.

To some, the crash stymied their great Antarctic adventure, but, on a continent, such as Antarctica, there would be more injuries and more deaths.

In preparation for air operations to the South Pole, it was October 25 before the squadron could get their planes in the air and as the weather improved, skis were put on the R4-D's as Lt. Commander Conrad 'Gus' Shinn and Captains Hawkes and Cordiner took off to scout the foothills of the mountains at the southern end of the Ross Sea Shelf and locate a proposed base to support the Pole operations.

Major General Chester McCarty, commander of the 18th Air Force, who just six weeks before had flown a C-124 Globemaster over the North Pole, made history making the first military air drop and the earliest flight over the South Pole.

His was the seventh plane to fly over the South Pole since Rear Admiral Richard Byrd, Col Bernt Balchen, Col Ashley McKinley and Cdr Harold June on November 29, 1929- almost exactly twenty-seven years before at almost exactly the same spot.

Major General McCarty's C-124 dropped about 10,000 pounds of equipment including a Grasshopper weather station to broadcast weather every six hours. The huge troop carrier climbed to 17,000 feet to avoid a whiteout in the high polar mountains and because the Globemaster wasn't pressurized for high altitude, the 43 passengers had to breathe from oxygen bottles, prompting Trigger Hawkes to tell his men. *'Better a headache than a broken neck'.*

That night the Admiral called a conference with the squadron aviators, together with the leaders of the special teams, who would build the South Pole base station. Hawkes and Cordiner reported there were several sites near the Beardmore Glacier suitable for a halfway base, as they had landed their ski plane in two locations but would take another look the next day before making their final decision.

The R4-D's could safely make the round trip from McMurdo to the Pole, as the same aircraft had previously landed and taken off from the soft snow of Greenland. With the high elevation of the polar plateau, it would be necessary to take off from the pole as light as possible and refuel on the way back, so the Beardmore Station would have to serve as an alterative airfield and a rescue station in bad weather. From there, radio signals would reach aircraft in flight from McMurdo to the Pole, and be able to send out regular weather reports.

'Landing with skis in deep snow was the most unusual experience', says. James Waldron. *'It was similar to landing on a deep bed of feathers, or conversely touching down on glacier ice was much like landing on hard rock.'*

Once the test landing was achieved at the Pole, the Task Forces operations would move into top gear. It was planned for Lt R Bowers of the US Navy's civil engineer corps, to be in charge of the polar base construction, as during the previous winter months at McMurdo, Bowers and his six teams, each of four men, lived and worked together in sub-zero weather. The master plan included two R4-

D's to land two teams first, followed by a train team of eleven dogs after the R4-D's had taken off and returned to McMurdo.

Bowers would locate the exact position of the South Geographical Pole by theodolite in case the plane's navigation system might be in error, then he would relocate to a position and radio direct to the USAF's C-124 Globemasters to drop the supplies and construction materials. Their first job would be to construct shelters, housing units, and workshops, establish power by way of generators just as would any construction gang. Next the USAF's Globemasters would air drop cargo by parachute which would have to be unpacked, making this by far the continent's most difficult airlift operation.

While the operation command wrestled with these operational problems, the C-124 Globemasters, having completed their tasks, would head back to the United States via Christchurch, and have the squadron's R4-D's stand by to fly in scientists and naval personnel for the first ever winter over at the pole, and evacuate those who had constructed the polar base.

The major possibility facing the command was that the sea ice at McMurdo would weaken and disintegrate before the season's programme was completed. Should the ice runway threaten to give way and be destroyed, the squadron would move their operations to Little America from where ski equipped aircraft could operate.

On October 31 1956, one of the most spectacular events in aviation and naval history was about to take place, when for the first time in the history of polar exploration; man was to land an aircraft at the South Pole.

The mission had its critics, the first occupation of the South Pole by the Americans were heterogeneous- some glowingly commented 'that the last frontier was about to be conquered, man has exploded an atom bomb, has broken the sound barrier, and was attempting to land a plane at the bottom of the earth '*while the more sceptic ones just shrugged their shoulders and remarked that, "Ah, well another crew of sailors going glory-hunting*'. These reactions were a little unfair.

What this group of doubters didn't know was that while aviation had made enormous technical and technological advancements, no plane had yet been performance tested at temperatures lower than 69 degrees below zero as no plane had been developed or specifically designed for cold weather operations, so the R4-D, while the first long-range and fastest aircraft to enter service with the Navy as an all purpose in the mid `1930's, was chosen to make this historic flight being flown by the barnstorming aviators of VX-6 squadron.

Two days before the planned assault on the Pole, the weather had deteriorated, requiring the two R4-D's servicing the Beardmore Station to return to McMurdo, and Lt Commander Mirabito was predicting unstable weather for the next day. The line crews, staggering from cold, fatigue and overwork, welcomed the Admiral's suspension of flight operations for twenty-four hours, giving them time to recharge.

Noel Eichhorn was scheduled to command the base at Beardmore but was taken seriously ill with the flu, so Chief Aviation Ordnance man Michael Baronick took over his duties. Dufek rated Baronick as intelligent, wiry and strong, as he had trained with his party through the Antarctic winter. Detail was such that every piece of equipment had been checked and rechecked and his men had been carefully selected. They needed to have food to last three months, radio equipment tents, sleeping bags, first aid supplies and a complete set of survial kits with every man carrying 55 pounds of cold weather clothing.

Preparations for the air assault on the South Pole and for the subsequent air operations, an R4-D *BuNo 17274* with Cdr Eddie Frankiewicz and Lt James Waldron, landed Michael Baronick and his men and equipment at the foot of the Liv Glacier to establish the camp. Their mission was the establishment of an auxiliary refuelling station at the Beardmore Glacier, for on route to the Pole.

With the weather closing in, Frankiewicz considered it prudent to wait on the frozen ground no longer than necessary, and after unloading the men with their gear he took off and seventeen minutes later the C-124 flew in to air drop additional supplies.

On his return to Little America, Eddy Frankiewicz said '*it broke our hearts to leave those guys there, and we had to almost push them out the door with their gear, and take off*'.

Lt.Cdr Cal Larsen, senior photographer, had gone to Antarctic aboard the *Glacier* in 1956, and arrived on the Ross Sea Shelf in mid October. He was on the first tractor train to Byrd Station as a driver and photographer, and flew with Eddie to set up Beardmore emergency Camp at Liv Glacier and recalls how with five others, all military were flown in '*with a disassembled Jamesway Hut in two R4-D aircraft. It was over 50 degrees below zero when we landed, and we started building or putting up our hut with considerable vigour. As I recall we had the hut heater going and poured our first coffee about three hours, later. The place was to be used as an emergency stop for planes going or coming from the South Pole.*'

Baronick and his merry men went about their tasks with determination, just as they had rehearsed a hundred times before, and with bad weather coming the gang were able to take a break in their cramped conditions. George Dufek again, '*I knew they were well trained and capable of taking care of themselves, as from their emergency radio set came periodic reassuring messages for us in our comfort zone*'.

On October 20th, four R4-D's and a C-124 piloted by Major General Chester McCarty took off from McMurdo. The C-124 was loaded with heavy equipment, while one R4-D was carrying personnel for Little America and equipment for Cdr Paul Frazier's trail party to Byrd and the three other R4-D's headed for Beardmore.

Aboard were four more personnel to complete the Beardmore base, with an Aewell hut for the air operations room, a radio shack and a Jamesway hut for sleeping quarters, primus stoves as well as stoves to thaw water and heat the tents. The carefully estimated supplies from kerosene lanterns to air mattress, whisk brooms to can openers, American flags to fire extinguishers and a various assortment of food including a turkey and tins of pineapple jams, were all aboard. All these supplies were dropped near a lonely tent pitched on the side of the glacier, and luckily only one drum of aviation gas was lost when the parachute failed to open.

A note on Beardmore Station, as this name is a misnomer, as the station is not located at the head of the Beardmore Glacier as *Operation Deep Freeze* publications reported at the time, but at the foot of the Liv Glacier, some 80 miles to the east of the Beardmore Glacier. The pilots of the first R4-D found the surface of the ice at the foot of the Beardmore far too rough for a landing, so Lt Speed scouted eastwards until he found a smoother surface, which happened to be at the foot of the Liv Glacier.

Cdr James Waldron remembers the time he and Frankie flew to Beardmore. '*I found myself once again amazed at the grandeur of the Antarctic continent. Our path took us over the Ross Sea Ice Shelf, which is flat and mostly featureless for over 400 miles, we kept to the western edge of the ice shelf where it meets the mountains that surround the continent. Heading southwards towards Beardmore Station, I had the magnificent ice clad mountains that bordered the continent on the right hand side of the aircraft- my side.*

These mountains held back the great mass of ice and snow of the continent's plateau. Since the air was so superbly clear, the mountains many miles away seemed much closer than they were, and although I knew that these icy peaks were extremely cold and forbidding for anyone to traverse on foot, still they looked from a distance wonderfully smooth and inviting. Like a beautiful painting you want to study in order to feel the vibrancy of the art, for these pearl like beauties caused me to stare at them for hours at a time, as we flew southwards.'

The flight from McMurdo to Beardmore was four hours in a R4-D and in Cdr Waldron's words- *'a lonelier site you couldn't imagine, two men had lived on this site for weeks at a time with nothing to look forward to except eating, sleeping, relying on radio messages and taking weather observations. Each time we shut off our engines and climbed out of our aircraft, I am amazed at how very quiet it is, especially when no wind is blowing. Since the snow absorbs most noise, you could hear the sound of your own breathing, and I marvelled at how men could stand living under these circumstances for weeks at a time. They enjoyed our occasional visit, especially when we brought them mail and gossip from McMurdo.'*

As late as January 1956, Marine Lt Colonel Hal Kolp had dropped several objects at the Pole from his R5-D and watched as they disappeared immediately, and reported the snow was 'very soft and powdery', as did Rear Admiral Byrd who had also flown over the pole and dropped objects in the late 30's in an effort to study the snow's density and hardness.

That night he wrote in his diary *'In the back of my mind is the haunting concern that the Russians will beat us to the South Pole, our press correspondents are with us and the world knows our plans and progress. We know nothing of what the Russians are doing, every delay caused by weather, every mishap that slows our operations makes me impatient, and it's difficult for me to sleep longer than a few short hours at a time. I too am getting the 'big eye'.*

The morning of October 30, dawned crystal clear, with unlimited visibility and clarity, with Mt Erebus as usual wearing a white plume from her majestic dome, some 13,350 feet above sea level, while across the Ross Sea, Mt Discovery appeared with her mantle of white snow gleaming in the Antarctic sun.

Later that day, on instructions from Admiral Dufek, Major Ellen took off in his Globemaster for a reconnaissance flight to the Pole and accompaning Major Ellen was Capt Hawkes who wanted another look at the surface of the polar plateau and decide where to put the plane down. At 3000 feet above the Pole, the temperature was 31 below, and the Pole's elevation was recorded at 10.400 feet.

From the Globemaster came the message from Capt Hawkes to his boss, *'if the weather holds, ceiling and visibility unlimited, surface hard and very rough. This is it!'*

At first Admiral Dufek offered the pilot's seat to his close friend and former Antarctic crewmates from *Operation Highjump.* He had decided two years previously, to include Trigger Hawkes as *'he was undoubtedly the most experienced and best qualified aircraft pilot in Antarctic flying in the history of this remote land, so I asked him to select his co-pilot, with his inherent modesty and fairness, he told me he would rather turn over the pilot seat to the younger generation and would have Lt Commander Conrad Shinn in the cockpit with him, while he himself would take the co-pilots seat. I knew he meant it and I liked and respected him too much to order it otherwise.'*

Subsequently the heaviest responsibility rested on the shoulders of the diminutive, yet serious, Lt Commander Shinn, who was also aware that his plane was not the first choice to make the historic flight, with or without Teflon coated ski's, but rather, the new Lockheed P2-V-7 Neptune with its turbo-jet power. Unfortunately it had not arrived in Antarctica, because of problems with its skis.

Finally the selected crew for the historic flight aboard the R4-D-5 *BuNo 12418* XD/8 were Cdr 'Gus' Conrad Shinn, ADJ2 John Strider, Mechanic Lt, John Swadener, navigator, AT2 William Cumbie, radio technician Capt, William Hawkes and Capt. Douglas Cordiner-the Squadron's Commander, and Rear Adm. Dufek completing the crew.

As VX-6's Aircraft Maintenance Officer Frankiewicz's R4-D was fitted with Teflon covered ski bottoms which Frankiewicz had located during DF11 while all the other R4-D's had polyurethane on the ski runners, *'which had a sheet like thing held in place by aluminium strip and mine was melted on and glued on the bottom, we found that the coefficient of friction was very light on the Teflon as opposed to polyurethane, which would flake off and pretty soon after a few landings, you're just landing on the bare aluminium of the skis.'* Commander Frankiewicz recalled.

On the morning of October 31, the plane's captain John Strider, a husky West Virginian had trouble getting down the hill to the Naval Air Facilities at McMurdo Sound where the USAF and Navy airplanes were parked. In true Boy Scout tradition, Strider carried a five-gallon water jug, sandwiches, and a pound of butter, some bacon and a large thermos of coffee. None of the weasel drivers were able to give him a lift with his heavy load, due to running errands for other plane captains, so John walked the two miles over the ice to his plane.

Strider was himself an Aviation Machinist's Mate Second Class, and as plane captain he must personally perform many tasks before the pilot arrives. Once on the line, he checked with the maintenance crew to see if the plane would be up to it. Strider was concerned with the R4-D's oil pressure, hydraulic and electrical systems as in October in Antarctica, he knew from experience that old planes such as the "Dak's" were allergic to the polar temperatures. Every item checked out, Strider joined radioman William Cumbie in the temporary line shack [on the plane line] for a cup of coffee.

The coffee break took a little longer than expected only to find on their return to *Que Sera Sera* that not only had the maintenance men installed and wired the 15 JATO bottles to the plane's underbelly, but more surprising was to see Rear Admiral George Dufek, Captain William Trigger Hawkes, Staff Air Officer, Lt. Commander Gus Shinn, pilot and Lt. John Swadener, squadron's navigator all standing beside the plane surrounded by newsmen with their notepads, microphones and cameras while Capt Cordiner leant against the plane smoking.

Feeling that the squadron commander and Task Force commander should share the greatest risk with the personnel at their command, it was no surprise that both men were on the flight, Dufek wrote in his notebook *'In the event of disaster, there will probably be criticism of my placing three senior officers of the task force in one aircraft. This will be unjustified, we have been planning the South Pole landing since 1954, we all shared in it and from the beginning I earmarked Hawkes for this task. If anything happens to Capt Cordiner, the squadron's executive office Cdr Edward Ward is fully capable of carrying on aircraft commandments [Cdr Ward was acting CO in Deep Freeze I]. My deputy Captain Jack Ketchum is fully qualified and capable of assuming the duties as Task Force commander. There is no indispensable man; I feel that as expedition leader, I should take as many chances as anyone but we don't expect disaster-only success- and with success no one ever quarrels.'*

Up to this point, John Strider didn't know where the plane was going, or that either him or Cumbie had been hand picked for the historic Pole landing flight, that hours later was to make aviation and exploration history with him being the first man in 44 years to set foot on the South Pole ahead of the Admiral, who historically claimed the glory of the first man.

John Strider had joined the Navy in 1948, and during the course of his career; he had become a plane captain in three types of aircraft- the R4-D, R4-D-8 and R5-D. Plane Captains in those days were responsible for the upkeep of the aircraft, heading the enlisted flight crew and serving as Chief Engineer while flying. Chief Strider had volunteered for *Operation Deep Freeze* in 1955 and received his orders the following afternoon. Reporting to VX-6 Squadron at Patuxant River, he was assigned as plane captain of a D4-D, flying across the Pacific to New Zealand as plane captain for the Squadron Commander Cdr Gordon Ebbe,

A Weasel approached the R4-D, pulling a sled load of cargo, including an American flag, [whose staff held a brass cylinder,] food, alpine axes, tents, stove, radar reflectors, extra clothing and pup tents. After all the survival equipment and cargo was loaded, a man could hardly walk from the cockpit to the passengers seat.

Further over on the taxi strip, photographers and reporters were casting lots to see who would be the lucky ones to ride in R5-D Skymaster and who would ride in the USAF C-124 Globemaster, that would hover overhead with the R5-D, ready to render assistance or drop survival equipment in case of a crash or inability to take off once Commander Shinn had landed on the Pole.

Reporters aboard the C-124 were: Walter Sullivan-*'New York Times'*, Ansel Talberi *'New York Herald Tribune'* Maurice Clutter *'United Press'* and Don Guy *'Associate Press'*. There was great disappointment among the news media at McMurdo, when the Admiral told them that no one would be travelling on the R4-D for the safety of the crew and the success of the mission. Plus an extra 500 pounds of survival gear was required and the plane had to land light and take off light.

The crew took along a number of cameras, both still and movie, from those reporters who were staying behind, so Bill Hartigan of NBC gave 'Trigger' Hawke a quick lesson in the operation of his movie camera and sound equipment, so he could pool this material with the other cameramen later.

Dufek turned to Hartigan and asked *'how much this equipment cost?'*

'Sixtyfive hundred dollars, Sir.'

'You must be optimistic about this flight', the Admiral replied.

'Its all in the game' he replied with a shrug,

'He was sorely disappointed that he could not be in the plane with us' the Admiral later wrote.

At 12.55 pm, on October 31st.with Admiral Dufek aboard the R4-D-5 # *12418*- the very old and weary aircraft, prophetically named *Que Sera Sera* with her gross weight of 34,000 lbs a huge 7,000 lbs. above the recommended maximum weight, started her take-off down the floating sea-ice airstrip at McMurdo gathered speed and took off without her JATO rockets.

With every historic milestone such as this flight, there were those playing a large operational part behind the scenes, such as aviator, Eddie Frankiewicz, Jim Waldron and their crew, who waited in the wings at Beardmore Station, as a rescue crew. They had landed their R4-D *Charlene* on the Liv Glacier, keeping *Charlene's* engines running for the better part of the day, in order to be ready at a moments notice in case the historic flight needed assistance.

Roaring up the Beardmore, however, 'Hank' Jorda's Skymaster *BuNo 56528 XD/3* developed engine trouble and returned to base, much to the disappointment of the reporters on board ready to record the event. While the Globemaster, under the control of Major Cicero J Ellen was able to overtake the slower Navy R4-D, he duly reached the Pole at 7.30 am, where he orbited for half an hour, determining the best navigational fix on the Pole.

Forty minutes before Cdr.Shinn reached the Pole, the breather line to the starboard engine froze and started to pump oil out of the top, causing such an oil streak on the wing, that Strider thought the plane's engine had lost all its oil, but later, on the ground, he discovered that only ten gallons had been shed.

'Gus' Shinn spoke to Major Ellen in the Globemaster as his red warning lights were flashing on and off as the pressure gauges dropped and the oil streamed out over the cowling of both engines, then Shinn made three low level passes to examine the surface and threw out smoke flares to determine the wind, and the direction of the sastrugi, *'it might have been the lack of oxygen or maybe our nerves, but we couldn't tell the wind direction'* Shinn said later. But then with the sun behind him he could establish depth perception by his plane's shadow.

Navigators on both planes agreed that when the R4-D reached the site just before 8am, they would be over the Pole. At this point Major Ellen flew a tight 360-degree circle to leave a contrail so the R4-D would have some type of target to land on.

There appeared to be no indication that this was an unusual flight, with a few wisps of white clouds to be viewed from the flightdeck, the pilots, navigators and radioman went about their tasks, with the occasional small talk over the intercom. Cdr Cordiner was slumped over some soft baggage, as he had just woken up, while Capt. Strider was making toasted sandwiches and a brew of hot coffee, Shinn continued to circle around- the two planes leaving heavy vapour trails.

Over the intercom Hawkes asked the Admiral if they should land now or request the Globemaster, flying above, to drop a marker onto the surface. As the C-124, with the news correspondents aboard, positioned itself high over the Pole providing navigational information, Shinn ordered Strider to drop the gear and then the skis, as the temperature outside was pegged at minus 50 degrees F, and the decision was made to land.

Shinn brought the plane down, bouncing over the sastrugi before coming to a stop at 8.34 am seven hours after leaving McMurdo.

Blowing snow churned skywards from the aircraft's skis and was fanned even more by its propellers, obscuring it momentarily from the Globemaster above where Ellen's crew feared the worst, but as the snow was so soft it had swallowed *Que Sera Sera* on contact. Jubilation echoed from the Globemaster's flight deck when the disturbed snow had subsided below, and they watched in awe as the R4-D glided to a smooth stop to minus 58 degrees F.

Once on the deck AD-2 Strider jumped out of the plane, crawled underneath and put the gear pins in the landing gear as the normal safety procedure after landing. The slipstream wind chill temperature was later estimated to be minus 80 degrees F. Radioman William Cumbie meanwhile had constantly kept the Globemaster in his radar scope, partly to avoid collision in the vapour trails left by both planes and also to test the performance of his own speed and to '*keep my mind off what were about to do*'.

John Strider had become the first man in 44 years to set foot on the hard crusty snow of the South Pole when he went to the cabin door and took out the passengers ladder so the others could climb down to take movies, even though his movie camera froze on reaching the ground just ahead of Rear Admiral George Dufek.

In a later interview, Newport News reporter Brian Shoemaker had spoken to Lt.Cdr 'Gus' Shinn to confirm that the AD-2 Strider was in fact the first man out of *Que Sera Sera* on that historic day, and he agreed that Strider was, as it was part of the plane captain's responsibilities to be the first out to pin the landing gear, so it wouldn't collapse.

This was confirmed by Eddie Ward, '*Yes, J.P.Strider was the first to step on to the South Pole. Two weeks after Brian Shoemaker interviewed Strider, he interviewed me and I reiterated that Strider did indeed jump out first. Of course this was never officially publicized, as in every expedition, it's the leader who gets the credit for the first man to do this. It's always amused me that Admiral Richard E Byrd, whom I knew and greatly admired, gets the credit for being the first man to fly over both Poles, whereas in reality, Floyd Bennett was the pilot on the North Pole and Brent Balchen was the pilot for the South Pole flight.*'

Admiral Dufek's participation was appropriate given that he had been a member of all the US Antarctic expeditions since he navigated Adm. Richard Byrd's flagship *USS Bear* in 1939-41. He told this writer later '*it was like going into another world, only after a few minutes I noticed Capt's Cordiner's face was white with frostbite.*'

Captain Cordiner stood with the Admiral as they planted the United States ensign with its brass capsule attached to it's staff, containing a certificate that the group of American aviators were the first Americans to stand on the Pole, but so hard was the snow, that the plane's survival axe had to be used to penetrate the surface.

Meanwhile Captain Hawkes assisted by Cumbie installed radar reflectors for future Polar flights and made some observations. Earlier, on the Admiral's instructions, all those on the ground were to work in pairs, so each man could keep a close and constant watch for any signs of frostbite on their companion, which was wise as Cumbie's hands froze to his shovel handle as he worked and he had to kick it free with the help of Hawkes.

Navigator John Swadener took a series of sun lines, which indicated the landing had been made within four miles of the exact Pole, in the direction of South America. When one considers that the R4-D flies with a six-to-eight-degree aileron tab correction, this was outstanding navigation.

After the flag was punched into the frozen surface to announce their arrival, Strider expressed grave concerns that his engines were leaking oil and his skis freezing to the snow surface, so after 49 minutes on the ice, Hawkes turned to Dufek, '*Boss, I can't move the fingers of this hand, I think they're frozen*'. The Admiral replied, '*Let's get to hell out of here.*'

Then drama: As Lt.Cdr. Shinn revved the engines nothing happened as the skis were frozen solid to the ice plateau and at 9,200 feet the engines weren't able to develop full power in the thin air. During the landing the R4-D's skis had heated a few degrees from the friction, causing the snow to melt then subsequently freeze to the skis. With the aircraft effectively frozen to the South Pole and the engines now turning at full power, Shinn fired four of his JATO's attached to the aircraft 's underside but even this failed to shake the Dakota loose.

The *Gooney Bird* shuddered, but didn't move an inch. Four bottles are equivalent to one 1,000 horsepower engine, for a thirty second burn. On the flight deck Hawkes voice crackled over the radio to Base *'McMurdo, we have a problem'*, as Shinn quickly fired four more bottles and the aircraft rocked and move forward slightly, so he fired four more - still no lift-off. He had four bottles left, and while Dufek was now considering spending the night at the pole, Shinn, with his fingers crossed, fired the last four bottles.

To those circling above aboard the Globemaster, *Que Sera Sera* momentarily appeared to have exploded and caught fire, as it disappeared in a swirl of flames, smoke and snow, bouncing involuntary over the rough ice surface, then staggering into the air at sixty knots. The flight deck's windscreen had completely frozen both inside and out, so Shinn was flying blind. *'Sixty knot's that's not bloody flying speed Sir'*, Strider said to Shinn.

'No' was the grim reply, as the 15 empty bottles were jettisoned to the polar surface *'but we're 2,500 pounds lighter now!'*

Strider recalled later that every damage signal on the instrument panel flashed on, *'it looked like a bloody Christmas tree'*. These danger signs could have been the result of the extreme external cold and the rarified atmosphere at the Pole's 9,200 feet elevation. It was impossible then to see how low or high the plane was above the ice surface of the polar plateau until the plane's defrosters had time to operate and remove the frost from the windshield. But another problem faced the crew when it was found they couldn't retract the landing gear.

Lt.Cdr. Gus Shinn recalled these events to this writer years later. *'Major Ellen was on top of us the whole time with his C-124 ready to drop supplies, and it was mightily comforting listening to him on the radio saying: If you can't get off the ground I'll crash-land alongside of you and you will have a house to live in. The nicest part of the whole flight was seeing his monster flying around up there'*.

Once airborne, the excitement wasn't completely over, as the faster Globemaster flew 'S' curves at 115-120 knots behind the R4-D all the way back to Beardmore Station.

Lt.Cdr.Conrad 'Gus' Shinn was recognized for his legacy of groundbreaking polar aviation during a ceremony at the Museum of Naval Aviation in Pensacola Florida in October 1999, forty-three years after his landmark flight, when the American Polar Society honoured him. In receiving the award, the retired Navy flyer joined the ranks of such Antarctic legends as Robert Scott's party, Richard Byrd, Paul Siple and Laurence. Lt.Cdr.Shinn became the 12th man to stand on the South Pole, behind his plane captain John Strider and Adm. George Dufek.

Dick Swadener was an outstanding navigator, hand picked by Admiral Dufek for the Polar flight, and Eddie Ward's navigator on his R5-D # *56505*. After returning to the States from Deep Freeze 11, he served with Eddie Ward aboard the *USS Albemarle* AV-5, a large Seaplane Tender in the Atlantic Fleet before retiring from the Navy as a Captain, after thirty years service. He then lived in New Orleans Louisiana as a ferryboat captain, and died in July 1996, to be buried in New Orleans.

According to his daughter Leslie [now Leslie Swadener-Culpepper] her Dad, who married two years after he returned from Antarctica, *'was one of those guys that never stopped for directions, and that became a running joke, as well as aggravating my mother from time to time. He spoke a lot about the navigational quirks of figuring out your location at the Pole, mostly related to the tightening of the longitudinal and latitudinal lines as you approached the Pole, and how compasses were useless at the magnetic pole.'*

He died from pancreatic cancer in 1996 aged 68. After he was diagnosed he tried fervently to start writing his adventures in Antarctica, but the sickness overtook him so quickly he never completed more than page 1. After his untimely death, his brother Marc with his wife's assistance, took up the torch and put together a stupendous collection of his photographs.

Among the media correspondents aboard the C-124 was an 18-year-old reporter for United Press [UP], Maurice Cutler. One of his assignments was to photograph the historic occasion and consequently one of his photos was used as the official US Navy photo of the landing. The youngest expedition member was a Civil Air Patrol cadet Robert Barger of Peoria III, who was aboard the C-124 on his third polar flight within six days.

'I made my first when I was 17, the other two when 18.' Barger said, explaining that he had celebrated his 18th birthday on October 29, two days before the historic Polar landing.

The South Pole landing gave the *Gooney Bird* the polar double, as on May 3 1952, an USAF C-47 landed at the North Pole, during the establishing of a weather research station there, with Lt.Colonel William Benedict and Joseph Fletcher at the controls.

On the three and half hour flight back to Beardmore Base where the R4-D's would top up with fuel for the final four hour leg back to McMurdo, the Admiral requested more coffee from Strider, who was having trouble getting the water to boil at the plane's altitude.

'I just leaned back and closed my eyes, only seventeen men in the history of mankind had set foot on the South Pole, and that included us seven, the first Americans to set foot on the South Pole. Fate and God had been good to us, the skill and faith of our men of VX-6 had been equal to the task,' recalled Admiral Dufek.

'We stopped at the Beardmore Glacier base for fuel then back to McMurdo, where the news of the South Pole landing had gone out by radio across the world and to Admiral Jerauld Wright, Commander-in-Chief United States Atlantic Fleet;

IN ORDER TO FAMILIARIZE MYSELF WITH CURRENT CONDITIONS OBTAINING AT SOUTH POLE I MADE A RECONNAISSANCE OF THE SITE THIS DATE WITH CAPTAIN D CORDINOR, COMMANDERING OFFICER, NAVY AIR DEVELOPMENT SQUADRON IN R4D AIRCRAFT PILOT LT. CDR CONRAD SHINN, CO PILOT CAPTAIN WILLAM HAWKES. LANDED GEROGRAPHICAL SOUTH POLES. DISEMBARKED AND OBSERVED CONDITION FOR FOURTY-NINE MINUTES.RETURNED MCMURDO VIA BEARDMORE CAMP.

To Task Force 43 stationed in Antarctica, to New Zealand, to Washington DC and to our ships at sea and those still in American ports waiting to sail, I sent this message of my gratitude.

THE SUCCESSFUL LANDING BY AIRCRAFT AT THE SOUTH POLE WAS THE RESULT OF THE SUPPORT OF MANY UNITS AND MANY MEN WORKING UNDER HARSH CONDITIONS. MY HEART-FELT THANKS TO ALL OF YOU FOR YOUR CONTRIBUTION.

John Strider recalled later *'I believe the take off from the Station where we refuelled for the return to McMurdo was harder than the take off from the Pole. There the control panel again became a Christmas tree, and I couldn't blame it on the minus 58 degree cold.'*

Eddie Frankiewicz recalled the plight of the plane after it landed at Beardmore. *'Gosh his plane was a mess; a lot of oil leaks, and as a matter of fact, his oil breather line on both engines had huge icicles coming out of them. His horizontal stabilizer was all battered in because as he fired his JATO it hit the snow and flung right into the leading edge of the horizontal stabilizer and dented it badly and the skin underneath too, but we refuelled him and he took of, so we followed shortly afterward flying escort for him.'*

So confidence had been the collective feelings of the men at McMurdo that the mission would be a success, that only a few turned out to meet the returning aircraft. The *Christchurch Press* in its Editorial on Friday November 2 1956 summed up the historic achievement headed "By Air to the Pole".

'*Rear Admiral George Dufek, the first man to stand on the South Pole for 44 years, must surely have reflected on Wednesday night how greatly his journey differed from those so arduously made by Amundsen and Scott. Amundsen's party, winning the race to the pole by little more than a month, had the benefit of dog teams, for generations man's best friend in polar travel. Scott's men had to leave their ponies behind and drag their own barest necessities, the fortitude with which Scott and his brave companions met the disaster that marched with them on their way home has made their expedition a legend overlaying the achievements of Amundsen.*

By comparison, Admiral Dufek rode in comfort above the snow in an aircraft piloted by Lt. Commander Conrad Shinn, whose name deserves to be remembered too. Yet for all the ease of the flight, it was incomparably easier than the almost incredible hardships of the earlier parties, but has not been quite as easy as it seems, as only months and years of planning and organization have made it possible. Nor has the operation, so carefully prepared, escaped the dangers lurking in the frozen continent. Already the crash of the Neptune and other accidents to wide ranging parties, have cost the lives of intrepid adventurers. Even the culminating flight had its risks when the engine gave trouble, and landing on windswept snow at that altitude on a field never before used by an aircraft, and taking off again must have called for steady nerves.

The world has moved at an astonishing technical pace since Scott, but Antarctic expedition still calls for some of the qualities of spirit linked forever with his name. Admiral Dufek stood at the Pole, not a lone conqueror, not even as the representative of his country, but as the representive of his century and his generation of brave men. His was a collective triumph, not a personal one, coming as a timely reminder that while there is much to divide the world, all men unite in acknowledgement of achievements in the service not of nations, but of man's pursuit of knowledge.'

After the historic South Pole landing, AD-2 Strider flew several missions to the pole with passengers and cargo for the base to be established there, returning to New Zealand on the USNS *John R Towle*. After arriving back in the United States, he was assigned to ANS Anancastia in July 1957. From there he made a number of flights to the Arctic, and on one such flight from Anancastia to Fort Churchill to Thule to the North Pole to Point Barrow, giving him the distinction of being the very first person to fly over both Poles in the same year. Strider retired from the Navy in 1974, after a very distinguished aviation career.

At the time of the landing at the South Pole world events overshadowed the moment, as the media were busy reporting on the fighting in the Middle East, Hungary's uprising, and the eve of the United States Presidential elections. In the Antarctic, the Navy and Airforce together with Task Force 43, were working for the purpose of peace, making the Squadron's victory a quiet one.

While the climax was approaching for this year's operations, other nations were also working to prepare bases, with the Soviet Union expedition ready to build a Vostok base near the Geomagnetic Pole and Sovietskaya near the Pole of Inaccessibility. The Russians would have a long hard journey, having to haul supplies by tractor train and by air transport similar to what had been done to get other bases established.

The Americans and Russians exchanged weather information, and by the middle of October the Russians had established three bases, the third being about 230 miles from the now Bunger's Post outpost. In 1947 during Operation Highjump, Lt.Cdr.Gus Shinn had discovered this ice-free coastline, which appeared to the flight crew as a land oasis, and the following year a Navy helicopter landed there with US Navy markers to prove their arrival, renaming the mainland near *Highjump Islands*, the *Bunger Hill*. In 1956, Russian and American scientist agreed to exchange observers for the 1958 Antarctic winter nights, with a Russian at Little America and an American at Mirnyy.

With the major objective of *Deep Freeze II* Polar landing by Admiral Dufek, successfully completed, McMurdo started to relax a little, but there was now the serious business of the enquiry into the fatal Neptune crash. Lt Commander Eddie Frankiewicz and USN's Medical Officer John Harris began to investigate the crash of P2-V-2N BuNo 122465 at William Field, McMurdo on October 20 1956. This followed an informal board of investigation, in accordance with the verbal instructions of the squadron's Commanding Office Cdr Douglas Cordiner on October 19.

It was revealed that all the aircraft's log books were lost in the snow but a 120 hour major periodic maintenance inspection had been completed on the Neptune by Squadron VX-6 personnel at the RNZAF Station in Wigram Christchurch during the week previous to take off. Neither fire nor explosion occurred before or after the impact, and the pilot had accumulated about 2615 hours flying time, the co-pilot about 40 hours, Lt Carey, 1064 hours, and the co-pilot, Kenneth MacApline some 127.2 hours.

Opinions of the cause of the crash:

[1] It was concluded that the pilot had no visible horizon during the portion of the executed low visibility approach. The maximum altitude was probably no higher than 300 feet lacking a visible horizon, coupled with a restricted visible ceiling, preventing the pilot from making a successful low approach, and a faulty gyro could have added confusion at this most critical time. He permitted the nose to fall during the right hand turn, thereby losing altitude to a point where the right wing tip and nose ski contacted the snow.

[2] Because he apparently did not change his altitude pr power just before the crash, it is thought that he did not use, or look, at his instrument panel during the last period before the crash.

[3] The nose probably started to drop when the pilot, in a right hand pattern, leant forward to look around the co pilot for the runway.

Misconduct findings:

[B-1] The crash did not occur as a result of misconduct of any person or persons.

[B-2] The crash occurred within the line of duty of those concerned.

AD2 Chifford Allsup told the inquiry that at the time of the crash, he was sitting in the navigator's compartment, not wearing a safety belt or shoulder harness, as required. Lt Carey was in the pilot seat on the left, Ens MacApline was in the co pilot's seat on the right, the plane's Captain Marion Marze was sitting on the deck just aft of the pilot's compartment and Staff Sgt Spann the navigator, was sitting next to him, with first Radioman Charles Miller in the radioman's seat, while Richard Lewis was also in the compartment.

'The pilot was making a GCA approach to the runway; I heard the pilot say over the radio that he had the field in sight and was taking over visually. We started to turn to the right at approximately 500 feet and a speed of 130 knots, but I couldn't see anything out of the window, and everything was white. I was watching the navigator's altimeter during the turn and noticed we were losing altitude. Immediately after the altimeter read zero, we hit on the nose ski and right wing and the plane started rolling over. The next thing I knew, I was standing in the snow trying to get Lewis out of the snow, then I saw a lot of people coming towards me across the snow.'

At the time, the state of their injuries did not permit either S/Sgt Spann or ENS Kenneth MacApline to be interviewed.

Because ATS Richard Lewis, the other survivor, was still in a state of shock, a statement was obtained from an interview between Lewis and three VX-6 Officers.

'He was facing aft, sitting in the radar compartment next to Capt Hudman, who was strapped in the radar operator's seat. He could see nothing out of the window, everything was white, and he had no indication that the plane was going to crash until he felt the impact with the snow surface. The next thing he knew he was in bed at the dispensary.'

Others to make statements were Lt James Bergstrom USN, LCdr J Donovan, USN, ACI Bryan Swartwood, AC1 Luther Rigg and AC1 John McCoy.

The inquiry board met on November 2 1956, and the Investigation Board's finding was reported to the US Department of the Navy in Washington.

The Task Force's next mission was the construction of the South Pole Station, and during his time on the polar plateau, Admiral Dufek considered the weather still too harsh for his men to work in sub zero temperatures at sea level, but not at 10,000 feet, so he delayed work on the base's construction for several weeks until the weather cleared.

Squadron commander Colonel Cresswell departed from Christchurch on November 10 in a USAF Globemaster, with one of the Weasel tractors tucked safely in its cargo hold, ready to be dropped at the South Pole. Among the crew that day were Capt Oscar Cassity, a member of the 1st Aerial Port Squadron and Capt Ronald Chambers of the RNZAF to assist the USAF technicians with the installation of short-wave radio transmission equipment at McMurdo. This was part of the Air Force dropping missions with 90 scheduled.

Finally the day of reckoning had arrived for Capt Cassity and his crew, and on November 19, he lifted his Globemaster off the ice shelf at Willy Field, with the D-2 Caterpillar tractor trussed up tight with parachutes attached, like some giant caged bird dominating the cavernous cargo bay, so now after days of testing and endless hours of preparation, this was the real thing.

After what seemed an eternity in the air, the Globemaster arrived over the drop zone. *'I took a deep breath, everything rests with this drop, and I lowered our altitude and slowed our speed. The big doors under the plane's belly opened, and the bundled up D2 ejected with a gigantic swoosh, leaving in its place, a blast of 50 below zero air gushing into the aircraft. Seconds later, I viewed one of the prettiest sights I've ever seen, as four 100 foot parachutes floated straight down to the target where they disconnected as planned.'*

Below us Antarctica, larger than Australia, stretched white and empty as far as the eye could see, with no living creatures great or small, anywhere.' recalled Oscar Cassity years later, as if it was yesterday, *'the ice encased continent, still largely unexplored, with its treacherous terrain of man swallowing crevasses and its weather of bitter cold, fierce winds and sudden blizzards, even during its short summer, leaves the adventurer no margin for error.'*

As Capt Cassity banked and circled back, on the ground below the bright yellow Caterpillar chugged across the frozen terrain carrying five navy crewman aboard, all yelling and giving the thumbs up.

Flying his way back to McMurdo, ready for a hot coffee and maybe a shower, Capt Cassity switched on his intercom and asked his navigator for a heading, *'how do we get out of here?'* he asked and the navigator's reply became an Antarctic classic *'Just head north, Sir.'*

The crew burst into tension relieving laughter as the navigator, turned comedian, finally asked his Commander *'which north?'*

The parachutes were repacked and rigged in order to carry out their task for numerous airdrops, and for carrying four barrels of drummed fuel for air dropping, a five-foot square, 18-inch thick plywood and honeycombed cardboard platform, was constructed to be stowed in the C124, able to be dropped at the continent's inland stations. These platforms were specially designed to absorb the shock once the cargo hit the snow, preventing the drums from bursting on impact.

Some parachutes failed to open, sending their contents smashing to bits or burying themselves deep in the snow on impact, often never recoverable, while on other occasions, the parachute would remain inflated but take off like a rocket, dragging the pallet like some monstrous motorized sled, and disappear over the horizon.

A serious tragedy was adverted ten days later, due to the courage and efficiency of VX-6 on the ground, when a Globemaster returning from an aerial dropping mission to the Pole, came short of the runway, hit a snow bank and caught fire. The Williams Field fire crash crews were at the crash site within minutes with extinguishers, pulling the crew down escape lines to safety, and the only injury was the pilot's broken leg. By this time there were three crashed Globemasters on the ice runway, all damaged while landing.

Seabee Charles Bevilacqua again, he and other Seabees were flown to the location of the South Pole on Christmas eve 1956 aboard # *17274 Charlene* piloted by Eddie Frankiewicz and James Waldron *'We were the first ones there, flying in a small underpowered R4-D-8 aircraft with flimsy skis, and as there was no landing field, the plane touched down but could not stop, for the skis would stick to the snow, so we all jumped out of the door and dived under the tail as it flew by.*

We did not even know the location of the pole when we arrived, and it took Lt Dick Bowers a few days to pinpoint the exact location of the geographic South Pole. After completing most of the Pole station, we turned it over to a new group coming in, but not before we were able to celebrate a most memorable Christmas, complete with an airdropped New Zealand Christmas tree and plenty of good cheer. It's good to be young!

When we returned to McMurdo, to wait our return home, as Deep Freeze II was taking over, those of us from DF1 had little to do, so a few of us went over to help Sir Edmund Hillary and the New Zealanders construct the original Scott Base. We stole much as we could from our Americans to help put in Scott Base and who could resist these jolly Kiwi's, it was a pleasure to work with them and to have a close association with Hillary'.

Eddie has clear recollections of landing for the first time at Beardmore:

'We flew two R4-D's to Beardmore to the foot of the Liv Glacier, where we wanted to establish an interim camp, but it was a total white out, and we couldn't see the ground at all, and we knew there were a lot of glaciers there and crevasses in that area at the foot of the Beardmore, so we just kept on going north and it was still a terrible white out, we couldn't see anything at all. Then I started praying real well, as I'm a Polish Roman Catholic. Nowhere else was there any sunlight but there ahead where we landed and it lasted long enough for Gus and me to land there, then it disappeared and I knew I believed in God.'

In February 1957 a message was received to fly urgent supplies to personnel at the South Pole Station after all the summer support had returned to Christchurch aboard the *USS Curtis* three days previously. A C-124C Globemaster was dispatched from New Zealand to fly surveillance and navigational cover for the R4-D and crew. Without skis the C-124C could only take-off and land at McMurdo, and going back to the Pole this late in the season was extremely hazardous due to below zero temperatures.

On February 21 Harvey Speed, was selected to fly in the R4-D- *BuNo 12418,* the only ski-equipped aircraft available, but as the R4-D was experiencing engine problems it was necessary to make three test flights, after having maintenance staff working round the clock to get the "old girl" back in flying order. The weather closed in as Speed left McMurdo, but he managed to land at the 10,000 feet high plateau, drop off his cargo and passengers, and then load seven passengers aboard for the flight back to McMurdo.

It was the last flight of the season, and two hours into the flight back home to Little America, Speed noticed a sudden pressure drop and observed that a serious oil leak was drenching his port engine, while below him the Antarctic terrain was mountainous, then came his greatest fear- he began to lose altitude.

The navigator gave him a new heading which would take him towards level terrain, but having fired his fifteen JATO bottles on takeoff from the polar plateau, Speed was somewhat reluctant to set his Gooney Bird down while still on the plateau but had little choice.

Had Speed not been able to get off the surface when he did, the standby crew at Little America would have had to fly to this isolated location with an engine heater, fuel, tools, survival gear and the necessary equipment to get him airborne again. It would have been an all or nothing situation, as the only other available flight crew was either in Christchurch or en route to the States, and it would have been many days to get them back to the ice. By the time assistance did arrive, the aircraft and crew would have been frozen solid on the windswept plateau. This was Antarctic aviation.

After three hours with his hands frozen and soaked with grimy oil, Miles managed to rob oil from the good engine to replace that lost from the port engine, and on takeoff, Speed raced across the virgin snow with his power settings at maximum and became airborn without JATO assistance. Byrd Station was secure and the last Pole landing of the season was on record.

After that experience, one would think a normal man would decide he'd had enough. But not the hale and happy Lt Harvey Speed, who wintered over at Little America ready for more search and rescue duty.

A year after the historic flight, a sophomore at Martinsville high school, VA, was inspired after she heard about the VX-6 aviators problem, and so the young Jane Gregory's somewhat ingenious, if not imaginative concept was born for making the skis slick, by laminating Du Pont 'Mylar' polyester film to the running edge of the surface, and for this idea she won two Science Fair prizes. While wondering what the navy was doing about the problem, which effected the whole Antarctic air squadron hourly, Jane gleaned the answer from Lt. Commander Gus Shinn, who by coincidence was home on leave, just 18 miles away at Leakesville, Spray, North Carolina.

The navy, he told Jane, was using skis surfaced with Teflon from the Du Pont Polychemicals Department, as it was particularly valuable where the material's low co efficiencies of friction and its apparent immunity to extreme temperatures made it invaluable.

The Task Force SLIDE had just demonstrated that Teflon did not adhere to snow or ice even under the weight of a large plane, when testing had been carried out on a frozen lake at Bemidji, Minn., using huge Lockheed C-130 propjet transporters. With Teflon on its skis, it had taken off with a record 111,000 pounds gross weight.

The big skis [the main ones are 19 and a half feet long by 5 and half feet wide] comprise a Ski-130 kit that can be attached readily to the aircrafts regular landing gear, making the plane operable on either snow or ice. Both Lockheed Aircraft Co and the US Air Force's Wright Air Development Centre developed the skid.

Meanwhile at West Trenton N.J, the Stroukoff Aircraft Corp had carried out the landing gear application of Teflon a little further, and using the new advanced Pantobase, a plane could operate on snow, ice, land or water. Installed on the multipurpose aircraft -YC-134, which Strukoff manufactured for the USAF, the Pantobase was a composite essentially for retractable wheels and ski lamination, with a sheeting of Teflon resin, because the Pantobase absorbs the strains of take-off and landing.

During Deep Freeze III, Lt Cdr Epperly took over command of Frankie's old Gooney Bird *Charlene,* flying a number of survey flights in the 'old girl' to remote locations, resupplying bases and traverse parties. *'It seems that my first month was filled with delivering replacement engines to Squadron aircraft that had suffered engine failure, one of these was another R4-D out on the Ross Sea, two helicopters and on to Cdr Frankiewicz at the Beardmore Glacier.'*

But most of these flights were non-eventful, however on one such flight hundreds of miles from nowhere, his co-pilot Ron Stone came down with kidney stones. *'He was in agony, poor fella, we got him back to McMurdo where we had an MD, but the flight was a slow agonizing one, then he was flown back to New Zealand aboard a Connie for further medical treatment.*

On another occasion we made a flight to Camp Rockford located 160 miles SE of Little American on the edge of the Ross Ice Shelf on the LA-Byrd tractor train trail, to fill a 10,000 gallon rubber bag with Avgas and set up an emergency fuelling station, but I don't believe it was ever used, at least not during my tour of duty.'

During *Deep Freeze II* the squadron sustained four more aircraft losses, the first on December 31, when a Bell HTL-5 assigned to *Staten Island* from detachment 31 Helicopter Utility Squadron One, was destroyed when its engines failed on takeoff, and it crashed on the flight deck.

On January 19 1957 the *Glacier's,* helicopter *BuNo 138595* from detachment 69 Helicopter Utility Squadron, crashed into the Ross Sea after its engines failed, and Lt Cdr Charles Costanza, pilot and Lt [jg] John W Erlewine co pilot, barely escaped before the helicopter sank quickly in the frozen waters.

The third helicopter was lost on July 12 1957- when a VX-6 HO4-3 *BuNo 138580* returning to McMurdo, crashed short of base due to the windscreen frosting and the visibility suddenly worsening from ice crystals. The VX-6 pilot Lt.Neil, who was on a routine proficiency flight, had just completed his basic helicopter training before being sent to the Antarctic.

Settling on its tail, the helicopter burst into flames, and while Lt.Neil and his front seat passenger escaped with only a few scratches, three of the passengers seated in the cabin suffered severe burns, and a third passenger AD2 Nelson Cole, not buckled in his seat was thrown into the tail cone when the Sikorsky impacted and was consumed by the resulting fire and died later. This crash also injured some VX-6 fire fighters.

On February 25th Admiral Dufek and his staff returned to Christchurch, New Zealand, placing the command in the hands of Captain Dickey, and from there on all the wintering over personnel had to exist on their own, as no longer would they be able to expect outside assistance, even in the event of an emergency. The squadron's tasks started with tying down some of the aircraft for the winter, and to do this, holes had to be dug in the ice then wooden anchors placed in the holes to freeze tight. Using ropes tied to these anchors, the personnel would then tie the aircraft to several secure points. Once the anchors had frozen, it would take a massive force to dislodge them.

Additional flights were still made to the Trail Party, Byrd Station and McMurdo, but these flights were on a somewhat irregular basis depending on weather permitting. On one such return flight, Lt Speed brought with him a Siberian husky, named *Clem*, who was to be the camp mascot at Little America for the winter months. It would appear that *Clem* was brought to the Antarctic to pull ski sleds out of McMurdo, but *Clem* didn't like the other dogs and refused to pull the sleds, so it was decided to get rid of him.

If Harvey had not taken him from his team and given him a boarding pass on his R4-D, the odds were that he would have been put to sleep, since the Navy could not afford to maintain a dog that had such an anti sled-pulling attitude. *Clem* was an extremely docile animal and since he was the only pet in camp, soon became the favourite of all the squadron, loving all the attention he received from the lonely gang at Little America and soon became the official welcoming party at the air terminal.

It was about this time that word was received that Rear Admiral Dufek had died. His death was quite a shock to all on the ice, since his exploration in Antarctica was a precursor to those in the squadron. A memorial service was held several days later, and on May 10 1957 Cdr.V J Coly was appointed squadron commander, taking over the command from Cdr.Cordiner.

On August 31 1957, the Squadron lost a UC-I Otter *BuNo 142426*. The aircraft had been tied down with double lines at Little America V, when an 80 mph wind opened the tie down rings blowing the Otter away. While the two R4-D's came through the storm in fine shape, it was the Otter that suffered when it had been blown about a quarter of a mile away, leaving the wings of the aircraft broken off at the wing roots, and the tail section [rudder, horizontal stabilizer and elevator] severed completely from the rest of the fuselage. The pilot's cabin, the engine, and almost the entire fuselage had carried on before being dropped upside down in one piece. There was no evidence of the aircraft having touched the ground on its journey, because the fuselage was largely intact.

Writes James Waldron *'I was quite depressed that one of the aircraft entrusted to my care was destroyed, but there was nothing we could have done to prevent this loss, short of leaving the Otter covered with snow, but as the aircraft was needed for summer operations, leaving it in the snow wasn't an option. Now we had to dig out our second Otter and have it readied for summer flying. After our two R4-D's and flight crews had departed for McMurdo, the remaining two R4-D's, three Otters and one helicopter were resurrected from the snow by the maintenance crews and readied for summer operations.'*

Evacuation of personnel has been a major function of VX-6- at times carried out during the Antarctic's extremely dangerous six month polar winter night. Cdr. James Waldron and Lt. Harvey Gardner can illustrate this best during the winter of 1957 when a Roosevelt Island Traverse party scientist, New Zealander, Mr. Peter Schoeck, was seriously injured after falling 60 feet into a crevasse, some 50 miles from Little America on October 31, and needed medical assistance. Following the evening's movie, a message was received that Schoeck was serious ill, but the caller said they didn't recommend a flight as the weather at the accident site, some 50 miles from Little America was too poor.

The base was told later of the events that when the Traverse Party was passing through a heavily crevassed field it had to stop for the night. Following the evening meal, Schoeck wandered outside the tent, and saw a strange shaped rise on the surface of the snow a few feet from where the tractors were parked, so walked over to investigate. Suddenly the snow he was standing on collapsed, sending him falling into a crevasse, where he landed on a ledge some 50 feet from the surface. The Traverse Party were able to rescue him from the crevasse, but Mr Schoeck suffered four broken ribs, damaged one of his lungs and ruptured his spleen, and the Traverse Party had no way of treating his injuries.

Lt.Cdr Cal Larsen, a photographer in the Antarctic during DF 11, at the time of Peter Shoeck's fall near Roosevelt Island, remembers the hours before James Waldron arrived. *'We put a line down the crevasse, and Hugh Bennett went down and basically tied Peter to himself and the five of us in the party started pulling them out, assisted by a track vehicle and a snow-cat, but it was still very painful for our New Zealand friend with such injuries.*

At the surface we awaited the rescue Otter and its two brave crew, and I went back on the plane with all the photos I needed. Albert Carry was the boss on that traverse, and the senior scientist on the continent, and a few days later Peter was flown back to New Zealand, where he was hospitalised and recovered. A couple of weeks after he left the Antarctic, I received a case of beer from Peter, and he wrote a note saying: 'You won the bet', Peter was always digging in the snow and I was bugging him just before he fell through, saying to him. 'Peter, I'll bet you that one day you'll dig yourself right through the ice bridge and into a crevasse'. That was Peter's story anyway. Actually, there was some truth in it.' Cal Larsen said.

Cal went back to Antarctic in 1969 as a navigator on a photo-mapping mission aboard a C-130, but was med evacuated out that time.

Commander Waldron recalled the rescue flight to collect Peter Schoeck. *'After a brief discussion with one of my pilots, we both headed to Kiel Field where our night time maintenance crew were readying an Otter # 142425 for the flight to Roosevelt Island. Knowing the weather at the accident site was marginal, we thought we would at least go to the area and see for ourselves. If it were possible to land we would do so, otherwise we would return to Little America and wait for an improvement in the weather, as the weather for take off at Little America was very good.'*

Homing in on a low frequency, brought Waldron right over the camp site, but landing on such a remote location was extremely hazardous at best, and as they approached the site, the visibility started falling off making it difficult to distinguish objects on the snow surface. They couldn't see anything smaller than the outline of men and red tractors and trailer vehicles, and dark streaks indicating the dreaded crevasses.

'A member of the Traverse Party told us that the crevasses were quite extensive, and if we decided to land, we should land in the area where his tractors had passed, but recent snow had made it

impossible, so I asked him to have the men he had with him to ski out from the tractors in the direction they had just come from, spacing each man about 25 yards apart.

Once they were all in place, I made an approach for a landing, as my radar altimeter indicated I was within 50 feet of the surface, visually lining up the Otter using the men as reference for my glide slope and direction. When I was next to the man most distant from the tractor my skis dug into the snow giving me a rather hard but non damaging landing, and we came to a stop just feet from the tractors and within a few minutes Peter Schoeck was loaded aboard the Otter.

I directed my co-pilot to turn the aircraft around and make a take-off, since we were going downwind the take off was extra long but the surface was so rough we bounced horribly. Poor Peter must have felt every bump that was adding injury to his fall.'

Both pilots were recommended for the Air Medal, and Waldron's medal was presented to him while he was stationed at Port Lyautey Morocco. Cdr.James Waldron recalled that while the rescue mission was anything but routine, over the months in Antarctica he had flown several flights under weather conditions far worse than the night they rescued Peter Schoeck.

It is interesting to note that Commander Waldron's co pilot that day, Lt. Lawrence Farrell and another Lt Gardner, were killed the following year while flying an Otter *BuNo 144673*. They had flown to a remote Antarctic site, and on take-off from the landing area, turned towards the mountains to the right of them instead of turning left, which would have placed them over open water. This misjudgement flew them into the hill killing both. Lt.Gardner received his Air Medal at Marble Point before he died.

Another VX-6 aviator to winter over during 1957 was Lt.Cdr Earl Hillis, who entered the NAVCAD Flight Training Programme, and was commissioned Ensign, receiving his wings in 1956, and his first tour was with VX-6. After picking up one of the squadron's Otters at the DeHaviland factory in Toronto, Earl with the Otter was shipped to Antarctica aboard the *USNS Joseph H Merrill*, escorted through the pack ice by the USS *Eastwind* to spend Christmas 1956 at McMurdo, before travelling to Little America where he was assigned to fly with Lt.Cdr Harvey Speed and Lt.Cdr Bill Schick as co-pilot and navigator, wintering over with *Que Sera Sera*.

Lt.Cdr Hillis flew as navigator with Crd.Waldron and Frankie on *Charlene* and in the winter of 1957 he and Jim Waldron flew together in the squadron's Otter. Jim described one frigid night when the visibility was less than good. '*We made a few takeoffs and landings and then we flew eastwards along the edge of the ice-cap for about twenty minutes. It became apparent after a while, that with every minute we were placing distance from our winter camp and any rescue, should our single engine quit, and at some distance we would reach a point where we would freeze to death before help could arrive. We were also losing radio contact with the tower so they would not be able to state where we might have gone down if our engine quit so we finally returned to Kiel Field and landed. Earl was very professional throughout the flight, as he was on all previous flights, and while we never became good friends, I presume that he had difficulty in associating with someone in authority, and since I was his supervisor, he held me in abeyance.*'

After leaving Antarctica in December 1957, he received orders to FASRON 102 in Corpus Christi, flying R7-D's for Project Magnet for the Naval Oceanographic Office in the Arctic, working out of Thule. In 1959-60 he was doing infra-red photography of the ice pack, and later flying ice reconnaissance for the submarine *USS Sargo's* winter transit through the Bering Strait in the Arctic in C-123's He flew over both the North Pole and South Poles.

The worst fear of aviators flying in the Antarctic were burns, which almost without exception were the major injury in an air crash, so besides beer, there was a considerable cache of brandy called *Old Methuselah* which the Navy had shipped to the ice, and fortunately the teetotal Medical Officer,

Doctor Unger was the controller of this 'issuance', so it was only on rare occasions that the men received a mug of the potent drink. Dr Unger considered wisely, that the accident potential could be rather high, and if personnel were able to consume social amounts of brandy it would not last long, and as it was a treatment for injuries rather than a social drink, the good Doctor kept it rationed.

As it was, during the long winter months when it was impossible to evacuate the injured to New Zealand for hospitalisation, many helicopter crashes and base accidents involved burns, with four severely burned personnel needing treatment over several months before they could be evacuated, and it was here the doctor dispensed brandy as a painkiller. At times his small clinic was taxed to its limits with several severe hand and leg injuries, and subsequently lots of brandy was prescribed making brandy drinking a rare experience for all those able personnel who wintered over during the long nights.

The final mission flown during *Deep Freeze II's* summer season, was the establishment of fuel caches along the Byrd Station trail to be ready for the tractor trains the next season, pressing all the R4-D's and a helicopter and two Otters into service.

Lt.Cdr Harvey Speed and Lt Robert Anderson the R4-D pilots in the wintering party at Little America learnt just how stark and naked the Antarctic could be. Lt Anderson described a moonlight 'high noon' familiarization flight from Kiel Field, Little America Five to McMurdo. '*We arrived at the strip and found the wings frosted. While the wings were being scraped, Herman Nelson heaters were used to preheat the engines. We knew after several hours that the engines were warm enough to start, but often as not after starting, the gauge in the cockpit showed no pressure because oil froze in the line between the engines and the gauge.*

Snow blew through the tiniest opening in the cabin, fuselage and wings, so we had to check carefully to be sure it was removed before we attempted a takeoff.

The runway was marked by flare pots which were very effective but in spite of all precautions, we had a heavily frosted windscreen during the first few minutes of flight, but by the time we climbed to 1000 feet, the temperature rose 20 degrees and the frost disappeared.'

Another first for the season was the parachute jump at the South Pole by Technical Sergeant Richard Patton, USAF of the 1710th Aerial Port Squadron on November 26 1956 Making the jump from a Globemaster, it was his 32nd jump during his 14 years military service, and he was also the first member of the USAF to stand on the Pole, and savours relating the story of how he had forgotten his toothbrush and had it delivered later by a C-124 airdrop.

The United States Antarctic base at Beardmore Station was officially disestablished on February 21 1957, the day before the USAF Globemasters squadron commenced their departure from McMurdo Sounds for New Zealand along with the CTS-43. With the support phase of Operation *Deep Freeze 11* officially over, the ships and aircraft departed the Antarctic, with the *USS Atka* and *USS Merrell* departing McMurdo Sounds for the US, while the last C-124 departed for Christchurch, and the last scientists were flown to the South Pole by R4-D to winter over, and so the curtain came down on *Deep freeze II*

CHAPTER SEVEN.

PAN AMERICAN AIRWAYS EXTEND THEIR SOUTH PACIFIC SERVICE.
THE FIRST AIRLINE STEWARDESSES ARRIVE AT MAC TOWN.

First commercial airline to land in Antarctica by Pan American
Airways, and the first females to visit the continent.
Operation Deep Freeze '59 continues.

In mid January 1957, after a 14 hour flight from McMurdo, a P2V-7 Neptune landed at Wigram airfield with only enough fuel left in its tanks for another hour of flying time. The Neptune was the first aircraft to leave Antarctica since December 18, when the USAF curtailed all their flights after high temperatures had made the ice runway unusable, but during this time, the ski-equipped Neptune's were able to continue to operate from William Field's ice ski-ways.

Describing his polar flights, Lt Commander Otti said that during his first attempt to reach the Pole, he was forced to turn back because of a propeller problem but landed on his second attempt, accompanied by the IGY scientist Mr William Housh, and spent two hours there before returning to McMurdo. Landing on the world's most isolated landing strip was an uncomfortable business, from the lack of instrument aids, and few contrasts in the white landscape, and it was necessary to maintain a high altitude because the Polar Plateau was about 11,000 feet above sea level.

Lt.Cdr Otti's co-pilot Lt A I Raithell said the Pole skiway was no great improvement on the strip at McMurdo, *'with alternate periods of cold and warm weather, the runway was constantly freezing and melting forming several large pools.'*

Weather forecasting in Antarctica in the early days of Operation Deep Freeze, had aviators relying on the Navy Meteorologist Commander John Mirabito who had been seconded from the Navy's Aerological Office spoke six languages and was to prove invaluable as an interpreter at the Paris and Brussels conferences during the planning for the IGY. His ambition was to be a professional baseball player, starting out as a pitcher with the Dodgers, but later became one of the most outstanding Navy aerologists who analysed the forecasts for the first flights to the Antarctic continent, earning a gigantic reputation among the Navy and Air Force pilots in the expedition.

'If Mirabito says we can go, then we go' would be their first comment.

'In 1955 when we first flew in from Christchurch, we had no weather reports from this side of the continent, we just had those five ships of the Task Force strung out in a line. Here at McMurdo Sound, there was no ground control equipment at the strip and behind it a million square miles of unexplored territory. As I look back now. [These comments were made in 1958] and know what could have happened, I get the chills.'

During the 1956/57 season, it was rather easier – there were three weather stations to cover a million square miles. This year, though with a net of about 40 stations all reporting in the weather to central at Little America, we can say with confidence that you can go a thousand miles from here and get back every time.'

He considers that flying in the Antarctica offers no more additional hazards than flying over the United States or Europe, for the weather in the Arctic is more severe, and the ground fog plagues aviators much more than the high wings do here. The difference in Antarctic that weighs the scales so much in favour of Arctic flying is that once a wheeled aircraft takes off here for the interior, there is only one airfield to which it can return-McMurdo- while in the Arctic there are many alternatives.

'The wildest storms in Antarctica are those which sweep down from the high central plateau. At the South Pole, although the temperature dropped to 102.1 degrees below zero in 1957, the average wind speed wind gusts, reached 40 knots. This makes the recovery of airdropped materials much simpler because it is not drifting over the brown snow to become buried out of sight.

Mawson used a can of beans on a string and a calibrated scale when he recorded a gust of 200 knots, but most meteorologists are inclined to doubt the accuracy of that reading. This year at the combined New Zealand and US base at Hallett Station near Cape Adare, the winds reached 99 knots in early December. At the French base at d'Ureville on the Adelie coast, the average wind was just 50 knots, yet gusts of over 120 knots have been recorded.

After the IGY, we should have a picture of the circulation of weather in the Antarctic, which will give meteorologists half the world over, a truer picture of their weather that they have never had before. New Zealand stands to gain considerably, as much of its weather originates from the Antarctic and the Southern Oceans.' Commander John Mirabito told this writer.

Maintaining vehicles in below zero temperatures is difficult when 20 grade oil freezes, making it impossible to lift the dip stick out or start an engine until it has been thoroughly heated for half an hour with aircraft engine heaters, and maintaining the water supply was another of the problems facing the group of Commander Roger Witherall's 34 Seabees who were stationed at the Naval Air Facility, McMurdo. With the first ray of sunlight showing over the horizon in late August, for the arrival of the austral summer, they were down on the iceshelf two miles from the station with D-8 bulldozers clearing the winter build up of snow off the runway in preparation for the arrival of the first flight from New Zealand. However, once this task was completed, the smoothing operations would continue every day to keep it free of snow, as it was a vital air link between Christchurch and McMurdo.

Repairing the 158 Task Force's vehicle fleet that varies from small weasels to huge bulldozers was a full time job for the Seabees in the motor garage. In temperatures this cold, metal becomes brittle so engines and other parts under repair take longer than is usual, causing vehicles to back up waiting for attention. All vehicles operating in the Antarctic climatic had an estimated life of just one third that of others in normal temperatures, owing to the vehicle being heated for half an hour, then left to run continuously over many hours. At the normal coffee, lunch or dinner breaks there would be dozens of bulldozers, weasels and trucks lined up outside the mess halls left idling until work resumed.

'Idling wears out the engines quicker than anything else, but the engines are placed under enormous strain every time they are started' says Commander Witherall, *'Because the base is isolated during the winter months, a huge supply of spare engines and engine parts are kept at the station to deal with any emergencies, with all spares catalogued at the beginning of each season, so that replacements can be airlifted or shipped in from New Zealand.'*

Earlier that year the Sir Vivian Fuchs and Sir Edmund Hillary led trans-Antarctic expedition had access to the spare parts pool from the United States stores for their utility vehicles, with other spares flown in from New Zealand so their journey could be completed. Rear Admiral Dufek had also come to their assistance when in late November Sir Ed decided the tractor train would go all the way to the Pole, even though that was not originally planned for.

This created a new problem, as extra fuel would be required, so Dufek allowed the extra fuel to be brought south on the ice breaker *Glacier*, and later when this had to be jettisoned during a storm just below 60-degree south, the *Deep Freeze* Commander then authorized 20 drums of fuel to come south by USAF Globemaster.

Until they journeyed to Antarctica in December 1955, the Seabees had had a short, but proud record beginning in 1941, when in December of that year, with an eye on the developing storm clouds of war across both oceans, Rear Admiral Ben Noreell, the Chief of the Navy's Bureau of Yards and Docks, recommended the establishment of Naval Construction Battalions, and with the attack on Pearl Harbour and the United States entering the war, he was given the green light. Their motto became *'We Build, We Fight'*, and following the Korean conflict which saw 10,000 men called up for the Battalion, they embarked on a new mission, that of providing assistance in the wake of the 1953 devastating earthquakes in Greece, providing construction work and training to underdeveloped counties. The Seabees became the Navy Goodwill Ambassadors and built or improved many roads, orphanages and public utilities in many remote parts of the world.

One of these Seabees was Frank Witty, who arrived in the Antarctic aboard the icebreaker *Burton Island* for *Deep Freeze III* in 1957-58. Frank remembers arriving at McMurdo the day after Christmas 1957 as a passenger aboard a Sikorsky to carry him the last 15 miles, as the icebreaker could move no further through the Ross Sea ice.

Their assignment was to erect four new 100 x 40 ft Quonset huts, with one of them to become McMurdo's first Navy Exchange building. *'We lived in a 20 x 40 Quonset hut with its own identity over the doorway. Ours was the 'Attic Annex', named after a little second floor coffee house, the Attic, in Christchurch, New Zealand. We kept our 3.2 beers on the floor beneath the bottom bunk, as there was no need for refrigeration. We would swap our diluted beer for the real 'stuff' from the Kiwis at the nearby Scott Base, but eventually trade barriers developed for whatever reasons, and we ended up making our own. One crew had a portable still brought to the galley, but while they were brewing some rice for sake, cooks were frying bacon on the grill and bacon flavoured sake was almost as bad as our weak Christmas cheer.'*

The Seabees had it hard at times but so did the pilots, as on a flight to Little America from Marie Byrd Station, with most of the 800 odd miles flown being routine, Cdrs.Speed and Waldron received a message saying they could expect deteriorating weather conditions on arrival. An hour before they were expected, the aviators encountered a heavy haze, making it extremely difficult to see where they were going, so to avoid crashing into the below zero white desert littered with unknown crevasses, Harvey Speed climbed to a thousand plus feet above the ice and switched to flying strictly by instruments, but by the time they reached Little America they had lost all visual contact with the surface below. As soon as radar contact was established with the tower at Kiel Field, GCA instructions were transmitted to Cdr. Speed, and if he couldn't make it the first time he would have to climb up to 1000 feet and make another instrument landing.

'Harvey Speed was on the controls during the approach to the runway and as we got close to the surface, I was to keep looking straight ahead for the first sight of the runway, the clouds we were flying through were quite dark and oppressive, and as we approached the two hundred foot altitude wave-off height, we still couldn't see the runway. With no other options available, Harvey added engine power and started his second approach.

In all we made three approaches to the runway and were never able to spot enough of the surface to make a safe landing, on one approach I did, for a moment, spot a vehicle below us with someone holding a lighted flare, unfortunately this glimpse didn't last and once again we re-entered the clouds. We were running low on fuel by this time, so Harvey decided that we should head inland, hoping to find a smooth place to land about fifty miles south of Little America. The weather over the Tractor Trail continued to be too poor for a visual landing, and as we looked eastwards we noted a glow towards the horizon indicating that the weather in that direction might be better, and since this was our only recourse, Harvey turned the aircraft in that direction'.

After about twenty minutes of flying they broke out suddenly into clear air and were relieved because being very low on fuel they either had to land or crash. Harvey turned the aircraft into the wind and made a landing in an area where no aircraft had ever landed before, close to the Ice Shelf and on a featureless plain of snow, which pitched slightly upwards towards the south. After Harvey switched off the engines they climbed out on to the snow, and found that the wind was blowing at a gentle ten miles per hour and the temperature was about minus 35 degrees F. '*Advising Little America by radio of our location we were told that fuel would be flown in, as soon as the weather improved.*

It was obvious to us now, that we had better start using some of those survival techniques which we had learnt back in the States, because we had no idea how long we might be stranded, knowing that after a few hours of minus 35 degrees F, we could expect that temperature to take its toll on us, even though we wore heavy winter clothing. It was obvious we couldn't expect to survive unless we took precautions. ' recalled James Waldron.

Eighteen hours after landing the crew were picked up by a squadron's Neptune and returned to Little America, but such was the Antarctic programme they were right back on the flight schedule and ordered to make a quick turn around within two hours, airborne on another mission.

The squadron's aircrews provided all types of logistic support, required for the various scientific parties where considerable flying hours were required moving those parties from selected spots to other locations for the checking of the composition of the earth below the surface of the ice. To accomplish this task the scientists would explode dynamite charges at short distances, and by measuring the recorded echo of the explosion, determine the location of the bottom of the ice and the depth of the ocean itself, and were able to assist the oceanographers to map the ocean floor. In the short flights for transporting these scientists, the VX-6 crew would see first hand what sort of terrain the parties might expect as they progressed slowly over the surface, so this also helped them plan their routes and enabled them to avoid any crevasse areas.

The sun had returned to the Antarctic sky, which had been starved of sunlight over the long winter months, and suddenly the gloom the crews had experienced evaporated. By August 17, they had successfully removed the last plane from its snowy protective envelope and prepared them for their initial flights, when six days later one of the R4-D's completed a short test flight. '*The landing gear refused to retract, so the test flight was cut short, but it was a start.*' recalled James Waldron.

On August 26 after a brief test of their R4-D # *17246* Lt Commander Waldron, Lt Harvey Speed and his crew completed a three and a half hour flight of the Bay of Whales, Roosevelt Island and the Tractor Trail out to the 20-mile cairn. The reconnaissance flight allowed the IGY staff to evaluate the sea and snow conditions to see the effect the winter weather might have on their upcoming operational plans.

'*The temperature on the surface was minus 52F at take off, but proved to be considerably warmer at cruising altitude*'. Jim Waldron said.

Pilots were ordered to fly supplies from McMurdo Sound to a site near the Beardmore Glacier where a camp was to be located. '*On September 3, both planes were loaded up and we departed on the first flight to for the season*'. Cdr Waldron continued. '*The weather was perfect for the flight, but I couldn't help but think that we were the only two flying within several thousand miles, and if any problem had developed with either R4-D's there was no help available anywhere. Other Antarctic bound aircraft and ships were weeks away from arriving on the ice.*'

They were warmly greeted after they landed on the snow runway at McMurdo Station particularly since they had brought some much-needed supplies for the camp.

Waldron again: '*we had hoped to start setting up the camp at the base of the Beardmore Glacier as soon as we could refuel at McMurdo. However, a radio blackout caused by the changes in sunspots, affected the Ionosphere, preventing the aircraft to communicate with the control tower, curtailing flights for a few days.*'

Cdr Waldron had a pleasant surprise when arriving at McMurdo and while having time on his hands until the blackout situation cleared, received an invitation for supper as guest of Sir Edmund Hillary, at their camp a few miles south of McMurdo. Cdr Flynn, the commander of McMurdo Station drove Waldron, Harvey Speed and Bob Anderson to the small camp. '*We had a delightful meal and an evening of contract bridge with Ed's officers. Ed Hillary was a great host and he made us feel welcome in an extraordinary way. I saw Ed several times afterwards as we passed by our work area on the sea ice with his team of sled dogs, and he always gave us a friendly wave of the hand.*

By September 9th the radio interference subsided, allowing both R4-D's to load up and take off for Beardmore Glacier and after a quick turnaround the aircraft returned to McMurdo for further supplies for Beardmore.'

Cdr Waldron wrote of their first flight to Beardmore campsite in August 1957 as a beautiful experience with visibility enroute of over 50 miles. *'As we approached the glacier we descended to about 100 feet over the surface and we were pleased to discover the surface of the ice to be relatively smooth and perfect for landing. The glacier was so immense in size ahead of us that it appeared we would fly into it when we were still five or more miles from its mouth. Harvey Speed, my aircraft commander, held his course until we were about a mile from the glacier before landing. Our cargo was quickly unloaded from the cabin of both aircraft and within a short while we were once again airborne for McMurdo.'*

The next day Wednesday September 11th started out as a normal day for the squadron, but quickly became a death defying experience for one of the R4-D crews. Two aircraft took off five minutes apart in sub zero temperatures, *# 17426,* was piloted by Lt Anderson, the other piloted by Lt. Commander Harry Speed. While flying to the Beardmore some 314 miles from base with 5,000 lbs. of supplies, Anderson developed a low oil pressure situation in one engine and returned to McMurdo for quick repairs by the squadron's maintenance crew. While on the ground they receive a radio message from Lt.Cdr Speed, saying he had had to make a forced landing on the bleak and lonely ice shelf on the Ross Sea, about 90 miles from McMurdo.

The port engine had quit in flight, but there were no injuries to the crew or damage to the aircraft, sending Lt Anderson and Commander Waldron to deliver two engine warmers to melt the ice from the fuel lines of the failed engine as snow had accumulated in one of its tanks during the winter months, and even though the squadron's maintenance crews and expended many days working to remove the snow and ice, some of the snow crystals had remained in the fuel tanks and dislodged, only to pass into the aircraft fuel lines and freeze at the engine strainer, thus cutting off the flow of fuel to the engine.

As quickly as possible the engine heaters were loaded and flown to the forced landing site, where they spent an hour on the surface while heat was applied to Speed's failed engine. Once Harvey had his engine running smoothly, Lt Anderson took off and returned to McMurdo, but five minutes after they left the site, the port engine again failed, forcing another landing on the sea ice.

Lt Anderson returned to the site with two heaters and a maintenance crew, and again the stricken engine was thawed out ready for take off, and after unloading his cargo onto the ice, Harvey's plane was light enough to fly smoothly on one engine, allowing both crews to limp back home.

Next morning, September 12, Harvey Speed made a short maintenance test flight where his engine appeared to be operating satisfactorily, letting him fly back to the site of his second force landing to recover the cargo he had dropped off. A few days later, with both planes loaded to the maximum with fuel and supplies, Speed and Anderson prepared to take off from the foot of the Liv Glacier. Harvey Speed started first, taxiing to the snow runway about a third of a mile from where Anderson was warming up his engines. Starting his take-off run, he appeared to have difficulty with his directional control, so he aborted.

Because he had a slight crosswind as the airplane started to turn into the wind, this may have made the aircraft more difficult to control on the ice surface, and being heavily loaded, caused him to leave the side of the runway.

Speed taxied back to the beginning of the runway and began another take off, but this time he applied the JATO rockets becoming airborne in the normal manner until the R4-D reached about 25 feet above the icy surface, then the port engine failed completely and his port wing dropped suddenly striking the hard icy surface and dragged along for over 20 yards. Lt Speed immediately turned off the other engine to level the aircraft, but moments later his port engine came back on with full power, lifting the left wing, thus dropping the right wing, so it too dragged on the surface.

All this time the JATO rockets were still firing, so taking the best action possible he added power to the right engine. The aircraft levelled itself and began to climb slowly to altitude, but six feet of his left wing tip was broken and was standing up vertically like a rudder, to appear an unreal version of an R4-D. Harvey Speed soon discovered that the ailerons were frozen in place, making it impossible to turn the plane around in the normal manner, and observers on the ground watched horrified as Speed fought desperately to keep his R4-D under control, with many hardened ground crew expecting the worst as the nightmare unfolded in front of them.

Since the ice surface directly ahead precluded a landing without totally demolishing his aircraft, Speed elected to attempt a return to the field, even with the outer six feet of his port wing tip broken and the starboard wing considerably damaged, he managed to level the aircraft and return to the ski runway for a safe landing.

Towards the end of September, while awaiting the 'new boys', those who had wintered over were preparing to leave for home. Both the squadron R4-D's flew to the campsite at the Beardmore Glacier and after unloading cargo immediately took off for the abandoned campsite at the foot of the Liv Glacier in order to move the fuel and cargo left there the previous summer. The old campsite was found intact with no visible damage from the severe winter that had just passed, and even the Christmas tree, which had been placed outdoors on a snow hummock the preceding December, had not lost its needles. It must have frozen while still green and as its sap had not dried out, its needles clung tenaciously onto the tree.

After retrieving 3,500 pounds of cargo, which included several drums of diesel fuel, they tried to extricate a snow kitten from the ice, but it was firmly frozen. *'We returned to the camp at the foot of the Beardmore Glacier, shut down the aircraft, planning to continue our resupply flight next morning.'* Cdr. Waldron recalled. *'Once again the weather closed in while on the surface at the new campsite, therefore missed being able to fly on out on the 25th, but the following day, the weather improved allowing them to fly to the old station at Liv Glacier. The gasoline pump was found to be intact but unusable, for over the winter months the rubber fuel tank had ruptured and most of the fuel had escaped. Lt Anderson and I returned immediately to the camp at the Beardmore, while Harvey Speed stayed behind and was able to extract 200 gallons of gas from the ruptured fuel tanks.'*

After Harvey Speed had returned to the new campsite it was decided that he and Lt Anderson would return to McMurdo since only his aircraft contained enough fuel for the return flight. Once he returned with a full load of fuel, it was easy enough to transfer fuel for both Gooney Birds to fly back to McMurdo-*'it was the first time in my tour on the ice I was left with nothing to do. Even during the darkest of the winter months at Little America there was always paperwork to be done, messages to be sent, or the evening movies and conversations with fellow camp mates. Now I was left behind on the Ice Shelf with two other men, and I had nothing to do but wait for Bob and Harvey to return to refuel my plane.*

Once both men disappeared over the horizon I was struck with the utter silence of my new world. The wind was still and the snow seems to absorb all sound, so I could hear my own breathing and even my heart beating made every thing seem unreal, like a new dimension had been added to my senses. I was literally on a fake desert of ice that extended westwards, eastwards and northwards for as far as my vision carried me. To the south my eyes were overwhelmed at the grandeur of tall mountains and Beardmore Glacier, the wildest river in the world. We were about five miles from the base of the glacier but the air was so clear and the glacier so immense that it seems I could have thrown a rock and hit some tumbled ice, making it descend down the glacier.

Geology books describe glaciers as frozen rivers of ice constantly on the move, endlessly flowing towards the sea. The surface was very rough and I knew that if I were a bit closer to the glacier, I could have heard the grinding of the ice as it slid towards the sea. Since the winter had just ended, the mountains were still covered with snow making them look like giant ice-cream cones, extending for about 12o degrees of our horizon south, while the Ice Shelf horizons occupied the remaining 240 degrees.'

Cdr Waldron and his crew's idyllic but lazy stay at the Beardmore camp lasted 48 hours. There was just one hut, a very small building serving as living quarters and workspace. It was dark and cosy in the sleeping area so one had no sense of daylight, even though outside it was 24 hours of daylight a day. James Waldron continues. *'I had removed my emergency sleeping bag from the aircraft and installed it in the hut. While on the campsite I managed to grab a bit of shuteye, and I slept so well in the warm space that it was difficult getting up at all. Those who occupied the camp for the summer ate a high calorie diet of steak, eggs and potatoes four times a day.*

It was nice for a day or two, but for me I believe I would have soon tired of it had my isolation been extended. Then Harvey and Bob returned with fuel for my near empty tanks and even 400 gallons for storage, and since they arrived late in the day, we decided to remain overnight before setting out for McMurdo again. On September 29th both aircraft returned to base, after having considered the camps outfitting was complete, and except for a few missing items and additional fuel, the camp was considered operational for the summer season.'

Soon Little America would grow in population as summer personnel arrived by both ship and aircraft, with some of the arrivals destined to become part of the VX-6 aviation detachment replacing the group who had spent the winter on the continent, and some would be assigned to bolster the stations personnel roster, while others would be IGY personal targeted for scientific studies of the ice cap.

With the squadron aircraft and flight crews about to leave their home port on the long trip from Rhode Island, the two R4-D's were no longer needed there, so Waldron, Speed and Anderson refuel both aircraft and flew them back to Little America where the crews knew how many missions to accomplish before they would be allowed to return to the States.

As the new season approach and with the changing of the guard, on May 19 1957 at Quonset Point, Rhode Island, Cdr Vernon Coley became the Squadron's fourth Commanding Officer.

Lockheed had solved the major problem of the Neptune skis before it delivered two new P2-V7's to the squadron, thus increasing its Neptune fleet to four, along with two new R4-D'S and three new HUS-1A helicopters.

The first fly in landed at McMurdo on October 1 to commence *Deep Freeze 111*. This included one P2V-7, one R4-D and a single R5-D with the remaining fleet due to arrive towards the end of the month.

While the squadron's R4-D's departed as usual from New Zealand's southern city, still at Wigram was Lt Commander Conrad 'Gus' Shinn with his Dakota grounded because of faults with its hydraulic system. The maintenance crews had already been working on it for about a week, but later that day he flew to Dunedin, then onto Antarctica behind Lt Commander Eddie Frankiewicz and Bob Epperly in *# 99853* who had flown out at 5.41 am.

There was hardly a breath of wind at Christchurch Airport as Lt Commander Harold Hanson took off in his heavily loaded R5-D *# 56528*, at 5.10 am on the morning of October 1 1957- the earliest flight to Antarctica to date. As the Admiral's plane roared down the runway in the early dawn, it gathered speed when the JATO bottles cut in, tailing a long white plume of smoke as he climbed into the southern skies over the city. Commander Coley left at 6.32am, his departure delayed when his radio had to be replaced from the RNZAF stores at Wigram station, where there was only a small knot of naval staff, friends and well wishers standing around to see the aircraft quickly disappear as the sun climbed over the trees at the end of the runway.

With the squadron about to depart Christchurch to commence *Deep Freeze 111*, on the flight manifest of one of the Neptune's was a *Miss North Kingstown*, a charming blonde seated rather gracefully in the gun turret of a ski-equipped P2V-7, though not exactly dressed for Antarctic conditions in her bright red and white bathing suit. She was in fact the second female to take up residence in Antarctica as the other was the striking *Irene* taken to the ice by Commander Eddie Frankiewicz aboard *Charlene* in October 1956.

Before departing the US for his deployment in 1957, ADI Harold Bracken conceived the idea of taking a mannequin to Antarctica with him, but with limited time and resources to locate a 'store dummy', Harry and his shipmates gave up on the idea. However, on his return to the squadron's home port at Quonset Point, Rhode Island, the ADI jocularly mentioned his idea to his wife Doris, who considered it was wonderful, prompting her to seek help from a local newspaper who's editor, apart from having a wonderful sense of humour, was himself an ex Navy man and expeditiously took up the challenge.

After a number of telephone calls, he was able to convince a North Kingstown merchant to make a donation of a window mannequin, and luckily it was just a few days before Harry departed from his good lady Doris. The prized dummy met the squadron's departure deadline receiving much more publicity than *Irene*, had. Harry Bracken's *Miss North Kingstown* and the whole Neptune crew were besieged by the media at every stop the plane made on its 14,000 mile trip from Rhode Island to Antarctic, with stories appearing in newspapers across the States and New Zealand. She even featured in the Navy Times and Yank Magazine.

Before departing from Christchurch on October 1 1957, which was the earliest flight south by the P2-V, piloted by Cdr Robert Boiling, the shapely 36-22-35, *Miss North Kingston* had been suitably fitted out in standard Antarctic survival gear for the cool trip, but once on the ice however, she refused to wear the standard polar kit, and instead as a morale bolster, arrived at the Pole Station [*Irene* never got there] as the first woman at the pole. Once given a place of honour in the galley, she gave the men that sense of having home comforts missed from loved ones they had left behind.

While the men lamented what she represented to them, the harsh polar conditions soon took its toll on the seductive, and at times outrageous *Miss North Kingstown*, and it was requested she be transferred back to McMurdo, but not before it had been agreed she would return to the Pole for Christmas dinner. I am informed by a reliable source that on her return to the Pole, her short blonde hair style had been replaced with a coiffeur of long blonde curls and gone was her red and white bathing attire, with instead an elegant sequined stole and a clinging seductive white silk gown fashioned from a parachute to transform this beauty.

From the moment she stepped off the plane and with the looks on the men's faces, she felt compelled to winter over with them and make up for all the hardships they were to endure, subsequently the alluring blonde was a gift from heaven. Later she became the resident hostess in the South Pole Station's *Bamboo Room Bar* now renamed *Rosie,* where she sports a new red wig, reflecting the bar name, and was dressed in a black velvet gown fashioned with a décolletage that would certainly have been classified as 'daring' anywhere on earth in the 1950's. It is rumoured that after *Miss North Kingstown* came the inflatable *'Judy Dolls'*, but that, it is understood, was many years later and in a different time frame with a vastly different morality.

After cartoonist Roy Crane, [the creator of the comic strip *Buz Sawyer,*] sent *Buz* on a tour of duty with VX-6 to Antarctica on December 31 1958, he drew a *Miss North Kingstown* into his strip. After carefully researching *Operation Deep Freeze*, he was very meticulous in his strip detail of Navy life on the ice, and subsequently introduced a Russian mannequin he named *Katrinka*, and that's where the problems started.

The squadron had a mannequin that's true, but she was not a gift from the Russians, and after Doris Bracken found out she fired off the first salvo in a letter to Crane demanding an apology. In reply, Crane feigned ignorance of any knowledge of Harry's sexy model, even with *Miss North Kingstown* arriving in early October and Buz on March 26 1959, it was entirely conceivable that Crane's character could have been conceived without any knowledge of the Blonde. Whatever the case, the squadron's CO Captain Slagle, presented Doris Bracken with a letter appointing her as honorary VX-6's Public Information Officer in recognition of her contribution to the morale of this command.

The letter, dated April 30 1959, points out the above details, and said that *'using your skills as a dressmaker and designer, you fashioned for her a bathing suit that did not detract from the pleasure of looking at her. You named her Miss North Kingstown, with a sash proclaiming her name. Having the upmost faith in your husband, she was assigned to his aircraft for the trip to the pole.'*

When *'Irene'* had departed from Dunedin on October 17 1956 in the cargo hold of the R4-D, a large crowd had turned up to watch Cdr. Frankiewicz and Cdr James Waldron take off in *Charlene*. Les Munroe, his wife Ruth and sons Barrie and Bobbie of Green Island were also there to see the pair off as they had given Frankie the attractive bikini clad mannequin, who was to adorn his Quonset hut for all to admire, and even after Eddie left Antarctic for good in 1958, *Irene* was still there out in the cold, apparently not minding the weather despite being scantily clad.

Operations became more complex during the third season. Scientists who had wintered over were now ready for evacuation, and their reliefs were just as anxious to reach their destinations as early as possible in the season. As tractor trains left Little America at first dawn and traverse parties were fanning out in all directions, each was clamouring for the limited air support the squadron could provide that early in the season.

On the first flight of the year to the South Pole on October 24 the P2V-7 became stranded, requiring an engine replacement. Cdr Vernon J Coley Jr, had just assumed command of the squadron between navy deployments and was flying one of the two new Lockheed P2V-7's to the Pole when on his second attempt to leave the ice after a normal 20-30 minute run up prior to take-off, he suddenly encountered abnormally high cylinder head and oil temperatures. An investigation found that in the super cold air of the Pole Station, Coley, made his mistake by turning the engine off while inspecting the Station, and then tried to restart the engine, cracking one of the cylinders which necessitated an engine change before he could fly back to McMurdo.

'Frankie and I landed at McMurdo, and for some reason Gus didn't arrive until some time later, but in time to ferry an engine to Captain Coley's P2-V stranded at the Pole Station' recalled Lt Commander Epperly. *'Frankie had started out earlier, but suffered an engine failure going up the Beardmore. I carried out an engine to Frankie in his R4D-6 'Charlene', as a P2-V engine would not fit into the older R4-D's, so we had to wait for an available R4D-6. After we changed the engine on Frankie's airplane, I escorted him back to McMurdo. That same replacement engine failed again a few days after being run in at maximum power.'*

This was the second P2V-7 to get into trouble, after one struck a radar reflector at Little America and required a propeller repair, while, during the same period Lt.Cdr Harvey Speed flying out of Little America, lost an engine in flight and was forced down on the Ross Ice Shelf. Two of the squadron's R4-D's were immediately placed on alert at Little America, should they be needed to get parts and men to the stranded Neptune.

During *Deep Freeze III* a dozen engines were changed in below zero temperatures, at times minus 50 degrees. While it took over a month to get a replacement engine to the 10,000 ft Polar Station, an engine change was accomplished on P2V-7 *BuNo 140439* by four men, in only four days.

Problems continued for the squadron, when a helicopter at Little America required an engine change and a few days later a P2-V piloted by Lt Robert Bolling, which had previously had a prop damaged, experienced a blown cylinder, which had developed into an engine fire a few minutes after leaving McMurdo on his way to the South Pole. Thus five of the squadron's fleet required engine changes almost simultaneously, with three of these at remote locations where no facilities were available for either aircraft repair, or living conditions.

Among the passengers flying to the Pole with Lt Bolling was a Mr P Mogenson, who was to return with four members of the Pole's wintering party along with Cdr.Coley and his crew, who were stranded there. Mr Mogenson had, only hours before that morning, returned to McMurdo with Cdr. Eddie Frankiewicz and his crew after the R4-D had made a forced landing at the Liv Glacier the day before, necessitating leaving his plane there while awaiting a replacement engine. This was Mr Mogenson second forced landing in two attempts to reach the South Pole.

Just when the squadron thought their problems were behind them and three damaged aircraft had been returned to service, the fourth, a P2V-7 had an engine fire, and was still out of commission due to lack of parts.

Throughout the course of the summer season, all VX-6's missions were completed despite handicaps and the hazards of Antarctic flying. During this period the squadron amassed upwards of 3,379 hours of flight; carried 2,778 passengers, and photographed 638,274 square miles of the continent. Having fulfilled all missions and tasks assigned, the summer support group was released on February and returned to their home base. Detachments were left at McMurdo Sound, Little America V and Ellsworth Station on the Weddell Sea.

However, an observation voiced by Cdr Coley, soon to hand over the command to Capt Slagle, provided a sombre note of caution to the future Antarctic aviators.

'We know more about the Antarctic and the operational hazards there, so we fear it less; but respect it more.'

When asked his views of Cdr Coley, the new commander, Eddie Frankiewicz with a board grin, said *'he was an enigma for a start, as he was a real nice guy, but then he got the problem of losing his engine at the South Pole through his own stupidity, or at least I thought that, and he was on the defensive from then on, and was really bitter.*

He was a pretty 'big boy' but he was stern, and in control of everything. Matter of fact, he was too much in control. I remember at Quonset Point one day he went out for lunch and it was raining and with strong winds, and one of our Otter's was parked right there on the sea wall with waves breaking over the airfield, splashing up and drenching that Otter with sea water. I ordered it to be moved, for its protection. When he came back, he looked out of his office window, and seeing the Otter wasn't there he called me up and said 'what did you do with the Otter Frankie?' I told him I had moved it to the other side of the hanger in the lee so it wouldn't get drenched and oh, he gave me hell. 'You didn't ask for my permission to move that airplane'- that was Cdr Coley.'

This was Eddie's last season in Antarctica before being transferred to flying Cougar F9F8 jets out of Kingsville, Texas, where he became the Aircraft Maintenance Officer and flight instructor. His reminiscence of his previous CO's.

'Cdr Coley followed Gordon Ebbe, a good leader of men and a quiet guy who never appeared to get rattled. While Douglas Cordiner was a special man who smoked cigarettes in a holder, he would listen to your request, then he'd reach up with his right hand, take that cigarette holder out of his mouth, blow the smoke out, look you straight in the eye and say 'NO' then he'd put it back in his mouth and that was it. No arguing or anything. Sometimes I didn't know why he would say no, but he must have had his reasons. That's why he was my Commanding Officer and I was his Maintenance Officer.'

A long range helicopter flight, which had been planned and executed during the previous year as a training exercise from Quonset Point, gave Cdr.Coley the opportunity of duplicating it under

Antarctic conditions, so with Lt Cdr Kenneth Snyder as pilot with Ltjg Murray Wright in the co-pilot seat and Capt R E Wallace AC2 flew the 410 nautical miles from Little America to McMurdo Sound to set a new Antarctic long distance helicopter record.

On one occasion late in the season the Air Force Globemaster Squadron and support crews were back in Christchurch preparing for their flight home to Donaldson AFB, when the base commander at McMurdo requested USAF Headquarters in Christchurch to prepare a C-124 and have it flown back to the ice to a fly surveillance and navigational mission as a cover for the squadron's R4-D and its crew.

The TSC had already completed 54 missions and airdropped over 690 tonnes of cargo but with the sudden deterioration in the condition of the ice runway at McMurdo so late in the season, it was very hazardous as the super cold temperatures struck the Polar Plateau.

Because the Globemasters did not have skis and were only able to land and take-off from the McMurdo ice runway, it was only feasible to paradrop emergency equipment, for if the R4-D broke down this would be the only emergency help available, except for relaying the situation to McMurdo by radio.

' Since the mission gave us no room for error, we hated to have this role placed on our small detachment; still it was a necessary flight and we were the ones capable of handling the situation.' wrote the squadron's administration officer of Air Development Squadron Six, Commander Waldron in his book The Flight of the Puckered Penguins.

Speed was the obvious choice and it was for him to select his crew for the dangerous flight. He opted for Ensign Schick as his co-pilot, Ensign Hillis as navigator, ACD Miles as plane captain and ATI William Cumbie; Lt. Bob Anderson would loved to have gone on the mission too, but he was the only other fully qualified R4-D aircraft commander on the continent at the time and it was necessary for him to remain at Little America, and make himself available for a rescue mission if Speed was forced on the ice somewhere desolate.

Before he could leave McMurdo, Commander Speed had to make three test flights on the R 4-D selected for the mission, so it was more important for the maintenance crews to check and double check, working round the clock. Soon after Harvey Speed arrived in McMurdo, the Antarctic weather closed in and it wasn't until February 11 that the weather had cleared enough for him to head to the Pole, where the weather at the polar station was good for that time of year, and he was able to make the landing without incident. Not wanting to waste time he dropped off his cargo and passengers then loaded seven other military personnel aboard for the flight back to McMurdo.

An hour after take-off he experienced low oil pressure on the engine which had thrown up a few problems before leaving Little America, a situation dreaded by all Antarctic aviators, so to avoid total aircraft failure, Speed made the decision to put his plane down on the polar plateau miles from any base and in uncharted terrain. His crew chief discovered that the oil line had frozen solid, so the crew pumped out the fuel tanks before landing on the ice for if this hadn't been done, the R4-D's engines would have frozen up in a few minutes, from a total lack of lubrication.

Working in sub-zero temperatures on an icy plateau, with the numbing wind racing across the continent, Chief Miles with only a few tools, repaired the frozen fuel line. After two hours stranded in well below zero the crew were fortunate that the engine experiencing the frozen oil line started. All those on the ice had fingers crossed, for their survival depended on Miles ability to fix the problem and for Speedy to get the aging 'Dak' off the ice, with vigorous shouts of sheer joy from the crew.

Harvey successfully restarted and made another take-off, heading for McMurdo.

'If Harvey had not been able to get off the surface when he did, those of us on standby at Little America would have had to fly to his position with engine heaters, fuel, tools, survival equipment and equipment to get him into the air. Since we were the last ski-equipped flight crew on the continent it would have been an all or nothing situation for everyone involved. The only available flight crews were either in New Zealand or en route to the United States and it would have taken many long days to *get any of them back on the ice if we had needed them. By the time they did arrive to help, we might have all been frozen solid on the windswept plateau.'* recalls Waldron.

During *Deep Freeze III*, a rescue mission with a difference, but equally dramatic, was flown by Lt.Cdr Ray Hall in late January 1958. Lt.Cdr Gus Shinn's R4-D-8 was en route to the Pole from Byrd Station on the Hollick-Kenyon Plateau, some 3000 miles from Byrd and 540 from Little America, when mechanical failure and a collapsed port landing gear forced him to land. Once news of the accident reached Little America, Hall loaded four air bags, two Herman Nelson heaters, an air compressor, two pneumatic jacks, new landing gear, along with hydraulic fluid, oil timers, 400 pounds of other gear and five mechanics into his R4D-5, then headed into the interior. Once landed beside the downed aircraft, after thirteen and a half hours after first hearing of his mate's distress call, the air bags were fitted to raise the plane high enough to install the new landing gear, and his mate was airborne again in twenty hours.

On Friday November 25th Cdr. James Waldron had just returned from a four hour flight in one of the R4-D's and having no further flights scheduled for the day and no ready available transport back to Little America, he started walking back from Kiel Field. It was a clear day, windless and the temperatures were relatively warm for that time of the year. So the one-mile stroll was no real problem for the aviator that had just spent the winter in Antarctica.

'Just as I started down the roadway to Little America, I heard one of the squadron's R4-D-8's approach the field, I had been expecting this flight because we had heard that R.Adm. Dufek and my new squadron skipper were due to inspect the base and our flying facilities. All of a sudden one of the R4-D-8's engines went to full power and when I looked upwards I could see that the right ski, instead of being parallel to the wing ski was pointed downwards. Normally there was a steel cable that kept the ski from pitching down and somehow this cable had broken.

Eddie, my aircraft commander from the previous summer, was the aircraft commander of the Gooney Bird, and with him he had our skipper Cdr.Coley, a non-qualified R4-D-8 pilot in the co pilots seat. With the ski pointed downwards it acted like a large air brake, slowing the aircraft severely on one side. This is why so much power had to be carried on one engine. Frankie would have likened it to having retracted the landing gear, but the rear of the ski was against the trailing edge of the right wing and it was felt that if the gear had been retracted that the ski would push itself into the wing, which would have ruptured the fuel tank on the side of the aircraft. That could have started a major in-flight fire with catastrophic effects. Minute by minute, as everything was considered on the flight deck and tried, Eddie became increasingly uncontrolled in his emotions and actions, as I learnt later from one of the pilots who had been aboard the aircraft when the accident occurred. I had noticed this trait of Eddie's time and again the summer before, that when things became extra difficult for Eddie, he seemed to lose control of himself.'

Whether or not it was a case of antagonism between Frankie and the Squadron Commander who knows, but at times there was a certain irritation and exasperation with each other, but things became more than a little cantankerous on the flight deck, and James Waldron wrote that Eddie's behaviour became more than apparent to Cdr. Coley. *'Because somewhere along the way he took over the control of the aircraft and told Eddie to leave the flying to him. This is a rare situation when an unqualified pilot would take over from a qualified pilot solely for the reason that the pilot became emotionally unqualified to continue.'*

After about 15 minutes of this high engine power situation, the right engine started popping and finally quit. It wasn't designed to carry maximum power indefinitely, so it just suddenly stopped turning. All Cdr. Coley could do was dive for the runway, and at the last moment level off as though he was going to make a normal landing. When the nose ski touched the runway it folded under the wing and the R4-D skidded off the runway coming to a sudden but undisciplined stop. None of the crew or passengers was injured, but the engine and ski were damaged beyond repair. Some minor fuselage damage also occurred during the landing, but this proved to be repairable with the aircraft remaining at Little America for several weeks before it was able to join her sister planes in the air.

'I wasn't privy to what the skipper said to Eddie after the flight, but Cdr. Coley told Eddie to remain in Little America for the rest of the season, and not be permitted to return to McMurdo until the squadron returned to Rhode Island at the end of the Antarctic summer.' recalled Waldron in his book 'The Flight of the Puckered Penguin'. *'Eddie then spent his time working out of his office at the base. Although he was senior to me in rank and fully eligible to relieve me as Officer in Charge of the VX-6 squadron Little America Detachment, the skipper chose to keep me in charge for a while.'*

Cdr. Eddie Ward remembers James Waldron recounting the story to him, as he knew Jack Coley very well, having been with him in the Arctic during Project Ski-Jump II [1951], *'He was a very likeable person but did have the tendency to be impatient and subjective, from hearsay I got from the boys in Deep Freeze III, there was a certain amount of dissension in the ranks, but then again, I wasn't there and there is always two sides to every story.'*

Bob Epperly who had flown down to the ice with Frankie aboard # 99853 *Wilshie Duit* in *Deep Freeze III* recalls *'After we had been a few days at McMurdo, the aircraft was out of action but soon after it was up and running, and Frankie started out with an engine for Cdr.Coley's P2V stranded at the South Pole. He lost an engine en route and landed at Camp Beardmore. I flew an engine out for him and assisted in changing his engine then flew back to McMurdo.'*

Following that, he flew to Little America with Admiral Dufek and Cdr.Coley aboard to inspect the base, and while approaching Little America, he lowered the landing gear but the right ski restraining cable broke forcing the ski vertical. He circled for almost an hour, after which, Cdr.Coley went forward to the cockpit and said *'we got to get this thing on the ground, the tail is going to shake off'*, the vibration was so bad. Just as Cdr.Coley got into the seat, the newly installed right engine, which had been under full power for the entire time, let go. Naturally, they were going down- including the Commander of Task Force 43- Admiral George Dufek. Reportedly Cdr.Coley flared by reading the radio altimeter. The plane did more or less a cartwheel with the right ski punching up through the wing, and at the time there was some overcast, but visibility was good, only the depth perception was very poor, and no one was hurt.

'After that Lt.Cdr Frankiewicz did not have an aircraft assigned to him, and I believe he left the ice early. I don't recall him being grounded, and I certainly wouldn't call him a cowboy, as he was a very cautious person, but somewhat excitable when things didn't go right.'

Ray Hall flew with Frankie during *Deep Freeze III*, in the co-pilot's seat, and said he didn't know why Eddie wasn't flying, but that he might have 'broken his plane'. Normally Dutch Gardner was Ray's co-pilot.

This was an incident on the ice that people down there didn't talk much about, however, reportedly it was suggested by some on the site at the time, that it was in fact Coley himself who was the culprit, and as the squadron's commander, directed that the accident investigation board exonerate him 'or else'.

Bob Epperly says that he never heard that it was Coley's fault *'yes he got into the cockpit at the last minute just as the right engine let go, and they naturally had to go.'* Chief Les Packman was Frankie's plane captain, T.Sgt Tom Southwick, who has since passed away, was the Navigator while Lushness was the radioman.

Bob did add a postscript *'the maximum speed for lowering the ski gear in the R4-D-8 was 140 knots, but I don't recall a maximum speed established when the skis were installed. There was only one forward restraining cable at the time of Frankie's accident, and the cable broke when lowering the gear, allowing the ski to go vertical. I always thought that the gear was probably lowered at 140 knots. Caution usually dictated to slow up much more when lowering the skis since there was only one restraining cable. In Deep Freeze IV, we had two restraining cables against the one that Frankie had.'*

Despite the best endeavours I was unable to gain access to the squadron's accident reports.

While Cdr. Waldron was waiting to be taken home from the Antarctic, he had time on his hands, and skipper Commander Coley was about to fly a local mission in his P2V-7 aircraft and suggested James go along as a passenger. *'I had never flown in that type of aircraft before, so was more than happy to accept his offer. Also this was my first joy ride since I had arrived on the ice and I knew I would find it unique to be able to look around at the glorious scenery and not be concerned about my flight duties. The P2V-7 was a powerful aircraft when compared to the R4-D and the Otter aircraft I had been flying. It cruised about twice as fast as the R4-D and its rate of climb was a marvellous experience for me.*

After take off I went up to the cockpit and studied the magnificent mountains which surrounded McMurdo Sound, I had viewed them for over a year, but seeing them at an height altitude in a fast moving aircraft gave me a thrill that I hadn't experienced when I observed them previously in a heavily loaded, slow R4-D. Soon Cdr. Coley told me that he was going to fly over the Dry Valley. This was a slope of rocks about two miles wide that went from sea level up to around 10,000 feet, and could have been a glacier at one time or another, and the constant winds coming down from the ice cap kept the area mostly clear of snow.

Cdr. Coley said I would have a better view if I were to sit in the glassed-in bombardiers seat in the nose of the aircraft, so I made my way forward to that choice location. It was here that I could put my face next to the most forward part in the aircraft and feel as though I was a free body rushing through the air and not enclosed in an aircraft cabin at all. Cdr. Coley lowered the Neptune to about 50 feet above the surface and with climb power on both engines we rushed over that jumble of giant rocks and debris from seas level to the top of the continent.

Once on top he turned the aircraft around and drove merrily down the dry gultch at well over 200 knots. It was at times quite exhilarating to say the least, and as a much qualified Aircraft Commander in the H-34 and H-3 helicopters, he attended school to become a Neptune co-pilot, helping him round off his flying career.'

Cdr. Waldron's last duty assignment was the Amphibious Operational Training Unit at Little Creek, Virginia where he as assigned as the Aviation Officer and later the Executive Officer. *'Our job in the Unit was to test the Atlantic Fleet ships in amphibious operations; I had a skilled crew of senior enlisted men who really knew their business. Unfortunately, it was a job without flying, and my only assignment where I had no place in the cockpit. During my one year at Little Creek, I received notice from the Bureau of Navy Personnel that there were no provisions for keeping Reserve Officers on active duty beyond twenty years; I was entering my twenty-second year of active duty so I was retired on June 30 1970.'*

During his 22 years in the United States Navy Cdr. James E Waldron was never assigned the same job twice. He flew about 125 different types of naval aircraft, operated off 13 aircraft carriers, two refrigerated stores ships, one aviation ordinance and refuelling ship. He flew as far north as the centre of the ice cap of Greenland and as far south as the South Pole itself. *'I was fortunate to see parts of North Africa, Europe, Japan, Central American, the Philippine Islands, much of continental America and New Zealand. Who could ask for more?'* Cdr. Waldron concluded.

The major objectives of *Deep Freeze III* were principally a resupply operation and the construction of seven bases on the continent, with over 4,000 personnel, ten supply ships and 44 aircraft, including 13 helicopters, made this operation one of the largest ever. It relied on the Navy Task Force 43's ships and aircraft for the movement of 22,650 tons of cargo, and 2.5 million litres of petroleum, supplying Antarctica in bulk for this mission, so greater use was made of the Naval transport aircraft consisting of thirteen R6-D's, the Douglas Liftmaster, from Naval Transport Squadron 22, VR-22 from Quonset Point, Rhode Island. Their airlift was once again supplemented by the USAF, consisting of six C-124 Goblemasters and 2 C-118's.

Another major shift in the operations administration at the start of *Deep Freeze 111*, involved Rear Admiral Dufek, who had previously spent the majority of his time on the ice, but now his health prompted him to move his headquarters to Christchurch, and to go south only when required. His staff functioned out of offices in the centre of the city, while the operational facilities remained at Christchurch International Airport.

He also took up an eighteen month lease on a property at 21 Snowdon Road, Christchurch, and moved his wife Muriel and two sons, David and George out from the States to become a Christchurch family.

The admiral did not make the first flight as in previous years, as he had caught a cold the weekend before, and because previously, several of the personnel who flew to McMurdo or travelled by ship caused an outbreak through the camp, claiming almost all those in the wintering over party to become infected due to a loss of immunity after several months on a germ-free continent. This year, the Admiral instructed that no man was allowed to go south while suffering from a cold, and he led by example.

With the commencement of *Deep Freeze III,* the R4-D5's and 6's left behind on the ice were dug out from under their snow blanket and returned to service. Among the new aircraft to arrive for the season were two R4-D8's *BuNo's 17219 and 17274,* that are a modified higher performance version, slightly longer, and with a larger fuel capacity. While similar in appearance to its predecessor, the 8's had a squared off tail assembly rather than a rounded one. Two additional 6's also arrived in the 1959/60 seasons, being: *BuNo 17246 and 39061.*

While they had operational advantages, pilots who flew both types of Dakotas preferred the R4D-5's and 6's as their engines were more reliable, easier to maintain, and their lower takeoff and landing speed were far less liable to incur damage in open field situations.

During *Deep Freeze III*, a different Globemaster squadron was assigned to the long-range logistic support mission, in association with the US Navy. They flew out of the same AFB in South Carolina and were the 53rd TCS also known as the Black Jack Squadron and operated C-124A's. The 52nd Troop Carrying Squadron returned for Operation Deep Freeze IV again in 1958-59.

While flying R4-D's in Antarctica, says Commander Jim Waldron, *'one was never without cold feet, even though we wore heaps of Arctic survival clothing and kept the cockpit as warm as possible, but the icy aluminium flight deck transmitted the outside 60 degree below temperatures directly to my feet. As a result they remained painfully cold from take-off to landing, with nothing at all to alleviate the pain so I constantly flexed my toes and ankles to ensure frostbite wouldn't set in.'*

'Buz' Dryfoose agrees; he recalled to me recently of a flight from Christchurch to McMurdo, that while the trip was uneventful, the heaters packed up, consequently the internal temperature of the aircraft became 30 below zero, and as they made a GCA at McMurdo the co-pilot and himself had to breathe alternately so the plane's captain could scrape the frost off the windshield after each exhale. *'This trip took twelve hours, and as for fears; we were all too young and invincible to have any fears but I would love to go back again some day, although not in a Dakota!'*

When the Admiral departed for the ice to commence the season, aboard with him in the Skymaster was Sir Herbert Wilkins who was to study the effects of extreme cold weather on men and equipment, and the effectiveness of protective clothing. Sir Herbert was the navigator on the first plane to make a flight in Antarctica on November 12 1928, and he was making his first trip back there since 1939. Five media correspondents were also aboard the Admiral's flight, three American and two New Zealand reporters.

On the first return flight of the season, and after battling strong headwinds for over fourteen hours, Lt Commander Harold Hanson touched his R5-D down at Wigram AFB with ten injured Americans on board, who had spent the winter on the ice. All were cheerful in spite of their injuries and the long wait for their evacuation.

Among those evacuated were five VX-6 crew of a HO4S-3 helicopter # *138580* which crashed while participating in a pilot routine proficiency flight, on July 12 on the Ross Sea Ice Shelf near McMurdo. Included were Lt Richard Anderson, who had suffered burns to both legs and had a possible fracture of his right leg, and Lt Bernard Fridovich who was suffering from a fractured spine, and burns to his hands. Three other crewmembers were slightly burned in the crash, and the five had to wait at the Antarctic for eighty-two days before they could be evacuated to Christchurch for treatment and then be transferred to the US Army General Hospital in Honolulu. The pilot of the downed helicopter, Lt McNeil the front seat passenger, was able to get himself free with only a few scratches.

When the doors of the Skymaster opened, the passengers who had not seen the sun for five months were treated to a bright sunny Christchurch day. Those with minor injuries walked down the steps and into the sun while the other five casualties, including Anderson and Fridovich, were stretchered to waiting ambulances. The body of the airman killed in the crash, AD1 Nelson Cole was brought back to Christchurch aboard a USAF C-124 Globemaster the next day, along with the luggage of the injured airmen. The Globemaster under the command of Captain Stianchi, had made the fastest return trip to Antarctica to date, even though on the trip south, he had been forced to fly half the distance without navigational aids, and it was not until Cape Adare that he encounter clear skies for visual navigation.

Following the 1956 Melbourne Olympic Games, Scandinavian Airlines [SAS] had proposed plans to fly a commercial flight to the Antarctic, having just taken delivery of their long range Douglas DC-7C *The Seven Seas*, in preparation for their scheduled North Pole service to begin on February 24 1957, as the first airline with a round-the-world service over the North Pole.

SAS purchased 14 of the DC-7C's in 1955, just before the jet age hit the world, for their impressive range, such as one delivery flight flying non stop from Los Angeles to Stockholm in 21 hours 44 minutes, a distance of 9,700 km. With this range it allowed the airline to plan its polar route next, however, that project was called off early in 1956 for reasons unknown, but Rear Admiral Dufek was also showing interest in such a flight, but by an American airline, and went ahead in discussions with Pan American, and Charles Lindbergh, who was at the time employed by the airline as a consultant.

By the early 1950's SAS had developed into one of the world's largest airlines with a global route network and a good reputation for safety, technical standard and service, however this was creating a few problems for United Airlines who had the US authorities demanding drastically reduced traffic on the North Atlantic run, arguing that many US passengers did not have Scandinavia as their final stop, but were continuing to other countries.

Subsequently with Scandinavia's geographic position in the far north with a relatively sparse population, the airline entered into agreements with a number of non American airlines, including Thai Airways, Austrian Airlines, and Gamsa of Mexico. Now American toes were being trodden on, giving additional leverage to Dufek and Pan American Airlines.

As Dufek was the first man to land at the South Pole, then any commercial flight to be made to the Antarctic should be an all American carrier not a foreigner, and Dufek's influence and pressure paid off. In Washington, Linbergh and Pan Am's President Juan Trippe saw the advantages of such an Antarctic flight and agreed.

The official government line was that now the Globemaster squadron were part of the Military Air Transport Service [MAT], the Navy might have to pay for their services, and for that reason, the Navy was interested to see if the commercial airlines would do the work for them, and asked the private carriers to bid for the contract, with a result that three were received, the lowest bid coming from Pan American.

Admiral Dufek told the *Christchurch Star* newspaper, '*That as only one commercial flight had been made over the Antarctic by a Chilean airline via the Palmer Peninsula, the passengers I think,* *paid $125 for their seats. It was a wonderful experience, but until a permanent airstrip was built at McMurdo, commercial air operations from New Zealand to Antarctica would continue to be 'chancy'.'*

The original proposal was that there be no women on the flight, and despite the fact that the airline had employed female stewardesses for some years, the austere naval man Dufek's stern, yet fair thinking was simple; the navy and Antarctic were men's domains, and should there be any hostesses they were going to be men! Already women reporters, writers, and pilots had placed him in an embarrassing position with requests from them flooding his office seeking permission to visit Antarctica. *'I try to say no as gently as I can, as I don't think we are quite ready for that yet,'* he said. *'Women will not be allowed in the Antarctic until we can provide one women for one man there.'*

Dufek's major concern was the lack of separate facilities for both sexes, while some close to Dufek at the time claimed he roared *'Women, women on the ice? There will be no God damned women on the ice while I'm Commander of this Task Force.'*

While his desire for no female stewardesses onboard the Boeing 377 was declined by Washington, he insisted at first they remain on board the aircraft while it was on the ice so Antarctica would remain 'women free', however, this time the Admiral did not get his own way.

On October 14 1957, the US Navy chartered a Pan American Boeing 377 Stratocruiser *Clipper America NC 1030V* under the command of Captain Ralph, a veteran of 23 years Arctic flying, and two of the airline's hostesses, Miss Ruth Kelly and New Zealand born, Miss Patricia Hepinstall, to fly 36 Navy Seabees from Davisville, Rhode Island, to Antarctica.

In Christchurch with seven USAF Globemasters on the airfield and one preparing to leave for McMurdo, a large crowd had gathered outside the overseas terminal to watch as the Pan Am Stratocruiser taxied in and the two slim stewardesses appeared at the cabin door, creating a lot of interest, but not as much interest as would be bestowed on them hours later when they stepped off onto the ice to be the centre of attention.

Movie people, television cameras, flashlights and tape recording newspaper photographers, greeted the girls as they were filmed and interviewed both by local media and US Radio and Television.

Before the airliner took off from Christchurch, the girls received a green and gold flag from Commander James Rofenkamp to be given to Rear Admiral Dufek, the flag coming from the City of Rockford, the Admiral's hometown. The Stratocruiser crew received a briefing from veteran Antarctic aviator Captain William Trigger Hawke, the US Navy's Senior Staff Officer in Christchurch, as to the conditions they may encounter on their flight south.

Describing the pending visit, Rear Admiral Dufek said:

'Beautiful and courageous have always been among the pioneers of a new frontier', explaining why Pan American Airways hostesses would be aboard the first commercial flight to touch down on the Antarctic ice, *'This was true in New Zealand as in America, and it will be true in Antarctica. My only reservation has been concerned with the necessary facilities for them, but in this case, a civilian airline proposes to take care of them as part of their regular crew in its own aircraft. It will be a pleasure to welcome them to McMurdo.'*

Included on the passenger list was the New Zealand's minister of Labour. Mr. J K McApline, the United States Ambassador to New Zealand, Francis Russell, and two correspondents, Charles Cordry, aviation editor of the *American United Press* and Mr B Jennings of the *American National Broadcasting Service.*

'With all those cameras here I feel like a film star' said Patricia Hepinstall. *'Only two weeks ago I thought my next trip was to Tokyo!'*

After flying into Christchurch at 7 pm, it winged its way on to McMurdo to become the first commercial airliner to land there with the first stewardesses to visit the Antarctica.

The *Clipper America* touched down on Willy Field at 8.14 pm on October 15 1957, with two girls who can claim the distinction of being the furtherest south of any other female, and to receive the red carpet treatment from men at the station, some of whom had not seen a women for over a year.

During their short turnaround time on the ice, one of their tasks was to judge a beard growing contest, and when one of the wintering over party was asked before the judging how he thought the sex appeal of the beards would be judged, he said ' *by touch I guess.* '

Before their arrival, Admiral Dufek went across to Scott Base to invite Sir Edmund Hillary to send one of his husky teams over to McMurdo as part of the welcoming party, so the girls could ride on the dog sledges to the base two miles away for coffee, during the two hours on the ice while the aircraft was refuelling for the return trip to Christchurch. With the Admiral joining in the festivities, he was asked for his appraisal of the events of this historic occasion, and he told the two stewardesses, '*you are about 500 miles closer to the South Pole than any other American women have even been before.*'

Commander Robert Epperly recalled the occasion with a certain gleam in his eye '*Yes I was on the runway when the Pan Am plane landed, and I ogled the two good looking stewardesses all the way to the mess hall and during their meal, like the rest of the hot blooded males on station.* '

The historic Antarctic flight created headlines around the round, partly because the airliner carried a large media contingent, and as Billy Ace Baker pointed out in a article in the *OAE 'Explorers Gazette'* '*Some newspaper journalists who should have known better, hailed them as the first women in the Antarctic. A common headline was 'Two Girls Invade Antarctica'. The reporters also erroneously reputed that it was hoped to use the ice runway at McMurdo Sound as New Zealand's Antarctic base and fly across the South Pole to Punta Arenas in South America. They couldn't get their facts straight, on how long the men have been on the ice or even how many men were there'.*

Then without stating who contributed the following, maybe with tongue in cheek he wrote: '*McMurdo is the Hub of Man's Land. Women may have briefly touched base at McMurdo, but Antarctica seems built for males. The age of tourism may appear to have arrived in Antarctica, but it's still a man's continent. A couple of venturesome airline stewardesses flew in here not long ago to become the first women to invade this male domain. The reaction to them was mixed, and their departure met with universal relief. To state it bluntly, many of the men are here to get away from women, and many are here just to get away from everything. This place will remain an exclusive boy's club forever. After the stewardesses, came the dignitaries, and many years later the new explorers came and they were women.*'

The Boeing commercial airliner and its eight crew members remained on the ice for four hours before returning to Christchurch; the visit also trailed the feasibility for Pan American Airways to operate commercial aircraft flights to the Antarctic.

The Pan American flight to Antarctica had both a New Zealand and VX-6 connection, for when Patricia Hepinstall retired from Pan Am she resided in Houston, Texas until her untimely death in 1998. She was related to Pam Landy [nee Hepinstall], her father's cousin, who married James [Jim] Landy, a VXE-6 flight engineer in early 1970 before moving to the States in 1972, and now lives in Pines Beach, Pensacola Florida.

Pam Landy recalls that at the time of the Pan Am flight to McMurdo, she was living in Rotorua, New Zealand, and her grandparents who lived just outside Christchurch at the time of the flight, sent her an article from the *Christchurch Press,* prompting her father to write to Partcia c/- Pan Am, then he received a call saying she would drop in on them on her scheduled flight into Auckland. Patricia made two visits, '*and as a youngster we were mesmerized by her thick southern accent and charm and beauty, plus all the 'goodies' she brought for us. After I met and married and came to the States, I corresponded with her for years.*'

About this time VX-6 Squadron were considering adopting an emblem, and were intrigued with the cartoons of a big Antarctic Emperor penguin that was decorating the wall in the Wigram airbase sergeant's mess hall, so they asked the artist, RNZAF Warrant Officer C.Cholcroft if he would paint them on the fuselages of their aircraft. Warrant Officer Cholcroft, himself a former commercial artist, agreed, and when the aircraft left for the ice, the squadron's new and unofficial emblem was emblazoned on the noses. Also freshly painted on the four aircraft were their new names. The Neptunes were *Amen* and *Tondemini* –the latter can be roughly translated from the Japanese word 'never happens'. The Skymasters were named after children of friends of the crews such as *Rosemary* and *Carole Jeune*.

Two helicopters from detachment 30, Helicopter Utility Squadron One [HU-1], assigned to the *USS Atka,* had been lost after HUL-1 *BuNo 143144,* caught fire and burnt three minutes after taking off from the flight deck. Flights were suspended until the wreckage was pushed over the side and the flight deck repaired. Two days later *Atka's* second helicopter the HO4S-3 *BuNo 138498* crashed on the Ross Sea shelf enroute to Little America and while there were no injuries, the Sikorsky was out of commission for the remainder of the season. To permit *Atka* to complete her assignments, a VX-6 helicopter was sent aboard as a replacement.

The weather also proved an operational problem for the squadron, as it was difficult to predict the Antarctic moods. All aircraft, except the Otters and Helicopters, were equipped to handle icing, but little could be done against fog, ice crystals, blizzards, blowing snowstorms and the infamous whiteouts. At times it was necessary to fly out just to evaluate the weather conditions. No accidents and very few mission failures by Vx-6, were due to weather.

During the 1957-58 season on the ice, the Task Force 43 commenced another initiative, that of locating a possible site for a solid airfield, enabling the commander to have year round access to their military operations to increase the feasibility of further commercial operations, after the earlier Pan American landing. There had always been some apprehension within the administration and the VX-6 Squadron, of the airfield's ability to handle heavier aircraft with safety. Previous air operations had been hampered by the deterioration and melting of the runway ice, particularly during December, which often put a stop to supply operations.

A promising site was located approximately 93km westwards across McMurdo Sound at Marble Point around 7.4 km from Cape Bernacchi, giving easier access by sea, and was affected by a minimum amount of fog. During late October, the UCNS *Greenville Victory* landed with two D-9 Caterpillar tractors, and 21 Navy Seabee's to construct a 1,200 foot airfield in just five days, after having to remove over 5,000 large boulders by hand.

When the weather was good, there was a scurry to get things done, and for the crews of VX-6 this meant exploration, so as the sun rose over Little America on Tuesday January 21 1958, what started out as an interesting, yet routine flight for Lt.Cdr 'Gus' Shinn and his R4-D-8 crew, later turned into a king-size adventure. The flight was scheduled over unknown territory between Byrd Station and the Amundson–Scott Station at the South Pole. Many flights in 1958 were over unknown and unchartered Antarctica.

Two hours out of Byrd, Shinn was cruising at 8000 ft in a cloudless sky with the crew going about their duties, when the flight mechanic noticed oil leaking from the port engine, and with the rugged Horlick Mountain range looming just ahead, he decided to return to Byrd Station.

While making a turn, Shinn noticed smoke coming from his port engine and immediately descended to ascertain the condition of the snow surface, which appeared to be reasonable enough to attempt a landing.

However on touching down he discovered that not only was his port engine heavily smoking but also his port landing gear had collapsed, so after the crew cut the engine, secured oil lines and electrical circuits and removed survival gear to a safe distance from the aircraft, a quick investigation of the engine found it could be repaired, but they needed a replacement landing gear. Radio contact was established between Little American, Byrd, McMurdo and the Pole Stations, and a repair crew at Little America stripped parts from an identical R4-D, loaded them into the rescue plane and headed out to Shinn and his crew now cast on a picturesque yet isolated part of Antarctica.

While waiting for their rescue plane, Shinn and his crew set up camp *Charger* named after the aircraft and a stuffed toy koala bear that they carried as a mascot. They constructed a snow block 'house' with a bright orange parachute for a roof along with the survival tents, and the commander assigned a stocktake of the rations on hand, just in case help didn't arrive soon.

When their White Knight in the form of the rescue party landed, they were greeted with enthusiastic shouts, and within minutes all hands began the task of removing the damaged gear and installing the replacement and checking it in the below zero temperatures. The only break in the 18-hour job was a quick one to consume a meal of hot beef and all the trimmings served at 'Camp Charger'. After the plane was repaired under the watchful eye of Gus Shinn, both aircraft took off with the assistance of JATO rockets and returned to Little America. All in a days work for the squadron aircrews and maintenance team.

There are a million tales of legendary polar aviators, and this is a tale of the early days on the ice, when total lack of communications or clarification, created a total 'can do' that was the spirit of the guys in the squadron; or with what the Kiwi's would describe as *able to do anything with a length of No.8 wire.'* [No.8 wire is used in New Zealand in building cattle fencing.]

One-day out of Little America-5 a tractor party was plodding their way cutting the road to New Byrd Station, designating their distances with bamboo stakes and red flags. This was not only to keep track of their mileage, but also to give them something to see should they have to backtrack. The position of the tractor party was given as 'mile such and such' on the trail. One day, in the galley at Little America-5, Lt.Cdr Harvey Speed was sitting at the table drinking coffee with his crew, when one from Ops came in and said someone would have to go out on the trail *'to pick up the welder'* at mile such and such, about 60-70 miles out.

Harvey said *'my plane is up; we'll go get 'em,'* after which he and his crew readied their aircraft and departed. They found the trail party, made an open snow landing alongside; and as Harvey got out he said *'Where's the welder?'* The leader of the trail party [a Seabee first class] said *'Right over here Sir'* and pointed to a 3,000 lb broken arc welder, not a person. This presented a small problem as they had no forklift or any heavy equipment with the trail party, except D-9 cats and a few Wanagan huts, so they got their collective heads together and proceeded to construct a ramp, as did the Egyptians when building the pyramids, except they used snow instead of sand.

They continued to pack the snow and made a ramp about 15-18 feet long rising up to the cargo compartment door on the old R4-D. After much drudgery, huffing puffing pulling and pushing, they managed with the use of a makeshift block and tackle, to get the welder up the ramp and onto the aft deck of the aircraft, only to find that they couldn't get it all the way or move it anywhere to get the cargo door closed. So being the ingenious people that they were, they secured the welder to the deck and threw a line around the cargo ring on the starboard side of the aircraft, then ran it across and onto the cargo door to keep it from flapping.

This completed, they did a rough weight and balance and found that they were so far aft that they were not supposed to fly, but the R4-D is kind of like the bumblebee and this bumblebee didn't have a pilot the likes of Harvey Speed.

Harvey managed to mile the plane into the air after a LONG take off run with an awful lot of forward tab to get the tail up. He managed to stagger back to Little America –5 and land uneventfully. He then proceeded into Ops [steaming under his collar] and asked them if they knew *'the name of the welder'*. Ops said they had no idea but *'did you get him?'* To which Harvey replied *'All 3,000 damn pounds of him. Now, YOU can get him off, but please don't break the plane because I'm going to need it tomorrow.'*

Harvey was once asked, while on the ice, what he was going to do when he got back to Christchurch, to which he's reputed to have said. *'If I get out of here with my hat, ass and overcoat, I'll be lucky!'*

He was a fantastic pilot, a most incredible man, and a polar aviation legend. Lt Harvey Speed was one of the 'old men who flew old aircraft in the new land of Antarctica' during *Deep Freeze I, II and III.* They didn't set new altitude records and certainly not speed records, but opened up new horizons in a hostile continent, flying the old faithful Douglas R4-D's which had entered naval service more than twenty years before the trio arrived in Antarctica. The planes had been on the navy's rolls, active or inactive since the second year of WW II.

Lt Conrad Shinn's naval record has been well publicized, from his Operation High jump flying to his history-making landing at the South Pole on October 31 1956. Lt.Cdr Roy Curtis signed up with his local recruitment office twenty one years before, and Lt.Cdr Eddie [Frankie] Frankiewicz, after flying for Pan American Airways, was commissioned an ensign 14 years ago, while Lt Harvey Speed was a relative newcomer to naval aviation in comparison after only 16 years.

They flew off an airstrip sitting on top of the 800 feet thick Ross Ice Barrier, without a doubt, the most unusual airfield under the US ensign, and sometimes these old experienced men knew just where they were going and what the landing strips would be like, while at other times they would not know what lay at the end of their mission. They just flew, setting the benchmark for the squadron's polar aviators to follow. They left the primitive airstrip at Little America to fly important supplies, parts and fuel out to trail parties blazing a safe trail through a path of crevasses. They were known more often to set their ski-equipped R4-D's down where man had never set foot before, making them the real pioneers of polar aviation.

Gus Shinn is an easy going, laid back friendly man, and outstanding aviator, who could be feisty should the situation warrant, according to the squadron's first CO Cdr. Eddie Ward. *'He's truly one of the most modest and courageous men I've ever met.'* Roy Curtis was a quiet, well-spoken unassuming Naval aviator, well liked by his squadron mates and was the most serious of the four, but resolute and totally reliable.

Lt.Harvey Speed was probably the most humorous, phlegmatic and likeable man in the squadron. Harvey was *a down to earth good old boy* as we say in the States, cheerful and fun loving. On the other side of the coin, put him in the cockpit and Harvey was no nonsense, all business. By virtue of his unsurpassed ability as an aviator, Harvey and his crew survived several almost fatal in-flight emergencies, as Jim Waldron described one of them, *'Only Harvey could have pulled that chestnut out of the fire.'*

Cdr. Eddie Ward wrote of the four in his memoirs. *'At this point, I would like to comment on the courage of the four R4-D plane Commanders, Lt.Cdr's Gus Shinn, Roy Curtis, Eddie Frankiewicz, and Lt Harvey Speed and their courageous crews. They were the men that made the South Pole history, making many perilous flights from McMurdo Sound to the Pole. They flew over the most treacherous terrain in the world, under the most adverse climatic conditions. These gallant gentlemen and their equally heroic crews carried out many hazardous missions with a perfect safety record. For their outstanding piloting ability, judgement and valour, they deserve the Navy's highest accolades. Congratulations to all for a job well done.'*

During the first phase of the trail operations, Lt.Cdr.Curtis, Shinn and Frankiewicz were flying from McMurdo, assisting in establishing the Beardmore Station, landing men, supplies and dogs to the Pole Station. While the advance trail parties had bridged the worst crevasses between Little America and Byrd Station, the first team at Little America were Speed and Curtis.

The priority of one mission was to fly 4,000 pounds of explosives to the crevasse area, another 4,000 galls of tractor fuel to the 250-mile point on the trail and pump fuel into 3000-gallon tanks for the advance party. When the tractor train carrying the materials to construct Byrd Station left Little America on December 5 on six large tractors and a weasel, the squadron's old timers had a 'milk run' on their hands, having to fly 5,000 galls of tractor fuel to the 250 mile point on the trail before the train arrived.

Flying 800 galls each trip, they achieved their projected target with time to spare, then their next mission was to fly another 8000 gallons to the same location to refuel both the advance party and the tractor train on their return trip, but their milk run didn't last as the weather turned foul, with blowing snow and white being the only colour every which way they looked.

A pilot can take off from Little America in clear skies with unlimited visibility only to find a fuel dump 250 miles away socked in completely, giving the pilot two options, to return to base or sit the aircraft down in the pea soup. Odds are they will return to base as the Op Plan says, but many times the base is also socked in so the aviator will set the old girl down wherever possible.

'In this case' says the first team fliers, *'you keep your descent to less than 200 feet per minute as if you were landing a seaplane on water, then when you hear the crunch of metal skis against ice you cut her.'* During the first five years in Antarctic several landings were made using this technique.

Aviators were faced with another headache, and one that caused Harvey Speed and his crew to spend a night on the trail, with the skis freezing to the ice. Sometimes, a plastic type covering is applied to the skis to lessen adhesion to the ice, as when placing metal in direct contact with ice, there is no more solid a marriage in all of physics. At other times the snow is just too ornery soft, sluggish, and sticky to take off from.

On this occasion when on a resupply mission delivering fuel to the trail cache, Speed was faced with the dreaded combination of broken polyethylene on the skis, and sticky snow. After powering the engines to their maximum, the aircraft didn't move, so he tried bouncing the tail but still no movement; so he lifted the wings alternately also without success. As his crewmen shovelled the skis free of snow, they immediately froze again giving him no option but to spend the night on the ground.

Now with Little America socked in, and Roy Curtis knowing of his old mates plight, he left word for the duty radioman to inform him immediately a break in the weather occurred, and then turned in. Next morning the weather report came in by voice.

'Weather CAVU [ceiling and visibility unlimited]' unfortunately, the radioman wasn't hip with this airdale lingo, and on calling Lt.Cdr Curtis reported, *'weather SNAFU'* so Roy Curtis awaited the weather break in comfort over another mug of hot coffee, while Lt Speed and his frozen crew dug into their emergency rations. Only after the misunderstanding was corrected, did Lt.Cdr Curtis fly out with enough JATO bottes to enable Speed to lift off and return to Kiel Field to have a new set of skis fitted.

Mid way out from Little America, Lt Speed had flown through almost perfect weather, then without any fore warning, a smoke like flog of a ghostly coppery colour, rolled in just minutes before the plane was due to land, so once more the no nonsense commander made another sea-plane landing in the soup alongside the tractors, which by this time where almost invisible from the air and once more found himself marooned on the frozen continent. With the weather closing in at Little America, he was ordered to 'sit and wait it out', but next morning it was still so soupy at Byrd Station that he had to navigate by radar bearings on fuel drums placed atop of snow cairns at 20 mile intervals along the trail.

Before a traverse party or tractor train travels from one site to another, the squadron would carry out reconnaissance flights with the exploration party on board to check over the proposed route. One such flight was made in late January, on a three-hour flight around the vicinity of Ellisworth Station, where it was discovered that the terrain was impassable by surface transport, as snow covered crevasses permeated the snowfields south for approximately 50 miles and westward beyond Gould Bay.

Here the crevasses ended in a rift about two and a half miles across and some 250 feet deep, but other snow covered crevasses and open pot holes began to show up on the surface about eight miles south of the Station. These had a honeycomb appearance and formed a network of dangerous criss crossed cracks that could spell disaster to the trail party and any aircraft having to make a forced landing there. As the R4-D skimmed low over the surface, the holes looked black, bottomless and damn ugly.

A closer inspection from the ground, disclosed snowy ramps about a mile wide crossing the rift, running north to south, these arch shaped ramps were heaved high into the air with the uppermost section shaped into triangular wedges, with deep canyons forming sheer walls 30 to 40 feet across. The exploration party came to the conclusion that even if a traverse party could travel through the multitude of crevasses to this point, those obstacles would prevent further progress south. Flights such as this one could save a traverse party on the ground many needless days travel or lives lost.

While on another reconnaissance flight from Ellsworth Station to probe the unknown area deep into Edith Ronnie Land, the crew, flying at 10,000 feet through rugged mountains, found previously undiscovered features unfolding, but encountered a haze bordering on a whiteout with visibility limited to 10 miles. Minutes later the haze suddenly disappeared, and there, towering in front of the crew, was a formidable mountain range, which seemed to spread a hundred miles or so in an east-west direction and extended south beyond the horizon to less than 400 miles from the South Pole.

The snow covered peaks, bare and lofty, rose to 11,000 feet and stood out as the twin engine Douglas flew along side the mightiest one. Their altimeter reading was that the foothills were at 5000 feet, but before the flight had ended, the exploration party aboard had discovered an easy trail in a southeast direction from the barrier rift.

On November 14 a traverse party travelling over the untamed Antarctica came to an abrupt halt when they hit a stretch of undetected and unexpected crevasses when one of their snow-cats simply fell through, coming to rest on the rear of its body, with it's pontoons dangling somewhat gracefully over a bottomless cavern which could easily swallow an airliner as large as a 707. Its walls dropped straight down into the dark and it was some hours later that the men succeeded in wedging the snowcat on to a solid surface again. Here the party discovered the vehicle's universal joint had been damaged beyond repair, so an SOS was sent out for a replacement.

The VX-6 aircraft, which ultimately arrived with the necessary gear, and quickly learnt the meaning of the somewhat stuffy phrase 'hazardous terrain', when one of the plane's crew casually walked a few feet from the aircraft to stretch his stiff legs, and the next thing he knew, he found himself in the crevasse some 20 feet below the surface, sprawled on a snow ledge with a huge black hole on one side.

Immediately a wire ladder was brought in to allow him to climb back to safety, completely devoiding him of any desire to check out other sights.

'Man these holes look bloody ugly, I'll fly combat missions anywhere rather than go walking around here.'

Little America in 1957 wasn't without its traffic problems and those that hooned along the mile long stretch of motorway had to watch themselves or the electric cop would nab them, and the offending squadron driver would have to face the stern faced judge, or talk themselves out of a fine, but in some cases the judge was the officer in charge of the base. The radar system used varied only slightly from that on route 66, and was just as effective, and used for GCA operations at Kiel Field to control the road between the main camp and the airstrip.

A speed limit was set at 10 mph and strictly enforced in order to keep the maintenance down on the tracked vehicles after it was found that higher speeds over the rough terrain had the tendency to snap their tracks. Punishment for hot-rodding aviators and maintenance crews alike was harsh, and their driver permits were in jeopardy with offenders faced with walking wherever they wanted to go, and in the Antarctic, that was, without question, as stiff a punishment as one could get.

The 53rd. TCS squadron's eight C-124's were deployed at Christchurch International Airport while their crews were stationed at Weedons, a base operated by both the RNZAF and the US Navy with 300 officers and enlisted men under the command of Lt Col Dixon J Arnold, USAF. Personnel from the 1710th Aerial Port Squadron were also deployed at Christchurch with their Globemasters as this squadron specialized in the preparation and loading of cargo for Antarctic airdrop missions.

Early in the season orders were given for a Globemaster to fly south with a load of pine trees for McMurdo. Brock Jackson [Ret] a 53rd TCS C-124 pilot recalls the occasion. *'When landing a giant aircraft, you can determine how high above ground you are by seeing objects, such as trees, power lines, buildings and other vertical objects, as you approach the runway. The trees did make a visual improvement, reinforcing the time-space theory of depth perception.'* A joke among navy aviators at McMurdo was Brock Jackson's idea of planting pine trees at the end of the runway, but with the ice approximately five and a half metres thick it was impossible for live trees to survive, and for this he bore the brunt of the jokes so his idea was discarded, as the pine trees only lasted about a week and all the needles blew off, making a replanting no consideration.

Captain Burnett USAF was flying a C-124 mission to the South Pole, with the objective of delivering a large D-2 Caterpillar tractor, and on arrival at the drop zone, the heavy bulldozer would be dropped from the Globemaster's belly on three 100 foot diameter parachutes, but as Captain Burnett approached the South Pole he encountered a high wind drift, making it more than a little difficult to judge the point of release. After 45 minutes, with the elevator doors open and the crew exposed to minis zero temperatures, the tractor was duly dropped.

Naval Lt. John Tuck the Military Leader at the Pole was on the ground at the South Pole Station observing the drop and in radio contact with the Globemaster above, and just as the load tumbled out of the transport, Tuck reported that. 'One chute opened, two chute opened. Oh Hell! Oh No'...then a pause.

The parachute's prolonged exposure to the extreme cold temperature had in fact chilled the load to the extent that the attached nylon straps had lost their tensile and elongation properties, so the impact of the 6.3 tonne plus load was too great for the straps that snapped as they took the full load impact. The C-124 crews and those on the ground could only watch as the tractor, now in free fall, landed outside the ring of barrels indicating the landing zone. The main body of the D-2 penetrated the ice by 35 feet, while the engine carried on to a depth of 80 feet. It was never recovered, suffering the same fate as a number of oil drums over the years.

It is understood that a meteorologist who witnessed the drop from the ground, described the impact as a snow quake that knocked him over.

Writing in the *NZ Antarctic Society Journal* Lt. John Tuck told how on opening some carefully packed eggs that had been dropped by the C-124, the men felt the Air Force had let them down because one of the eggs was cracked. *'They looked again and saw written on the egg surfaces. 'This egg was cracked before we dropped the damn thing.'*

When one scrutinizes the VX-6 pilots road map to Antarctica the Antarctic Strip Charts 16384/3 and 4, from Christchurch, New Zealand to Scott's Island, the mind boggles at the great expanse of frozen water and the staggering fact that not one aircraft had to be ditched in the southern ocean en route to the ice runway at Williams airfield.

[The author] I was privileged, in fact honoured to witness first hand the skills of the squadron's navigators who did the impossible, as I sat behind the flight crew to Antarctica in 1984, when I was flown to the ice to redesign the Officers and Enlisted Men's mess's at McMurdo.

Bob Nyden was a navigator with VX-6 along with Bob O'Keefe from 1971 to 1974 and thanks to Bob Nyden with his insight into Polar Navigation and its application to Antarctica, I am indebted to him for this enlightened story about flying from Christchurch to the Ice, having reached cruising altitude and turned on course abeam of 4YA the New Zealand radio station at Oamaru East.

'Now it was time to switch over to grid navigation. Over most of the world the familiar magnetic compass, when combined with suitable corrections for local variation, is perfectly adequate. But as one aproaches the poles, the magnetic compass becomes less and less reliable and the corrections larger and more frequent. So as a convenience the charts of the Polar Regions have been overlaid with an artificial square grid, which ignores magnetic influence and eliminates another bother of standard charts, the convergence of lines of longitude at the poles.

This grid is arranged so that north and south lie along the great circle which creates the Greenwich or 0 degrees meridian, and 180 degrees meridian which roughly creates the International Date Line through the Pacific Ocean.

On a C-130, our gyro-driven compasses, which were normally tied to the magnetic, were reset to align with the grid system whenever we headed south to Antarctica. As a matter of convenience and safety the conversion usually took place just after passing the last reporting point associated with New Zealand, namely Oamaru East. Thus if anything went wrong with the compasses during the switch, we could easily return to base using the backup magnetic compass.

About the only problem with grid nav was that it relied on a very stable gyrocompass, one that processed [gained error] very little. Normally ours could be depended upon to vary only one degree an hour, but our only reference to the outside world was usually by taking a sight on a celestial body that could verify that the gyro was holding the proper grid heading. I was hoping that we would be able to take a sight within a few hours, because for every degree of compass error that I couldn't detect, we would drift four of five miles off course every hour.

An ironic result of the arbitrary alignment of the grid system was our southerly true course became a northerly grid course. In fact the course to McMurdo now was 354 degrees grid, almost dead on 'north'. It always amused me to watch visitors to the flight deck as they sorted through the imposing array of instruments until they found the compass, only to discover that somehow to go south you had to go north!

Grid nav was really great- much easier than using the magnetic compass because you didn't have to worry about magnetic variation corrections, with the grid printed in nice regular 30- nautical-mile increments [half a degree of latitude]. I think the Air Force used grid nav all over the world; certainly the nav charts all have the grid printed on them. Celestial worked much the same as in the real world because the grid is aligned to the same true north. Estimated positions for calculations were still the standard latitude and longitude. The trick was in calculating the direction, and you had to point the sextant to find the celestial body, that is the azimuth angle (Zn). What you did was add your east longitude, or subtract west long,. to the normally found azimuth angle and use that and your grid heading to find the bearing to the body. This is akin to the rule for converting magnetic heading to true heading: magnetic to true-add-East [variation] but here it's true-to-grid-add-East [longitude.] [a similar calculation is done to find the local hour angle [LHA] when computing the sextant altitude [Hc], whether you're using grid or not]. It is easy [and important] to check the gyros for precision by calculating the bearing where the Sun should be relative to the airplane and comparing that to the actual azimuth angle. At the Pole, it is necessary to use the skiway alignment as a reference to check the gyro because there was no way telling what line of geographical longitude you were on.'

'Buz' Dryfoose recalls another story.

'Picture a navigator trying to operate a periscope sextant or complete a nav chart wearing big bunny mittens. At one time in the cockpit an engine-driven fuel pump stopped pumping and we had to use the priming switch to keep the engine running, the switches on the overhead panel were so close together we could not operate them with mittens on our hands. So once again, the pilot would hold the switch on for 30 seconds then the plane captain would hold it, while the other warmed his hands until the next turn of holding.

We flew this way for two hours- bloody enjoyable.'
And another R4-D flying yarn, from Buz Dryfoose:

'It happened one day that old Doc Hedbloom [Captain USN and Senior medical officer on the ice at the time], went to Little America with me on 853. He had heard of the aircraft and its problem through my complaining loud and long to all available ears. About an hour and a half into our four and half-hour flight, he came forward and yelled. 'Buz, why the Hell don't you turn the heaters on.' 'They're working as well as they have for the last month' I replied. He spun around, went back into the cargo section and returned momentarily with a little brown box about 8 inches by 9 inches by 4 inches. Upon opening the box, he produced two ounce bottles of 'medicinal brandy', which he gave to me, my co-pilot, plane captain, loadmaster and navigator and said,

'I am a Navy Captain and outrank all you poor bastards. Now DRINK THIS!' which we did, then we had a second round, by which time, the warmth was coming back into our hands a little bit, and we continued merrily on our flight. One of the most enjoyable flights we'd ever had really.

When we returned to McTown, Doc Hedbloom went down to the maintenance shack and raised hell about our heaters, finally, they were repaired and worked for the rest of the season.'

'God Bless Doc Hedbloom!'

Another R4-D barnstorming story from the Buz Dryfoose files :

'My shortest flight in the Antarctic was 1/10 of an hour on the yellow sheet. A six-minute flight, that came about in this fashion; # 99853 was sent out to supply an IGY trail party taking seismic tests. They needed some more dynamite but not being able to carry dynamite and blasting caps in the same plane, we looked the other way and put the caps in the tail cone and the 1,000 lbs. of dynamite in crates in the cargo section.

As luck would have it, in the early days, there were always some VIP's around who wanted to impress their constituents and it happened that Sen. 'Scoop' Jackson from WA or OR [can't remember which] wanted to go on a flight and we were it. We threw a blanket over the dynamite crates and strapped a seat belt so he had somewhere to sit, having no idea what composed his bench.

Starting, taxiing and warm-up were uneventful, but on take-off at about 200 feet, the sump warning light on # 2 engine came on, indicating metal filings in the oil. We turned immediately and while feathering the engine, called the tower for a downwind landing [only 5-knots of wind] and proceeded to land and taxi back onto the line.

The senator meanwhile, had brushed the blanket off one of the crates and as the crew departed the aircraft, a very white -face senator was trying desperately to get up from his seat. As I passed, I said, 'Senator, it works much better if you release the seatbelt'. He did and exited the plane in one hell of a hurry.

Maintenance found some cylinder head bolt threads in the sump and that was all. We refilled the oil, started the engine and had the OK for the flight. Upon inquiring about our passengers, we were told it was like he vanished from the ice. He was nowhere to be found, so we proceeded without him, but I'll bet he had stories to tell when he got home. He probably said' they sat me on DYNAMITE and would've had me fly out to the trail party in that condition. These men are just crazy down there!'

Towards the end of February the Ross Sea began to break up rapidly due to the southerly winds and tides, and when this happened the men at McMurdo found the open waters extended out from the base of their camp around Cape Armitage to within a few hundred yards of the 5000 foot runway at the New Zealander's Scott Base and to a point a mile and a half from the Cape. Despite sub zero temperatures, a large crack began to develop on the skiway, so the squadron employed two large D-8 tractors to hastily construct a safe parking area for their R4-D's along with a 1200 foot emergency airstrip for the Otters on the fast ice which covered the volcanic beach behind the Kiwi's base.

Portable fuel tanks were laid while R4-D crews shuttled 7000 gallons of fuel the four miles from the now deteriorating McMurdo airfield to Scott Base, while the squadron's helicopter moved fuel lines and radio gear and the last remaining material to the camp. Finally the GCA tower, generators and two refuelers were sledged by tractor to Black Island. This sudden deterioration of the ice runway caused the evacuation of the USAF's Globemaster well ahead of the planned departure date, and the squadron moved their aircraft over to Scott Base, which took on the resemblance of an International Airport.

With banners and flags flying, the nine piece marching band dubbed *'McMurdo Philharmonic'* were fine tuning preparations for the arrival of the British explorer Sir Vivian Fuchs, who just before 2pm on March 3 1958, with their four snowcat and sledges, finally reached their destination at Scott Base to complete their historic trans-Antarctic crossing. The two great polar explorers Fuchs and New Zealander Sir Edmund Hillary stepped down from the lead vehicle to a rousing welcome from Kiwis and Americans alike.

When the party arrived, at the end a 90-day trek, they became the first men to ever cross the Antarctic continent overland, so the NSF at McMurdo declared a public holiday to mark this historic occasion.

Before the season drew to a close, the USAF special Electronics Test Unit from Bolling AFB in Washington DC visited the Antarctic. Under the command of Major James Lessiter, it was deployed to the continent via South America with two ski equipped C-47's. The unit was based at Ellsworth Station and its mission was to test a new electronic positioning system, and to complete their flights by mid January, after surveying and photographing some 100,000 square miles within 400 miles from Ellsworth.

Just before the Admiral and his staff returned to the States, the President of the United States announced that the American Antarctic Research Programme, while it was to continue indefinitely, would be on a reduced budget as the following year *Deep Freeze IV,* would signal the end of the IGY, and see the closing down of Little America V in December 1958 along with handing back the custody of Wilkes [Casey] and Ellsworth Stations to Australia and Argentina respectively.

When the festivities for the end of season parties and the historic British Expedition had died down, the departure from the continent gathered pace. A message was passed along to the naval men, reading:

'Ross Sea Ferry Boat Company has announced tentative schedule of the last seasonal sailing of the diesel packed ship 'Glacier' with stops at Little America, McMurdo and Hallett, and requests to be ready and waiting. Subject to acts of God and the restraint of princes and R.Adm.Dufek, the management intends holding to schedule.'

At precisely 1506 on March 21 1958 in the dim Antarctic afternoon, the ensign of the United States Navy was lowered from atop a flagpole at the geographical South Pole at the exact time the sun went down, or rather went below the theoretical horizon, and the group of men left behind at the South Pole to winter over stood to attention during the impressive ceremony in a 16-knot northerly wind blowing powered snow. With traces of red and purple in the sky and the temperature dropping below minus 52 degrees, the men reflected that as the sun comes up and goes down only once a year, they were able to say to their families back home in the United States. *'We will be home tomorrow, in the morning.'*

CHAPTER EIGHT.

THE TRAGEDY AT CAPE HALLETT.
THE 'CITY OF CHRISTCHURCH' C-124 CRASH.

*On October 15 1958, a USAF C-124 Globemaster,
the 'City of Christchurch' crashes into the slopes above Hallett
Station killing six personnel –a tragic day for
the 52nd TCS in support of Operation Deep Freeze.*

On July 12 1957, a helicopter was lost, when a VX-6 HO4-*3 BuNo 138580,* crashed while attempting to land at McMurdo. During the morning it had made a number of landings in the course of an inspection of the main airstrip, but later after participating in a routine pilot proficiency flight, was returning to the hanger at Hut Point, when two miles from Scott Base to refuel, frost and ice on the windshield caused the pilot to misjudge his altitude. It was observed to hit the ground then bounce into the air and make a temporary recovery before hitting the ground again, settling on its tail and bursting into flames.

Of those aboard, Lt.Anderson USN, with his clothes on fire, was thrown out of the copter, while Lt McNeil USNR who had just completed his basic training, and Captain Pullem USMC, managed to get out unaided to extinguish the flames on their clothing. These three men then dragged Lt. Bernard Fridovich USNR, from the blazing wreckage, throwing themselves on top of him to smother the flames in the snow that had started falling heavily. When AD-2 L.L Scarborough managed to extricate himself, he found Lt. Anderson was alight for the second time.

AD-2 Nelson R Cole USN who was not buckled in to his seat was thrown into the tail cone of the Sikorksky and from the resulting fire later died.

Commander James Waldron, as president of the Aircraft Accident Board wrote of the crash, that Lt. McNeil was piloting the base helicopter getting some night experience when the accident occurred. He was not a highflying helicopter pilot, having just completed his basic training immediately before being sent to the Antarctic. *'Considering the extraordinary weather conditions and extreme cold of the Antarctic, he had been left as the only helicopter pilot at McMurdo Station during the winter season.*

Lt. McNeil's accident occurred on a clear, windless evening when visibility was very good. He had been flying out over the sea ice, performing takeoffs and landings with a non-pilot sitting in the co-pilot seat. When Lt. McNeil had completed his practice over the ice, he proceeded to return to the heliport situated on the hill next to base. During the flight the moisture from the breaths of the two men in the cockpit must have frozen on the windshield, because the pilot couldn't see ahead. As he approached the heliport, he was a bit low resulting in his wheels hitting the surface unexpectedly.

Lt. McNeil must have panicked when this happened because he pulled back on his cyclic pitch control and up to his collective pitch simultaneously, when pulling up on the collective pitch would have been sufficient. The helicopter went into an extreme nose high attitude as the aircraft gained considerable altitude suddenly, and with the pilot unable to return the aircraft, it settled vertically on its tail and crashed.

The helicopter immediately caught on fire. Lt. McNeil and his front seat passengers, who had been seated in the helicopter, escaped with only a few scratches, while three of the passengers who had been seated in the helicopter cabin suffered severe burns. The third passenger, who had not been buckled in his seat, was thrown into the tail cone when the helicopter impacted with the ground. The resulting fire consumed him. Our accident report board of inquiry determined that McNeil had exceeded his flying ability when attempting to fly during the winter months. He also reacted improperly when his wheels contacted the ground as he approach the heliport. The Board also thought he was assigned as the base helicopter pilot without adequate helicopter flight experience. It was my understanding at the time that Lt McNeil had received separation from active duty order after he reported for duty on the Antarctic continent. He was asked for an extension of his active duty time to allow him to complete his wintering over period, this request was granted.'

In a quite moment of reflection, Lt.Cdr Robert Epperly recalled the joys of flying in the Antarctic, and one of the fun stories of his early flights from Little America during *Deep Freeze III* which was non-eventful except for a young pesky reporter authorized to board at the last minute. The crew were a little aggravated. *'We sat him down in the canvas bucket seat near the cabin door directly over the external JATO bottles and we purposely didn't tell him that we were going to fire the rockets for take-off. He was terrified at the sudden noise since it sounded like the hammers of hell. In any case, word came down the line, that in the future we should brief all passengers.'*

Soon after getting settled in at McMurdo and becoming accustomed to his role, he and his crew took the Para rescue team on a short flight in the local area for a re-qualification jump. Lt.Cdr.Epperly was more than a little concerned about the low overcast at just 800 feet, but the grizzly old Master Gunnery Sergeant assured him that it was ok.

Unfamiliar with the regulation and procedures, the young Lt.Cdr didn't check. When the 'stick' of six jumpers exited the aged R4-D, the static line in the overhead pulled loose from the bulkhead. The info was immediately relayed to Epperly, who thought that he was responsible for the death of six jumpers, knowing that he was far too low for the expected free fall jump over the Antarctic continent. However, the story had a happy ending, as fortunately the flange on the end of the static line was intact and had snagged the chute static rings, opening their chutes, a big sigh of relief when all six jumpers landed safely.

Bob Epperly recalls a flight out of McMurdo that was an attempt for an Aerial Traverse trial, instead of pulling sheds by a sno-cat they would use an airplane. After loading up his R4-D-6 with IGY personnel and their equipment, they headed up the Victoria Plateau about 9,000 feet above MSL. The sastrugi was unusually hard and rough, and even though they had carefully made several low passes to pick out the seemingly best spot to land, they still experienced a very rough landing, spending several hours waiting while the scientists did their routine. Every hour or so Bob and his crew had to start the Herman Nelson Heaters to keep the engines warm, as it was very cold with the wind blowing about 20 knots, reducing visibility with blowing snow.
In the mid afternoon, much to their dismay, the Herman Nelson heater caught alight with a big ball of flame emanating from it. Acting quickly they pulled it away from the aircraft before any fire damage occurred to the plane, and advised the scientists that they would have to depart within an hour, but while starting the auxiliary power unit to start and warm the engine, the generator shaft sheared. With the extreme cold and the time that had expired since the Herman Nelson Heater fire, it was doubtful if they could get an engine to start on the batteries alone.
The plane was loaded up, scientists and all, and as Lt.Cdr. Bob Epperly tried the starter, low and behold the right engine started with one-quarter rotation of the propeller, and after a rough take off over even rougher sastrugi, they flew back to McMurdo, and as far as Bob knows the Aerial Traverse was never tried again using R4-D's in either *DF III* or *DF IV*.

On one occasion when engulfed in the festive spirit, Epperly on a rather uneventful flight, [aircraft wise at least], flew a thanksgiving dinner with all the trimmings to the two lads, a radioman and an aerologist who manned the isolated Beardmore camp.

His passengers were two psychologists who were along to study what made the aviators tick. The aircrew spent the night at the camp, enjoying the delicious dinner in the warm Jamesway Hut, and later the psychologist insisted they sleep outdoors in their personal pup tent; well- that was until about midnight when the wind started howling and they asked to come back into the warmth of the hut. Incidentally, the same two lads at the camp had hosted maintenance personnel and Cdr. Frankewicz's crew, after Frankie had landed there due to engine failure while enroute to the Pole with an engine for a stranded P2V.

On a routine flight one morning from Little American to Byrd, Bob's navigator Tom Southwick called up on the intercom and requested rather formally. *'Sir, request permission to execute Lost Plane Procedure'* Tom replied *'I didn't think we were lost-are we?'* but he only wanted to do a practice procedure, whereby he would merely advance a sun line through the destination, turn one way or the other about 30 degrees and DR to the line, then turn down the line to the station. The procedure worked perfectly.

The plane that wound up with a vertical ski at Little America, the R4-D-8 # 99853 was shipped to the States at the end of the *DF.III* season in January 1958. It had had a couple of memorable moments for Lt Commander Robert Epperly, namely when he asked the CO if he could stop off in Auckland on the way home. *'Sure'*. *'And after a nice time in the city of sails, we proceeded out to the RNZAF base at Whenuepai for a flight planned for Nandi, Fiji. On attempting an engine start, the left magneto was completely dead so I telephoned the Squadron in Christchurch and had one sent north posthaste via Air New Zealand, and took the opportunity for another night on the town, rescheduling my departure for the next morning. About ninety minutes out we were in torrential rain, I asked by co-pilot to hand me the weather folder but he didn't have it so I asked the navigator but he didn't have it either. It was then I realized that we had started out on a long water trip and no one had checked the weather since the previous morning, but since we knew the Kiwi's gave very accurate wind forecasts, we received them by radio and proceeded on, but never got out of that torrential rain.*

We had received the Nandi forecast; it seemed doable even though the instrument runway at Nandi was unusable due to reconstruction for the advent of the forthcoming Jet Airline Age. Using the Kiwi's forecasted winds we navigated directly to Nandi, but by the time we arrived, the weather had deteriorated with a 50 knot quartering tail wind and a low ceiling. Several NDB approaches were made to the runway for a circling approach. Never saw a thing! Finally the good people of Nandi set up a portable homer right on the end of the runway, and we let down to about 50 feet over the ocean, headed straight to the homer and landed in a 50 knot tail wind.

The first 1000 feet or so of the runway was uphill, but after cresting the hill the other side was a veritable lake, so we easily ploughed to a stop in the lake resulting in a deluge of water loosening the mounding on the leading edge of the flaps [as I recall about 3 feet of mounding on the inboard of each flap was loosened and bent back and had to be reattached] in any event we made temporary repairs with the assistance of a local metal shop.

Had we been an hour or two later, the rain would have subsided and the ceiling lifted enough to have made a circling approach to Runway 17 more or less into the wind instead of downwind on Runway 9, also a lot of water would have drained away from the runway, but the landing was much more exciting the way it happened- but definitely not recommended.

After a two night stop at the Mocambo Hotel at Nandi Airport, we started up next morning and found that the engines would barely run. The ignition harnesses had dried out in the Antarctic and the long flight in the torrential rain spelled their demise. We got to spend several days in Nandi awaiting the shipment of ignition harnesses from Oaklands CA and had a very enjoyable time drinking local beer and playing water polo with a QANTAS Airways crew. The bad weather was caused by a typhoon, centred round Noumea. I always felt something was amiss for not checking the weather; the only excuse is that I must have gotten out of the habit in Antarctic [very few places to check with] but the rest of the flight was uneventful after changing ignition harnesses. There was some concern with turbulence going through the equatorial front, and because we knew that the aircraft had had damage to the wing, we always tried for smooth air.' Bob Epperly recalled.

After a brief stopover at Alameda, CA they proceeded to Los Angeles enroute to Jacksonville Overhaul 7 Repair Facility, but as the aircraft was climbing out of LAX on a standard instrument departure to 13,000 feet the crew experienced both engines cutting out for no apparent reason. Now flying in very light icing, they returned to LAX, but could not find anything wrong and tried again with problems. *'I ran into this again during the fly in of DF 1V. The air intake to the engine had been modified in such a way that any icing sloughing off from the propeller dome would go straight into the carburettor even though in alternate air. Didn't necessarily figure this out until much later and felt rather stupid after it occurred at the start of the next season, while enroute to Antarctica from Invercargill. In fact I had forgotten about it, icing was rarely a problem in the Antarctic, except for one incident which occurred in Deep Freeze 1V.'*

July 7 1958 Captain Slagle was appointed Commander of the Squadron, the first of only three Captains to hold the role [Capt Douglas, Capt.Cordiner, and Capt William Munson.]

The fly in to New Zealand in 1958 wasn't without its problems, for as Admiral Dufek arrived at McMurdo, a turbulent Antarctic storm broke, keeping all flights grounded at Christchurch until the storm blew itself out. As the Admiral's R5-D was fighting head winds on its journey south, the *USS Brough*, half way between New Zealand and Antarctica was being buffeted by a severe storm, encountering 35 foot seas which damaged its hull and carried away an 80 foot antenna.

Cdr. Frank Kimberling and Lt.Cdr Robert Epperly departed for New Zealand along with the fleet, from Quonset Point for the planned fly in on October 1, but their flight to Christchurch wasn't without its complications, in fact it was rather problematic of the R4-D aircraft, as the evening they had planned to depart Alameda for Honolulu, Epperly's Chief Joe Long, the Plane Captain noticed a small hairline crack in the nose of the right engine on *Negatus Perspirus*.

A nose case was not available but an engine was, so the crew changed the whole engine and departed the following day for Christchurch. Cdr. Kimberling had already departed, but returned after only a few hours as his position reports indicated that he was below the 'red line' on the Howgozit chart, so Pac Flt Op Control ordered his return.

In his next attempt he experienced a rough running engine and again returned to Alameda, and during the following attempt he experienced an engine failure an hour or so out, so again had to return to base, but Lt.Cdr Epperly and his crew aboard *Negates Perspirus* after the engine change at Alameda had an uneventful flight to New Zealand.

Commander Frank Kimberly this time finally made it to Honolulu, Hawaii in his R4-D8 after flying for 14 hours and 55 minutes- the trip while uneventful, was wearying on the crew.

Suffering slight fatigued, the thought of a cool bear and a warm bed was heaven after a night without sleep and the incessant drone of the Gooney Birds engines – at least he now had two running smoothly.

After some shut eye and loaded with 10,000 pounds of cargo for the Antarctic operations, plus an additional 500 galls of fuel in the fuselage tanks, Commander Kimberling turned his plane around at the top of the Hawaii runway and awaited control tower clearance.

It was 6.35 pm and with the aid of 15 JATO bottles he blasted his Gooney Bird off the runway, and watched by hundreds of interested locals, he headed into the South Pacific sunset to Canton atoll in the Phoenix group of Islands some 1,670 miles, hoping all the gremlins were out of the system or would Murphy's Law kick in?

Generally, all was serene aboard the 'jinxed' Douglas transport, with some playing cards, while others slept as the two co pilots, Norman Davis and Reginald Simmons settled down for the long monotonous flight across the South Pacific. It was a little after midnight and still 620 miles to go, when all hell broke loose, and their hours of boredom was disrupted by a sudden terrifying whine of the port side propeller and the 'old girl' started to run out of control. Kimberling looked out to see his port engine on fire illuminating the midnight sky, so he immediately tried to feather the engine as per the flying manual, but to no avail.

Now with both Davis and Simmons in the cramped flight-deck, matters got worse as the propeller speed governor malfunctioned. Knowing they could shut the engine down would be an option but would the whirling steel blades then fling loose and rip through the fuselage like a giant power saw.

Nothing Cdr Kimberling did could reduce the engines rpm, so now he saw only one course of action, to cut off the fuel to the port engine, thus allowing the dead propeller to windmill until it froze from lack of oil.

Before the emergency, he had been cruising at an altitude of 8,000 feet, but by the time the oil had stopped flowing to the disabled engine, the Gooney Bird had dived 7,000 feet and was heading straight for the cold waters of the Pacific, but with the good engine now wide open, the plane was in a skid from the excessive weight and drag on the port side, caused by the spinning propeller of the dead engine. How far could he fly on one engine was the question he asked himself, thinking that the situation could have been worse as he could have been over the frozen waters of the Antarctic ocean.

Kimberling had heard the story of US Marine Corps pilot, Major 'Skip' Kimball, a member of SCAT-South Pacific Combat Air Transport Group, when he flew a Douglas C-47 from Pearl Harbour to San Diego.

Having just passed the half way mark, at a point nicknamed 'Jones Corner', Kimball's stomach sunk into his flying boots, when he lost power to his port engine and had to feather it. His choice now was either going back to Pearl or heading to the United States West Coast- either way the distance was the same- he headed for California.

Just how far would his Gooney Bird fly on a single engine?

It soon became apparent that he could not maintain his altitude unless some of his cargo was ditched in the Pacific so the crew jettisoned it by kicking it overboard and from there Kimball flew into San Diego without further problems and set a record for flying a C-47 on a single engine for more than 1,100 miles.

An encouraging thought for Cdr.Kimberling who had to fly only 800 miles with just his starboard engine, and at this point he ordered his crew to jettison cargo- *Throw out everything you can get your hands on* he shouted from the flight deck. So into the Pacific went toolboxes, personal gear and pay records. The crew needed no prompting- it was the cargo or their lives, however, to their dismay, the 'jump door'- a small door which can be drawn inside the plane while in flight and closed again after a parachute jump or supply drop, had, for reasons unknown to the crew, been riveted shut.

Now with time the essence and without panic, the only alternative was to rip the pins from the main cargo door and push it overboard.

The entire 10,000 pounds of cargo was then unceremoniously dragged to the wide doorway and shoved out- piece by piece, as the cargo followed the steel door into the blue waters of the Pacific. At the time, none of the crew were wearing cold protective gear to guard against the midnight air that was now engulfing the cargo hold.

'Throw out everything'

Kimberling shouted while every ounce of his body was pushed to its limits to keep the Old Girl airborne, while the rest of the personal gear went out along with the radar set, navigational equipment and tools.

The situation was becoming serious by the minute, as Lt Norman Davis, whose weight was less than 200 lbs started to drag the six 280 lbs JATO bottles to the doorway and toss them out, not realizing at the time just how heavy they were.

For the next six hours Cdr Kimberling battled on, struggling with the controls, and not helped by the drag created from the windmilling dead propeller and the yawning gap left by the missing cargo door. He applied the right rudder trim, while he and his co-pilot took turns holding the right rudder all the way forward with their frozen feet.

Now the Commander had the R4-D-8 in a skid airspeed down to 89 knots- barely above stalling speed. The radio operator Mike Ortege had managed to flash a Mayday message on the liaison set, at the first sign of trouble aboard the Gooney Bird, that was Ortege's first trip to Antarctica.

Radiomen in Christchurch listened as the pilot told Canton Island of their plight, until a QANTAS Super Constellation piloted by Capt John Connelly, who had just departed Honolulu on a scheduled flight, headed for the disabled machine.

Flying at a maximum speed Connelly soon managed to catch up with the crippled VX-6 Squadron transport some 130 miles out of Canton, and as the British dispatched an air-sea aircraft from Christmas Island, two USAF aircraft took off from Pearl Harbour.

When the QANTAS Lockheed Commercial plane located the R4-D-8 the instruments on the stricken Naval airplane were showing the plane was running out of fuel, so Kimberling radioed his fuel concerns to the QANTAS pilot, who acknowledged the transmission and relayed it to the Navy on Canton who dispatched a rescue boat from the Island, powered by an outboard motor.

Thirteen miles out from Canton, Kimberling reckoned he had only twenty gallons of gas left, and when five miles out the gauges read empty.

'Somewhere there is a tape of the communications involving the QANTAS aircraft that escorted him a good part of the way,' recalls Bob Epperly. *'I did listen to the tape many years ago; I've always had a theory that for some reason, their centre of Gravity was too far forward. The R4-D-8's had a very forward CG near the forward limit when not loaded with other than fuel. Too far forward would result in having to use 'UP' elevator to hold the nose up resulting in increased drag. At the weights they were, I thought the aircraft should have flown at about 115-120 knots with less than maximum, except Take-off [Meto] power, but I wasn't there, so who am I to say- the aircraft never arrived on the ice that year.'*

Questioned on his arrival at Canton, the exhausted commander told reporters *'I'll never know how we made those last five miles, but we did, and just as we touched down the Starboard engine sputtered and died*

We had flown for five hours and forty minutes under the most difficult drag condition any pilot even had to contend with just to stay aloft. Believe me, I've flown lots of hours in lots of planes and had my share of near misses, but of all the airplanes in the world, only the faithful Gooney Bird could have done what we asked of her today' he said.

Three of the passengers were sent to New Zealand and the fourth, a naval metal smith, joined the crew in repairing the Dakota. Two new engines, new crew records, radio, and new clothing for the crew were flown in from the US.

The repaired plane arrived back in Christchurch on October 20, after its forced stay at Canton from September 29, but even its return from Canton after nearly two months waiting to reach New Zealand was not without further mishap.

The jinxed Gooney didn't make it to Antarctic that season, but during an exploratory flight over the Horlick Mountains in Ellsworth Land the following season, *#17219 Semper Shafter,* ran out of luck, when it crashed without lost of life, and today Commander Frank Kimberling's old Gooney Bird lies buried beneath thousands of tons of snow and ice in Antarctica.

Maybe someday, when the world's aeronautical engineers fail in their endeavour to produce another small twin-engine airplane to replace the Douglas built Dakota the Prince of Aviation, some scientist exploring in Antarctica may dig up Kimberling's plane and fly it again.

At 2-30 pm NZ time, just as Cdr Kimberling's R4-D-8 was approaching Canton Island, the US Navy's Antarctic Advance Headquarters in Christchurch reported that Admiral George Dufek's Skymaster #356528 was on it's way on the first flight south for the season, and had reached McMurdo.

In the latter section of the flight, the R5-D had struggled against strong head winds, with the flight taking two and a half hours longer than scheduled.

Forecasters at McMurdo were forecasting storms of 25 knots south of New Zealand and on the flight path to McMurdo.

Lt Cdr Robert Epperly's flight to Antarctica wasn't without its complications either; in fact it was the rather problematic and idiosyncratic R4-D-8's, that were creating additional frustrations after arriving in Invercargill from Christchurch on October 3. Starting out from Invercargill for Antarctica they had to turn around after experiencing both engines cutting in and out, just an hour into the flight south.

'We were experiencing some icing but were already in alternate air for the engines so suspected possible water in the fuel. It was actually caused by the modification to the engines carried out by National Airways engineering staff and VX-6 maintenance people so as to accommodate the ski installation. In any case I descended and returned to Christchurch, and our maintenance guys. I left next day for McMurdo from Christchurch while the rest of the fleet including the four C-124 Globemasters had departed on schedule on October 9, so we were now flying non-stop from Christchurch to McMurdo alone, not a good feeling, but that's Antarctic aviation I guess.'

After experiencing an excellent tail wind, and when almost abeam of the Balleny Islands they had a voice radio message from Admiral Dufek personally, to return to New Zealand, but Epperly replied *'negative', do not have enough fuel to return to New Zealand against the wind',* explaining to the Task Force Commander that he would land at Cape Hallett to which Admiral Dufek agreed. Upon arriving over Hallett, Epperly let down through an overcast sky over the sea until below a ceiling of about 1000 feet, and by radar to a point of land near Hallett Station, then turned down the 'fjord' searching for a smooth area of ice on which to land.

'At first the ice was broken up and appeared to be very rough with small icebergs etc. With distances being deceptive in the Antarctic it appeared that the 'fjord' may be far too narrow to turn around if that became necessary, so we turned and re centred along the west side, and the further we went in, the better the ice looked. About half an hour in, we came upon a full 9,000 feet of ice as bare and smooth as a billiard table'. Now tired and slightly stressed from the flight down from Christchurch, Lt.Cdr. Epperly and his crew were happy to have landed safely, and then radioed McMurdo to report in.

Bob Epperly and his weary crew were still in their aircraft having a well earned mug of coffee and a quiet cigarette before venturing into the sub zero temperatures of the isolated station, when they were notified that four giant C-124 Globemaster's were heading their way after just having completed air drop flights to the South Pole and Byrd Station. When the weather deteriorated at McMurdo they had been directed to fly onto and land at Hallett Station. Their crews were planning a gear up landing out on the Ross Sea Shelf as they were almost out of fuel, but fortunately for the four transports of the 52nd USAF's Transport squadron they heard the joyful news that a Navy R4-D was on the 'deck' there and would assist their hazardous landing on the stations emergency seven foot bay ice airstrip some 450 miles from McMurdo.

As McMurdo was being stung by a 40-knot blizzard, the cloud forming the ceiling was dissipating, and extra time was not needed to get underneath the overcast. Lt.Cdr. Epperly positioned his aircraft # *17154* so its lights were at a point where the good ice started, and suggested the Globemasters land abeam or beyond, and talked the aircraft down while also in constant radio communication with McMurdo, where Rear Admiral Dufek and the USAF Squadron Commander Lt Colonel C J Ellen personally directed the operation.

The hospitality of the 16 Americans and New Zealanders manning the IGY station were severely strained by the arrival of the unexpected 50 guests, including Col R J Barnick, officer commanding the 63rd troop and Cdr. John Mirabito, the Task Force's meteorological officer. As the 'guests' had to remain at Hallett until the VX-6 R4-D's had delivered fuel from McMurdo once the weather had cleared there, it meant sleeping in shifts at the station's limited living quarters.

While the four giant USAF Globemasters and Cdr Epperly's lone twin engine Navy R4-D sat on the remote and isolated Hallett Station's make shift airstrip, the indignation from ten thousand plus Adelie penguins was directed at these foreigners who dared invade their territory, as the small loveable penguins had only just arrived back to their rookery for the nesting season.

The scenery at Cape Hallett is magnificent, black cliffs are the backdrop for the small station, with the white peaks of the Admiralty Range jutting skywards with the 10,000 foot Mount Sabine. The air is rich with the fishy smell of the Adelie rookery, where thousand of the small birds return annually to spend the months of spring daylight at the Cape. Here Americans and New Zealanders work side by side, while biologist study the chattering penguins and other scientists continue their programme in geomagnetism, ionosphere physics, aurora and meteorology.

Prior to 1957, the Adelie penguin occupied almost every square inch of the spit on which the base was built, taking ownership of all the small pebbles for their nesting materials. The site is a natural nesting ground, being composed of glacial moraine and just 16 feet above sea level. Penguins always return to the exact geographical spot they nested in the previous year, and according to one squadron member *'when that spot has been pre empted by something else, the penguin will do its best to retake it. They seemed to have had a GPS thing down there long before civilization did, and they didn't need electronic satellites.'*

Anyone who has grown up in the rural country, could appreciate the sights, smells and sounds of the penguin rookery, for with an excess of 50,000 penguins as close neighbours, you would experience, and feel at home on Hallett with that hen house smell, and those early morning barnyard sounds, only here going 24 hours a day. When the weather gets warmer and with the arrival of the sun and constant daylight, the ice begins to melt, so imagine as the top layer of 'soil' starts to thaw, the cool air is heavy with the smell of a chicken coop, turning the beautiful black and white penguins grubbier and grubbier by the day. They sure didn't look like their loveable postcard images.

With the warmer weather, the bay was soon clear of solid ice, enabling the penguins to bath, wash and feed without having to travel miles to find open water, but the squadron had lost their ice runway.

For the Adelie colony of breeding pairs and their chicks, the personnel had to be careful not to frighten them off their nests of pebbles as they sat on their eggs, or the patrolling skua birds would swoop down for a meal. It was their nesting area, and Cape Hallett was their precious territory, so to most on the station, it was the Penguins who were the good guys, the skuas the bad.

Hallett Station is the unforgiving site where its warmest annual temperatures average minus 40 F, where strong winds create snowdrifts throughout the camp, while the violent surf smashes against the shores. Air operations from the ice runway six miles southwest of the camp are limited to 10 weeks because the Ross Sea action breaks up the field in early December.

Jointly operated by New Zealand and the United States from the beginning of the IGY in 1957 until February 1973, the eastern side of Cape Hallett was operated as a year round research station until 1964, when the main scientific laboratory was destroyed by fire. Hallett was then operated as a summer only research station until 1973, when it closed. The station was primarily used to study biology and the Adelie penguin in particular, so a joint American and New Zealand team completed an environmental survey of the former Antarctic research station, and recommended steps be taken to safeguard penguin chicks at their nearby rookery from melted pools contaminated with oil.

Under the auspices of the USAP, measures were required to assess a complete clean up of the station, where the source of the contamination appeared to be petroleum residue in a dozen or more small melt pools on the site, so clean up work was started in the mid 1980's by a four man New

Zealand team. While the station is no longer an active research station, Cape Hallett is visited by several tour ships annually, drawn to the area because of the Adelie colony.

The station provided communications and weather reporting for the air route between Christchurch and McMurdo, in addition it served as an alternate landing strip when Williams Field was closed. However, since the fire in 1964 and the advent of jet powered transport, it lost its reason to exist, encouraging American and New Zealand to reclaim the 22-hectare site to its original pristine environment, but costs were against the proposal.

The Dakotas used the Hallett ice strip early in the season before the ice broke up as an emergency area when coming in from New Zealand, but this was the first time Globemasters had landed there. Their landings were made particularly hazardous because the long narrow bay is land locked by high peaks on every side, giving the pilots of the huge transports no second chance if their first approach was faulty. Later Admiral Dufek remarked that the successful landings were *an excellence display of teamwork between the Navy and Air Force.'*

Little did either Admiral Dufek or Lt Colonel C J Ellen know that tragedy was to strike the operations ten days later, when a USAF Globemaster *The City Of Christchurch* was to crash at Hallett when making an emergency landing, killing six of the 12 crew and passengers onboard.

Shortly after finally arriving at McMurdo, the squadron needed a pilot for the famed *Que Sera Sera,* so Lt.Cdr. Epperly recommended his First Officer Harvey Gardner, who was qualified and most eager to have his own aircraft, so he was assigned. Unfortunately the aircraft needed parts that were unavailable at McMurdo, leaving him grounded for a time, and Larry Farrell continued as Epperly's co-pilot, making a number of routine flights. Farrell had been trained in P2V's but had been in an accident in a squadron P2-V involving a vertical ski at Burbank CA.

'He was very content to be in an R4-D and felt more secure, but the squadron now needed a P2-V trained co-pilot and assigned him to a P2-V crew over our objections, although he was terrified of a P2-V. I was assigned another co-pilot and Larry turned in his wings, and while he was awaiting transportation back to the States for re-assignment, he went with Dutch in an Otter to Marble Point where they were to deliver 'goodies' to the Seabees working there, and upon departing they turned towards the glacier. Both he and Dutch were killed and the Chief Petty Officer seated behind them was seriously injured. It was indeed a sad time for us all.'

Lt Commander Epperly: *'We were really gutted by the news, I believe I was on a flight out of Little America at the time; news travelled fast by HF radio and dispatches.'*

Early in the season Lt.Cdr.Epperly was assigned to make a recon flight over the proposed route of a traverse party to Byrd. The flight started out routinely, but the aircraft heater failed, and being dressed warmly on the flight deck, they continued on with the flight. Onboard the plane was a hot plate on which to prepare steaks, coffee etc, so the crew were confident of being able to continue the flight despite the 50 below cold.

Their only problem was a reporter, whose religion did not allow him to drink coffee, so he became chilled and rather comatose, but after getting some hot soup into him, and by placing chemical heating pads into his trousers and a sleeping bag cover, he thawed but the flight was cut short to drop him back to Byrd, where the Officer in Charge was an MD. However, their journalistic passenger had some influence with the 'high command', and before long orders were circulated which forbade flights without an operational heater, *'we never had another heating problem while I was on the ice.'* recalls Cdr. Bob Epperly with a degree of smugness.

A later flight that he vividly recalled was out of Byrd towards the Palmer Peninsula and back several hundred miles westwards from the Peninsula along the coast to Little America. By this time in the season, with the warmer air along the coast, icing conditions could occur. The first part of the coastal leg was in reasonable weather and routine, as well as being scenic, but after awhile the aircraft # *17154* with Cdr. Bob Epperly in command, began to encounter cloud, which thickened as they flew westwards and became lower and lower along the coast.

Epperly had a good radar picture all along, but they started getting a vibration from the left engine, which was obviously caused by ice accretion on the left propeller. The prop de-ice/anti-ice was on and while revving up the engine helped some, the crew knew they had a problem with the ice building up on just the left propeller but not the right. Instinctively they knew that they needed to get as much cold air as possible, and that clear air would most likely prevail north of the coastal range.

Bob Epperly takes up the story. *'We were barely able to climb, but turned inland directly across the coastal mountain range, wondering if we had enough altitude to clear the terrain. Our radio/radar man Operator Bill Burkhart threaded our way thru the relatively low peaks by radar with at least 500 feet to spare above the terrain. Our navigator, Sgt Tom Southwick, navigated us directly to Byrd, and as soon as we crossed the mountain range the weather began to clear and the ice disappeared. Investigation revealed that a 20-gallon alcohol tank was partially filled with cigarette butts, obviously left there by maintenance men in Jacksonville. In those days everyone smoked and the alcohol tank located under the decking near the cabin door was a handy ashtray during the overhaul process. In any event, the alcohol line to the left propeller became plugged with cigarette residue.'*

Epperly recalls a story about himself and Lt Ron Carson during DF 4, when the pair started out from Little America one afternoon with a load of cargo for Byrd Station, and the weather turned really lousy; Ron was in his R4-D-6 and Epperly in a much faster R4-D-8.

'Enroute, Ron's radar went out and he wound up making a precautionary landing near the plateau rather than searching futilely for Byrd. In the meantime, I landed at Byrd, unloaded and started wondering where Ron was. The radioman at Byrd thought he had heard a transmission that Ron was landing, but did not have a position on him. After completing unloading and pumping fuel aboard from 50-gallon drums, I took off, flew out in the direction where I thought he would most likely be, and started an expanding square search.

We located him finally by means of fade-build up on the VHF radio when about 10-20 miles away by radar. He had restarted his engines, so took off and joined us in the overcast, following us back to Byrd, and flying in close formation during our radar approach to the oil barrels at the end of the skiway. We were in solid cloud during the approach, visibility on the surface by this time was zero or near zero as we made our routine 200 feet per minute descent, and when about 200 feet above the surface on the radio altimeter, I waved off so he could land first. After insuring he was clear of the skiway, I made another radar approach and landed.

Actually the expert in all this was the radio/radar operator Bill Burkhart. Incidentally, we still had our charts, and where Ron had landed, the map showed a tall mountain nearby, but it was a reflection caused by a temperature inversion of a distant mountain that had been drawn by somebody in an earlier expedition. The CO sent us an 'Attaboy', one for Ron for doing the prudent thing and yours truly and my crew for locating his aircraft.

Before I forget,' Rob Epperly continued with his usual 'Yankie' humour *'On one occasion, we flew a visiting Congressman, a reserve Rear Admiral from McMurdo to Little America for a visit. He wanted to fly out to our base and Buddy Krebs offered to fly him in an Otter so the congressman was loaded aboard, and Buddy started up, and headed out. There was overcast with good visibility, but with 'white out' conditions. The pilot system in the Otter had frozen up, but Buddy continued anyway and while nearing LA IV, thinking that he was about a thousand feet above the surface, touched down. He was surprised but turned around to the congressmen and said 'Well Admiral, here we are'. He had intended to circle to land, but the congressman was happy and never knew the difference.'*

The high number of R4-D accidents during the season caused the command concern, with the only R4-D –8 in the fleet going through the season free of engine malfunction, was R4-D-8 *BuNo* 99853 under the command of "Buz" Dryfoose. Included in his crew was his pet German Shepherd named *Utz*, who soon became popular with the crew. *Utz* spent the season on the ice with his master and on returning to the States, the R4-D-8 was loaded aboard the *USS Ticonderoga* with *Utz's* kennel and despite heavy weather, *Utz* suffered no ill effects. Dryfoose flew the R4-D-8 back to the Antarctic the following season with a different crew, but no dog.

'*I acquired Utz in Germany in 1955, when he was 18 months old. I had no problems with the Navy taking him to the ice, but there was a problem with customs in New Zealand, where I was told the dog would have to be destroyed, and since this was a border trained dog who'd become a rich part of the fabric of my life, I replied that they would have to shoot me first! The powers that be quarantined Utz to my aircraft and I stayed aboard with him in Auckland until I reached Christchurch where he was then taken to a vet and placed in quarantine where he rapidly became the pet of the kennels. The employers would fight amongst themselves to see who was going to take Utz to the park for play that he so badly needed. He was the gentlest, most even tempered dog I have ever owned and by far the most loving and loyal.*

He came from Garmisch /Partinkerschin part of Germany and was trained for border patrol by Gernat Reeidel, who was the noted trainer in Germany. Utz was born and bred to show and was completely police trained for obedience and fighting, he was a small dog only 125 pounds.'

'Buz' told me that Utz slept at the foot of his bunk on a discarded sleeping bag and rode on the floor next to the navigator's station on every flight he made that year. The only trouble 'Buz' ever had with his friend in Antarctic was that everyone wanted to feed him, so rules had to be set down.

'*He loved nothing more than playing in the snow and would run upwards of four miles from McMurdo to the airstrip at Williams Field behind the snowcats and weasels when the crews were going to fly. Upon opening the aircraft door, he would immediately ascend the ladder and take up his position perfectly contented.*

As soon as my aircraft landed at outlying stations such as Cape Hallett, the Pole or Byrd, the rear hatch would open and wintering over personnel would stick their heads and say 'Where's Utz'. Even some of the huskies that had befriended him that year, where sadden at his absence.

When I left VX-6 in 1962 and was transferred to Morocco, it was clear that he would be unable to stand the trip, as at the time he was totally blind and about 10 years old. The hardest thing I have ever had to do was to take him to a vet and have him put down.'

Lt.Cdr Robert Epperly reminisced of the wintering over crew at LA V in *Deep Freeze III*, who had travelled out to LA IV and dug tunnels and buildings about 20 feet below the surface- [a few telephone poles could be spotted sticking out of the snow] Vast stashes of food were stored in these tunnels, so the squadron's crew at Little America always had a supply of delicious steaks and food that had been perfectly preserved. '*We always had a box of steaks aboard our aircraft that could be cooked on the hotplates*' recalled Cdr Epperly.

'*We had quite a team at Little America. Major Foster and his crew in the second R4-D-8, Ron Carison and his crew in the R4-D-6; Buddy Krebs manned an Otter and a helicopter, and there were others whose names escape me right now. With a small portion of the squadron that year, we flew a large portion of the squadron flight hours, and as far as my crew goes, a lot of credit goes to the Plane Captain Chief Joe Long, Radio/Radar Operator Bill Burkhart, and navigator Sgt Tom Southwick, not to mention the co-pilots assigned, Lt John Douglas, Lt Frank Wasko, Dutch Gardner, Larry Farrell, Ron Stone, and others.*

Some of these were with me in DF-3 and DF 4. Lt Ron Carlson flew me on the final flight of Que Sera Sera on the ferry back to McMurdo on December 18 1968, actually, we had it pretty easy at Little America, and we had a minimum of paper work to do. The paper work consisted primarily of sending a SIT REP [situation report] every morning to McMurdo, advising them what we did the day before and what we were going to do that day. Incidentally, the third R4-D-8 that year was based at McMurdo and manned by Buz Dryfoose and his crew- and of course his German Shepard dog Utz.'

Flying with Lt Cdr Dryfoose was a real treat in the words of his radioman Larry Sharpe aboard *Wilshie Duit* his trusted R4-D-8 # 99853. '*He trusted his crew to do their jobs and didn't interfere.*

AD2-Jones was the plane captain and was good at it and he wintered over that year. Master Sgt Art De Bolt was the navigator, and I was the radio/radar, and also maintenance man for all the electronics on # 99853, maintaining the communications gear and radar.

We all worked together, in the true spirit of the squadron. Buz had a great sense of humour and we always had Greek jokes for our co-pilot Lt Janulis. Buz could play the piano and always played at parties, and I for one was sorry to see them go, because after they left, I stayed on with # 99853 and got an assortment of pilots. Didn't really like all of them, several of them didn't have any previous experience in the R4-D-8's nor experience in flying to the various bases.

Buz knew his plane, and flying in the Antarctica with a crew who worked well together is essential, with the Antarctic presenting many problems from rapidly changing weather to false readings on the radar altimeter- 'Buz' was the quintessential Antarctic aviator.

Meantime in New Zealand the then Prime Minister Mr Walter Nash feared that continuous American operations would prejudice New Zealand's International relations and specifically his fears were of being under American control. While on the other hand, Operation Deep Freeze command was looking hard at transferring the operation to Hobart, Tasmania, Australia, and this move would have been disadvantageous to the city of Christchurch in monetary terms, and not giving the Task Force ability to operate with efficiency and flexibility.

The *Christchurch Press* wrote a strong editorial on October 3 1958, that the Christchurch City Council must do all it can to provide reasonable facilities at Harewood for the US Navy's Antarctic exploration. Quite apart from the friendship and good will that had been built up over the past three years. '*Christchurch has sound economic reasons for welcoming the presence of the Americans. They have given trade in the city strong support, and the use of Harewood has directed its attention to the merits of the airport. Citizens will agree that the Americans have been most acceptable guests with an extraordinarily high standard of behaviour for a military formation so far from home.*'

Fears were that their constituents might see the American's as squatters, and that the giant Globemasters and other VX-6 aircraft might interfere with commercial and civilian air traffic. Little did the Labour government and its 'cloth cap' minister and their sanctimonious followers realise, that the ex Royal New Zealand Air Force buildings were never meant to be a permanent feature on the city landscape, having a limited lifetime, which had now passed.

'*In any case the government was only too happy at the end of the war to relinquish any responsibility for other permanent housing, leaving local authorities to cope with the difficult task of making temporary homes for families in need.*

As for the possibility of American flying interfering with civilian operations, the analogy with Whenauapai is false. It is true that the Globemasters are service aircraft, but they are not using Harewood as a military base. If the airport could not cope with the relatively small additional traffic, it would not be a civic asset that citizens know it to be. In another 19 years it may have to handle many more overseas movements than the Americans account for now.

It may be that the American operations mean much increased work for civil aviation officials, but this had surely been taken into account in the unwritten agreement by which the Americans and British in the Antarctic give each other mutual support, with the balance heavily on the Americans side. Possibly the Prime Minister [Mr W Nash] fears that continued American operations from New Zealand soil would prejudice New Zealand's international relations and specifically his hope to bring Antarctic under international control. Although much of the work is purely scientific, the American expedition is organised through the armed services because they have an agreement.

If Mr Nash wished to keep the American soldiers and sailors off New Zealand soil except as occasional guests, his case would be respected whether we agree or not. But he could hardly adopt such a policy at this stage after he has encouraged the Americans to go through New Zealand and has permitted the acceptance of American favours in Antarctica. To provide reasonable facilities for peace time exploration is a friendly gesture New Zealand should make to a nation with which it is bound in alliances. If the gesture is to be made, it should be made freely and without reluctance.'

Almost half a century later, the left wingers still cling to their anti American idealisms, for what ever ideological reasons; forgotten are the sacrifices made by the United States, and in particular the Marines for defending both New Zealanders and Australians during WW11, if it wasn't for the 'yanks' who turned the tide of the Japanese relentless match down through the Pacific in the *Battle of the Coral Sea, Midway* and *Guadalcanal* in 1942, many of us Australasian could have been captured and heaven help us, we needed all the help we could get from the Americans.

Due to a progressive and strong willed local council at the time, the US Navy remained in the city until 1998, during which time Harewood was the local US naval base outside the United States and when the USAF Air National Guard took over Operation Deep Freeze, Christchurch remained the operational base.

During the fourth season of the operations, five aircraft were lost, killing eight men. The first accident was a P2V-7N *BuNo 140434* a modified patrol bomber during an acceptance flight in California, where the aircraft was destroyed. On October 15 1958, an USAF C-124C *SN 52 1017* from the 52nd Troop Carrier Squadron, departed from Christchurch for McMurdo Field. Aboard the giant transporter were a crew of nine, four passengers, general cargo, mail, timber for the building of the Pole Station, and provisions to be air dropped at Hallett Station enroute to McMurdo. The C-124C *The City of Christchurch,* formally named by the then Mayor of Christchurch, Mr. R M Macfarland in November 1956, crashed into a mountain near Cape Roget.

A Globemaster commanded by Major Herbert Levack, had left Christchurch shortly after 6pm, and on board was its only passenger, Ian Howell, the *Christchurch Press* correspondent with the American Antarctic Expedition. Major Levack picked up a mayday message from the downed C-124 giving its approximation location, so once the weather had improved, Major Levack's Globemaster left McMurdo after taking on limited fuel, and flew to the known area. But with the sun down behind the mountains and a heavy fog engulfing the Ross Sea Ice Shelf, he was unable to pin point the location of the C-124C, so he brought his plane down to a low level, and the wrecked aircraft was sighted.

A P2V-7N Neptune had failed to locate the crash site before the weather closed in during the initial search, so rescue was impossible until the following evening. An Otter and helicopter were dispatched from McMurdo to Hallett Station, to the crash location, with two weasels from Hallett manned by New Zealanders, Mr J King and Mr J Salmon.

Major Levack radioed that he would drop survival gear, but they informed him they had sufficient food and blankets, so the Globemaster continued to circle the area and at 7.25am a ski equipped VX-6 Otter was in sight and for more than an hour the navy plane's pilot tried to land away from the crevasses, but the plateau was too steep, prompting him to radio for helicopter assistance.

The C-124C was resting on a 2400 ft plateau surrounded by crevasses and with steep cliffs on nearly every side. The only visible parts of the aircraft were the tail and wing portion, as the aircraft on impact had ploughed forward for 280 metres before coming to rest in three parts, littering the area with lumber. The survivors were sheltering in the tail and wing portion, while well away lay the nose section with the remains of the bodies scattered everywhere.

The seven survivors, three of them seriously injured, spent some 25 hours in the wreck before being rescued from temperatures of minus 20 degrees. All six personnel in the cargo hold were killed. The aircraft's commander Major George Bone was on the radio at the time of the crash talking to Cape Hallett when the next he remembered he was hanging upside down in his straps and his co-pilot saying *'Are you alright boss?'*

Although dazed, those who had escaped were the six men in the crew section. When Major Lavack had radioed them to drop down survival gear, their immediate problem was their footwear, as they were only wearing ordinary boots and now suffering from frostbite.

Major Bone said it was bitterly cold 1500 feet up on the hill as there had been a blizzard that night and the next morning items left outside were covered with snow, and for the first time his men had the experience of seeing petrol from the shattered tanks freezing as it flowed down the hill. There is a deep twilight at the Cape at that time of year, which almost amounts to night.

A rescue party had left Cape Hallett on Thursday for the crash site about 30 miles north of the station, and were able to approach within four miles of the spot, but the nature of the country described as 'inaccessible and hostile', prevented them from reaching the survivors, even though they could see the flares from the wreck. As the party crossed the heavily crevassed country en-route, two of their weasels were lost in crevasses, and despite being so close, they were forced to make a detour, which took them seven miles from the crash scene.

When the survivors arrived back in Christchurch, Major Bone told a press conference, that when the Globemaster crashed the crew compartment was sheared off in one piece and hurled 150 feet forward from the main wreckage. At the time of the crash he said, they were descending through the clouds to get into position for the air drop for Hallett Station, and had the flaps down and the airspeed reduced when the crash occurred, and the 80 ton aircraft carried along the slope and turned over, tearing the crew section off and landing on its roof. *'We had no warning of the impending crash'* reporters were told.

The survivors made the wrecked tail section their temporary home, and even though their hands were frozen were able to light a fire in the toilet casting to keep warm. During their time on the ice, radio contact was carried out with McMurdo, but with the severe cold the crew could not stay outside the aircraft for longer periods than necessary. *'Within a minute of talking on the radio my breath had frozen up the mouthpiece, so we had to go back inside to warm it'* said Major Bone.

While three of the crew in the cargo compartment had been strapped in their seats, the other three were not as the plane was not coming in for a landing, only engaged in preparing the cargo for the drop at Hallett to then carry on their return trip from Christchurch. Neither were they carrying survival tents or stoves, and only the sturdiness of the Globemaster's construction saved the six men in the crew compartment when the machine smashed into the hill.

Captain Walter Chapin, whose Globemaster flew south an hour before *City of Christchurch*, said some of the men had been transferred to the other C-124C because his aircraft would be carrying frozen foods, and he could not have his heaters going on the flight deck so they were moved to the other Globemaster, which was carrying the timber and had heating for the twelve hour flight.

Captain Chapin said that as he had travelled to the airport with one of these men *'He was telling me about his wife expecting their child in a few weeks.'*

Killed in the crash were:

Technical Sergeant Iman A Fendley, Technical Sergeant Nathaniel Wallace, Staff Sergeant, Leonard Pitkevitch Wallace, Airman First Class Richard J Angelo, Airman Second Class Robert L Burnette and Airman Second Class Kelly Slone.

The survivors, apart from the pilot Major George Bone were Billy Weir, Raymond Potter and William Meadows.

Later the small Chapel of the Snow was packed for a memorial service conducted by the stations chaplain, Father Harold Heaney. After conducting an interdenominational service, the bodies of the men were flown back to Christchurch by USAF Globemaster.

When Lt Commander Edgar Potter landed his helicopter on the plateau he could not recover the sixth body that had been trapped under the wreckage. While it was first thought that the sixth body may not be recovered until January when the snow started to melt, just three days after the crash, the body was located, and flown to McMurdo in a VX-6 R4-D with the official Navy investigation team.

Soon after Lt Commander Edgar Potter had recovered the survivors, a heavy blizzard set in with snow covering the wrecked Globemaster, *'Five of the six bodies were recovered, resulting from a map drawn by survivors, giving positions of all the bodies enabling Lt Commander Potter and his crew to recover them a few feet from where they were marked on the map.*

When the returning Globemaster with the survivors aboard was four hundred miles out from Christchurch, it was expected it may have to be diverted to the RNZAF base at Ohakea, north of Wellington due to a low cloud ceiling in Christchurch, but the skies cleared to a bright clear blue as the Gobemaster, piloted by Lt.Colonel C J Ellen, the Commander of the 52nd Troop Carrying Squadron, touched down. As the rear hatch doors swung over, there was a shower of snow, carried 2000 miles from Cape Hallett spreading onto the dusty grass. Within half an hour of the Globemaster's arrival, the injured and other survivors, all showing signs of their 25-hour ordeal and the long flight, were driven straight to their base at Weedon where they were able to speak to their families in the United States, over the Air Force's powerful Mars radio transmitter.'

Apart from this tragic setback to their operations, the 52nd completed its season's commitment in record time, and after their first air drop on October 8th four days after arriving at McMurdo, they had carried out their entire mission 39 days later. During this period the C-124's made 33 missions to Byrd, dropping 433 tonnes of cargo, and 30 missions to the South Pole Station dropping another 371 tonnes. In all the squadron carried out 33 missions from Christchurch to Antarctica.

However, these missions weren't problem free for with high winds at Byrd, often the loads were carried away with many pallets lost. On October 9 a 30k W diesel generator was dragged across the Rockefeller Plateau when two of its parachutes failed to open. Aircrews were asked to look out for the lost cargo, and when the generator was finally located it was 37 km away from the drop zone, and it was nothing to locate missing pallets as far as 174km away. With Hallett Station acting as an emergency landing strip for the first time that season, by October 9 nine Globemasters had been ordered to divert to Hallett after blizzard conditions closed McMurdo.

Eddie Frankiewicz recalled the occasion he flew into Hallett, *'I flew there in Deep Freeze 111 in an R4-D-8 en-route flying on instruments weather, my radioman had the radar on and says ' weve got land dead ahead' but it's real low', and just then the clouds opened up and there was a huge mountain directly in front of us. We only had time to bank out and around, so again God was our co-pilot. We landed at Cape Hallett runway that they had marked with oil drums and it was at least 300 feet wide and 8000 feet long on glare ice.*

Just great, but that basin of ice at least 8 miles in any direction, was white, not blue ice.[Sea ice.] Well, yeah I think it was sea ice. And you can land any which way you wanted to, but we were the first ever to land there. We went into the camp and the radio operator asked me to come into the radio shack. He said, 'The C-124 coming back from the Pole has lost an engine and has just made two GCA's at McMurdo and can't get in.'

I said. 'Let's tell him to come here' So I got on the phone and called McMurdo and said 'Gee the weather here is great, send the C-124 here, 8000 foot runway, wide open, good visibility and all that', so they diverted the Globemaster to Cape Hallett. I went outside to go down to my plane so I could talk the plane down in, when I saw it was now a vicious blizzard, just like that, so I turned around and went back inside and said, 'Don't let the plane come here, its awful'. The Air Force C-124 pilot made a couple more GCA's at McMurdo and made it on his third attempt.

I had a number of interesting people on that flight to Cape Hallett, a couple of Naval Captains, an old Antarctic explorer and Father Darkowski. 'My VIP passenger list included the famous Sir Hubert Wilkins, who didn't come into the station, just wanted to remain in the aircraft, and spent the night there in his sleeping bag, and he just loved Antarctica so much that he just wanted to get on with it. The next morning we were ready to take off, but the wind as I remember was 40-50 knots and we had to take off down wind, which was nothing because I had plenty of power and 8 miles of runway ahead of me.

But there was a mountain upwind and I couldn't take off that way so I had to turn around, but it was glare ice and I could not turn around using maximum power and full rudder and aileron control so we got a weasel, tied a line on our tail wheel to the weasel and he pulled me around and now I was facing downwind, when I told him don't let go because I'll weather cock again and told him that when my engines are revved full power, then release the line. We took off downwind in about 40-50 knots of tailwind and got off the ice OK- but an interesting experience, if that weasel wasn't there, I'd still be.'

Two UC-1 Otters were lost during that summer, the first *BuNo 142427* was initially reported as an aircraft accident, but later classified as a ground accident. The Otter was supporting a scientific party taking observations on the Ross Ice Shelf and after the scientists had taken their observations, the Otter taxied to another site for more observations, but during the 'trip' the fuselage cracked, although able to return to McMurdo, the single engine plane was not repaired and struck off the squadron's roster.

The second Otter *BuNo 144673* crashed after take-off from the Marble Point dirt runway, the location of a newly constructed all year airstrip 50 miles from McMurdo. The pilots were on logistic support from Williams Air Facilities to the Marble Point Camp of the Naval Construction Battalion Reconnaissance Unit. After unloading their cargo, they took off for home and were making a steep turn towards a glacier, when the mission went tragically wrong. Caught in a strong cross-wind gust, the crew realized their danger, and the pilot made an heroic effort to recover, but the wing hit a small knoll and the aircraft cartwheeled and crashing, killed both pilot and co-pilot. Investigators were unable to determine the cause of the crash.

Those who died were Lt Harvey E Gardner USN and LTJG Lawrence J Farrell USN and although rushed back to McMurdo by helicopter for emergency hospital treatment, the pilot died four hours later, the co pilot Lawrence Farrell died almost immediately.

The United States Naval medical officer Lt. Frederick Ackroyd who had spent the previous winter at McMurdo, and a medical orderly, flew from Christchurch to McMurdo aboard a R5-D Skymaster # *56528* piloted by Lt Commander Harold Hanson, leaving Christchurch at 10.57 on a twelve-hour flight. In the meantime at the base hospital at McMurdo, a doctor and medical staff were caring for the injured that were flown there by a VX-6 helicopter. Those injured in the crash were Chief Aviation mechanic Joseph Bratina, who was suffering from a possible pelvic injury, photographer's mate [second class] Richard Bundy with multiple bruises and lacerations, and journalist James Donald, having fractures and lacerations.

The previous season, a scientist had fallen into a 60-foot crevasse at Roosevelt Island, so the traverse party leader warned that the patient was in the middle of a crevasse field and advised against an aircraft landing because the visibility was extremely poor and such a landing would be more than hazardous, but despite this warning Lt Commander James Waldron, and Lt Harvey Gardner took off from Little American in an Otter # *142425*, where they carried out a most remarkable rescue mission. Using men as markers, Waldron landed his Otter in the heavily crevassed field, picked up the injured scientist and rushed him back to McMurdo. More old fashion virtues of honour, duty, comradeship and sacrifice, by the men of VX-6.

For an interview as part of the American Polar Society, and the Byrd Polar Archives of the Ohio State University, Brian Shoemaker went to the home of Eddie Frankiewicz in San Diego, and asked Eddie if he kept in touch with his old shipmates from that era of Operation Deep Freeze.

'Regretfully, too many of them have died. Jack Torbett, Charlie Ottie, he's one that killed himself in the Otter over the Dry Valley across from McMurdo. I never could understand that. He made a landing there, and then instead of turning right to go over the bay ice, he turned left into the incline of the mountain and smacked right into it.

I never could understand it as he had made a number of landings there. When I was without an airplane at Little America, I went flying with him once and we went exploring the area. We went on the ice shelf and took a look at the hundreds and hundreds of seals down there, and when he was 10 feet above the snow and there's a whiteout I was very uneasy about his flying. That was very dangerous and sure enough, he got clobbered, I went to his funeral up in Alameda.'

Rear Admiral Dufek made his first flight to Antarctica for the season later than normal due to his health, and it was the first time a flight from New Zealand had flown south without the *Brough* being on station 1000 miles south of New Zealand, as she had been each year since the first fly in to the Antarctic in 1955. A few days before though, a squadron's C-121 Super Constellation had made a turn around flight without the *Brough*.

The Admiral's Skymaster piloted by Lt Commander Harold Hanson departed from Christchurch at 7am and touched down at Invercargill to refuel before heading to McMurdo with a cargo of Christmas trees for the men of the US stations plus, 2500 pounds of mail.

In December 1958 pipes sounded by Bosun's Mate E F Kingen shrilled out as Rear Admiral David M Tyree stepped from Navy's R5-D Skymaster *# 56728* that had brought him from Awckland, in preparation to taking over command of *Operation Deep Freeze* on April 15 1959, and he was greeted by Rear Admiral George Dufek.

As he was on a familiarisation tour, he was driven out of the RNZAF Station, past a guard of honour to his hotel.

'I am looking forward to the job, but I realise it will be tough taking over from a man like George, who has done a great job. He is an old friend of mine since we passed out of Naval College at Annapolis together in 1925.'

He departed for the Antarctic aboard the *USS Wyanot* on December 15, staying on the ice for three weeks making an extensive familiarisation tour of all the Antarctic bases, and expressing grave concern on his return that he considered there were some 'very tired' aircraft in VX-6's fleet, and that scrapping some of them would be one of his priorities once he returned to Washington.

Apart from the squadron's aging transport fleet, some of the stations were beginning to show signs of wear from having been established in the mid fifties when they were originally set up for a limited duration only, with both Byrd and the Pole stations starting to display signs of being crushed by the build up of snow and ice. Admiral David Tyree also had firm views of the Task Force's command and supply organisation within the United States Navy system, and suggested that personnel could be rotated to support a longer operational term,

On the morning of December 18 1958, Lt Commander Robert Epperly and Ron Carlson flew *'The Grand Old Lady of the Antarctic' Que Sera Sera # 12418* now without its original landing gear, from Little America to McMurdo.

'The trip was rather a memorable one' recalls Bob Epperly, *'because the landing gear could not be raised, we knew that before taking off, the right generator was inoperative [the good engine] and the left engine constantly cut in and out every few minutes as I recall, due to a faulty blower seal internally. I believe that the weather was good and otherwise it was an uneventful flight, so we were the last to fly the 'lady', who was then shipped back to the States and later presented to the Smithsonian Institute.'*

Larry Sharp who was assigned as a radioman to 'Buz' Dryfoose's R4-D *# 99853* was given the task of escorting *Que Sera Sera* on the New Zealand leg of her last journey to the States aboard the *USS Wyandot* in January 1959. Before leaving McMurdo her wings and rudder were removed, and after arriving at Port Lyttleton in Christchurch, she was loaded onto a road transporter and taken to a waiting USAF Globemaster for her final journey back to the United States.

Sharp remained with Buzz and *# 99853* until the end of February 1960, when he returned home as radioman on a P2-V *# 140436* piloted by Commander Lloyd Newcomer, later returning for the summer season of 60-61 with the support detachment in Christchurch. He recalls the story of the 'no beards' order, when the squadron's XO issued an order that all VX-6 personnel were to be clean-shaven.

One of the advantages of going to Antarctica was the possibility of growing a beard. '*At the end of the beard spectrum was my dozen or so whiskers and I: and at the other end of the spectrum was Lt Ribose and his full faced, gun blue beard. Signs appeared the next day with a bald headed penguin moving to the North Pole 'no beards allowed' and 'Slagle's Slickies-Semper Vitalise', so we became the laughing stock of the South Pole region, as Seabees and scientists alike made fun of the 'no beards VX-6'ers.'*

On February 12 1959 a Sikorsky HRS-3 helicopter *BuNo 144257*, that was assigned to the *USS Glacier* as part of Detachment 69 Helicopter Utility Squadron Two, crashed. Lt. Cdr. Russell was only a few minutes into a test flight after an engine change, when the engine failed and the 'copter crash landed on the rough ice some 2,000 yards from the *Glacier,* smashing the blades on impact, and due to the crash site's inaccessibility, it was not recovered. The helicopter had been called to aid the British Antarctic supply ship *John Bisco* and was an essential part of the icebreakers equipment in polar waters, used in the main for locating the most suitable passage through the pack ice.

The American's decision to continue their Antarctic Research Programme necessitated the United States Navy Support Force Antarctica to locate a more permanent headquarters in Christchurch. Since the time they arrived in the city to commence *Deep Freeze I,* Task Force 43's Advanced Headquarters had operated out of an old disused brewery in Kilmore Street, Christchurch, while VX-6 Squadron and other naval units where based at the RNZAF base at Wigram, Harewood airport, and the Air Force weather station at Weedons, so it was decided to base the whole operation from Christchurch International Airport.

Deep Freeze-IV, the Admiral and his command staff arrived in Christchurch and during the following 1959-60 season, they moved into their new Advanced Headquarters at Christchurch International Airport, followed by the Navy's VX-6 Squadron's move from the RNZAF Station at Wigram to Harewood on December 11 1959. The Squadron were to move into two reconstructed barracks consisting of two enlisted men's quarters [BOQ], a wardroom mess and the main mess, with all buildings being internally heated and decorated. The new accommodation would house some 400 personnel.

These buildings had been used during World War II as wartime accommodation for the Royal New Zealand Air Force, and post war, were converted into transit housing units. Contracts were let in late January 1959 for the conversion of the old YWCA building into Operation Deep Freeze headquarters and were officially opened with the United States flag rising on March 31 1959.

On the land adjoining the airfield on Orchard road, the Navy began the construction of a 27,000 sq foot prefabricated hanger, with the Christchurch City Council planning to develop a paved parking apron for the Squadron and USAF aircraft in front, so they could use the main airport runways, thus bringing together all the various military and civilian agencies supporting the Antarctic operations. So at last all the various military and civilian agencies and groups supplying the United States Antarctic programme were concentrated on one site.

During the 1958-59 operations, the Navy's fourth on the ice, VX-6 introduced the Lockheed R7-V Super Constellation to its Antarctic operation fleet. This aircraft *BuNo 131624*, was to provide the main passenger airlift of personnel between Christchurch and McMurdo, and being equipped with a tri-camera system for aerial photographic survey work, it replaced one of the Squadron's R5-D's.

With the change of command from Rear Admiral George Dufek to Rear Admiral David Tyree, it proved the importance of having the United States Department of Defence and the US Naval Command operations in Christchurch, where it was to become the largest US Naval base outside the United States.

With the decision to continue the Antarctic programme, serious consideration had to be given to a second supply line, for until then the operation had been simplified by concentrating on a single supply line from New Zealand to the Ross Sea area, using Christchurch as a staging post. Planning had to take place in Washington to establish a second supply line into the continent with the planned opening of the Palmer Station on the Antarctic Peninsula, proposed for *Deep Freeze-65.*

A major task for the Admiral, was to established and implement a new supply and command organisation within the Naval system, for in this way, personnel could be rotated in and out of various units if the operation was to be long term. This rotation would also apply to the command itself with Rear Admirals being replaced every three, and later every two seasons.

The commander's post of Naval Support Force, Antarctica, was downgraded from Rear Admiral to Captain on September 6 1972. Rear Admiral L B McCuddin USN was the last of seven Admirals to hold the post, when Captain A N Fowler USN replaced him.

During the year that New Zealand established their Antarctic base as it was their government's contribution to the IGY, with the New Zealand observers given the task of electing a site this went to Sir Edmund Hillary, and the base was finally chosen, but not without its difficulties. Observers first went to McMurdo in the summer of 1955-56 with the base to be built the following summer.

One of the important site considerations was the position of the base in relation to the Polar Plateau through the mountains on the Western shores of McMurdo Sound, since the New Zealand support party were to lay supply depots on the high plateau between the Pole and McMurdo Sound. After a thorough reconnaissance, often involving men hauling sledges up many miles of glacier, Butter Point was selected. This area is at the mouth of the Ferrar Glacier and straight across the sound from Hut Point, and to Sir Edmund it offered the best features of approach by sea and across to the plateau.

To transport the New Zealand expedition to Antarctica, the New Zealand government purchased the *John Biscoe,* a supply ship of the Falkland Island Dependency. Unfortunately, when the wooden ship, renamed *HMNZN Endeavour* reached McMurdo in the summer of 1956-57, her engine power proved inadequate for penetrating the massive flow ice accumulated on the western side of the sound and the rough ice surfaces between the ship and the proposed building site, precluding the transport of construction materials over the ice surface within the available time.

So Butter Point was 'out', and it was commander Rear Admiral George Dufek who came to the Kiwi's rescue in providing a helicopter in which Sir Edmund Hillary could reconnoitre further and he finally chose Pram Point, so named by Scott's 1902 expedition when they kept a Norwegian 'pram' dinghy there to get from the shore of the Ross Island to the Ross Ice Shelf on the eastern side of the Hut Point Peninsula.

The Royal New Zealand Navy frigates *HMNZS Pukaki* and *Hawea* escorted the *Endeavour* from Dunedin as far as the pack ice, while the *Endeavour* carried some of the personnel and part of the supplies for the New Zealand expedition, the rest of the base construction material and operational stores brought south in the US Naval ships of *Deep Freeze II* and by VX-6 squadron aircraft. Despite valuable time lost, the base was completed and their scientific programme began on schedule with much credit going to Sir Edmund and the US Navy.

New Zealand had had aircraft in Antarctica in the early years, and when the RNZAF took over from the Royal Air Force, one of the RAF Austers [*WE563- later redesignated NZ1707]]* was purchased by the RNZAF for their Antarctic flight in from Christchurch on May 1 1956, under the command of John Claydon, one of two pilots, a radio operator and a mechanic.

The Auster was later flown to Mt Cook, in the South Islands Southern Alps [NZ] to carry out ski tests, however during manoeuvres a ski dug into the snow and its rail came up overturning the small aircraft. The accident occurred at 5,000 feet causing considerable damage to its wings, tailplane, a bent propeller and a smashed canopy. Repairs were carried out on the site but the ill-fated Auster's run of misfortune was not yet over. Loaded aboard the *Endeavour* at Lyttelton for its voyage south, a special cradle was constructed for it on the stern of the ship, but as the vessel pulled away just after midnight on December 18, the stern of the *Endeavour* swung around and made contact with another ship moored alongside.

Because the Auster's wings overhung the sides of the ship, the starboard wing got badly damaged, but once the ship arrived at Dunedin, the wing was removed and flown to the RNZAF Station at Taieri for inspection. As a replacement wasn't available either in New Zealand or Australia, the expedition decided to set sail for Antarctic and have the wing repaired in the US.

A second aircraft, a De Havilland Canada Beaver was purchased new from donations and assembled at the RNZAF Station at Hobsonville near Auckland.

After arriving in Antarctica, an airfield was chosen on the sea ice between Cape Armilage and Pram Point- half a km from Scott Base, where it was decided to construct the aircraft parking area under the shelter of an ice cliff near the end of the runway. The crate in which the Auster was transported to Antarctica, was later used to construct a workshop in real Kiwi style, while an old wartime military truck became the operations radio hut.

At the beginning of October 1957, the Beaver *[NZ 6001]* was reassembled after being taken south aboard the *HMNZS Endeavour* and one of the Beavers first missions was an operational medivac to the Ross Ice Barrier to evacuate Dr George Marsh who had become ill while with a trail party making this the first landing away from their base.

The *USS Curtiss* brought the replacement wing for the Auster south and after being assembled and test flown, both planes were engaged in many supply and reconnaissance missions, and on February 9 they made history by landing at 8,200 feet on the Polar Plateau. This marked the successful traverse of the Skelton Glacier after landing to establish the first supply depot on the Polar Plateau by air.

The Beaver flew throughout April including some night flying, right up until the end of May when all flying ceased for the winter. At the beginning of October, it was reassembled and test flown in readiness for the Trans-Antarctic Expedition.

After the purchased of an Otter, the Auster was loaded on the *Endeavour* for the trip back to New Zealand, and the Beaver was prepared for transport aboard the *USS Glacier*. However, it remained at Scott Base for the winter after encountering damage as it was being loaded at McMurdo and was later shipped back to Christchurch aboard a USAF C-124 in October 1958.

One of the RNZAF's significant aviation achievements during *Deep Freeze III* was carried out after the arrival of the TAE Otter at Scott Base on January 6 1958. Piloted by Squadron Leader Lewis RAF, it made the 1,250 miles from South Ice [the British party's inland base] in just less than 11 hours, remaining at Scott Base to assist the Beaver with supply operations until sold to the US Navy at the end of the Expedition.

Two RNZAF pilots, Squadron Leader J Claydon and Flying Officer W J Cranfield had visited the South Pole in December, courtesy of VX-6, when they hoisted the RNZAF Ensign at the pole, the first British flag to be flown there since Capt Scott's fateful visit in 1912. The first flight by an RNZAF C-130 was made on 28 October 1965, a further two flights were made on a turnaround system during that season and this schedule continues today.

In January 1957, sledge dogs went south in support of the Commonwealth Trans-Antarctic Expedition, with the original pack of 60 drawn from three sources. The majority and the best, coming from Australia's Mawson Station where the breeding line of these dogs dates back through to those held at the French station in Adelie Land, then through dogs from the Falkland Islands Dependency Survey's, Hope Bay Station [about 1948], to the original bred on the west coast of Greenland.

New Zealand's Auckland zoo provided 16 others descended from Admiral Byrd's United States Expedition of 1939-40, with a further 12 purchased from the Danish Administration coming directly from Greenland and arriving in New Zealand aboard the *Endeavour*. In view of suspected inbreeding and lack of balance in ages, new blood lines were introduced in 1960, with 12 dogs chosen by Mr W Herbert in Greenland. These dogs were flown direct to New Zealand by the USAF MAT's C-124, and a breeding programme was then carried out at Scott Base.

By the completion of *Deep Freeze –64*, the geological and topographical survey of the Ross Dependency no longer used dog sleds teams, so the size of the dog population at Scott Base was reduced to 20 with enough dogs to provide two nine man teams.

Towards the end of the season Commander Bob Epperly flew *#17154 Negatus Perspirus* back to the States in a flight which was more than normal, even for the squadron's aging R4-D fleet. While not a typical VX-6 Dak flight, it did however, underscore the squadron's 'just another day at the office' professionalism when faced with keeping the *Gooney Bird* in the air.

Bob had gone down to the ice for the first time in 1957 as Eddie's Frankiewicz's co-pilot in a R4-D-8, a couple of months after joining the squadron. On reaching the ice the R4-D was down for some maintenance items and he took over *Charlene*, which Eddie had flown the previous year. After several flights in *Charlene*, Commander Epperly was ordered to fly her back to Jacksonville, Florida, as Frankiewicz had already left Antarctica.

On arrival at McMurdo from Little America, the crew removed the skis and placed them inside the cabin, then gassed up and blasted off heading for Christchurch. On board the flight were Lt John Douglas [co-pilot] CPO Joe Long [plane captain] Sgt Tom Southwick [navigator] Bill Burkhard [Radioman] a helicopter pilot Lt.Cdr Buddy Krebs [the Officer in Charge at Little America that year] who rode as a passenger and one other. *'Buddy Krebs, was a very active jovial Officer with whom it was my pleasure to serve.'*

About 75 miles out of McMurdo the crew heard an unusual noise emanating from the left engine, and fourteen hours later when the aircraft landed in Christchurch, they had a firewall very hot but still holding. *'We felt pretty lucky as the aircraft, at least during the first third of the trip, was much too heavy to fly on one engine with Maximum except take off power. The skis, due to size and weight were all but un- jettisonable, but the much-reduced power used on the left engine was enough to carry us through very nicely.*

Our course from McMurdo was direct to the RNZAF station Wigram Aerodrome where the squadron was based at the time, so we altered course a few degrees to put us closer to landfall. As a result, we ended up flying over the South Island for quite a while before landing at Wigram. We didn't really consider diverting to Invercargill since we were doing so well and were very light by the time we had reached lanffall. If we had to shut down the engine completely, we would have survived.' Bob recalled.

Returning to the US after his tour of duty had been completed Lt Commander Epperly received a most unwelcome message from the operations Headquarters in Christchurch, saying that the three R4-D's were to be loaded aboard an aircraft carrier for transport back to the West Coast.

'I was dumbfounded! I sent confidential messages back appealing the decision, but to no avail. Buz Dryfoose was named to escort the three aircraft on the carrier, which he did along with his dog Utz. I was so disappointed in not taking 'Negatus Perspirus' home that to this day I do not recall subsequent events in VX-6 before leaving the squadron in the spring for another assignment. Notwithstanding family commitments, I probably would have stayed for another tour or two.

I somewhat childishly did have the name 'Negates Perspirus' removed from the aircraft. Looking back it was probably a prudent decision in light of past engine problems in the R4-D-8 fleet. Captain Slagle I believe thought he was doing me a favour and got me a Washington assignment, but the last thing in the world I wanted to do was to fly a desk in Washington, but that's life. I guess everything turns out for the best, some months or years later, I was saddened to hear that my ex 'Negatus Perspirus' had crashed while making a 200 ft min radar approach to Byrd, I suppose she is still there buried in drifting snow.'

Why the name *Negatus Perspirus?* When asked, Bob Epperly replied with a mystical smile, *'I don't know, strictly made it up myself, thinking it sounded better than 'No Sweat', I never studied Latin, but it sounded real good, no sweat!'*

Two aircraft, both R4-Ds crashed during that season. The first an R4-D5 *Takahe* BuNo 17163, on September 15, while making a landing on the ice at Cape Hallett, when the starboard landing gear collapsed, making the aircraft a strike and not economical to repair due to its age. Then, on Christmas Eve, an R4-D8 BuNo 17154 crashed while attempting a landing at Byrd Station during a whiteout. No injuries to crew but again a Douglas aircraft were destroyed. *Takahe* was name by Roy Curtis in Deep Freeze I after the well-known flightless bird of New Zealand.

Some in the squadron said this was not an example of a newer pilot being inexperienced in Antarctic flying in the R4-D-8's but blowing snow. On this mission when Lt Garland Regenar left McMurdo to fly to Byrd Station, the weather report he was given enroute was to expect fair weather, but when he and his crew arrived there was snow blowing, but from the air the surface of the snow looked solid and he wasn't aware of the blowing snow.

He stalled the airplane thinking he was landing on the skis, and although Regenar applied power and used his rudder to compensate, when the aircraft stalled and fell 50 feet to the surface, the right wing hit hard, breaking the back of the aircraft, and luckily there were no serious injuries. A sad end to Commander Robert Epperly's pride and joy- Negatus Perspirus, the aircraft he named that had served him well.

The tour in Washington for Robert Epperly wasn't too bad as he got quite a bit of extra flying in an R4-D, R5-D, T-28B and T-34, when he could break away from the desk in the Bureau of Naval Personnel to go pick up Reservists for weekend drill etc.

Retiring from the Navy as Captain in June 1964, Robert Epperly started flying Super Constellations on non-schedule flights as co-pilot and then on a number of non-schedule services including DC-8's and later flying Cessna 310's part time, until the owner went out of business in 2002. Bob hasn't flown since.

Lt Commander Epperly recants a story regarding the Navy aviator's distain for reporters and a 'run in' with a journalist from the New York Times, *'I suppose there was a little vice- versa in this disharmony, as they were strange bedfellows. Anyway, while waiting for a cylinder replacement to be sent to us at Byrd Station, a very long dispatch was copied by the Byrd radioman from the reporter. I sent the dispatch [Reference UR dateline; Request fairtrain (first available air transportation) three pounds of whatever you're smoking.] Another time after unloading at a traverse party, a photographer/ writer would not get back in the aircraft even though he was not authorized to stay, and we parted company shaking our fists at each other! Plenty of excuses were found not to pick him up for a week or so, but he did take some wonderful photos of the nearby mountains, and was ready to return when we did finally arrive with another delivery. The traverse parties had only limited accommodation for overnight visitors.'*

On July 21 1959, Captain William H Munson took over command of VX-6. from Cdr Jerry Barlow, who held the post for ten weeks.

CHAPTER NINE.

THE CHANGING OF THE GUARD:REAR ADMIRAL DAVID TYREE REPLACES GEORGE DUFEK AND THE INTRODUCTION OF THE 'HERK'S.'

Rear Admiral David Tyree takes over Task Force 43 command
From Dufek - The first mid winter medical
evacuation mission from Antarctica - The first C-130
Hercules arrives.

In *Deep Freeze-60*, the designation of the USAP's annual expedition was changed from Roman to Arabic numerals to reflect the current fiscal year, with VX-6 deploying 21 aircraft, the USAF's 9th Troop Carrier Squadron deploying ten C-124s, and the 61st Troop Carrier Squadron out of Stewart AFB, brought seven ski-equipped and one wheeled C-130 Hercules. The introduction of the USAF's *Project Iceflow* added a new dimension in Antarctic logistics.

The decision to continue the *Deep Freeze III* programme meant the supply situation would be simplified by concentrating on a single supply line from New Zealand onto the Ross Sea area. Following Admiral Tyree's earlier inspection, it was agreed to shore up and strengthen the old huts at both the Pole and Byrd Stations, having most of the structural material delivered by naval ships, to be available on the ice before January 1960.

The Navy ordered four ski equipped Lockheed C-130 Hercules transporters to be part of the new command's equipment, as they realized the longevity and testament of the turboprop aircraft designed for Antarctic operations. By replacing the R4-D *Gooney Bird* that had been their polar workhorse since 1955, the navy believed that Lockheed's design team lead by Willis Hawkins, and the mighty Hercules, as it was aptly named, was the right replacement.

By the 1970's the C-130 was already a legend, and soon aviation writers and pilots alike had run out of superlatives to describe its achievements and exploits. It was able to undertake a greater variety of missions than any other aircraft, ranging from military conflicts around the globe, to the transporting of food and medicine on humanitarian relief operations, and being able to operate from almost any airfield in the world, this aircraft would be the best for polar operations.

The ski-Herk or ski-bird, as it is often called, was actually the first C-130 derivative off the production line. During the cold war, the Distant Early Warning Line constructed in the 1950's, was a chain of manned radar sites spanning the Arctic from Alaska to Greenland, and these sites were built to serve as North American's first line of defence against a feared Soviet attack from the North Pole region. Subsequently the USAF's Tactical Air Command needed an aircraft with the ability to not only resupply the radar bases, but more importantly, to land and take off on snow covered strips.

The Air Force opted to have skis attached to the normal landing gear of the C-130's, so the 48th C-130A off the Burbank line was modified and fitted with skis in late 1956, and the first ski flight followed on January 1957 with successful tests in Bemidji, Minnesota and a few weeks later in Greenland, confirming to both Lockheed and the USAF that the Hercules could be adapted for polar missions.

With Lockheed modifying their assembly line and after twelve C-130A's came off the line as C-130D's, the first of these were assigned to the 61st Troop Carrier Transport Squadron based at Sewart AFB, Tennessee and landed in the Arctic in early January 1959. Two more were modified and later eight of the D models were converted back to standard Herks, with the remaining six assigned to the 17th Airlift Squadron at Elmendorf AFB, Alaska between 1964 and 1975, when the Arctic resupply mission was assigned to the New York National Guard's 109th airlift wing. The D models were retired in 1984.

Navigators often had hairy missions assigned, and this manifested itself more in Antarctica than in any other part of the world, and in particular during the 1950's, with navigators digging deep into their experience for possible solutions, especially when the solutions were very hard to come by if there was no precedent established, and one they never encountered at navigation school. In Antarctica the navigators had to learn and learn fast to survive, so then they could pass that knowledge on.

James MacDonald JOC wrote of an actual case in the *Naval Aviation News,* September 1959. '*A party of 10 scientists is exploring a patch of Antarctic terrain some 1200 miles from their home base, McMurdo Sound and they are in a critical need of food, fuel, spare machinery and medical supplies. To reach them overland would take months, so weekly air support is absolutely necessary for survival, but the Navigators are confronted with several distracting factors:*

The terrain over which the plane will fly is unknown, existing charts frequently are inaccurate. Altitude is anywhere from 5,000 to 25,000 feet. The best information the aerologist can supply is an honest guess based in reports from stations hundreds of miles apart.

Visibility will be zero to 75 miles. Icing may be light, moderate or heavy at all levels. Temperatures at flight level at times dips to 60 below. Winds drive from any direction at the force of 5 to 100 knots.

Location of the exploratory party is known, but only within 40 miles. The plane will take enough fuel to reach the party and return. Cargo load will bring the total aircraft weight to the maximum allowed under emergency combat operating conditions. There's no reserve holding fuel available, for theses men need all the supplies that can be carried.

There is no room for error so obviously the navigator is the key man in this operation. He has only the sun to go by – if of cours he can see it!

VX-6 has faced up to these problems through four Deep Freeze operations and was now in its fifth season on the ice with more and more complicated daily navigational problems to solve.

Over the years in Antarctica, Marine Corps navigators have compiled a full bag of tricks, which would flabbergast the ordinary navigator accustomed to routine standard navigational problems. Their repertoire so numerous as to be usual and they have been solely responsible for returning their fellow crewmembers as well as the aircraft back safely at the completion of another difficult mission.

VX-6 navigators, the majority of whom were US Marines who had volunteered for the operations in Antarctic, are indeed a very special breed of man who has always been hand-picked and well experience, but not necessarily in polar navigation. Many a squadron crew have owed their life to them.

At NAS Quonset Point the Squadron established the only Antarctic Polar Navigation Course, conducted at squadron level, ordered into existence by its Squadron's CO Cdr Jerry M Barlow. When a new navigator is ordered to the squadron, he immediately commences a specialised two-week course, which in 1958 had no counterpart within the US Navy. The course is highly advanced for qualified navigators as its subject matter is presented from the standpoint of practical polar application. Every problem, every lecture, every trick in the book is based on the hard won experiences of four years in Antarctica.

The navigator's classroom curriculum consists of a thorough indoctrination into such subjects as polar Celestial Navigation, Free Directional GYRO Steering, Polar Grid Navigation and peculiarities of Radar Navigation in the Antarctic.

Information critiques on various flights are conducted in order to give the students the benefit of another man's experience in outwitting the Antarctic's inherent traps for the unwary. Equipment used in the demonstration is the actual equipment used during an Antarctic deployment for realism proposes.

The two men responsible for the administration and instruction of these 1958 courses were MSgt Bill Barker and TSgt Tom Southwick, both with more than fifteen years navigational experience, several of which had been in the Antarctic. These Marine instructors passed on their hard learned know-how of how to deal with the various problems arising from extreme cold and long Antarctic twilight conditions. It has been necessary to place these requests on a quota basis, and Com.Nav.Air.Lant, through whom appropriate applications must be made, handles all arrangements.

'The most gratifying reward a commanding officer can experience' says Cdr Barlow, *'is to report on an exceptional job completed under difficult circumstances by his men.*

Our navigators have certainly done this and even more. No matter how difficult the mission, no matter how impossible the conditions, they pull us through safely and fast. Although instructors, they are still students, for each operation in the Antarctic present a new problem or a new variation of an old one. They store up experience and, in the squadron's polar navigation course, pass them on; they help make each successful Antarctic operation a safer one.'

Flying into Invercargill to commence *Deep Freeze-60* on October 1, the first to arrive en-route to Antarctica was Lt Commander 'Buz' Dryfoose flying his old faithful *Wilshie Duit # 99853* who made a circuit above Innvercargill airport and then swept in quickly from the east for a landing. The north-westerly wind assailed the aircraft viciously as the pilot made his approach, appearing to have initially touched down on one wheel only.

The second R4-D *# 17217* flown by Marine pilot Capt Maurice LeBas and his all Marine crew, arrived a few moments later and appeared at first to have no difficulties until, when only feet from the tarmac lurched in flight as a sudden gust of wind hit, dropping its wing perilously close to the ground. From 'Buz' in his own words, *'my memory bank is growing increasingly thin. Actually there were so many cross-wind landings, this one doesn't stand out in my memory, as landing on one main mount is standard operating procedure in any crosswind landing.'*

The incidence provided a graphic illustration, as flights by N.Z. National Airways into the city had been cancelled that evening due to Civil Aviation regulations of no landings with cross winds gusting to 25-30 mph, but the American aircraft which were due to leave for Antarctica later that evening were not similarly restricted.

'What boy from the age of six to sixty-six can fail to be enthralled by a Deep Freeze take off from Invercargill Airport; what boy can fail to be imbued with a sense if longing and envy as runway lights gleam, navigation lights flash, engines roar, JATO bottles rent the night and the big grey and orange planes blast off for the polar icecap?' - so wrote the *Southland Times* on October 3 1959, as Buz Dryfoose and Marine Captain Maurice LeBas and their crews entertained the city folk prior to taking off from the world's most southern city.

When asked why he joined the Navy in June 1946, Lt Cdr. Buz Dryfoose who hails from East Greenwich, Rhode Island, married, and at the time with two children under five, said since Admiral Byrd's book 'Little America' was read to him by force while he was at school, he found it still bugged him after he left, so he followed this continuing interest to Antarctica.

Acting MSgt W H 'Hooch' Clarke, who was about to become a grandfather at 40, in 1959, had been in the Marines since 1942 and was in New Zealand during the war. *'A change of duty stations and talking to other radio operators, I decided to join. I guess I just wanted to go to Antarctica.*

Like the other squadron members, 'Hooch' couldn't understand why in NZ *'your pubs closed at 6 O'clock, when your beer however tasted fine, but couldn't it be chilled a little more?'*

The baby of the two crews was twenty-one year old Larry Sharp AT2. *'I joined the navy after leaving school because all my mates did.'* Larry signed up as a radio operator for *Deep Freeze, 'just to get out of where I was, for new experiences and new places to go I guess; hell, I'm no glory hound, I'm just a plain little old sailor.'*

Navigator acting MSgt Art de Bold, the man with probably the longest military services of the two aircraft's ten crew members, joined in 1942, aged 36, having the urge to see Antarctica and the prospect of the thrill of being able to navigate his plane there and see the South Pole. He signed up with *Deep Freeze 'as an aerial navigator, as it was a challenge to my ability that I wanted to take'.*

For Marine Captain Le Bas, when asked of his interest in Antarctica, said *'it was my mother and her friendship with both Admiral Richard Byrd and his brother, Sen Harry F Byrd that I got interested when I was very young, so I suppose it was just natural that I signed up.'*

The night before the take off for McMurdo acting USMC MSgt Charles Jewel *'and I ain't ever been cold before,'* who hails from Miami Flordia, was pouring over his flight charts in his hotel room in preparation for the flight south, *'I signed up because I just wanted to try navigating down there'.*

Other squadron members included Marine crew Sgt Andy Holzemer, Lt George Janulis, Capt Joe Walker, and AD2 Billy Jones.

The two R4-D's departed, blasting off with the assistance of JATO rockets through the receding dawn's ground mist, rocketing away to the west before swinging on their southerly course to McMurdo. A Rescuemaster DC-4 left Christchurch and trailed them to the halfway mark, then the US navy weathership *Peterson* went on alert some 1000 miles south of New Zealand. The flight took the pair 11 hours 7 minutes, a pretty typical length of time for flights to Antarctica from Invercargill.

The Admiral's Tyree's C-121 departed from Christchurch, after a short meeting with the US Secretary of Defence, Neil McElroy, then flew to Invercargill, where he was honoured with a civic reception and dinner with the city fathers.

It was the second visit to the city of Invercargill by a Commander of Operation Deep Freeze, a tradition set by Admiral George Dufek. Invercargill was only one of three New Zealand cities to host the United States Antarctic Expedition, so it was a goodwill visit and to thank the city for its assistance and hospitality as well as for flying the flag for the United States Navy.

In the meantime weather reports were being received by Morse and over the teleprinter services from Campbell Island, McMurdo Sound's Air Facility, Cape Hallett, the destroyer *Peterson* and other shipping in the vicinity of the flight, and from these reports, the Task Force's meteorologist Cdr W S Latterman drew up weather maps and briefed the pilot Cdr J A Henning on conditions and the tail winds encountered for the flight that would be the best recorded yet in the region.

As zero time approached the following day, Commander Henning and his crew prepared their final checks for the long trip, and at 9.15pm Rear Admiral Tyree arrived with his executive staff and boarded the plane, which taxied to the southern end of the runway, and after its final checks, Cdr Henning moved the aircraft from its stationary position as the large crowd which had gathered started to cheer, but were quickly drowned out by the noise of the JATO bottles igniting as the plane gathered speed.

A final burst from the bottles gave the aircraft a sharp lift, as the Admiral and his staff soared quickly over the lights of the city at a 45-degree angle and were on their way, and as the plane turned onto its southerly course for Antarctica, thousand of spectators began to leave, causing traffic jams from the airport.

There was jubilation at McMurdo, as the long Antarctic isolation was broken when Admiral David Tyree, stepped from his Super Constellation with Captain J Eady, chief of staff, and the commander of VX-6 Captain W M Munson, and not far behind was Lt. V Colonel Roy Frost commander of the USAF's 9th ATC and Major J Mitchell the USAF operational officer, Their C-124 had left minutes behind the Admiral's and touched down with the first outsiders for six months, with the temperature at McMurdo at minus 2 degrees F some 50 degrees cooler than Christchurch International Airport.

The first ski-equipped turbo prop C-130 to arrive in Antarctica touched down at McMurdo, after an eight-hour flight from Christchurch in January 1960, and on January 25 flew its first test mission to Byrd Station. Two days later the Hercules piloted by Lt. Colonel Wilbert Turk made the first landing of a four engine plane at the polar plateau, with the Admiral accompanying that first historic fight, just as his predecessor George Dufek had done aboard *Que Sera Sera* in October 1956.On the flight, Rear Admiral Tyree took with him the American flag that Admiral Byrd had carried on his historic flight over the north and south poles in Lt.Col Turk's aircraft *Frozen Assets #* 570495.

None of Lt.Col 'Will' Turks crews, similar to the crews of the 61st TCS, were strangers to the harsh polar operations, as the majority of them had operated on the Greenland icecap in support of the DEW line early warning radar system, but the Antarctic proved to be more harsh on the aircraft and required more rigorous disciplines for the crews than that experienced in the Arctic. The 61st continued into 1961, providing C-130 D as the largest ski- equipped aircraft built, its main skis alone were 6.25 metres long and 1.7 metres wide, with the nose ski measuring 3 metres long and 1.7 metres wide, and the overall weight of the ski equipment a staggering two and a half ton.

The turbo-prop flights proved their feasibility to the VX-6 squadron chiefs, and during its period on the ice, the squadron delivered 400 tons of fuel, timber and other building materials, making twenty-eight landings at Byrd and 30 at the Polar plateau. Although the C-130 D could not carry as much cargo as the old faithful C-124 Globemasters, it flew faster and higher and could land alongside the various inland stations rather than having to do air drops, thus saving the operation over $US 1 million a year in parachutes, and millions of dollars in lost equipment.

Named the *Green Hornet* in both Greenland and Antarctica, Col Wilbert Tuck and his 61st Squadron from Stewart AFB brought seven ski-equipped C-130D aircraft to the ice, as well as a wheeled C-130-A which did not venture south of Christchurch. The squadron made a total if 28 flights to the Pole and to Byrd Station plus a number of field camp support missions between January 25 and February 5 1960.Their statistics were impressive with a total of 128 ski landings, average flight /days 7, total flight days 1104, cargo carried, 407 tons [Pole and Byrd] with 131 crew members, 10 flight crews and an average of 7.3 missions/ flight crews.

Said Col Wilbert Turk *'The emergency airlift was essential, as the two US stations in Antarctica would be abandoned unless essential equipment and supplies could be provided for the wintering over party. Remember at the time the Antarctica treaty had not been agreed to and if the US abandoned its bases, other nations [eg.USSR] would occupy them.'*

Col Turk was correct about the Russians taking over, after all, they had made their first land traverse to the Pole only a month before the Air Force aircraft had shown up in Antarctica, but it is now known that the USSR could not have resupplied the Pole for winter operations.

It's interesting to note from the Cruse book photos and other documentation that the arrival of the USAF aircraft seemed to be a last minute plan, as the Public Works folk had to scramble to prepare a new skiway for the aircraft at short notice, and at least from the quantity of cargo delivered, it is not inconceivable that the inland stations would have lacked adequate supplies for the winter if the extra aircraft had not happened.

Col Turk later wrote to the magazine *Aviation Week* regarding Mr Norwall's coverage including many interesting facets of the area as well as many of the military units that have played, and will continue to play, an important role in the exploration of the continent with one important exception. *'The exception is the 61ˢᵗ Troop Carrier Squadron, which in January and February 1960, made aviation history when it demonstrated the feasibility and capability of conducting sustained aircraft operations into remote areas of Antarctica- the synopsis of our mission was as follows.*

From March to October 1959, the 61ˢᵗ TCS with twelve ski-equipped aircraft assigned, operated on the Greenland Ice Cap as part of the Dew Line extension project. In the late summer of that year, the squadron was ordered to prepare for an emergency mission to Antarctica in January 1960.

After resolving serious logistic problems with our cooperative Navy hosts, the first mission was flown to Marie Byrd site on January 25ᵗʰ 1960, just twenty days after leaving our home base and three days after touching down on the Williams snow strip. Thus modern aircraft was introduced to Antarctica and the cumbersome inefficient airdrops by C-124 Globemasters was elevated with those two landings. So the 61st mission continued all vital supplies delivered with 30 missions to Byrd and 28 to the South Pole. VXE-6 assumed the aircraft mission the following year.

My interest in the subject is personal as well as professional. You see I had the honour and indeed privilege of commanding the 61ˢᵗ squadron for the Greenland operations and for the Antarctic missions. Without a doubt it had the most talented, professionally qualified and dedicated personnel one could ever hope to serve with. They were the finest of the finest and I don't want their accomplishments to go unrecognised.'

Pressure from Admiral Tyree had the first four new ski-equipped C-130BL Hercules diverted from the original USAF contract to the Navy's VX-6 Squadron in August 1960. They were similar in appearance to the C-130A apart from their four bladed propellers, and Lockheed incorporated major improvements giving them greater performance. The 'B' also had more powerful engines, greater fuel capacity and greater structural strength, allowing them to operate at higher gross weights, which resulted in the squadrons improving their Antarctic operation's payload range. The ski assembly was the same as the C-130D's, allowing the plane to land on either skis or wheels.

The first C-130B *BuNu 14831* arrived in the Antarctic on October 29 1960, commencing polar operation the next day. This aircraft was later buried in the ice for sixteen years before it was recovered and returned to Antarctic service with the New York Air National Guard.

Cdr Elbert B Binkley averaged better than 308mph in setting a new speed record for the flight from Christchurch to McMurdo on the initial fly in, in a C130 BL, flying at 24,000 feet and carrying a five ton load of spare parts and ground support equipment.

One of the USAF 1608ᵗʰ Air Transport Wing's [ATW] C-130-E was deployed to Christchurch with 18 personnel during November and December 1962, and while there the aircraft # *62 1785* made its first proving flight to the ice on November 29ᵗʰ.

During the season major structural work had to be carried out on the deterioration of Byrd Station that was one of the first stations constructed in *Deep Freeze I*. While major bracing had been carried out earlier, Washington could not delay the station's replacement any longer.

Following consultations with the US Army who had recently built a new scientific station on the Greenland icecap, the Navy consider the same radical building approach at Byrd. The new buildings would be constructed inside deep trenches with arched roofs that allowed the snow to blow over them. With the station buried below ground level, the Navy envisaged that as occurred in Greenland the drifting snow would simply blow across the level surface and not accumulate. The new Byrd station was built over six miles from the original site.

However in order to dig these tunnels 9 to 12 metres wide and six feet deep, the navy had to have snow milling machines delivered to the site. To deliver these *'Peter'* snow machines from France, the USAF deployed the largest cargo aircraft at the time to land at Christchurch - the two Douglas C-133 Cargomasters that could lift 24 tonnes of cargo over seven thousand km.

The largest assembly of giant transport aircraft ever seen at one time in New Zealand, attracted thousands of locals to Christchurch International Airport on October 15 1960 the USAF's Douglas C-

133C, Cargomasters, with a payload of 117,000 lbs, and weighing in at over 100 tons, arrived. The two aircraft *[59 0523, 59 0527]* were each carrying a giant 'Peter' snow-moving machine, which had been transported from France for the special construction project at Byrd Station. The Douglas Cargomasters could lift 24 tonnes [52,000 lbs] of cargo over 7,408 km at a cruising speed of 520 kph [323 mph]. The C-133C was eight metres longer than the Globemaster, and could be converted to carry more than 200 troops fully equipped, or used as an ambulance. They carried a wingspan of 179 feet, a fuselage of 157 feet and were 48 feet to the top of the tail. These huge bellied aircraft were specially designed for military use in the guided missile age.

While on the tarmac at Christchurch, the two transport giants were parked alongside eight C-124 Globemasters, four VX-6's LC-130's, two squadron Rescuemaster's, a C-121 Super Constellation and two P2-V Neptune's, becoming the largest assembly of giant aircraft at any one time in New Zealand. Each of the C-133, unloaded 30 tons of machines, spares, and weather station equipment.

The total cost of the nineteen America military aircraft was estimated in 1959-dollar terms at approx $40 million.

Misfortune continued to plague the USAF'S Troop Carrier Squadron. Two giant USAF C-124's made an emergency landing on October 16 1960 after the aircraft had covered two thirds of the flight from Christchurch to McMurdo, when Captain Wilcox received a radio message to return to Christchurch because a blizzard had closed in the ice runway at McMurdo. He had reached the point of safe return, but running into headwinds of 60 knots on the return trip, the fuel began to run dangerously low, and at 1.30am, Invercargill airport was requested to stand by for an emergency landing.

At this point *Deep Freeze* Headquarters in Christchurch had the USAF's four-engine Douglas SC-54D Rescue master # *0-72567* airborne by 9pm, intercepting the C-124, 9000 feet above the Southern Ocean shortly after midnight. The SC-54D was equipped with a nose-mounted APS-42 search radar, large circular observation windows in the rear fuselage and an anti-skid braking system. It also carried four rescue flares, which could be air dropped to crews in distress and with each kit was included a 140kg 40 man life raft. Major H Eubel, deputy commander of the 9th Troop Carrier Squadron was the only passenger aboard the transport on his way to inspect the air facilities in the Antarctic.

With the headwinds gradually decreasing, the Globemaster flew north with its Air Force escort, but its fuel was running treacherously low, prompting Captain Arsenault the navigator to consider other arrangements as it was going to be touch and go whether they could reach Christchurch. Radio operator Staff Sergeant Owen informed Christchurch of this and both Invercargill and Oamaru airports were placed on standby for an emergency landing. South of Dunedin, the fuel gauges were registering 'very low' and at this stage it was critical every drop of fuel was needed, so the plane's commander turned the aircraft west and touched down at Invercargill at 2.46am, with the fuel gauges indicating it had enough fuel for half a hour flight and so would not have reached Christchurch.

Nor could the heavy aircraft have landed at Dunedin airport as there was no night flying facilities installed at the time, and no sealed runways, and the weight of the C-124 would have sunk it into the grass and caused major damage to the undercarriage.

The co-pilot Captain J Stihl commented, *'I would rather ditch at sea than land on a grass runway with this machine.'*

On deck to welcome the aircraft was Invercargill Mayor Mr A Adamson, who was informed of the emergency landing by airport officials at 4.30 am and immediately went to meet the deputy commander of the 9th Troop Carrier Squadron.

Six minutes later the Rescue Master aircraft landed, in case the 61 ton Globemaster's cargo had to be removed to allow the giant transport to get off the 4000 foot runway after taking on 1400 gallons of fuel to get it back to Christchurch.

However, its commander did not think it necessary and after refuelling departed for home at 5.53 am after being on the ground for a little under three hours. On making the emergency landing

Commander Wilcox and his crew had been in the air for 14 hours and 45 minutes and had flown 2800 miles.

The other three Globemasters in the flight returned to Christchurch safely early on Saturday morning, while Capt Wilcox and his crew were refuelling at Invercargill. The four fully loaded C-124's remained at Christchurch until the weather picket ship *Wilhoite* returned to take up her station at 60 degrees south. Only a VX-6 Super Constellation managed to fly south with scientists and American and New Zealand media aboard.

The squadron was honoured in 1960 by the scientists they were supporting, by naming a newly discovered 3000 foot mountain peak 'VX-6 Mountain.' There are over 132 VX-6 aviators who have been immortalized in Antarctica, with mountains, glaciers, bluffs, hills, spurs and peaks named after them.

The lifeblood of Polar flights was avgas, and with the induction of the Lockheed C-130 Hercules during *Deep Freeze –60* under the command of Captain William Munson, the squadron had its fair share of fuel supply problems.

One afternoon in the office of the CO, a weary group of VX-6 commanders were relaxing over a cup of coffee at an informal briefing on the dwindling fuel supply. '*Howizit?*' the Captain asked, '*Forty-four thousand gallons*' said Cdr Lloyd Newcomer, the squadron's operations officer and acting exec officer for the deployment, '*and this fuel has to be divided between the South Pole, the remote Byrd Station and the NSF base at McMurdo.*'

Captain Munson shook his head thoughtfully, while he sipped on his re heated mug of coffee. '*If the 'Alatna' doesn't arrive on time we're out of business.*'

Few US Naval Air Facilities are confronted with these logistical problems with an air facility 2100 miles from civilization and more than 12,000 miles from the United States, perched on the volcanic rock of Ross Island and the Ross Sea Ice Shelf which is shared with the New Zealanders a few miles away at Scott Base.

The fuel logistics facing Capt Munson and his senior officers were no different to his predecessors, except that this time there was the addition of the C-130's to the squadron's fleet with their insatiable demands on avgas and as McMurdo can only be resupplied by sea, it is compounded further by the relative inaccessibility of McMurdo Sound throughout most of the year. While planes flew from Christchurch in the early days of October, the task of resupplying the base by November or December each year relied on the tanker and cargo ships with the assistance of the icebreakers getting through the pack ice before that time.

During the first months of *Deep Freeze I* in 1955, the initial assault on Antarctica, the F E squadron's Neptune's and Skymasters would taxi up to the tanker *USS Nespelen* to refuel before launching their long range assault on the Antarctic interior, while two storage tanks were constructed at Hut Point near the camp, and two YOG's were towed through the *Roarin Forties*, the *Furious fifties* and the *Shriekin Sixties*'[latitudes] to locate the permanent anchorage off the Point. While fuel storage has greatly improved since the trial and error days of Task Force 43, annually fresh cries are voiced for better and more modern facilities.

Towards to end of *Deep Freeze –60*, the giant C-130 Hercules was first used with the USAF flying to Antarctica for the first time in February 1960, adding to Capt Munson's problems. With the aircraft encountering good weather, more flights than originally projected were flown in and this increased pressure on the already limited fuel supplies, so the supply of JP-4 fuel decreased proportionally and by early February only 70,000 gallons remained in Antarctica.

This caused concern for the squadron's senior chief aviation boatswain's mate Bob McKain who had wintered over. '*When we get that close, we need to watch our daily sitreps*, [situations reports filed by the tanker *USS Alatna* at that time en-route to Antarctica] *with our bloody fingers crossed'* he said.

With the introduction of the Hercules the navy had constructed an additional two 250,000 gallon tanks to store the JP-4, but even so the mighty Lockheed planes thirst for fuel increased daily. Now the Task Force was giving greater attention to opening more and more remote areas for scientific studies, and greater emphasis being placed on aerial mapping, and added to this was the unusual requirement of the squadron flying their Otters on a daily basis on '*bug runs,'* the aerial sweeps of the McMurdo area in an effort to collect airborne insects in nets protruding from the underside of the plane. Also, increased activities by the squadron's helicopter flights to Marble Point, Cape Royds, Taylor Dry Valley, Cape Crozier, Minna Bluff and many other locations near McMurdo Sounds where entomologist had established stationary nets to catch the tiny winged Antarctic bugs.

Outlying stations at the Pole and Byrd received their avgas and other fuel by drums airdropped by C-124's, but with the C-130, the Globemaster airdrops became unnecessary, as the ski-equipped Hercules could land on soft snow, whereby the C-124, required a hard landing strip for wheel landings and these areas are unavailable in the interior of Antarctic.

'And none too soon, was the general attitude of men at both stations who must take on the arduous job of locating, picking up and hauling the heavy pallets of fuel and other cargo to base' says Capt Munson. *'On 28 consecutive days in October and November last year the Globemasters flew over both stations and dropped drab-green parachuted pallets to the men below. Tractors and weasels would warp and weave over snow, battling four to five foot sastrugi in an Antarctic imitation of a wild west cowpunching.*

You see why fuel is such an important item in Antarctic operations as very few of the scientific studies could be conducted without it and as a direct result of its availability and expense, we are particularly careful to combine as many missions as possible.'

But as careful as planners are, both on the ice and in Washington, some fuel is wasted, not by irresponsibility, but by the capricious nature of Antarctica itself. The greatest loss occurred in *Deep Freeze 1*, when the tanker *Nespelen* loaded on fuel at Norfolk, then travelled to Antarctica via the Panama Canal, and after berthing briefly at the Port of Lyttelton to top up her tanks, she then challenged the polar pack ice obstructing the sea approach to McMurdo, where a slab of ice smashed into her hull, tearing a hole below her waterline causing 140,000 gallons of avgas to be lost.

While forty-one flights were made over the Pole during the season, dropping 538 tons of cargo, the men at Byrd chased down and collared 900 pallets of air dropped goods. Retrieving these pallets was especially hard at any high altitude as anyone who has engaged in this task knows all too well, that strenuous movements are sheer bloody agony, and frequent exertion is a danger to the lungs, even for the physically fit and able bodied man.

Richard Kramer, AD2 assigned to VX-6 at Byrd during the airdrops said retrieving was an all hands on with all rank being equal, '*the first few days were sheer hell, I think it was the altitude that made it so tough [Byrd Station is 5095 feet above sea level]. That, along with the cold, made your chest ache when you tussled with the cargo, but after awhile we got to pacing ourselves and that made the job a little easier.*

The hardest thing to handle was the parachute itself, as it weighed well over a hundred pounds and seemed heavier, then the wind would catch it sometimes and tear it out of your hands'.

Transporting drummed avgas to either the Pole or Byrd was expensive, achieving a value out of all proportion to its costs in the US. One official compared the cost in Antarctica, taking into account transportation costs, man hours and other variables, and concluded that plane commanders would have to shell out about $US 4.50 per gallon if they were to pay for it at the pump.

Senior Chief aviation boatswains mate, Bob McKain made a discovery in 1960 when he discovered that the extreme cold of Antarctica at times had a deteriorating effect on avgas. He sent avgas samples to New Zealand where tests were carried out that proved that the extreme cold of the

Antarctic winter actually lowered the octane content through stowage freeze, causing all the avgas tanks to drop in octane ratings below the acceptable standard.

'Almost all of it was saved by mixing the sub standard tank proportionately with acceptable fuel from another. There was a 500-gallon remainder in each of two tanks and this was contaminated gas, spoiled by water and sediment that normally we'd leave as a bottom and pump fresh gas on top, but this year, VX-6 wanted it.' Bob McKain said.

The squadron found an unorthodox use for this contaminated fuel for one of the veterans of the R4-D fleet *Charlene* after she had reached retirement age and was withdrawn from operational service after useable parts were removed and the stripped aircraft was hauled to the foot of Observation Hill.

During the previous year, transportation to and from the strip had got bogged down on the muddy road when the influx of the summer party arrived, and the base population quadrupled. Concerned at the number of its winter strengths and having the weasels experiencing breakdowns occurring faster than the maintenance personnel could repair them, the situation became critical, and as Capt William Munson viewed that situation he turned his entrepreneurial eye towards the stranded and abandoned *Charlene,* and reached a decision.

The aircraft was pulled from her parking lot, where metal smiths chipped her wings off and tightened her body; electricians checked her wiring, and maintenance crews readied her engines. On November 30 she was taxied out for her first 'flight' and renamed the *Wingless Wonder* taxi, lumbering across the snow for the four mile journey to the bay ice, covering the stretch in eleven minutes, compared to the weasels who on a good day, took half an hour.

She was now *#17274 The Great Antarctic Taxi* and the star attraction each time she made one of her runs, that was indeed a strange sight. Bob McKain explained that she runs on contaminated avgas that turns the engines all right, and if they decide to conk out, all that has to be done is to change the filters.

While the USAF Globemasters conducted their round the clock airdrop missions into the interior, Bob McKain and his crew ran an avgas pipeline built in 300 sections of 50 foot hose, a little over three miles from Hut Point to the McMurdo ice landing strip. This line fed one 15,000 and two 10,000-gallon reusable rubber bladders supplemented with two 5000 and one 2000-gallon bladder and one 2000-gallon ski mounted tank truck.

Later in the season as the day long Antarctic sun weakened the bay ice, the landing strip was moved further inland on the Ross Sea Ice Shelf, making every day a challenge for McKain and his crew, as the avgas and JP-4, like the mail, had to get through, a single pipeline was run over the saddle formed by two hills leading to the ice barrier from nearby Scott Base.

Six VX-6 aviators missed death by a foot at Invercargill airport on October 12 1960, when their R4-D's twelve rockets failed to fire.

It was just before 10pm on a cool Invercargill morning, after the crew had enjoyed a hearty Kiwi breakfast that the R 4-D pilot Commander J .W Weeks, started his plane down the runway. His normal procedure for the JATO was to fire the first bottles when he had covered approx 1000 ft of runway, but as the aircraft sped down the runway it showed no signs of rising with the already roaring engines belching red and its landing lights turned on. As the airport's lone fire tender crew raced some distance behind, they saw the aircraft raise slightly but gain no height. Several seconds later, the plane's command radioed the control tower in a calm voice that the rocket bottles had failed to fire, a few seconds passed as he neared the end of the runway when he again radioed 'OK'.

The next message from Commander Weeks was that he had jettisoned the JATO bottles not long after clearing the runway, and asked the controller if they were likely to cause any damage to property, to which the controller, Mr Benfell replied that stock could possibly be grazing in the area and asked the pilot if they were likely to have a delayed action explosion. The pilot radioed back. *'I don't bloody know'*, his concern was that if the unexploded rocket bottles were still attached to his plane they would explode on him.

With the fire crash vehicle scouring the area for the bottles, Commander Weeks radioed back that the bottles would not jettison when he pushed the button, but his crew were still checking. A collective sigh of relief in the Invercargill air traffic control tower when twenty minutes later Commander Weeks radio back to say that the bottles were still attached, and he would jettison them in the sea near Stewart Island. One local was heard to say, *'No one was meant to die last night'*.

Commander J Butcher, at flight operations in Christchurch, when told of the near tragedy commented that they were very lucky, while a senior VX-6 officer believed that the pilot would have calculated the take-off in the event of the JATO bottles not firing. He would have calculated his all up weight, the length of the runway and other factors, and from this he would have known whether he could have taken off, and with a 4000 ft runway and 40,000 pound load, he should have made it, and he did.

On November 25 1960, a US Marine Corp R4-D-8 BuNu *17219* JD/9 [the Squadron's fleet side numbers were changed to JD-Jig Dog], named *Semper Shafters,* while flying over rugged Antarctic terrain from Byrd Station, landed on a rough snow surface in the Horlick Mountains, suffering serious landing gear damage. After temporary repairs were carried out the undercarriage was patched up sufficiently to limp back to the McMurdo Air Facilities. On her return flight, she was overtaken by another Gooney Bird R4D-5 *BuNu 17246* XD/8 *Little Horrible-Korora II* who escorted her home, the R4-D-8 was later loaded aboard a Navy ship and sent back to the States.

Chief Petty Officer Whit Whitney sent this yarn of his days at the Barrier in 1960- the Barrier was an emergency fuelling station at which four VX-6 personnel lived at a time, each day one person was the 'duty house mouse' whos tasks were as cook to melt snow for the group's water and washing supply, having all this carried out on a pot belly type stove. Sleeping in the Jamesway Hut, they could lie on their bunks in a double mummy sleeping bag on the top bunk and never need to zip it up as one would roast, but conversely if they placed a case of beer on the floor, the bloody thing would freeze in minutes.

Hanging on a peg right behind the stove was the 'picture frame' [loo seat] which was wrapped in towelling to protect your butt when you used it, and using it in times of need took more than courage. *'I relate this because an R4-D called in one day to drop off a doctor who was going to inspect the station'* relates Whit. *'The plane was going on to New Byrd and would pick him up on the return to McMurdo, but a whiteout condition occurred so the doc had to spend several days with us. By the time he left he had no comment to make as to our living conditions and handling of food, we kept the meat in a box outside the door, we used a wood saw to cut slabs from the frozen hamburger rolls and an axe to cut roasts of beef to the required size rather than thaw the lot, and upon entering the hut he noticed the picture frame and with a medical voice said it was not a sanitary thing to be hanging so close to the cooking stove.*

So he removed the towelling and set the picture frame outside the door in the snow and Antarctic blizzard conditions. We just looked at one another, stunned and in utter amazement thinking OK we will see who is the first to make THAT TRIP to visit Uncle Tom, and as it happened it was our medical man who had to respond to the call of nature, and stepped outside.

The loo was sheets of plywood with a door and on the inside was a wooden platform with a hole cut to put the picture fame on, when the turd tree built up and we couldn't sit down, all we had to do was dig another hole and shift the unit over. Needless to say, when the good doctor returned to the hut he came in with the picture frame in hand and proceeded to wrap the towelling around it again and hang it on the peg behind the stove, but we did notice he didn't sit for quite a spell. We reckon he must have taken some hide off his butt as the temperature on the Barrier that day hovered around 50 below zero.'

During the season, aviation storekeeper Richard Goodell won the title of Mr Deep Freeze hands down because he had participated in each of the Antarctica operations since they began in 1955 and the only man left of the original compliment. A year ago there were just five 'plankowers' left in the squadron, when yeoman Jerry Potter went to the Exam Centre at Great Lakes, photographer Walter Long went to NAS Brunswick, Main, Aviation Bos'n Jerry D Cole transferred to Seabees and reported to Port Lyautey and Chief Aviation Ordinance man Michael Baronick departed VX-6 for a new duty assignment, leaving Richard Goodell as the 'Last Plankower' in Antarctica.

Many developments in the Navy are predicted by chance and to some degree-by need, but the induction of the Lockheed Martin C-130BL Hercules into the Navy inventory is one of those chance occurrences for which LTjg Irving J Morrison, then an Ensign must take full credit. Ensign Morrison had just completed two months of schooling at the Limited Duty Officer's School at Newport, RI, successfully bridging the ranks between officer status and enlisted men. Morrison had the 'itch' for overseas duty and a touch of adventure within, and soon after being commissioned, he requested and received orders for deployment with VX-6 Squadron.

Before departing the States, Ensign Morrison decided to spend his leave with his sister in Marietta, GA, on his last R & R before following his mates to the Antarctica, and that was where the links in the chain of these strange circumstances began to weld together.

His brother-in-law worked as a Field Service Analyst Engineer at the Lockheed Martin Marietta Division, and took him to see the company's newest type cargo aircraft, the Hercules being modified by the USAF for snow landings.

After a coffee conference and a movie shown on the Hercules A model which had been in operation with the TAC's 463rd. Troop Carrier Wing since December 1956, the young enthused Ensign left the plant 'loaded down' with literature on the aircraft.

With his leave over, Morrison reported to VX-6 at NAS Quonset Point with all the aircraft's material tucked away safely in his new officer's briefcase and over the next few weeks was kept busy with orientation and training programmes in preparation for the ice, however one day with a group of other officers, including Cdr Jerry Barlow, then the squadron's executive officer and a Task Force 43 Commander, Morrison had an attentive audience who all appeared more than interested with his impromptu sales pitch for Lockheed. That week when the staff officer returned to Washington, he took with him all Morrison's literature, and as far as he was concerned, that was the end of the matter as the Department of the Navy had never before taken on board ideas of a recently commissioned officer.

His deployment hour had arrived and the Antarctic adventure he had wanted had begun at McMurdo as a member of VX-6 Alpha. No sooner had he arrived than he was called into Cdr Jerry Barlow's office, after a thanksgiving dinner *'Seems you've got something generated in the C-130 plane'* the Cdr Barlow said, *'and as you've already got your foot in the door at Lockheed, and if you want to take over the project, I'll have your wintering-over orders cancelled.'*

Surprised, Morrison took very little time to accept the assignment and returned to Quonset by the first flight available out of McMurdo, picked up his new orders and flew to Marietta to attend a series of conferences and subsequently became an active member of a Support Guidance Committee, which would direct the introduction of the Lockheed Hercules into the Navy's aviation supply system.

The off the shelf acquisition offered the most expeditious means of delivering the planes, and four were eventually ordered in time for *Deep Freeze 61* seasons. The Navy's version was configured according to the Navy's specifications and designed for Antarctic operations, and was obtained by the Navy 'off the shelf' from the USAF making it the first C-130 built for polar flying.

Since this was a completely new type of plane, the aviation supply system had no spare parts in their bins, which was essential for polar operations, providing the Navy with a serious new problem. The Bureau of Weapons [then BuAer] solved this by using a new system called Special Aeronautics Requirement [SAR] 398, and the induction of the Hercules with VX 6 was a test case of this system.

Basically SAR 396 called for the contractor to provide support until their own normal logistics support could be effected, subsequently speeding up delivery of the aircraft spare parts. This was the first application to an operational squadron, and also its first application of contractor support while the squadron was on deployment with the VX-6 at the bottom of the world.

In order to properly steer the direction of SAR 398, LTjg's Support Guidance Committee met monthly, and it was during these regular meetings that problems were raised, solution proposed, responsibilities delegated and deadline dates assigned for action. The System remained in effect until September '61, where at this point, the Navy's own supply systems caught up.

In the meantime Cdr Jerry Barlow and the squadron's assistance maintenance officer Joseph Moore flew to Greenland to observe the Air Force C130A model in polar operational conditions, and when the pair returned to home port were both impressed and jubilant at the prospect of the plane's potential in Antarctica. After more discussions in Washington, at Stewart AFB, at Wright-Patterson AFB, and Quonset, VX-6 crew training was now on the agenda, as with the acquisition of a new type of aircraft that was so radically different, demanded they had to concentrate on this aspect of the programme, so over the next few months the Field Service School of the Georgia Division of Lockheed received many of the VX-6 men set for deployment in *Deep Freeze 61* at Marietta, with many attending more than one course during their training, depending on the requirements of the individual.

On August 4 1960 a large crowd gathered at ANS Quonset to watch the first two of the four C-130BL's touch down, and to watch their arrival and attend a ceremony conducted by Rear Admiral Benjamin Moore, were Rear Admiral David Tyree and Capt William Munson.

The day was a proud one for LTjg Irving J Morrison, as he watched *#148321* touch down and stop outside the VX-6 hanger- his dream had come true- eight-five days later the Hercules would make a ski landing at McMurdo to commence its operations, leaving for its first Antarctic flight the following day.

The Commander of Task Force 43 Rear Admiral David Tyree addressed the gathering.

'Since the early days of the 20th century, man's mode of travel has progressed through several stages from the primitive to the most modern. Scott's tragic march is a monument to courage and perseverance. Since that time [1911-12], travel on the ice and snow has seen the use of dogs, ponies, wheeled and tracked vehicles and a variety of aircraft. Today, we are privileged to receive C-130 Hercules inaugurating the latest in Antarctic travel.'

Capt Munson added: *'These planes will enable VX-6 to increase and improve its support of the Antarctic bases and the US Antarctic Support Programme, as they will fly higher, faster and will carry many more times the payload of our current aircraft.'*

His words were indeed prophetic, for by the end of the Deep Freeze 61, the squadron's three Hercules racked up a staggering tonnage of airlift materials, while the fourth C-130 was used soley for testing. They operated later into the season than any other aircraft had in the past before they returned to the US, and would be used for mercy dashes to the ice during the Antarctic winter and to begin regular mid winter flights.

By the end of the first season they carried 1700 tons to the South Pole and Byrd Stations, while two of them made a 2800 mile round trip from McMurdo to Eights Coast, across the frozen continent, this proving to be the longest logistics flight in the history of air operations within the Antarctic continent at the time.

With the commencement of *Deep Freeze 61* the Task Force 43 Command placed emphasis on improving the station's living conditions, operational safety, communications and weather forecasting, 1960-61 was the first field season conducted under the Antarctic Treaty, again providing the bulk of aviation support with 21 aircraft and assisted by the USAF's 9th Troop Carrier Squadron, with 10 C-124C's and 2 C-54's.

On October 31 a Lockheed WV-2 *Warming Star BuNo 126513,* and Lockheed *No 4467*-also know as EC-121K a specially configured Super Constellation previously used in Project Magnet, flew in from Christchurch, but because of a crack in the runway at McMurdo, the Connie attempted to land instead on the cross runway at Williams Field. Commander Bandy landed hard about 100 yards short of the runway, bounced in the air and landed again 50 yards short, its landing gear collapsing as it veered into a snow bank, tearing off one wing and breaking the fuselage behind the wing. Only one of the 23 men aboard was seriously injured.

At the time of the crash the plane's commander was occupied with a landing gear warning light, while his co-pilot was at the controls. Wreckage was strewn over quite a portion of the runway, causing another C-121 piloted by Commander D L Reckling, which had left Christchurch two hours after '*Project Magnet'* to remain in the air over the base for over an hour until the wreckage was cleared away.

The Lockheed WV-2 was not a VX-6 Squadron aircraft, its mission, and why it was in the Antarctic is still a mystery, even those on the ice at the time 'were kept in the dark' as to its appearance. The only comment was that the cold war still existed and the Russians had a base at Vostok near the Geomagnetic Pole and Sovietskaya near the Pole of Inaccessibility, so it was rumoured to have been a covert operation.

The C-121 used was a virtual flying magnetic observatory. *Project Magnet* was one of the major scientific studies. The Super Connie *El Paisano,* operated by the Navy's Hydrography Office, had completed a number of spectacular missions in the study of magnetic forces within the Southern Ocean. Seven days before its demise at McMurdo, the Connie had just completed the first non-stop flight from Antarctica to Australia, on a route from McMurdo via the South Magnetic Pole to Hobart, Tasmania, a distance of almost 3,700 miles in just 16 hours. A week later the $6 million flying laboratory lay scattered over the ice at Williams Field, *El Paisano's* next scheduled flight was to have been another record-breaker from McMurdo to Perth Western Australia, and then on to South America.

Immediately after the crash, a VX-6 helicopter flown by Lt. J Hahn and Lt. G A Hickley with three doctors aboard was on the ground, making three trips to carry the injured to the stations hospital, and although this was the first accident at McMurdo that season, it had not involved men employed in the American programme.

Immediately after the crash, the navy's priority was to remove all the scientific equipment considered to be sensitive, from the crippled plane before attention was given to the injured.

The seven men [six of whom were stretcher cases] were flown back to Christchurch aboard the C-121, piloted by Commander Reckling with the flight back from McMurdo, in 8 hours 35 minutes. The resident naval surgeon, Lt. J W Potter, who had flown to McMurdo to escort the US Naval Surgeon-General Rear Admiral B W Hogan around the Antarctic bases, accompanied them.

The only other VX-6 Squadron C-121 to crash in the Antarctic was during *Deep-Freeze 70,* when *BuNo 131644* JD/1 -[Lockheed Serial No4145] *Pegasus* was destroyed while landing at Williams Field on the first day of the summer season. With 68 aboard including a crew of 12, it was the seventh aircraft to depart Christchurch for the Antarctic that season. Some half-hour before arriving, the weather suddenly deteriorated to zero visibility in a blinding snowstorm, but with no alternative airfield, and the aircraft low on fuel, the pilot made several low-level radar controlled approaches all unsuccessfully. On the last attempt, and with almost no fuel, he landed, veered off to the right of the runway leaving the C-121 seriously damaged, but without any crew injuries. Rear Admiral D.F Welch told this writer at the time, that having it crash so close to the runway with only one wing attached and in full view of aircrews and incoming passengers is not good for the morale.

Another C-121J- *BuNo 131624* JD/6 [the sides change to JD from the original XD] named *Phoenix* was flown back to Davis-Monthan AFB in 1968 after 13 accident free years service with VXE-6, and was retired on March 16 1971.

A Sikorsky HRS-3 *BuNo 139162* crashed in a heavily cravassed area in adverse weather while flying off the Eights Coast on February 15 1961.Assigned to Detachment 12 on board the *USS Staten Island* [AGB-5] the helicopter's engine caught fire and exploded injuring two of the crew and the HRS-3 was declared a strike.

1960 marked a milestone for the squadron when VX-6 personnel received their LC-130BL Hercules from Lockheed, which arrived at their base at Quonset Point on August 1, and planned to commence operational missions that season.

Early in *Deep Freeze 60,* a young twenty-year-old Navy photographer/ journalist, Robert Woods was to arrive at McMurdo for a two-year tour of duty, including wintering over at the Pole Station. However, after arriving in Christchurch he was forced to spend almost a month there, giving him time to get romantically involved with a young Kiwi lass as many of the yanks had done, before heading to the ice.

It took the Navy three attempts to get him to the Pole, but he finally flew south in the USAF's C-124 Globemaster. Half way there all onboard were instructed to get into their Antarctic gear as the temperature in the aircraft was to be turned down, so when they landed, our young photographer was still in his bulky clothing and very naïve as well.

Wanting to relieve himself in a hurry, there he was as cold as hell, trying to get through all these layers of US Navy cold weather clothing, which measured four inches thick, and of course the cold weather had shrunk his 'you know what' to an inch in length, so there was our intrepid photojournalist trying to have a 'wee' through four inches of clothing with a shrivelled up one inch peter - hard to do at the best of times.

On arriving at the main camp at McMurdo he headed for the photo lab, to be told to quickly repack his gear and catch the first plane to the Pole, his first experience of Antarctic interior travel. This was the first aircraft to land at the Pole that year, and at minus 86 degrees such were the conditions that the Hercules almost never made it as the skis froze to the snow from the heat created by friction on landing, and then there was difficulty getting two of the engines to start. To anchor the Herk while it revved up its engines enough to get the other two started, a D8 was brought in to hold it steady through this operation.

Our newcomer photographer was sucked in by his new mates on the first day he was there after he foolishly asked directions to the photo lab, and was told to go out the door of the mess and turn north. They had him 'hook line and sinker' for no matter what direction he went in it was always north, but on his twenty-first birthday he walked around the pole 21 times. *'I was feeling good that day, as the Station's doctor broke open a case of miniature brandy bottles for myself and a scientist whos birthday was the next day'.*

He later recalls spending the summer support season in the photo lab at McMurdo while the other squadron photographers were flying mapping the continent. He was sent back to Christchurch for the Christmas break before heading back to Antarctica as the winter set in. *'We all had cars, I had an old Austin and all the guys would go out to where the R5-D's were parked and fill our gas tanks with 115/145 avgas- Boy did these little cars fly down the Christchurch streets.*

After we had all left McMurdo for home, the squadron had the task of rescuing an ill Russian scientist, so a C-130 landed at McMurdo then flew off to Byrd Station to pick him up. The crew at McMurdo worked in freezing sub zero temperatures hand carving the ice runway, setting out drums with pots on the top for lights- it was dark and cold- bloody cold. The Hercules made an emergency seaplane landing that is dropping 15-20 feet levelling off again then dropping again until the pilot touched down on the ice. We were having some kind of a whiteout at the time.'

One task in which the entire camp assisted was as a chain gang for removing an R4-D's engine which under normal conditions would take about eight hours to change, but not in Antarctica in the winter months. On this occasion the aircraft was located near New Zealand's Scott Base, and as they could only work two hours a day, even the cooks put meals on hold and helped by passing the tools to the squadron's mechanics.

'In the squadron hanger, we hung a fur lined toilet seat over the heat stove, if you had to use it, you removed it from the peg and went out to the outhouse, did your business and rehung it back for the next guy. The stations outhouses had five seats each, and sometimes all seats were taken, so the best way to hurry them up and quicken their operations, was to open and close the doors many times, creating cold drafts- they finished fast then!' Robert Woods remembers even after 40 years.

The first Hercules to arrive, were the ski-equipped LC-130F/R models. The Navy's LC-130 were based on the C-130H, but powered by 4,910-esph T56-A-16 turboprops, these were the second ski-equipped sub-type to be operated by the in the Antarctic. Five aircraft were delivered in November 1968, BuNo's XD 155917[Lockheed No 4305] 159129/XD05 [4508], 159130 /XD 04 [4516] and 148318/XD 00 [3562].

The first to enter Antarctic duty BuNo *XD 155917* was totally destroyed in a crash at the South Pole in 1973. After the Navy took delivery of the BuNo XD 155917, the National Science Foundation funded the remaining five on order from Lockheed, while the US Navy flew all five.

The following Hercules carried Lockheed production numbers *45519* /XD07 [3564] *148320*/XD06 [3565], *14831* /XD03 [3567] and *148331*.

During the 1961 season, three C-130's completed the longest flights in Antarctic history when they flew a 2,730-mile roundtrip from McMurdo to Ellsworth Highland without refuelling. A C-130 with a VX-6 Squadron crew flew from McMurdo to the South Pole and down to Greenwick Meridian to a point where the peaks of Princess Martha Coast were visible, bettering this flight on February 22 1963 without incident.

On February 8 1961, Rear Admiral David Tyree, with the assistance of his aide Lt.Cdr Douglas Madison, raised the first 50 star American flag at the South Pole, *'Don't asked me why it took so long to get a new 50 star flag down there'* commented the VX-6 veteran Bruce Raymond. The 50th star was added to Old Glory when Alaska was granted statehood on January 2 1959, and the flag is now on display at the Smithsonian Institute in Washington DC provided by Rear Admiral Furlong, USN [Ret].

'In VX-6 a house is not always a home- it is sometimes a shop, believe it or not,' the Navy Aviation News reported in October 1961.

Necessity the mother of invention, had another blessed event at the squadron's spaces at NAS Quonset Point – she gave birth to ten metal house trailers, with all ten resting glumly, briefly and so very beaten up, but otherwise usable to anyone with 'do it-yourself' skills, like handyman Tim Taylor, at the end of VX-6 camp near Land Plane Hanger Four.

Why you asked? The squadron is hard up for housing- not uncommon in the armed service.'

During last season's operations at Williams Field- Antarctica International Airport, the squadron's maintenance department was pressed for shop space- especially since the main camp at McMurdo is located some four miles away with to and from transportation at a continuous premium.

So LTjg Harold F Buchberger, the squadron's assistant maintenance officer came up with a solution to the problem facing the men. He suggested the procurement of ten manufactured cargo sheds; this idea was turned down flat, because among other things, of the cost involved.

Then last July, someone spotted a Navy surplus catalogue lying around the room which listed 60 house trailers up for tender at Melville, Rhode Island trailer Park. LTjg Buchberger jumped at the idea as just 'what the doctor ordered' with the thought of acquiring ten units being the answer to his prayer. Subsequently his bid was successful and before long the house trailers were delivered.

Squadron personnel started to cannibalise the units with gusto, tearing off such unnecessary accoutrements as screen doors and furniture, returning these items to the surplus stockpile. Usable stoves and sinks remained, and a group of welders from MCB-1 Davisville, welded steel frames onto the bottom of the trailers running the length of each unit, to work as elongated skis.

The trailers were then hauled to Davisville where they were loaded aboard cargo ships for their journey to Antarctica and then offloaded at McMurdo to be used for maintenance shops, storage and also as personnel quarters to provide much needed emergency sleeping accommodation for the large number of men who would be participating during the following season- the Navy's seventh.

In Antarctica, fire has always been the biggest fear for personnel, due to the lack of water, and knowing how fire spreads at an alarming rate the squadron members are always on alert to detect the menace which they know can occur at any time.

Late in the evening in February 1961, a major fire fanned by 25-35 knot winds, broke out in two Quonset Huts, hampering the efforts of fire fighters and causing over $US200,000 damage. Both buildings, housing a parachute loft and an aviation electronics shop, were burnt to the ground, resulting in the loss of expensive electronic equipment required for maintenance repairs of VX-6 aircraft and diminishing the potential of the Squadron's para-rescue team.

When the fire was first discovered at 10pm, it was feared that Richard Spaulding Parachute Rigger Second Class was in his bunk in the parachute loft, but he was in fact the first on the scene when the alarm sounded.

In late March 1961, word was received that a Russian scientist was suffering from a bleeding ulcer, which led the United States to launch a mercy flight that was to become an historic first, by piercing the Antarctic winter darkness.

Mr Kuperov was first admitted to the routine list by Lt Donald R Walk, UC, USN, Officer in Change and Medical Officer at Byrd Station on March 19, after he had complained of nausea, vomiting and intense pain in his abdomen. After tests for appendicitis proved negative, and with no background as to the patient's history, Dr Walk's first diagnosis was that that Kuperov had an upset stomach, but soon realized that such an obviously acute abdominal condition was much more serious.

By March 22, following a period of rest, Kuperov appeared to be on the mend, but four days later, he could not get out of bed nor eat and was convinced that he had a 'frozen kidney' due to the cold conditions at Byrd. During the late evening of March 27, Mr Kuperov was in constant pain, and with a language barrier, an attempt was made the following morning to make contact with Mirnyy to have their doctor talk to him, with the Soviet doctor diagnosing his illness as a sore on the stomach walls, and suggested urgent treatment.

On March 31, after a voice radio conference with Lt Jack W Potter, MC, USN the decision was made that Mr Kuperov's condition was becoming a chronic problem with the possibility of further complications, so on April 1, Rear Adm David Tyree ordered the already alerted C-130 # *148312* aircraft, under the command of Lt.Cdr. Lloyd Newcomer, to begin their mercy dash, departing Quonset Rhode Island on a 26,500 mile, 69 hour return flight. It was to be the first winter flight undertaken by VXE-6, and a test for other such dangerous winter flights to the Antarctic. [This mission was superceded three years later, when in June 1964 a C-130 # *148321* returned to McMurdo to evacuate a seriously injured US serviceman back to Christchurch.] Aboard the C-130 #*148312* with Lt.Cdr Lloyd Newcomer were 16 personnel, including a spare crew, a linguist and medical officers and a second back-up C-130 under the command of Lt Ronald F Carlson.

They reached Christchurch on April 4, but weather delayed the aircraft's departure from Christchurch for four days. The icebreaker USS *Staten Island* made a dash from Lyttelton, leaving New Zealand on March 31 and arriving at the ocean station 60 degrees south at 0700 on April 5th in order to cover the rescue mission, while a second C-130 Hercules was on standby at Christchurch as SAR aircraft.

On the ice, the Seabees at the Navy Air Facilities at McMurdo, and the party at Byrd, had readied navigational aids, ground control approach equipment, fuel for the aircraft, and had the skiways ready for the rescue operation at both stations by April 5, with the aircraft scheduled to arrive that day.

By April 6, Mr Kuperov's diet had been increased to include oatmeal and small amounts of plain spaghetti, this slight improvement in his condition allowed for a consumption of large amounts of milk. Haemoglobin studies on the following day showed no change, and the question continued to exist as to the cause for his loss of blood.

Meanwhile back in Christchurch, the weather in Antarctica was giving the flight planners some concern, delaying the mercy mission three times before finally at 1250 on April 8, Lt.Cdr Newcomer and his double crew including passengers, photographer PHC Frank 'Kaz' Kazukaitis, Cdr Price Lewis, Representatives of the Chief of Naval Operations, Lt.Cdr James Corley Legal Officer US Naval Support Force Antarctica and Lt Jack Potter US Naval Support Force Medical Officer and a passenger to McMurdo Cdr James Broshahan, Commander Antarctic Support Activity, Naval Air Facility, McMurdo.

Remaining in Christchurch were the back up crew lead by Lt Ronald Carlson, all knowing that with the austral winter darkness rapidly approaching, and temperatures in Antarctica steadily falling, speed was of the essence if the injured Russian scientist Leonid Kuperov, who by now had lost fourteen pounds, was to be rescued. It would be a race against time for the VX-6 crew, knowing that by April 25th, only two weeks away, twenty-four hour darkness would shroud the continent, and the crew didn't particularly care to winter over in the Antarctic dark.

Special pre-flighting was conducted prior to the critical 917 miles from McMurdo to Byrd Station, and the Hercules was given a thorough going over with a fine-tooth comb. Recalled Don Angier, *'At that time of the year, we still had a five hour window of murky twilight at Byrd Station, and we had to time our arrival with that window.'* It must be remembered that while on the mercy mission from Christchurch, the crew had no navigational aids, only celestial shots with the sextant.

The C-130 remained at Byrd Station only long enough to pick up Kuperov and get him back to Christchurch to be hospitalised, thus proving the feasibility of such winter flights and the ability of the Navy's Penguin Airlines to operate in the darkness, so Antarctica no longer needed to be isolated seven months of the year.

Airlifting back to the edge of the continent, the C-130 was refuelled for the eight-hour flight back to Christchurch, taking on 45,000 lbs of fuel, eight JATO bottles and several boxes of equipment they needed to backhaul.

The Hercules commander Lloyd Newcomer taxied the 70-ton aircraft and began his take-off ski run across the white expanse of ice and snow. *'I fired the JATO bottles at the stagnation speed and attempted rotation, but the plane would not get airborne',* recalled Bill Smith, Lockheed's marketing representative who was at that time Lockheed's technical representative assigned to Navy's VX-6 squadron on the mercy flight from Christchurch.

'We skied and bounced almost four miles across the snow- about 20,000 ft- trying to rotate, but we just couldn't get into the air. Cutting new tracks in the virgin snow was just too difficult for the aircraft to surmount.'

The crew joined in the barnstorming session when Smith suggested they taxi up and down for about a mile and compact the snow and ice into a ski runway. He also urged that the flight deck be cleared of everyone except two pilots and the engineer, getting the other 20 personnel to the rear cargo hold. This done, another take-off attempt was made, and this time the giant plane broke free of the snow at 4,000 feet and leaped into the cold air for the flight back to New Zealand. With the aircraft in the air for 23 of 48 hours from the time it had left Christchurch until it arrived back again, some of the crew had not slept for 26 hours, and upon arriving at 12.51 am on April 11, they were met by Rear Admiral David Tyree, who congratulated the crew on their historic achievement in breaking the traditional winter isolation in Antarctica.

The *USS Staten Island* left her station on April 10 and sailed for Wellington ten hours after the rescue mission was completed. Lt. Carlson and his crew, who had stood by in case of an emergency, left Christchurch for Quonset Point, while Cdr Newcomer and his crew rested in the city for two days, before they loaded cargo and passengers and began the flight back to the States.

On April 11, the Christchurch Star in an editorial *'A Flight To Remember'* wrote.

'Gratitude and admiration are the sentiments aroused by the successful completion of the world's most notable mercy flight. When the United States Navy's ski-equipped Hercules left Christchurch International Airport, manned by a complement of brave men, it was to face something never before encountered by flying men, so it is little wonder that those left behind had anxiety mingled with pride in what men will attempt to succour other men.

Over long miles of water and ice, on a route not previously traversed so late in the season, flew the Hercules, bound for McMurdo Sound, and then for Byrd Station, where lay the sick Russian scientist. Not only did those aboard face the normal hazard of Antarctic weather: they were also heading towards a land where the hours of daylight are few.

Now that it is all over, modest tendency is to regard the flight as more or less routine, but that in no way diminishes the value of this arresting example of the oft-repeated and several times proved phrase, that among those who face the perils of the polar regions national barriers mean nothing. There may be other flights like this, but there can never be one quite the same. It is something to remember as a stirring example of the call that humanity can exercise in the world where so much stress is apt to be laid on inhumanity.'

A few years ago I had the privilege of meeting up with Don and his lovely wife Joan at the Airport Plaza in Memorial Ave in Christchurch, a popular drinking hole for Squadron members as they passed through to take in the beauty of the South Island. Don recalled the historic flight over a cup of coffee, how the deep virgin snow and his aircraft's heavy payload almost prevented them leaving Antarctica. *'Of course on the whole mission from Christchurch the crew had no navigation aids and no en route weather forecasts. We flew by grid navigation and celestial shots with a sextant.'* VXE-6 squadron personnel who flew the evacuation mission were;

Cdr Lloyd Newcomer USN C-130 – Commander, Capt William Munson USN -Co-pilot and the squadron Commander Lt Donald Angier USN - VXE-6 Capt Richard Johnson USMC - Co pilot MSgt Henry Brown USMC - Co-pilot GV Sgt Fred Streitenberger USMC - Navigator. ADC Howard Murray USN – Navigator.AD1 John Beiser USN – crew Chief.AD1 Howard Hoffman USN – Flight Engineer, ADI Robert Parry USN - Flight Engineer.AE1 Charles Kovach USN - Mechanic. AMI Adrian Behrens USN – Electrician, AMI Franklin Daughtery USN – Metalsmith.AT2 Kenneth Starr USN – Metalsmith.At2 Joe McKinnis USN Radioman.

After the mission Leonid Kuperov returned to the Soviet Union and disappeared from public view, but in light of his condition reported to be improving one moment and serious the next, Antarctica was awash with speculations and rumours, by now a fertile breeding ground for conspiracy theories. Was the Russian really sick and what happened to him once he reached home? One theory was that the scientist wasn't really ill at all and that because of the cold war between the two super powers at the time, the Kremlin just wanted him back.

A recipient of the Distinguished Flying Cross, Commander Newcomer retired from the Navy in 1962, later working as a flight instructor at Jefferson County Airport in Colorado and as the chief research pilot at Boulder's National Centre for Atmospheric Research. Lloyd E Newcomer died from respiratory failure on December 18, 2003 aged 85, and his lasting memorial in Antarctica is the Newcomer Glacier, named in his honour for the accomplishment of that first winter landing there.

Cdr Martin Demetrius Greenwell took over the Squadron as their CO on June 17 1961 at the squadron's homeport hanger at Quonset Point. Turning to Capt William Munson, he said '*I relieve you, Sir*' followed by the usual cutting of the cake, to become the squadron's eighth commander.

Born on October 6 1917, at Morganfield Kentucky, Martin Greenwell's naval career spanned 33 years. Joining the service in 1941, he completed Naval Air Training at Corpus Christi Texas, and received his commission in August 1942. During his naval career he received the American Defence Medal, the Pacific/Asian Medal, WW II victory medal, the China Service medal, the Korean Service Medal [5 stars] and two Naval Commendations- even an Antarctic glacier was named in his honour. Martin flew rescue squadrons in the Pacific during WWII, participated in the Inchon Invasion during the Korean War before being promoted to Commandeering Officer of VX-6 Squadron.

After his Antarctic service, Cdr Greenwell headed up the war plan group for the US Atlantic Fleet and served as a US Navy representative to NATO forces in Iceland. Despite such lofty credentials, the now Captain Greenwell was always a humble hero, who passed away on September 16 2003 and was buried with full military honours at Arlington National Cemetery.

His long time friend, Columnist Dave Gibson of the '*American Partisan*' wrote his obituary. '*As the raindrops fell, the band fell silent, and a lone bugler played 'Taps' against a grey November sky. My eyes drifted between the solemn faced young men who were carefully and precisely folding the flag which draped his coffin and the tombstone which surrounded his grave, as I read the names and the wars in which they had given so much, I was overwhelmed and humbled by the very ground on which I stood. As the Captains flag was handed to his grieving niece, my eyes welled with tears. I was overcome not just from the sadness of a lost friend, but because he was safe and will always be with heroes. I am richer for having known him; he was a model of an officer and a gentleman. He will be sorely missed though his presence will forever remain. Farewell Captain- Farewell.*'

Attached to squadron VX-6 the P2-V7 *# 240437* became the first aircraft to fly over both Poles referred to as 'four-three-seven', piloted by Lt Little D Player and his eight man crew who accomplished this extraordinary feat on May 28 1961 during the Antarctic winter season, with another Neptune out of NAUD South Weymouth, Mass, who was at the time, operating in the Thule-Albert area as a backup search and rescue plane. Acting as a lifeguard for the North Pole, Lt Player and his crew had this sudden irresistible urge and sought permission which was duly granted for the flight over the North Pole- thus chalking up another first for the squadron.

Much in the way of scientific research was accomplished on this operation, as aboard the South Weymouth plane, which was equipped with wheels and not the skis it was fitted with for Antarctic operations, was using special equipment which mapped and uncovered details of the submerged ridges and mountains that both planes flew over.

The South Weymouth plane and VX-6's 'four-three-seven' operated in the far northern region from May 19 to 28th. Upon completion of the North Pole flight, VX-6 aircraft followed the other Neptune to Point Barrow, Alaska, where it continued more scientific missions. Lt Player and his crew returned to Quonset Point on May 31 to be greeted by their Commanding Officer Cdr. M D Greenwell.

The rest of crew were WW Weeks, R R Quain, D D Griffins, J Schohert, J M Ileardes, J T Jackson, J L Gary and J D Adams.

During *Deep Freeze-62* the squadron were operating three R4-D-8s and a lone R4-D-5, the 8's having spent the winter at McMurdo to be reactivated at the start of the season. While the other two made the long flight back to the states, as in previous seasons, the R4-D's carried out tasks principally for traverse and field party support flights to inland stations, setting out automatic weather stations and searching out proposed landing sites for Hercules.

They also flew weather probes in advance of the photo- reconnaissance missions of Michigan glaciological team who were investigating the valley glaciers that feed the Ross Sea. During the early part of *Deep Freeze –62* the party from the University of Minnesota engaged in geophysical research, were assisted by two of the Squadron's R4-D's from McMurdo, which carried the team to the foot of the Nimrod Glacier on October 30, then a few days later Dr Edward C Thiel was picked up and flown back to McMurdo so he could carry out an airborne magnetometer survey, but sadly he was killed in a Neptune *#140439* crash at Wilkes Station five days later.

The remainder of the party completed their 174 mile journey to a site in the vicinity of the Beardmore Glacier.

Antarctica is littered with the skeletons of man's endeavour to explore its forbidding surfaces with airpower and another was about to be added to its hostile environment, when on November 7 a Lockheed P2V-7P Neptune *BuNo 140439*, a former patrol bomber, modified with two jet engines and a metal bomb bay fuel tank, named *Bluebird* arrived at Wilkes Station under the command of Lt Eli Stetz. It had just made a magnetic survey of the little known eastern Antarctic by way of the Soviet Station Mirnyy, and Wilkes Station,. which had recently been handed over to Australia by the Americans. The project course was 3,500 miles and would at the time, set a new interior distance record from McMurdo by way of Mirnyy, with all going well until the stopover at Wilkes Station.

Bill Burch, a member of the Wilkes team at the time, recalls how the Neptune P2V crew and some of their team had driven back to their base to party, leaving Bill and a few of the volunteers to refuel the ex-bomber. Numerous 44-gallon drums of ATK were hauled to the airstrip on an Athey wagon behind a D4 driven by Max Berrigan, the PV-2's mechanic.

The most engaging feature of Max, which has stayed in Bill Burch's memory, was his teeth, an absolutely perfect set, always visible through a mouth that rarely closed as he chewed gum and talked simultaneously, *'A tricky manoeuvre which demands great facial mobility.*

He was in every way the epitome of what the movie and early TV had taught me to think of as the 'All American Boy', six foot something, crew-cut hair, big beaming smile, looked to be barely twenty. His mother must have been proud of him.

I think he was an aircraft mechanic and he and eight of his companions had just landed after a flight from Mirnyy, the final stop before McMurdo. Somehow almost of all the rest of the crew and ours, had hopped into the Weasels to go back to base, leaving just a few of us 'volunteers' to refuel.

'I remember too,' continues Bill in the story in *Aurora* *' feeling more than a little miffed when one of the first things he said after our self-introductions was 'That was one hell of a rough landing strip you guys have- nearly as bad as Mirnyy.'* Poor old Max had ploughed up and down with his D4 for hours, knocking off the tops of the sastrugi and making a strip as smooth a surface as he could, for there was not really a strip at Wilkes, just a slightly flatter area of plateau defined by survey pegs. But still it was a very happy meeting, being the first visitors we had seen all year, and this was November 7. The dog team was a big hit as of course there's nothing like animals to break the ice, if you pardon the metaphor.*

One can imagine refuelling the aircraft, as in those days it was pumped from drums with a single hand pump could be well compared with one of those crude parallels about porcupines and hot butter but what was more galling for me as my arm began to seize, was the fairly brisk flow out of some drain holes aft of the bomb bay area in the fuselage where the huge auxiliary tank had been mounted to give the aircraft its long range capability. After being assured by his mate, after questioning this curious exercise of pumping ATK out on the snow via the aircraft, my new found comrade dismissed it as 'pretty usual spillage'. He should know. I'd never even been close to a specialised aircraft like this before, let alone help refuel it.

So eventually the work was done and Bill trundled back to the station to join the party. Lofty, the cook had excelled again in the pastry department, [it was the only department in which he really excelled.] 'Eat it or wear it' attitude was his common riposte; fortunately the station's visitors had brought some meals on wheels in the form of fresh vegetables and meat, so Lofty's vernacular changed to 'we pigged out'.

The following morning, some of the ground crew who had not blown themselves away at last night's party, escorted the nine visitors back to the aircraft, to see them take-off.'

In the cockpit, the crew's comfort was much better than that of the passengers, who were plopped around the cramped passenger accommodation in jump webbing seating, mainly sharing its belly with the long-range fuel tanks.

Lt Commander William Counts and his co pilot Lt Romauld P Compton started the Neptune with a whine; this somewhat ungainly looking bird appeared to waddle over the wind blown snow waves like a pelican with outstretched wings to the edge of the more or less flattened sastrugi at the Wilkes airstrip, and it was away before the zoom lenses of Bill Burch's 16mm camera were released, so he had to follow the whole takeoff sequence with the long lens.

'The engine pitch rose to a scream making the propellers tear frantically into the still air, and a huge fluff of snow billowed out as the plane began to roll. Right on cue, I saw the JATO rocket flames spit rearwards, seeming to paint the side of plane in fire.

Hey, hang on! It didn't 'seem' at all, it WAS suddenly burning right into the tail and the plane was now well into the air, thrown there by the JATO's thrusts.

The sharp edged JATO flame had vanished, no long flaring from the bottle, but the P2V was engulfed in flames all over its rear section, and as it turned into a sharp left bank, I could hear some frantic garbled shout over the nearby Weasel's radio, about fire and smoke and not being able to see anything. I kept my camera rolling, but a nearby rise in the plateau screened us from the remaining drama.

I am sure we all hoped in those few seconds that somehow the pilot had succeeded in any kind of safe return to earth. But then a black geyser of smoke above our snowy screen signalled immediately that he had not. For the next few minutes it will forever remain the memory of all those on the ground, as the nightmare sequence of events unfolded.

Imagine riding pillion on a D4, going flat out across the sastrugi at about 10 mph trying desperately to cover perhaps a kilometer in case we could help. The Weasel beat us of course, and when we came over the brow of the rise we saw through the thick smoke, three shadowy figures staggering to the Weasel, all with their hands over their heads. In fact four had escape but the other five could neither be seen nor heard, while the heat from the burning wreck prevented us getting closer than 20 metres of the fuselage, which was largely intact, while the rest of plane was scattered over a wide area.

Apart from severe burns to exposed areas, those who escaped were only lightly injured. It was agreed that the five others must have perished and our priority lay with getting the injured back to base as quickly as possible. Max and I were asked to stay back and record the wreck site as well as we could, in case a blizzard wiped out vital evidence for the crash investigation, and locating bodies of the others for later recovery. For over forty minutes or so we paced and photographed all we thought was relevant and now the centre of the burnt out metal bird was cool enough to approach closely. Knowing where most of the crew had been sitting, it was obvious where they should be and led by the faint sickly smell of badly burnt flesh, we found a jumbled mass of almost unrecognisable bodies, all but one.

He was fixed in the remains of the exit doorway, his hands on what must have been the release lever- I knew who he was- my friend of less than a day ago.'

Five of the nine men aboard were killed. The subsequent investigation reported that the Neptune was subject to stress from exceeding the design limits of the aircraft during take-off from a very rough runway. At the time this Neptune had to land on a makeshift airstrip eight miles from

Wilkes Station, and while most of it was mainly smooth, it was covered by sastrugi between six inches and a foot high in places The Neptune had left McMurdo on Monday with two objectives, one was to deliver an American exchange scientists Dr. M E Pryor, to the Russian base at Mirnyy and the other was to carry out scientific research on the magnetic variations for a study being made by Dr. Thiel of the University of Minnesota.

They arrived at the Russian base about 1500 miles northeast of McMurdo on Monday, where they were delayed and didn't arrive at Wilkes until the Wednesday, to evacuate an Australian tractor mechanic who was suffering from a nervous breakdown.

Those killed were Lt Cdr. William D Counts USN, Lt. [junior grade] Romauld P Compton USNR, Petty Officer William R Chastain, James L Gray USN and Dr. E C Thiel a United States Antarctic Research Programme scientist. The survivors were the pilot, Lt. Stetz, Lt Hands and Petty Officers J.C Shaffer and C C Allen.

Dr. Thiel received immortality by having the Thiel Mountains named in his honour and as he was the chief seismologist at Ellsworth Station from 1956 to 1958 and the leader of the traverse party which discovered a submarine trough in the Weddell Sea, that too was named the Thiel Trough at the insistence of Dr Albert Gray, whom the trough had been originally name after.

Lt Cdr William Courts also had two Antarctic features named in his honour- Mount Courts and later the Courts Icefalls. Ltjg Compton has the ice filled *Compton Valley* named after him and for Petty Officer Chastain the *Chastain Peak,* and Petty Officer L F Gray – *Grey Spur.*

Billy-Ace Penguin Baker wrote *'It was only fitting that all of the landmarks honouring the men killed in this crash are located together in the Thiel Mountains. They died together and they are immortalized together. Not even a rock, nor a nunatack was named to honour the two known survivors, not then, and not later were they so immortalized.'*

Two theories were advanced for the crash. One blamed the jarring loose during take-off of an auxiliary fuel tank located in the Neptune's bomb bay, spilling the contents, which ignited and caused an internal explosion.

The other was that a JATO bottle stored at the rear of the plane had been shaken, impacted and ignited. *'In either event'*, writes David Burke in *'The Story of Antarctic',* an explosion ripped through the plane, filling it with flames and smoke, blind and choking, Stetz and his co pilot fought to bring 'Bluebird' down, but lost control and smashed into the plateau ice. Five passengers died in the fiery wreck, four of them navy men. The New Zealand Army provided a guard of honour for the bodies of the deceased crews on arrival at Christchurch.'*

In December 1961, two Russian aircraft landed at Christchurch Airport for the first time, enroute to Antarctica to service their base at Mirnyy Station. However, the aircraft had to fly via McMurdo, as there was a lack of weather data which would allow a direct flight. On the trip south each aircraft, an Antonov-12 and an Ilyushin-18, had a VX-6 pilot on the flight deck to assist the Soviets on the flight south. The Russian aircraft returned to Christchurch direct from Mirnyy on January 25 1962, and returned to Christchurch the following season.

On the morning of December 7, a squadron's R4-D picked up a three man glaciological team moving them to a location some 30 miles to the north of the Amundsen Glacier, leaving with them two motorized toboggans, fuel for 300 miles running and enough food for six weeks, along with their camping, surveying and glaciological equipment.

Three days after the Neptune crash at Wilkes, a VX-6's R4D-8L *BuNo 17219* was declared unsalvageable, after it crashed while landing three scientists from the Minisota University, who were to conduct bedrock geological surveys in the Sentinal Ranges and establish their camp site. The R4-D was operating about 450 miles from Byrd Station when it struck high hard sastrugi as it landed, collapsing the starboard landing gear and throwing the aircraft on its wing, resulting in substantial damage. Immediately news of the mishap reached Byrd Station, a R4-D set out to pick up the eight crew and passengers, but bad weather forced the flight back having another Dakota dispatched to the crash site.

During *Deep Freeze –62,* the squadron were engaged in a new type of traverse, one that was to grow in importance in the years to come to support a topographic survey by the United States Geological Survey, when the army sent two turbine-powered helicopters to Antarctica. These machines had the huge advantage of being able to carry topographic engineers to high mountain altitudes, but were limited to only relatively short range missions, subsequently the Task Force command were limited in their principal function of supporting the survey parties.

Fuel caches had to be laid out, supplies had to be brought in and campsites had to be moved, so these operations were carried out by the R4-D's who in a few days were able to lay out fuel caches between McMurdo Sound and Beardmore Glacier to the south and McMurdo and Hallett Station to the north.

The squadron's four R4-D's flew 980 hours, carried 450 passengers and 183 tons of cargo, but this was not achieved without mishap, as one mission which did not get into Cdr Greenwell's report, was a landing beside a heavy traverse, carrying supplies and equipment, which had been salvaged from the former Little America V to Byrd Station. One R4-D-8 lost its tail wheel, so those on the ground simply hoisted the plane's tail with the boom of a D-8 tractor, fixed a new pin, and the plane's commander took off.

In 1962 came the sad demise of the iconic R4-D # *17274 Charlene* the now wingless taxi, after being left for disposal on an ice flow in the Ross Sea.

James Waldron recalls he brought the then damaged aircraft back around the snow skiway and executed an excellent and truly professional landing, but it was the last time Eddie Frankewicz 'baby' ever flew. That night after the movie a real Antarctic storm broke, bringing high winds and snowstorms to the airfield.

'One of the ground crew in checking the two R4-D's, found that one of them had broken free from their tie downs and had moved 'somewhat' from where it had been parked by Harvey. He ordered a small crew together and re-tied 'Charlene'. They noted that her wingtip was broken from when Harvey Speed landed and the starboard wing had dug into the snow after his starboard engine had again failed, striking the hard surface and dragging some distance in the snow.

He located me and says that the flapping wingtip was getting violent and that he thought we [him and I] should go out with a stepladder and a hacksaw to cut the wingtip free from the aircraft, he said it was far too dangerous to ask the maintenance crew to do the job that we, as officers, should do instead and I agreed.

So with the ladder and hacksaw in hand we started out to the aircraft. The blowing wind and snow was so blinding, we had to walk to the aircraft with only our internal sense of direction telling us the way. We spent much time zigzagging back and forth until we practically walked into the side of the R4-D without seeing it until the last second.

Harvey had me climb the tall stepladder and hold the wingtip with the weight of my body while he sawed away with the hacksaw. After a long period of sawing, Harvey said that he was almost finished cutting and that I should hold on tightly as possible to the wingtip. Well, when the cutting was done the 50knot wind that was blowing, jerked the wingtip from my hands as though I had not been holding it, and the entire wingtip [6 ft x 5 ft] disappeared downwind and we never saw it again.

Well, getting back to camp was a lot easier than finding the two aircraft had been, all we had to do was walk with the wind to our backs and in a short while we were back to the hill leading up to our quarters. Later, we flew back to Little America in BuNo 17246 and picked up a replacement R4-D and returned to McMurdo to continue setting up Beardmore Camp for the summer ahead. After that I'm told she was converted into a Taxi- a wingless R4-D taxi.'

Buz Dryfoose recalled later, that the cruise book-DF-60, showed *Charlene* in all her fine glory, but wingless, *'I drove her on her maiden run with Captain Munson, our skipper, and she was a good source of transportation, it took her four to five minutes from Mac to Willy Field.*

After she was written off the books as a viable aircraft, we just got in and loaded it up with Pax and firewalled the go handles. When the tail came up and I had the rubber control we were off and running! Slowing down and stopping was more trouble, but we managed. We drove through the snow about twenty feet off the roadway from Mac to Willy- lots of fun to say the least.'

Charlene was not the first or only 'wingless bus or taxi'. The OAE's life Director and Historian Billy-Ace Baker Penguin tells that it was indeed an Australian who first achieved the feat with an old Vickers with a 45 foot wingspan and was sent to the Antarctic without wings for the purpose of being used as an air tractor. It was wrecked in Australia prior to the deployment of the Mawson's 1912 Antarctic expedition to Commonwealth Bay- but that's another story.

[Note from the author.] As I write this chapter, I have just learnt, from his wife of 57 years, that my old mate Eddie Frankiewicz passed away on May 9 2003 of pneumonia and heart failure.

While I never met Eddie, I feel as if I have known him personally for years. I am so very indebted to this pioneer polar aviator in the writing of this book, his contribution was immeasurable, his willingness to provide material, personal press cuttings and photos. Eddie trusted me enough to copy and return the material to his home at Buena Vista Street, San Diego. Like all old OAE's Commander Edward Frankiewicz is now flying with the angels, and was truly a quintessential naval aviator.

'Rest old mate, I can imagine the yarns being recounted with your old flying mates. 'Gus' Shinn, Jack Torbett, Harvey Speed, Charlie Ottie, 'Dutch' Gardiner and many others. Rest in peace Eddie. Rest in peace.'

No man in the squadron knew Frankie better than his co-pilot Cdr James Waldron, his recollections of his old friend and veteran polar aviation, were related to me last year *'If someone works closely side by side, with another person for six difficult months, there should be reams of information that might be elicited about that relationship. Frankie and I flew together in good weather and in bad, we covered a good part of this globe, we lived on everything from Rhode Island to the Greenland Ice Cap and later to span the United States and much of the Pacific Ocean and that incredible flight from New Zealand to McMurdo Sound. We spent around a hundred hours of flying over the Antarctic continent, even landing twice at the South Pole.*

With Frankie it was always a love hate relationship. When we were not flying, Eddie was the soul of compassion and friendliness; he always would ascertain that I would get maximum enjoyment out of what we did and what we observed. I had not, up until then, experienced the Pacific environment and he was always ready to present the best of what there was for areas we visited. Of course these areas included San Francisco, Hawaii, the Fiji Islands and New Zealand.

The other side of Frankie was his persona in the cockpit, as he was a very experience multi-engine pilot and I wasn't. He knew his aircraft's capabilities and was always aware of the situation that existed as the flight hours added up. Eddie knew that my experience before we met were those of a single engine fighter and helicopter pilot and flying missions off aircraft carriers.

I had never flown a large multi-engine aircraft, so it must have seemed to him that he was to venture off onto the most dangerous mission with a pilot beside him who didn't know the basics of the aircraft we where to fly halfway around the world and then venture into unmapped lands where little was known as to what was ahead.

Initially, if he had little or no trust in me as a pilot, I could accept that, however, as my flight time built up in the R4-D, I would expect he would have given me a bit more credit than he did. Eddie, most of the time did a creditable job as aircraft commander of the R4-D, flying to remote areas of

Antarctica, selecting landing areas where no aircraft had landed before and successfully completing mission that were long and arduous.

On several occasions, when events arose that increased danger of various kinds, I observed Eddie becoming very tense and erratic, and at such times Eddie was a danger to himself and the entire crew. Fortunately, we survived these situations, but the uncertainty of the moment was still a matter of concern for us all. Around 1967, I was on a trip to San Diego from my base in Japan, and spent an evening with Eddie and his wife. It was a glorious evening, knowing our history together was all behind us, and the hidden fear that sudden death might overtake us, was no longer there to envelope us. Eddie died recently and during the last few years of his life, he and I exchange several e-mail messages and we managed to remain friends although he knew how I felt about those few difficult flights over the ice.'

Cdr Eddie Ward, the squadron's first Commander added *'as Jim points out, when you fly many, many hours together over some of the most treacherous terrain, it brings out the best and worst in people. Amen.'*

If by some remote chance anyone has all copies of the Navy's Antarctic paper *'The Ross Island Review'* the *'The McMurdo News'* to the *'Navy News'* and its successor *'Sometimez'* through to the present, *'Antarctic Sun'* they would without doubt, have a complete chronicle, not only of VX-6 Squadron, but of all those men and women who played their part in Antarctic exploration.

Today's publication is issued on-line as part of the United States Antarctic Programme, funded by the NSF and published by Raytheon Polar Services from building 155 at McMurdo, and is a far cry from that first issue in the mid 1950's as *'McMurdo News'* so eagerly awaited by those VX-6 Squadron members over 12,000 miles from their loved ones. Daily they read about themselves, their idiosyncratic behaviourisms and their moods that reflected their life in Antarctica.

During the IGY year, the paper had a change of format and was renamed *'The Navy News'*, then in the 1960's was renamed to be *'Sometimez'*, a name was derived from the group of volunteer radiomen who were working on it at nights, and in the early days if time permitted, sometimez it met the 'news stands' by breakfast, and 'sometimez' it didn't.

Originally it was just a few pages of news and sport, copied from radio news beamed in from New Zealand, Australia and South America, with little news from the States, *'At times we made up sport results, and in the later years it was a weekly we called the 'Sometimez Sunday'. During this period we were able to get people outside the communication department to contribute to the paper and we had a number of regular columnists for sport, scientists, religion, 'wanted' ads and other featured articles'* says Billy-Ace. *'When the JO's took over, they put out a few pages every day during the summer season and later they even went to a weekly issue.'*

Even though Billy-Ace Penguin Baker was not a member of VX-6, he was with the ASA and later the NSFA, and was an iconic Antarctic figure, as symbolic to OAE's as penguins were to the world, when he arrived at McMurdo in 1962. The radiomen at the station were publishing the paper daily, small in size, consisting of a few sheets of text composed on a teletype, then printed off.

'During the winters of 1967 and 1971, management exercised its authority and bureaucracy reared its ugly head'. Billy Ace Penguin Baker wrote in *The Antarctic Sun.*

'Censorship was a real nightmare to all of us who worked on the paper. Even though we produced it on a volunteer basis and usually in our free time, we still had to bow to the might of authority, because of the inclusion of the official weekly calendar, the paper was considered a house organ with official status.'

Additionally, the paper was produced using government equipment and supplies, and after all most of the staff were members of the US Navy. *'Looking back, I wonder what all the fuss was about. Most of the objectionable material related to US involvement in Vietnam and to a hippy-like guru named Mehar Baba. In 1971, in addition to the censorship board, a military advisor was assigned to prevent controversial editorial material.'*

Billy Ace was appointed a military advisor, but in each edition of the paper, some of the offensive and anti-military material still managed to get past his critical eye.

With no women wintering over during Baker's tour of duty, the Operation command's censorship board deemed any material which was slightly risqué, sexy, demeaning or in poor taste, to be bad for the men's character and morale. Yet despite this, its distribution continued to increase with copies being dispatched to all the bases, Williams Field, the Kiwi's at Scott Base and any ships in port.

'Sometimez' was Billy-Ace's first experience in the field of journalism and continued until the Navy's JO's took the paper over in the 1970's, when the NSFA replaced the ASA, and the Navy's journalist was spending more time on the ice. As the JO's didn't winter over, the radiomen like Billy-Ace took over until the Juno's arrived back in the spring. The *'Sometimez'* continued until well into the 80's when the NSF began publication of the *Antarctic Sun Times*, which was later renamed its present masthead as the *Antarctic Sun.*

In October 1972 a new platemaker 'recovered' from the Washington Navy Yard was taken to the Antarctic along with other journalistic materials, and an old Jamesway hut, which had served as work space and a doss house for visiting media, was converted into the most southern production room for a daily newspaper and was naturally and effectively named *'Pressheim'.*

According to Billy-Ace, after many hours of frustration, delays, frozen chemicals, brittle plates, and an eternity, the first edition of the newspaper rolled off the printing press and was delivered to the mess in time for breakfast on the morning of November 5 1972. The long hours of frustration paid off, with the entire fourth estate dedicated to producing the paper.

The Navy journalists had managed to salvage a photocopier, or was it 'liberated' from the stores? Either way, with that equipment, the entire task of producing the daily newspaper was by the navy journalist as they resumed the production and publishing of *'Sometimez',* which contained overseas and national news from the USA. The squadron's pilots would fly the 'paper round' to get copies to remote field parties each day, and as they flew their flight plans they would drop into the office to pick up a bundle of *'Sometimez'.*

'By October 1974, the newsroom and production office was moved to Building 155 from 'Pressheim', and was then located adjacent to the radio and television studios' recalled Billy-Ace.

Two years later, despite no longer using the plate making machine, the paper continued to make its daily deadlines during the austral summer, and the format changed very little between 1974 and 1980, with the exception of a new masthead being introduced. On February 9 1997, the Navy journalists continued to published the paper with the old 'cut and paste' method and changed the name to *'Antarctic Sun Times'.* By now though, the use of computers and digital cameras had arrived, and while it was still available on the old fashion print copy, it also had a worldwide distribution via the World Wide Web and e-mail.

After the Naval detachment and the squadron's decommissioning on February 20 1998, the Antarctic Support Association assumed full control and responsibility for the most southern newspaper, and its name was shortened to its present masthead *'The Antarctic Sun.'*

On July 17th 1996 Billy-Ace Baker of Pensacola, Florida legally changed his name to Billy-Ace Penguin Baker. A unique penguin lover whose claim to fame is that he is the only person to have wintered over four times during *Operation Deep Freeze* in the 1960's and 70's, at McMurdo Station.

When he first decided to have his name changed to Billy-Ace Penguin Barker, he was thwarted because someone else already had the name, but when that person died, it was now his big moment, so Billy again made his way to the US Navy Legal Services Offices at NAS Pensacola and had them draw up the appropriate paper work, and with this done and papers in hand, Billy made an appointment with the circuit Judge at the local county court house, where Judge Geeker heard his petition and performed the ceremony.

'The day of my court hearing, I wore a tuxedo and was quite a hit in the waiting room which was full of women who were going before the Judge to reclaim their maiden names. I was the only guy there and I was cool, but out of place. However, the Judge granted my petition and I became a 'Penguin'.

Billy is a charter member of the American Society Polar [Penguin] Philatelics and has one of the world's largest collections of penguin stamps and postal covers. The OAE 's Historian and editor of the Association's *'Explorer's Gazette',* is often referred to as the Director of Penguin Affairs, and is a frequent contributor to the *Penguin Post.*

Known as the Strip Rats the VXE-6 air control and maintenance crews proudly became known as SNATCH being the Southernmost Naval Air Traffic Control Headquarters.

From the first landing on the ice in December 1955 during *Deep Freeze 1,* the ice runway/ skiway had been located on the sea ice about four and a half miles southwest of Hut Point, with the surface prepared by bulldozing the snow to the edge of the runway. In time this snow formed ice beams, which quickly accelerated with the accumulation of drifted snow. By *Deep Freeze –62,* these beams on the inland end had grown to over six metres in height tapering upwards of 60 metres and running 200 plus feet on either side of the runway. At the end of each season, the ice to this area broke off and drifted out to sea, so destroying most of the runway.

Work started on a new runway / skiway system at Williams Airfield two, that is directly south of McMurdo and in preparing the new runway, the Seabee construction gangs had to bulldoze both sides of the runways which had been buckled by pressures ridges. Once referred to as Williams Field, it was now known as McMurdo Station where the previous season, temporary living facilities were established at the field with the air and maintenance crews living at the airfield along side the flight line.

The new system allowed upwards of 200 personnel to be accommodated at the strip, thus saving the time previously lost when crews had to be transported to and from McMurdo for their shift and flying duties. When flying was relocated from the sea ice to the skiway, the accommodation was also relocated to that new site.

During this period a helicopter hanger was constructed from an old converted jumbo size Quonset hut with a mezzanine floor that allowed the helicopter's to be stored during the Antarctic winter, and doubled as accommodation for construction crews during the summer months.

In 1993, as a means to provide for an extended use of larger aircraft, such as the Lockheed C-141 and C-5A cargo transport, a new blue ice runway was constructed closer to McMurdo Station, and named *Pegasus* after the Lockheed C-121 Super Constellation, *BuNo 126513* which had crashed on the sea ice runway, where the wreckage was dragged to now rest just off to the west, as a memorial on the Ross Ice Shelf. *Pegasus* runway was carved out of hard glacial ice 30 meters thick, and is 1830 meters long, 91 meters wide and 6km closer to McMurdo than the Williams Air Facilities. Between November and December when the airstrip is not in use, its surface is covered with several centimetres of snow to protect the ice from melting.

Providing permanent and reliable airfields in Antarctica has always been a major problem for the military command, before the construction of the blue ice runway the only other runways regularly maintained for both ski-equipped and wheeled aircraft were located at Williams Field on the Ross Sea Ice Shelf. The USAP command were looking to the year 2000 and beyond, and the introduction of an all jet transport logistical, and a proposed 1400 km road between McMurdo and the Pole Station, which would eventually mean a reduction in the number of C-130 flights.

In 1962, the US Department of Defence ordered all services to adopt a uniform system of aircraft designation for Navy aircraft in the Antarctic. R4D-5 to LC-47H - R4D-6 to LC-47J- R4D-8 to LC-117D-C-130BL to LC-130F - P2V-7N to LP-2J -R5D-3 to C-54Q - R7V-1P to C-121J - UC-1 to

U-IB- HRS-3 to CH19E- HUS-1L to LH-34D - HUL-1 to UH-13P-HTL-7 to TH-13N and HU2K-1 to UH-2B.

The summer season was marked by the establishment of Eights Station, at the base of the Antarctic Peninsula 1400 miles from McMurdo, and as research expanded deeper and further into Antarctica and further away from the Naval Air Facilities, the Task Force 43 command found it increasingly difficult to supply the necessary air support with the limited resources available to the command, so this concern was reported to the Chief of Naval Operations with another emphatic request of more C-130 aircraft for VX-6 Squadron.

On November 22 1962, R4-D-8 *BuNo 17188* crashed when its ski landing gear collapsed while landing at the Sentinel Ranges of the Ellsworth Mountains, where the plane was on a supply flight to a geological survey party working in the area. Carrying a crew of six, they had to wait aboard for 60 hours for a rescue R4-D to arrive from Byrd.

Also lost on the same day was VX-6's helicopter LH-47H # *15719* piloted by Lt Cdr. R H Spencer that practically disintegrated while landing in the Wright Dry Valley in McMurdo Sound. As the helicopter was setting down on the ice, it 'rattled itself apart' by what is known as ground resonance [an uncontrolled vibration set in motion on landing]. The helicopter was being used to transfer a field party from one location to another with two geologists onboard at the time. The two scientists and the helicopter's co-pilot J Buckman, managed to extricate the pilot, who suffered serious scalp lacerations, and placed him in a sleeping bag before communicating with McMurdo to request assistance.

On November 25 1962, the crew of R4-D LC-47H *BuNo 50777* were making a jet assisted take-off from Davis Glacier, and accidentally released a JATO canister, but before it stopped firing it hit the aircraft's propeller. Only a split second prevented the plane from cart wheeling onto its wing, which dug a long scar into the runway before the aircraft settled at right angles to the flight line. The JATO rocket canisters continued to flame as the aviation fuel trickled onto the snow, but the 30-degree frost prevented any ignition. The R4-D lost an engine and was considered a 'strike' and not recovered.

At the time of the accident the pilot was taking off from a makeshift runway near the head of the Davis Glacier some 145 miles north west of Scott Base. To say it was miraculous that the crew escaped serious injury because the petrol failed to ignite would be an understatement, but also had the starboard wing dropped, the aircraft would have ploughed through the camp possibly killing both men and their dog teams.

New Zealand's 14 man field party were evacuated by two VX-6's helicopters and an Otter seven hours after the crash, making this flight the second of two by the same aircraft, after picking up the scientific party travelling by motor toboggans in company with a four man dog team survey party.

While waiting for the rescue helicopter and the Otter, the crew dined on steak and eggs salvaged from the aircraft, and later Scott Base leader Lt Colonel R Tinker guided in the rescue mission.

The final loss for the season occurred on December 23 1962, when LH -34D *BuNo 144658*, had difficulty taking off from the McMurdo helicopter pad and crashed. The engine oversped, exploded and burnt on impact with the ice.

On February 1 at Byrd Station, a R4-D-8'S JATO bottles failed to ignite after the crew had retracted its landing gear, causing an unscheduled belly landing, leaving the plane repairable, but as the accident occurred so late in the season, it was decided to let it lay there until *Deep Freeze 63*. Eventually the aircraft was picked up and flown back to McMurdo, then stowed aboard ship to Christchurch for repairs.

The Lockheed Constellation became a vital weapon in the Squadrons stable during the sixties, a second R7V-1 named *EL Patchep Up O # 131659* was loaned to VX-6 during *Deep Freeze 62*, due to the withdrawal from service of the unit's only remaining R5-D # *56528,* but she returned the following season when the operation command required an SAR aircraft to be based at Christchurch. However, this was to be her last season with VX-6, being replaced the following season with another C-121J # *131644* name *Pegasus*. This aircraft became the squadron's main photographic aircraft, after being fitted out with the more powerful R-3350-42 engines.

When the squadron flew into their homeport of Quonset Point, wife's sweethearts, parents, sons and daughters met the bearded men who in some cases were holding their latest arrivals for the first time, and later while 'supping suds' at their local pub, related stories and tails about life at the coldest place on earth. If they spoke of 'cross winds' while landing or taking off from frozen airstrips, they were not just blowing smoke or being a little unfaithful with the facts, as the average wind velocity on that barren continent has been recorded in excess of 200 mph, playing havoc with the aviators and the shipboard sailors who supported their mates.

The guys who manned both the support ships and icebreakers often encountered 30-50 foot seas along the Antarctic coast, so while at home on leave they were able to recall over the months, blizzards, and white outs, in a land where the actual snowfall in some locations is less than 10 inches a year.

While seated on a bar stool, the storytellers talked of the 'lake that never freezes', which to the casual listener, pondering over his glass of beer says *'pull the other one'*, but there is such a lake in the Wright Valley which never freezes even during the coldest winter months. Scientist have determined that its waters are eleven times more salty than normal sea water which accounts for this strange phenomenon.

But for those squadron boys not coming back for another six months their stories will keep until once again they can listen to their proud children talking about their fathers in fur-lined boots, and stranded aircraft, and pour over the photos of their hero Dads months in the Antarctic in search of adventure.

On his return to the US the squadron's commander Greenwell stayed in the Navy until his retirement in 1974. Always the dapper gentlemen, he never left without his trademark porkpie hat, built his own boat named the *'WEEZIE'* after his beloved wife of 17 years, Louise. After she suffered a series of strokes resulting from a car accident in the mid 1980's, he eventually left his job at the Consumer Protection Agency for Norfolk, to care for Louise full time.

His devotion to her was incredible, she slept in a hospital bed in the front of their house, and he slept in a chair beside her, so when she passed away in the mid 90's the 'Skipper' was heartbroken. He spent more time on his boat then always eager to share his Kentucky bourbon with friends.

For those embarking on another deployment in Antarctica, it's back to work. Above all it's back to their physical stamina, plus gaining knowledge of ditching and survival at sea, of learning how to keep alive on a continent covering 55.3 million square miles, covered by a cloak of ice upwards of three miles thick. And so the squadron prepares for its seventh year of *Operation Deep Freeze*. Finally as interest begins to build up and departure day approaches, the new men are talked to by their Commanding Officer and shown a 16mm film taken on a *Flight to the South Pole* and what they will encounter there.

By performing the same tasks and types of missions as they did the previous season, the R4-D's flew 1,319 hours on 260 flights. At the beginning of the season only two of an inventory of four aircraft were operable owing to LC-117 still lying on her belly at Byrd Station awaiting temporary repairs so she could be flown to McMurdo and later loaded aboard ship. Also the LC-47 that had wintered over at McMurdo, was damaged by a mid winter storm and now awaited spare parts. More aircraft would be acquired during the season so that despite their losses, VX-6 ended the season's operations with one LC-117 and three LC-47's- all of which were left in the Antarctic for the following winter.

CHAPTER TEN.

THE FIRST FLIGHT FROM AFRICA TO ANTARCTICA.

Another first for the US Navy's VX-6 Air Squadron.
The historic non-stop flight from South Africa to
Antarctica.

With the Navy planners continuing to push the Hercules to their limit, it was decided to bring personnel down early, in fact the earliest fly-in to date, but when *Deep Freeze 63* got under way on September 16 1962 with temperatures in Antarctica between minus 50-58 degree F.

The idea of the early start was to carry personnel to assist in the construction of the new ice runway and two new summer weather stations. This gave the command and in particular the squadron, a new headache, as the extreme cold so early in the season had an effect on the aircraft causing serious mechanical problems for both aircraft and equipment. So it was decided to abandon the programme on September 20th, when the aircraft returned to Christchurch, but it highlighted the difficulties of operating the C-130's when the temperature was below minus 40 degrees F, and finding after four days on the ice that the aircraft became 'cold-soaked', causing hydraulic failures and cracked windscreens.

This season the squadron's Hercules pioneered a new method of inland fuel delivery, and in February 1963 a ski-equipped LC-130 made the first ever bulk delivery of JP-4 fuel to Byrd Station, when it carried 13,627 litres [6,600 US gallons] in removable internal tanks. The system had been developed for the US Marine Corps for air-to-air refuelling of strike aircraft, but the tanks could also be installed in the Lockheed transport, to increase mileage.

Although the system was purely experimental during *Deep Freeze 63*, it wasn't until the following season, that full-scale bulk fuel delivery was accomplished and proved satisfactory, thus allowing the squadron to bulk store fuel at inland stations. During Deep Freeze 64 a total of 1,890,000 litres [499,300 US gallons] of diesel and JP-4 were delivered to both Byrd and the Pole Stations. Of this total only 257,400 litres [68,000US gallons] was delivered in drums, whereas previously this quantity would have required a little under 10,000 drums, involving R-4D's and a great deal of manpower and valuable time.

It now took only one person to fill or discharge the new bulk tank in a little under fifteen minutes, while previously it took two hours to unload or load the 50 drums, using an 18 tonne sled with a bulldozer and three men. The squadron soon discovered the value of the new system, when the weight of the drums could be replaced with fuel, a saving of 378 to 1200 litres, or about 300 US gallons per flight. All four of the squadron's LC-130's were filled with the necessary plumbing to carry the new style fuel tanks, and at the end of each season, the tanks were returned to Christchurch for storage and in case there were any other mid winter emergency flights to Antarctica.

Soon after arriving at McMurdo in October 1962 to commence *Deep Freeze –63*, under their new commander Cdr Everett, the first obstacle for the squadron was the annual uncovering of their main living quarters, at a time when Antarctica was experiencing its worst storms in years, hampering VXE-6 flight operations for the first two months with the minus 40 degree temperatures, freezing the hands of the aircraft mechanics, and those assigned to unloading and loading the slippery aircraft.

The season had scarcely got under way, hardly a few hours old, when a tale unfolded of a village appearing out of left field 500 miles from Byrd Station only to disappear five days later. But the village held little mystery for the aviators of VX-6 who, after being forced down in below zero temperatures with winds screaming across the snow, the crew of the LC-130 hastily erected a survival tent village of high blocks of ice with tent roofs resembling a small community.

The Hercules was forced down due to contaminated fuel, and consequently water was located in the aircraft's fuel causing the engine strainers to clog up. To correct the problem it required a week of living out in the open with the cold and tedious task of draining the aircraft's fuel and filtering it, then transferring it back into the fuel tanks. When this was accomplished Major Leslie Darbyshire, USMC and his crew took off for home. The area was named Darbyshire and later served as an emergency landing strip for other squadron crews.

While mechanical repairs in this part of the world represent a monumental task, in Antarctica, although covered with ice, is as barren and dry as the deserts of North Africa. Metal does not rust or deteriorate rapidly in this environment, and it is a rare day when the wind does not blow, so repairs carried out in the field, as with Major Darbyshire's fuel problem, are never easy or comfortable, as another of the squadron's helos forced down near the area found when subjected to an open field engine change, forcing the small repair crew to live in survival tents and remain isolated until their task was accomplished.

Against all these natural hazards, the squadron's personnel delivered over 4,000 tons of cargo and 4,500 passengers, while logging some 4,000 hours in the air during the season. Delivered over 2 million pounds of supplies and carried 850 scientists and military personnel to their various destinations during a two-month period.

Working 12-hour shifts, seven days a week, the squadron carried out 382 missions, flew over 1,300 hours in less than seven weeks; While the aircraft did create numerous problems for the maintenance crews working under extreme frigid conditions, the ski operations on the ice surfaces caused many more as their landing gear brackets failed, causing several of the giant Hercules to be ferried back to the Lockheed plant in Georgia for repairs

November 26, 1962, was a cold Antarctic day, just 34 below zero, as eighty six scientists, naval personnel and media stood shivering on the lofty ice capped polar plateau, under a cloudless Antarctic sky, to watch the changing of the *Operation Deep Freeze* command. In a simple ceremony at the bottom of the world, Rear Admiral Reedy assumed command of the US Naval Support Forces from retiring Admiral David Tyree. The two parka-clad admirals saluted each other, read orders, saluted again and shook hands. Among those also shaking hands on that Antarctic afternoon, were the president of Notre Dame University, Theodore Hesburgh and Dr Lawrence Gould, who had been Admiral Byrd's second in command at Little America. After the ceremony all boarded the C130 to head back to base.

Reedy was fifty-two when taking up his first Antarctic assignment. He was born in Cleveland, Ohio in 1910, and like many naval aviators, received his flight training at the Pensacola Naval Air Station, being awarded his wings in 1935. Reedy served as a dive bomber instructor at Texas's Corpus Christi NAS, before commanding a bomber squadron conducting search and destroy missions against German subs in the Atlantic during World War 11.

Exceptional service, earned him the Air Medal, Distinguished Flying Cross and the Bronze Star and after the war he advanced to become a Rear Admiral in 1961, a few months before taking over the command of *Deep Freeze 63*.

It was rather ironic that on February 17 1999, the day the squadron gathered at their Christchurch Headquarters awaiting the arrival of Commander David W Jackson, the squadron's last CO, piloting the last Squadron aircraft to depart the Antarctic before decommissioning, that word of the death Admiral James R Reedy, came down the line from Frank 'Kaz' Kazukaitis.

In 1955 the US Navy flew for the first time, four aircraft into the Antarctic from New Zealand, and in 1962 Reedy's predecessor was involved in the decision to fly a VX-6 C-130 from McMurdo to Punta Arenas, Chile, by way of the South Pole. No long-range flights were flown across the bottom of the world between South America, Australasia or South Africa; in fact no plane had ever made long-range flights that would connect two or even three continents to the vast icy expanse of Antarctica.

In 1963, Reedy decided it was time for such a flight to be carried out by VX-6 squadron and began planning for a flight from Africa to McMurdo. His plan called for the use of two squadron C-130 turbo-prop ski-equipped aircraft to fly 4,700 miles across the widest ocean in the world, from Cape Town South Africa, through Australasia, over the Antarctic Ocean and then across Antarctica by way of the South Pole to the US base at McMurdo, and from there the last 2,400 miles to Christchurch- thus completing the longest first flight from continent to continent, over the width of the south polar plateau, crossing many areas unseen by man.

The objectives of the proposed flight were to ascertain the possibilities of such long-range flights in the first instance, and to prove the feasibility of a new commercial air route linking Africa to Australia and New Zealand, similar to that of the north polar routes used by the majority of commercial airlines. Currently airlines were flying by a long and circuitous route, leaving conventional aircraft to swing northwards across the Middle East to India and southeast to Singapore, over the Timor Sea to Darwin, and south to Australia and then onto New Zealand, a distance of 13,705 miles, taking around 35 hours. Flying from South Africa to New Zealand halved this time and distance.

From a military objective the flight would enable the exploration of uncharted territory, and investigation of the mysterious auroral belt, which caused atmospheric interference with radio communications in the southern ocean and between South Africa and the Antarctic coastline in the Ross Sea.

Reedy took his ideas to a meeting of *Operation Deep Freeze* staff officers one afternoon, arguing his case as a conversational trial balloon idea, after strongly outlining his arguments in favour of this long range flight proposal.

One officer a little stunned, suggested that we are now talking about the unknown, *'No one has ever flown directly from South Africa to the South Pole from the mainland of either Africa or South America.'*

Reedy's reply was simple- saying that until December 1955 no one had ever flown from New Zealand to Antarctica, and reflecting on aviation's achievements in Antarctica since Sir Hubert Wilkins and Ben Eielson became the first men to fly over the south polar region in 1928, the aerial conquest of the Antarctic had moved ahead steadily overtime, gradually pulling back the mantle of Antarctica's mysteries.

Another officer with certain misgivings, said *'Plenty of flights have crossed distances just as great, but not over 4700 miles of empty ocean and a continent covered with ice. You'll be flying above the most inaccessible and bloody inhospitable areas on earth.'*

Convinced his idea would receive positive support from the majority of his officers, Reedy turned to his senior officer of VXE-6, Commander George R Kelly and asked him direct.

'But can we do it George?'

His Irish indignation rose at the mere suggestion that naval airmen couldn't carry out such a simple task, and as he looked his boss straight in the eye said *'Yes Sir, I think we can'*. Kelly's positive response and a show of hands carried the day, and within a few weeks preparations for this historic flight were in full swing.

Two VXE-6's Lockheed transporters were placed on special detail and crews selected, with both planes to be equipped with special landing skis and wheels, which could be interchangeable according to the terrain, and September 30 1962 was the date set for the squadron's two LC-130's to depart with the jumping off point from the small Malan Field on the outskirts of Cape Town.

Early in September Admiral Reedy rang Lowell Thomas the famous American radio commentator, lecturer, and author of 'Lawrence of Arabia', and at the end of the conversation, almost as a postscript, Lowell inquired of the Admiral *'was there anything exciting happening in your world?'*

To Lowell's surprise he was told of what the Navy were planning and asked in hope, *'Don't you think I ought to go along.'* Reedy explained that they were flying two of the squadron's LC-130'S that would be flying gas tanks with virtually no extra space, but being a newsman, Lowell never gave up hope of experiencing such an historic flight. Next day to Lowell's astonishment, Reedy rang. *'Lowell, old boy, we've decided to drop one of the pilots and take you instead'*, so to his sheer delight he was to be one of the first to fly from Africa across Antarctica to New Zealand.

Here was the man, who after being depressed by the brutality of the war on the western front, had set off to film General Allenby's historic entry into Jerusalem, where he met a man who was to make them both famous. He was a diminutive British army officer in a borrowed uniform, named Captain Lawrence.

On September 19 1963, two squadron ski-equipped C-130F's *#148318, The City of Christchurch* and *# 148320* named *Puenta Arenas* or *'Pete'* were flown to Andrews Air Force Base near Washington to pick up Admiral James.

Reedy flew from Quonset Point, then onto South Africa, via the Azores, Cairo, Nairobi, finally landing at Malan Field on the outskirts of Cape Town, were the Admiral was attending the Scientific Conference on Antarctic Research.

When Cdr Bill Kurlak had prop trouble out of Nairobi he had to put #320 down at Johannesburg for repairs, so #318's stay in South Africa was extended to allow Kurlak to catch up. Luckily with the South African Air Force operating C-130's, they were able to make repairs there for the flight to McMurdo and onto Christchurch.

For two weeks in between breaks, the navy crews had worked on the two Hercules engines, checking the communication systems in preparation for a September 30 take-off, for when fully loaded, the two C-130's would weigh 145,000 pounds, almost 10,000 lbs more than recommended by Lockheed, but the two commanders anticipated little if any take-off problems.

Each plane had 9,600 US gallon of JP-4 jet fuel, providing 17 hours flying time, with part of this loaded inside the C-130's cavernous cabins. Both aircraft were stripped down to allow for the additional fuel, and all but excess gear, including the crew's liberty clothing and all personal items, were crated up and shipped back to the States.

The South African government and the Navy fully co-operated with the history making mission, and the South African Navy's frigate *Transvaal* was stationed 1,200 miles from Cape Town in the Antarctic Ocean as a safety measure, to be on emergency standby and to set up navigation beacons if required.

The lead plane C-130 *# 318* was piloted by Lt.Cdr Richard G Dickerson of Pocatello and the squadron's Commander George Kelly from El Dorado Illinois, with co-pilot 'Art' Herr, and passengers Rear Admiral James Reedy, Professor L King of the University of Natal, representing the South African government, and the *National Geographic* staff photographer Otis Imboden. Lt Cdr William Kurlak of New York City piloted *# 320*, with Jack Stitch and Andy Huggins on the flight deck along with Ally Baum, a photographer/ reporter from the *New York Times*.

Later recalling the flight, Art Herr said with certain pride, that Dick Dickerson who died several years before, had *'taught me everything I needed to know about polar flying; he was one of my heroes whose entire life was worthy of a book, as he was a truly great man for adventure and an intrepid naval aviator.*

As a lowly USN Lieutenant I had to defer to all the brass as far as seat time, but did get my share and one of the Air Medals that were subsequently awarded, plus membership in the Explorers Club.'

Cdr Richard Dickerson was one of the great polar pilots of the 1960's and 70's who completed three tours of duty in Antarctica before retiring from the Navy and VXE-6 in 1964, moving to

Fairbanks, he joined the Naval Arctic Research Laboratory where he was test pilot for eleven years, then after moving to Point Barrow with his wife Betty, he flew DC-3 into the Central Arctic Ocean in support of multi-twin disciplinary research, before flying Cessna ski-equipped 180 aircraft and twin Otter.

Cdr Dickerson flew combat missions against the Japanese during *WW II,* before being transferred to VXE-6 squadron, where he served in a series of training and logistic programmes and began his Antarctic operational duties flying Neptune's in 1960, during the time the squadron acquired their first ski-equipped C-130 Hercules. Dick become the first VXE-6 pilot to transition to the Lockheed Martin aircraft, and as his ability was such that accordingly he 'wrote the book' on Hercules operations.

During his time in the navy after leading the longest flight in history from South Africa to McMurdo, Cdr Dickerson flew the first State Department Antarctic Treaty inspection team into the Russian Antarctic Station of Vostok in the spring of 1964, the same year he flew in support of SUBICEX where two submarines surfaced together at the North Pole, and operated C-130 Hercules out of Thule, Greenland, to carry out ice reconnaissance for subs.

Always modest of his own achievements, and reluctant to speak of himself, he often down played his own personal achievements; but from Captain Brian Shoemaker; *'I used to fly with him in the Arctic, when I was the Commanding Officer of NARL and he was always a strong silent type who seldom spoke and when he did, never minced his words. He is one of the very few people I know that never brags and has a tendency to downplay his past.'*

A brisk dawn broke on Monday September 30 with clear skies, and at 2pm with the aircraft thoroughly checked, they took off watched by several hundreds of South Africans who had waited since early morning to witness history being created. Many of them had never seen a giant Hercules before and marvelled at the idea of them flying non-stop across the Antarctic continent.

Commander Dickerson taxied *# 318* to the end of the runway, leaving many on the ground to ponder if the two C-130's with their wings actually drooping under the weight of fuel and with the nose angled up so very slightly, would make it. Commander Kelly remarked *'Dickerson opened the throttle and we began to move, sixty knots, ninety knots, one eighteen! The wheels got the message and gradually began leaving the ground with Commander Kelly calling the air speed.'*

' Man, she looks like she'll do it' was Dickerson's only comments, so the words *'wheels up'* was real magic to his ears as the C-130 lifted off in the last few feet of the 8,500 foot runway and slowly, ever so slowly as the landing gear began withdrawing into its housing, second by second continued to gain altitude.

However while the old girl's nose wheel and its ski had retracted into the housing, it had apparently failed to be securely fastened into place, pointing to a problem with the hydraulic gear. Such was the progression of the squadron's crew that after Dickerson set his course towards the South Pole, the landing gear was lowered again for another try at pulling it back into place. A return to Cape Town was being considered on the flight deck, but as the plane climbed higher, Dickerson set it on course for the South Pole, still trying several times to retract the landing gear, and moments later the red lights flashed with the welcoming signal indicating *'wheels locked'.*

By the time Lt Cdr Bill Kurlak was airborne in *# 320* he reported that he was on course and holding visual contact with Table Mountain that is second only to Gibraltar, as an outstanding landmark and he too headed south across the Antarctic Ocean. Two hours out, and the exterior temperatures were now 24 below zero with a tail wind of 50 knots. Flying out over the Antarctic Ocean, Commander William Hogg, the skipper of the *Transvaal,* signalled with a radio message to Rear Admiral Reedy *'GODSPEED'.* Reedy thanked him and his crew for their escort.

By 7pm, the temperatures had plummeted with the first blast of cold air reaching them from the southern ocean and polar cap, and that was when the crews began adding their special Antarctic clothing, as the two Hercules approached the Point of Safe Return just 2,300 miles off the South African coast. At 8.45 pm and flying at 30,000 feet, a thick frost was now forming on the windscreen, but there was now no turning back.

Plotting their course with their sextant, having only the planet Saturn and the stars of Antares, Canopus and Altair as their guide, navigators Don Miller and Marine Staff Sergeant Arthur King, droned onwards towards the South Pole with the Sor Rondana mountains to the left and the Wohlthat Ranges stretching almost into infinity. All eyes lit up when the crackled voice of the South Pole Station came through, replying to a message from the commander of the Russian's Mirnyy Station, offering their congratulations, adding that they would be welcome to 'drop in on our landing facilities', which was a little on the small size to accommodate the Hercules.

Some of the mountains were known to the Americans as they passed over the Pole at 10.30 pm before flying across uncharted regions of Queen Maude Land, the polar plateau of Antarctica and on to McMurdo. Reedy remarked that he would love to return someday for another look at the rugged frozen terrain in clearer skies as now the weather was deteriorating.

Dickerson received a message from Captain Roy Shults from McMurdo that the weather at the base was closing in and that the Pole Station was experiencing a strong, wind blown snow storm that had reduced visibility to less then 400 yards, and the ground temperature gauges showing minus 28 degrees 'Typical day at the Pole,' remarked Dick Dickerson, 'hot and dusty'.

At 12.30 am, the midnight sun was beginning to rise as the two aircraft reached the Amundson Scott Station, and at this point those on the flight deck of # 318 saw Bill Kurlak's # 320 fly along the port side as both aircraft could faintly see the outlines of the Station's airstrip below. Their thoughts were with the 22 men who were wintering over, dug down in their tunnels, so Reedy radioed their greetings, assuring them that a plane would return to pick them up within a few days.

With the sun now well up in the Antarctic sky, the crew donned their sunglass and with the Pole well behind them, the forward weather at McMurdo's Williams Air facilities was getting worse, with visibility continuing to deteriorate by the minute causing the commanders to give serious consideration to an alternative landing field, with returning to the Pole Station a possibility if visibility didn't improve. But by now their fuel supply was only marginal, and there was still the probability of landing the giant transports on rugged ice without ground control, but the conditions at McMurdo were near whiteout, and less than one hours fuel remained.

After a brief discussion on the flight deck the decision to press on to McMurdo was made at 4am by Lt. Commander Dickerson, who was too cool an aviator to let a whiteout condition bother him. While on its high frequency homer beacon, with the undercast growing thicker every mile, McMurdo reported that both planes were on their radar and gave the crews new bearings.

With the snow now blowing fiercely, it made it impossible to see the McMurdo ice runway even though it was directly below them, so ground control began talking the C-130's down to within a few hundred feet of the runway, allowing the lead plane to zero in between the rows of oil drums lined up on either side. Commander Kelly shouted 'we've got barrels!' then added with a large smile, 'we've got threshold.' meaning he could see the end of the runway.

Swiftly the Hercules skis touched down on the hard snow packed runway 14 hours and 31 minutes after leaving Cape Town. It was now 4.31am.

Stepping down from the lead aircraft, Rear Admiral J R Reedy spoke that the flight itself was a great success 'All right boys, you're all a bunch of ruddy heroes.'

A few minutes later Lt. Commander Bill Kurlak brought # 320 down and was greeted by over a hundred base personnel, including the leader of New Zealand's nearby Scott Base, Colonel Ronald Tinker. After a short stop over at McMurdo and having delivered a large consignment of fresh South African steaks, the crews sat down to a banquet in one of the squadron's Quonset Huts. New Zealand's Antarctic commander Colonel Rob Tinker was in speech making mood, as after all he was one of the hosts, but in the words of Lowell Thomas, *'I don't recall what he said, for once started, his speech went on for what seemed hours after he had gotten underway, so I headed for my bunk. Even at 4 o'clock in the morning as the storm continued to howl outside, I could hear the eloquent Kiwi commandant- and he was still going strong.'*

Later the aircraft took off on the final second leg of their flight of the 2,400 miles to Christchurch .New Zealand.

Asked by the waiting media to comment on the first continent to continent Antarctic flight and what it had accomplished, Rear Admiral James Reedy replied *'We proved our communications could satisfy requirements for regular flying into and over the Antarctic from Africa, and I have no doubt that the day will come when planes will fly this route across the South Pole, just as transports routinely fly great circular routes across the top of the world.'*

Co pilot 'Art' Herr didn't continue on to Christchurch and Australia. *'I was left behind at McMurdo Ops to monitor the flight to Chi-Chi, since the rest of the squadron had not yet been deployed to the ice'*, at the time, another disappointment for me as the junior officer who got the *'short end.'*

Lowell Thomas wrote of the flight. *'Finally at last, comes the aerial adventure that inspired my book, the flight that brings to a close one of the major eras in the life of man. The flight airmen have talked of and dreamed of for more than half a century, the circumnavigation of the planet within the earth's atmosphere, by both the North and the South Pole.'* Thomas died in 1981 in New York at the age of 89.

The flight was featured in the March issue of *The National Geographic* magazine, and in a book by Lowell Thomas, *The Last Great Flights.* Both crews subsequently received the Navy Air Medal, rarely awarded for non-combatants, and were inducted into The Explorer's Club.

While the helicopters were kept busy during *Deep Freeze-63,* the four squadrons LH-34D logged over 800 hours carrying 2,000 passengers and 145 tons of cargo. Fitted with JATO, the UH-1B's were able to perform their short-range missions, which in turn freed up the LH-34D's and the remaining LC-47's for other flights.

This prompted the squadron's new commander for *Deep Freeze 64* Cdr George Kelly to write. *'As Antarctic operations expand, it becomes increasingly apparent that turboprop aircraft are mandatory to complete assigned missions.'* He expressed concern at the aged C-121-J's, LC-47.'s LC-117's and the LH-34's that were getting old, and the increased requirements being placed on these aircraft. His concerns became more justified as scientists moved further inland to uncover the mysteries believed hidden on the continent and the proposed programme of the NSF.

'Buz' Dryfoose recalls BuNo # *148318* was the first test bird fitted with 1500 strain gauges that were installed during it's construction and were subsequently used to test the airframe at the increased weights from the A model. All aircraft # *318*, # *319*, # *320*, and # *321* were accepted by the squadron and first deployed on the ice in September 1960, when # *318* was taxied off the runway in a whiteout at McMurdo on February 15 1971 rupturing a wing, and causing a fire which destroyed it. It was the only one of the original four that is not in existence today, although # *321* had a recess of 17 years buried in the snow at the Dome, but is now back in business. Buz Dryfoose was the first Navy pilot qualified in a C-130 on March 31 1960 and flew all four 'originals' by October 1960, the first season of their deployment with VXE-6.

Taxiing in at the South Pole, the Ski-equipped LC-130, would slide to a gentle stop on the prepared skiway, fine snow and ice crystals whipped up by its four powerful Allison T56-A-7 turboprops, and four bladed Hamilton Standard propellers, almost obscuring the hooded parka ground crew in the minus 60 degree F air. Once the fuel and cargo was off loaded, the aircraft refuelled and reloaded, ready to continue on the resupply mission to the Pole.

One C-130 crewmember related to me how some might appear a little frustrated having to wait sometimes for hours for warmer temperatures or acceptable weather patterns, only adding to the tension on the flight deck. One his crew sat at Christchurch airport for three days while another for two at McMurdo, until the weather improved at the Pole Station. One Commander of a NYNG C-130 said landing at the Pole was sometimes *'like landing a ping-pong ball, or threading a needle,'* so he had more than admiration for those guys in VX-6, and in particular those aviators flying the underpowered Gooney Birds.

Open field landings are a hallmark of their versatility, being able to land anywhere to facilitate the movements of the scientists and their equipment to and from remote Antarctic locations. Naval procedure requires the aircraft's commander to make several flyovers at various altitudes to determine the presence of crevasses and once the area for either the establishment of camps or resupply is visually determined to be crevasse free, then the crew performs 'ski drag' to open up any hidden crevasses, in preparation for landing. For ski dragging the pilot makes a normal approach and touchdown, so when the aircraft's main skis maintain contact, he holds the nose ski off the snow and with power full on, the aircraft maintains this attitude and slides for one minute.

The crew conducts two drags adjacent to each other in a straight line, and after each drag performs an additional visual survey of the landing area, and if the area is crevasse free and snow conditions are favourable, then they make a full stop landing.

Take-off is a rather unique evolution too as after taxiing to the end of the skiway continuous movement is maintained until take-off power is applied, for if stopping, the aircraft could freeze to the surface. Once the rudder becomes effective, the commander requests his co-pilot to set full power and at 60 knots he must compress or 'pump' the yoke forward, and with the nose lurching downwards, gives a forceful yank, then brings the yoke full back. Now, the nose slowly rises and is adjusted, and while the slide continues, he builds up speed until the aircraft reaches take-off velocity and slowly 'floats' skywards.

Getting the Hercules airborne is a difficult task, as take-offs from the snow are triumphs of hope over physics; *'the object is simple'*, says one VXE-6 pilot *'get to sixty knots and get the nose up off the snow, for once we get the nose up, it will fly'*. This is not always easy as the nose attitude during the slide is critical for with too much nose high the aerodynamic drag may prevent the aircraft reaching recommended take-off speed. Great care must also be taken to prevent the nose ski from settling back on the snow for if the snow is soft and wet it acts like glue, and may require a series of pumps to break the nose free.

'One golden rule for take-off,' observes Captain Norman, a NYNG 109th pilot, *'we can try different flap settings, move the cargo to the back of the aircraft to change the centre of gravity, or stop and unload some of the cargo, we have left scientific equipment on the ice in order to get off, but we try and put things in our favour.*

It is the loadmasters who really earn their money, for as soon as we stop, often at places that may be as high as 10,000 feet above sea level, they are out there in minus 40 degrees F, off loading JP-8 [fuel], unloading cargo manually or using tracked vehicles to pull the load off. When we are on the ground, the aircraft's engines are kept running in the cold, or they might not start again, and this prevents the aircraft and crews getting stuck, so ground times are minimal.'

Lt Commander Lanzer emphasized that all LC-130 pilots must practice whiteout landings, and they must requalify each season they arrive on the ice. Although the training is carried out in reasonable weather conditions, instruments are used to simulate an actual whiteout landing.

'I know pilots with up to 5,000 hours of flying under their belts, who have never performed or practiced a whiteout landing before they came down here, mainly as its something that is not done anywhere else. Landings are particularly challenging, especially when flying in Antarctica, and carrying out remote open field landings when LC-130's try to land adjacent to a massive Antarctic

glacier to offload or unload passengers and cargo. Pilots try to steer clear of the glacier, because of the crevasses. In order to do this safely, pilots follow a set of safety procedures developed over years of polar aviation' he said.

CHAPTER ELEVEN.

THE DEPENDABLE 'HERK' AND ITS INFLUENCE ON ANTARCTICA AND THE DEMISE OF THE 'DAK'.

The Hercules to replace the Gooney Bird as the
Squadron's new Antarctic workhorse.

Deep Freeze 63 saw the departure of the C-124, the USAF prime mover, from the Antarctic programme, leaving Christchurch locals saddened to see them go, as the sight of these giant pregnant elephants had been a familiar part of their life for over seven consecutive seasons.

They were easily recognizable in the city skies, and during their last season associated with the Antarctic operations, they carried 503 tons of cargo and ferried 592 passengers to McMurdo, back loading 179 tones and carrying 273 passengers; airdropping almost 1400 tons of cargo, mainly fuel to the operations inland stations, with their final drop on December 11 1962. The various USAF squadrons, flying these *'wonder birds'* suffered only one fatal accident after thousands of hours in the air.

Due to the capping off of the financial budget for *Deep Freeze 64,* came the last season for VX-6's remaining two ski-equipped LP-2J Neptune photographic aircraft and the withdrawal of the squadrons SC-54 Rescuemasters, of *Deep Freeze 63.* With the withdrawal of the Rescuemaster from SAR duties at Christchurch airport, arrangements were made for its return the following season if the need arose. During its deployment with VX-6, the C-54 # *56528* had amassed over 20,000 flying hours.

Withdrawal of the C-124, meant the elimination of airdrops that had been the backbone of the Operation's support logistics since 1955, but now the USAF were no longer required to operate a wheeled aircraft over the continent's interior where they had flown dangerous missions with only Hallett Station as their alternative landing field.

The USAF added to their fleet the Boeing C-135A aircraft powered by four jet engines and configured to carry a crew of 10 with 75 passengers and baggage, and in Washington it was planned that *Deep Freeze –64* would be the first season of total C-135 involvement. The planned but not yet constructed runway extension at Christchurch airport necessitated the chartering of commercial C-121's and a Canadair CL-44 from Tiger Airlines, to augment their commitment to the Antarctic programme. So with the US military command committing its C-135 fleet to transport 14,500 troops for military exercise, the planned additional 525 metres to Christchurch airport runway was brought forward in time for DF-64, allowing the Boeing jets to fly direct from Honolulu.

The squadron lost a further aircraft during Deep Freeze 65, an LH-34B *BuNo 150220,* its recovery was a heroic and physical exercise involving both the squadron and the crew of the *USS Staten Island* which had been pounding the pack ice of the bay, but things were to take a dramatic turn of events for the ice breakers crew who's morning, had started out as normal when the VX-6 helicopter pilot Lt Charles Montag, took off from McMurdo on a routine flight to evacuate four scientists and a news reporter from the foot of the continents only active volcano, before an impending storm struck.

As Lt Montag was manoeuvring his Sea Horse onto the ice at the foot of Mt Erebus his position was surrounded on three sides by sheer ice cliffs rising hundreds of feet in the air and when one of the copters crew ADR1 William Leoffler prepared to drop a smoke flare to determine wind direction for a landing, and the flare went off prematurely, filling the helo with dense smoke reducing cockpit visibility to less than six inches. Lt Montag now unable to see let alone read his instruments was not too anxious to risk flying into the nearby ice cliffs so he elected to make a forced landing.

Touching down on the ice firmly on the port main mount his chopper tilted, striking the rotor blades and coming to rest on its port side leaving Leoffler and a third crewmember AE1 Keith Smith shaken but unhurt as they hurriedly abandoned the crippled craft. Mean time back at McMurdo, the Squadron's CO Cdr Frederick Gallup had just taken up his duties as SAR commander when word reached him that the Lt Montag's helicopter was overdue, so he directed his senior helicopter pilot Lt Cdr Jim Brandau to search the Erebus Bay area for the missing crew, while he continued a communication check with ships and aircraft in the area.

In less than an hour Jim Brandau spotted the three men, and returned them to McMurdo, as by now the Antarctic storm had hit with all its fury, with blowing snow and strong wind gusts. After the storm had abated Cdr Gallup was faced with a problem of salvaging the damaged Sea Horse in order to return it back to McMurdo and then on to an overhaul facility in the States. Consulting his senior officers they considered many proposals - some totally bizarre but in the end he accepted the assistance of the stout men of the *USS Staten Island* with their indestructible spirit.

The icebreaker with VX-6 crew and a set of R4-D tail skis aboard manoeuvred to within four miles of the downed aircraft, and once the skis were attached to each of the landing gear, and long lines secured to mooring points along the fuselage- the hard toil commenced.

As dawn greeted the Antarctic, and after a hearty breakfast and strong coffee, every available man aboard the icebreaker walked the four miles to the copter and heaving on the lines began the long trek back to the ship. Four hours and four miles later, after many solid navy grunts, groans and many cigarette breaks, the damaged Sea Horse was man hauled to the icebreakers crane which lifted it aboard and set sail for McMurdo.

Cdr Gallup sent his warmest words of praise to the captain and crew of the *Staten Island*. *'The admiration this command has held for our surface shipmates, has just been enhanced by the professional performance of the VX-6 helo recoverer operation by the crew of the USS Staten Island. The spirit in which the event was completed at the expense of a well earned holiday, is deeply appreciated and will long be remembered.*

While all aspects of the operation were impressive, particular note is taken of the men who physically towed the aircraft several miles across rough snow and ice of the deteriorating ice shelf in a display of the ability of the Navy's most vital commodity- manpower.'

For the men aboard the *Staten Island* who spent the majority of their time pounding the ice in both Polar Regions, and who seldom got ashore during their deployment, this was a great adventure and earned them an extra toddy of rum to boot.

During *Deep Freeze- 64,* the USAF strengthened the squadron by deploying the 1608th Air Transport Squadron [ATS], with three C-130E's flying out of their home base, Charleston South Carolina. The squadron carried out a punishing schedule of one mission a day for the first twenty days of their deployment, after which one mission every second day was established.

The first C-130E [62-1814] carried out the first of its 40 turn round missions on October 14 and more than one mission was scheduled out of Christchurch every second day.

With a fourth aircraft positioned in Christchurch for SAR coverage from October 22 to November 2 it did not participate in the airlift.

There was one emergency landing during their first season, when a C-130 # *62.1814,* low on fuel after a fly in from New Zealand had to make an emergency landing on the ski runway in zero visibility on December 13. While the weather remained reasonably good it was at the final approach that weather conditions deteriorated, with the pilot having to be held over the base for over four hours waiting for an improvement.

After dumping his cargo of mainly Christmas mail, [less than 10 percent was not recovered] the pilot was talked down by McMurdo's tower. With snow now blowing across the runway and a 30mph crosswind, he made his landing, but when the Hercules pilot brought his plane to a stop, its wheels had ploughed a 24-inch furrow through the hard snow suffering only minor damage, with no injuries to the crew.

Due to the efforts and assistance from VX-6 and Navy Seabees, the C-130E was recovered, repaired and returned to Christchurch within three days for further maintenance by Air New Zealand engineers.

The USAF 1501st ATW also visited Antarctica, making a flight between McMurdo and Christchurch via the South Pole, a distance of 7,037 km [3,800nm] in 12 hours 52 minutes

So for the first time a pre-season airlift was accomplished by using two Lockheed C-121's, with the addition of a second Constellation named *Pegasus # 131644*. The first named *Phoenix # 131624* had been fitted with the more powerful R-3350-42 engines part way through the previous season, these engines gave it increased performance, allowing for cruising to altitudes of 25,000 feet on these missions. The C-121 had now become the squadron's main photographic aircraft since the retirement of the P2-V Neptune's from Antarctic service.

While the safety factors were also considered, the C-130E's with their shorter take-off run and greatly improved three engine performance, were ready in the event of a sudden emergency, and being pressurized could fly above the weather thus avoiding icing and turbulence.

Commander Sid Wegert, a LC–130 aircraft commander flew with the Puckered Penguins for two years from 1966-68, flying on the ice on an average of 100 hours a month.

'It comes to you in the autumn, with the feeling manifesting itself because that's when we'd be preparing to leave our stateside base for Christchurch, and, ultimately for the season in the Antarctic.

The squadron's working year was split into half with five months spent deployed in Antarctica and the remainder stateside for other logistic operations, and until 1973 we were based at Quonset Point NAS, Rhode Island, then moved to Point Mugu, Calf.

In the Antarctic, we were divided into A and B crews, flying the same aircraft, on for 12-14 hours, then off for the same length of time. On each duty period we'd usually fly double shuttle for example, and we called the McMurdo-to-Pole run rickety rack to the Pole and back, and we'd fly it twice in that time frame. We kept all engines running at the Pole of course, and were usually on deck for about 15 to 20 minutes offloading supplies.'

Commander Wegert, a veteran pilot who had logged more than 5,500 accident free hours in jets and turbo props had flown a number of aircraft, and said the LC Hercules have proved well suited for the squadron's operations in the Antarctic and have been successfully operated in a climate where the mean temperature is thirty below, *'in fact we operated in temperatures up to minus 65 degrees, but below that, the hydraulic and oil seals become brittle and failed.*

Actual instrument conditions occur about 20 per cent of the time, and about one of every three approaches is made in IFR-type weather which could feature low flying scud clouds or blowing wind.

If zero conditions existed at Williams for example, the aircraft would be vectored to a pre-surveyed whiteout landing zone, where there were no obstacles to flight within 20 miles of the flight path, then following pre-established whiteout procedures, the pilot would commence a 100-200 fpm rate of descent with landing skis and flaps down, the minimum rate of descent were not to exceed the 200 fpm limit.'

Cdr Wegert said pilots would fly a seaplane type approach *'at about 50-100 feet above the terrain, ground effect would occur and cause the aircraft to level off, and you had to resist the temptation to nose over and instead squeak off some power and re-establish a rate of descent. This required some finesse.*

During unusual flying conditions like flying on the ice required adjustments, because between late October and early February, when the Antarctic has its perennial daylight, sleeping time had to be regulated as all personnel had difficulty getting some shut-eye. Most personnel experienced what in Antarctic jargon, is called 'Big Eye' but I was lucky, I had little trouble getting to sleep, despite the continuous daylight hours.

The Hercules have adapted well to Antarctic flying conditions and it's winterised role' said Wegert who flew number # *148319*, the *Penguin Express. 'We had to be careful landing with the skis because the nose ski in particular was vulnerable to damage, as stress on it was excessive, so in both taking off and landing we kept it raised for as long as possible.*

You have to be flexible because of the limited weather information available, quite often clear weather which had been forecast would disintegrate to zero-zero in minutes.

Those days were exciting, gratifying and uplifting, I know I'll probably never get the opportunity to return to the ice but I'm very happy to have had the chance to experience the wonders of flying the Antarctic.'

After his tour of duty Commander Wegert served for a time with the USAF at Air Training Command HQ, Randolph AFB, Texas. In the *'Naval Aviation News'* in 1975, when asked if he still 'feels the season coming on' he replied without hesitation;

'Absolutely, when the leaves turn, I pack up and head towards the bottom of the world. I suppose part of the motivation stems from the explorer instinct in all of us. It's an intriguing sensation flying over places that only a handful of people if any, have seen before. I have great respect for that continent it can be so unforgiving as it is remote and beautiful. It's sort of like the last terrestrial frontier. It always amazes me to be able to fly from McMurdo to the Pole in three hours, a journey which took Captain Robert Scott of the Royal Navy 78 days in 1911.'

Deep Freeze 64 saw only one aircraft lost, a CH-19E *BuNo 144255*, which crashed during a whiteout four miles from McMurdo, leaving both crewman injured and the helicopter destroyed, on November 28 1963.

Cdr F Gallup assumed command as CO on May 6 1964. In late September 1964 VX-6 achieved another historic first, described by Rear Admiral Reedy who was aboard *'the last great long distance flight to be made on this earth connecting two continents,'* when a single LC-130 departed from Melbourne, Australia on September 30 to Byrd Station, via the South Magnetic and Geographic Poles, a distance of 4420 miles in just over fifteen and a half hours.

When the ski equipped LC-130 piloted by Commander Frederick S Gallup, [a native of New Haven and a naval veteran of more than twenty years] reached the South Pole, some 3,300 miles from"Melbourne, the exterior temperature had plummeted to minus 85 F. To those at the South Pole, the monotonous drone of the C-130 flying overhead at 5000 feet must have seemed like an angel from heaven, as they stood in the frozen darkness and fog waiting for the 50 pound mail sack to be parachuted to them, for among the mail were copies of the *'Sydney Morning Herald'* and other Australian newspapers, and this was their first mail and newspapers for nine months.

After leaving the Pole, the weather deteriorated to such a degree that Admiral Reedy needed to alter course for Byrd Station, 900 miles further south. At Byrd the Hercules landed, but after the failure of the automatic locking device, heavy chains were needed to hold the nose ski in position. Over Mc Murdo, Commander Gallup brought the 65-ton plane to a skilful halt, with the main skis bearing the plane's weight as the C-130 touched down, completing a three-flight assault by VX-6 aircraft. Two

Hercules which had left Christchurch the night before, landed at McMurdo at 3.17 am, a few hours before a ski-equipped C-130 from Punta Arenas Chile reached McMurdo, followed by Commander Gallup who arrived at 5am.

On board the aircraft were two Australian journalists, David Burke and Phillip Law, who reported that the flight which was expected to be routine, turned out to be quite eventful *'after arriving over the South Pole, but being unable to land because of the low temperatures-just minus 85F, and while dropping mail and fruit to the Station's personnel, the sliding doors, open for the air drop, then jammed and would not close.*

We shared the inhalation of oxygen from a couple of cylinders as the plane crossed over the Queen Maud Mountains, and a radio message then informed us that the weather had closed in at McMurdo, so we change course for Byrd, but on arriving there the nose ski could not be lowered, and after a half hour struggle to release it, Cdr Gallup decided to land without it. What a fine display of Antarctic flying and it was a very relieved group of men who emerged when, after slewing around when the nose finally dropped onto the snow and the aircraft came to rest.'

The crew of #*318* was Cdr. Gallup, Lt A Dick, C/P, Lt G Hitchcock, P/C, Lt.Cdr B Taylor, Lt G F Wright Navigator, W S Bow AMSC Metalsmith, L Campbell, AT1, Radioman, and R C Blummer ADJ2 Flight Engineer, Del Nelson, ADJ1, Flight Engineer, Z Zimmer ABHC Loadmaster, SGR M Hester, R Berth AE2, A Cox ADJ2, Bob Owler ADJ1 Flight Engineer.

A few weeks later Cdr. Gallup few out of Christchurch to commence *Deep Freeze –65*, after a four day flight from the squadron's homeport at Quonset Point, with stop overs at Hickham AFB, the Canton Islands and Fiji. Before departing from Christchurch, the message from Antarctic indicated the weather to be normal for October, and the winter over personnel had completed the last task of their stay in preparing the ice runway, digging the last of the R4-D's out of their winter entombment and test flying them in sub zero temperatures.

On October 22 when VXE-6 was flying in support of a UH-1B geodetic survey team on the Lillie Glacier, LC-47H *BuNo 12407* while taking off with JATO assistance, had one of the canisters inadvertently fire while being jettisoned, causing one rocket to strike the left propeller knocking the engine off and forcing the left ski into a vertical position. The aircraft was a total loss and subsequently written off the books.

On November 8 1964, one of the Army's UH-1B helicopters # SN12544 crashed while attempting to land near the summit of a 13,800 foot peak in the Admiralty Mountains off Victoria Land, about 38 nautical miles from Hallett Station. It appeared that the helicopter lacked sufficient power for a controlled landing at such an altitude, and while there were no injuries, the unit was destroyed.

On December 5 1964, a UH-13P helicopter *BuNo 143146* assigned to the *USS Staten Island* detachment 43, Helicopter Utility Squadron, crashed while making an emergency landing, with the helicopter catching fire when the main rotor blade struck the tail assembly during the hard landing, leaving it totally destroyed.

A little over a month later on January 12 1965, the fourth Squadron accident occurred when LC-47J *BuNo 50778* was on it's landing rollout to the skiway, and one of its skis struck a large but unnoticed sastrugi, striking its propeller, tearing off the port engine, and twisting the fuselage.

During *Deep Freeze 66*, VXE-6 squadron was tasked to support the establishment of a Polar Plateau Station, which would be as near to the centre of the Antarctic continent as possible with the estimated altitude of the station at 13,000 feet. At the time the station was the smallest, coldest and without doubt the most inaccessible of all the United States Antarctic scientific stations situated 1,350 n-miles from McMurdo Station. Cdr S F Kauffman had the task of building the station which consisted of five pre fabricated vans that were assembled, making a building 25 by 75 feet with an additional van and Jamesway hut as emergency shelters The additional building was projected to be constructed by the Seabees from NCBU-201 the following year, for housing between 4 and 8 wintering over personal at any one time before the station was closed in January 1969.

The story began on a cool overcast morning of December 13 1965, the squadron's CO Commander Moe Morris, once again proved his flying skills when he took off from McMurdo in the *City of Christchurch # 148318,* for the first flight to the polar plateau station, to prepare for the unloading of the building materials.

They were the first group of VXE-6 aviators to set foot on the Polar Plateau Station, which is the highest point in Antarctica located on the rim of the earth's curvature, with the landing site being 600 miles beyond the South Pole. This was one of the most unusual missions for the *Puckered Pete* mob since the 'bug' runs started on February 12 that year, after a C-130 transported a special load of Penguins and Seals to the United States zoos, prompting one squadron member to say '*We can deliver anything anywhere, anytime.*'

Prior to the polar plateau flight the squadron had made several exploratory flights in an endeavour to locate the ideal spot for a scientific station, finding an area some 600 miles from the South Pole. Preparation for the mission began by off loading all that was not required, to lighten the plane due to the difficulty of taking off from that altitude in soft dry snow, but two rounds of JATO bottles were loaded onboard to assist if necessary, for flying from McMurdo to the Pole Station required a refuelling stop, as the Plateau station was another 800 miles further on.

Aboard this flight was NSFA chief of staff Captain D.Bursik, the stations first Officer in charge, Lt. Jimmy Gowen [Medical Corps] and Rear Admiral Bakutis the Commander of *Task Force 43.*

Landing on the polar station is well documented, as the ski equipped Hercules slid to a gentle stop, with the props whipping up fine ice crystals that almost obscured the lineman wrapped in a heavy hooded parka. Once the ramp and cargo doors are opened the minus 60 degree polar air quickly rushed at the crew in an icy blast, taking their breath away. By now it was mid morning with the winter sun shinning brightly through the thin air, making physical activity particularly exhausting.

Two flags were placed some distance behind the aircraft to outline the pathway for the crews manning the heavy equipment, as it had become a man made blizzard from the props back wash. [Similar to the situation that killed crewman Andrew Burl Moulder when he was crushed between the LC-130F and a cargo sledge, on February 13 1966. Andrew was an experienced navy personnel loader, who had done a lot of unloading at the South Pole Station.]

Once unloading was completed, Cdr 'Moe' Morris and his crew left for the 800mile flight to the Polar Plateau, being a first for the squadron and once the area was visually determined as crevasse free by performing ski drags to open up any hidden crevasses, they prepared to land.

'*After landing we looked for footprints and when we could not find any, we surmised that we were in fact the first people who had ever been here,*' recalls Lt Bob Owler the Flight Engineer. '*The planting of Old Glory and the station's flags were accomplished and following congratulating handshakes, the USARP personnel and cargo were unloaded to begin the establishment of the Plateau Station.*'

While on the virgin landing strip Cdr Morris was more than concerned with the take off, as surface temperatures were approaching 40 below, and with the low angle of the midnight sun, could warm to 20 below near midday. Fuel lines were always in danger of freezing but this coupled with the drag of the soft snow was a greater fear, and the Squadron pilots realised that the first flight to leave the Plateau Station would experience difficulties. The veteran polar aviators knew that with each landing at the Plateau Station they would experience these problems over and over again as if for the first time.

'Once the initial camp was established and the first personnel were secure in their tents with their equipment and supplies, the aircraft prepared for take off to McMurdo. The soft snow, which had yielded so readily to the flag, now became a clinging mass on the Tafton-coated skis of the straining LC-130. In addition, the thin air at this elevation could not satisfy the power requirements of the aircraft's turbo-prop engines' wrote the aircraft's commander in the *Antarctic Journal of the United States.*

Then it was time to take off, preparation for which had been rehearsed many times before leaving McMurdo, and with all the eventualities having been covered the crew loaded the JATO rockets to the aircraft. Their first obstacle was that at 13,000 feet, *'the Jatos felt a lot heavier than at sea level'* said Bob Owler, and with the crew hyperventilating, walk-around oxygen bottles were needed to help them increase their strength to complete the job.

As is normal in open field and soft snow procedure, Commander Morris taxied back and forth many times in an endeavour to pack the snow down to a hard base, but the powered snow would not compact with the snow's water content being absent, and all the time they were burning off vital fuel, however, this resulted in lightening the aircraft too.

Then 'Moe' gave the instructions *'let's give it a go'.*

Bob Owler again *'on the first try, which felt like 11 miles long, we achieved about half of what was required as take off speed. On the next try the order was given to fire the JATO rockets, so when our top speed was obtained, the JATO was fired only to find that the elevators in the full position were not enough to keep the nose up nor the nose ski from digging in the snow and slowing us down.*

All during this time I had the four-engine bleed air valves closed to get more power and that made it very cold in the cockpit, yet we all began to sweat profusely. The second and last round of JATO bottles to be loaded felt even heavier than the first, but as always the VX-6 crew got them on the bird.

Now the remaining fuel was down to approximately 8,000 lbs, which happened to be the minimum required to reach the nearest gas pumps at the South Pole Station. I must now tell you that I for one was not about to walk the 800 miles to the South Pole. Now came the time to fess up to the skipper as to what had to be done to give us more power in an emergency, for one does not always tell the skipper what you have done, up until one is forced to, and I guess I can reveal this 40 years later.

Before departing McMurdo, the Temperature Datum [TD] fuel control valve null orifices were manually repositioned to the full open setting that would give us more juice if needed, so I suggested that on this take-off attempt we switch the electronic TD switches to null in case we could not get more power, also advising not to look at the engine turbine inlet temperature just put the throttles to the fire wall.'

The second ski run also seemed too long, but with the planes increased speed to top speed, the very nervous order was given to fire the last round of JATO bottles and with a big bounce of the nose ski the *City of Christchurch* as airborne, hardly flying, but off the soft snow.

'After skimming the snow for who knows how long or how many miles, we began to gain some altitude and our thoughts turned to what a great time it would be to have a stiff drink - I can't remember if we dank that 40 oz bottle of Jim Beam that was in my survival kit or not. The throttles were pulled back, the TD's returned to auto and bleed air valves opened. The remainder of this historic flight was uneventful, after all, we had had enough excitement for one day on the ice' says Bob.

Cdr. Morris recalled *'repeated take off attempts were made until finally the rapidly diminishing fuel load reached the point were one more try would tell the tale. If not successful, the newly established Plateau Station might very well be provided with an all alumimum ski-equipped 'building.'* We taxied, reaching 14,000 downwind then turned around and lined up with our tracks, after an agonizing, fuel consuming, 15 minute wait to allow the tracks to solidify, full flaps were lowered and all available power applied to the engines, using full throw of the controls to steady the aircraft as it *began to 'lope' in its tracks, accelerating ever so slowly, calling for the JATO as the airspeed crept past the 60 knot mark.*

Instantaneously the eight JATO bottles fired to give an additional 8,000 pounds thrust and the Hercules was muscled free of the snow at 75 knots, far below its design performance of over 100 knots required for take-off.'

Bob mused *'The over temp's did not hurt our old faithful Herk T 56 engines at all, we knew that we had to go back to the Plateau, but how could we get a skiway that would support routine?'* he relaxed as much as he could on the way back to the warmth of his McMurdo home. *'It was determined that our old and beloved D2 cat Linnus with her cut down LPG tracks would need to be taken to the Plateau Station within days to drag a skiway at this god forgiven place. Linnus had travelled all over Antarctica with us, but we knew that we would never be able to lift her back out of the station. She did her job and regular flights began to the Plateau Station.'*

The Plateau outpost station had Linnus remain there as a memorial to its sacrifice to better the Antarctic scientific endeavour, at the most inaccessible part of Antarctica. For the new boys, life at the Plateau Station was quite difficult, for apart from becoming accustomed to the abysmal weather, the total isolation and accepting one's fellow mate's company, they also faced altitude sickness that gave them the classic feelings of a 'hangover', along with huffing and puffing and keeping their food down.

When this sickness struck it usually lasted a week or more; *'when you tried to sleep, you would sit up in a cold sweat with your heart pounding. Your lungs gave incredible chest pains; you would breathe in panic as though you would never be able to breathe again'*, said a squadron's veteran of the Plateau Station winter over party. *'At about 13,000ft above sea level in the polar regions where the atmosphere is thinner because of the drawing of air to the equator on a spinning earth, we only had 60 per cent of the normal oxygen content.'*

For those poor unfortunates stationed there during the winter, and without the diurnal sunrise and set, there was no forcing mechanism to control fluctuations; storms would break the inversion and they could watch as the broken inversion brought temperatures to 50 below down to ground level. Shortly after a storm passed the temperature would fall between minus 110 deg F to minus 116 deg F almost routinely, leaving one to only imagine these extreme temperatures.

'As we came in for a landing, I was allowed in the cockpit behind the co-pilot and could see a lone Jamesway Hut and a scattering of freight crates all over the place.' recalls Martin Sponhoiz in his Book *'Among the Magi'* Research Tracks in the Desert Snow. *'I was immediately self centred with the concern that a region of the snow might have been left untouched for my delicate radiation measurements and drift experience.*

Even the invasion study assumed a snow surface relatively undisturbed, but if tracks and crates were strewn all over I feared losing that purity. The pilots on the other hand, were concerned for our safe landing on a still uncompleted landing strip. The big traxcavators needed to pound the snow surface for a hardened skiway were not yet delivered, as these flights would follow in the next days.'

Martin Sponholz described one phenomenon, *'as he spat speculatively, there was a sharp explosive crackle that startled him, so he spat again and again into the air, but before it could fall to the snow, the spittle crackled. He knew that at fifty below, spittle crackled on the snow, but this spittle had crackled in the air, so undoubtedly it was colder than fifty below. Could this be true!'*

At the Polar Plateau, it remain true that 80 calories must be lost for every gram of liquid water to solidify to ice, and that always takes time; wrote Martin Sponholz. *'Granted, the colder the temperature outside, the more rapid the cooling effect. The moisture of your breath did build up as frost all around your face, balaclava, and cloth material of your parka. For some reason the frost of your breath did not build up on the wolverine fur ruff of the parka. If you were outside for an hour or longer, this frost would become so thick you needed assistance when you came back to the camp to be gently cut of your parka and it was for that reason beards were most convenient. A razor blade could easily remove a little chin hair rather than sacrifice the valuable parka.'*

Another story of life at the Polar Plateau Station in those early years is written by an unknown author and printed in the *'The Lutheran Educator'* in 1983. *'The greatest difficulty of life at the Plateau was the loneliness - no mail, no radio, no church, simply nowhere to go. Some of my glacial work took me about a mile from camp, and I can recall it was always especially clear day or night, the same thing, but without the sun, with bright stars of the Southern Hemisphere overhead. The snow was swirling and screeching constantly as it drifted from nowhere to anywhere, and I was overcome with fear and trembling.*

I wanted to reach for my rifle or a club or a sword or anything. But there was neither person nor creature to fear for over 600 miles. No natural life exists anywhere within the interior of the Antarctic. Our exploring team was the intrusion, but yet it was frightening. It was never easy to hike out that distance and fear was always with me. But by this time, in dark winter, I was fully acclimatized and the cold was acceptable. Earlier in the summer the scientific leader, the camp construction engineer and I, had surveyed the region for deep crevasses and found none. We had learnt to deal with the unpredictable weather and took proper caution with beacon lights and lifelines for walking to remote scientific sites.

These were not reasons for fear. Yet alone, I was terrified. How I can say that to be alone in nature with God, the Holy Almightily Creator of all, a sinner is most fearful. I can understand why, when the angels made the announcements to men they always started with 'Do not be afraid'. A glance at the Southern Cross would ease my fears. The Southern Cross has a red star at its side, and that little reminder of my savoir was always present, even in the unexplored polar wintry night.

But a reminder of human interpretation is never enough. Without God's clear Word of the Bible, the only comfort this continent gives is a bitter cold death. Others losing their senses to the fatal chill of a barren land also cursed the beauty praised by early explorers. In the Antarctic there was no church [except at McMurdo's Chapel of the Snow] but Christ's Church was everywhere. The Bible gave sermons, and my bunk was the pew. As a child I did not like to memorize hymns for my teachers, but in the Antarctic, those that I could remember, I sang to the wind until the frost build-up on my parka closed my mouth.'

As the last weak shinning light had disappeared from the Antarctic sky, the United States flag was ceremonially lowered and removed from the flagpole for the duration of the cold winter plateau darkness. The camps CO Jimmy barked out his command with full military fluency, Jerry Damschroder a Naval personnel, and mechanic trained as a heavy equipment operator, lowered the flag, while Bill Ludlow and the CO saluted, while the four civilians stood at attention in the cold

Fifteen thousand gallons of diesel had been airlifted onto the Plateau before darkness had set in, more than twice the amount needed, straining the Navy's method of keeping the supply warm, but this was necessary in case the next summer proved to be colder or having more violent weather restricting the re supply flights getting through. Historically in Antarctica, a few re supply efforts were cut off by bad weather leaving the wintering over crews expecting to be relieved, but instead left stranded. This was not in the American experience, but still a contingency that needed to be accounted for.

Likewise, nearly three years supply of food was airlifted by VX-6 Squadron and stored in two different locations at the Plateau Station. One years supply was stored in a special food cache at the emergency camp and the other two were stored near the main camp with a snow barrier dividing them.

With fire being the major fear, planning and placement of these caches had to be carefully considered, as in a desert of snow and ice, fire had to be attacked without water, with the French losing an entire station a few years ago, Jerry Damschroder trained and retrained the whole station's party routinely in fire fighting tactics.

It is hard to explain the severity of the cold weather at the Plateau Station. Martin Sponjolz writes. *'It was severe. The Great Antarctic Inversion was in its extreme glory most of the winter. The snow surface was always colder than the incredible 100 degrees F below zero temperatures except when a storm would pass over the icecap plateau. The wind would pick up and the turbulence would break the inversion, pulling down the warmer air above the surface to minus 50 degrees F. This happened on five separate times when the several storms would last more than a day. One way to describe the cold is to say that on these few days of minus50 degrees F in the depths of winter it felt very warm in spite of the winds and blowing snow.'*

The Plateau station was operational by January 30 1966, and after a two-day delay awaiting the arrival of the fuel tanker from New Zealand, the VX-6 aircraft delivered some 66,000 gallons of fuel, taking full advantage of the favourable weather. The squadron flew 24 hours a day often completing 65 squadron hours each day before the operation shut down.

On December 28, one VX-6 C-130 crew flew 22 hours and three other Hercules joined the effort to give the squadron a record 85.5 hours, and during the 24-hour period the aircraft delivered 267,000 pounds of cargo, over 17,500 total miles. The squadron supplied and supported the existing Antarctic Stations but their major task was the planned construction of the new Palmer Station on Anvers Island.

Each season after the squadron returned to home station for the northern summer, they were engaged in a number of operations apart from training for their next deployment in Antarctica. In April of 1965, VX-6 squadron became involved in a military airlift when the political conditions in the Dominican Republic deteriorated with a communist led rebellion to overthrow the military government, who had ruled the Islands since September 1863. The rebellion caused President Lyndon B Johnson to authorize the American intervention with 140 LC-130's from the United States military units involved in the massive aerial transport operation for the airborne invasion, in preparation for the landing in the Republic.

VX-6 aircraft, now back in their base at Quonset Point Air Naval Station, Rhode Island, preparing for the next Antarctic season, were ordered to join the aerial armada, transporting US Marines to San Isidro.

Cdr Marion Morris took over the squadron as CO on May 5 1965 from Cdr F S Gallup [now deceased]. Cdr 'Moe' Morris entered the navy in March 1944 and after receiving his wings reported to a Pacific anti-submarine seaplane squadron, VP-47, qualifying as Patrol Plane Commander while still an ensign, his first crew included an ensign co pilot and a midshipman navigator.

Over the next 30 years Cdr Morris served primarily in the Pacific theatre starting with the occupational forces in Japan. During the Korean fighting, he was assigned to V-48, where his area of operation was the South China Sea and the waters off Korea. Other significant assignments included participation in the first thermonuclear test in the Bikini area in 1953, Combat Information Officer aboard the seaplane tender, *USS Albemarle* [AV-5], VX-6 *Deep Freeze 64 - 65* and *66* as Operation Officer, Exec Officer and CO and Commander Antarctic Air Group.

He earned a BS in Nautical Science while attending the US Navy Postgraduate School and later as MS in International relations while taking the Senior Course at the Naval College, joint staff duty, including, contingency planning at CINCLANT and finally NORAD.

After completing his naval service Cdr Morris was active in general aviation, then put his talents to writing and has had seven novels and two non fiction books published.

When the squadron departed their NAS Quonset Point on September 18, two C-47's [R4-D's] almost never made their destination to McMurdo in time, indeed there was speculation they would make it at all. Fifty days later at 2.05am. Lt Don Kahler touched down on the ice runway to win the official transpacific air race, thirty minutes later Lt.Cdr. Dennis Olson brought his aged aircraft to a halt some 20 yards behind the victors, then the C-117 which had been delayed in Christchurch for an engine change.

The aircraft set no records in their half way around the world flights that the squadron had been making since 1955, and like all other previous transoceanic hauls they were without major incidents. However the 12,000 mile flight from the American's west coast to the bottom of the world would sap the strength of the Navy's finest as this flight was beset by maintenance problems and extremely poor weather en-route, as the two R4-D's battled their way to the Antarctic with what Lt Kahler described as *'Plenty of guts and a multitude of prayers.'*

As the crews made their way towards Antarctica from Rhode Island, engines failed, the radio quit and malfunctioned, their radar equipment stalled at times, JATO rockets misfired, tail winds made sudden switches to head winds, while the dreaded icing was most prevalent on the last leg to McMurdo.

Lt Don Kahler recalls one harrowing instance occurring midway between Rhode Island and Hawaii, when a chip detector light began to flicker indicating that one of the aircraft's engines was about to fail. With equal time point already reached, it precluding any thought of a return to California, leaving the Gooney Bird to plod on to Hawaii with the crew prepared to ditch at any moment.

'Nothing happened luckily' commented Lt Kahler, *'but I got so sick of looking at that blinking light I just reached down and unscrewed it, and after that the crew and me just sat back and relaxed'.* This was surely the understatement of the season.

Another point where the plane's capability was stretched was on the leg to Christchurch. As they flew over the mountainous ranges of the South Island approaching Christchurch, the cloud obliterated everything in sight, and with more than considerable skill the crew were able to climb to 12,000 feet, exceeding the theoretical limits of the plane by 1500 feet. Once the weather cleared and they were above the jagged snow covered Alps, Lt Commander Olson recalled *'that it was touch and go for a few minutes.'*

Normally the last leg of the flight from New Zealand to Antarctica is the most dangerous and unpredictable, but on this trip surprisingly, both planes experience the easiest 14 hours of the total of 106 hours actually spent airborne.

While the flight was high on their list of 'unforgettable memories', their stopovers in Hawaii, the Fijian Island and New Zealand's southern city Invercargill, was remembered for the hospitality from the townsfolk welcoming the navy aviators and taking them into their homes, for meals and lodgings.

It was during *Deep Freeze –66* that the Kiwi's displayed some of their innovativeness, when the first flight by a Royal New Zealand Air Force from Christchurch to Antarctica arrived on October 17 1965, under the command of Wing Commander B A Wood, of No 40 Squadron, who completed the flight in seven hours fifteen minutes.

'We made a very small modification to our C-130H # NZ 7033', said Flying Officer J Kelly, the RNZAF's Engineering Officer-in-Charge of the seven servicing personnel at Scott Base, after extra air was pumped into the oleos before leaving Christchurch, but perhaps the most novel modification was placing a coil of rope around the nose-wheel oleo to overcome the shock of landing on hard rough ice. The RNZAF'S Antarctic operations were code named *'Ice Cube'* and the operation continued every season afterwards, supporting the Americans / New Zealand supply pool.

The RNZAF No 40 squadron flights varied largely depending on the finances available, and considered the three to four flights each season to be training flights, with additional flights funded by Antarctic New Zealand. During *Deep Freeze 68,* the squadron made three airdrops to Vanda Station in the Wright Valley.

During the 1960's a Christchurch resident Bob Bull became a friend of the squadron in more ways than one, as Paul Panehal remembers, *'the diminutive snappily dressed locksmith was a frequent caller to VX-6's hanger in Orchard Road, armed with a hand full of tools, wire, and electronic parts to repair all their locks. He always had a smile on his face, and usually a good Kiwi joke to boot. I met him first in '65, as he came to the AT shop a couple of times a week and we became good friends over the years. After I was drafted back to the States, we corresponded regularly until in the mid 1990's when he passed away with cancer.'*

Bob would regularly be 'summoned' from Christchurch to McMurdo on a fast return Herk flight to the ice just to open the safe containing the men's wages, this often happening at odd times. Bob had another talent, as in his small brick Opawa garage, he made hundreds of wall plaques for Squadron and Task Force 43 and Deep Freeze personnel, and for this author, I was honoured to have known Bob and his wife Joyce, who were personal friends and neighbours for over 38 years. Bob would do anything at all for everyone.

During *Deep Freeze 66*, the Task Force 43 constructed a new runway on the Ross Sea ice shelf at Williams Field and built the Plateau Station as well as the very high frequency longwise antenna substation in Marie Byrd Land. VX-6 deployed 21 aircraft and 3 C-130E's from the USAF's 1501st Air Transport Wing and 8 helicopters from the four USN Icebreakers two squadrons.

Again the LC-47's heavy workload was taking its toll in the Antarctic operations. The squadron lost three aircraft during the 1965-66 season. On October 6 a LC-47H *BuNo 17239* crashed on the Ross Sea Ice Shelf while practicing open field landings. Two months later LC-47's BuNo *17107* had the main mount collapse while landing in the Horlick Mountains, having the investigation board report the cause as material failure from the mount not being strong enough to withstand the pressure of the sastrugi in the landing area.

The morning of February 2 1966 dawned a normal day for the crews of VX-6, when after breakfast, the aircrews met in the operations room. After being briefed they discussed their various missions and weather conditions and both Lt Morris and Commander Olson were aware of the low visibility over the Ross Sea Ice Shelf at the time, but little did they know tragedy was about to strike that close knit community. A catastrophic chain of events to the mission and crew of # *50832* was to grievously change the lives of six families forever, in just a few short hours.

Lt Harold M Morris and his crew approached their R4-D that their ground maintenance crew had prepared and fired up ready, and together with a LC-117 BuNo *99853* flew out of McMurdo on a routine mission along the 60-mile tractor trail from Little America to Bryd Station to pick up a scientific party. The LC-117 *BuNo 99853,* under Cdr. Dennis Olson and Lt. Stan Jones landed safely in extremely limited visibility.

However the crew of the #*50832* named *Spirit of McMurdo* wasn't so lucky, for when approaching camp on the Ross Sea, named Mile-60 [70deg 50'S/159DEG25'E], some 380 miles from McMurdo, the D4-D stalled due to severe icing from a partial whiteout, while at about 200 feet above the surface. As the right wing dropped, Lt. Harold Morris lost control and the aircraft hit the ice while almost inverted, breaking the fuselage in two places, but before rescuers could reach the aircraft, leaking fuel caught fire igniting the eighteen JATO canisters aboard which continued to explode for several hours after the accident. Except for the tail section, the R4D was destroyed leaving the twisted wreckage lying in a giant hole in the ice, some 40 ft wide and over 35 feet deep.

A scientist less than a mile away at the time of the crash, reported, '*it plunged to the surface making a violent impact with the snow, the front part of the aircraft was compressed by the force of the collision while the centre section and both wings tore loose and the rear section ripped free. Before rescue operations could start, leaking aviation fuel caught fire, subsequently igniting the JATO bottles, and continued to prevent any effect to remove the remains of those onboard. The entire aircraft, except the extreme empennage and portion of the outer starboard wing panel, was consumed by the flames, leaving the twisted wreckage rested in a giant hole over 35 feet deep. No evidence exists that any of the crew members attempted to escape.*

All six crew aboard died on impact and it was more than six hours before the burning wreckage could be approached as Dennis Olson and his crew watched helplessly as their friends and buddies ended their final mission in this way.'

Only a few months earlier Lt Morris had been Dennis Olson's co-pilot on LC-47H *BuNo 17017 Deep Freeze Express* flying all the way from Quonset Point to the ice the previous November on an 80-hour flight. *BuNo 17017* was lost on December 5. Another member of Olson's 4-man crew, Lt. Ken Buel was later killed on a mission during the Vietnam War, and Jones later made his first whiteout landing at the same site.

The dead squadron crew were Lt. Harold 'Hal' Morris, pilot, Lt. William 'Bill' Fordell co-pilot, Lt Commander Ronald Rosenthal the navigator, Petty Officer Richard 'Dick' Simmons radioman, and Petty Officer Wayne Shattuck, and Petty Officer Charles Kelly, the planes captains. It was the most tragic accident in the Squadron's history. The bodies were brought back to Christchurch aboard a C-130F and transferred to a C-121J *'Pegasus'* for return to the United States.

Commander Fred Schneider, then the squadron's Maintenance Officer, was the senior member of the accident investigation team, and the following D.F.67 season, he was appointed Exc. Officer and Squadron commander, stressing that it was not the purpose of the accident board to affix blame, but to find out what actually happen so it might be prevented the next time.

'There were two R4-D's taking a field party out for research projects. White out conditions prevailed, and it appeared that the first aircraft had landed while the second one #50832 came in at about 200 feet, he went inverted and crashed into the snow - it is believed that the pilot Commander Harold Morris neared the onset of the stall and thought he had in fact landed, pulled off the power and crashed.

The pilot of the second aircraft had time to start up a snowmobile and go to the crash site. The tail section was separated from the aircraft, so he had time to access the rear cabin, then there was an explosion, which hurled him about 30 feet, luckily he was uninjured. The whole structure, engines and cockpit ended up in a hole some 40 feet deep. All the 14 JATO bottles also exploded in addition to all the avgas. They burnt horizontal holes in the ice, since both ends of the R-4D blew out, we lost six men, -3 officers and three enlisted men, it was a very depressing time for us all.'

Dick Simmons was the radioman on # *17017* the R4-D that went down in January 1965, after it caught a wing tip on landing. Wayne Shattuck had taken Red Auxfords place on that flight.

Doc Holik [Captain Hedbloom USN-senior medical officer] an iconic figure on the ice, was considered by the squadron to be their own Florence Nightingale and Angel of Mercy. Paul Panehal remembered the crash and the hours leading up to it at 0942 hours Zulu on the Ross Ice Shelf.

Paul Panehal believed that Wayne Shattuck was a normal member of the Otter crew. *'For this reason, this accident has been etched in my memory, since Dick and I were good friends. He and I had dinner together the night before the accident, and he helped me with my binary [which seems odd today] and we discussed electronic theory.*

A short time after dinner Wayne wasn't feeling well and had gotten sick in his stomach, he thought something he had ate didn't agree with him and went straight to his rack. The following morning [the day of the crash], I was coming down out of the AT shop at Willy Field and caught my wedding ring on the door as I went, I slipped down the steps onto the snow, taking with it a good bit of skin, I remember being on my hands and knees for some time digging in the snow trying to locate the ring, while all the time my finger was bleeding like crazy.

After some time I found the ring, wrapped my finger in a handkerchief and headed for the sick bay post haste. Just as I was checking to see Doc Holik, the radio went off, announcing the plane crash and instructing an emergency medical crew; a C-130 was standing by to fly Doc Holik and his party to the crash site.

Everything went into top gear, the equipment and personnel were already out the door, and it may have been half an hour or longer before everyone settled down enough to take care of my bleeding finger. I'm sure Doc and his group were out there within minutes of the call, but all of us were concerned about the extent of the accident. All the information was not known, as those in the know had cut-off circulation of all information. I think the reason I was told, was due to our friendship. I was sick when I discovered Dick was aboard, they also reported that Doc Holik was dedicated and relentless, he would not give up in his efforts, although others resolved there was nothing that could be accomplished.

Doc Holik was highly revered even before this situation, and became almost legendary afterwards. I have never known a more dedicated Doctor in my 30 plus years in the Navy. My hat has, and always will be off to the 'Real Quack' of VX-6 and many things he did on the ice to make that everyday fatigue disappear. Those who served with him will always remember the picture on the door of the sickbay with a duck dressed as a doctor and the words 'VX-6 Quack' – THANKS DOC.'

AT2 Jimmy Clark, who was the radioman on # *17832* during his pre C-121J days with VX-6, was there at the time and reported that due to the exploding JATO rockers, the intense heat destroyed all but the tail section.

Cdr 'Moe' Morris was having lunch in the Hill galley, when he was informed of the accident. He said while it was '*Lt Morris's first flight as an aircraft commander, he was a fine, experience and fully qualified pilot. Unfortunately, he encountered unusual weather conditions for Antarctica; clear skies. We seldom encountered that, as it was normally too cold for such accumulation of frozen moisture. Rime ice, somewhat less hazardous, was the norm.*

On his landing approach, he was most probably unaware of the additional weight of the ice and may have used too slow an airspeed. In any event, the A/C stalled and one ski went vertical when a bungee support cord broke. The resultant drag caused a deeper stall and spin. He applied full power but was unable to recover and they went straight in, nose first. Explosions and fire followed. It was daylight, of course, but whiteout conditions prevailed so there was no horizon or surface definition. One of our Herks had preceded him in landing and witnessed the event.'

The words of Rear Admiral Richard Byrd to a family of another who died in Antarctica, could well have been said that day. '*He served and died for his country, just as devotedly and with as high a purpose as if he had died fighting to preserve freedom. The mission for which he had volunteered and on which he served is, and will continue to be, an effort to unlock further the secrets of nature in that vast area Antarctica, and put them to the use of all mankind.'*

'*As for the R4-D's*, said Commander Schneider '*well I was glad to see them leave the Antarctic since I believe that a bunch of lives would have been saved, although there was some sadness since it was the close of an era, the Hercules did a much better job in the field and could do the work of 4 even 5 Gooney Birds'*. As VX-6'S Maintenance Office he considered them too difficult to work on and keep in the air, because of the cold weather the metal became brittle. '*We had to keep the tools inside or they would break, I recall that we tried to change a spark plug [in the hanger] and the plug broke off, and it took the better part of 24 hours to get the shank out of the cylinder, even with the heat of the engine.'*

The squadron's fourth loss of the season occurred on January 11, 1965 at Camp Ohio high up on the Shackleton Glacier, when LC-47J named *Gotcha*, [delivered to the Navy in October 1944 and added to the squadron's fleet in October 1962.] was at landing rollout on the skiway when one of its main skis struck a high but unobserved sastrugi. The ski turned vertical and struck the propeller, tearing off the engine and twisting the fuselage.

Following these loses the Commanders of both the Task Force and VX-6 decided the LC-117/LC-47's had a limited life on the ice, and expanded the Lockheed LC-130 Hercules' role. Also that season, the remaining UC-1 Otters were retired after their final flight on January 16 1966.

Another airfield was established on a barrier approximately five and half km from Pram Point during *Deep Freeze 66*, this time on the permanent ice about 13 km across the sound from McMurdo.

It was intended to act as an emergency cross wind landing field for wheel-operated aircraft, for when the ice runway deteriorates late in the season. The Americans commenced construction in November 1965 and a VX-6 LC-130F evaluated it on February 11 1966 after making a successful first landing.

So ended *Deep Freeze '66,* and home at last for the squadron, to be greeted on arrival by families and friends at Naval Air Station -Quonset Point.

Back at their home port carrying out pre deployment training for *Deep Freeze 67,* Lt Brian Shoemaker and PRJ Jim McDonald were out on a routine training flight at an altitude of one thousand feet, when they sighted an upturned boat and two elderly fishermen swimming towards the nearest land some four miles away. The pair had got themselves into difficulty and were struggling in the rough seas, so by manoeuvring their helicopter, Lt Shoemaker along with ADR2 Claude English and ADJ2 Larry Lister, plucked them to safety and flew the pair to Quonset Point's Naval hospital for treatment and a check up.

Commander Daniel Balish had relieved Commander Marion 'Moe' Morris as the Squadron's CO on June 17 1966 to become the squadron's 15th Commanding Officer.

This season will also go down in history as the year of accomplishment for VX-6, as by the end of June, some 1,080 visitors had visited the US Antarctic Museum that had been established by the squadron, and during the Wickford Art Festival, some 6,500 people were able to view the squadron's display of coloured photographs relating to Antarctica and the meet the squadron's mascot- the stuffed penguin - in a sidewalk display.

As the rest of the squadron were readying themselves for their season on the ice, Lt Cdr Thomas Schanz [SC], the officer in change of the Para-Rescue Team, reported they were ready and operational for deployment. On the morning of September 9th the Task Force was notified that an ailing scientist, Armand Spitz was suffering from acute peritonitis at Byrd Station.

While wintering over at Byrd Station, Dr. Larry Spitz became ill, and it was comforting to those Naval personnel and scientists to know that their countrymen half a world away where about to undertaking a hazardous rescue mission. As one scientist remarked *'I will never again cast disparaging comments towards the US Navy, even though they often referred to us as 'sand crabs'. Because Larry Spitz is alive today, is an example of the full scope of the military and VXE-6 Squadron.'*

At 2300 local time on September 4, the Washington duty officer of the US Navy Support Force Antarctica received a phone call from Davisville, Rhode Island. The duty officer at Davisville HQ had managed to pick up a very garbled message from the amateur radio operator at Byrd Station, but with an Antarctic magnetic storm raging, communication was almost inaudible, and to make matters worse, the Byrd operator couldn't hear Davisville at all. Fortuitously, the ASA operator heard enough of the Byrd transmission to relay that an American scientist was stricken with what sounded like acute appendicitis, and that Byrd was not only requesting immediate aerial evacuation, but that they were already preparing a skiway for a landing.

It was hoped that while Dr Spitz was being treated with antibiotics, he would respond sufficiently to the treatment to be able to wait for the scheduled October 1 fly-in. At first all was going well, but early on September 9 Dr Robert Hunt the doctor at Byrd, reported his patient's rising temperature, so that afternoon Rear Admiral Bakutis, Commander of *Deep Freeze* requested and obtained approval for a medical evacuation flight.

Immediately preparations began for this early flight, as at this time of the season Byrd Station was completely under snow and not normally accessible to aircraft during September. The evacuation aircraft *Penguin Express # 319* piloted by the Squadron's CO Cdr.Daniel Balish departed Quonset Point with orders to push straight through to Christchurch with minimum time on the ground, and then to proceed to Antarctica as fast as weather permitted with the back up aircraft *# 321* piloted by LCdr Anderson to provide a search and rescue role, departing Quonset Point 18 hours after Commander Balish.

As Cdr.Balish crossed the Pacific, personnel at both Byrd and McMurdo Stations where instructed to make surface synoptic weather observations every three hours, and to take upper air soundings every 12 hours. The Australian and New Zealand stations at Macquarie and Campbell Islands were also requested by the Navy to make upper-air soundings at the same intervals.

Meanwhile Antarctic personnel were engaged in skifield preparations, setting out emergency runway lighting, reactivating navigation aids mothballed since early March, and checking out all equipment, while the Christchurch detachment of the Naval Support Force were asked to have fuselage fuel tanks ready for installation in both Hercules.

Commander Balish arrived at Christchurch International Airport at 1125 hours on September 11th, and the following day at 0959 after a rest in Christchurch, the Commander and his crew flew out of the city, only to face head winds upwards of 140 knots. Poor weather at McMurdo and Byrd Station forced a delay of several hours until the weather conditions cleared sufficiently to carry on to Byrd, even though the skiway there could be best described as poor.

Dr Hunt reported that while Dr Spitz was resting comfortably, his general condition was gradually worsening, but the emergency, while real, was not considered acute. Dr. Spitz was evacuated and taken back to Christchurch, with a stopover first at McMurdo, arriving with another ill scientist on the afternoon of the 14th. After diagnosis at the Christchurch Public Hospital, it was decided that surgery for an infected appendix could be delayed for three months while treatment with antibiotics continued. Once again the VXE-6 'Angels of Mercy' had lived up to their motto of *Courage, Sacrifice, Devotion.*

With their Commanding Officer Balish on *# 319* were Lt Kahne, Lt Serba, Lt Muckenthaler, Lt.G Bland, Lt Cdr Short, Lt Lusk, Lt Holik, Ltjg Pope, ATN2 Wailda, AMH3 Hyndman, AE2 Stackhouse, PH2 Eley, ADRI Lingo, ABH2 Johnson, ADJI Herring, ADJ1 Poorman and ABHC Boleen.

Cdr Balish received the Air Medal, and his crew were awarded letters of commendation from the Commander-In-Chief, US Atlantic Fleet.

As the mercy flight was in progress, the remainder of the squadron were in final preparation for their deployment, packing supplies and equipment and saying their last farewells, with the first aircraft departing Quonset Point on September 20th, the first ever airlift of personnel to be transported by commercial DC-8, seven days earlier than R.Adm Bakutis and his staff aboard their C-121 Connie.

Commander Balish remained in Christchurch to await the Admirals arrival, due at midnight on September 30th in a C-130 *# 319*, with the CO at the controls. The Admiral flew out of Christchurch for the traditional first of October fly in with three other Hercules -# *319* –Cdr Schneider, *# 320*- Lt Simpson and *# 321* Lt Cdr Anderson, all following at two hour intervals.

Cdr. Balish joined the US Navy after graduating from Scranton Central High School in a cadet programme in March 1953, and was designated a Naval Aviator in November 1954, first flying PBY-5A Catalina's on submarine patrols in the Aleutians. His first tour of duty with VX-6 began in 1964, serving as both Operations Officer and Executive Officer, prior to his assumption of command. He completed three tours of duty of Antarctic flying, and in 1965 was awarded the Navy Commendation Medal for his participation as a crewmember on a C-130 which made the historic rescue flight to McMurdo in the dead of winter to evacuate and save the life of an injured US sailor.

On March 17 1967, he also received the Air Medal for meritorious achievement as the pilot and aircraft commander of the Herk, during the emergency evacuation of a critically ill scientist from Byrd Station.

During October Lt Cdr Schanz's Para Rescue team underwent five days of extensive ice survival training conducted by members of the New Zealand Federated Mountain Climbers Association, being taught ice traversing, crevasse recovery, igloo building, rescue techniques and the use of the equipment. In addition during their Antarctic deployment, they made a total of 131 practice jumps, and AE-2 Henry B Thomann Jr a member of the Squadron's Para-rescue team made the first ever parachute jump at the South Pole.

After being assigned to storage at Air Naval Station Litchfield in April 1948, an R4-D-8 was assigned a new Douglas serial number # *43381* and entered active service with the Navy when assigned to VX-6 in 1966 as LC-117D. On November 28 1966, 71 tortuous days after departing their homeport at NAS Quonset Point, Lt Cdr Clifford Moran and his weary crew stepped down from their aged # *17092* onto the cold skiway at McMurdo amidst a cheering welcoming party.

The crew had been beset with mechanical failures by the aircraft and obstinate weather conditions. Their long flight over the Pacific Ocean was via the tiny atoll of Canton Island, which was in American possession and located in the Pacific Ocean near the Equator, then onwards via Fiji to Christchurch. The flight to Canton Island required twelve hours of flying over water, mostly in darkness with no moon out, as their Douglas transport trouble 'bugged' the crew until they finally reached McMurdo, having to fly with pitch upwards and nose steeply downwards.

But as Lt Moran struggled with his decrepit C-117D displaying all the signs of her advancing years and almost at the end of her life, one story must have rung in his ears about the flight of Commander Frank Kimberling in October 1957 in *Deep Freeze III*, when forced to land on the isolated atoll after losing both engines, one of which gave up the ghost 629 miles short of the Island forcing him and his six man crew to jettison everything moveable including their personal gear, baggage and records.

Landing there was a lottery, recalls Cdr. Waldron. *'Because there was no moon and no surface lighting except for the runway lights, everything beneath us was inky black. Using cockpit instruments, I was able to tell my attitude, airspeed and altitude, however, when I looked outside the cockpit the runway seemed like a tiny spot in a black void, and there would be almost no visual clues to help me land until the aircraft crossed over the end of the runway. The ocean below us must have been glassy smooth because I could see no whitecaps to assure me where the water began.*

As I approached close to the airfield I slowed the aircraft, lowered the landing gear and the wing flaps and gently lost altitude. Still it seems that we were not moving, but that we were suspended in midair with the runway still a long way ahead of us. Finally, after what seems a small eternity, the runway started getting larger, giving me some idea of what I could do to affect a landing. After I finally got the aircraft on the runway, I realized that it would take a lot of practice before I could consider over water nightime landings as being for me a routine event.'

The crew of *Would You Believe It*, apart from Lt Cdr Clifford D Moran, were radioman ATR2 Jim Clark, the plane captain/flight mechanic AS1 A.M 'Red' Auxford, Navigator Ltgj K Buell, and Co-pilot Lt Cdr R E Sorne. Auxford was an ADR [aviation machinist mate reciprocal -radial engine] but changed, as his rating was closing and the chances for advancement were better in the aviation support equipment rate. He was a member of the C-47 crew that went down on 1 February 1966, the day he swapped with AD2 Wayne Shattuck who needed flight time, which spared Red's life.

The story of Lt Cdr Clifford Moran and *Would You Believe It* goes back to February 1966 with Deep Freeze –66 drawing to a close. Paul Panehal returned to Christchurch aboard the *USS Wyandot* along with R-4D [C-47] # *17221 Mutha Goose,* back to Christchurch from the ice so that it could be overhauled by New Zealand National Airway's [NAC] workshops in Christchurch to check out its electronics, have its wing root bolts replaced and other structural work done. Paul returned to home base ANS Quonset Point Rhode Island.

With the work by NAC completed in May, both Paul Panehal and ADR-2 Jim Wright flew back to Christchurch with their Skipper Cdr Moe Morris and passengers in June, to accept # *17221* from NAC and prepare the aircraft for its flight to Antarctica in November, upon Lt Moran's arrival. Some of the preparations the two performed were installing the two 450 US gall and one 200 US gall fuel tanks inside the fuselage, tuning the engines, repairing and checking all the electrical and electronics equipment, not to mention waxing the aircraft in order to gain a few extra knots flying speed. *'After the aircraft was assigned back to VX-6, waxing was almost a weekly routine that became a passion with Chuck Ratliff, much like most folks waxing their car.'* Paul Panehal recalls.

On the arrival of the aircraft's regular crewmates to Christchurch, the acceptance test flight was carried out.

'The acceptance flights really caused a stir with NAC engineers, as it would appear that someone overheard Jim and I discuss [just loud enough for them to hear] that the commander, Cdr Ray Berger, would take her [# 17221] up for a couple of pitch and roll tests, a couple of stalls and do at least one loop. Some time later Cdr. Berger chewed us out for scaring the wits out of some of the passengers. At first there were a lot of NAC folk volunteering to make the test flight, then some somehow decided not to make the flight. Basically the C-47 was never designed to perform acrobatics and the very thought gave the uniformed a cold chill up the spine. Jim and I informed most of the passengers that day, that we were only pulling their legs.' Paul's memories of his time in Christchurch come flooding back to him.

Piloted by Cdr.Ray Berger, the Officer in charge of VX-6 Detachment Christchurch and a Leutenant from the RNZAF, # *17221* made a number of round flights between Christchurch and Invercargill.

According to Paul Panehal, Ray was a delight to know and fly with, his Det consisted of nine enlisted personnel whose skills were required to maintain and replenish the equipment and spaces after the squadron departed Quonset Point for New Zealand, with these folk being hand picked to serve a three year assignment in Christchurch.

As soon as their regular crew arrived from Quonset Point, Lt Berger carried out a number of training and familiarization flights around New Zealand in readiness for their flight south. Part of these flights was the number of round trips to Invercargill to build up the survival gear, food and large numbers of JATO bottles for the eventual flights south.

'The Goonies could load 15 JATO rockets under the fuselage starting near the main wing joints in two banks –8 and 9. We had stored all the stuff at the Invercargill Airport Fire Station and that must have been the biggest secret in the town, as nothing went missing during our periodic flights. What is surprising today about the airport was its security to the field where they had a few turnstiles attached to a three-foot high fence. You could walk on the runway and use the restroom day or night, I don't ever remember them being locked. During those days most people were very trusting.' Panehal recalls.

When Lt Moran arrived, both aircraft attempted a number of launches from Invercargill, but unseasonable weather prevented their departure, so they had to wait in the southern city for a break in the weather between Invercargill and McMurdo and the AG's [weather guessers] forecast was bleak to say the least, and the best they could predict for Lt Moran and his crew was for the week following Thanksgiving '66.

Suggestions were made by some members of the squadron, that the race to Antarctica should be dubbed 'The Great Gooney Bird Race' – then the bad news.

Paul Panehal again *'On Thanksgiving Day, after many false starts, I was informed our aircraft # 17221 was scrubbed from the launch to the ice, and that Moran and his LC-117 crew would be launched to make the flight south alone. We were told the choice was made to send # 092 as it had slightly better engines and a better chance of making the flight successfully.*

Jim and I were really disappointed at having our flight scrubbed as we started shipping the entire excess store back to Christchurch that we had previously flown to Invercargill. Our last back load was the heavy one, mostly crated JATO; we loaded the bottles under old #17221's wings and made a JATO ourselves. Jim and I flew # 17221 for the remainder of the season.'

While the regular pilot, co-pilot and the navigator of # *17221* were sent to the ice, Paul and Jim remained in New Zealand and flew about the country with Lt Cdr Ray Berger for the remainder of the season. After returning to Quonset Point in February 1967, Paul Panehal was informed he had been selected to be transferred to VX-6 Det. Christchurch, and resume crew status on *# 17221* until July 1970.

From the time it entered service with VX-6 in 1963, *# 17221* carried the side number JD 14 and was named *Mutha Goose*- the artwork was a Goose with a long neck, but this artwork was removed prior to leaving the ice as it was considered not appropriate for public display.

During Deep Freeze-67, both Jim Wright and Paul Panehal worked on coming up with a new name for *# 17221* to replace the nose work assigned from 1963 to January 1966, when it returned from the ice for the last time. Seated having a quiet cool beer at the White Heron [now called the Sudima Hotel Grand Chancellor] in Memorial Ave, near Christchurch Airport where they were staying, they discussed a new name for the plane affectionately known as Dirty Duck by VX-6 personnel.

Eventually the *Kool Kiwi* was selected and used as the nose art, so Lt Cdr Berger had a small Kiwi bird on skis painted just aft of the nose radome seal, port side, at a point about midway from the top to bottom- it was accompanied by the words *'It ain't no big thing'*- a favourite saying of the commander. Assigned to VX-6 on the ice, the side number JD-4 was changed and renumbered to JD 14 as one of the squadron's hellos on the ice was already using the number JD-4.

Paul Panehal again: *'During 1966-69 # 17221's crew was Pilot Clifford Moran made Captain and retired in Minnesota. His aircraft # 17092 was returned to the US in January 1968, and stored at Davis Monthan AFB until sold minus its engines in October 1974.*

Going back to Canton Island for a moment, which is important as the tiny atoll Island in the Phoenix group was a vital link, in fact a lifeline, for the squadron's planes who had to land to refuel on the pork chop shaped island, while en route to Antarctica via Christchurch. An island whose beach is composed alternately of coral sand and broken fragments of reef rock. It's best described by Cdr. James Waldron in his book. 'Flight of the Puckered Penguins'- 'at night it was not a very intriguing place to say the least. Except for the runway and a few adjacent buildings there seemed to be little except sand and palm trees. The air was heavy with humidity and except for two or three Polynesians who helped us fuel, it might have been a deserted atoll island anywhere in the tropics.'

Canton Island the largest and most northern of the Phoenix Group, is also known by its Kiribati name of Kanton or Abariringa, an atoll made up of a low narrow rim of land surrounding a large shallow lagoon, and is just four and a half miles wide on the west, from where it narrows to the southern point which is nine miles from the northwest point. The rim of land varies in width from 50 to 600 yards and its height from 5 to 20 feet, with the ocean beach rising steeply from its fringing reef, to a crest this is fairly smooth and level.

The island was discovered independently by several ships, mostly American whalers, and with its fair anchorage off the southwest lagoon entrance, it provided a haven for these whalers despite its lack of water and coconut groves. After a variety of suggested names, including Mary Swallow and Mary Balcout, the name Canton came late, but stuck because of the dramatic circumstances. On March 4 1854, the New Bedford whale ship *Canton*, with Captain Andrew J Wing ran ashore on the reef, and after a brief stay he and his crew took to their open boats and arrived in Guam 50 days later. Eighteen years later in 1872, Cdr R Meade of the *USS Narragansett*, surveyed the island during his efforts to bring a certain Capt William 'Bully' Hayes to justice, and he named it Canton to commemorate his adventure.

Although claimed by American guano diggers, Canton does not appear to have been worked by them, while the John T Arundel Co between 1885 and1886 dug a little guano, in 1899 the island was leased to Pacific Co, but was not developed. In 1916, it was among the islands leased to Captain Allen of the Samoan and Trading Company, but aside from planting a few coconut palms, of which only ten survived, the company made no use of the island.

Canton broke into world news in 1937 when the American and New Zealand 'eclipse expedition' selected it as a spot from which to view the total eclipse of the sun on July 8, thus producing enough radio and press media coverage to place it on the map. But more than the eclipse of the sun was observed, when both British and American noted that here was a splendid lagoon on which seaplanes could settle as well as a flat rim for aircraft to land, with the advent of seaplanes as a new type of romantic commercial travel, so both parties made a monument displaying the flags of the nation.

Prior to this, the British had taken pains to reassert their jurisdiction over the Phoenix Islands, with officials landing on Canton from the *HMS Leith* on August 6 1936 and erected a sign asserting sovereignty in the name of King Edward VIII. On June 3 1937, *HMS Wellington* stopped and a second sign was nailed to a coconut tree in the name of King George VI. Meanwhile on April 8 1937, the Phoenix Islands had been placed in the hands of the Gilberts and Ellice Island Colony [now Kiribati and Tuvalu] and its administrator added his sign, in October the same year.

During 1938 and 1939 Pan American Airways laid out and developed an extensive airport, deepened and cleared the lagoon and initiated flights to New Zealand using Canton as one of its ports of call. This was indeed an interesting 'call' by the American carrier using Canton as an intermediate stop for airmail, and passengers. A barren coral atoll, it had no human inhabitants and practically no vegetation, but it afforded a convenient location with the central lagoon furnishing an excellent harbour for their Clippers. To make an ocean air base, *Pan American* established a community on the island, built quarters, and installed water supply systems, an electric power system, built a dock for disembarkation and a hotel for the use of passengers in transit. Every item of material had to be transported from the US by ship. Hillary Kerrod, daughter of the islands District Officer, wrote her recollections of growing up on Canton in the 1950s and 1960's, of the Pan Am hotel, now disused and how with her brother use to play in it, climbing in through its tiny high up windows.

The island is remembered by veteran US Navy airmen Ken Barber as having only one tree and one landing strip, located at the northwest corner of the island. *'I suspect that a B-25 we lost on December 5 1944 is in that lagoon somewhere, as I recall he [the pilot] would have been headed south as I was going in the opposite direction, when I saw him buzzing the strip'.* While Quartermaster third class Charles Martin, from the *USS Natchaug AOG-5* recalls, *'yes I remember that tree, we took a jeep for a joyride, if I remember it was getting dark and I hit this tree a glancing blow. That was my only claim to fame aboard my ship, and of the entire twenty-two islands in the Pacific I visited, and this was one of the worst. No liberty, just nothing to do, we would only spend a day or two unloading oil and gas, then head back to either Guam or Pearl Harbour.'*

Erik Abdal recalls *'My grandfather told me that the island had occasional Japanese fly over at night, but only once was there an attack from such planes, and I recall him saying it was very brief and was one plane, and no casualties. Without intent, my grandfather left me interested in the Central Pacific war topics.'*

But whatever, this tidy barren coral atoll was not only strategically useful during the US space age testing programme, it was a lifeline to the squadron's R4-D pilots enroute to Antarctica- a refuelling stop after twelve hours of flying over water, the first feel of land after leaving their home port.

For the remainder of the season # *17221* was used to ferry Naval staff around the country, including the staff of US Secretary of State Mr Dean Rusk and President Johnson's staff during the pair's visits to New Zealand. During one such state visit that year, a press photographer request Cdr. Berger to fly over so that he could get a good picture of the plane and the ship, not realizing how high the ships antenna tower extend above the Carrier.

On another occasions, they were flying a squadron of Marines to Wellington for their Ball, or flying the squadrons baseball team to Invercargill, or the trip to Dunedin when the commander and a passenger had business in the city and left Paul and Chuck to stay with the plane-then ten minutes after they left in a cab, the two decided to walk into Dunedin to look around the city and didn't have a cent between them. Yes if that old bird, now resting at the Christchurch Ferrymead Historic Aeronautical Park could only talk and relate her stories, she would have some interesting tales to tell.

Paul Panehal remembers acquiring and wiring up speakers to the main cabin, so they could send local music back to the passengers, he is sure that had they had a longer tour with *# 17221*, they

could have done more than glue a rug to the sheet metal and screw it over the corrugated deck in the old Gooney Bird, although the table, curtains and the C-121 seats were better than the long troop seat along both bulkheads from the front to the rear door. They also installed an electric stove, the source of so many pots of good black coffee, and a number of dinners, with it operating off the 28 VAC power bus.

During the mid sixties, the United States Seabees in Antarctica were buzzing, transforming the remote Antarctic capitol from the appearance of a mining town into that of a little village. The navy's construction unit worked around the clock, some of them putting in upwards of fourteen hours a day, confounding the experts who had expressed doubt that the project could be completed that summer. On the office walls of Lt.Cdr H A Tombari, the commanding officer of the Mobil Construction Battalion 6 out of Davisville Rhode Island was a critical path chart, giving every job its place in the over-all scheme and displaying to the Seabees how to be ahead of their schedule by four per cent.

The Seabees had to build the first road in the Antarctic continent and in order to achieved this, they had to scrape some 100,000 yards of brown material off the hills directly above the camp, crush the rocks in a pre-fabricated crushing plant, and construct the road's foundation with a six inch layer of stones and fines. Construction in the Antarctic is onerous and downright uncompromising at times causing the Washington based engineering experts to be sceptical about the very possibility of constructing the road across one section of permanent ice.

However, Lt. Commander Tombari himself an engineer, along with his professional team built the road over the hill, constructing three large culverts to take the summer melt under the impervious rock layer, and had it in use by late 1965. This road cut down the time required in unloading ships from upwards of 13 days to between 3 and 4 days.

Another project of theirs was a bridge that took the road across the low point with it ending at the beginning of the track across the frozen sea to Williams Field's air facilities. The starting point for the pipeline was the pumping station at Hut Point, which ended at the Winter Quarters Bay, where previously flexible hoses had run from the ships to the 15 inshore fuel tanks. Manpower was no longer required for this vigorous and freezing task that had not been looked upon with joyful appreciation by personnel moving aviation, motor, and diesel fuels for winter storage. Both road and pipe lines were completed the following season.

The third major project undertaken by the MCB-6 and their first in Antarctica was the water distillation plant that turned salt water into fresh, thus making the tedious carrying and melting of thousands of tons of snow, a thing of the past. It stands on Observation Hill, overlooking MacTown like some guardian angel watching over the isolated base, where the water is pumped 350 ft from the sea to the distillation unit that is capable of producing over 14,000 gallons per day.

The plant is also the sewerage system, which until its operation, Rear Admiral Reedy described as a twentieth century power plant and a seventieth century toilet system.

During that year, the MCB-6 started work on two new warehouses, completed as the earth science and glaciology lab, and the other a science warehouse, with new quarters completed for senior scientists. They then commenced work on a new ten bed dispensary with operating room and dental facilities, while a new tunnel and other facilities were built at Byrd Station, and new buildings at the Pole Station with a generating plant at Cape Hallett, and the new Anvers Island Station which was built on the Palmer Peninsula.

By the end of 1967 the *MacTown* camp had changed completely with the completion of an officers club, recreation facilities, new gymnasium, barracks to house 259 men, with laundry and drying facilities, and a new science centre. Yes! The men of Mobile Construction Battalion really laid it on that year with their 200 specially trained and devoted personnel transforming the village.

During *Deep Freeze 67*, VX-6 were involved with two aerial photographic reconnaissance projects, the first code-named *LITTLE SARRECCO* [South American based Reconnaissance] with the concept being to photograph the ice conditions around the northern ice surfaces of the Antarctic Peninsula, with a view to determining the feasibility of operating a research trawler during the Antarctic winter.

One of the squadron's R7V-1 [previously C-121] *Pegasus* the Flying Horse # *131624*, was flown back to Burbank by Lt Cdr Phillip Griffith, where prior to its deployment Lockheed installed a special new internal fuel system. This consisted of two 500 US gallon and one 2000 US gallon, fuel bladders and associated plumbing which was located in the main cargo compartment, increasing the total fuel capacity to 9,559 US gallons. Overall it added some three and half hours to its in-flight endurance.

With a fifteen-man crew to operate the photo-configured C-121, which also carried eight additional observers, the mission took place from August 8th to the 15th 1966 from Chabunco Airport, near Punta Arenas in Chile, but the project was plagued with bad weather, having the first two attempts aborted before the successful flight was carried out on August 11, allowed them to take weather recorded data over sixty-five per cent of the planned route, but when the bad weather continued in the Antarctic Ocean the project was abandoned.

Two days after the first supply mission to the South Pole Station was completed on October 19, Lt Cdr Griffith in his photo configuration Super Connie # *624* departed from Christchurch for Punta Arenas via McMurdo, where the crew made a two day stopover before flying across the continent to Chile on October 24 1966.

A second project, code-named *Santop* [South American Antarctic Topographic Photo] was conducted during October and December 1966, and was again based in Punta Arenas, using the same long-range fuel system aircraft that carried a crew of fifteen and eight observers. It differed from the first, by being a topographic mission that involved photo missions over Palmer Land covering 129,350 square miles in 23 photo lines. While the time frame had been extended by two weeks, only about eighty per cent of the intended area was covered as the project was abandoned due to bad weather. On December 29, the programme terminated, and Lt Cdr Griffith and his fifteen weary crew, returned to Christchurch for some well-deserved R& R.

The crew of # *624* who flew the mission with Lt Cdr Griffith were; PH2 Schmidt, AMS3 Beier, Lt Cdr Sallis, Lt Phillips, PH2 Beard, AT1 Gray, AE3 Ross, Lt Riley, LCdr Philo, Lt Cdr Morrison, Ltjg Suarez, ADR-2 Perkins, PH1 Lee, ATN2 Burkett, DR1 Newland, AE2 Hammond, PH2 Springer, PH2 Eley and Mr MacDonald.

Task Force 43 commenced *Deep Freeze 67* with VX-6 providing the majority of air power from their 15 aircraft and the additional Army, Navy and US Coast Guard's UH-1D Helicopters.

The Air Force had attempted their first flight to Antarctica on November 10-11, but the aircraft had to overfly McMurdo and return to Christchurch due to the extreme crosswinds on McMurdo's ice runway, but had more success on November 13 when Captain Howard Geddes touched his C-141 [65 0229] down on the ice for the first time in more ideal conditions. After circling the airfield for some 20 minutes, he made a perfect landing using only 1220 metres [4,000 feet] of the available 3,050 metre [10,000 feet] runway, five hours and 52 minutes after leaving Christchurch. The VX-6's C-121 took ten hours to cover the distance, while the C-130 Hercules flying time was eight hours.

It wasn't until *Deep Freeze-69* that Starlifters were used in the United States Antarctic programme full time, with two C-141 from the 438th MAW making eight Antarctic turnaround missions between October 29 and November 10 1968, with each flight carrying an average of 18 tonns [40,000 pounds] of cargo, thus taking a huge burden off the shoulders of VX-6. By this season the USAF's C-141 were also carrying the bulk of the United States and New Zealand missions.

The squadron suffered two helicopter crashes during *Deep Freeze 67*. A Bell UH-1D [serial number *65-9741]* from the Army Aviation Detachment, Antarctic Support, crashed in a whiteout on November 5 1966 at Marie Bryd Land Camp 1. Major B D Hawkins the detachment commander and pilot with five crew had just made an aerial check of a marooned topographic party, and while the party was safe the bad weather prevented the helicopter from landing.

Returning to camp in heavy turbulence, he was preparing to land when the weather deteriorated to whiteout conditions and Commander Hawkins lost visual reference causing his UN-1D to land hard. None of the crew was injured, but the Bell Helicopter was severely damaged and abandoned after the removal of radios and special equipment.

The second helicopter accident occurred on January 1967, when a HU-13P Bu*No 143135* assigned to the *USGGC Glacier* [WAGB-4] detachment 55 Helicopter Utility Squadron One [HU-1], crashed on a glacier tongue while supporting a seal counting mission from Couling Island to Edisto inlet.

The helicopter was making a precautionary approach to the glacier tongue after a sudden loss of power, when the pilot, Lt. Commander Allen B Callison reported a loss of surface definition in a near whiteout and landed on the nose of the helicopter, which rolled end over end, and with Commander Callison still strapped in his seat he was thrown through the canopy on the first roll and while he was not seriously injured, his helicopter was destroyed.

From *Highjump* days the US Coast Guard's icebreakers had assisted in opening up supply sea channels into McMurdo, but it wasn't until a trial program in 1967 that their helicopter support detachment proved feasible. Based at Mobile, Ala, the Polar Operations Division's officers and enlisted aviators flew Sikorsky HH-52A's with each detachment deployed to an icebreaker, consisting of two helicopters, four pilots and 12 enlisted personnel. These detachments were self-sufficient, and while deployed to maintain and repair their aircraft, they were not dependent on VX-6 as rescue capabilities rested entirely with the individual icebreakers as they operated from remote locations far from the populated areas.

The three remaining LC-117's saw only limited use during the season, and while two were used as backup, only one remained operational, *# 17092 Would You Believe* delivered to the US Navy in May 1943 in scientific support, making the very last Gooney Bird flight in Antarctica on December 2 1967, on a flight from Hallett to McMurdo.

On January 3 1967, a party from the National Aeronautics and Space Administration [NASA] headed by Dr Wernher Von Braun arrived at McMurdo for a ten day visit, and it was the squadron's job to transport the party on an investigation tour of the dry valleys, which were thought to have features found on other planets.

On January 29th two of the squadron's C-130's remained in Christchurch due to geomagnetic disturbances, causing a radio communication blackout between all stations, and lasting eight days. Not only was this the longest blackout of the season, but it also created a backlog of air movements and a subsequent delay in the Task Force's operations. A few days later on February 7th with communications back to normal, the last scientific field party from Beardmore Glacier was returned to the comforts of McMurdo Station, and at the same time another Hercules landed at the Plateau Station, marking the official closing of Deep *Freeze 67*. After supplying all outlying stations, the Pole Station was closed down on February 16, with Brockton on the 19th and Byrd two days later. From then on, the squadron's C-130's were shuttling back and forth between McMurdo and Christchurch as the bulk of the personnel were taken off the ice.

With the aid of USAF's C-141's and a commercial DC-8, all the men flew back to their families at Quonset Point, after the Skipper, Cdr Daniel Balish and the crews of four C-130's bade farewell to Christchurch and headed home.

Operation Deep Freeze 67 was over.

After being relieved as the squadron's Skipper, Cdr.Balish reported to Washington DC for duty with the Bureau of Naval Personnel, and on March 17 1967, he was awarded the Air Medal for meritorious achievement as pilot and aircraft commander of the C-130 during the emergency of a critically ill scientist from Byrd Station.

Operation *Deep Freeze-68* got underway with a change of command ceremony at Quonset Point on April 6 1967, when Cdr Fred Schneider assumed command from Cdr Daniel Balish, to become the squadron's new commander. Born on December 21, 1928 in Clare, Mich, Cdr. Schneider entered the Navy under the Holloway Aviation College Programme in June 1946, after attending several flight training schools, and received his gold wings in June 1948 to be commissioned as an ensign in 1955. In February 1965 Cdr Schneider received C-130 flight training at Sewart AFB, Tenn. before reporting to Air Development Squadron Six in April 1965, serving as Maintenance Office and Executive Officer before assuming Command.

Another aviation milestone in the programme of Antarctic research and exploration came when Rear Admiral J M Abbot Jr. took over the command from Rear Admiral F Bakutis. He described participations in Antarctic flights to McMurdo as '*a great step forward*,' adding he could foresee the day when winter aircraft missions would be a regular procedure in Operation Deep Freeze.

'*With winter flights*' said Admiral Abbot, '*the United States can apply the talents of scientist who would normally not be available because of teaching demands,*' however, the prime objectives of the June flights, named *Project WinFly* were to add seven new members to the 200 man winter community of scientists and naval personnel at McMurdo Station.

For the June 1967 mid winter flight, planning had started months before in Washington, with the necessity of getting scientist onto the ice. The blueprint was presented by the National Science Foundation's Office of Antarctic Programme to the US Naval Support Force, and plans were being developed for *Project WinFly*, with the *City of Christchurch* LC-130F selected for the mission, flying to McMurdo as soon as possible after June 16, when the moon would be in its three quarter phase and approaching full. Both Hercules departed from Quonset Point, Rhode Island on June 12, for Miami, and would fly to New Zealand three days later, making stops in California, Hawaii and American Samoa.

Admiral Abbot along with several of his senior staff officers had set out from Washington aboard another C-130 a few days earlier, and would remain in Christchurch on standby to provide search and rescue, if necessary. The C-130 arrived in New Zealand several days before the scientists had departed Christchurch for Antarctica.

Operation Deep Freeze Control, a communication and monitoring flight centre in Christchurch was activated at Harewood International Airport with communications between Christchurch and McMurdo excellent. Accompanying the Admiral to Christchurch was Lt Commander Ralph Sallee, assistant staff meteorologist with the US Naval Support Force, Antarctica, to establish a weather control centre expected to remain open throughout any mercy mission.

The loading and final preparation of the aircraft began early Friday morning as VX-6 crewmen installed internal fuel tanks in both planes. The fuselage tanks were required for the *City of Christchurch* because of a possible low altitude return flight from McMurdo during the evacuation of two Navy men, Chief Radioman Ronald Hilton, and Corpsman First Class Lloyd G Goodrich.

Providing the reserve Hercules with an internal fuel tank was precautionary for the aircraft's commander Lt Cdr F A Prehn, who wanted maximum fuel available in the event he had to conduct any search and rescue mission.

Wrote Lt.John Hoshko: *'By Friday, the opening of Williams Field and the preparation of the skiway for incoming Hercules had been completed. The winter-over continent of Antarctic Support Activities at McMurdo had worked in temperatures ranging from minus 40 to minus 60 degrees F to open buildings that had been nearly covered by blowing snow during the proceeding four months. Generators, heaters, snow movers, communication equipment, air navigational aids and the GCA [ground control approach] radar had been reactivated.*

Along the 8,000 foot skiway, which is 300 feet wide, a large snowplough first cut then graded the surface, and two 35-ton low- ground- pressure D-8 tractors with 150 feet of anchor chain between them dragged the strip twice to ensure smoothness. Through the first 1,000 feet, the skiway was equipped with electric lights, while the remaining length was marked with Coleman double-mantle gasoline lanterns placed every 500 feet whereas for the previous winter flights into Antarctica, drums of burning oil were used as runway lights.

On Saturday evening, June 17, a tentative decision to launch the flight was made. Commander Fred Schneider, the Commander Officer of VX-6 and the commander of the 'City of Christchurch' planned to take off from Christchurch in the early morning so as to reach McMurdo in the early afternoon. While Commander Schneider would arrive in the darkness- it would be just three days prior to Midwinter Day, the time when the least sunlight falls on the Southern Hemisphere, the early afternoon in Antarctica would be the time of nautical twilight, when the sun is at its highest point on the meridian of McMurdo. The command considered that the combination of twilight and moonlight would provide the best visibility at this time of year.'

Activities at *Operation Deep Freeze* Support Force Headquarters in Christchurch reached a peak by 0200 on Sunday June 18, with aircraft being loaded and prepared for the flight. By 0400, meteorologists were evaluating the expected weather along the flight path to McMurdo letting # *318's* crew be briefed, and an hour later the crew and passengers gathered by VX-6'S hanger in Orchard Road, opposite the now new Antarctic Centre.

Thereafter WinFly became an annual event in Antarctica. Of the cargo, six were passengers, along with several tons of mail and fresh provisions timed to arrived before Mid Winters Day on June 18, and for the wintering over party isolated from the world since February, while the 5,000 lbs of mail was a godsend.

Commander Fred Schneider was also involved with a previous emergency flight in June 1966 *'we carried a National Geographic photographer with us on the flight and he got a lot of good pictures for us- his story appeared in the November issue of the magazine entitled 'Flight into Darkness'. On the take off from Christchurch, I used 8 JATO bottles since I was 10,000 lbs over gross weight with mail, provisions etc, having to taxi slow and make wide gentle turns so as not to damage the landing gear.*

It was a dark morning in Christchurch, no wind but with a wisp of fog in the air. There was an aircraft [old bugsmasher- didn't know what type of aircraft it was], ahead of us and he told the tower that he would like to see the Herk take off since I was using JATO. I understand that the heat from the Herk and the heat from the JATO bottles fogged in the runway and he had to wait 20 minutes for the fog to clear.'

Lt John Hoshko wrote that the weather along the flight track to McMurdo was so good that the *City of Christchurch* enjoyed a clear sky all the way; so the first sight of Antarctica was spectacular with the jagged features of the continent outlined in the blue white moonlight.

'The plane's Teflon-coated skis touched down on the ice skiway at Williams Field-the time 1421 in a relatively mild temperature of minus 39F. Unloading operations began as soon as the four

turboprop engines were shut down and the scientists and the Admiral were transported by helicopter to 'the hill' as McMurdo Station is known.

> *The Admiral spent nearly six hours at the station, conferring with various unit officers, inspecting the winter construction and maintenance projects and speaking to the members of the winter-over-party assembled in the general mess hall, about the significance of winter flights. He also discussed with the Navy men their prospects for duty assignments upon relief at the beginning of the summer support season.'*

Those returning to New Zealand aboard the C-130 were four passengers, including Chief Radioman Ronald Hilton who had suffered a collapsed lung, along with his attendant Corpsman Lloyd Goodrich, who was in worse shape than his patient due to an infected gall bladder. Chief Hilton carried an oxygen bottle to help keep his lungs inflated via a plastic tube inserted through an incision in his chest. The *National Geographic* staff photographer aboard the flight had asked Chief Hilton to exit the plane again so that they could get photos of him and his oxygen bottle. When Hilton asked if he would receive payment for the photos and received a negative answer, he refused to cooperate. The other passengers on the homeward flight were a Navy builder third class Steve Zacravecz who had departed the Antarctic on emergency leave, and a USARP civilian worker Mike Kulis, who had been drafted into the US Army.

By midnight, activities at *Deep Freeze* Control Christchurch were on alert and awaiting the aircraft as problems arose just three hours from touch down when thick fog descended on the Canterbury area closing the airport. Commander Schneider and Harewood air traffic control had to consider alternate airports to reach, with the other major alternates as Dunedin and two North Island airports, Auckland and Wellington, but all reported fog and rain.

Fortunately the fog lifted from Christchurch airport greatly improving visibility and allowing the *City of Christchurch* to land at 0337 on Monday morning, less than 24 hours after beginning its mission. Both sick men arrived in Christchurch in a satisfactory condition experiencing no adverse effects from the normal altitude flight.

The crew of *The City of Christchurch* on Operation WinFly, were Task Force 43 Commanding Officer R.Adm Abbot, Lt. Braddock, Lt Cdr Short, AT1 McKinnis, AMS1 Brewster, ABH1 Falone, Ltjg Hunter, Lt Serba, ADJ1 McClinton, Lt Hotik, Sgt Corley, PHC Reiner and AE2 Maddox.

The second schedule WinFly flight in 1967 was piloted by the squadrons Executive Officer Cdr.Eugene Van Reeth who return to McMurdo on September 3 with several tons of supplies, mail and fresh provisions and picked up the three scientists taken there on the June flight. Again *The City of Christchurch* was used for the mission, which also evacuated two naval personnel, Lt Brian Shoemaker and Petty Officer J Muzzer, who had sustained injuries.

Accompanying Cdr.Van Reeth were ATI McKinnis on his second mercy flight of the year, AMH2 Lopez, ADR1 Houghton, AEC Richards, ADRC Daley, Captain Wegert, Lt Cdr McLin, Ltjg Clark, Ltjg Fuller and ABH1 Johnson.

One of the first tasks of Cdr. Fred Schneider's command was the decision back in Washington to explore the feasibility of constructing a new South Pole Station. By Christmas that year over 6 metres of snow covered the station and despite constant and costly maintenance, it was only a matter of time before the station would be uninhabitable.

A design life of 15 years was specified for the new building which would have to withstand extreme temperatures of minus 112 deg F, winds up to 24 metres a second and drifting snow of approximately 6 metres per second. This structure had to be able to cope with all the elements and the building had to accommodate eight to nine scientist and equal numbers of support naval personnel, doubling that in the summer season. Also the materials had to fit inside an LC-130 and weigh no more than 9,000 kg.

The task facing the squadron was the transportation of the materials required, so the construction gangs could build the structure within a 75 day window, from mid November to early

February, working in conditions with temperatures averaging minus 25.5 deg. F. The new station would consist of eight separate modular units and two control units, a geodesic dome 50 metres in diameter and 16 metres high that would cover the main complex of three two storey buildings. The NSF's think tank studies indicated that this type of design structure would reduce snow drifting, thus ensuring its longevity and cost effectiveness.

On October 3rd. Lt Cdr F A Prehn Jr a veteran polar pilot with 21 Navy men aboard, made the first flight into Hallett Station, in *# 320*, to open up the season that proved to be an adventure, or in his own words. '*It was probably the most difficult I had to make in the Antarctic*' after he had to make three landing passes approximately 50 feet above the skiway prior to setting the aircraft down safely.

The same day a helicopter crew preparing for their initial Antarctic flight of the season had their first mission of hauling cargo and scientists to several sites in the McMurdo Sound area, along with the regular ice reconnaissance flights. Two of the crews had aided New Zealand scientists during the construction of the winter over quarters at Lake Vanda, and part of their mission was to recover some 27,000 pounds of cargo dropped by USAF Globemasters that had scattered over a large area. Due to the efforts of the VX-6 crew members, Lt Cdr Locke, Lt JG Goldsmith, AMH2 Tipper and ADJ3 Murphy, they saved the New Zealanders several weeks of delay in their construction programme.

On December 5 1967, a C-130 under the command of Cdr. Fred Schneider flew 1,500 miles from McMurdo to the British Halley Bay Station near the McDonalds Glacier off the Caird Coast to evacuate a critically injured English Doctor. On arriving at the base off the coast of the Weddell Sea, he requested them to indicate on the ground the wind direction with something, as he didn't have the best of radio contact. '*To my surprise, they made an arrow out of cocoa on the snow, as they had nothing else to mark their makeshift landing strip with. I had an aircraft carrying out photo work in the area a few days later, and we dropped several cases of 'Swiss Miss' that mixed with hot water or milk and was really good, to replace their cocoa. They offered to trade all their cocoa for our Swiss Miss.*'

Others on this flight with the Commander were Lt Cdr. Sorna, Captain Noll [USMC] Lt Pope, and Lt Holik. Ltjg Spencer, ADJ1 Bourgeois, ABH1 Tamplet, ADJ2 Waltkin, PH1 Richards and HM2 Kleim. Cdr Schneider was awarded the Distinguished Flying Cross for the mercy flight, while the rest of the crew were awarded the Air Medal.

On December 30 the *Penguin Express # 319* under the command of Cdr Van Reeth with Lt Cdr Wegert on the flight deck, flew on a routine resupply mission to Byrd Station, thus logging its 10,000th flight hour. Two other C-130's passed their 10,000 hour mark during January 1968, while the remaining Hercules had logged more than 9,800 hours before the flag was lowered on *Deep Freeze '68*.

But before the season ended Lt Cdr Prehn and the A crew of *# 320*, flew to Eights Station near the Antarctic Peninsula in an attempt to locate and gain entry to the station which was abandoned in 1966. The site was finally located using a fascinating scientific method, for after landing Lt Cdr Prehn fell into the station through the aurora dome while walking about the area. Earlier on January 13th he and his crew completed a 24-hour flight with one stop at Byrd on a photo mapping mission of the Thurston Island area of Antarctica.

Many weeks of close study of ESSA and Nimbus satellite weather pictures went into picking the day and time for this mission which had defied all other photo-mapping efforts for the squadron over a number of seasons.

Flying 14 aircraft, of five different types supplemented by the USAF, the Douglas C124C transporters were making their last appearance in the Antarctic, assisted by C-130E. This year RNZAF's 40th Squadron provided a C-130H- *NZ7001* the first "H" model off the Lockheed Marietta, Georgia's production line, number 4052, it was also the first season since 1955, that the Antarctic weather ships were not on duty to provide communications and weather data to VX-6 aviators on their isolated and weary twenty odd hour flight to McMurdo.

Operation Deep Freeze 68 was the second accident free season for VX-6 and the first year free of accidents for the whole Task Force 43 operations, but tragedy struck for the old warrior *BuNo # 99853 Wilshie Duit* or *Divine Wind* the veteran of ten years service to Antarctic, while being loaded aboard the USN *Pvt. John R Towlle,* she slipped from her sling falling 25 feet to the quay and being badly damaged in the mishap.

The LC-117 was abandoned, but did not give up easily. Like the six original R4-D's left on the pack ice after *Operation Highjump* in 1947, *BuNo 99853* was pushed out on the ice of the Ross Sea to drift away and sink peacefully in the frozen Antarctic water, but a year later she was still there clearly visible from McMurdo station, before the icy waters swallowed her.

Two other LC-117D'S *BuNo's 17092* and *12441* were struck off VX-6 's register and delivered to Davis-Monthan AFB for storage at the Davis Monthan junk yard in the desert.

The *LC-47/LC117* had limited capabilities and as a result of Command and Squadron discussion, the aircraft would operate only from established skiways or in areas where the snow surfaces were known to be safe.

This decision meant that the squadron's C-130's would support most scientific parties in the field, because of the added function given the Lockheed transporters, requests were made to obtain one or two more Hercules. In the meantime the squadron's R4-D inventory would be retained, with the possibility of having them overhauled in New Zealand at Air New Zealand's engineering workshop, and those lost would not be replaced.

On February 6th the R4-D *The Spirit of McMurdo # 50832* piloted by Lt Morris, appeared to have stalled to the right, then after briefly resuming level flight stalled sharply to the left and plunged to the ground killing all aboard, and was the only *Goonie Bird* to claim the lives of men in the Antarctic Rack This aircraft was almost rebuilt from parts cannibalised from other R4-D's such as *Charlene,* but after this fatal crash the Goonies were mostly used for cargo flights and the majority of these shuttled between Hallett Station and McMurdo- the 'Rickity Rack.'

'The R4-D was asked to do more and more, particularly in the areas of open field operations. Then we lost one and its crew [DF66] to clear ice, which was a rarity on the continent. The increased logistic demands called for heavier loads while the R4-D was better, the polar plateau really strained the capabilities of the old bird. We had at the time considered the twin-Otter but it was not quite a suitable replacement- money was also tight.' 'Moe' Morris said.

'While the C-130 could do anything the R4-D could do, and as we used it, it was found to be a better open field aircraft. I flew the old bird on each operation and must admit I enjoyed it but there were times when I felt it was obvious we were treading the edge of the envelope, I felt it had reached the end of its usefulness except for a few tasks- but then the sleds and dogs had theirs also.'

The venerable *Gooney Bird* used in the first decade of *Operation Deep Freeze* will have many agree that the ambitious programme and strict timetable of the International Geophysical Year could never have been successfully completed without them or the adventurous pioneering aviators of VX-6.

Cdr W.H Everett, the squadron's *Deep Freeze 63* CO had commented that the R4-D was the best aircraft available for medium-range logistic support, because of the nature of the missions, *'it was the type most often called upon to make open field landing and was, therefore, the most susceptible to damage. This susceptibility was compounded by the fact that replacement aircraft could be drawn from the 'mothball' reserves and when received by the squadron, already had up to twenty years of flying and thousands of hours on their airframes. I recommend that a light to medium weight transport aircraft be obtained as their replacement.'*

When Rear Admiral James Reedy relieved Admiral Tyree in November 1962 as commander of the US Naval Support Force, Antarctica, he was at the time very outspoken to the point that he recommended the Dakotas together with the Otters and the H-34 helicopters be replaced *'as soon as possible'*. He predicted that the loss of one or more R4-D's could be expected each season thus losing their good Naval aviators.

While nothing over the previous seven years with the tens of thousands of miles flown by the R4-D's appeared to support this gloomy prediction, it was true that five Daks had been damaged but without any loss of life or even serious injury to aviators or passengers. Of these five losses, two had occurred in Deep *Freeze 60*, two during *Deep Freeze 63* and one during *Deep Freeze 62.*

While the other four seasons of operation were accident free, it was possible in all cases to have the planes back into service again, due to the excellence professionalism of the squadron's maintenance crews, who had toiled tirelessly to avoid any loss of flight time. This more optimistic analysis appeared to have been borne out by the events of *Deep Freeze 64,* when six Dakotas, five LC-47's and one LC-117 flew 248 missions covering a total of 1,190 miles carrying 458 passengers and 142 ton of cargo, without any significant mishaps.

So many stories have been told and retold about the squadron's 'Goons' and those who flew or were associated with them, with one such story related to me by Richard Anderson, a flight engineer who had joined the US Navy in January 1959. Soon after enlisting Dick was ordered to CIC School at Brunswick Georgia NAS.

'I was pissed because I didn't join the Navy to go to Georgia! Every week I submitted a request chit to go someplace else, and I was a real pain in the ass to the Navy. Finally I hit pay dirt and got accepted to 'Operation Deep Freeze'. I left Georgia one year to the day after arrival. Glynco was a training command and really chicken, we had an admin inspection just before I left in preparation, and we had personnel inspections about every week before the 'real' inspection. Just after my arrival the Marine Captain that I check in with [think his name was Lasecki or something like that], said I did not have to stand inspection since I was so sharp. I already liked this outfit! But before I checked into VX-6 I had to undergo a screening at the Naval Station at Washington DC.

As I recall, only about 20% of the folk who came to Washington went onto Rhode Island and VX-6, those who didn't make it went back to their units, but we underwent extensive physical and mental exams. There were five shrinks of whom one was a female, and if you showed any unusual sexual tendencies you got to go to the female shrink- that's how we saw it anyway. They showed us ink spots and asked us to equate them. I saw one that was a dead ringer for female genitalia, but not wanting to go to the female shrink, I said it was a rowboat in a small pond and it worked-no female shrink for me, so I went on to Quonset and the Antarctic.

I wintered over the first season, with Hene Whitehead, can't recall any flight problems- all the VX-6 Det Alfa were a class act, as were the folks who didn't winter.

Working on a 'Goon' floorboard one bloody cold morning- colder than a well diggers ass, I can recall a shipmate saying, 'Make some room so I can give you a hand.' When I got to VX-6, our maintenance Chief was a guy named Mihalcik, my 'Goon' was # 399853, some 'Goons' were on the ice, so we had to share with other crews, but # 99853 'Wilshie Duit' was the premiere 'Goon,' and we took offence to any others not respecting our status.

Well, one day, continued Flight Engineer Dick Anderson, *'one of the other crews took # 99853 up for a spin and they griped about my LORAN. The AT was a guy named Bannister, he said my APN-4 LORAN was inop; I checked it out and found it just fine. I surmise Bannister was not aware of the 'On-Off' switch on the box under the Radioman's table. In those days the 'yellow sheet' was just that- only one copy and you signed off the gripe on it.*

It was late and after hours and I signed off the LORAN gripe as 'Turned on On-Off- check ok- check next flight-time 10 milliseconds'. Next morning the Maintenance Chief, Chief Mihalcik, summoned me to his presence and invited me in his office. He vigorously counselled me on the merits of not being a 'smart ass'. In those days, 'vigorous' literally meant he bounced me off the walls a fair bit. He continued his counselling for months afterwards.

I worked on all the squadron's aircraft-R4-D's-R5-D's and P2-V's, whatever. On many occasions I can recall being all on my lonesome on the back line working a gripe and all of a sudden the power would go off, I would vault out of the plane to see what's wrong and there would be my boss, AT1 Larry Sharp [he would shut off the NC-5 to get my attention] and would say that Chief Mihalcik wishes to see me. I would go to Maintenance and the Chief would shove a coffee pot at me and say, 'I need coffee, boy', now that's character building and leadership- he really liked me- tough love.'

With the phasing out of the Gooneys, it made a number of the 'Goon Crews' who lived in Hut 7 at Willy Field during their time on the ice, a very congenial lot. They were somewhat unemployed as the LC-130's were taking their place on the ice. Richard Anderson recalls. *'Some of our crews even left us for the Herk crews- guys like 'Dangerous' Dan Dompe and AD2 Bob Capling, couldn't really blame them, the Herk was the future-the 'Goon' wasn't. Humorous events and happy times took place in Hut 7, I recall one of our Mechs was gravel-voice AD1 Red Auxford, we were celebrating November 19th- I don't know what, but we were celebrating, and these occasions were usually accompanied by beer, steaks and cards in our lounge adorned with a parachute canopy, and before retiring Red took a stroll outside to get some fresh air.*

He slipped and fell into a snow bank which elicited some 'expletive deleted'. He weathered this mishap okay and retired to his rack. During the night, we were awakened by groans only capable of Red Auxford. He was obviously in great pain so we got up to see what his problem was. He said his arm was killing him, we readily determined the cause to be his watch, which had a special Speidel band and had slipped up his arm to his elbow and was acting as a tourniquet, cutting off the blood flow, which had caused him so much pain.

We had another mech, who I won't name. I will only say his nickname had religious connotations. Our Flight Surgeon Doc Holik set a goal of circumcising all who had not received this purifying rite,' and Richard Anderson recalls a 'spoof' picture of the good Doctor with hedge clippers preparing to perform his rite. *'Well, our Mech got clipped, and he was obviously in a fair bit of pain, but he just loved to read 'Old English Novels' that aroused him, thus causing excruciating pain. His remedy for this situation was a Number 10 can of snow placed next to his rack. When he got to a place in his novel that aroused the poor fellow, he would reach into the can and take a hunk of snow and hold it on his 'member' to discourage enlargement and deaden the pain.'*

By the end of the 10th season, Admiral Reedy renewed his plea for a long-range turbo-powered helicopter, including a report from the squadron's CO Cdr George Kelly. This was a thoughtful analysis of the problem of air support for scientific field and traverse parties. Scientific activities he said, were being conducted at ever increasing distances from the established camps more frequently and at greater altitudes. *'The number of participants was growing, along with the greater quantity of equipment and supplies required,'* concluded Cdr Kelly in the Admiral's report to government.

Operations in the Pensacola Mountains during *Deep Freeze –64* had been at the extreme range of the LC-47 [1200 miles] and almost that of the enlarged LC-117 [1400 miles]. The loads required had made the Douglas aircraft almost a detriment to efficient field support, and these developments pointed to the superiority of the Lockheed C-130 turbo-prop Hercules. In addition the redesigned ski landing gear of the Navy model had proved superior to the earlier Air Force models, thus making it possible to lift many of the restrictions the USAF had placed on the Hercules as a result of its Greenland operations, as the C-130 Hercules could land wherever the Dakota could.

Looking back over his season as Squadron's CO during *Deep Freeze-62* Cdr M C Greenwell reflected that handling cargo in and out of the R4-D's was extremely difficult, as was the refuelling with hand pumps, and that extensive preheating was required to get the twenty year old aircraft started, and like his predecessors, preferred the R4-D-5 to the R4-D-8's. All of those were however, comparatively minor when one compares the all-round usefulness of this type of aircraft, about which Cdr Greenwell expressed himself so eloquently in a report to this bosses.

'*The R4-D has again proven herself a valuable friend and the 'Grand Old Lady' of Antarctic operations was economical and durable, and her versatility in short range open field ski operations remains undisputed, it is not difficult to foresee the day, perhaps in the near future, when an equally versatile, long range, greater-payload, higher flying turboprop replaces the old warrior, but until that day comes, treat her kindly, keep her warm, push the right JATO buttons, and navigate clear of all obstacles'.*

Deep Freeze –67 was virtually the last Antarctic season that the twenty-year plus Dakotas were operational within the squadron; in fact their demise was signalled in December 1966. To justify the purchase of another Hercules the Commander of the US Naval Support Force Antarctica, and supported by Cdr.Morris, argued that not only was it to increase safety, but of the savings in personnel and operational expenditure if the R4-D's were removed from the program and the squadron's fleet. With the approval of the Hercules purchase from Lockheed Martin, the days of the ancient aircraft were numbered with the commencement of *Deep Freeze 68*. Maybe Cdr Martin Greenwell was reading his tarot cards, because the new workhorse Lockheed C-130 Hercules was soon to make her debut in Antarctica and reinvent polar aerial logistical scientific support.

CHAPTER TWELVE.

VX-6 HELICOPTERS IN ANTARCTICA
HEROS ALL.

*Heroic stories of the Squadron's helicopter aircrews in
Antarctica and the major role they played in support
of Operation Deep Freeze.*

Flying helicopters in Antarctica is an unparalleled experience for pilots on active duty on the vast ice continent, but everyday is just another day *'except that operating here is a little less carefree than in the office'* for the helo aircrews of VX-6 squadron.

This is best summed up by Lt Daniel Keohane a VX-6 UH-1N helicopter commander, *'helicopter pilot and crew face stern challenges in Antarctic aviation, the most obvious are the hostile climate and adverse temperatures, they make operating here a little less carefree than in an area with more temperate climate, in this extreme weather, and while nothing can be taken for granted, you're always concerned about the simple things such as whether the helo's engine oil is going to be warm enough or whether various drive shafts are going to rotate freely and not be frozen.*

Just landing a helo, especially on snow or ice is different from surfaces you find elsewhere. In the Antarctic there is a 'squat check', before each landing the pilot will land lightly on the skids while the crew chief, looking through the open side door will tell him the shreds set well and the ice is thick enough to bear the weight of the helo. There has been a time when a helo has had an entire skid or both skis on a snow bridge over a crevasse. These snow bridges are false surfaces and cannot hold much weight.'

Adding to this, Chief Aviation Structural Mechanic [Hydraulics] 3rd Class Bradley Peterson mentioned poor visibility *'Sometimes we land at a site to offload scientists and there is so much blowing snow that as soon as our passengers walk 20 feet from the helo, we can barely see them. If there is a high wind and we land in a rocky area and slip on the rock, the wind combined with that of the helo's main rotor can throw us down and send cargo all over the place.'*

Another problem facing the copter crews at times is the wind whos direction often had very little correlation with the surrounding conditions. A smoke flare is the only safe method of determining wind direction, and while the pilot must at all times be vigilant and prepared for an erratic wind shift when landing his helicopter, it's during this final phase of the helicopter's approach over light powdery snow, that the strong blast created by his rotor blades whips up snow into such frenzy that his visibility is almost non-existent losing all visual references and landmarks at this critical time.

'The pilots only solution is to maintain altitude fly by the gauges and settle the craft smoothly on the ground and pray,' says one veteran pilot.

'Even with the helicopter on the ground, the situation may be anything but safe, what may have looked like a solid snowfield from the air, or low attitude, can conceal any number of dangerous crevasses. Just when the pilot thinks that the landing is complete and all is well, a gear may suddenly crash through the frozen crust into a 1000-foot void. The aircraft is then in danger of rolling over and beating itself to death.

There is seldom a day on the ice that these versatile aircraft are not flown.' said the Commander of VX-6 in *Deep Freeze 61* Captain William Munson, *'without them, many of our operational commitments could not have been met and more importantly, there are a number of men breathing today, who owe their lives directly to the skill and courage of our VX-6 pilots. In 1959, they flew 373 helicopter hours in support of civilian scientists within a four month period, and would have flown more had weather conditions been better.'*

It was Rear Admiral Richard E Byrd who recognised the importance of the helicopters in Antarctica and their operational ability. During his 1933 Antarctic expedition, his party had used the predecessor to the modern helo, the Kellett autogyro for short-range reconnaissance flights and high altitude aerological missions. It was given the nickname *Pep Boy's Snowman,* and it's success had even Bryd surprised, as in just one month's operation it had carried out nine major flights in the Little America area, flying at an average altitude of nearly 9000 feet, carrying a specially fitted aero-meteorograph mounted on its fuselage to record the temperature, pressure and humidity of the various strata, but it's Antarctic missions came to an abrupt halt on September 28 1934, when it crashed on takeoff.

The honour of the first helicopter pilot in Antarctica went to US Coast Guard pilot Lt. James Cornish assigned to the icebreaker '*USCG Northwind* during *Operation Windmill.* In December 1946 in an almost obsolete helo, he flew south of Scott Island for a reconnaissance flight, but by the time the *Northwind* had reached the Bay of Whales off the coast of Little America, he had assisted in escorting the convoy through 700 miles of pack ice. ·

As it was Byrd's intention to fly his four R4-D's off the deck of the *Philippine Sea* to the Little America base, he ordered the *Northwind* to a SAR station between Scott Island and the Ross Sea Ice Shelf, and as the icebreaker entered the heavy pack ice, Lt. David Gershowitz was sent aloft to scout the best passage. He was just six miles out when he sent a distress call, saying his rotor blades were icing and he was losing altitude fast.

With the *Northwind* altering course, Lt. Gershowitz feared his pontoons would freeze to the ice if he landed so instead chose to land on a small water pool, setting his HNS-1 down so that he was later able to takeoff and then return to the deck of the icebreaker. While the use of the helicopters proved to be an added value to the operations, many of the aerial photographs taken from them were declared to be worthless, mainly as they lacked specific ground control points with which the photos could be identified. Some navy cartographers suggested that ground control points could be established if the helicopter airlifted surveyors based on the icebreakers.

So the helicopter came of age and in the following season of 1947-48, helicopters were deployed aboard the Navy's icebreakers *Burton Island* and *Edisto* to Antarctica.

On their first aerial reconnaissance missions from the *Burton Island,* Cdr Paul Frazier flew out to chart the ice fields with the senior helicopter pilot aboard manoeuvring the aircraft. On reaching Drygalski Island, the two icebreakers separated, the *Burton Island* headed for Haswell Island, while the *Edisto* sailed some 40 miles to the West.

The aircraft were grounded by 55 plus knot winds, which abated by midnight, enabling shore parties from both ships to be landed. However, severe solar disturbances resulted in blocking out communications for the next few days, so when communications were eventually re established the disturbing news was that the *Edisto* was unable to make contact with the shore parties whom they hadn't heard from for two days, so orders were to launch the helicopters which located the men a few miles from the ship. This resulted in another operational decision, that ground control points would be established for exclusive helicopter use when transporting parties who where out of sight of the ship.

The use of helicopters in Antarctica continued after *Operation Highjump* but were absent in Antarctica until the summer of 1954, when they returned carrying the insignia of both the US and Argentina, when the *General San Martin* sailed to the eastern part of the Weddell Sea and launched helicopters to photograph the vertical ice cliffs and establish a base at the head of Filchner Ice Shelf.

The same year, the Antarctic claimed its first helicopter life when the *US Atka* arrived at Little America and it was witnessed from the air that large sections of the Ross Sea Ice Shelf had broken off and floated away, leaving Little America 1, 11 and 111 still there, but gone was half of Little America

1V. Initial air reconnaissance was led by chief aviation pilot Albert Metrolis, who after buzzing Little America 111, headed north until antenna masts of LA 1V became visible. The half section of camp that had broken off carried with it the nine R4-D's left on the ice during Operation Highjump in 1947.

Before continuing her search for an adequate base site, the *Atka* remained in the area to conduct a series of scientific test, and it was during one of these flights that Lt JG John P Moore lost his life. He had just transported Father Daniel Linehan the world famous seismologist to the ice, and was on his return to the *Ataka* when he crashed after losing the horizon. A second copter piloted by Metrolis, didn't see the actual crash, only the wreckage, so setting his helicopter down he lifted Lt Moore from the twisted machine but he died three hours later.

Information brought back to Cdr.Glen Jacobsen, the ship's commander, enabled him to inform *Deep Freeze* planners that the Bay of Whales was not fit for a new Little America Station, so Kainan Bay was recommended.

When planners sat down in Washington on 17 January 1955 Cdr Edward M Ward was commissioned to command the new Air Development Squadron Six - VX-6. The first squadron plane to check in at their Pax River home was a HU-2 helicopter, piloted by Lt Cdr Robert G Graham and Lt Harold Todd. Drawing on the enormous experience of the two previous Antarctic expeditions and the first *Deep Freeze* operation, the icebreaker *USS Glacier* had a detachment of 60 aboard and two HO4s-manned by four pilots, one ADC and eight naval personnel, with the helo's sharing the deck space with a UC-1 Otter.

By the time *Operation Deep Freeze 1*-summer support activities ended, pilots operating from the new icebreaker had logged 383 flights, the majority in far from ideal flying conditions. Their first operational mission was to scout a possible landing strip for the squadron's long-range aircraft, which at the time were being prepared in Christchurch for the flight south, and about 35 miles up McMurdo Sound the *Glacier's* helos located an ice landing strip near Hut Point.

Two days later after a landing strip was marked out for the squadron's arrival, the helicopters flew their Antarctic search and rescue flight from the *Glacier* after two men had been reported stranded for 36 hours in a Weasel which had partially fallen through the ice. After the rescue, the crew flew in Rear Admiral Richard Bryd to see what was left of his Little American 1V then continued on reconnaissance missions, scouting suitable landing sites for the establishment of Little America V Station, which was to become the headquarters of scientific exploration effected by the United States during the IGY. Location was found in Kainea Bay, allowing the ships to begin unloading.

With her own off-loading completed, the *Glacier* transferred one helicopter with pilot, crews and spare parts to the cargo ship *Arneb* then went on an exploratory and scientific survey of the Sulzberger Bay area near Little America.

The *Edisto* arrived at McMurdo just as the *Glacier* was leaving Little America, and the VX-6 planes arrived from Christchurch that evening, so the pilots and crews were flown aboard for hot food and a rest before beginning their exploratory flights. Just as the *Edisto* was underway the following morning to rendezvous with other Task Force ships near Scott Island, they learnt of the crashed Otter on the Ross Sea Ice Shelf and returned to render assistance.

On Christmas Eve, *USS Edisto* arrived back at McMurdo, but a blistering gale kept the helicopters firmly tied down to the flight deck. Subsequently the Otter crash survivors were reached overland by snow tractor and hauled back to Hut Point, and when the weather had eased by midnight on December 26, it allowed the injured to be flown aboard for treatment.

By January 1956 the *USS Eastwind* had transferred one helicopter and crew to the air facilities at Hut Point, and by the middle of the month, the icebreaker reached a point between Cape Adare and New Zealand to provide SAR potential to VX-6 planes returning from the ice.

One of the big stories of the operation's first season on the ice concerned the incredible chain of events following word that an Otter was missing on the ice cap in Marie Byrd Land with seven VX-6 Squadron personnel aboard including the pilot Lt Cdr Lathrop.

At McMurdo, three attempts were made to fly an Otter to Little America but they were frustrated by weather, so the Skymaster in New Zealand was ordered to stand by. Three members of the trail party who were scheduled for a second VX-6 Otter flight to Little America were ordered to backtrack and search for the missing Otter. *[Both events being covered in an earlier chapter]*

In *Deep Freeze II* VX-6 again operated with three Sikorsky HO4S helos, keeping one at McMurdo, and the second sent to Little America V Station to support a traverse party setting out to establish Byrd Station, while the third was lifted aboard the cargo ship *Wyandot* who steamed off to the Weddell Sea area to establish Ellsworth on the Filchner Ice Shelf.

When the *Glacier* arrived at McMurdo on October 28 1956 to commence *Deep Freeze 11*, they found the bay ice in Kainan Bay was split by a six foot crack, thus necessitating the offloading operations to be accomplished by the HU-2 detachment, who also airlifted JATO bottles for the VX-6 aircraft and 4000 pounds of high explosives used by the trail parties to blast crevasses.

Once the VX-6 HO4-S arrived at Little America they operated a tight schedule, the helos turnaround flights were scheduled every twelve minutes. First Lt Leroy Kenny, USMC carried out 97 flights to guide a trail party through a seven and a half mile area of snow bridge crevasses. When one was spotted from the air, an ice expert was strapped to the hoist of the hovering helicopter and lowered so he could mark the crevasse with a flag.

Once the surface crew had planted explosives inside the crevasse, the group would withdraw and set the charge off, opening up the crater. The snow was then scraped into the yawning hole and packed so they could then move on to the next crevasse. Such was a day's work for the helo pilots.

The icebreaker *Staten Island* sailed into the Weddell Sea to establish Ellsworth Station, escorted by the cargo ship *Wyandot,* to unload the sections of 18 buildings. In late December the ships's helicopters took to the air for reconnaissance runs that convinced the pilot that neither Cape Adams nor the Bowman areas were suitable for a station site, and it was on one of these reconnaissance missions that a Bell HTL-5 crashed onto the *Staten Island's* flight deck and was decided a strike. After salvaging parts of the copter, they pushed the skeleton overboard, and from then on the spot was referred to as *Helicopter Hill.*

While in the Ross Sea area, Marble Point emerged as a focal point of scientific interest, and during March 1957, a two-year programme to study the feasibility of creating a permanent land runway began. A VX-6 helicopter flew a party of six to Cape Bernacchi, four miles south of the Point, where the survey started. '*Throughout the entire project*' Admiral Dufek wrote in his report for the Chief of Naval Operations, '*the UC-1's [Otters] and the helicopters fulfilled the valuable mission of liaison, reconnaissance and short range transport in both the Ross and Weddell Seas. Helicopters proved indispensable in ice reconnaissance and the ferrying of priority cargo.*'

With a glacier in the backyard and icebergs off the front porch, Marble Point became the loneliest helo gas station, which does not appear to be much of a duty assignment, but the residence soon got to like the place and its remote location even if their visitors were only the helicopter crews. While the facility's isolation may lead to boredom for its three residence, it had an important role to play as being the last gas station for the squadrons helo's who's range is 200 miles, and with the round trip of 120 miles from McMurdo to the continent, this refuelling point was vital.

It was the only gas stop in Antarctica to support the Task Force's operations to the continents remote camps, and being banished to such a site may appear to be the Navy's sense of the macabre, it was almost a threat to those within its ranks '*one more screw up and you're being transferred to a gas station in Antarctica.*' Their only neighbours were the skua birds that nested nearby, and since this remote place is their home rookery, they regularly made co-ordinated attacks on the intruding humans.

Days at Marble Point could be dull and monotonous until the buzz of an overhead helo signalled another customer or another soul escaping civilisation. On a busy day, six or seven helicopters could call in, but during the quiet times fuel bladders and pumps were checked and weather observations taken. These facilities were manned from the beginning of the austral summer beginning in September until the middle of March, being supported each year by a series of bulldozer drawn traverse bringing more than 30,000 gallons of diesel fuel from McMurdo 60 miles away.

Marble Point was the site of the fatal Otter crash # *144672* that killed Lt Harvey Gardner and Lawrence Farrell in 1959, and was first christened on January 21 1958, when the squadron's Otter carried Rear Admiral Dufek and Sir Edmund Hillary, there.

Joseph Madrid [a native American and VX-6 helicopter crew chief during Deep *Freeze 79-80,]* has vivid memories of life at Marble Point and of those foul tasting 'avgas' sandwiches-

'We would normally visit the Point two or three times a day, depending on your flight schedule, we sometimes would use it as a rest stop and eat our box lunch, but not until after the 'bird' was refuelled and given a quick check.

The refuelling was done by hand, and a small hand pump was all that was there and had to be attached to the bladder and stowed away again once the operation was completed. Of course after this you always smelled of jet fuel, a fine smell to go with your box lunches; not real meals, normally a spam sandwich [two pieces of bread with a piece of meat] washed down with a can of juice or maybe even some fruit if the cook felt generous, but a great hearty meal for one who had been flying and working since 5am till 6, 7 or even 8pm.

There were days that we flew for over 12 hours, and that was just the flying part of the day, as we had to fuel up, move cargo, stop at one camp, go to another, retrieve whatever there, and move it over here. There were even times when us crew chiefs were left behind at the Point because there was no room in the copter. It wasn't a nice place then- pretty barren.'

What was a normal day for a VXE-6 crew chief at Marble Point?

The day began early when the crew chiefs were flown out to the fuel train where they would unhook the bladders from the sleds and then wait for one of the helos to come overhead, attach the bladder to the 'bird' and fly it to Marble Point. Once there one of the crew chiefs would begin to empty the small bladders into the large one, then all the empty bladders were put into a net and sent back with the helos at the fuel train.

'Of course we had all hoped that the train would make it to Marble Point by themselves, but as life goes-nope. So there we were working our tails off in the freezing cold, bladders coming and going, fuel being moved from one point to another. I am not sure how much we did in a day, but it took all day. Little did I know that next time I was at Marble Point I would be pumping fuel again, and again it would be by hand. Each Helo holds about 212 galls and with a small herdy girdy it seemed to take forever, and ofcourse the pilots just took a nap while the work was being done.

And so the day went on, until Sunday October 17 1979, after we completed the transfer of the fuel and all was well. The fuel train headed back to McMurdo and the Helos were ferrying back all the empty bladders, and it was then that the crew chief and I realised we had been left behind! No radio, no food, no water, but plenty of fuel. We had to wait for several hours before we were missed and they finally returned for us. When we returned, the chow hall had finished carving dinners, and all that was there was hot dogs and chilly. Yum ! said Joseph.

After retiring from the Navy, Joseph Madrid, now living in Tucson, immersed himself into his native culture. He has his own native drum group and conducts cultural ceremonies while participating in others and teaching children the native culture of his people.

When the ships returned for the summer in support of *Deep Freeze III* [1957-58], helicopters from the *USS Glacier* and VX-6 had their work cut out, after the *Glacier* had powered her way through the ice cluttered waters to Marble Point with tons of supplies and cargo to support the survey parties. VX-6 helicopters flew out from McMurdo to assist the icebreakers own copters, which hovered over the flight deck while netted cargo was hooked underneath to be flown ashore.

By then VX-6 was operating three HUS-1A's and an HO4S in the McMurdo area, two HO4S's at Little America and another at Ellisworth. The season was to be one of intense activity for the IGY which commenced on the first of July and ended on December 31 the following year.

Helicopters from HU-1 and HU-2 were assigned to the icebreakers, with one HO4S and an HUL placed on the *USS Atka*, two HUL's on the *USS Burton Island,* while HU-2 provided HRS-3's on *USS Glacier* and two HUL's on the *USS Westwind.*

The *USS Atka* suffered a casualty on December 1 1957, when one of her HUL's launching from her flight deck, attempted a takeoff before all the tie-downs had been released, causing the aircraft to crash and catch fire, injuring two passengers and as it was a strike it was pushed overboard.

Meanwhile over at Little America plans were underway for an historic event on December 7, when it was declared *'the day of the helicopter',* in honour of the bird's contribution to the operations. Capt William Munson, the Squadron's commander during Deep Freeze *61* told the *Naval Aviation News* that there was seldom a day on the ice that these versatile aircraft were not flown. '*Without them, many of our operational commitments could not be met- and more importantly, there are a number of men today who owe their lives directly to the skill and courage of our pilots.'*

Lt Cdr Kenneth P Snyder, who had joined VX-6 in July 1956, boarded his HU-2 copter and made a 440 mile non stop dash from Little America to McMurdo in four hours 40 minutes, with an Otter to provide cover in case of an emergency, but the Otter had only covered 50 miles before returning to LA V, so Lt Cdr Bob Epperly took off in his R4-D and covered the entire flight riding shot-gun, but there was no emergency for the two crews.

While the squadron's helicopters were not flying at Little America, there was to be a tricky flight rescue before the winter set in after a scientist who had been studying the ice barrier, was standing on the cornice of an ice cliff which could not support his weight, plunging him down into the floe-cluttered water. Uninjured, he managed to lift himself onto a small flow as two men launched a small rubber raft, while the third man raced for assistance.

After reaching the scientist and dragging him aboard, the raft was caught in the tide and with gale force winds they were swept close to the barrier and the sea. Cdr John W Franks, a HO4S pilot didn't have a great deal of room to manoeuvre his helicopter, so his plane captain, Don Foreman AD1, swung out of the Sikorsky and radio directed Commander Franks until all three men were brought aboard.

In *Operation Deep Freeze IV,* the squadron flew a HUS-1A at Little America, which theoretically should have been their last year in Antarctica after eighteen months of concentrated activities. The squadron should have been out of a job and probably disestablished, but later with the formation of the United States Antarctic Research Programme, they got the nod from Congress assuring the continuation of scientific studies on the continent. As the sun rose briefly on August 1958, air operations had already begun with several helicopter flights to the ice landing strip.

On the second day of sunlight Lucre Frank D'Andrea and Ltjg Murray Wright along with three passengers and the plane captain Henry Barnes AD2, flew their helo to Wilson-Piedmont glacier, opened a specially packed lunch basket complete with a bottle of wine and had a picnic, basking in the warm rays of the polar latitude. After spending the winter in total darkness and isolation, it broke the monotony of the long nights and certainly boosted the men's morale.

At Ellsworth during October, the helicopters made frequent reconnaissance missions to gather data on projected trail operations, and at Little America the centre of activity was focused on the two over-snow traverses to Byrd Station, and to McMurdo, with Army Major Merle Dawson leading one of these trail blazers, but on approaching McMurdo, they entered a heavily crevassed area where two sleds were lost injuring two men.

The *USS Glacier* en route to McMurdo from Terra Nova Bay in company with the USS *Staten Island* encountered ice up to 20 feet thick, keeping the shipboard helicopters on round the clock reconnaissance flights in an effort to untangle the ships from the pack ice. The pilots flew to sea and returned to radio directions to the officer on the deck as to the leads they had sighted.

For as long as OAE's relate their stories of Antarctica and the helicopters of VX-6 Squadron, the name of Lt Commander Edger A Potter stands alongside a select band of VX-6 aviators like Harvey Speed, Gus Shin and 'Jack' Paulus. In an interview with a naval magazine in 1960, he recalled that one day as he stood at the window of his Jamesway hut at McMurdo, he eyed the wind-whipped snow which had restricted visibility and grounded his helicopter. Suddenly, he spotted a petrel swooping through the air, slicing a wavering arc towards Observation Hill.

'Hey' he said to his fellow aviators, who were trying to relax in their hut, 'look at that big bird.' 'But how' asked a somewhat mystified and disbelieving voice in the background, 'can you see a white bird against the white snow?'

And from that day on, despite an undisputed and hard earned reputation as a crack chopper pilot he will always be remembered by many, as an expert on the subject of the white birds of Antarctica and when the Otter failed to locate the crashed C-124 at Hallett that killed six, without hesitation Lt Cdr Potter volunteered to fly his HUS-1A to the crash site and evacuate the injured, flying in company with an Otter from VX-6. He flew the 350 miles to the Bay Ice at Hallett and was the first at the crash site, from where he shuttled medical personnel the 30 miles to the scene of the tragedy, then transported the survivors out of the mountainous terrain where his only landing area was on an angle on a steep sloping glacier.

With all the injured airman flown out to another waiting C-124 parked on the bay ice, the weather was now well below zero but Commander Potter returned to the mountain to rescue one of the two land party, whos attempt to reach the crash site was prevented when their weasel crashed into a crevasse.

In May 1960, Lt Commander Edger Potter was called to 'front and centre', after the squadron's personnel inspection at their Quonset Point base. Before the assembled officers and en-listed men, the Squadron's Commander Capt Munson read out the citation from the Secretary of the Navy, which had awarded the helicopter pilot an Air Medal for meritorious achievement in aerial flight during Operation Deep Freeze in Antarctica.

Two months later, in January 1959, Rear Admiral David Tyree, who had just been appointed to relieve Rear Admiral George Dufek, made an inspection trip of Antarctic bases. Commander Potter was flying the Admiral to Marble Point, when he received a crackled message on his radio that one of the squadron's Otter's # *144673* had crashed during take-off from the dirt runway at Marble Point.

Turning his helicopter sharply, the squadron's intrepid aviator headed back to camp where he made a series of shuttle flights between the crash site and McMurdo. Two aviators died in the crash, Lt Harvey Gardner and Lt Lawrence Farrell the co-pilot, while the Otter was on a logistics support mission from Williams Air Facilities at McMurdo to the camp of the Naval Construction Battalion Reconnaissance at Marble Point. By January 1959 conditions at McMurdo had deteriorated so the squadron's long-range aircraft were sent back to Christchurch leaving the helicopters and Otters, together with the R4-D's, to continue to assist by flying wintering over parties around the frozen continent until darkness and weather grounded them for the season. Lt Commander James R Lacoix and LT Richard Fuller made the last helo flight.

In *Deep Freeze 60* McMurdo sent out an urgent S.O.S for an additional helicopter, resulting in a Sikorsky HUS being flown in from Charleston AFB, to Quonset Point where it was dismantled and stored in the belly of a C-124 transport then flown the 12,000 miles to McMurdo. It's true that Commander Potter's skills with helicopters are legendary, but when the replacement Sikorsky arrived in Antarctica, he tried his skills as a D-4 forklift driver. As the copter was pulled out of the C-124's womb, Potter aimed his machine at the stern of the helicopter to assist in its unloading, however, his 'forklift report card' was down marked when he damaged the helicopter, causing minor damage that was later repaired by the squadron's maintenance crew.

On November 19 1959 during *Deep Freeze 60* a New Zealand traverse party were investigating the Cape Selbourne area when a sudden Antarctica storm blew up as they entered a heavily crevassed field and a snow bridge collapsed under the weight of their Snocat, killing a New Zealand Army Armoured Corps Lieutenant, Tom Couzens and seriously injuring two scientists when they fell nearly 100 feet.

The distress SOS was sent to the Victoria Land party some 200 miles away and that message was then relayed to a VX-6 R5-D with Rear Admiral David Tyree onboard, while making its first flight to the South Pole for the season. They then passed the message onto operations at McMurdo, and an Otter and a squadron's HUS, piloted by Commander Potter were dispatched to bring the injured out, with the Otter waiting at the site until the dead New Zealander's body could be recovered.

In late October, Commander Krebs, along with Commander Potter had flown to the Skelton Glacier area in response to a trail party who were winding their way up the Glacier. After their first cache entered a heavily crevassed area the caravan had stopped to radio VX-6 for help. On arriving at the site, Potter's helo flew at a high altitude giving instructions to Cdr Krebs who was hovering over the crevasses while Mr Toney, a USARP representative and AD2 David Maguire fluttered 12 foot bamboo poles with black flags attached as a guide for the party to proceed with safety.

A few weeks later Commander Krebs experienced a case of a 'hiccupping helicopter' when he was re supplying the same land traverse party from his HUS, but on his return flight his helicopter developed engine trouble while still a hundred miles from McMurdo.

His plane captain Dave Maguire, attempted some on the spot maintenance repairs, but with the temperatures at minus 45 degree F, the oil cooler wouldn't permit the oil to pass freely causing the oil to overheat, so with Maguire unable to undertake a successful repair, Krebs decided to attempt to fly the sick helicopter back to base.

To get back home he found that by landing every 10 to 12 miles in order to allow the oil to cool, had them finally arriving at McMurdo an hour and a half later. This was the same helo that arrived at Antarctica in a C-124 Globemaster. *'We usually run into little problems, its just not used to cold weather.'* said Maguire.

Two days earlier, the flight may have been more than an embarrassment, as the same helicopter was making a local inspection in the Ross Sea to ferry a VIP party on an inspection tour of the McMurdo area. Aboard were, nine star Admiral Herbert C Hopwood, Pacific East Commander; Vice Admiral W M Beakley, Deputy Chief of Naval Operations. Rear Admiral Tyree and Admirals Hopwood and Beakley were observing the operations.

While the helicopter's engine cooler was operational for the VIP flight, it did have its moments when the starboard hatch cover popped off with an ear splitting noise, swinging out from the ship, and nicking the tips of one of the rotors. The military brass aboard accepted the incident with total equanimity, but the newspaper reporter on board to cover the inspection considered it exciting stuff.

In early January 1961, with the arrival of the cargo ships, the speed of off loading became increasingly important with the Bay ice deteriorating rapidly. VX-6's Lt Ben Hooper sped up the activities of airlifting working parties and stevedores from base camp to shipside and back again, cutting these runs to four hours of the working day. Helicopter pilots at Hallett Station also undertook similar cargo shuttles with two-hour turnarounds.

In *Deep Freeze 60,* the Icebreaker *USS Atka* was the first in and last out of Antarctica, and in late March in what Lt Hooper described as stinking weather, with blowing snow, winds gusting at 60 knots, poor visibility and minus 20 degree temperatures, it made flying a 'dangerous cocktail' to get the mail of the season through. When Lt Hooper shut off his engines a short time later, he received word that a tractor train laden with last minute cargo was lost, so he launched again and found the train a mile and half from the ship but with the weather so bad he had to return to base to await better weather conditions.

A few days earlier he flew another hairy mission reminiscent of Cdr.Kreb's 'hiccupping helicopter', as on that occasion his mission was to resupply a small over snow traverse being carried out on the Ross Ice Shelf. The party was embarking on a mission to investigate an area known as *Discovery Deep* and to test out two new and specially designed SnoCats for Antarctic operations. Discovery Deep is a spot on the floor of the Ross Sea, discovered in a previous season.

When ten miles into the return leg, Lt.Hooper's oil supply overheated, forcing him to return to the traverse site to make emergency repairs, but when this proved to be fruitless, and both his VHF and UHF radios in his helicopter malfunctioned, he requested the party to radio the problem to McMurdo with intentions to return to base in a 'leap-frog pattern'.

Spotting the trouble with the oil flow, he secured cabin heat for the five hour hopping flight of five to ten minutes flying and then landing until the oil cooled, and in order to conserve fuel, turning the heat on only at brief intervals to defrost the windscreen. Unbeknown to Hooper, the traverse had also developed radio communication difficulties, and could only send the occasional garbled and intermittent messages to McMurdo.

Nearing McMurdo, he was forced to land more frequently with his helicopter landing 18 times in a 90 mile stretch, with the last thirty over a deep crevassed area with light powdery snow and with the strong blast from his rotary blades his visibility was near zero, but still he managed to coax his wounded helicopter back to McMurdo, and landed just as a Squadron's Otter was taxiing to search for him.

'The scariest I got', recalled the plane's captain AD2 Charles Steven, *'Was when we were forced down in a small patch of ice and snow surrounded on three sides by crevasses, I don't remember when I was so cold or so nervous.'*

There is a story told and retold of the Squadron's ADRC, Howard Humphrey. Work in Antarctica was routinely miserably cold and what made it more intolerable for Humphrey were the frozen raw eggs, which had to be shelled like the hardboiled kind and then mashed in a frying pan with a fork to be able to cook them, so he tried to solve the problem of sunnysiders by thawing an egg under his armpit.

Well it nearly worked! As the egg reached that tender stage, one of his mates called him and on turning quickly and without thinking, he knew he had a sticky problem and that the egg was no longer suitable for scrambling.

Another irritating incident happened when a downed helo that was perched precariously on the Ferrar Glacier some 60 miles from McMurdo Station, was waiting to have its engine changed.

It all began when a VX-6 aviator flew into the Royal Society Range, Antarctica to pick up a two-man New Zealand trail party. As the flyers were preparing to depart with the Kiwi's, one noticed that the sump warning light had come on. Shutting down his machine, he radioed McMurdo but it would be hours before a helo arrived to evacuate the group.

A maintenance team, which included Humphrey, was flown in next day to inspect the downed helicopter and found an engine change was necessary but the surrounding crevasses forbade the landing of a fixed wing, even by those equipped with skis, so a helicopter was needed to transport the engine out.

There was an A-frame on hand at McMurdo, but it was too bulky for the helo, so a 400- pound rig was designed and built, but there were delays as the original plan called for two three-man crews working in12 hour shifts.

A torque wrench, tossed to the party from a U-1B Otter hovering at an altitude of 100 feet, was immediately lost in the surface snow never to be found, so another had to be flown in but the equipment proved too heavy for three men and the two-shift system and had to be abandoned.

The sled holding the defective engine froze to the surface, so preheaters were used to loosen it, but this in turn caused the snow and ice under the downed helo to melt, so a good size hole was dug under the forward wheel so that the 15000 pound helicopter could be moved by simple man-power.

The four days of actual work on the engine passed, but not quickly enough for the gourmets on the maintenance team who said of their sometimes duty cook, an ADJ2 that he '*even burned the bloody frozen stuff*'.

Larry Lister recalled the time an H-34, the only one in the squadron's 1965 fleet on the ice that had a hydraulic throttle, was parked in front of the hanger awaiting maintenance. During the engine start, recalled Bud English and Walter Smith, it had an over-speed which flung the engine cooling fan blades, cutting a fuel line and starting a fire. As it happened, there was a Seabee with a D-8 parked there, so when the fire couldn't be brought under control, he pushed the helo over the side of the bank.

Larry also tells the story that occurred towards the end of the '69 season, when the US Air Force were trying to load a Navy's VX-6 UB-2B from one of the ice breakers into a USAF C-124 Globemaster but couldn't seem to get the thing loaded. '*So Charles Nordyke, AM-1 [called UGH] and I got the job of loading the damn thing.*

With Lt Elliot Freeman [Helo Officer] in charge of the loading, we were having a little problem getting it in, so we improvised! With a 16 pound sledge hammer, fire axe and hacksaw, I removed the tail rotor blades and hub and gained enough clearance to stuff the helo into the C-124, but when Lt Freeman saw how I was doing it, he just shook his head and left saying he was going for a cup of coffee but never came back. Never did understand why!'

As I stated earlier in this book, many stories vary from the actual facts, and in the intervening 50 years, stories often retold and second hand are coloured and enhanced.

Lt John Colson a squadron helicopter pilot, who joined VX-6 in the summer of 1957, went south with Buz Dryfoose and his dog Utz, and the second year he hitched a ride with a US Icebreaker from Christchurch and back as passenger cargo.

On one occasion he had to fly out to a crevasse field near Little America with Tom Austin one of the scientists, to take measurements in the ice through the crevasses, but because the ice was broken into pieces too small to put his copter down, John had to hover over the spot for Bill to jump onto the ice, then fly away for a few minutes so that measurements could be taken.

'*Sometimes getting him back into the helicopter was a mite difficult and we would have to lower the hoist and pull him up that way. He didn't like the hoist so we usually tried the jump first. On one occasion, he determined not to ride the hoist and made a huge jump into the passenger compartment- and made it. However, the crewman reported to me that Bill's crampons [2 inch steel spikes strapped to his feet for walking on ice]- had punched holes in the floor of our helicopter so we had to hightail it back to camp because we knew there were fuel tanks located under the floor.*'

There was a valley of crevasses between Little America V and the edge of the barrier ice where the Navy ships tied up, and in order to keep it safe for vehicles, the Seabees would used explosives to blast the crevasses closed. John Colson writes, '*one little Adelie penguin was exceptionally curious and appeared to sense when they were going to blast. He would come as fast as his little flippers would let him and try and get right on top of the snow pile where the dynamite was buried.*

The Seabees guys tried to chase the little fellow away when they were ready to set off the blast, but often he was still close enough to knock over and ruffle a few feathers. However, once he snuck up the back side and was right on top when they set off the dynamite, it blew him about 50 yards with the crew fearing the worst for their adopted little feathered friend, and rushed to the little guys assistance to see if he was alive. As they approached he stood up, shook his feathers and headed straight back to find out where they had 'buried' the next charge, but by now he was showing the scars of battle with some scorched spots and his feathers sticking out all over. The Seabees adopted him as 'Ol Joe' and from then on, it was bloody harder than ever to keep him away from the explosions.' There are very few ways to get your kicks in Antarctica.

Another story from our helicopter pilot friend, *'after dropping off some scientist to carry out studies at a penguin rookery, they requested that I take my 'copter away for several hours to allow the penguins to settle down a little. As we were flying away, I asked my mechanic Alsup if he had anything he wanted to do, he replied that when he had any spare time at home he always went fishing but here he didn't have any fishing gear, and at this point we spotted a rather large killer whale below us. In a flash Alsup pulled out a sharpened replacement hook for the helicopter's hoist and a thawed steak from our emergency rations. He wanted to go fishing for killer whales for hell's sake and had come prepared to do it. For an instant I gave the idea serious consideration, but quickly decided that I wouldn't know what to do with it if we in fact managed to hook one, I also didn't know if the helicopter could handle it and probably the scientist and my commanding officer would probably have taken umbrage too.'*

Lt John Colson also related a story about the dangers of whiteouts, crevasses and ice crystals in the fuel, but there was another in his opinion, feared more by VX-6 aviators and ground crews alike in the Antarctic, the more rare 'Ice Fog'. This is similar to regular fog in that it is made of exceedingly tiny particles, but the particles are ice crystals rather than water droplets.

As with regular fog, they are so small that they remain suspended in the air rather than falling to the ground. These crystals stick very tightly to anything they touch and walking a short distance in this kind of fog results in being coated with a thick layer of ice crystals so that one could easily pass for a snowman! They stick to clothing, beards, hair and even the skin although they melt after a short period on bare skin.

'I once drove a snow cat in from the airfield stopping every few yards for the defroster to clear the window, but by the time I reached the 'city' the radio's ten-foot antenna had a build-up of ice crystals on its front edge, showing that such a build up would cause an aircraft to be unable to fly due to loss of lift on its wings or rotor blades.'

In 1939, a 30-ton Snow Cruiser was a big disappointment to the Antarctic expedition as it had in fact been expected to be able to carry an aircraft on its back for 5,000 miles and to cross fifteen feet wide crevasses. Actually, the huge tires could not get enough traction and its electric motors couldn't provide the required power, so subsequently the giant was moved a few hundred yards from the ship to West Base that remained its final resting place.

In 1958 Lt.Colson flew several scientists to its location that had been determined magnetically. *'My crew and I assisted them to dig about 20 foot of snow from its top hatch. Inside many things were perfectly preserved by the constant low temperatures of minus 40F. A 35 mm film was still good after 20 years, a side of bacon and other food was taken back to Little America V where it was eaten as if it had just came from the store. Also several hundred overly optimistic 'Snow Cruiser Reaches the South Pole' envelopes were retrieved along with a stamp intended to be post marked at the South Pole. Some scientific papers and materials were also retrieved'* related Colson.

In January 1995, two helicopters from the US Navy's Antarctic Development Squadron six completed another first when the helicopters flew more than 300 miles from their deployment base at McMurdo to a remote location on the polar plateau to recover a lost $US 6 million Long Duration Balloon [LDB] and its valuable scientific equipment.

The LDB was carrying the Japanese/American Cosmic Ray Emulsion Chamber Experiment [JACEE], which was organized and run by a collaborative group of 35 senior scientists from eleven institutions from the United States, Poland and Japan. The scientific experiment was headed by Dr R

Jeffrey of the University of Washington and fully funded by NASA, and the balloon was launched from McMurdo on December 22 1994, and had made two revolutions of Antarctica at an altitude as high as 131,000 feet- or more than 21 miles.

The purpose of the project was to carry a cosmic ray detector above the earth's atmosphere for 10 to 20 days on a flight duration much longer than that of any other flight in the US. The balloon and its payload was brought down by radio control from a VX-6 LC-130 on January 3 1994, but at the time the ski-equipped Hercules was unable to land on the plateau to recover the 6,000 lbs payload due to ground fog. Six days later with an improvement in the Antarctic weather, a second ski-equipped LC-130 was sent to the area, however, when the crew attempted to land, they found the hard snow surface unsafe due to high winds and high hard mounds of snow. Later a NSF contacted a Twin Otter to attempt to land but they found the conditions hadn't changed.

The helicopter pilots of VXE-6 the *Ice Pirates* determined that recovering the 'booty' would be of benefit to science, but that meant the squadron would have to go over twice the normal range to recover the gear and require refuelling and working with the Italian Antarctic Programme.

Next day the flight of two helicopters began at 6.30am with a balmy McMurdo of 20 degrees F and clear skies, while in front of them were four hours flying over featureless terrain and a fuel stop where the crew had to hand pump the fuel from 55-gallon drums. Arriving at the site around 9 am at a pressure altitude of 8,800 feet, the temperature had dropped to minus 18 degrees with a wind chill of minus 55 degrees.

Before recovering the payload it had to be disassembled for transporting it back to McMurdo, giving the crew from the National Scientific Balloon Facility [NASA] along with Steven Peterzen, a monumental task, which took them four hours. LTJG Eric Vosler of VXE-6 said '*The ice formed on our faces and clothes, so we all worked hard to stay warm, wrestling with a 600 lb parachute, which had been filled by driven snow and was pulling us around in a 25 mph wind. Before the work was done, everyone was suffering from a mild form of 'mountain sickness' or hypoxic hypoxia, caused from working so hard at such a high altitude and in such weather.*' The effects of the altitude were definitely felt as their muscles fatigued and their heads ached from lack of oxygen.

Taking off again, the two VXE-6 helos took the payload down to a suitable landing site so the balloon could be reloaded into the Twin Otter where once again they had to hand pump fuel before leaving en-route to their home at McMurdo, landing at 9.30pm under cloudy skies and ending the crew's fatiguing 15-hour day working in subzero temperatures.

The NSF Station Representative Dwight Fisher said the recovery was largely due to the assistance of the helicopter crews on the ground and their true skill of flying was a great consideration to the success of the mission. The Antarctic Support Association [ASA] Helicopter Coordinator Robin Abbott said of the mission. '*These helicopter crews are the greatest! They constantly amaze everyone with their teamwork and action, in making it happen.*'

Lt Daniel Keohane best sums up flying helicopters in Antarctica in an interview with '*All Hands*' in April 1988. '*If a helo must land and spend the night, the crew can survive the harsh environment in relative comfort. Aside from wearing their cold weather clothing whenever leaving the confines of McMurdo, the crew of each helo maintains on board a survival bag containing gear for three men for five days. This includes a radio, tent, stove, fuel, sleeping bags and body protection. Similar survival aids are also carried on the LC-130's and every air crew member, whether serving on board a helo or LC-130, has been trained in polar survival techniques.*'

For Keohane, his whole Antarctic experience has been, as he expressed it, '*Great! I've seen places down here that would rival the Grand Canyon in scale. Yet more important than the rugged beautiful scenery is the education for a pilot down here that is tremendous. To venture a guess, I would say that a flight hour down here in the conditions we have to operate in is worth two flight hours anyplace else.*'

A chapter on the helicopter squadron without acknowledgement of AOI Raymond Skinner-enlisted pilot and OAE, has the best of these stories come from Cdr. Ray Berger, who was the Officer in Charge, Christchurch Detachment in the 1960 and an R4-D pilot.

'*We are old shipmates from the ferry squadron days, VRF32, San Diego. In 1954 three of us 1ˢᵗ class aviation pilots, AP's- [running mates, party animals] were ordered to take the chief exam by our skipper, a direct order. Bill Longley AD1, Ray Skinner AO, and me an ALI – all AP's. Bill and I MADE IT, Skinbean [as we called him] didn't. But that's OK- AP's don't cry. Then in June-July 1955, 331 of us were given commissions. Again Ray Skinner didn't make the cut because he had landed an F6F Hellcat wheels up early one morning in Dallas, while on a ferry trip. Ray was a hard charging pilot and was up and away from El Paso, while the rest of us were nursing a hangover.*

He got to Dallas before the wheel watch was at the end of the runway, in any case, while I was having them crazy brass bars hung on me in 1955 at Sanely Point in the Philippines, Ray was preparing to go to the ice, having gotten orders to VX-6 squadron out of the blue sky. He tells me he was virtually the only helo pilot on the ice, and operated mostly out of McMurdo. They all lived in tents, apparently there was a detachment from a helo squadron there but they were either afraid to fly or couldn't keep their aircraft in an up status.

He told me how he was inadvertently left behind on the ice after the squadron had returned to NAS Patuxent River. His wife Katie was there to meet him, as were all the other wives to meet their men, but no Ray Skinner, even the skipper Gordon Ebbe didn't know where he was. Actually they had left him behind, so he had to bum a ride on the USS Glacier to South American than caught a MATS flight to the states, arriving some time after the rest of the squadron was home. So much for being an enlisted pilot! But he has no sour grape, says he saw more of Antarctica than most up to that time, and when his enlistment was up Ray retired and flew for the FAA in gooney birds as a route navigation facility checker, and after that he retired.'

Ray Berger claims he was in the right place at the right time that got him into the enlisted pilot programme, his class was one of the last classes to graduate from the programme in 1947, '*In 1955 there were 621 of us left; enlisted pilots in the navy goes back to 1921 after WW1, when each country was allowed a certain number of naval aviators, and we [the US] came up with a programme of naval 'aviation pilots'. At one time in the 1930's we flew off carriers and the famous fighter squadron-Flight two, the 'top hat' squadron were all enlisted men, except for the CO and XO, including seamen first class who did mess cooking between flights.*

They won every fleet award in gunnery and formation flying at the time. Later in WW2, we were relegated to transport patrol squadron, overhaul and repair test piloting, operations pilot, ferry squadrons, and embassy pilots- you name it. We had many in PMY Blackcat Squadrons; one became famous for 'sighted sub sank same'. I was originally a boat pilot-the PBM's landing boat at night that's just like landing a ski plane in a whiteout at Byrd.

It was good training. There have been many AP's and ex-AP in Antarctica, an early pilot in Operation High Jump was Chief Harvey Speed and AP first class Raymond Skinner, a helo pilot aboard one of the icebreakers in 1959-60. Some of my predecessors were ex AP's, Lt Cdrs Johnny Ogden, Don Miller, Bill Kurlak [Mr Deep Freeze, we called him] who made four trips, and I'm sure there are many more. In 1955 they commissioned 321 of us, we were sort of a thorn in the officers side, because all we had to do was fly airplane and they had desk jobs as well, anyway, we drew all the shitty flying jobs and thereby became some of the best pilots in the navy. The marine and army air force had flying sergeants also. Well 'nuff of that.' Recalls Cdr. Ray Berger,

The United States Army had been called upon on various occasions during the early years of the *Deep Freeze* seasons to assist in difficult Antarctic projects, where they had gained previous experience and were able to offer the Task Force specialist advice. When the Navy encountered difficulties with their initial overland reconnaissance to the Byrd Station site in *Deep Freeze 1*, the

Army's expertise, based on their long experience in the Arctic, came to the fore, but it wasn't until *Deep Freeze 62* that the first US Army Aviation unit visited Antarctic for a project involving three topographic engineers who were tasked with the triangulation and positioning of 68 control stations over a distance of 2,222 km in the Trans Antarctic Mountains.

As the sites to be occupied were at elevations upwards of 3,050 metres [10,000 ft], VXE-6 own HUS-1A piston engine helicopters were questionable at that elevation, so the Army was called in to assist. Although the Bell HU-1B Iroquois, a turbine powered helo that was chosen for the operation, had never been operated in the polar regions, it had an excellent low temperature starting capability which in short, required little or no pre heating. It was also able to operate up to 4,000 feet with a payload of 2,000 lbs and had a range of 231 n/miles, with another plus that it could be transported to Antarctic inside both the LC-130 and the USAF C-124 Globemasters.

The Army detachment consisting of nine personnel and two helicopters departed from their base at Fort Eustis, Virginia and arrived at McMurdo in October 1961 aboard a C-124. After a short period of rest, the squadron were briefed on their operation which would be divided into two phases starting with '*Topo South*', which was to be supported completely by air, concentrating on the area from McMurdo to the head of the Beardmore Glacier with VX-6 aircraft establishing fuel caches and transfers of necessary equipment from site to site.

With this phase completed by early December, the second phase called *Topo North* was then commenced. When this phase was originally planned it was envisaged that the helicopters would be operating from the US Icebreakers, but when the ships were damaged while clearing a channel in the pack ice and had to return to New Zealand for repairs, the project became land based with *Operation Topo North* concluded on January 12 1962. The operation proved more than successful, with accurate data being recorded over 100,000 sq miles of previously unmapped territory.

The Army's Bell copters, like the VXE-6 C-130's proved remarkably suited to Antarctic operations, even with one Army Iroquois having to have an engine changed on the 10,500-foot Mount Discovery. It was returned to the States at the end of the season, but returned for the following Antarctic season in *Deep Freeze –63*, along with three UH-1B's for another topographic project operation.

Again in Deep Freeze 63, this time with additional aircraft, the Army deployed three UH-1B's on another topographic mission which had been planned and broken into two phases. The *Topo West* project was a continuation of *Topo North* in the Cape Hallett area to the South Magnetic pole and parts of McMurdo Sound. While *Topo West* which had commenced on December 2, was an easterly extension of *Topo South* from the Beardmore Glacier to the Eastern Horlick Mountains.

After completing both phases, all three UH-1B's were positioned in the Mount Weaver area and prepared to launch a mission to fly to the South Pole. VXE-6 LC-130's had delivered fuel to the area and the Hercules would accompany the Bell helicopters as a navigational platform to act as SAR in case the Army encountered problems. All three helicopters set out on February 4 on their 342 km [185n/miles] flight and landed at the Pole at 5.15pm local time, a few hours later they were returned to McMurdo by VXE-6 Hercules.

When the Army helicopters first arrived in Deep Freeze 62, there was no intention of Antarctic support beyond 1962, however by Deep Freeze-64, the Bell helicopter had become such an integral part of the support programme that the Army agreed to the NSF's request to continue their involvement, subsequently the unit was redesignated the 62nd Transportation Detachment [Medium Helicopter] and came under the operational control of VXE-6 while operating in Antarctica.

At the end of Deep Freeze-64, two of the helicopters remained at McMurdo in the stations helicopter hanger for their first winter on the ice. VXE-6 LC-130's also airlifted the UH-1B's to remote Antarctic campsites for the first time during the season, an activity that was to become commonplace in subsequent seasons on the ice.

The Army suffered their first loss but no injuries during Deep Freeze–65 when a UH-1B crashed just below the summit of a 13,800-foot peak of the Admiralty Range, Victoria Land. During Deep Freeze–67 three more powerful models of UH-1D arrived at McMurdo to begin the season, but one was lost when the pilot lost visual perception on his landing approach at a Marie Byrd Land camp on the Arthur Glacier in almost whiteout conditions. This helicopter was extensively damage and abandoned on the site after being stripped of radio and communication equipment- again none of the crew suffered injury.

CHAPTER THIRTEEN.

"PEGASUS THE FLYING HORSE BITES THE DUST."

*The last R4-D leaves the ice. The squadrons
involvement with Little Sarecco and a C-121
Super Constellation 'Pegasus'
crashes while landing to commence Deep Freeze '71*

Deep Freeze- 68 was over, and preparations began for *Deep Freeze-69.*
The first commercial jet airliner, a Convair 990 N-5615-named *Polar Byrd,* owned by Modern Air Transport, made its historic flight on November 22 1968 carrying 60 tourists on a 26 day round-the world charted flight. The Convair had made the flight down from Christchurch in four hours, thirty-two minutes and then after refuelling, departed for Christchurch later in the day.

During the season a fifth Lockheed Hercules was added to the Squadron's fleet, being an R model *#155917,* named *'Ao Te Aroa'* and like the F's it was modified to take 3,600 US gallons and could operate on both wheels and skis. The Squadron's photo-configured LC-130F #148320 operated from Punta Arenas, Chile and Byrd Station into Graham Land, Palmer Land and Ellisworth Land and in December 1968 despite merciless weather the crews like the Squadron's Puckered Penguin predecessors managed to cover 40 per cent of their intended targets. For this mission # 148320 was re named *Ciudad de Punta Arenas* having had additional fuel tanks installed.

The Air Development Squadron Six, or VX-6 changed its name on January 1-1968 to Antarctic Development Squadron Six with a shorter designation VXE-6; the change was made to accurately describe the Squadron's Antarctic missions.
Deep Freeze-68 was also the last season to be covered by the US Navy's Antarctic weather picket ships, with the *USS Mills* and *USS Calcaterra* sharing the last season in the cold Antarctic waters. Since 1955 picket vessels and their crews had endured the worst of Antarctic weather and sea conditions to provide weather data and communications for the Squadron aircraft on their long and at times lonely flights to and from Antarctica.

The original Destroyer Escorts were DER type radar pickets in 1960/61, as these vessels extended their radar intercept range to around 148 km [80 miles] and the UHF voice communications were also installed in Christchurch and McMurdo Station. These picket ships and the USAF aircraft gave the Task Force a greatly improved result in this notoriously bad reception area. The SSB system was extended to other Antarctic Stations and all the Squadron aircraft in 1962.

For four seasons, *Deep Freeze–62/65* New Zealand provided Lock-class antisubmarine frigates the *HMNZS Pukaki* and *Rotoiti* in the picket ship role, and with the introduction of increasingly more reliable weather satellites and the use of the turbo prop Hercules and later the imminent introduction of jet aircraft, the need for the picket was reduced, thus saving the United States Antarctic Programme millions of dollars annually.
The Destroyer Escort Radar [DER] was modified for destroyer escorts, but after the second world war many of the serving destroyers were mothballed, then in 1945 and later in the 1950's DE's were converted to radar picket ships. This conversion allowed the ships to operate as ocean going radar

and communication platforms until state-of-the-art radar, navigation and communication equipment was installed on the DER's and they then took their picket ship stations around the world.

The challenges of these '60 degree South' pickets were many, and normal shipboard operations and activities were always interesting, especially while bobbing about like a cork in the wind blown Antarctic Ocean. The wear and tear on the equipment, not to mention the crews, always kept everyone busy, and one radar electronics technician was always amazed that the SPS-8b's antenna [height finding radar] never broke off its mountings. The lateral forces on the antennas parallel to the horizon, was nothing less than surreal.

'In my mind, I can hear the motor generators and the platform stabilizing motors complaining loudly as they responded to the ship's pitching and rolling, while the antenna itself was whipping about in the opposite direction to the pitch and roll of the ship. It's been 32 years since my last picket ship duty- but it feels just like it was yesterday.

Bobbing around in the vicinity of 60 degrees South, 158 degrees East, these picket ships spent most of their Antarctic tour on the stormiest seas on this earth, observing atmospheric conditions and reporting weather. Being diesel powered these vessels were capable of covering great distances before the need to refuel.'

The DER's mission was multifaceted including measuring upper atmosphere weather conditions for the aircraft flying between Christchurch and McMurdo, establishing a Tactical Air Navigation [TACAN] presence for navigational purposes and in an emergency, to act as a SAR platform in the cold Antarctic waters. The very thought of ditching in the frozen waters and the chance of survival if they did as the last resort, could be the very reason why not one aircraft ever ditched.

On July 14 1968, Commander Eugene Van Reeth assumed command of the Squadron. After graduation from Mount Carmel High School, he enlisted into the Navy and served as an air crewman, and after the war he attended Loras College at Dubuque, Iowa, until recalled to active duty as an Ensign. Selected for Command on July 1 1965, Cdr Van Reeth began his Antarctic tour of duty with VX-6 in May the same year, serving both as maintenance then Operations Officer, prior to assuming the role of Executive Officer.

The first historic attempt to land a jet on the ice was made on November 10-11 1968, but the jet had to overfly McMurdo and return to Christchurch due to strong cross winds on the ice, the C-*141 # 65 0229,* piloted by Captain Howard Geddes, USAF, headed south again and made the first historic pure jet landing in ideal Antarctic conditions after circling the station for a little under a half hour then touching down to a perfect landing using only 4,000 ft of the station's 10,000 ft runway. The USAF C-141 made McMurdo in five hours 52 minutes and began regular operational flights between Christchurch and McMurdo during *Deep Freeze-69,* having the two giant jets making eight return flights between October 29 and November 10 with each carrying 40,000 lbs of cargo.

The old runway spread atop 95 inches of ice could be used until it began to soften, melt, and finally have cracks appear before it dropped into the 900-foot deep waters of McMurdo Sound, during the waning days of the Antarctic austral summer.

Nature begins the rebuilding job in the early days of the autumn from March to June, when by that time the severe temperatures and winds of winter subside, leaving the ice at the runway location a sturdy thickness again capable of accommodating aircraft with a gross weight of more than 250,000 pounds. Ice boring determines the actual thickness and provides the signal for the wheeled aircraft of the USAF to begin their airlift role of resupplying the vast scientific operations of Antarctica.

On cue, activity at the Antarctic stations blossom when a tremendous amount of work by VX-6 squadron and the USAF must be accomplished, climaxing the start of *Deep Freeze –69* with the C-141

Starlifters arriving in October and continuing until the McMurdo Sound airstrip is closed down for the season The lifespan of the airstrip is determined by the weather; as a hot summer [with temperatures reaching the high 30's] can cause an early closure.

The Squadron mission route to McMurdo from the Atlantic Coast covered more than 11,000 miles including stopovers at Andrews AFB, Maryland's, Travis AFB, California, Hickam AFB, Pago Pago to American Samoa and Christchurch before the final flight to the ice. Crews for the flight to the ice are on a turnaround mission with time on the ground just long enough to off load, refuel and obtain other basic ground support and take off back to Christchurch with retrograde cargo.

The crew include the aircraft commander and two other pilots, two navigators, engineers and loadmasters, and there is only one especially imposed qualification, that the aircraft commander must have participated in a previous flight to the ice, and if the commander has not made a previous flight south, then on his initial flight he is under the supervision of an ice-qualified flight examiner.

Air Force pilots admit moments of anxiety as they touch down, despite repeated assurances from the Navy's pilots who say there is little difference from regular landings, giving the air force boys great respect for those VX-6 Pilots. They also have praise for the Navy's ground crews at McMurdo, with the runways damagingly rough one day and smooth the next, but constantly maintained by efficient crews who continually scrape the rough spots and then blow over three to four inches of snow that acts as a slowing agent, so full reverse thrust is seldom required to halt the rolling airplane, in fact, power must frequently be applied to taxi off the runway.

A combination of GCA, TACAN and the airborne radar computers go into action to guide the large jet transporters onto the ice runway, while the return flight to Christchurch is like a bicycle ride in one of the city's beautiful parks on a warm Sunday afternoon.

November 1969 witnessed another Antarctic first when accompanied by Rear Admiral David F [Kelly] Welch, the commander of Naval Support Force, Antarctica, came the first women to arrive at the South Pole. The party included Lois Jones, [a geologist at Ohio University, who obtained her Ph-D by studying samples obtained from the Antarctic], Eileen McSaveney, Terry Tickhill, Kay Lindsay, [a New Zealand biologist] Pam Young and Jean Pearson the *'Detroit News'* science writer, who had the Commander arrange for the all girl's historic trip to Antarctic. Once the C-130 landed, the women were instructed to wait while the cargo ramp was lowered from the belly of the Herk and the bay doors opened wide, thus allowing the six girls to set foot at the Pole together.

With cameras clicking, all six women walked down the ramp abreast, and arm-in-arm with the Admiral, because the news agencies had been pressing him to tell them the name of the first woman to step onto the South Pole ice. Fortunately the rear ramp of the Herk was wide enough for all to step off at the same time. Lt Jon Clark USNR, the Admiral's aide, retired from the naval reserve as Captain, and later practiced law in Denver.

In the late 1960's it was still unthinkable for female scientists to actually travel to the ice and work in its harsh conditions, and up until then the Antarctic was a total all male club, but things changed with Lois Jones submitting a proposal involving field work in the Dry Valleys with an all girl team. Jones proposal was accepted, dispelling the Navy's opposition to females in the field, and leaving them to fly to McMurdo and onto the shores of Lake Vanda for the 1969 and 70 seasons, but before the girls made it to their research site, they were put on the passenger list as tourists, which came with all the usual media hype as every step was recorded, and after a symbolic mirror topped 'Pole', the women were photographed shaking hands with Admiral Welch. After a guided tour of the station and lunch with the men at the station, they all boarded the VX-6 Hercules again and returned to McMurdo. The only other women scientist in Lois Jones' party, Christine Mullier-Schwarze who was studying penguins at Cape Crozier, declined the South Pole trip.

Barbara Land wrote a book, '*The New Explorers, Women in Antarctica*', published in 1981 by Dodd Mead & Company chronicling Lois Jones' scientific work in Antarctic, and Jean Pearson wrote a series of articles in the *Detroit News* from January 27 through to February 6 1970.

Once again the annual down under exodus was underway at the squadron's home port for *Deep Freeze -69* the squadron's fourteenth of Naval support, officially beginning on October 8 with the first flights departing from Christchurch. The Admiral's Connie departed home base earlier on a four day 5,500 mile trek to the squadron's jumping off point for Antarctica, with the squadron's new CO, Commander Eugene Van Reeth, but first stopping in Washington DC to pick up the Task Force's Commander Rear Admiral Lloyd Abbot Jr.

Before departing Quonset Point, all the men of VX-6 squadron on this deployment, had embarked on a rigorous training programme for the bitter cold of Antarctica and the disciplines required for their task ahead, a programme that followed each pre-season. Apart from blood tests, physicals, spending time in a low pressure chamber, night vision examinations, dental care, swimming, wet ditching drills and endless lectures in first aid, survival, public relations and New Zealand left hand driving, they would have attended 67 onsite training courses and 61 offsite schools, with half the squadron's personnel receiving some form of special schooling.

During the months at Quonset, the squadron maintained an operational status with VX-6 aircraft making logistic and photo mapping flights throughout Europe and the Arctic, and during the weeks leading up to their flight to Christchurch, there was a round-the-clock maintenance in hanger two for the regular night check operations, with operation and administration staff all working well into the night.

Five commercial Douglas DC-8's assisted by a USAF C-141, moved passengers and cargo from Quonset and Christchurch between September 27 and October 22, with the 'big push' coming between September 27 and October 5, when over 90 percent of the squadron left their home port, and the squadron's deployment airlifted scientists of USARP, the CTF-43 staff and navy men from the Davisville based Antarctic Support Activities and NCBU-201.

One of the squadron's International tasks was to transport Norwegian and British field parties during their geological studies of Queen Maud Land, and to assist this squadron's fifth ski-equipped Hercules that arrived during the season.

More than 2,000 men from the Navy, Coast Guard, Army, Air Force and Marine Corps participated in *Deep Freeze 69*, along with nine countries announcing their plans to operate active stations during this season.

Highlighted by eight round trips by the USAF 438th Military Airlift wing's C-141 Starlifters, again with support from the RNZAF's C-130H's, it also marked the transfer of three US Army's UH-1D to the Squadron, as it was the Army's last season on the ice after fourteen years in Antarctica. A new summer station, Siple, was established at Ellsworth Land, and updated fuel tanks were constructed at McMurdo where resupplying and maintaining remained the squadron's prime logistic function.

The Squadron's accident free record ended on November 19 1969, when a LH-34D helicopter *BuNo 150220* crashed, some 57 nautical miles west of McMurdo. The helicopter's engine failed while landing on the slope near Mt McLennan and it slid down and caught fire. The LD-34D was destroyed, killing the American scientist and New Zealand television cameraman Jeremy Sykes.

For his act of bravery, Lt. Mabry, the Marine helicopter's co- pilot was awarded the Navy-Marine Medal for his action following the crash. The Citation from President Richard Nixon read in part.

'Realizing the remote possibility of being located by search and rescue forces, Lt. Mabry, with complete disregard for his own personal safety and fully aware of the danger involved, unhesitatingly walked 12 miles in the Antarctic wasteland to summon aid and guide rescuers.'

The Squadron spent much time devoted to crew training in Antarctic SAR techniques, including flying and navigating in some of the worst weather conditions and hazardous terrain they would ever encounter.

Organized in 1956, the squadron's Pararescue Team was almost unheralded until January 11 1969, when it placed its name in the records with an unusual feat, as Petty Officer Dick Spaulding completed a jump from 20,500 ft, with that record remaining until PR1 Harry Gorick also jumped from 20,500 feet.

It wasn't until the squadron lost a UC-1 Otter when it crashed into the mountains, 125 miles northwest of Little America Station during *Deep Freeze 1* that the Task Force command realised that of all the hundreds of men on the ice, only one was qualified to parachute into the icy wilderness, causing the think tank in Washington to realise they had overlooked this vital position in their meticulous planning, even though Marine Captain Rayburn Hudman, the loan parachutist with VX-6 in *Deep Freeze I* had formed the Squadron's first special 13 man Para rescue team.

Each season since its inception, the Pararescue men of VX-6, had trained at becoming experts in Antarctic survival, and to prepare themselves for any emergency the men were trained in crevasse walking, deep crevasse rescues and ice trailing, with each member of the team having to complete this phase of training before qualifying as an Antarctic Parachutist.

Deep Freeze –69 was the final season for the involvement of the US Army detachment in Antarctica. In April 1969 the USAF Globemaster transport squadron delivered three UH-1D's to VXE-6 homeport, at NAS Quonset Point enabling the Navy unit to take over the Army's aviation mission in the Antarctic.

Late in 1969, while all the remaining C-47's and C-117's had been crated up and shipped back to the US for disposal, Cdr. Ray Berger's C-47 [R4-D] at the time the only aircraft of its type still in operation with the squadron, was about to be handed over to the New Zealand people as a 'thank you,' on April 28 1969 by the then America Ambassador Henning- a memento of the early days of VX-6 and its very close bonds between the squadron and the people of Christchurch. The Government handed the historic aircraft over to the Ferrymead Aeronautical Society as custodians on behalf of the City of Christchurch.

A radio message from Paul Panehal the radioman aboard # *17221* as the R-4D approached Christchurch airport one afternoon: *'Christchurch tower this is Operation Deep Freeze # 221..radio from Paul.. Roger... understood.. land on western grass taxi to Ferrymead.. roger Paul.. call ops boss and see if it's ok to taxi down Memorial Avenue ..ARRKKK... Roger.. break. Break..break..operation deep freeze control.. 221..ovah..."*

Prior to the handover, the aircraft was renamed '*Yankee Tiki Au Hau*' [loosely translated means, *Yankee good luck charm of the air,* and the names of the Memorial Crew were painted on the aircraft as a silent memorial to all those friends who died when their R4-D crashed while making a landing approach at Mile-20 on the Army-Navy trail on the Ross Ice Shelf on February 2 1966.

Pilot Lt. H M Morris.
Co pilot W D Fordell,
Navigator Lt.Cdr Ronald Rosental,
Plane Captain ADR3 CC Kelly.
Plane Captain ADR3 Wayne Shattuck [on board only for flight time]
Flight Radioman AT1 Richard Simmons. [A very close friend of AT1 Paul Panehal who had spent the previous night studying for a rating exam.]

The then secretary of the Ferrymead Aeronautical Society Denys Jones said the historical VX-6 aircraft would join their National Airways Viscount, *The City of Christchurch* and Admiral Byrd's Fokker Universal from the ice. He told me several years ago that the only log book they had for #

17221 was Number 5, but despite writing back to the US, I have not been able to obtain any earlier log book data.

The log is vague to say the least, merely having pages for each month of the years 1963-69 and the odd entries on various dates recording solely flight hours, with no records of flight destinations etc. The log has all the equipment cards and by virtue of its physical construction is not an easy item to copy as it is some 5 inches thick.

This grand old girl of Antarctica, # *17221 Kool Kiwi*, was towed the 20 km to her new home at the Ferrymead Museum via downtown Christchurch with her slow journey creating a great deal of interest for the people of Christchurch who had been used to seeing the bright red tailed aircraft of the squadron in the skies over the city, but they had never seen one on their streets before.

ATN-Radioman Paul Panehal was first assigned to # *17221* by ATC Glenn Hunt, the squadrons avionics shop chief in late December 1965 and started flying crew training in March 1966 after the squadron had returned home to Quonset Point. He returned to the US in July 1970 then received orders for Glynco, Brunswick, Georgia, leaving behind many good dart mates, close friends and drinking buddies at the Russley Hotel, a downtown Christchurch pub. With many fond memories of the garden city of Christchurch, he resolved to come back again some day and bring his lovely wife Pansy.

Deep Freeze 70 saw the first season where the US Coast Guard Aviation Detachment were assigned to their icebreakers, replacing the Navy's VX-6's units, with both detachments being equipped with the Skorsky HH-52A Seaguard turbine-powered helicopters

On June 24 1970 in the Seaplane hanger 2, Cdr David B Eldridge took over the Squadron's command relieving Cdr Jerome R Pilon a veteran polar aviator, who on October 3 1967 had flown the 380 miles to Hallett Station with 21 men aboard his C-130 to prepare for the opening of that station. The mission and its landing proved to be an adventure for the aviator when he had to make three passes approximately 50 feet from the surface, before setting his C-130 down safely. Cdr Pilon became the squadron's 15th CO, and after his Antarctic tour of duty, he reported to the Naval War College at Newport.

Both Cdr Pilon and Cdr Eldridge were native sons of Maine and both graduated from the Maine Maritime Academy. Cdr Eldridge was commissioned an ensign upon graduation in 1953 and entered the Navy the following year, with his first assignment being that of gunnery officer aboard the destroyer *USS C T O'Brien* at Newport. He entered flight training in January 1956 at Pensacola, completing his jet training at Corpus Christi, Texas, then served an 18-month tour as a formation flight instructor at Whitting Field, Fla. then serving as maintenance officer and patrol plane commander in the P2 Neptune with Patrol Squadron 23 deployed in Iceland, Newfoundland.

Cdr Eldridge began his tour with Antarctic Development Squadron Six in February 1966 when he was the Squadron's CO for the winter-over detachment, and operations officer during *Deep Freeze 68* and Cdr Pilon's executive officer the following year, before assuming command.

What type of guy was Dave Eldridge?

One Old Antarctic Explorer summed him up in the season prior to him wearing the Skipper's Hat and writing under the name Ah-Yuppp, he writes, '*Dave Eldridge was a pleasant person of wide knowledge and a better role model than I had previously been following. He came to our Connie crew 644 and was a smooth pilot, not jumpy or unsure. He would let me pickle the autopilot from the right seat and we commenced 100 credit hours of 'what is what' talk while I practiced straight and level flight on instruments across the Pacific.*

I thought of him as when we had been boring holes in the sky out of Quonset Point [NCO] and over Mass, Maritine Academy. I thought of him again and how he must be doing, as I heard he went on to become a skipper of VX-6, later retiring as a Captain and spent some time in Washington DC. He

had graduated from Maine Maritime and told me that after a very good education, he was ready to attend Navy Flight Training and go onwards and upwards.

Sure sounded cool to me. We had these Flying Red Horse caps with our names on the back. Jerry Pladko, Gordy Williams, Hank Moorehead, George King, Jim Frazier, Fred Overson, Earl Rudders and others- all good mates like the Skipper. We all had too much fun and settled down later.'

With the start of *Deep Freeze 71,* the squadron entered the new decade with 15 turbine powered aircraft in their fleet, two C-121 Super Constellations, a single LC-130 to transport passengers and military personnel from Christchurch to McMurdo, four LC-130F's and three turbine UH-1D'S previously operated by the US Army, on intercontinental missions

1971-72 brought management changes to the Antarctic program, after President Richard Nixon reaffirmed the US national interest in Antarctica and directed the National Science Foundation to assume management and total budgetary control. Subsequently a change was made to the funding procedures and management by consolidating those responsibilities of the National Science Foundation.

The statement read in part. *'Because the United States in Antarctica is primarily scientific in nature, and in order to achieve maximum effectiveness in developing funding for a national programme, the President has decided to consolidate funding and programme management responsibilities for all United States activities in Antarctica within the National Science Foundation.'*

Similar to the commencement of *Deep Freeze II,* when a VX-6 Neptune *Boopsie # 122465* crashed on landing on the ice runway at McMurdo in 1956, tragedy, while not fatal, again struck the squadron's Super Connie *Pegasus* in Oct 1970.

Just before 9am on a dull cool Christchurch morning, hundreds of well-wishers had gathered to watch the Squadron's fleet depart for another season on the ice. Lt. Cliff Greau, a veteran of two previous Antarctic seasons roared his C-121J into the southern skies and headed south. Appropriately named *Pegasus* the flying horse, she was on her seventh season of Antarctic missions to open up *Operation Deep Freeze 71* with her destination Williams Field, McMurdo.

Carrying a crew of 12 and 68 passengers, including a technician from Lockheed, plus cargo and mail for the wintering over party, she was the first aircraft to get away just after midnight, as was her sister craft *Phoenix,* followed by five C-130 Hercules.

The aircraft's second navigator Robert O'Keefe on his inaugural flight to the continent was unknowingly a matter of hours away from his grim introduction to Antarctic flying. That day, October 8th 1970 is still firmly etched in his mind.

Arrival at McMurdo was scheduled around 8pm where weather was marginal at best, and with a large storm approaching, their arrival, and that of all the other aircraft flying south, was of paramount concern as there was no alternative landing sites available to the crews once they had passed the point of safe return, although each aircraft was in regular contact with ocean control until they were handed over to McMurdo Centre.

Says Bob O'Keefe, the second navigator aboard, *'As we reached the point of safe return, it was 4pm, we had learnt that McMurdo weather was deteriorating and visibility at Williams Field was ten miles with winds at 13 mph so we commenced a conference, and Lt. Commander Greau made the call to continue the flight south.*

We really didn't discuss it much, everyone on the flight deck had their thoughts, but we all said a silent prayer as thoughts flashed back to the loved ones we left at home.'

Between 6 and 7pm a violent snowstorm developed, with visibility at McMurdo now reduced to zero and winds gusting to 40 mph. The 'Connie' utilized a slightly longer route into McMurdo than the Hercules did, and because of the mountains and the Ross Sea, it required approaching aircraft to stay above Mt Erebus elevation, and then drop rapidly for the approach into Williams Field. The C-121 route required skirting the Ross Sea and Beauford Island, and then to proceed straight into Willy Field.

'I can remember being able to see Williams Field from about thirty miles out as we descended for our approach, the front of the storm was like a great white impregnable wall just to the south of the ice runway as we flew almost directly over the airfield's buildings, racing to beat the storm, but we got lost.' Rob recalls.

Deep Freeze Headquarters in Christchurch were alerted to the situation, and contingency plans were implemented, with the local radio station beginning half hourly details of the flight, assuring listeners that the plight of the aircraft and those aboard was not serious.

Meanwhile back on the flight deck the commander was receiving vectors from the radar approach, while the crew secured everything aboard the aircraft, and briefed the passengers on evacuation procedures should the landing attempt be unsuccessful.

'We made six or seven ASD radar approaches and after each abortive approach, our flight engineer reported to the commander of our fuel status, and on the sixth approach came the news we didn't want to hear', recalled O'Keefe, *'only enough fuel for one more approach, and only fifteen minutes of holding remained until we were out of fuel.'*

He tells of Cdr Greau informing the crew that he was descending to 100 feet and if Cdr Avery, the first pilot could see any part of the runway, he should assume control of *Pegasus* and land the old girl. If they could not see the ice runway, they were to climb to 500 feet and intercept the Precision Approach Radar Glide Path for the ski field at Williams Field some two miles away, and retract the wheels for a 'wheels up landing' on the skiway normally used by the ski-equipped C-130's, being there was not enough fuel for an approach.

'We began with a certain apprehension, the adrenaline was pumping and I had responsibilities to carry out in an emergency. We all tightened our seat belts a little tighter and made sure that there was nothing in our shirt pocket to scratch our faces. The Commander caught a glimpse of the runway at about 100 feet above the ice and called for control of the aircraft.

I can remember vividly that he had completely idled the engines and dived for the ice runway, where we landed very hard and would probably have suffered little or no damaged, had several frozen snow drifts not formed on the runway while we were making our first approach.'

Unlike the Hercules, the 'Connie' did not have skis, so when touching down on the ice the 'Connie' straddled a three to four foot high and eight-foot wide snowdrift between the nose and main landing gear. Immediately on hitting the ice, Cdr Avery placed the four engines into reverse just as the right main gear impacted the snowdrift, causing the aircraft to veer rapidly to the right and turn about 210 degrees clockwise and slide backwards to the right of the runway. Then the main landing gear ran into a massive snowdrift and came to rest in the middle of it with the gear twisted and sheared off just below its pivot point inside the gear well.

O'Keefe recalled the right wing tip contacting the ice, *'as it slid backwards I remember watching with absolute horror number 4 propeller spinning off the engine, moments later number four engine ripped off its mount as if by some giant hand, followed by number 3 propeller, then number 3 engine, then the entire wing. While I recall it as if in slow motion, I doubt that the whole chain of events took more than a few seconds.'*

When the Connie finally stopped the two left engines were still running at full power in reverse, as the control cables from the flight deck had been severed. At this point Cdr Greau switched off the magnetos to secure those engines.

'A very eerie temporary silence ensued' recalled Bob O'Keefe, *'hardly a word was spoken on the flight deck, then seconds later a rapid evacuation on the left side of the aircraft put all our endless hours of emergency training to work. At 8.10 pm the Connie finally slid to a stop on the frozen ice surface where it was only half a mile from the aircraft parking lot and cargo staging area, but it took over three hours for anyone to locate the crashed aircraft.'*

Five crew were injured, suffering from lacerations, bruises and back strain. The OIC of the VX-6 wintering over party, Lt. Koening was at the runway awaiting our arrival from Christchurch, together with a large military terrain stakebed truck with a canvas top, and two large four-wheel buses, used for transportation between McMurdo and the ice runway at Willy Field.

Evacuating the crew and passengers was made via the left and forward crew cargo doors, as the rest of the crew assembled the passengers away from the aircraft. One of the loadmasters stayed behind with O'Keefe to get as much as possible of the aircraft emergency equipment unloaded with the fear of fire breaking out being foremost in their minds.

'We were able to off load all the equipment, which included several tents, that we felt could shield the passengers and crew from the now extreme wind, blistering snow and severe chill factor, that was now effecting us all, recalled O'Keefe.

But with a 50 mph wind blowing across the ice, it was impossible for the crew to erect the tents, and as half the passengers were not properly dressed, it was considered they would be better off inside the 'Connie', for with no fuel in the tanks, the likelihood of fire was low and at least they would be out of the freezing winds and 50 plus below zero temperatures, and we could utilize the tents and as much of the other gear as possible to keep our passengers warm.

The GCA radar at Willy Field was frantically working with Lt Ken Koening to locate us and get us back to safety and shelter. Ken had radar on the top of a four-wheel drive vehicle and was able to talk to radar operators via a radio in his truck. The radar operator could see the 'Connie' on his screen and directed Lt. Koening towards the crashed aircraft, but by that time the visibility was less than 50 feet, and with snow now driving harder than ever nothing could be heard for more than a few hundred feet from us.

He could neither hear us nor we hear him, and when he finally discovered our position, he radioed our status to the radar operators back at Williams Field, who then radioed the information to the squadron back on the 'hill', while a support worker with the ICO he had brought with him, walked behind the truck, planting flag poles to which he attached a rope and flags.'

This operation took over 30 minutes to get back to the staging area, then they had to drive the truck to evacuate the first of the passengers and the injured crew.

Bob O'Keefe was the last of the crew to leave the crash site, being transported to the staging area then transferred to the heated buses for the slow ride up the hill to McMurdo, which to the standing only crowd, appeared to take forever.

'I couldn't believe that it took so long to locate us, after a couple of hours, the numbing cold began to work its will on us so we were just concentrating on staying alive.

The harsh Antarctic storm lasted until the following day, and by the time I was able to get down to view my beloved 'Pegasus', the snow had drifted up against the left side almost to the top of the fuselage. The main landing gear was still sticking straight up out of the snowdrift, which had ripped it off the aircraft, and one could literally follow the trail of parts that had been ripped off as we slid backwards down the runway.'

Bob O'Keefe remained with VXE-6 in Antarctica until March 1973, later attending the squadron's decommissioning at Point Mugu Naval Air Station. After this mishap a major change was made to the C-121 minimum weather operational criteria for flights to McMurdo, and the decision was to retire the only remaining C-121 *Phoenix # 131614* at the end of the season. She made her last flight to Antarctica on December 13 1970, after which she was transferred to Naval Air Systems Command for deactivation and retirement.

Paul Panehal's recollections of his first and only landing were '*Neat*' - at least that's the way he looks at them now. It was his first or second C-121 flight to the ice in Sept/Oct 1965;

'I was on C-121J # 121624 and the approach was straight and smooth in the pitch blackness of the Antarctic day for one of the first flights to the ice, and it was a pure text book approach, then the wheels touched down and the aircraft started to slide sideways down the ice runway, an interesting

feeling when you are sitting aft of the main wing on the starboard side. I know I could see lights as runways markers; I guess I slowly oriented them into my view before I realized I could see the markers or lights on both sides of the runway. Just about everyone was calm, even though they could tell we were sliding sideways.

After we stopped moving nearly everyone got up and started towards the rear of the aircraft. Then I notice another phenomenon. The tail of the aircraft was starting to rock backwards. The weight of all the bodies moving to the rear of the plane had off set its centre of gravity, and this is when the shouting began 'Get back in your seats! Move towards the front of the plane!'

Between the intercom, Jimmy F and the rest of the crew shouting, you couldn't tell what they were saying, but they were sure upset about something. Then, I saw Jimmy grabbing people and pulling them towards the front of the plane and telling them one by one to go all the way forward and not to stop. By now it was teetering some, and then it settled back on the nose wheel. I remember finally getting off the plane and asking about the tail support, which by now hung from the tail towards the ground.

The other thing which was very apparent was that it was pitch black, and each of the folk who met the aircraft had flashlights, and I wish I had had mine where I could get it. Not so mind jarring was the ride from the strip to the Hill in an enclosed duck, so in my book, making a flight to the ice in a Connie was sufficient. To make the trip as many times as the crew did deserves a special medal. That was a hazardous day!'

Also on the ill fated Connie flight was passenger Dave Hazard, who was sitting over the wing that sheared off after they hit the deck, recalling that the crew knew we had a problem after passing the point of safe return with the weather at McMurdo taking a turn for the worst.

'It's my understanding from one of the crew, that we could only take 25 knots of cross wind to land the 'bird'. On our last attempt, the wind was moving us sideways, because we didn't have fuel for another attempt, and the wheels no sooner hit the ice when the wind spun us around and we hit a snow burn and the right wing snapped off, number one and two engines caught fire but were extinguished by the aircraft fire bottle. I remember clearly all exiting the Connie and attempting to erect tents, but to no avail, the wind was far too great. What seemed like an eternity – two to three hours, maybe more before finally being picked up by the lads at McMurdo.'

Another explanation for the crash, which could or could not have been avoided, was that if Cdr Dave Eldridge did not want to make such a big PAO deal of flying all the squadron aircraft to the ice on the same day, operations at Christchurch would have instructed *Pegasus* to turn around at the PSR. Some members of the squadron referred to their commander as an egomaniac, sort of like Captain Finn Ronnie, a noted American Antarctic explorer, or at least this was the opinion of Billy Ace. Ronnie was to command the Weddell Sea base when it was established, and had been selected by the USNC-IGY to head the scientific programme there.

He holds the distinction of being the only leader of the America bases in the Antarctic in command of both scientist and military personnel. Cdr Eldridge wintered over in 1967.

On January 9 1971, the US Coast Guard suffered their Antarctic loss when HH-52 # *CG 1404* lost power in flight and crashed on the eastern slope of Mt Erebus while on a mission en route to Cape Byrd. The four man crew were unjuried and were found seven hours later on the summit of Mount Erebus, to be rescued by a VXE 6 helicopter, with the damaged Sikorsky being abandoned due to its location.

The season ended on a sad note with the loss of *The City of Christchurch* a VXE-6 LC-130 # *148318*. The Hercules had just taken on 7000 gallons of fuel for the return trip to Christchurch when it burst into flames as it was taxiing around the GCA building. Its left ski went over a five and half foot snow bank causing its right wing to hit the ground and break between the two starboard engines, leaving the nine crewmembers and a single passenger to make a hasty exit.

The fire, fed by fuel and high winds, soon destroyed the C-130 and crash crews who were hampered by blizzard conditions were unable to control the fire. The Hercules had earlier developed minor technical problems and was heading back to Christchurch for repairs, when the accident occurred.

BuNo # 148318 was also named *The Penguin Express.* Its commander in Antarctic was Lt Cdr Sid Wegert, who served with the *Puckered Penguins* from 1966 to 68. With the loss of # *148318* and the loss of one C-121 and the withdrawal of the remaining Connie, a heavy workload was placed on the USAF, the Kiwi's and the planned reconstruction of the South Pole Station. The opening of Siple and Brockton Stations and the closing of Byrd Station had all contributed to the increased cargo movement.

Another first for Antarctic was the arrival of a Douglas C-133A cargomaster # *54-0135* on October 21 1970, which was carrying one LH-34D and two UD-1D helicopters. This cargomaster which had made its first flight on April 23 1956, was the first off the Douglas Aircraft's production line, as Douglas never made a prototype.

In a colourful ceremony Cdr C. H Nordhill took over command of the squadron from Cdr Eldridge on 24 June 1971, knowing that the problems facing him once he arrived in Antarctica were enormous, but well within his capabilities.

Cdr.Claude Nordhill was the first outsider with no previous Antarctic experience to be chosen for the billet, and all subsequent CO's were selected the same way, unlike those before him like Gene Van Reeth and Dave Eldridge, both having joined the squadron and flying C-121's for two years before assuming the position as Operations Officer.

Cdr Claude Nordhill said *'I joined VXE-6 in 1969 and assumed the duties of Operations Officer; Cdr Jerry Pilon was the new CO, and Cdr Dave Eldridge was the Executive Officer, while Cdr Gene Van Reeth was the previous CO that Jerry relieved. Pilon had served as Van Reeth's Exec Officer and Eldridge had been his Operations Officer.*

Each of these officers was serving in VXE-6, when they were selected as C0's. Someone within the Dept of the Navy had determined that the progression to serve as Commanding Officer in VXE-6 required that these officers serve one year as Operation Officer, then a year as Executive Officer, before assuming command. I can only assume that this was due to the unique mission of the squadron and the environment in which it operated. In other words when an officer was elected to command the squadron, that officer would serve a minimum of 3 years within the squadron.'

The role of Commanding Officer, along with the Operations and Executive Officers are the three most senior billets within the squadron. The Commanding Officer is responsible for all aspects of the squadron, which includes training, flying, administration, safety, and maintenance etc, and whatever happens within the squadron is his responsibility, while the Executive Officer handles the squadron's administration for his CO. VXE-6 is a large squadron, and in *Deep Freeze 72* there were 65 officers and 450 enlisted personnel. The Operations Officer handles all aspects pertaining to flying operations, including flight scheduling, composition of crews, co-ordinating requirements with the science community, while other officers are assigned responsibilities for training, maintenance, supply, communications etc.

Entering the Navy's training programme in February 1952, Cdr. Nordhill received his wings and commission the following year. His first assignments included two tours in Patrol Squadrons flying P2-V Neptunes, flight instructor in the advanced training command, Assistant navigator on the *USS Ranger* [CVA-61] student at Command and Staff College, Military Secretary on the Joint Chiefs of Staff, operational flying in a special mission squadron in Vietnam, faculty at the Command and Staff College, VXE-6 student at the naval War College, followed by duty as a Professor of Strategy and Policy at the War College, Commander of US Naval Support Force Antarctica and Commander Task Force 199, and lastly assigned to the staff of Commander of Chief Pacific [CINCPAC]. Cdr

Nordhill retired from the Navy in 1981, and holds a Bachelor's Degree in Political Science and a Masters Degree in International Affairs.

Operation *Deep Freeze-72* marked the end of an era in naval aviation with the retirement of the last reciprocating engine aircraft in support of science in Antarctica. Under Cdr Nordhill, all navy air transportation within Antarctica would be provided by turbo-prop ski equipped LC-130 Hercules and the twin turbo-prop UH-IN Iroquois helicopters.

Cdr Greenwell's dream had materialized with the change from a mix of turbo-prop powered and reciprocating engines, to pure turbine powered aircraft that simplified the squadron's support and maintenance, and only one aviation fuel, JP4 would be needed, while spare parts would no longer have to be for four different types of aircraft, leaving maintenance crews needing only to be qualified in turbine engines.

Cdr Nordhill led the flying from Christchurch on October 8th followed two days later by the first of 40 USAF C-141 Starlifter's turn around flights between Christchurch and McMurdo.

The first obstacle the squadron faced when they arrived on the continent was the annual uncovering of their living quarters, but severe Antarctic storms hampered their early flight operation schedules for the first two months and the minus 40 degree temperatures froze the hands of aircraft mechanics and made footing dangerously slippery for personnel loading and unloading aircraft, resulting in serious injuries and broken limbs. Despite these hardships, over two million pounds of supplies and 850 scientists and military personnel were delivered to their remote destinations, keeping the squadron working around the clock seven days a week, and flying over 1,300 hours in less than seven weeks.

Even without the early season storms and below zero temperatures and wind chill factor, maintenance has always be problematic for the squadron, and with all work being performed outdoors procedures had to be developed to compensate for the Antarctic temperatures. Engines were pre-heated prior to starting, with the aircraft's ground power units fitted with NiCad batteries to defeat the energy sapping cold. These effective systems were an improvement on what the squadron had to use in the mid 1950's, when a cessation of all aircraft operations became effective as soon as the temperatures reached minus 65 degrees, the time when the seals in the aircraft [LC-130's] started to lose their reliability.

Air operations were suspended on October 24 for four days when a massive storm struck McMurdo, covering the area with more than 24 inches of snow, which produced a wind-chill factor of minus 109 degrees. As the after effects of the storm were cleared and normal flights resumed, the back-up of both priority cargo and personnel from Christchurch resulted in ten flights being made from New Zealand.

Although VXE-6 had operated the LC-130 for ten years without major mishaps, this decade would prove to be disastrous in terms of serious Hecules accidents.

On December 4 1971, an LC-130 aircraft J D #321, piloted by Lt Cdr Ed Gabriel was damaged during take off from a site named D-59, some 125 miles south of the French station of Dumont d'Urville approximately 850 miles from McMurdo Station. The aircraft had just completed the second of five supply flights to the French traverse party who were part of a combined US/French glaciology project, and was on its way to the Soviet station Vostok from Dumont d'Urville, when at an altitude of approx 50 feet, two of the JATO bottles broke loose from their attachment on the left rear fuselage, resulting in one going up the tailpipe of the number 2 inboard engine and the other striking and shattering the number 2 propeller, with several large pieces entering the cargo compartment.

Since the Hercules had just become airborne, the sudden loss of power from engines #1 and #2, left engines #3 and # 4 still at maximum power, causing the aircraft to yaw hard left with the right wing coming up rapidly. Lt Cdr Gabriel rolled the aileron full right wing down, applied full right rudder and closed the throttles.

He managed to get the Hercules straight and level just prior to the impact, which collapsed the nose ski. He then resisted the urge to power the plane out of its problem, which would have resulted as he struck the snow, in an extremely left wing down attitude, whereby the plane would have cart wheeled itself to pieces undoubtable with loss of life. For this brave action the commander was awarded the Air Medal for his amazing presence of mind.

Although no one had been injured, the ten man crew had to live in a survival shelter for more than 3 days until the weather had improved enough to allow a rescue plane from McMurdo to land.

The Navy personnel who arrived to inspect the aircraft and investigate the accident determined that salvaging it was far too dangerous, costly and out of the question, leaving the salvage crew only an hour to retrieve the most valuable instruments before the aircraft was left to be buried by snow, where she remained in her icy grave for sixteen years.

The accident investigation revealed a disturbing chain of events, after the painters at Aero Corp, the company that carried out the last overhaul on the first C-130 to have entered Antarctic service with VXE-6 on October 26 1960, had painted over the slider mechanisms on the latches. This could have caused binding and jammed the release mechanism. This was the first year that the company had carried out overhauls of VXE-6'S Hercules as prior to this Lockheed did all rework and no paint was ever applied to those areas. One good result from the investigation was a modification to the JATO mounts so the bottles could no longer be jettisoned while in the air.

Writing of the air operation facilities in Antarctica in the *Naval Aviation News* in 1972, Captain Peter Anderson [USAF] who was assigned to the Task Force as a technical editor for the Antarctic Journal wrote, *'unique airfields are made of ice, hangers are non-existent and while both Byrd and the South Pole are equipped with precision approach radar [PAR] landings are made on 14,000-foot prevailing-wind skifields. At Siple and Brockton Stations, open field landings are made with the only available aids, radar corner reflectors. Hallett Station has a 6,000-foot skiway with minimum markers and a low frequency homer.*

Williams Field consists of a main skiway on the ice runway, where seals bore through the ice in late December and early January, and there is an emergency runway on the ice shelf at Outer Williams Field. Both the main skiways and the Otter Williams Field are serviced by PAR; the ice runway has airport surveillance radar; Tacan and ADF radio homers are available at Williams Field runways and skiways.

When intense storms hit the McMurdo-Williams Field areas and normal landings are impossible, a ski-equipped Hercules can make an instrument landing on pre-surveyed clear areas of snow 20 miles long, and after landing the aircraft and using internal radar and Tacan, taxies to Williams field complex.'

Other factors test the abilities of VXE-6 aviators, including a lack of weather reporting facilities. There were only 30 weather-reporting stations on the continent in 1972 to cover an area the size of the United States and Mexico combined. Pilots flew by pressure patterns and sun lines with the polar grid, artificial systems that designated the Greenwich Meridian as north regardless of where you are on the continent.

The squadron delivered over 4,000 tons of cargo and 4,500 passengers, while logging some 4,000 hours in the air during this season.

Prior to *Deep Freeze –73,* Task Force 43 was reorganized with its headquarters in Washington eliminated, and many of its senior positions integrated with Antarctic Support Activities, which then became the US Naval Support Force, Antarctica. Other basic operations remained the same, and Task Force 43 continued its support role with its Advanced Headquarters remaining in Christchurch and the Squadron continuing to be entrusted with its role of aviation support.

Four student scientists from the University of Canterbury in Christchurch were out on a boating expedition on the Ross Sea looking for a school of rare Antarctic fish, when their engine failed, so when the party failed to turn up at their base, a five day air search got underway with VXE-6 and RNZAF aircraft searching the area.

The squadron's helicopter piloted by Lt Jeff McComas and Lt Allan Costlow and their crew, AMS2 Richard Nelson and ADJ2 Kenneth Moncrief, found the scientists and hovered over the party now stranded on a large iceflow far too fragile to sustain the weight of their helicopter. The men had survived their ordeal eating penguin meat and rations taken from their disabled boat.

Looking back over his command of what Cdr Nordhill described as 'the most unique squadron'. *'No two seasons were ever the same, each season seemed to bring problems to cope with that no previous squadron commander had experienced, and in my case it was a rash of cracked windscreens in the Hercules. Routine flights would suddenly be interrupted by one of the cockpit windows cracking for no known reason. It was quite disconcerting to the pilots, but luckily none of them ever blew out.'*

As the Commander recalls, the squadron experienced 14 such incidents. *'We never did figure out what caused this and it just ceased as suddenly as it started. We finally chalked it up to the Antarctica adage, or Murphy's Law: to wit, if something can go wrong in Antarctica – it will go wrong.'*

Probably the one thing that has remained in his memory over the years was the attitude of the personnel that served in VXE-6. Flying in that harsh environment was a piece of cake compared to the hardships that the squadron's maintenance personnel confronted on a daily basis. *'For whatever reason, winds and cold temperatures seemed to bring the best out in these young men and they seemed to revel in accomplishing the most difficult tasks under the most arduous conditions. I still tip my hat to them, the United States Navy has never had another squadron similar to VXE-6 and we were all proud to have been part of the traditions and accomplishments of the Antarctic squadron.'*

The change in the command of the squadron saw Cdr J B Dana assume the position of CO from Cdr Nordhill on June 30 1972 with a *'Welcome Aboard'* from the squadron at Quonset Point, Rhode Island. Cdr Dana, a veteran of seventeen years naval service, was in his third season in the Antarctic when he assumed command of the Squadron, having been Operations Officer, and the previous year as Executive Officer under Crd Nordhill.

The two Commanders had met earlier in their naval careers when John Dana had been Project Officer for one of the systems installed in the aircraft Cdr Nordhill was flying in Vietnam. *'He came to Vietnam to learn first hand how the system was performing and flew many missions with us, not as a pilot but rather as a gunner. This was typical of John's attitude and aggressiveness, as he was a highly energetic and capable officer who passed away far too early in his life.'* Lefty Nordhill spoke of his close friend.

Soon after arriving in Christchurch for the season, the squadron co-hosted with the Naval Support Force, one of the biggest air open house days ever observed in the city, with more than 30,000 people attending the show to view the exhibits and watch as the aircrews of the *World's Southernmost Airline,* the Puckered Penguins displayed their skills. The Task Force has put on many shows like this before and since, but the 1972 display was by far the biggest, being part of the goodwill to Christchurch and its people. During the Sunday afternoon Cdr John Dana received a proclamation from the city's Mayor Neville Pickering.

Although VX-6 had operated the LC-130's in Antarctic for 10 years without a major accident, this decade would prove disastrous for the squadron's turboprop Hercules, an aircraft, in all due respects like the hero Hercules of Greek mythology.

A series of mishaps to their workhorse fleet of C-130's, first occurred on November 13 1972 when a LC-130R # *155917* was delivering a field party to the Ferguson Nunataks, near the Lassiter Coast, when it damaged its port landing gear while making an open field take off, but after fixing the gear in place with chains, they took off for McMurdo, later sending it to Christchurch to have the repairs completed before returning it to Antarctic service.

AMCS Thomas Eaton remembers the aborted take off in # *917*, *'We shot ourselves in the foot, a JATO was no match for the ice that day and after making several passes just couldn't reach take off speed, and after installing more JATO, started another run, but one rocket left its secure and slammed into one of our engines, we made a spin then stopped-then the rescue C-130 arrived.*

After several passes over the snow to pack it down, the pilot decided to porpoise the Herk in an attempt to gain the extra speed required, we gained some speed, but not enough, so the C-130 lost air, coming down hard on its nose ski with the ski, lower strut and attach points departing the aircraft. We came to rest with all four engines still burning and turning and we departed the plane from the paratroops doors as the crew was in front of the engines.

With the engines still turning, the pilot ordered us to bail out, but there was a lot of snow blowing back on us as we jumped, not realizing we were higher off the ice than the main skis which were still lowered for ski operation.

The jump looked like between 8 and 10 feet, as I recalled today, and we hit the ice and were blown back by the prop wash, and when I recovered, I looked back and all I could see was white, I was behind the nose ski and was looking at white Teflon from the bottom of the ski. I thought the plane had disappeared, so I repositioned myself and looked back at the aircraft which was still on the ice with its props still turning. I only suffered bruised knees as I jumped from the plane.'

On January 28 1973, the same aircraft was involved in a much more serious accident while making a control landing to the South Pole Station. Control waved the plane's commander away for its final approach to the skiway, however the fuselage hit the snow skiway so hard that its wing touched the ice, causing the landing gear, outer wing tail section and engines to disintegrate, and the C-130R become engulfed in flames.

Most of the cargo was salvaged from the crippled C-130R, apart from a 500-gallon bladder full of motor fuel, which was tossed out on impact and ignited on the ice some distance away. Much of the credit for the number of crew and passengers not injured went to the loadmaster who had secured his 20,000 lbs of cargo so well it hadn't moved on impact.

Lt. Commander Dave Crouse remembers the fateful flight.

'The final flight of # 917 was routine from the pre-flight to take-off and climb out, but at this point in time I don't remember if the flight was scheduled to be double shuttle or not, as it turned out, it was not'.

Lt Cdr Dave Crouse was on his 8th VXE-6 L/R mission on January 28 1973 in # *155917*, when it crashed at Ferguson Nunataks so he has 'first-hand' recollections about the way that that particular flight ended. As a new pilot to the squadron and relatively new to the Hercules, he felt it his duty and his privilege to hop on almost every flight departing Williams Field air facilities in an effort to spend time in the aircraft and at the same time, learn about the mysterious ways of the Antarctic continent.

'I was allowed to sit in the left seat for the boring part of the flight over Beardmore and onto the Polar plateau. This part of the flight was very uneventful, and on our first radio contact with 'Old' Pole Station, we were informed that they were in and out of white-out conditions, normal procedure as I recalled, so we were to make a GCA approach to the field and if unable to land, to remain in the local area for a safe period of time. If a safe landing could not be made, the flight was to return to McMurdo.

With the possible white-out looking at us, the Commander took the left seat and I returned to my station on the flights lower bunk with harness. I was sitting next to the navigator instructor for the remainder of the flight while we each monitored the GCA via our headsets.

The let down and the approach went well up to about a mile from touch down. The GCA controller gave me the hand written recap of the GCA instructions that were transmitted to the aircraft; "On course-on glide path/ on glide path on course, 018 your heading/ on glide path at 2 miles from touchdown/on glide path/turn right now at 020, on glide path, right turn now at 022, picked up a sight left drift/on glide path centre line is very slightly right, I mile from touchdown/ on glide, centre line is slightly right correcting slowly, / on path coming up on course, left to 020/ on glide left to 018/on course now going above/slightly/above/slightly above, above glide path.

Take a wave-off, too far above glide path, /climb out straight ahead, upon reaching 11,000, standby for further clearance." Inside the cockpit, the pilot, who had been following the directions of GCA, shifted his scab to the outside of the aircraft which, in retrospect, was the wrong thing to do.

The pilot spotted one of the black marker drums at the approach end of the skiway, at which time he said words to the effect, "I have the runway, I have the airplane." At this time, of course, the co-pilot had started to throttle forward took the control and closed all 4 throttles and started a transition back to the landing altitude. All of this took place in a short period of time and in my position on the bunk behind the pilot, I saw one of the marker barrels pass underneath the left wing.

From the records of the people at Pole Station they know # 917's descent was excessive, and if my memory serves me correctly it was over 1000 feet per minute. The pilot made his transition to the landing altitude just at the time we contacted the skiway. The landing was very hard, but did not seem excessive to anyone on the flight deck. Our altitudes changed rapidly.

The aircraft was moving towards the left side of the skiway, but had a slight tilt at this time. The co-pilot was attempting to correct the left drift by using the entire right rudder he could muster, and in the process, pushed so hard with his left foot on his right that he bruised his right foot and nearly collapsed his arch. None of us, and certainly the co-pilot, was aware that the tail had separated from the aircraft and his effort was accomplishing nothing.

After the fact, we know that the plane touched down at about the 850 foot mark from the end of the skiway and nearly in the centre. The force of the landing caused the wings to flex all the way to the skiway surface. It was a matter of discussion that, had it been a concrete runway, the wings might have survived, but because the skiway is only hard-packed snow, the wing tip dug into the surface and broke away from the main wing just outboard of the inboard engines. The wing separated from the outboard engines and went their separate ways. The force of the landing crushed the main landing gear and the skis tearing free went their separate ways.

The tail broke free of the main body at the head of the ramp, the tail section followed right behind the main fuselage and came to a stop about 8-10 feet aft of the fuselage. The main section of the aircraft continued at a slight drift from the skiway centreline and continued down the skiway, coming to rest, almost level, just past the large plywood '8' [8,000 feet remaining] marker on the port side of the runway. Total distance covered from impact to stop was approximately 1,150 feet.

From the cockpit, things did not appear too dissident from the landing, with the exception that we started a very slight port side roll. This was our first clue that things were not normal, and when the aircraft came to rest, everyone knew that we had NOT made a normal landing. The flight engineer went down the steps to open the door but it would not move. At this point the loadmaster had moved to the bottom of the flight deck steps and was saying something about a 'FIRE'. To emphasize his statement, smoke was drifting from the cargo area up into the flight deck.

As we came to rest there were no signs of panic, however with the idea of fire, we were all a little eager to leave the aircraft. When I saw the flight deck wouldn't open, I reached up and opened the overhead hatch above the upper flight deck bunk, and at this point I was ready to 'lead' the troops to safety via the open hatch, unfortunately, when you open the hatch, it comes into the aircraft and must be moved out of the way. Since I opened the hatch, I was the lucky one to have to find a place to 'stow' it. I could not tell you where I put the item but it did get stowed.

Everyone exited the overhead hatch to the sight, but no sound of the aircraft burning. The wings were just 'stubs' and the ends of the stubs were dumping all of the remaining fuel from the ruptured fuel tanks. Either the hot engines or the friction of the tearing metal had ignited the fuel, with the flames consuming most of the fuel as it fell to the surface. There was a tall column of smoke rising from both wing stubs into an even bigger column of smoke that was left from the 'burning fire ball' of the aerated fuel that had been sprayed from the separating wings

This 'fireball' was what the people at the station had seen. In order to depart the aircraft, it was necessary to slide down the side of the cockpit and make the drop of a few feet to the skiway surface, but for whatever reason, the student navigator tried to slide down on his stomach and ended up straddling one of the blade radio antennas. Looking back it was funny but at the time it was something that was slowing us down.

The one person that did not believe that we were in trouble was the pilot. With the aircraft burning, we did not know if there would be an explosion or not, but it seemed like a good idea to leave the area. The pilot would allow himself to be pushed out and dragged for a few feet, but would then turn and stare at the burning aircraft in shock and disbelief. Everyone else was eager to get as far from the aircraft as possible, including our two passengers who were Seabee hard hat drivers wanting to say they had been to the South Pole. Boy they got their wish and then some!

The outside temperature at the time was minus 57, to my knowledge, but no one ever talked about the wind chill, even though the wind was usually blowing anywhere from 10 to 30 knots and often even more than that. What difference does it make if it's minus 57 or minus 90 with the wind chill-cold is cold.

At the time of impact, the only people that were wearing their parkas were the loadmaster and the passengers, because they were the only people planning to leave the aircraft. Of the rest of the flight crew, only the flight engineer and Navigator Instructor were smart enough or calm enough, to retrieve and wear their parkas. The rest of us were leaving with standard waffle weave or flight suits, and because of the adrenaline rush, no one noticed the cold for quite some time. We began our transit to the Pole Station en masse, and after about 1000 feet, we were picked up by a D-8 Caterpillar that was heading back to the station. The driver was totally stunned to find a crew walking on the skiway.

At the station, manned by a total of 8 personnel, we found the remaining members packing body bags on sleds, and to say they were surprised would be an understatement, they were shocked! From what I could see, the rising fireball and the instant silence from the radio had them believe that there were certainly fatalities – believing us all to have perished. The aircraft had, in addition to a lot of miscellaneous cargo, three fuel bladders holding engine fuel for the reciprocating engines on the station's equipment.

One of the bladders was secured to the ramp and was pulled free when the aircraft broke in half, and the bladder caught fire from either friction or from burning fuel from the wing stubs. It did burn for hours and made a hole close to 100 feet deep, with the smoke rising from the hole for several hours. I don't think anyone got any sleep during the time we waited for a rescue flight from McMurdo. I was part of the group that went back and walked through the crash field before the rescue and accident investigation team arrived. From the time of the crash until our rescue return to McMurdo was 18 hours.'

Sitting next to Lt Commander Dave Crouse, was the Squadron Admin Officer at the navigation station, up on the flight deck with Clarence 'Joe' Wiebelhaus and trainee Lt.jg Bruce Mead 111, as they made their approach on that day.

Sadly Joe passed away in June 2004 in his hometown of Camarillo.

A member of the crew when # *917* crashed thought he was bullet proof. *'It has been some time now that I have thought about it. For many years afterwards I relived the crash, knowing it will never go away. I sensed something very wrong on the decent that day. I was in the cargo compartment and having made enough ice landings, you have that sixth sense that kicks in that something's up. The support personnel were rather shaken up with the landing to say the least. I guess we all were.*

We couldn't go through the rear cargo compartment because of the smoke, I remember the details very distinctly, I watched the tail separate and the rubber mo gas bladder lift up and shoot through the opening between the tail and main cargo section, it seems like an eternity before the plane stopped sliding.'

The cargo was salvaged, so much of the credit has to go to the professionalism of the loadmaster David Hazard, who had secured the 9 tonnes [20,000 lbs] of cargo in such a manner that it did not move.

David recalled later that the only cargo lost was the ramp load, which went out the starboard paratroops door, *'the crash tore the bladder from the 4631 pallet it was cinched to with 10,000lb chains. The D rings were torn out of the pallet, the rear of the cargo section looked like Dante's inferno when the fuel from the wings ignited and pushed the centre escape hatch inwards. The ramp section broke lose at flight station 737 at a diagonal direction rather than straight across, We slid approximately 1800 feet before we came to a stop, the reason the crew entrance door couldn't be jettisoned was that the bars holding the equipment under the galley floor jammed the mechanism.'*

Hazard had experienced a harsh introduction to the ice, when he had flown south on the ill-fated Connie # *131644 Pegasus* when it cashed on landing on October 8 1970. What a start to a tour of duty in Antarctica, and he remembers clearly the day they loaded # *917* at McMurdo for the first of two shuttles to the South Pole that they called a double shuttle. Together with his in-flight scanner AE3 Pat Yoas, the loadmaster started their pre-flight tests two hours prior to take-off and then started to load the aircraft of the 20,000 lbs of cargo, two 500gallon bladders of mo gas and three pallets of general cargo and mail. The pair commenced to load the three pallets one by one, and when all were loaded, they placed a ten thousand-lip bridle on the lower portion of the pallet. These pallets placed on grocery store rollers were not the usual wooden type, but were made of aluminium measuring 88 x 108 inches that could handle a ten thousand pound load.

David recalled *'We had eleven people on the LC-130R that day, nine crew and two passengers, one Seabee going to the Pole and a Coastguardsman along for a sightseeing trip. The Coasty made a remark after # 917 came to rest 'are all your landings this rough?' then we told him we had crashed.'*

The wreckage of # *917* was later moved off the new skiway, but was still fairly close to the station, on January 7 1975 two days before the dedication of the doomed station, # *917* was moved by forklift to its present position as a radar marker about a mile upwind of the McMurdo end of the runway. The tail and fuselage were moved separately and assigned as they had been after the crash. The wrecked Herk was lined up with the runway coordinates to serve as a radar beacon.

The same day a fire fighting truck from the Hill at McMurdo on its way to the permanent ice strip at Williams Field crashed and was a total loss, and just to complete the most expensive day on the ice, one of the ice cutters clipped another ship causing extensive damage, making it: one ship, one fire tender and two crashes at Dome Charlie.

An engineering team from the Naval Air Systems Command and Lockheed Martin Company along with representatives from the Naval Air Renwork Facilities were flown to the site to inspect the two damaged LC-130's during 1975, and after a series of planning meetings, a number of salvage options were considered.

One of these was to carry out temporarily repairs in the field, then fly the aircraft to a repair facility, which would mean the construction of a camp and ski-way near the site. Initially # *159129*, the newer of the two aircraft, was concentrated on and many of the required components and a new wing were ordered from Lockheed for # *319*, and these salvage operations would be deemed top priority over other Antarctic projects during the season.

This was the third Hercules accident in 21 months leaving things looking grim for the squadron, who were ending the season with only two LC-130F's and six UH-1N's, but their situation was eased somewhat with the arrival of three new LC-130F's. These and the first LC-130F were owned by the National Science Foundation and ordered, back in 1967 at a cost of US$19.4 million. The first # *148319* flew in October 1973 arriving in Christchurch on November 3 before flying onto Antarctica the following day while the second arrived in late November and the third in February 1974.

When the squadron returned to the United States after completing their 18th season of Antarctic operations on March 1 1973, they were again on the move, transferring from Quonset Point to NAS Point Mugu, after an eighteen-year stay at Rhode Island. This move involved some 700 navy men and their families. Although October 1 1973 was the 'paperwork' date in the homeport shift from Quonset Point, many of the personnel being transferred were already in the Point Mugu area, as more than 200 officers and enlisted men and approximately 80 families of VXE-6 personnel had already settled in Ventura County. The move by VXE-6 was part of the Defence Department's realignment and reduction programme whereby many US bases and military units were being relocated or closed down.

On June 30th 1973 Cdr Vernon W Peters from South Joseph, Michigan, relieved Cdr John Dana as the squadron's 22nd commanding officer.

Cdr Peters, a veteran naval aviator, who distinguished himself both in war and peace, entered the Navy in 1954 and was commissioned a naval aviator two years later. In June that year he reported to Airborne Early Warning Squadron Twelve [YW-12] at Barbers Point, Hawaii for his first tour of duty as assistant administration officer and legal officer. Cdr Peters began a two-year tour of duty at the US Naval Post Graduate School. In October 1968 he was assigned to the Commander Second Fleet/Commander Strike Force Atlantic Fleet staff onboard the *USS Springfield* and the *USS Newport News* as the staff electronics warfare Officer.

With a crew of 35, the C-130 piloted by Lt Commander 'Art' Herr and carrying the squadron's new CO together with Naval Captain Alfred N Fowler, who commanded the Navy's Support Force Antarctica, departed their new homeport on the logistic mission to Antarctica. Normally these early flights are referred to as WinFly, as the supply mission to the Antarctic to bring out many of the 300 Navy men and scientists who had been isolated since February, and to deliver equipment and much awaited fresh food and mail.

During a two-day stopover in Christchurch, the crew were fitted out with special cold weather clothing, and boarded eleven New Zealand scientists before setting out on their second leg to McMurdo Station to be welcomed by the 156 Americans who had wintered over.

Operation Deep Freeze –74 had begun with the United States Navy's Air Squadron starting its 19th year supporting *Operation Deep Freeze.*

During November it was a common sight to see squadron aircrews digging their living quarters out from under tons of snow, and equally routine to see ground support personnel and crews sliding down through narrow holes in the ice to see their work. However, despite all this, the squadron managed to haul some 10,600 pounds of materials during the month, where most of the materials were delivered to the South Pole station for the Seabees who were constructing a massive geodesic dome similar in size to the Houston Astrodome.

In the Antarctic, the Christmas festive holiday season lasts only a day and it is the one day in a short Antarctic summer support season when the tight operational schedules are placed aside, aircraft stand a silent vigil at Willy Field, and a twenty-hour period when the incessant noise of pre heaters are not heard letting the men and women [some sixteen of the latter] rest from their battle with round the clock re supplying the isolated stations and camps.

Christmas trees emerge from storage to be decorated in the traditional style, complete with lights and ornaments. Parties and gatherings take place in various huts, with the annual Christmas service performed in McMurdo's *Chapel of the Snows* and as at other inland stations, the cooks work around the clock to provide what is the traditional fare.

Snow blanketed the whole continent, with McMurdo and the interior getting from two to thirty inches of snow on Christmas Day 1973, and for the seasoned OAE's wading along High Street, it was easy to spot the newcomers who found walking difficult yanking their boots high in the air and squishing down again, making very slow progress.

Unpredictable Antarctica weather plagued VXE-6 throughout the austral summer season, with violent snowstorms, and hurricane-force winds brought air operations to its knees on many occasions, ceasing flying vital and much needed supplies inland '*It was miserable for awhile, but we made it*' says Lt Thomas Preato, a squadron's navigator.

The weather did warm up in late December to record one of the warmest months in Antarctic history to date, with the highest temperature recorded at McMurdo occurring on January 2, when a balmy 47 degrees F above zero was reached.

Besides their own problems the squadron assisted other international units in trouble, including a Canadian civilian pilot who flew off course when en-route to Byrd Station after his inertial navigation system failed while the aircraft was still 600 miles from Byrd. '*We located the aircraft while we were on our way back to McMurdo and led him back to safety*' said Lt Cdr Floyd Eldridge the VXE-6 pilot who performed the airbourne rescue mission [not to be mistaken for Cdr C.D. Eldridge the squadron's CO in *Deep Freeze 71.*]

In a joint project with the British Scott Polar Research Institute [SPRI] to investigate the ice thickness of Marie Byrd and Ellsworth lands, VXE-6 provided a photographic LC-130F # *148320* fitted with a 35MHZ radio echo sounder and antenna in the summer of 1969, the programme which continued into 1971, was at times unsettled by Antarctic weather, but they were able to survey 4,500 miles, flying 230 hours.

The origin of the remote sensing radio echo-sounding mission was begun under the direction of the Danes in Greenland back in the early 1970's, with a Professor Dr Gudmansen of the Technical University of Denmark [TUD] in charge. Up until this time various squadron aircraft with only basic wing and fuselage configuration had been employed until the mission was given to Cdr Arthur 'Art'Herr in 1973.

His crew eventually took *#148320* to the Naval Air Weapons Development facility at Warminster, Pennsylvania for the aircraft to be completely dedicated to becoming an exclusive 'Remote Echo Sounding' aircraft. With a crew of US Navy volunteers, together with the SPRI and TUD scientists, the aircraft departed from the US in late November arriving back at McMurdo the day before Thanksgiving on November 24, 1974.

From that day until the squadron returned to the States, 'Art's squadron members Al Mayo as Flight Engineer, Bob Nebry and Jimmy Wishart as alternate AC's, Charlie Snodgross as navigator and around eight other USN shipmates airmen and the scientists of the UK and Denmark completed more lines and maps than ever before or since.

The crew began flying virtually round the clock for ninety-two days straight, sometimes clocking up eighteen hours a day and all done at very low altitude in all types of weather, including numerous whiteouts, with refuelling often done at either the Pole or the old Byrd Stations.

The concept of the mission was the study of the ice, its properties, movement and formation which had been the mission of the International Antarctic Glaciological Programme, a ten year long programme carried out primarily by Australia, France, the USA, England and Russia. This was a vast project as 95 per cent of the world's permanent ice is in Antarctica, some seven million cubic metres of it, making Antarctica the highest of all continents with an average elevation of 7,500 feet. The crews of VXE-6 squadron covered over 80,000 miles of ice sensing flights over the continent, discovering two lakes under the sea at the East Antarctic Plateau, and surface bedrock on the plateau was also studied during these missions.

On the ice sensing missions over Marie Byrd Land, detailed soundings were conducted to tell just how the ice is 'streaming' [flowing in streams] towards the Ross Sea Ice Shelf from Byrd Station, while another area of investigation was the aspect of glaciology of the ice on the Ross Ice Shelf. Here using equipment developed by Chris Neal of the SPRS, the scientists studied the bottom of the ice shelf by the echoes received. The principle Investigator for the Project was Dr David Drewry, later Vice Chancellor of the University of Hull in the UK.

The initial design of the external antennas and much of the internal sensing electronics and operator stations for # 320 was a TUD/SPRI function with the actual fabrication, installation, testing and trouble shooting accomplished by the skilled work of the Naval Air Development Centre. The ice sensing mission flown by VXE-6 C-130's was fitted out with an array of antennas suspended beneath the wings. These antennas on a bar shaped trapeze 60MHZ and pylon mounted disc 300MHZ were connected to transmitters, receivers and recording equipment inside the aircraft, with the antennas being designed and manufactured by the Electromagnetic Laboratory of the TUD in consultation with the US Naval Air Development Centre in Warminster, Pa.

'The research has been productive and a whole new continent has been discovered. In the three previous seasons of ice sensing, mountain ranges 10,000 feet high, a valley 400 feet below sea level, extensive plains and lakes have been found' so wrote Art Herr in VXE-6 'Familygram' February 1974. 'Scientist have been able to locate these areas by flying low over the ice sheet, usually at about 300 feet, sending signals down to the sheet. These waves bounce back from the surface from the internal layers of the ice and from the underlying continent, and this way it is possible to continuously measure and record the geophysical features of the continent below.

Because of these missions, the Scott Polar Insitute has been able to construct a relief map of East Antarctica, and with the additional information acquired this past season the Insitute will be able to show more detail of this complex area, and construct an initial map of Marie Byrd Land.

Also included in the ice-sensing missions were sophisticated photo mapping equipment which records the surface features of Antarctica. The use of photographic and electronic readings, afford the scientist an opportunity to closely study the surface where the usual readings were recorded.'

When Cdr Herr retired from the Navy in 1975, Lt Cdr Bob Nedry continued as Mission Commander in LC-130 # 320 in addition the squadron's LC-130 # 131 were used to finalize RES until 1978. 'Satellites and other technologies had made RES obsolete, at least for ice sensing. I believe that NWC China Lake did only minor work for the NSF and that the so-called ADRS platform was originally done at Warminster for #320 and transferred to #131 at the end. All of this can be accurately confirmed by SPRI as they have very good records' recalls Art Herr.

The follow up in Antarctica was collaboration with TUD and SPRI scientists, funding coming from the Office of Polar Programmes thru the NAF. Air and logistics support was courtesy of VXE-6 squadron under various Commanding Officers, most significantly Commanders Claude 'Lefty' Nordhill and Fred Holt, both having entirely separate tours of duty.

The squadron's Mission Commanders and highly qualified navigators and C-130 crewmembers were actively involved; two of the more notable were Art Herr and later Jim Wisehart, now a senior Captain with American Airlines.

Captain Nordhill recalled that it took a day to install the antennas inside the aircraft, as the Herk was used for other supply missions. 'To ensure navigational accuracy, which was critical to the success of the project, the aircraft carried two LTN-51 inertial Navigation Systems, the latest state of *the art navigational equipment available at that time. The aircraft was also configured with an internal tank and I believe the capacity was around 3600 gallons as this gave the aircraft considerably more flight time for longer missions. All the tracks were laid out by the scientist who was conducting the project, and mostly the flights were very routine and more often times boring for the crews, but the results were remarkable.'*

The programme was halted towards the end of 1975 when the LC-130- *#320* was abandoned after a mishap in DF 76. During a take off a JATO bottle broke free from its mountings causing serious damage, so a seventeen man VXE-6 repair maintenance crew arrived and in three days had changed its engine and propeller and completed temporary repairs to its electrical system. A crew wearing oxygen masks flew *# 320* back to McMurdo, and then on December 28 the plane was flown to Christchurch for more extensive repairs before entering service again in February 1976.

On March 31 2001, a reunion was held for the British members Scott Polar Research Institute science project, the group which had mapped much of the under ice geographic features of the Antarctic continent back in the 1970's to honour the Director of the endeavour Dr Gordon de Robin, an organization still active in maintaining fellowship with all his former 'Old Antarctic Explorers' fellows.

Commander Fred Holt and others sent Art Herr as the sole USA delegate to the reunion with credentials to commemorate the twelve years of ice sensing done between the USA's NSF, the US Navy and the UK's SPRI. It was indeed an honour to both Art and the VXE-Squadron, and modest as always, Arthur Herr never boasted of his achievements in the RES missions. *'We should all receive equal glory for an extraordinary undertaking. I was fortunate to be the AC in # 148320 in 1973-75.'*

One of the attributes to the squadron's camaraderie, cooperation and desire to complete a worthwhile task was Art's personal honour of being inducted into the British Antarctic Club in 1990, *'this honour is, however, really one for all the Navy crewmembers and the UK and Danish science guys, who are always the most deserving and least recognized. It seems appropriate that while we sailors were just doing our duty once again, some of us remember who it was that made it really possible. I just made a few ski landings on the Great White Continent, and had the fellowship of some great men'.*

Brian Shoemaker wrote of his dismay as to how little recognition the United States tendered to members of VX-6 squadron for this project and in fact other magnificent flying programmes in Antarctica *'If one looks at a map of the continent in 1955 when the squadron was formed, one can see that it was about 80 per cent unexplored.*

Then look at the map ten years later and all of the spaces have been filled in an area larger than the United States, discovered mostly by VX-6, or to put it in another perspective, more than Scott, Amundsen, Mawsen and all other great Antarctica explorers of note put together. More than Lewis and Clark and other noted explorers in American history, in addition the squadron supported all the great traverse and field science programmes that have explored much of the continent on the surface and the scientific mysteries of the place.

Of these scientific programmes, the Radio Echo Sounding Project was the most magnificent, conceived by Dr Gordon and Dr David Drewry and others at SPRI, but carried out by VX-6. To their great credit the British led by the Scott Polar Research Institute, laud VX-6 for their pioneering working in Antarctica much better than were ever honoured by the U.S. Dr Robin who was Director of SPRI from the early 1950's to the 1980's was the champion of that recognition and Dr Drewry who followed him as Director has continued in that tradition.'

The National Science Foundation was keen to modify one of its own LC-130R's to add to its scientific potential and for its logistic support role. The following year modifications were again carried out on the system, fitting a pallet-mounted data logging system to # *159131* called Airborne Research Data System [ARDS] and connected to sensor probes and apertures on the aircraft.

The system originally designed for the US Navy hurricane reconnaissance aircraft, could receive, display and print data from a number of sensors, with the ability of recording upwards of 100 channels of information. VXE-6 conducted flight trials in Antarctica in January 1977, flying 12 missions in 9 days to a total of 67 hours. The system was designed so it could be quickly and easily removed and not compromise the C-130's main logistic function.

In 1977 the NSF wanted more modifications following the earlier trials in Antarctica, so *#159131* was again the test bed with three new research tools added: an air-sampling manifold and exhaust ports for air chemistry research, and coaxial cables were installed in the plane's wings for radio echo-sounding systems.

Before some of the equipment was transferred from # *320* to # *131*, a new dipole array had to be constructed on the wing configuration of the 'F' model. The equipment included a 10-foot detachable tail mounted airborne magnetometer, which was tested on a deployment flight from the United States to Christchurch, however, bad weather delayed the initial Antarctic deployment but two series of research flight missions were completed over the continent during this period, with the equipment later being stored at Christchurch.

In the months prior to *Deep Freeze –79* the squadron's aircraft # *131* had a vertical camera bay fitted and during that season the aircraft carried out air sampling, radio echo-sounding flights, aerial photography and air magnetometry and radio echo-sampling missions.

These cameras shot through heated optically ground glass windows in the planes fuselage, and in addition, several Otters and R4-D's were configured to accept a single vertical camera mount and viewfinder and a special side photo door, which could be opened in flight.

The history of the squadron's aerial photographic mapping of Antarctica began in 1955 in support of the IGY, with the cartographic aerial mapping of the exposed Antarctic land mass assigned to VX-6. In order to accomplish this phase the squadron photo configured several of their aircraft-the PV-2 Neptune's and R5-D'S Skymasters with a Trim trogon aerial camera mount utilizing three six inch focal length Fairchild T-11 CA-14 cartographic serial cameras which provided a horizon to horizon coverage. One of the first people assigned to the task was the late John D Reimer.

The enlisted photographers of VX-6 who photo mapped nearly 600,000 square miles of frozen continental terrain, were more than just photographers as they were also airman and technicians with a little explorer thrown in for good measure. The six-man team of aerial photographers based at McMurdo first used a single engine Otter to fly exploration flights preliminary to the actual mapping mission in the larger four engine Skymasters.

While very little mapping was carried out in *DF 1,* due to the short season among other factors, in *DF.11,* the squadron received four ski-equipped P2V-7's, two of them equipped with the Tri-Metrogon mount located in the nose or bombardier's compartment, that gave an excellence view down the flight lines, and two more mounts installed in the aft section behind the wing. In the R5-D's the photographer's panel was located in the passenger/cargo area back near the rear entry doors, with the mount in the aft cargo bay reached by a hatch to the deck.

The processed film, flight logs and prints were taken back to NAS Quonset Point at the end of each deployment where the VX-6 Photo Division assembled rough mosaics, annotated the many rolls of 9 inch aerial film in preparation for shipment to the Navy's Hydrographical Office in Washington DC.

As training and preparation for *Deep Freeze III* was underway, an improved aerial mapping programme was assigned to VX-6 to map various mountain ranges and other land mass areas of Antarctica. The Photo Division prepared flight line charts, overhauled and tested equipment and carried out a training programme for flight crews, including training with VAP-62 at NAS Norfolk for photographer mates assigned to the flight crews preparing for deployment in Antarctica in September.

Cartographic aerial photographic mapping missions were flown at 15,000 feet above sea level, that required 60 per cent forward overlay that was determined by the aerial mapping technician, utilising a radio altimeter and an intervalameter which electronically triggered the three cameras at the correct intervals, depending on the altitude above the terrain and the ground speed, while the navigator kept the course down the flight line.

Once landing on the ice or ski runway at McMurdo, the photo tech would unload his magazine from the aircraft for transportation up to the photo lab on the hill. Most mapping missions used three sets of film magazines on the T-11's, the magazine held a 390 foot roll of 9 inch aerial fame which would produce 440 exposures of 9 x 9 inch negatives.

One of the first aerial photographers Petty Officer Reimer was lucky enough to have his wife Janice and their two young children- aged 6 and 2 accompany him to Christchurch during his second tour of duty. John had married Christchurch girl Janice Cameron, in 1961 and after a short stay in Christchurch, took his new bride back to his hometown, Norfolk, Virginia where he served at the NAS and aboard the aircraft carrier *USS America*, before returning to New Zealand in August 1966.

Like all Squadron wives, life was tough when always on the move and having to adjust to their new surroundings and often being without their man. Janice Reimer was an exception as she was working back in her home city in Christchurch operating the switchboard at Deep Freeze Advanced Headquarters at Christchurch International Airport, and while John was in the Antarctic she and her children lived with her parents in St Albans.

Her photographer husband was supervisor at the Antarctic Photographic Centre at McMurdo, and was responsible for many of the Official Navy Photos sent to the *Deep Freeze* public affairs office for release to the news media, and with Janice as the office receptionist she was usually the first person to receive them.

One of PHC John Reimer's last missions to Antarctica was onboard the *City of Christchurch # 148318* on the first ever WinFly flight to McMurdo from Christchurch on June 4 1967. John Reimer passed away on April 22 2002 at Stafford.

Despite blinding snowstorms and aircraft maintenance problems facing the squadron during its 18th season of Antarctica, flight operations still had to be solved by ground crews in that freezing weather.

When the squadron arrived in Antarctica in October from Quonset Point, they were immediately faced with the problems of removing thousands of pounds of snow and ice that buried the main living quarters.

In the earlier years of Operation Deep Freeze it was the aircraft, namely the R4-D's and the Otters which wintered over in Antarctica that had to be dug out of open storage to ready them for the summer season due to it being impractical to fly them back to Christchurch. Some of those Gooney Birds at times, under took the long and arduous flight back to the States for overhaul, maintenance and modifications that were unavailable at either McMurdo or Christchurch repair facilities.

'As soon as we would dig the houses out, a snowstorm would cover them again within hours' describes BMC James Burns.

The Antarctic weather also created problems for pilots and maintenance support personnel- *'October was a bad month, as soon as we would get ready to fly again, the 'Hawk'- an Antarctic snowstorm, would drive us back indoors for several days, and at times it could be disconcerting when the wind drives you backwards,'* says Milton Ducharme.

On many occasions during the season the aircraft encounter a number of mechanical problems, which tested the crews, and on one such flight they were tested to the limit. After delivering a cargo of supplies to Byrd Camp-one of the United Station's isolated sites, on take off the aircraft on entering the overcast had the inertial navigation system fail and the compass started to spin wildly and rotate with attempts to stabilize it unsuccessful. *'Sure I was bloody scared'* said one crewmember when describing his feelings as the pilot's attempts to correct the malfunctioning compass failed and the aircraft continued on an unknown course.

Being above the overcast, a return to Byrd was not advisable as there are no approach aids, radios, fuel or adequate shelter available, so a return was not an option. Ahead some 800 miles was McMurdo, but there were no en-route navigation aids in between and no visual reference on the never-ending snow below.

The challenge would task even the most experienced polar navigator, and Lt Commander Joe Wiebelhaus immediately realized a major problem of no heading reference. The magnetic compass, constantly moving was of little use since variation changed 75 degrees during the trip and the unstablized radar indicated relative bearings only. The only way to determine the aircraft's bearings was to continually check the sun's azimuth.

So for three hours he computed and observed celestial data on the sun once every three minutes thus determining the aircraft's heading, while the pilot maintained a heading by attitude gyro along with corrections made between sun shots, bringing them to within 40 miles of McMurdo. During the three-hour flight the aircraft's position never deviated more than 20 miles off the desired track.

A few fixes obtained en route were a result of Lt Cdr Wiebelhaus's past knowledge of a certain peculiar radar return from snow to crevasses along the flight path. A McMurdo TACAN lock-on 40 miles out provided the final assurance of his navigation, and the pilot made an uneventful landing on the skiway.

Gunner Mike Subritzky, with four other gunners from the New Zealand 161st battery sent to Antarctica on a tour of duty in October 1973, as part of VXE-6 Squadron at McMurdo, recall those months with the 'yanks' at Willy Field. Along with Brian 'Gott' Eggerton, Dick 'Maori Dick' Wilson, Lance Bombardier Warren 'Snow' Berkett, they were the first members of the 161st battery to serve in Antarctica.

Mike did 13 tours overseas in various places throughout the world, but going to the ice was a vast new avenue for him and his unit and he is still in touch with many of the Americans he met. He sent me this story: *'A Gunner's white Christmas.'*

'At first we worked in the cargo yards at Christchurch and then, once we had reached a proficient standard in using the American equipment, driving on the wrong side of the road etc; we were flown to the ice aboard a C-141 Starlifter.

Just before we left we were given several briefings by a VX-6 Officer, and at one such lecture we were asked if we had any questions, 'Snow' Berkett put his hand up and asked the inevitable 'What about females in Antarctica sir', to which the squadron's Lt Commander replied. "Don't worry about women down there, Kiwi, because there's one behind every tree!"

It wasn't until we arrived on the frozen continent and had been there a week, that it dawned on us that there wasn't a tree on the entire bloody continent.

There were about twenty New Zealanders in the contingent accommodated in a Jamesway Hut out on Williams Field beside the ice runway, and with the Task Force operating two runways, an ice runway and a snow runway at the same time, the groups task was to operate as Aircraft Loaders, working in 12 hour shifts-12 on and 12 off, unloading and loading C-130 Hercules, with supplies.

'The long hours and hard work kept us very busy and as it got closer to December 25, Captain A N Fowler USN, the Task Force Commander decided that the 'Ice' would close down on Christmas Day. Captain Fowler also decreed that each and every sailor, including us Kiwi's, could purchase one bottle of spirits and a bottle of wine, but there was no restriction on beer. Now for about a week out from Christmas, the New Zealanders at Scott Base invited us to a home-cooked meal of roast lamb, spuds and cabbage.

After eating the rich American food that we had been living on, the down-home Kiwi 'tucker' was much appreciated and it was also good to talk to fellow Kiwis and catch up on news from home.

The beer drunk that evening were cans of Budweiser and Schlitz and it was free! Now that's strange I thought, so Snow Berkett and I waited until everyone was very happy and then quizzed 'Tich' the Postmaster of Scott Base about the free beer. He explained that is was old stock that the Americans wouldn't drink and that the Chief of the PX [American for Garrison Club] sold it at a much cheaper rate than normal.

So two days before Christmas day, Captain van Draanen the New Zealand Officer, and Staff-Sergeant Sam Bigg-Wither, called a meeting of all of our contingent and it was decided that they all put in $US10 and buy a case of beer each for the Christmas celebrations. It was also decided that a truckie called Noel Burgoyne and I should drive to Mactown and pick up the 'Kiwi Express'. Now the 'Kiwi Express' was a large US Army 'Duce and a Half' truck with oversize tyres and chains, and it had a Kiwi painted on the side wearing a pair of army combat boots, and as the contingent had each put in ten dollars, the Kiwi Express was large enough to carry twenty cases of beer.

Just before we arrived at Mac Town I remembered what Tich the Postmaster had told Snow and I, and so instead of driving to the actual PX we drove up to the last large warehouse which Tich had described to us when we were at Scott Base. We turned the truck around and backed it up against the loading ramp and presently an American Chief Petty Officer came outside and asked what we wanted, and after explaining that we had come to buy some of his old beer, he said "Kiwi, that shit tastes like swamp water but if you want it, you can have it, so how much do you want." Twenty dollars worth I said "Goddamn Kiwi!!" the chief yelled. "That's one shitload of beer!"

We had already started loading, when it suddenly dawned on me to ask how much each case of swamp water was going to cost. "This old stock sells for a quarter a case son and I think that it's going to be too much for this beast, so best you call for some backup."

In Antarctica a single can of beer in 1973 sold for a quarter [about .25 cents] and here the Kiwi's were getting 24 cans for the same price, a real bargain by anyone's standards. It was the Gunners equivalent of winning the lottery, and doing a quick mental maths he reckoned 24 cans to a case, 4 cases to a dollar, 4 cases worth times $US20 equals?

Here the gunners gave up, the Chief was right, it was a shitload of beer no matter who's counting. In a short space of time the eager Kiwi lads fill up the *Kiwi Express,* including inside the cab, then radioed up for another vehicle to come and assist. 'Snow' Berkett arrived in a Dodge Power Wagon which was also filled up, and the remainder was uplifted by our 2 IC, a young Territorial Officer who was somewhat staggered by the situation.

'When we got back to Willy Field, we swore the young Territorial officer to secrecy and then split the beer in half, hiding 200 cases in and around the Jamesway Hut and the other half in and around the VX-6 Squadron Bar. The American tropias told their officers that it was ours, and Captain van Drannen that it was owned by 'Yanks'. Next, before anyone in authority could become interested in our beer purchases, God himself very kindly intervened on the Kiwi's behalf by sending a 'Herbier' [whiteout], and it was considered too hazardous for flying operations so the whole of Operation Deep Freeze stood down and began to celebrate the birth of Jesus. It was December 23 1973.

We stacked as much of the 'swamp water' as possible inside the Squadron's bar so that it could thaw out, and once it was liquid again, we placed it in the chiller to cool it down a little. The Squadron's Bar was about 30 odd feet below the top of the ice and the cases of beer were piled all the way up the steps, and then we hid the remainder under a heap of snow on top of the Bar's location. The chores completed, we began to celebrate!

Two days later when Christmas arrived, our American comrades who had steadfastly refused to drink the 'swamp water', had partied so hard they ran out of their own spirit and wine allowance, and it was only then that they decided to gingerly taste last years vintage of Budweiser, in fact the beer was actually pretty ok; there was the odd slimy green stuff on the inside of about one can in ten, but they gave those cans the 'deep six' and carried on.

Next day was the 26 December and as we Kiwi's staggered to our feet and began to get ready for the next shift out on the cold Antarctic ice runway, the sky was clear and the wind was still, so obviously a perfect day for flying. It was then explained to us that 'today' was in fact Christmas Day in the States and the only true Christmas Day, so it was off with their 'Bunny Boots' and 'Bear Claws' and back to party mode. American Christmas!! How we Kiwi Gunners Battery loved every moment of it.'

By December 27 [NZDTG], without having drunk all the swamp water, the Kiwi's were back on duty at Willy Field, loading and unloading planes and assisting in the construction of the buildings of the New South Pole Station, '*In fact it was the only time in my military career of 25 years and about five different uniforms that I ever actually built something, as in the Gunners, virtually everything I ever looked at I either put a hole through, or simply blew to pieces.*' recalled Mike Subritzky.

'*VXE-6 Squadron US Navy was probably the most professional military unit that I ever had the honour to serve with. Nothing was ever a bother to them and they would willingly give you the 'shirt off their back,' and in fact on numerous cases that's exactly what they lost as well as baseball caps, flying jackets and aviator sunglasses. The squadron's motto was ' If it will fit, it will fly' and it was that dedication to duty, that their comrades serving in the numerous scientific outposts and situations that dotted Antarctica at that period in history, knew they could always rely on. We finished all our beer, and when Ben Ngapo and the relief team arrived in January 1974, they inherited all the beer that we left.*' So wrote Lance Bombardier Mike Subritzky.

Between July 21st through to August 15th. 1974, VXE-6 crews were operating in Greenland where their main objective was ferrying scientists and their equipment to 'study some scientific advancements'. Dave Crouse recalled the missions were pretty much routine except for the number of open snow landings and take off's' with *# 320,* and one in particular still sticks in his head because of the composition of the Greenland snow being wet and sticky, as compared to the dry snow in Antarctica.

On one particular take-off, after a couple of very poor tries, Lt Commander Crouse made several taxi passes to pack the snow to a consistency that would allow a regular take off, and yes, it worked! Some of his crew had been trying to figure out how they could survive until rescuers arrived and located them, let alone pick them up. '*I didn't know about that until we arrived back at base.*' he recalled later.

On another occasion when called to rescue a French party travelling with six snow Skidoos, Dave Crouse was convinced their trouble would be fuel, but to their surprise found it was engine oil. Skidoos don't do too well at that altitude and temperature without large quantities of engine oil, and before setting out on their cross-country trek, they had not made allowances for carrying additional oil. The squadron's mission was to deliver the oil without landing as they were in an area of poor snow with some heavy crust flaws, so it seemed like a relatively safe mission. They had two 55gallon drums of engine oil and only needed to get one of them close enough for the French party to retrieve, the other they could locate, once the Skidoos were again operational.

All went well until the first pass, a little high and a little too fast, '*We did have the skis and flaps down on the Loadmaster, but while very good and very knowledgeable, forgot his physics about bodies in motion. We were ready to roll the drums off the ramp, but whenever we slowed, the drums wanted to roll forward and not off the ramps as intended - so much for preparation. A couple more test runs set us up for the drop runs, and I figured the slower and lower we were, the better our chances of getting the drop closer to the Frenchmen watching from the ground, ready to retrieve it.*'

To the crew's surprise the first drum 'exploded' on the second or third bounce, and almost had the contents inside the plane's compartment. The Loadmaster said that the flash of oil into the air was very petty and colourful.

'After that one, I figured I would have to get in lower and slower, the second pass worked, the drums held together and as we departed the ground party could be seen chasing their mid winter Christmas Present and a few days later I was introduced to the French expedition leader who was very grateful and gave me a great bear hug. Unfortunately he was just off the snow and had not had a bath for weeks, and if you have ever been close to that situation you would have known that odour instantly if not before.' Cdr.Dave reliving the moment.

After retiring from the Navy in 1975 aged only 38, Lt.Cdr.Dave Crouse moved to a new neighbourhood, only to find that everyone had a problem that only 'you can fix'- but that's another story. He then spent the next fifteen years as a Bank Manager, which is a far cry from polar aviation- maybe he reached both poles.

Cdr Fred Holt assumed command of the squadron on July 18 1974 from his predecessor Cdr Vernon Peters.

Cdr Holt entered Navy School of Pre-Flight in 1957 as a Naval Aviation Cadet, graduated from Naval Air Advanced Training Command a year later and reported to Patrol Squadron 16 [VP-16], at NAS Jacksonville, Florida for a four-year assignment. After a colourful career, he reported to VXE-6 as Operations Officer, following transition training in Lockheed C-130 Hercules at the US Little Rock AFB Arkansas in 1973, and completed *Operation Deep Freeze-73* deployment in that role as a C-130 commander.

The Executive Officer, Cdr Bruce Willey who was to assume command of the squadron in 1974, elected not to accept the assignment, so Fred Peters was moved to the Executive Officer's slot under the command of Cdr Vernon Peters for a few months, before assuming the command in 1974. The change of command was held at Point Mugu, and he led the squadron through all of *Deep Freeze –74* and half of *Deep Freeze –75.*

When Cdr Holt handed the command over to Cdr Dan Desko it was not at the squadron's homeport, but in front of the Rear Adm. Richard Byrd memorial at McMurdo, on December 11 1976. R Adm James B Stockdale Commander, Anti Submarine Forces, and Pacific Fleet, extended Cdr Holt's tour of command for the purpose of providing continuity and experience during a time when the government intended to rescue two C-130's from the ice, - the aircraft that had become disabled at Dome Charlie.

Early on in the operation, after the third Hercules had crashed while supporting the rescue mission, the Cdr asked R.Adm Stockdale to allow him to turn over the command to Cdr Dan Desko his Executive Officer. Cdr Holt told me. *'The story of the recovery of these aircraft should be told, it is an epic of 'Courage, Sacrifice and Devotion', such as is seldom seen, and these heroes deserve recognition.'* He had pride in the men and women of the squadron he had the honour to command.

When Cdr Fred Holt assumed the position of the Squadron Officer on July 74, little did he know before leaving the States that his two year tenure would be complicated by a number of incidents involving the Hercules. A qualified Aircraft Commander in the C-130 during *Deep Freeze- 74*, Fred spent the entire season on the ice, primarily supporting the construction of the new South Pole Station.

Says Cdr. Holt: *'The flight to the Pole station takes around three hours from McMurdo, depending on the winds encountered aloft, after crossing the Transatlantic Range at an altitude of 26,000 feet, while below is a series of mountains and glaciers rising from the shores of the Ross Sea to an elevation of the plateau at 10,000, with the skyways at the pole consisting of a snow surface while smoothed by bulldozers and marked by red flags, when your aircraft touches down on the surface, the altimeter in the cockpit reads a little over 9,000 ft above sea level and the outside temperature can reach upwards of 40 below zero.*

Landing a C-130 on the skiway is not all that different than landing on an asphalt or concrete runway. When the landing gear handle is placed in the 'DOWN position and the SKIS DOWN' switch is activated, the wheels lower as for a hard runway surface landing, and the massive skis drop to just below the bottom of the tires. The nose altitude at the touchdown is critical, lest one dig the nose ski in before landing, the weight of the plane is on the main landing gear. Once all of the skis are solidly planted on the surface, the four turboprop propellers are placed in reverse pitch, causing a 'snow storm' to appear across the flight deck's field of vision. These were times when the only way I knew for sure that we had stopped was when the airspeed indictor registered zero knots!

The old station was completely covered over in snow and ice and it had become dangerous to continue operations from it. Every sheet of iron and the nuts and bolts that joined the sheets into the dome shape that rose above the Pole surface had to be transported by the Herks and then be assembled by the Seabees, so the new station was placed into operation by the NSF in January 1975.'

The fairer sex was now becoming established in Antarctica and a common sight around McMurdo during *Deep Freeze 76,* when the largest contingent of women brightened up the frozen continent. Four women officers and seven enlisted Navy women, along with two civilian navy employees and numerous women scientists were deployed. Still the navy made up the largest proportion of the inhabitants, while the rest of the summer colonies on the continent were scientists, civilian contractors and the US Air Force.

Williams Field is unlike any other airport in the world, as the field has no hangers or fuel tanks, fuel being kept in huge rubber bladders sitting on top of the ice ready to be loaded aboard the squadron's LC-130'S and transported to outlying remote fields. The control tower, with its great red and white chequered radar dome resting on skids, can be moved a considerable distance, and each year the tower makes the trip to Willy Field in mid December then back again, as the Antarctic winter approaches.

In mid December when the temperatures rise causing the ice runway and passages from the ice to land deteriorate, the skiway at Willy Field must then be the one to use. Since the USAF'S C-141's are not ski equipped they can no longer operate from that time on, so almost all air missions are carried out by VXE-6 LC-130's and helicopters.

During the normal operational season, the ice runway is preferred over the skiway at Willy because according to Lt JG Don Chine, VXE's scheduling officer during *Deep Freeze 88. 'A plane landing on the ice runway at Willy must be accomplished with skis, a plane landing on skis has a maximum cargo payload of 8,000 pounds less than one which lands on wheels.'*

Whether one lands on ice or snow, polar flight operations have a distinct quality, as Lt Commander Bradley Lanzer explains, '*some of the differences in flying in Antarctica is that the weather here changes more rapidly than any other place I have known, everywhere we fly is remote, one example is every round trip to the Amundsen-Scott South Pole Station carries an LC-130 and its crew over 1,650 miles of rugged snow covered mountains, treacherous ice fields and glaciers laced with crevasses.'*

There was not a lot of US Air Force presence on the ice during Commander Holts tour of duty, when only an occasional C-141 Starlifter would visit regularly during the early part of the season, as only they could land on the ice runway, and this was the times the VX-6 aviators could often see the seals sticking their heads through the ice runway.

Commander Holt relates a humorous story of airdropping a Caterpillar Tractor by a C-141 Air Force crew over the Pole. '*Their crew had bragged to us in the mess over a quite beer on the previous evening that they were the only folk in the world who could make such a delivery, and I was impressed. That is until next day, when I witnessed the tractor leave the Starlifter's rear ramp and plummet several thousand feet with no functional parachutes to retard the fall. The tractor's engines were started while still in the cargo bay of the C-141 because it was feared that its oil and hydraulic fluids would freeze. The last view I had of the new tractor after the Air Force's special mission was at the bottom of a very deep hole, with its exhaust stack still emitting a steady stream of white smoke! The Air Force crew didn't have a lot to say that night in McMurdo.'*

Deep Freeze 76 actually kicked off in late August when the first group of squadron members and other Naval support staff left on flights leaving Point Mugu between August 28 and September 5, when two ski equipped Hercules brought over 20 tons of cargo and 144 passengers.

During the briefing before departing from Christchurch on September 3rd Cdr Dan Desko and Lt Commander E A Cushing were told they could expect marginal conditions at McMurdo with the prospect of a whiteout. The first aircraft, piloted by the squadron's exec Cdr Dan Desko, had to make two attempts before he could touch his C-130 down, while the second Hercules piloted by Lt Cdr E A Cushing could not find the field's skiway, but landed safely amidst swirling snow in the whiteout area several miles from the field, ready to deliver the first fresh food and some 2,900 pounds of mail to the 54 men who had wintered over at McMurdo and nearby Scott Base. The two aircraft made five round trips in the coming weeks.

This was the start of Task Force 199 [previously known as Task Force 43] and the twenty-first year of Antarctic operations. The Task Force is composed of the Naval Support Antarctic [NSFA] with their home base at Port Hueneme, VXE-6 operating out of Point Mugu, NSFA Detachment Data a forward staging base located at Christchurch New Zealand, and NSFA Detachment Alfa, including the wintering over party-headquarters at McMurdo, Antarctica.

According to historian of OAE's Billy Ace Baker Penguin, *Task Force 43* was changed to *TF – 199* when CNSFA moved from CBC Davisville Rhode Island to CBC Port Hueneme in 1974. At that time CNSFA was chopped from the operational control of CINCLANTFLT in Norfolk, Virginia to the operational control of Commander Third Fleet in Honolulu Hawaii, the change being effective on July 1 1974, and at some point after 1980, CNSFA stopped using the Task Force designation altogether.

'As a matter of trivia' recalls Billy Ace, *'there was a change of command [COC] ceremony in Davisville Rhode Island on June 25 1974 in which Captain Eugene Van Reeth relieved Captain Al Fowler. The COC brochure lists the name of the command as Commander US Navy Support Force Antarctica and Task Force 144. Task Force –43 apparently became Task Force 144 on September 2 1972, when the Navy realigned the command of the Antarctic Task structure.*

The Antarctic Support Activities at Davisville R I and the Naval Support Force Antarctica at the Navy Yard, Washington DC were both disestablished. The two commands were centralized and relocated to Davisville and at that time the command billet was downgraded from Rear Admiral to Captain and the new command came under the auspices of the Atlantic Fleet Commander. Prior to that, the Antarctic Support Activity at Davisville was a Seabee command and the auspices of Naval Facilities Engineering Command.'

In addition, Coast Guard icebreakers and military Sealift Command supply ships joined the force during the summer season, completing the logistic body, along with the support of the USAF, New Zealand Air Force and Navy. But again, as in the previous twenty-two years, it was the Antarctica Development Squadron Six who provided the major support.

The US Navy in recognition of the difficult and dangerous working environment that their personnel faced in this hostile southern frontier, has, since 1946, awarded the Antarctic Service Medal to personnel deployed on the continent. An act of Congress authorized the medal on July 7 1960 and made it available to personnel for services in Antarctica subsequent to January 1 1946, and continues its issue to date.

With the establishment of permanent Antarctic stations, the government soon realized that the past method of awarding medals designed for each expedition would no longer be appropriate for recognizing Antarctic service, so it was decided that the best course of action would be the establishment of one medal, which could be awarded to all personnel who undertook Antarctic service. The US Heraldic Office carried out design work on the medal in 1961, when two designs were submitted to the Commission of Fine Arts for evaluation and subsequent approval the following year. Both designs were almost identical and after some refinement by the US Mint, the Antarctic Service Medal was approved.

During the northern summer of 1977, two of the squadron's LC-130's operated in Greenland assisting the NSF's scientific projects. The VX-6 Hercules carried out three missions to Sondrestrom from the United States, ferrying scientists and equipment during July and August. *Deep Freeze –78* was an all LC-130 R season, with neither of the squadrons two 'F's remaining at their home port, as the squadron operated the National Science Foundation's two newest acquisitions, the LC-130R's # *16740* and # *160741 –Spirit of Oxnard.*

The season concluded with two helicopter crashes, the first on January 7 1979, when a UH-1N # *158239* crashed at the Gawn Ice Piedmont at the foot of the Darwin Glacier, when the aircraft had flown into a ridge destroying it on impact. All the crew and passengers aboard including four injured were evacuated to McMurdo by other squadron helicopters and a LC-130.

The second accident occurred in the United States on February 17 at Naval Air Station North Island, California just after the helicopter UH-1H # *158241* had became airborne and was hovering a few metres from the ground, when a mechanical malfunction cause the Bell to go out of control and crash. While none of the crew suffered injury, the helicopter was written off, so as an interim measure, the US Marine Corps loaned two VXE-6 UH-1N's helicopters they had had in storage for the last four years.

The Antarctic has a reputation for giving up its secrets grudgingly, making exploration a great personal risk for those attempting to unlock the frozen continent's mysteries, sometimes with fatal consequence, but credit to the professionalism of the men and women assigned to VXE-6 squadron and Operation Deep Freeze when the season was completed without loss of life or serious injury. Once *Deep Freeze –78* was completed, the squadron departed Antarctica and New Zealand and headed home for the northern summer.

On May 31 1978, Cdr Jeager handed over command to Cdr W A Morgan.

During the Antarctic winter, on July 14th 1979 the USAF made their first mid winter airdrop using a Lockheed C-141A Starlifter *[66-0130]*. Previously all mid winter flyins were carried out by VXE-6 Hercules and in order to keep the costs down, the NSF sought to utilise the C-141A that the USAF had stationed in Christchurch on supply missions.

The exercise was designed as an emergency resupply for McMurdo and Scott Base during the Antarctic darkness, and the Starlifters already in Christchurch on their annual supply missions, were utilised and became a morale booster as well, for personnel left on the ice over the long Antarctic winter nights thus saving Operations pre-positioning costs.

The jet left Christchurch at 7am on the supply mission, arriving over the drop zone at 11.30pm, having to make five passes over the runway at McMurdo's airfield that had been litup by flares positioned every 76 metres. All the lights at McMurdo and New Zealand's Scott Base had been switched on to illuminate the area to assist the aircrew, which dropped 24 separate bundles totalling 4.2 tonnes. Chemical lights were attached to each bundle to make them easier to locate as the extreme cold at that time of the year could affect the fresh produce if it was not located within a short time.

Also included in the airdrop were mail, medical supplies and critical spare parts for Scott Base. The crew of the C-141 included three New Zealand Army parachute riggers from the 5th Terminal Squadron.

When the squadron arrived in Christchurch to commence *Deep Freeze 79,* with their new commander Cdr W A Morgan, little did they know it was to be a season which was marred by tragedy and disruptive incidents that would stretch their resources to the limit. Air operations were hampered by extremely bad weather, maintenance problems caused by the cold, and a number of emergency medical evacuations, which began when a C-141 had to limp back to Christchurch with a damaged undercarriage and the cruise liner *Linblad Explorer* grounded on the northeast end of Wiencke Island on Christmas Day.

VXE-6 and the US Navy's *Operation Deep Freeze* had been in Antarctica for twenty-four years and when Cdr D A Srite assumed command of the Antarctic naval squadron VXE-6 on May 11 1979, from Cdr Morgan at Point Mugu, little did he realise that he was to inherit an Antarctic catastrophe on a scale never before witnessed on the continent; a tragedy not military, but commercial.

CHAPTER FOURTEEN

'PHOENIX' # 148321 RISES FROM AN ICY GRAVE AFTER BEING BURIED IN ANTARCTICA FOR SEVENTEEN YEARS TO FLY AGAIN. THE 'HERKY BIRD' IS PLAGUED BY MISHAPS IN THEIR FIRST DECADE.

*The greatest aircraft recovery in polar history
after seventeen years buried at Dome –59 on the Polar
Plateau.*

The successful recovery of the two LC-130's which had crashed at the remote Dome Charlie, the east Antarctica site near Dome 57 in the austral summer, renewed interest in the recovery of the multi million dollar *# 321*, so in 1978, four engineers again visited the site to examine the aircraft that by now was under approximately four meters of snow.

They considered its damage was less than originally thought, and recommended a $US20 million recovery during the 1979-80 austral summer, but with budget restrictions and other major problems facing the NSF budget managers, the project was subsequently put on hold, with no further plans made until June 1986, when the National Science Foundation announced its intention to recover *# 321* if at all possible. Programme [DDP] began collecting data on the condition of the C-130 and the crash site.

An engineering team out from the Air Naval Systems Command along with technicians from Lockheed-Martin and representatives from the Naval Air Rework Facilities, were flown to the crash site to inspect and appraise the two crippled Hercules, subsequently planning meetings and a special think tank were set up to consider various salvage methods to recover the damaged aircraft and it was decided to carry out temporary repairs 'in the field' and then fly them out.

A field camp was set up and a special ski-way constructed with the salvage operations concentrating on *#159129,* as it was the newer of the two the aircraft and its degree of damage the least. A new wing centre was ordered for *# 319*, but in 1976 when thoughts of recovering her were abandoned, VX-6 recommended cancelling her from military operations after first stripping all reusable components, but now its salvage still looked feasible and planning commenced for it to proceed. When the salvage camp was evacuated in January 1975, the buildings were left in place along with *# 319*, on the polar plateau.

Chief Petty Officer in Charge John Speck was head of the salvage operations of *BuNo 159129,* and *# 148319* and another C-130F *BuNo 148320* which had suffered a similar mishap in 1975 but was not so badly damaged.

Says Speck, *'It was very difficult carrying out the recovery of the three 'herks" while working on the aircraft at an altitude greater than 11,000 feet in an open area. The cold winds, the high altitude, the reduced oxygen, and the cold soaked aircraft all combined for tiring days, and because of these conditions we could only work 20/30 minutes at a time.'*

Working in freezing sub zero temperatures using airbags and hydraulic jacks, the crews nobly displayed their professionalism.

As the first of its kind, *# 129* became the first Hercules ever to be salvaged in Antarctica, after an all volunteer crew headed by the Squadron's CO Cdr Desko flew to Dome Charlie to recover 'the lost one' and fly her back to Christchurch via McMurdo. The crew included Lt James Wishard, CPO Thomas Davidson, Petty Officer Billy Keeler and Petty Officer Victor Potts.

The recovery operation was completed in seventeen days by working in two shifts 24 hours a day, with work being completed one day less than a year after the accident. A complete lower nose section, including the landing gear assembly had to be fabricated in the United States, and the aircraft was certified for flight on January 20 1976.

A period of bad weather delayed # 129 for two days at McMurdo, and on Christmas Day Cdr.Desko, broke a bottle of champagne on the nose ski before it was flown back to Christchurch, but as the LC-130 was not pressurised, Cdr Desko had to fly at a greatly reduced height. After repairs in Christchurch the C-130 was flown onto Lake City, Florida in January 1976, having completed the recovery in just 50 days, some 30 days ahead of the scheduled time.

The newspaper 'Christchurch Star' carried a photograph of # 159129 [nicknamed Cripple Pete] at Air Zealand's Engineering Workshop at Christchurch International Airport while she was being repaired. Someone had painted just aft of the newly fitted nose panel: OVERHAULED BY CRABS, BEE'S & ONE ARMY PUP. Also written was 'McMurdo or bust- CH-CH or bust'. Air New Zealand had been carrying out repairs and overhauling LC-130 ski aircraft since 1981 and had an ongoing contract with the National Science Foundation and the New York Air National Guard.

Back at Dome Charlie and working on # 319, the fuselage was righted to remove the No 1 engine and the left outer wing section, and by the sixteenth day, in spite of working in almost inhumane weather conditions, they were able to tow it 3km back to the camp site where the original plan was to have the Seabees erect industrial scaffolding across the wing and centre section.

However as the C-130's wing is over 16 feet from the ground the required scaffolding would need to be over 33 feet by 36 feet, so to simplify the operation and reduce the amount of scaffolding required, Chief Petty Officer John Speck organised a trench be dug 200 feet long by 20 ft wide and 6 and a half feet deep in the snow. A D-8 Caterpillar towed the damaged aircraft onto the surface where the wing section was raised 3 feet vertically before it was moved horizontally and lowered to the surface using trolleys and winches suspended from the erected scaffolding.

A brand new wing was fitted in 32 days, and after all four engines were replaced, # 319 was towed from the trench to allow the propellers to be fitted and substantial repairs to be carried out to the fuselage.

The recovery of # 319 was the most extensive salvage operation ever attempted in Antarctica and had been completed in 34 days by a team of 50 personnel after it had been buried at its frozen site for 709 days. It was during the salvage operation that the squadron flew 34 flights to the Dome, carrying 122 tons of cargo and 101 passengers.

In 1977-78 VXE-6 mounted an assessment survey mission to evaluate the feasibility of recovering the C-130BL # 148321–Phoenix. Four engineers recommended recovery, which was originally planned for the 1979-80 austral summer but budget restriction canned the project. With the crash site being directly south of Dumont d'Urville and on an annual traverse route, the aircraft was a landmark on these trips, and in 1982-83 Mike Savage accompanied one of these traverse parties as part of the NSF automated weather station [AWS] project. Savage was probably the first American to visit # 321 since 1977, and as a result of Mike's pictures and the report submitted to Brian Shoemaker, planning for the aircraft's recovery started again.

Throughout the early 1980's work progressed, then in December 1985 a French traverse party which included an American Bob Flint visited the site at D-59 to gather information about the plane and make observations as to the feasibility of landing a rescue C-130 close to the buried plane, together with the reports of VXE-6 crew members who had attempted to land at the site earlier that year.

This information confirmed that before a squadron's LC-130 could land safely at the site, an adequate ski runway would have to be prepared, as by this stage # 321 was now almost completely buried in snow, with only the top two metres of its tail jutting above the snowline, suggesting to the NSF that no more detailed information could be provided until excavation work was commenced.

Despite these reports, interest in salvaging the $US30 million aircraft continued at NAS headquarters until April 1986, after the ITT Antarctic Services submitted a recovery proposal to NSF which was reviewed, revised, reviewed again and later discussed at a US Antarctic Programme logistics and support meeting at Port Hueneme, California. Once all the programme's participants [NSF, NSFA, VXE-6 and the ANS] had studied the plan, it gained the final seal of approval from the National Science Foundation, and James Mathews was duly appointed as project manager, who recruited five other personnel needed to complete the complicated project.

Throughout the summer of 1986 Mathews and his team worked closely with VXE-6 Commanding Officer Cdr. Joseph Mazza and the squadron's aircrews and maintenance personnel. They studied the operations of the LC-130's ski/wheel landing gear at the squadron's base in Point Mugu California, discussed with Roger Biery the ITT/ANS heavy-equipment operator, to identify any special attachments required for the heavy equipment selected for the recovery project.

James Mathews and his team including M Brashear, the cook/medic/radio operator and weather observer, arrived at McMurdo in early November 1986 to be greeted by two other members of the team who had prepared all the heavy equipment for the project. To shelter the recovery team while they worked at D-59, Mathews had designed a special living module with the base personnel beginning to build it while Mr Biery constructed a ski cradle, and when the basic structure was completed it was moved to the Williams Field ski runway to be finished and tested before being flown to D-59

During the last week in October, the Expedition Polaires Francaises traverse party, led by Pierre Laffont arrived at McMurdo Station at Mathews's request for the party to inspect the module and verify that it could be successfully towed to D-59 and D-21 as Laffont and his party were the only ones who knew the terrain well enough to give advise. By November 2 1986, all essential cargo for the project had been prepared for shipment and stationed at the sea-ice runway.

The following day along with the French traverse team, Mathews and his party departed for D-21, to the selected landing site some 22 km inland from the French station Dumont d'Urville, with a second VX-6 C-130 following the same day carrying skiway construction gear.

The wintering over party from Dumont d'Urville had prepared a rudimentary skyway for the first two flights, and as soon as the ANS crew received their equipment they began to improve the skiway landing surfaces to take a LC-130 carrying upwards of 135,000 pounds of cargo and fuel. With this task completed the team was ready for the next flight on the morning of November 5 1986.

The party was now ready to begin the traverse led by the French Expedition who were highly organized and established in polar trekking for the 220 km overland to D-59, which involved navigating between metal poles spaced at 10 km intervals from a location known as Carrefour [D-40] to terminus at D-120, approximately 800 km inland.

The terrain between D-21 and D-59 is a series of rolling hills and valleys, which gradually ascend towards the polar plateau. In this area snow accumulation is low, and in some areas, snowfall is zero, but katabatic winds create sastrugi patterns and near D-59, winds and precipitation change the landscape annually, so when the French party approached the site in 1986 they encountered sastrugi that ranged from1.5 to 11.2 metres high. In order to compensate for the time lost at D-21 they travelled at least 12 hours each day, while about one kilometre ahead the French navigation vehicle led the tractor train which was in turn led by one of the US vehicles, a low ground pressure D-6 bulldozer pulling two ten ton sleds.

The Bulldozers improved the ground conditions for the other vehicles in the party as it had sufficient power to raze a road. By November 23rd, less than four days after leaving D-21, the party reached D-59 to find at the crash site only the top meter of the vertical stabiliser of # *321* incongruously visible above the ground.

After selecting a campsite, the group prepared for a scheduled airdrop of 7,500 litres of diesel fuel [DFA] and 2,200 litres of mogas. This airdrop went better than expected with only eight drums of diesel being lost when two parachutes failed to open. As the party now had sufficient to last them two weeks, there were no great concerns and work could continue even if supply flights from McMurdo were delayed.

With the weather at McMurdo sometimes marginal, it caused the delay of a number of VXE-6 flights into D-21 over the next two weeks, forcing the team to reconstruct the D-21 skiway completely, but nine days after the storms abated on November 27, came the second air drop. The first aircraft to land at D-29 since January 1978 touched down the next day bringing additional diesel fuel, and over the next few days three more Hercules brought in supplies and equipment.

By December 1 all the equipment needed to complete the project had been delivered, with only a delivery of fuel scheduled for later in the month, and the French party had departed for their D-10 camp, although their radio operator Didier Simon remained with the US team for the season to both observe and to assist with snow shovelling.

On November 26, experimental digging around # 321 began, but it wasn't until three days later, after a tracked caterpillar loader with blade and bucket arrived at the site, did the team seriously begin removing the packed snow from around the aircraft, using the heavy machinery and the hand powered shovels.

In early December the weather was generally windy, consequently during the first 3 days storms interrupted them from any form of exterior work to be carried out, but when the weather cleared the team of six Americans and a Frenchman toiled hard in the cold to unearth *Phoenix* from her ten-metre deep grave, working in shifts removing the snow from around the plane. The first test digging to discover a way to prevent further damage, was after due consideration, selected in an area near #1 engine which had been damaged when it crashed, and it was during this early digging that the team discovered that # 321 was covered by between 6 and 7.5 metres of compacted snow. Earlier it had been presumed to be upwards of only 4.6 meters, but once digging commenced and they had reached 3 metres, they found dense compacted snow with melt around many of the aircraft's surfaces, and for a week the team worked to uncover the upper surfaces and to open a way into the plane.

Such was the weight of the compacted snow that they discovered while digging, the plane would rise noticeably when large amounts were removed.

This observation suggested that the snow loading over the plane's whole structure was indeed significant, for if uniformly distributed it would probably not have damaged the airframe, so to prevent further damage other than caused by the crash, it was decided to remove the snow from the centre wing section and forward fuselage last.

By December 10, the team were able to enter the aircraft for the first time, and while the forward fuselage was intact, there was some damage to the two escape hatches and some cracked windows on the flight deck. With all the top surfaces now free of snow, the recovery team began the construction of a ramp onto which the aircraft could be towed out.

To construct the ramp, the team first had to trench backwards from the ten metre snow wall to the aircraft, and this one hundred metre long ramp took a little over a week to complete. On December 16 the crews were now working ten metres below the surface, and began to uncover the fuselage and to remove the snow from between the engines. To make their task easier, the crews used one of the tractors to move the snow and a chainsaw to remove snow inaccessible by the tractors. Once the pressure was released the plane rose, and consequently the amount of manual labour by using pick and shovel to free the Hercules was reduced.

The entire LC-130 rose out of her frozen tomb at an average of 5 to7 cm each day, but to their sheer delight the most dramatic rise occurred when the left wing tip rose 80cm over the next 5 to 6 days.

By Christmas Day 1986, after a successful attempt early in the morning, the ANS crew towed Juliet Delta *# 321* out of her snow pit and onto the snow surface of D-59, allowing the interior to be cleaned in preparation for the planes inspection by experts from the Lockheed Corporation and the US Navy.

The ski equipped Hercules *# 321* the squadron's first C-130BL which had made her first operational Antarctic mission on October 30 1960, with an initial flight to the South Pole, now sat on top of the snow at an isolated site in East Antarctica [68 degees 20'5 137degrees 31'E] 190 km from the coast, about a hundred meters away from the 9 meter trench which had been her icy tomb for more than fifteen years.

 # 148321, which had rolled off Lockheed Martin's Georgia production line in 1959 with the manufacturers production number 3567 and Lockheed s/n 282C-6B in January 1987, awaited a five man VXE-6 maintenance team to arrive from McMurdo to further assist in removing the four engines and three propellers and fly them back to McMurdo for evaluation, and then on to the US for repairs and refurbishment.

Lockheed Martin Georgia Corporation flew their engineering team to the crash site from McMurdo to begin repairs to the plane prior to replacing the rebuilt engines, propellers, and flight controls. The project also required repairing the main nose gear, nose gear landing struts, instrumentations and radome, along with the left side of the fuselage, damaged when the props ripped through the hull. Salvaging the engines and propellers alone paid for the cost of the entire project many times over.

After inspection of the plane's structural and electrical components by personnel from Lockheed and the Naval Air Rework Facilities in Cherry Point North Carolina, the groups preliminary conclusion sent in a detailed report to the NSF, was optimistic, and their assessment was that *# 321* could be flown from the site.

On January 8 1988, Mr Jim Herman, the official inspector from NAD, certified the Hercules as ready to be flown back to McMurdo after VXE-6 flight crews ran their final tests. On January 10 1988, Commander Jack Rector, VXE-6 Commanding Officer who had flown to D-59 earlier to ready *# 321* for its flight back to McMurdo, would have to fly on three engines, as number four engine had been disconnected to prevent oil leaks.

A second LC-130 piloted by Cdr. Bradley Lanzer as the escort, revved its engines so the wash from its props could activate *# 321's* propellers, and it was considered that a high-speed taxi be carried out in an attempt to isolate any problems at take-off speed. All was set for her 'maiden flight', and at 6-10pm, the salvaged of *# 321* was almost complete as she set off under escort on her flight to McMurdo. The escort Herk acted as a navigation and communication platform as these systems were only partially functional in the re-born C-130.

Just before 11pm local McMurdo time on January 10 1988, under a cloud-filled sky above the Ross Island, a group of both civilian and military personnel most of whom had been involved in this most remarkable aircraft recovery project, heard the familiar sounds of a C-130 echo over the airfield.

The group had been waiting expectantly for over an hour for the planes to land, and moments later the second C-130-*Juliet Delta 321* landed safely on the ice shelf with its crew being greeted with cheers from the welcoming party.

While on the ice at McMurdo, more repairs were carried out and a second inspection completed. Cdr Rector likened the recovery of the plane to the rising phoenix of Egyptian mythology, *'I think that's what we're going to name the airplane'* he commented.

On the flight to Christchurch, and because of additional drag, it had to be flown at a lower than normal altitude and slower, subsequently carrying an extra 3,600 US gallons of fuel.

After the transporter was handed over to the Air New Zealand engineers, they carried out extensive repairs in preparation for the flight back to the United States, departing for Point Mugu on July 2 1989, and delivered her to the Naval Aircraft Depot at Cherry Point for further modifications with considerable updates to its communications and navigational systems. In October 1989, C-130BL # *148321* was finally handed over to the National Science Foundation.

Fifteen years previously it had been considered to be too costly and a logistically complex and dangerous mission, but now that it had been accomplished, it defied all logic and had shown to cause minimal disruption to the US Antarctic Science Programme. The reasonable costs was a credit, not only to the people who carried out the work, but from the co-ordination of other Antarctic treaty signatories and those who had sponsored the recovery project, with special thanks to the French Expeditions Polaires Francises Traverse Party at Dumont d'Uriville for their dedication to International Antarctic co-operation during the years that # *321* was entombed at D-59.

When # *321* entered service again with Operation Deep Freeze, it was due to the combined efforts of the personnel from ITT/Antarctic Services, the Naval Support Force Antarctic, VX-6 and the National Scientist Foundation's Division of Polar Programme. Ironically when *The Old Grey Mare* did fly again in the Antarctic it was with the New York Air National Guard's 109th Air Wing- not VXE-6 squadron.

According to Dr Peter Wilkniss, director of the NSF Polar Programme, the cost of recovering the stricken Hercules its repair and modernization was approximately $US10 million, compared with purchasing a new one at a cost of $US 38 million.

The B model sent to Antarctica that year had carried out ski assembly tests in Antarctic conditions, tests which established that the restrictions placed by the USAF on the earlier 'D' models were no long necessary, and that take-off and landing were now possible on unprepared surfaces. So adaptable was # 321 and her two sister ships, that on December 10, two C-130BL's were placed with a geological party consisting of nine people and 9 tons of equipment in the fields over 2,408 km from McMurdo- a task which would have been impossible with the Air Force's D models. They performed beyond all expectations that season, and succeeded in moving more than four times the quantity of cargo originally allocated to them.

As most of the USAP temporary camps consisted of Jamesway huts that were easily assembled and transported by LC-130, they were again provided for the excavation crew at D-59 and gave the designers the opportunity to test the air-transportable mini stations as shelter and support in those remote and temporary camps.

When the module was fully assembled, it was required to be strong enough to withstand a possible 240 km overland traverse, and on reaching the selected site would have to provide power, heat and water immediately, and although the module would be a prototype, it would have to be reliable enough to continue to provide service throughout the season.

During the early planning period, the designers realized that with a single generator house in the module, they could consolidate the supply power for the entire camp, as well as providing many amenities not usually located at temporary campsites. Generators and other appliances required for the module were investigated in detail, and besides items that might be available at McMurdo, they also selected a 20-kilowatt marine-rated generator as the most likely one to meet the recovery team's needs. After all preliminary work was completed at McMurdo, the Project Manager George Cameron commenced design work on the module.

The D-59 camp comprised of the 30-foot prototype module and a 36-foot Jamesway, which was used as sleeping quarters for the crew. Although a roughly designed prototype, the mini station included such features as flush plumbing, hot showers, a washing machine and dryer and cooking appliances, as these amenities improved the health and productivity of the crews working seven days a week and upwards of 12 hours a day.

Additionally, the module design included an electrical plug- in system for the tractors so the crew could shut the equipment down at night and start them up easily in the morning, which significantly improved the vehicles continuous performance and reduced the chance of them breaking down.

CHAPTER FIFTEEN

TRAGEDY ON EREBUS.

*Air New Zealand's DC-10 flight 901 crashes into Mt Erebus
November 28 1979, killing all 237 passengers and crew aboard
and the part VXE-6 Squadron played in search and recovery.*

It was 5am on August 22 1978, when the fire alarm shattered the early dawn of McMurdo Station.

The news spread faster than an Antarctic 'herbie' when the little timber church, the pride of the station, built in 1955-56 and named the *Chapel of the Snow* was engulfed in flames.

The fire had started at the rear of the heating room, and while the station's fire crews gallantly fought the blaze, the chapel's interior with a sudden flare up, indicated that the fire had spread between the interior and exterior walls and along to the ceiling space, so despite the efforts of the fire crew the whole chapel was soon engulfed.

Concerned that the fire could damage the communication cable strung along near the front of the burning Chapel, a front-end loader was used to push the chapel's front wall inwards, but when the roof of the adjacent building began to smoulder, a bulldozer isolated the piles of burning sections by dumping snow on top of them, restricting the sparks being fanned by the strong wind and stopping them from spreading to other adjacent structures.

The fire came under control by 7.40 am but the southern most parish was destroyed, except for the chapel bell discovered later in the rubble, but all the chapel's contents were lost, including historic memorabilia dating back to *Deep Freeze I.*

The Chapel of the Snow which had served the station and the nearby New Zealanders at Scott Base for 22 years, had been built under the guidance of the base's first Chaplain, Father John C Condit and volunteers from the construction battalion who had gradually gathered enough material to build what was to be Antarctica's first church.

Before the McMurdo Station was completed, this neat little church complete with its steeple, stood on a ridge overlooking the camp and was later given a bell procured from a small gasoline tanker. When plans for the original station were drawn up in Washington, the Department of the Navy did not include a chapel for the Operations first chaplain Father Condit, who was then conducting Sunday services in the station's mess hall.

It had always been the quintessential dream and yearning of Father Condit to have his own church in which to conduct his Sunday services, and since his appointment as chaplain his resolve was to get his chapel. After continued pressure, the Catholic priest received the Ok from Rear Admiral George Dufek who, as if by divine influence from above, saw a mysterious pile of lumber, planks, nails, Quonset hut sections and assorted materials begin to pile up on a knoll overlooking the camp.

Before going to the Antarctic in 1955, Father Condit had a little parish in the Ozark Mountains where people did not care much for going to church, so he had to learn to play the piano, accordion, mouth organ and organ. Organizing a band and singing groups, like the pied piper he led the mountain folk into his little church for prayer. When he was assigned to winter over at McMurdo, a Protestant Chaplain Peter Bol also went to Little America, to assist Father Condit.

Within hours of the fire, volunteers began converting a nearby Quonset hut into a temporary house of worship to serve as the site for the station's religious services, and a new Chapel was built as part of the National Science Foundation's plans to refurbish McMurdo Station using materials salvaged from older structures that had been demolished during the NSF seven-year rebuilding programme.

A new Chapel had seating for 80 personnel and was the third chapel to be raised at the station, again situated on a knoll overlooking McMurdo Sound and the peaks and glaciers of the Transatlantic Mountains. This new chapel was dedicated on Sunday January 29 1989.

The hour long dedication ceremony attracted an overflow crowd with personnel from both the American's base and Scott Base, with bible readings by Lt. M Brad Horton, chaplain of the US Naval Support Force, Antarctica. Also attending the dedication service were Captain Dwight and VXE-6's CO Commander John V Smith, Neal Terry, personnel co-ordinator for Antarctic Services [NSF support contractor], with the guest speaker being Father Gerard Creagh from Hoon Hay Parish in Christchurch.

This was the second time Father Creagh had participated in a ceremony to dedicate a site for religious services at McMurdo since he had been the invited speaker in 1979, when the small southern community gathered for a similar service recognizing the makeshift chapel after the 1978 fire. Concluding, he noted that *'Another chapter in the history of a unique operation is about to begin in peaceful co operation and co existence on the only continent that has no weapons, has no known class struggles or wars, and from which nuclear explosion and waste are banned by the treaty.'*

It was, perhaps a season marred by omens, not only by the McDonald Douglas DC-8 tragedy and the loss of two helicopters, but by the number of disruptive incidents which hampered the American's Antarctic programme, placing pressure on the personnel and others.

First extremely poor weather conditions on the ice causing a build up of traffic and supplies, continuing maintenance problems with cracked windshields to the LC-130 dominating maintenance work, the grounding of the cruise liner *Linblad Explorer* at the northeast end of Wiencje Island on Christmas Day, a number of emergency medical evacuation flights, a serious landing mishap of a UFAF C-141 at Christchurch Airport on a return flight from McMurdo and then the tragic crash to the lower slopes of Mount Erebus, on November 28 1979.

On January 7 1979, one of the squadron's UH-1N helicopters # *158239* was reported lost at the Gown Ice Piedmont at the foot of the Darwin Glacier. It had apparently flown into the ridge and was totally destroyed on impact, injuring four who were later airlifted back to McMurdo by one of the squadron's LC-130's. The second helicopter crash didn't occur in Antarctica but at the Naval Air Station, North Island, California on February 17 1979, when a VXE-6 helicopter # *158241* had just become airborne on a training flight, and a mechanical malfunction caused it to spin out of control while hovering a few feet above the tarmac.

The helicopter, which was due to be shipped to the Antarctic via Christchurch within a few weeks, was extensively damaged then written off the Navy's books, so the US Marine Corps squadron loaned the Navy two stored UH-1N's for four seasons to assist the Antarctic programme over their loss.

This was the squadron's second loss of a helicopter on home soil, as on July 28 1987, six aircraft and a UH-1N BuNo *158255* were conducting a training flight in Southern California with the cause of the crash as pilot error, while he was making an unauthorised manqué. Those killed were Lt Commander Joseph Dale Cerda, Lt Commander Stephen Bernard Duffy, Aviation Machinist Mate Chief Senior Kevin Michael Kimsey and Aviation mate Airman Eric John Kugel.

In 1978 six Royal Australian Air Force [RAAF] crews became associated with their New Zealand counterparts as part of the Kiwi's Operation Ice, and the following year they brought their own C-130 [A97-005], as part of a combine tri-partite agreement thus making their contribution to the New Zealand-United States aircraft pool.

The Australian government and the RAAF had been considering such a programme for a number of years, and in exchange Australian scientists would move onto the Antarctic continent by

VXE-6 aircraft. During 1978 the RAAF's C-130 made four return flights from Christchurch to McMurdo after the crews had undergone regulation snow craft and survival courses. At first the aircraft were crewed by Kiwi's who made their first flight on December 1 1978 with some 24,300 lbs of cargo and 10 passengers.

The following year the Aussie's operated their own flight programme to Antarctica in an operation code named 'Snowflake', during which time they made six turnaround missions, with the Australian army handling all cargo. Additional flights were made in December 1979, assisting the New Zealand government and Air New Zealand with the recovery and transportation of bodies from Flight 901.

Only a few weeks before the tragic Air New Zealand's Flight 901, all the emergency services had been placed on alert as a USAF C-141 Starlifter # *0249*, returning to Christchurch in the early hours of the morning of October 31, was trailing its undercarriage landing gear that had been damaged when leaving the ice. Approaching Christchurch airport for an emergency landing after a demanding seven hour flight from McMurdo, the crew's greatest fear was the marginally low fuel situation and being unable to retract the landing gear.

A radio ham operator Mr. R Bowater just south of Dunedin picked up a message from the crippled transport, which he relayed to *Operation Deep Freeze* at Harewood for the first *'mayday'* call. Dunedin and Invercargill airports were placed on emergency, but both were unsuitable for such a large aircraft so an RNZAF Orion was placed on standby at Whenuapai, Auckland, while accident & emergency doctors were summoned to the Christchurch airport to wait. Twelve St John Ambulances and nine fire tenders were dispatched, while six-air traffic controllers talked the cripple plane down.

'With our fuel position crucial and the drag of the trailing wheels, we had doubts we could make landfall, but had to head for Christchurch or 'ditch', as we would not have been able to reach any other fields,' recalled Major Colley the 30-year-old USAF Military Airlift Command pilot who had been flying C-141's for seven years.

Just after 1 am, Christchurch weather was marginal for landing as heavy drizzle was falling as the crew struggled to keep the giant jet transport in the air. Local radio stations broadcast a minute-by-minute update on the crippled jet saga as it unfolded, which brought inquisitive locals out in the cold early morning and the police, who set roadblocks making it impossible to get near the airport for a closer view.

There was only enough fuel to barely reach Christchurch, and not enough to make an aborted landing or to allow for a low level flyover to allow the ground crew to make an appraisal of the damaged undercarriage, and this was the city's first major potentially disastrous situation.

Two RNZAF Iroquois helicopters dispatched from Wigram, loomed out of the mist and were positioned half way along the runway, but well clear in case they were needed to reach the crippled jet if it ended its journey off the runway.

All available emergency services both professional and volunteer, were ready for the worst possible scenario landing of a large jet with a crew of nine and eleven passengers, and the fear of fire. As many as 50 emergency service vehicles crowned the tarmac, while the fire service dispatched nine fire tenders and media photographers were banned from using camera flashes as officials feared they could distract the aircraft crew as it made its final approach.

The plane came in slowly out of the south in a 10 knot wind limping through the air, reminding one of returning RAF Lancaster bombers returning from a raid over Germany *'Coming in on a Wing and a Prayer'*, but this time it was a lame refugee from the Antarctic. The C 141 appeared to float onto the tarmac then slid along for several hundred yards wobbling in the strong wind, giving the appearance it would pancake but the wheel held up for about 300 yards before collapsing gently with a spray of sparks over the tail as the machine settled and stopped. It was 2.10 am.

The crippled aircraft sat on the runway for eight hours while the airport was closed to local and international flights, and was later towed away to VX-6'S maintenance base to have its damaged starboard wing and mutilated undercarriage repaired before it returned to the US.

When Captain Jim Collins arrived at his home, his wife Marie gave him the letter of his Air New Zealand advance roster, and although somewhat surprised that he had been assigned to the Antarctic flight 901 on November 28 1979, he was also thrilled.

When VXE-6 lost its two first helicopters in January 1979, the United States Antarctic Programme and the air squadron were unaware of the momentous role they would play ten months later on the treacherous concrete hard slopes of Mount Erebus. The continent's only active volcano was struck when an Air New Zealand's DC-10-30 flight 901 from Christchurch, with 257 people aboard on a sightseeing excursion to Antarctica, ended in tragedy a few miles from the New Zealand and American scientific bases when all aboard died instantly.

As the Douglas jetliner was about to crash into the mountainside, the passengers, all modern day Antarctic explorers were unaware of their fate as they crowded the windows to capture through a murky cloud, the icy wonderland of Antarctica.

Together with his first officer Cassin, he called at Air New Zealand flight dispatch at Auckland International Airport fourteen days before, where the flight plans of the airline's previous Antarctic flights were produced. Noting down the co-ordinates for his flight plan, Jim double-checked them on the map at his home the night before he was due to take 901 down to the Antarctic.

One hour before take off as Collins and his crew went over their pre flight checks, a normal procedure they had carried out hundreds of times, Collins thoughts where slightly more apprehensive than normal as he was to fly a route he had never flown before, even though he had familiarised himself with some aspects of the journey.

Air New Zealand had discussed tourist flights to Antarctica as early as the late 1960's, with a team in charge of investigating the feasibility of such flights in the restricted daylight hours, and the implications to the men on the ice should there be an accident, as they could not refuse to assist, even if it meant the suspension of normal operations, scientific support, the deployment of personnel and time lost, all coming at a cost to them. In short they didn't want starry-eyed tourists invading their domain.

Air New Zealand flight 901 was the airline's third Antarctic flight, with its inaugural fly down made on February 15 1977, followed by the second seven days later.

The Australian National carrier QANTAS had established Antarctic tourists flights during the same period with two in February and one in March, and following its success they flew nine more flights in 1977- 78 and 79.

ANZ flight TE901 ZK-NZP, departed from Auckland at 8-17 am, its flight plan was south via the Auckland Islands, Balleny Island and Cape Hallett on its approach to McMurdo, planing to fly around Mt Erebus and return via Cape Hallett and Campbell Island with its first intended landing point at Christchurch. On the flight deck was a crew of five, ten cabin crew and the official commentator, Peter Mulgrew, known to many Americans on the ice, as he had been a New Zealand member of the Trans-Antarctic Expedition.

[ZK-NZP was manufactured by McDonald Douglas in 1974 and purchased as new by Air NZ, arriving in Auckland on January 27 1973 under the command of the airline's chief pilot Captain P F Le Couteur.]

On that same fateful day, Senator Harry Flood Byrd was aboard a USAF Air Command C-141A Starlifer # *64-0643* on its way from Christchurch to McMurdo under the command of Major B L Gamble, leaving Christchurch about 45 minutes behind Air NZ Flight 901.

While Byrd was retracing the air route of his famous uncle Commander Richard E Byrd, this flight was arranged to commemorate the 50th anniversary of Richard Byrd's historic first flight over the South Pole on November 29 1929. Also aboard the Starlifter was Dr Laurence M Gould noted geographer and geologist, second in command on the first Byrd Antarctic exploration, and with him was 74 year old Norman Vaughan, who had been in charge of the Byrd's party of five dog teams, and who was making his seventh visit to Antarctica, while on the flight deck the co-pilot was Vaughan's son, Captain Gerald Vaughan.

When the DC-10 was about 140 miles north of McMurdo, the Air Traffic Control Centre MAC Centre transmitted a weather forecast, advising the crew of Flight 901 that the Ross Sea was under a low cloud with a base of 2,000 feet, visibility of 40 miles, some light snow, with a clear passage approximately 139 miles northwest of McMurdo. At the time a VX-6 LC-130 was approaching Williams's air facilities from the south west, and was expected to land at 1:30pm, while the USAF C-141 was flying directly behind the DC-10.

Captain Collins told his passengers, as the jet was in its descending orbit, northwest of Mount Bird on Ross Island. *'Captain again ladies and gentlemen, we are carrying out an obit and circling our present position and will be descending to an altitude below cloud so that we can proceed to McMurdo Sound. Thank you.'*

Passengers caught glimpses of the Antarctic coastline, checking their cameras to capture the snow and ice through the cloud ceiling, and at 1.49 pm the DC-10 was down to 2000 feet.

'What's wrong' someone on the flight deck asked, *'make up your mind soon or....'* followed by Captain Collins voice. *'We might pop down to 1500 feet here'*. Moments later Collins *'Actually those conditions don't look very good at all- do they?'* 00-49-04 [Mulgrew] *'I don't like this'* 00-49-25 [Collins] *'have you anything from him* [control tower]. [Cassin] *'No'* 00-49-30 [Collins] *'we're twenty six miles north, we'll climb out of this'* then follows a discussion by the pilots as to whether they should turn left or right. Then GPWS sounds at 00-49-44 and the impact into Erebus occurred six seconds later at 00-49-50.

The two underwing engines and the rear underside of the fuselage slammed into the rock hard layer of ice on the lower slopes of Mount Erebus with such a massive force it left a deep indentation in the shape of the aircraft, as the lower panels of the DC-10's fuselage tore away carving deep into the ice. The ungainly hulk, cracked and gaping in five sections was tossed all over the snow like some helpless and cripple bird.

The force of the impact ruptured the wing fuel tanks and the 70 tons of aviation fuel ignited almost instantaneously raining down the mountain like a raging hellish storm, engulfing the aircraft, but avoiding the cockpit, already smashed and only recognisable from the mass of dials, wires and columns, protruding from the nerve centre of the world's most sophisticated control systems. The Douglas DC-10, which departed from Auckland only hours before, now lay torn and twisted with its burned and blackened pieces scattered over an area of 2000 by 500 feet, and close to two large crevasses.

Passengers blasted out of the wide body cabin were killed instantly and some were still strapped in their seats, while the cockpit and front galley section broke off on impact from the main fuselage, throwing the captain and his co-pilot over 200 feet from their controls. The crumpled fuselage was twisted like a plastic toy with the large main cabin with its wing roots still attached ending up at the head of the wrecked tail section.

The tangled remains of Air New Zealand's pride and joy was now spread up to 1900 feet above sea level, leaving its footprint to history and 257 passengers and crew dead.

On the flight south of the USAF's C-141, its commander Major Bruce Gumble had been talking to the crew of flight 901 since they left Christchurch, he had heard Captain Jim Collins report to McMurdo that the DC-10 was going visual and making a descent, and as the Starlifter neared the McMurdo air facilities, Gumble tried to contact flight 901 in order to determine its flight path.

He didn't get a reply so he tried a second time as he began his own descent onto the ice runway. This failure to make contact over twenty minutes was very unusual, so Gamble at first surmised there was a communication break down, but McMurdo had also failed to make contact with flight 901.

Landing on the ice at 2.52pm, Major Gamble's last contact with the DC-10 was at 1.45 [NZ time], meanwhile back at *Operation Deep Freeze Head* Quarters at Christchurch Airport, the navy's public relations chief Mike Hatcher was relaxing in the clubroom, having a few quiet beers while catching up with some mates who had just returned from Antarctica. Suddenly he received urgent instructions to return to his office a few yards away. A large naval man handed a teleprinter message to Mike as he rushed in the door, grasping the message which read, *'A commercial airline, Flight 901, was overdue, last contact with McMurdo was just before 1.45pm [NZ time]'*.

November 29 1979 was to have been a day of celebration as it was the 50th anniversary of Adm.Richard Byrd's flight over the South Pole, and en route to Antarctica were United States Congressman and other distinguished visitors but the 'party' was ruined by news of Air New Zealand's flight 901.

Mike Hatcher noticed the message was timed at 4.43pm as two US Navy's VX-6 Squadron helicopters and a C-130 Hercules were about to begin a search out of McMurdo. It was now 5pm and Mike knew he was in for a long night, as apart from monitoring messages coming through from McMurdo, local, national and international media would soon besiege him, so he set up a media centre at *Deep Freeze* Headquarters.

The US Navy VX-6 helicopter Squadron accompanied by RNZAF aircrews, flew virtually around the clock, with only minimum rest periods while they were involved with the rescue and crash operations, while also attending to their normal duties of supplying the various scientific field parties scattered over the continent. While having very little spare time to themselves at the best of times, this was over and above their call of duty, and they must have been on their last legs, so no praise was too high for these *Puckered Penguins*.

VX-6 launched a LC-130 Hercules with Lt Commander John [Cadillac Jack] Paulus to begin the search for the DC-10's last known position 38 miles from McMurdo, and he was joined by two of the squadron's Sikorsky UH-1N helicopters. After a short turnaround the USAF's C-141 departed McMurdo on its return flight to Christchurch and backtracked along the DC-10'S route from its last reported position.

Aboard the VXE-6 C-130 that morning was Flight Engineer Jim Landy, preparing the Herk for a supply mission to the South Pole, but unwittingly the day took on a special meaning for Jim Landy and his fellow crew, Charlie Swinney, the load master, Jack Ward, the navigator and the pilot John 'Cadillac Jack' Paulus, when the Hercules would fly on the exact navigational path flown by Admiral Richard Byrd commemorating the 50th anniversary of that historic flight *' Not in my wildest dreams did any of us anticipate the tragic event that was about to unfold'* Jim Landy told Mike Subritzky of the New Zealand Antarctic Veterans Association on the 25th anniversary of the crash.

'We flew to the Pole and after spending the standard 'on deck time' we headed back to McMurdo along the route we heard Mac Centre on High Frequency radio attempting to raise the DC-10. We had become accustom to the 'tourist flights' and initially thought nothing out of the ordinary was occurring, as in this part of the world HF communications sometimes perform poorly.

But as we drew closer to McMurdo, Mac Centre contacted a C-141 that was inbound to McMurdo asking if they had sighted the DC-10, the thought was that the Air New Zealand flight had possibly turned around and was heading back north, and still we gave little thought that anything was amiss then Mac Centre contacted us and asked if we had seen the jet, so now we began to realize something was wrong - terribly wrong.

Mac Centre requested our onboard fuel load and wanted an estimate how long we could stay airborne, as at this point we were fairly close to McMurdo and onwards past Beauford Island along flight coordinates normally used by air traffic. Some thought was given that quite possibly the aircraft had ditched in the sea or made a forced landing on the ice shelf. However our commander Lt Commander Paulus, expressed misgivings about this theory. As much as he hated to think about it, he believed the aircraft had crashed somewhere on the backside of Ross Island

As the weather was fine across most of the area, there was moderate to heavy cloud cover on the north side of Ross Island extending far out to sea, and after flying back and forth past Beauford Island for a period of time Lt.Cdr Paulus changed course and headed to the north side of Ross Island, where we maintained altitude to remain above the cloud tops and occasionally could see the terrain through breaks in the cloud cover. After a while, we saw it- the crash site.'

Load Master Charlie Swinney continues the sad story.

When we got near the suspected crash site we put everyone on board in the windows to have as many eyes as possible on the look out, but still almost didn't see it because we were looking for something that resembled an airplane and there wasn't much left that looked like one, only the wheels and that piece of tail section. We kept circling low over the site looking for survivors, but of course there were none. We stayed in the area until one of our helos got there, and I will never forget the devastation we saw on the side of the mountain. I don't remember much more about that day other than the absolute sick feeling of helplessness and frustration at such a huge loss of life.'

Jim Landy again: *'It is difficult to explain my initial thoughts as it simply didn't seem real. There far below us was the wreckage of what was once a jumbo jet that we could see, but what about the people onboard? Good Lord, what about those people! O heavenly Father, grant them eternal peace.'*

Sighting the wreckage, the Hercules's crew were astounded at the sight below them on the northern side of Erebus as the DC-10's wreckage was nothing more than a long black smear extending hundreds of yards up the snow covered slope of the mountain. Some of the larger pieces of the wreckage could be seen clearly near the top of the 'smear', but from their flight deck it was difficult to see anything of any size, and as the crew scanned intently for any signs of life they couldn't find any movement or see any survivors.

After locating the wreckage site, the crew of the VXE-6's C-130 radioed, notifying of the location of Flight 901, which was received in New Zealand in time for the morning news, while overseas media carried the news of the tragedy in their afternoon editions.

The RNZAF Orion # *NZ 4204* from No 5 squadron departed from Auckland late in the evening of the 28th and after refuelling, followed flight 901's flight path with instructions to search the known filed flight plan 30 miles either side of the route taken. However, when approximately 600 miles south of Dunedin, it was recalled after the crew of a VXE-6 LC-130R *#159131* had sighted the jet's wreckage on Erebus.

Christchurch police constable a passenger on the RNZAF's C-130, was Alistair Windeburn who remembers flying around the crash site as they approached McMurdo, *'It was just like cigarette ash on the snow, a big long black mark that stood out and it wasn't until you got close that it got bigger and bigger.'*

The squadron attempted to land a VX-6 *UH-1N # 158278*, but owing to strong blowing snow and a 30-knot wind creating severe turbulence, and the 35-degree slope of the mountainside, the mission was unsuccessful. Another attempt was made to drop three experienced Christchurch mountaineers, Keith Woodford, Hugh Logan and Daryl Thomson near the crash site, but they were unable to reach the actual site by foot.

Bob Thomson, the head of the New Zealand Antarctic Division, DSIR released a statement to the media in Christchurch on the morning of November 29, based on information received from Scott Base at 10am, advising that the crash site was *'almost inaccessible by foot or helicopter.'*

After being dropped, the three mountaineers reached the site by foot only to find strewn around them in the snow the 257 bodies, some burned and mangled beyond recognition, but some unscathed by the violent impact. They began their grim task in complete silence, as roped together they combed their way circumspectly through the wreckage to avoid the crevasses.

At the point of impact the jet had bounced on its underside ripping a hole four metres deep in the ice surface, and then carrying on up the side of the mountain. They signalled to a hovering VX-6 helicopter crew indicating that no one had survived, then pitched their tent on a relatively stable plateau and began their recovery task.

While the Air New Zealand's tragedy on the slopes of Mt Erebus was lugubrious for New Zealanders, as few Kiwi's gave the VX-6 personnel a passing thought as to the grim task enforced on them, and even fewer considered the heartbreak and long lasting effects the accident would have. One of the first on the crash site was VXE-6 helicopter crew chief Joseph Madrid, whos memories of that day are indelibly engraved in his mind after he set down the New Zealand mountaineers onto the site to determine if anyone was alive.

'This day I will never forget' wrote Joseph. *'I was woken at 0600 by Becker, who told me I had to fly on standby today, so I dressed in my flight gear and went to the hanger and got my Helo ready. After a few of us went to breakfast I learnt that the DC-10 had been found, Hector and his plane tried to get there but the winds were too bad to attempt a landing, so we just hung around loose until the weather cleared. Meanwhile I went to the Red Room for a coke then on my way back to the hanger I saw my 'bird' tuning up, so I hurried over. The co-pilot was doing his engine checks, as I took over, and after we got started the three Kiwis' showed up and we flew to the crash site wondering just what we would find.'*

Another squadron helicopter went with them with navy photographers aboard, while a C-130 flew over the crash site keeping the helo pilots informed on the weather. *'When we approached the crash it was a grizzly site, it first looked like a great dark stain on the white snow, but as we closed in on the site, we could see bits and parts that were once an airplane and people. When we arrived and hovered over the site, the slope was very steep and in noway could we land normally.*

We had to stick one skid of our Huey into the snow, drop the climbers, and down rotor that is away from the high side of the mountain otherwise they would run into the rotor blades. As we looked for a spot to stick the skid I was looking down and we passed over many bodies while trying to locate the right place. When we did, I remember one body looking up at me, it was strange for the head had been turned all the way around and he was laying on his belly, yet he was looking at me.

When we got the skid in and were stable enough for the New Zealand mountaineers to exit, with each one I received an electrical shock due to static electricity from the rotor blades turning. But we got them off and departed.

You see at that moment it was still a rescue operation so we flew to one of the rookeries and waited an hour. When we returned to the crash we retrieved the New Zealanders, and their faces were ashen and so very silent, so we returned to base, landed near the helicopter hanger and the pilots and Kiwi's went to a special headquarters set up to debrief them on what they had found. In the meantime I was bedding down the helo, and it was then that I notice that there were tables set up by the gym with food, coffee, water and all manner of foods. Of course this was for the crash survivors, which by then we knew that they would not be arriving, yet there were these tables, filled with all the hope of life.' Jos related with tears in his eyes.

The New Zealand government had a clear list of priorities that could be perceived as a cover-up, but Air New Zealand staff should never have been allowed on the site and there was no room for the media.

Did Air New Zealand officials already have knowledge of the prime cause of the tragic crash? Did they already know of the wrong co-ordinates that had been programmed into Flight 901? The many unexplained mysteries including what happened to the air crews flight bags, Capt Collins empty ring binder notebook, Miss Kennan's diary, and the airline files, among many others, prompted Chief Justice Peter Mahon's now famous quote of the airline's report as an *'Orchestrated litany of lies'*, that still reverberates down the years.

Justice Mahon levelled the charge of an attempted cover up by the National Airline and the then Prime Minister Rob Muldoon, who refused to table Mahon's report, only rebuking him. Many New Zealanders came to his defence, and even now over 25 years on, the aviation industry remains sharply divided on the issue.

His son, painter Sam Mahon remembers so clearly the night before his father's report was released. *'So it was surprising that as soon as his report on Erebus was signed and delivered he should make a rare visit to the hills, don his worsted greatcoat and loiter amid the willows of a cold autumn evening listening again for the sibilant whisper of wings. I remember the wind rippling the black pond and the restlessness of the trees, I remember him lighting a cigarette in the niche of his lapel, the shotgun broken in the crook of his arm, the brief smoke shredding in a wind pouring from an empty sky. 'Tomorrow' he said, 'old hell's going to break loose' and it did.'*

Some believe that Erebus unravelled his health that took his life too soon. That maybe so, says Sam, *'But he was an artist in his own way and Erebus was his masterwork.'*

Mahon's book *Verdict on Erebus* is a calm and objective story of the sad events, and the conclusions he reached startled the public, airline management and the government, when he cleared the aircrew of any responsibility and accursed the airline of a 'pre-determined plan of deception'. Perhaps that is why the news media were made unwelcome on the ice and at the crash site, leaving the world ill informed of the truth.

The only woman who visited the crash site was US Navy Flight-Surgeon Sandra Jan Caroline Deegan, who was flown in by helicopter on December 3. Over the next twenty-four hours her mission was to view every body visible and every obvious piece of human form, to certify that life was extinct and that no one survived the tragic crash of 901.

This event affected all the Americans on the ice at the time, like personnel Jules Ulberuage, who was in the communications room at the South Pole, *'After the news broke at the Pole, the NSF representatives had a situation meeting and burst into tears, as we all did'*. Later a heavy-equipment operator at McMurdo, Rob Robbins got the sad news while working in the Berg Field Centre, and a McMurdo driving co-ordinate recalled that night, *'I don't think there were many people in town that held out much hope. The chapel overflowed with McMurdo residents offering prayers for the passengers on the plane.'*

Robbins and other general field assistants were hurriedly put to work at the ice runway constructing a Jamesway to act as a temporary morgue, and for six days body bags were transported by helicopters before being loaded aboard an RNZAF C-130 for New Zealand.

Another American, Brian Vorderstrasse, a member the squadron's Para-rescue team and jet mechanic of the C-130's who had been trained by New Zealand mountaineers, assisted on the crash site with body recovery.

'Mostly I was a labourer moving aircraft parts, and placing bodies in bags after they had been recorded. I also marked bodies and body parts with flags after them being photographed, then we would place the bags in a cargo net, loading on an average 10-12 people, when the helicopter at McMurdo came and took the victims back to Williams field.'

Vorderstrasse tells of the time during a white out, when they were stuck on the cold mountainside for several days drinking an unbroken bottle of champagne from the DC-10.

'We also took a makeshift cross up to the saddle between Erebus and Mt Terra Nova that was later replaced with a permanent memorial.'

On the funny side, and to relieve in the grim undertaking in the extreme weather conditions, Brian told this writer the discovery of a prosthetic leg with a shoe still attached.

'You asked how this could be funny, well there where shoes everywhere around the crash site as it seems all the victims lost their shoes, even those wearing boots. On one part of the recovery mission I found this 'leg' that appeared to still have a shoe; it was big news and everyone came to have a look.

While moving debris, the artificial leg was just lying there, so the joke was on the person who had not only lost a shoe, but their leg too - although it doesn't sound so funny now.'

Brian who also swam in Lake Vanda, parachuted into the South Pole Station, trained C-130 and Helo flight crews in Antarctic survival, later worked as a fire Lieutenant and Paramedic with the Albany Oregon Fire Department.

Joseph Madrid recalls: *'Those on the mountain had a task that was far more grotesque than for us in the hovering helo. They loaded ten bodies into a net that we slung beneath our machine as there really wasn't any other way to do it. Anyway clear bags were being used, why -who knows? The thing was, as we pulled up and the net tightened around the bodies, heads, arms, legs, whatever would just pop out of the net, not falling out, just protruding from the net. Of course, as the crew chief you have to lie on your stomach and watch the whole operation, as your job is to make sure all goes well when you lift the load. There again, we landed at McMurdo, unhooked the nets and waited for the guys on the ground to remove the bodies, then we would fly back to the crash site with the same net for more.*

There lies a problem as the bodies left little pieces in the nets, and this was no big deal until they started to warm up inside the helo. God what an awful stench that was of bodies, jet fuel, and burnt flesh.'

Recalling the above was not easy for Joseph, opening up old memories *'I didn't drink much in those days, but I think a long stiff drink is called for after writing all this down, life has been hell from time to time, as with this crash, so be thankful that there are so many other good things to off set this.'*

God bless you Joseph and all other VX-6 ers involved in those dark days of New Zealand aviation, for the country will forever be indebted to you and others for your *Courage, Sacrifice and Devotion.*

On the 25th anniversary of the Erebus crash Joseph Madrid sent an Indian medicine bag down to the ice to be placed in the memorial at the NSF building at McMurdo, as the medicine bag carried spiritual and significant items. Such was his feelings for those souls who lost their lives on what started out to be a flight of a lifetime. Joseph's compassion was symptomatic of his fellow squadron members who's task it had been to help where death had reached out, in Antarctica.

VX-6 squadron's aircrews flying between New Zealand and the Antarctic had always considered ditching was not a survivable option, as would have been the case with Fight 901, and at the later inquiry, Communications Commander Coltrin and Chief Petty Officer Priest both expressed concerns over the unreliable nature of communications with the New Zealand Civil Aviation Links, although there had been correspondence on this matter over the previous two years.

The United States Navy Controllers at McMurdo had no control over civil aircraft, believing themselves not to have any function except on a simple advisory basis as far as the movement of civil aircraft were concerned. However, McMurdo Air Traffic Control acting in the interests of their own aircraft either flying to or from New Zealand or within the continent, did have the paramount duty of separation of traffic for both civil and military aircraft, but the base's commander acted on the sound proven and long-standing principle that they could not, and would not, direct the flight path of civil aircraft.

An article prepared for the October 1997 issue of *Topic Air* a month before the Erebus Tragedy, written by a US Navy journalist, James M O'Leary;

'Aviation in the Antarctic has not been without its setbacks. The bodies of over thirty American fliers and crewmen attest to the hazards of flying, serving as a constant reminder that man is still subject to the caprices and whims of Antarctica's beautiful but treacherous nature.

No one knows what the future in Antarctica holds, but aircraft and aviation will be intertwined with the future, tempered and balanced by the hardy souls of pilots and crewmen who challenge it constantly.'

Scott Base personnel bewildered by the tragedy of Flight 901 began to think that November was proving to be a 'hex' month at the base, as on November 19 1959, Lt.Tom Couzens of the Royal New Zealand Armoured Corps, lost his life at Cape Selbourne in a snowcat accident.

Exactly ten years later to the day, Mr. Jeremy Sykes of the New Zealand Film Unit died near Mount McLemman in a US Navy VX-6 squadron helicopter crash. There were no accidents on November 19 1979, but with the Base's personnel aware of the 'hex' and the significance of the date, were taking that little extra care as they went about their duties- but nine days later came New Zealand and Antarctic's worst aviation disaster.

Even now, a quarter of a century later, New Zealand public opinion, and the aviation industry are divided as to the real reasons it became the countrys and Antarctic's worst air accident.

CHAPTER SIXTEEN.

BACK TO NORMAL ON THE ICE AFTER EREBUS.

*There was a life after the Erebus tragedy for the squadron
as they entered a new decade of Antarctic exploration
with a reduced budget and the USAF playing a greater role, and #321 flies
home.*

The *Erebus* disaster left a profound and lasting impression on New Zealand aviation, that in turn had a domino affect on the tourist industry for many years, stunning New Zealanders who are by the nature of the country's small population, knew of someone who had died on those cold slopes.

It left an indelible influence on the Americans on the ice at the time too, particularly members of VXE-6 who played such a courageous part in the search, rescue, and body recovery from the mountainside.

The squadron's C-130'S committed 24.8 hours and the UH-1N's spent 102 hours they could ill afford with the Continent's limited daylight hours, to achieve their support and supply programme. The Operations medical officers and their assistants spent over 325 man hours in the investigative efforts with body recovery and identification, while many additional hours were spent by terminal operators, also involved in the recovery operation.

The weary squadron returned to their homeport with a heavy heart, having been through what would be their most distressing Antarctic season. Commander Sprite handed over the command to Commander V-L Pesco on May 30 1980, with Flight 901 problems still lingering on in Antarctica. The squadron knew that they couldn't have done more so their discipline and confidence was high, but it was the basic fact that a foreigner had chosen their space and created a tragedy, leaving those personnel so involved with the search and rescue and body recovery, that it was now Cdr Pescos task to bring tranquillity back to the ice.

Antarctic aviation history and VX-6 Squadron have produced many aviators who have been honoured for their exploits, and another was added to the 'Antarctic hall of fame', the retired Lt Cdr John F Paulus, known affectionately to OAE's as Cadillac Jack. There were many rational reasons why this veteran got his nickname, but the one that seems to have originated came during one of the squadron's bull sessions where someone was reported to have remarked *'Jack Paulus is so smooth that flying with him is like riding in a Cadillac.'*

Pilots, crew and every support personnel together were quick to concur in this assessment, and from that day on he was know to all who plied the Antarctic continent as Cadillac Jack.

A veteran of nine Antarctic deployments, there would be no man in the squadron who was more knowledgeable and skilful an aviator, and none would have contributed more to Antarctic aerial exploration than Jack. Making his first Antarctic deployment in Deep Freeze 69, under the command of Cdr Eugene Van Reeth, he then proceeded to amass more than 2,250 hours of cold weather Antarctic flying in his LC-130 until his retirement in 1980. During his tour of duty the Lt Commander worked under nine Commanding officers, a record for any VXE-6 aviator.

During his unequalled time with VXE-6 in Antarctica, Jack Paulus piloted several historic flights. In December 1969 he commanded the first flight to land in the field some 2,250 nautical miles from McMurdo that was later known as Siple Station and he transported the first group of women scientists to the South Pole, then during *Deep Freeze-80* carried two medical relief missions from the

Russian scientific stations and airlifted a terminally ill Russian Scientist from Antarctica to Christchurch.

In 1974, Lt Cdr Paulus flew his LC-130 from McMurdo to Christchurch for nine hours over open seas with one of the aircraft's propellers feathered, and his Flight Engineer Lamar recalled another incident that illustrated the veteran's familiarity with the terrain. After closing down the summer research camps and transporting the scientists and other personnel and their equipment back to McMurdo, the Hercules was operating independently in the absence of navigational stations along a route where he had to navigate visually to a site located in the Lagorce Mountains. A rather low scud layer shrouded the surface obscuring any referenced landmarks which would show the aircraft's position but Cadillac Jack, thoroughly familiar with the remote mountain ranges, descended a few feet and spotted a glacier whose distinctive features he had years earlier committed to his computer like memory and immediately oriented himself.

On landing on the rough ice surface, the personnel were quick to heap praise on the Commander, but Jack just shrugged his shoulders. *'No big deal'*, but just to try landing in Antarctica without navigation aids and where one snow-covered mountain appears to look like every other, is no mean feat.

His ability to deal with the harsh Antarctic continent on its own terms during those nine years has made him a legend of his time amidst the cold weather aviators, a contribution to some degree largely unheralded throughout his distinguished career, although the United States Navy officially named the skiway at the Pole Station the Jack Paulus Skiway in his honour, and as a tribute to this remarkable aviator.

During *Deep Freeze –82* the US government slashed the NSF Antarctic operational budge from $US.71 to $US.66 million, in line with across the board US budgetary restrictions. President Ronald Reagan released a memorandum on Antarctic policy which read in part that the United States Antarctic Programme should be maintained at an acceptable level as to provide an active and influential presence in Antarctica, while designed to support the range of United States Antarctic interests on the continent.

The Presidential memorandum read in part:

'This presence shall include the conduct of scientific activities in major disciplines, year round occupation of the South Pole and two coastal stations and the availability of related necessary logistic support. Every effort shall be made to manage the programme in a manner that maximizes cost effectiveness and return on investment.

I have also decided that the NSF shall :

 # Budget for and manage the entire United States national programme, including logistic support activities so that the programme may be managed as a single package.

 # Fund university research and federal agency programmes related to Antarctica.

 # Draw upon logistic support capabilities of government agencies on a cost reimbursable basis.

 # Use commercial support and management facilities where these are determined to be cost effective and will not, in the view of the group, be detrimental to the national interest.

Other agencies may however, fund and undertake directed short-term programmes of scientific activity related to Antarctica, upon the recommendation of the Antarctic Policy Group and subject to the budgetary review process. Such activities shall be co-ordinated within the framework of the National Science Foundation logistics support.

The expenditure and commitment of resources necessary to maintain an active and influential presence in Antarctica, including the scientific activities and stations in the Antarctic, shall be reviewed and determined as part of the normal budget process. To ensure that the United States Antarctic Programme is not funded at the expense of other National Science Foundation programmes, the OMB will provide specific budgetary guidance for the Antarctic programme.

To ensure that the United States has the necessary flexibility and operational reach in the area, the Department of Defence and Transportation shall continue to provide, on a reimbursable basis, the logistic support requested by the NSF and to develop in collaboration with the Foundation, logistic arrangements and cost structure required for effective and responsive programme support at minimum cost.

With the respect to the upcoming negotiations on a regime covering Antarctic mineral resources, the Antarctic Policy Group shall prepare a detailed US position and instructions. These should be forwarded for my consideration by May 15 1982.

Ronald Reagan. President
United States of America.

This heralded the slow transfer of *Operation Deep Freeze* operated by the navy since 1955, to the New York Air National Guard and the USAF who were involved with the NSF's Arctic operations and the withdrawal of VXE-6 squadron from Antarctica after 44 years.

Resulting from the review of the Antarctic programme, carried out in Washington, the operation budget was increased by 7.3 % at a time when the US Navy was downsizing their involvement. In addition VXE-6 were maintaining communications, weather forecasting and air traffic control at McMurdo while maintaining other stations in Antarctica, the NSF had let contracts to a private civilian contactor to operate and maintain Palmer, Amundsen-Scott and Siple stations until the Siple Station in Ellsworth Land was closed in Deep Freeze-87. As well as operating the research vessel *Hero,* the private contractors provided construction and support facilities and functions while operating the scientific laboratories and the facilities at Williams Field.

This was all part of the Reagan administration objectives of creating a polar 'one stop shopping' while making considerable cost savings. With the Antarctic programme budget increased the navy would, until 1999 maintain communications, weather forecasting and air traffic control, while progressively handing over the its air transport operations to the NYANG.

VXE-6 began the *Deep Freeze –81* season operating fourteen aircraft of three different types, the five LC-130R's operated by the squadron were owned by the NSF, while VXE-6's two LC-130E's had been transferred to the NSF in October 1979 and were still in their fleet, along with the Navy's seven UH-1N helicopters.

Other major changes where made to the operation with the National Science Foundation entering a new decade by changing the system for transporting personnel to and from the United States to New Zealand, for until now the bulk of military personnel used US commercial airliners for the transportation of civilian workers, scientist and some military personnel.

The new system first used for *Deep Freeze-81* was to book personnel on scheduled commercial flights from American's west coast to Christchurch, while personnel travelling to Palmer Station on the Palmer Peninsula, flew via South American - a system operative ever since.

The only C-141B to get stuck at McMurdo occurred in early October 1980 while making a routine flight, its sixth for the season, as it was about to return to Christchurch, when the No 3 engine would not start, but before a maintenance crew could be flown in from New Zealand, the weather at McMurdo deteriorated, standing the jet transport on the ice for days.

On the morning of the eleventh day it was realised that if the aircraft wasn't moved quickly failure of the ice under it could occur, as by this time the giant jet was buried in five-foot snowdrifts. The task crew and VXE-6 maintenance personnel were called on to start digging out the Lockheed transport so it could be towed to a safer, firmer parking area for repairs to be undertaken. These repairs were completed in four hours even with the team being hampered by the 70knot wind sweeping in from the Ross Sea, but the aircraft had shown little effects of the low temperatures and had suffered little damage.

Under the command, another NSF initiative was the purchase of its own 20-foot shipping containers with the ultimate aim of pre-containerising cargo at movement centres in California's Port Hueneme. The first of these containers arrived at Lyttelton during *Deep Freeze –82* on their first leg of the circuit to Antarctica on a journey that would take them to McMurdo one winter and return them to California the following year to start the cycle again.

Each season more containers were progressively purchased, thus ultimately reducing the ever recurring cost of leasing and these containers were shipped to Lyttelton for the first time after using commercial shipping lines since *Deep Freeze- 63*. Two years later during *Deep Freeze-85* the *M/V Green Wave* was the first commercial container ship to join the USAP, and commenced transporting the containers to McMurdo Station.

The squadron continued to carry out missions with the photographic and scientific equipped C-130F # *159131*, flying extensively on aerial mapping missions in the Cape Royds, Cape Evans, Hut Peninsula and Mount Erebus area, but # *159131* had had a chequered career in the early 1980's, while carrying out work measuring the ozone and aerosol concentrations on its regular trans-Pacific flights from California to the Antarctic via Christchurch.

Its first mishap was at the South Pole Station on November 11 1982, when it sheared a nose landing gear strut, and became stranded at the Pole for 16 days. It flew its last mission in December 1987, after crash landing at D-59 while carrying an engine, propeller and starting equipment for # *148321 The Old Grey Mare*, killing two passengers. This was a huge blow to the Foundation as it was the only aircraft with a sole photographic configuration that had been rigged for scientific data collection.

More mishaps came when two VXE-6 C-130's became stuck on the Starshot Glacier some 444 km from McMurdo, but fortunately the aircraft # *160740* was only taxiing at the time of the accident, and the extensive damaged was repaired taking two weeks before it could be flown from the site. The other C-130R # *3160741 The Spirit of Oxnard* was returning to the States from New Zealand in February 1985, when it was extensively damaged by fire after a turbine failure while on the ground at NAS Barbers Point Hawaii, and did not return to its base at Point Mugu until mid May 1985.

In August 1983, the squadron under their new CO Cdr Jim Radigan had to cope with one of its most difficult WinFly operations, as during this assignment the typical mid winter Antarctic weather caused two of the squadron's three C-130's to be diverted to Auckland, after one had one of its four engines shut down.

A few days later the last of the mission aircraft were past the PSR, with all three C-130's committed to landing at McMurdo where winds were gusting at 60 knots and visibility was zero. As they circled the McMurdo skiway with no hope of an improvement in the weather and their fuel level critically low, they were forced to make a landing in the whiteout conditions, for which the commanders of the three C-130's were later cited by the navy and awarded Air Medals for their achievement.

When the squadron arrived with the main body of men to commence *Deep Freeze-84*, the squadron aimed to provide a warm welcome as they touched down, so despite the frigid temperatures McMurdo Station manager wore a short sleeved colourful Hawaiian shirt as he met the planes, '*the ground crew who taxied us in were wearing a tuxedo and a top hat*' remarked Cdr Jim Radigan.

Describing a landing that day, JO2 Mike McKinley wrote in '*All Hands*':

'*On the icy snow-covered runway, the engines roar increased momentarily as the props are reversed and you are gently pushed forward in your seat as the plane slows to the taxi speed. Settling back comfortably in your seats you hear a friendly voice over the intercom 'Ladies and gentlemen- on behalf of the entire crew, I would like to welcome you to Williams Field, McMurdo Station, Antarctica, the last place on earth. The local time is 4pm and the geological time is Pleistocene Epoch –the ice age.*

Please remain seated, with your seat belt firmly fastened, until the plane comes to a complete halt.

For those of you who are terminating your flight at McMurdo, we thank you for flying with us, and hope you enjoy your stay. For those of you who have connecting flights to Byrd Station, Siple Station, the South Pole Station or various glaciers on the continent, our friendly agents at the terminal operations will be on hand to assist you. Again, we thank you for flying with VXE-6-the World's Southernmost Airline.'

Operation Deep Freeze commander Captain Brian Shoemaker, said that, *'You'll never feel more welcome anywhere else in the world as when you step off a VXE-6 aircraft into the arms of folks who have been cut off from civilization for eight months.'* The weather however, refused all common courtesy with the thermometer hovering at 68 degrees below zero.

On May 25 1984, Cdr Dwight Fisher assumed command of the VXE-6 to be the squadron's 30th commander. While at college, he applied for the Navy's nuclear engineering programme that was his first perceived failure, as the engineering programme turned him down. Disappointed, Cdr Fisher took flight training instead and liked it so much that he stayed in the Navy, flying surveillance aircraft P-2's in the Navy's anti-submarine warfare division for sixteen years with his goal to command his own squadron.

'My greatest failure in my life turned out to be something that changed it' he told the paper. In 1982 he was offered a squadron, but not flying P-2's, for it was to be with Antarctic Development Squadron –6 in LC-130 Hercules making him feel he was being sent to the ends of the earth. *'I didn't want to come here, I knew hardly anything about the mission and I tried my damnest to get out of it.'*

Then he began to hear from his predecessors that the Antarctic assignment might not be so bad, and once he arrived he was caught up in its spell. *'I've never experience more exciting flying than I did here'* said Fisher, who had flown all over the continent *'you would just literally take an airplane to a place no one had ever been to before and land this big airplane on a glacier.'*

Cdr Fisher rose quickly from operational officer to executive officer to Commander Officer in three years, setting a new goal for himself to become a captain, but didn't make this goal for thirty years.

When the Navy was downsizing in the early 1990's, Fisher was working as the Dept of Defence liaison to the NSF from an office in the NSF's Washington DC headquarters, and figuring he'd be asked to retire early, he resigned after 26 years in the Navy and applied for an opening at the NSF.

The association between the Squadron and the Royal New Zealand Air Force's no. 40 Squadron personnel, was a special one going back to the early 1980's when the squadron's aircrews were attached to VXE-6 for operations on the continent, with this association made more congenial by the closeness of the Kiwi's Headquarters just a few miles away at Scott Base.

The same exchange scheme of personnel continued in *Deep Freeze 86*, about the same time that the Kiwi's deployed helicopters to their Antarctic operations, but when a Bell UH-1H *[# NZ3808]*, arrived it became the butt of American jokes who nicknamed the orange/red painted Iroquois *'The Orange Roughy'* [which is an ocean fish, eaten in N.Z].

With special arrangements between the famous New Zealand cartoonist Murray Ball, and the NZ Antarctic Society, the RNZAF had Ball's famous cartoon character *Dog* painted on the starboard front door and it was flown to Antarctica aboard a RNZAF C-130 on October 27 1985, after removal of its rotor head. It was reassembled on its arrival at McMurdo and code named *'Snowbird'*. The UH-1H with its six man crew and nine maintenance personnel were under the command of Squadron-

Leader B H Phillips, and during its six weeks on the ice the copter flew just under 100 hours in Antarctic support, before returning to Christchurch on December 8[th.]

A second UH-1N of No 3 Squadron was deployed in November 1989 with the Kiwi's continuing their exchange role with VXE-6. This association exchange scheme continued with 12 personnel from the 5th Terminal Squadron of the Royal New Zealand Corps of Transport who were deployed to assist in the loading and unloading of ships at McMurdo and the Kiwi's and VXE-6 became closer in 1986 when it was revealed that the VXE-6 Cdr Paul J Derocher USN, had a New Zealand connection as he had previously served with the RNZAF as an exchange officer, flying Orion's with No 5 Squadron.

There has always been a long running 'conflict' between the Navy pilots and the USAF aviators who flew the *milk run* between Christchurch and McMurdo as the Globemasters aircrews could conduct a relationship with the local Christchurch girls, while the Navy pilots were confined to the rigors of the Antarctic's 'no female zone.'

With the introduction of the New York Air National Guard the relationship with the 109th Air Wing, as part time aviators, gained a little more acceptability with the Naval aviators than had the Globemaster pilots, however, there was still that inner service antagonism in the nicest possible way, knowing that they were about to take over what had been established when the Antarctic was uncompromising and demanding on the air crews, so a response from the Navy guys was swift when the U S Air Force Reserve was to replace VXE-6.

There were discussions about the impracticability of this new arrangement, and recalled Flight Engineer Richard Anderson. '*We used to look down on the Air Force folks who worked with us on the ice because of their short stay and requirement to be home for the holidays. I remember an incident with an Air Force type before I joined the Navy. I played the trumpet and worked myself through a Boy Scout Camp called Camp Cachalot in Massachusetts by playing my bugle, and additionally, I played taps at many funerals for veterans.*

For some reason, maybe aloneness, I had my bugle in Hut 7, and one night I saw this Air Force guy returning from the showers and decided to play colours and see what he would do. It was bloody cold and he didn't have much on, and as I played colours he dutifully came to attention with his douche kit at order arms and faced the colours at attention until the music ceased, but the problem was the flag stayed up and the music went on and on and on until I finally felt sorry for the shivering Air Force puke, and finished playing colours. He did not figure out that in the summer the sun doesn't go down on the ice and so the flag does not come down either - poor chap!'

Another such story related, while second hand, by a VXE-6 helicopter pilot Lt John Carson, [maybe Buz Dryfroose can confirm this —who knows!] But Carson writes, '*The Air Force C-130 aircraft bring in high priority items to the ice runway at McMurdo Station, and not being ski equipped, it was important to keep the runway clear of snowdrifts, sastrugi and pot holes. In January, the sun had been up for weeks and the pothole repair operations were a very major job.*

On one occasion a USAF C-130's nose wheel was broken off when it hit a large pothole, a minor incident with no injuries, and the pilot did an emergency shut down and had his crew evacuate quickly, but just as he started to get out of the giant plane, it shifted a little and he thought the whole plane might go thru the ice. Since everyone else was out of the Hercules, he decided to use his emergency exit, which calls for him to pop out his side window and climb down a knotted rope stored in a pouch above the exit window.

The window is 14 feet above the ice, even with a broken wheel, so he took the rope's end firmly in both hands and jumped and that one mistake gave him two broken legs. Can you guess what he was thinking as he fell? Oh my gosh what else have I done wrong!'

On December 1986, a KC-130T BuNo *163023* from the US Marine Corps Unit, VMGR-234, based at Glenview, Illinois, touched down at McMurdo on a special feasibility mission as the Hercules was fitted with a new type of radar system designed for aircraft having to make landings without ground control approach radar assistance.

          This first USMC Hercules ever to visit Antarctica, spent two days testing the special equipment on the ice before returning to Christchurch on December 8th with the satellite tracking equipment onboard. A second Marine Hercules, a KC-130R # *160019* made a turnaround visit to Antarctica in late 1989.

          In *Operation Deep Freeze 87-* for the first time since December 1955, the Icebreaker *Glacier* was not part of the American Antarctic Support Task Force 43, as she was now retired from active service and had been replaced by the Coast Guards newest acquisition the icebreaker *Polar Star*. Its deployment meant a single icebreaker was considered sufficient to break a channel into McMurdo Station and to escort the supply vessels in and out through the Ross Sea Ice field. It was Operation Deep Freeze Command's decision to operate the new state of the art icebreaker from Christchurch to Antarctic, but events beyond their control involving the New Zealand government's new anti-Nuclear Act that had just been passed into law, prevented that.

          The USSCGS *Glacier,* who had an illustrious career, has been restored by the Glacier Society, through arrangements with MARAD facility at Suisun Bay. Several teams of volunteers worked on the old girl restoring her interior and carrying out minor repairs before transferring her onto the West Coast shipyards dry dock for a major overhaul at its engineering plant, and then sailed under her own power to a permanent homeport of Connecticut.

          The Coast Guard graciously provided the Society with a surplus Arctic Survey Boat, while the Navy gave a nine foot long builders scale model of the *Glacier* on loan. When commissioned on May 27 1955, she was the world's largest and most powerful icebreaker; 310 feet long with a beam of 74 feet and a full load displacement of 8,915 tons, making the *Glacier* capable of breaking through ice 6 feet thick. From 1955 to 66 the 'Mighty G' served with the US Navy on Antarctic duties, acting as the late Rear Admiral Richard E Byrd's flagship in 1955-56.

          In 1966 the US Coast Guard assumed responsibility for the United States ice breaking missions, and all the Navy's icebreakers were transferred to the U.S.C.G.S, with their hulls now painted bright red. The *Glacier* was nick-named *The Big Red* during her thirty years of Antarctic service, and she carried out 39 expeditions, 29 trips to Antarctica and 10 to the Arctic, steaming over one million miles in icy waters, to open up the polar sea ice for the Navy supply ships.

          On one occasion she rescued from the ice the beset Danish vessel *Kista Dan*, which was carrying the veteran British explorer Sir Vivian Fuchs, and on another occasion on her way back to homeport Boston, assisted in flood relief near Forteleza off the coast of Brazil.

          When she was decommissioned on July 7 1987, ex shipmates formed the US Glacier Association whose mission was to restore the *Glacier* as a living operation tribute to those who helped expand the knowledge of the Polar Regions. Despite her and other icebreakers significant contributions to the United States in polar exploration, there is, according to the Society, no museum in the US dedicated to recognizing the military personnel and civilian scientists who made Antarctic exploration possible to ensure the sacrifices and accomplishments made by so many are remembered. For years the motto of the *Glacier* was *'follow me'*.

          As the news was received in New Zealand of the US *Polar Star's* visit, it sent the late David Lange led fourth Labour Government into a tailspin, as they had just passed their 1987 Nuclear Free Zone Disarmament and Arms Control legislation which placed a total ban on all nuclear military ships entering New Zealand waters. The Act demanded that any Navy ship must declare if they were carrying nuclear weapons, and since the United States government would neither admit nor deny this and would not yield for obvious military reasons, the result was a breakdown in New Zealand and American relations by an ideology that had triumphed over common sense.

While David Lange received huge credit for the now emotive nuclear policy and subsequent legislation, it was common knowledge that initially he had no great personal passionate convictions on the issue, however, being a spin doctor rather than a great politician and Prime Minister, he saw this issue as a winner with the misinformed public, and could gain political mileage, so he leaped on the bandwagon.

Personally, I could never see why the local media continued to thrash his one-liner uttered during the 1985 Oxford Union debate, when Lange, leaning forward to face the United States fundamentalist Christian Jerry Falwell, quipped ' *Hold your breath just for a moment, I can smell the uranium on it.* '

Once on his anti-American 'soapbox', Prime Minister Lange set out to wreck our military relationship with the United States and Australia and the ANZUS treaty [Australia- New Zealand and the United States] established on September 1 1951 Against the views of his Cabinet colleagues and certainly against the wishes of normal New Zealanders, he withdrew New Zealand from the treaty in a speech made in the States, after he had changed his speech notes moments before delivering his address. While it greatly enlarged his ego, it shocked his colleagues and New Zealanders as they read their morning papers over coffee and toast.

At the time of the 1984 election, which swept the Labour government into office, over 75 % of the country favoured the retention of our military ties with our two military partners. With this clear and increasing marjority was a clear mandate to his government that he would have substantial difficulties in selling his 'I'm vehemently opposed to nuclear powered ships' so his spin-doctors devised a 'muddy the waters' campaign from the 9th floor of the Beehive with a nuclear crises that was conceived to convince the country at large, despite vehement U.S rhetoric.

The legacy left by David Lange, apart from his acerbic humour, is two decades of strained United States- New Zealand relations brought about by his ban on nuclear powered ship visiting.

Current Labour Prime Minister Helen Clark says New Zealand has gained international recognition over the past 20 years from its nuclear free policy.

'Part of our international personality is the very strong advocacy for nuclear disarmament. This is an issue that New Zealand and America have put to the side for 20 years and we have worked together with them, both militarily and diplomatically.'

But this fluffy slipper philosophical thinking doesn't put food on the table, and the bottom line is that N.Z. is a trading nation and the loss of the US Icebreakers berthing there has cost Lyttelton and Christchurch millions of dollars and a huge amount of business annually. The USCG would like to come back to New Zealand, as it is understood that it would save $US 5m a year in fuel costs alone by operating out of Lyttelton rather than from Hobart Tasmania. The US Embassy Deputy head of mission, David Burnett says the icebreakers are still US military ships, and even though there would be savings for them, while the visit ban was in place this benefit was not possible.

It seems improbable that a gesture by the N.Z. Government of removing the legislation ban and reinstating a policy ban alone would not win over the minds in Washington. The environmental movement was then as it is today, resolutely opposed to nuclear power both civil and military, but as a US Senator once said. *'God invented environmentalists to make economists and politicians look good.'*

Nuclear ships have an outstanding safety record, and if indeed radiation leakage spooks people, one only has to reflect on the fact that in a normal hospital, the radiation emission is greater than that of the entire United States warship fleet. In reality, time has overtaken the 1987 anti-nuclear legislation as nuclear weapons are not on the surface of United States Navy ships, and the majority of their ships are not nuclear powered either. The only nuclear powered icebreakers in the world are in the Russian fleet, with four in all.

So for the first time since the icebreakers and support ships of Task Force 43 sailed into Lyttleton Harbour in early December 1955 to an overwhelming spontaneous Christchurch reception before they set off to Antarctica to commence *Operation Deep Freeze 1,* anti nuke opponents of all things nuclear, yell out in unison agreeing with Lange, their argument mainly based on misinformation. New Zealand's nuclear free status has to be reviewed which specifically outlaws nuclear weapons, but does not legally prohibit the presence of nuclear propelled ships in their ports, as with Danish law.

The camaraderie between the United States and Canterbury and the benefits associated with the visits is lost, while the 'Yanks' are welcome in Hobart Tasmania, Lyttelton has lost something which added to the flavour of the port and the vibrancy of the city of Christchurch. The loss of regular visitation is disappointing if only for reasons that we are the Antarctic gateway since before Scott.

The mayor of Lyttelton, Bob Parker remembers the excitement of those childhood visits from the US Coast Guard Icebreakers on their way to and from Antarctica. *'Our parents would have these little bottles of scotch and the Americans would have great flagons of the stuff from the PX store, and to us they seemed rich and incredibly tall, I guess that was a view of a kid. They were definitely part of our community and I would love to see that happen again.'* Mayor Parker reminisced.

The US coast guard ice-breakers and supply ships were just as much a part of Lyttelton as the red tails of the VX-6 aircraft and the giant USAF Globemasters were in the skies over Christchurch for twenty years.

At the peak of the *# 321* recovery project at D-59, tragedy again struck the squadron when on December 9 1987, a ski equipped LC-130R1 *# 159131* crashed while attempting to land near a remote site in East Antarctica. The aircraft, owned by the National Science Foundation and operated by VXE-6 was totally destroyed, and was the only NSF's LC-130 which had been configured for aerial photography and other scientific projects, so it's loss was a huge blow to the Foundation who had to charter a Kenn Borek Air Twin Otter instead for their photographic mission on the Siple coast during *Deep Freeze –89,* using a Zeiss-Jena LMK camera with an 89mm super side angle lens.

Two navy personnel on board the Hercules were killed, Lt Cdr Bruce Bailey and AK2 Donald Beatty, with eleven injured including one seriously in the crash. The plane was making a routine supply delivery to the field at Dome –59, where Navy personnel, Lockheed employers and personnel of the NSF' Antarctic contractors ITT/ Antarctic Services Inc, were working on the recovery of *# 321.*

The squadron had been flying regular missions to the site bringing in supplies and heavy equipment, and a witness reported seeing the wing of the Hercules hit the snow, veer off the skiway, overturn and catch fire. First on the scene was US Navy Corpsman Second Class Barney Card, who was the only person at the camp qualified to provide medical assistance, and Lockheed employers Brad Honeycutt and Johnny Howard.

'I heard shouts of the crash, it was just before 8.30 am, and I immediately jumped into a snowmobile to get to the skiway some distance from the camp where all that could be seen was heavy black smoke and twisted metal.' Card said.

'With the danger of the JP-5 fuel exploding, it made the extrication harrowing and I was scared, I knew that it could blow at any minute and wanted to get everyone away from the plane.'

One of the survivors recalled later that *'he literally gave me the shirt off his back; he also gave me his parka and gloves and continued to work in sub zero temperatures in just his thermal undershirt.'*

While Johnny was rendering first aid, Honeycutt began searching one side of the cockpit of the burning aircraft looking for trapped survivors inside while Howard searched the other side.

With fuel beginning to leak and the electrical power still switched on, the site was a powder keg, when finally a small hole in the flight deck area was spotted. Howard was first to see one of the crew struggling to get out of the aircraft, so he and Honeycutt began pulling the survivors out one by one. The three rescuers together with the rest of the recovery team, who had made their way to the crash site knew they had very little time with the fuel leak increasing.

All the survivors, the two dead crew and some of the cargo were moved to snowmobiles for the mile trek back to camp, but they had only moved about fifteen feet from the wreck when the first explosion rocked the burning aircraft.

The injured under the direction of Card were taken to a makeshift emergency room where Corpsman Barney treated them. *'Back at camp in my make shift 'hospital' I assigned a person to each of the injured to sit with them while they kept an eye on them and to let me know what was going on.'* He moved from one to the other evaluating the seriousness of their injuries and got them stabilized, found and provided the minimum he needed to do as bad weather at McMurdo had delayed the rescue flight for eight hours. *'The guy was just superb, he was like the calm in the eye of a storm.'*

Robert Johnson, a corpsman on the medivac flight with the doctor Lt Kermode, recalled the incredible job Card did in the enormous odds, as Card had nine cases, four of them serious, to care for. According to Lt Kermode, *'here was a situation which would have tasked any hospital emergency ward, and one of the injured would have died had Card not kept his wits about him.'*

LC-# 159131 had a long, proud and somewhat chequered history with VX-6, since arriving in Antarctica during 1973. In May 1976, the NSF were keen to modify one of its own LC-130R's to add additional scientific capability to its logistic role, and carried out modifications by fitting a pallet mounted data logging system.

Her photographic /scientific mission continued during *DF 81* and was used extensively for aerial mapping in the Cape Royds, Mount Erebus, Cape Evans and Hut Point Peninsula areas. It was also involved in a mishap at the South Pole Station on November 11 1982 when landing, and became stranded at the pole for sixteen days after it sheared a nose landing gear strut. Now the warrior lay in a heap of twisted metal.

Two other LC-130's were involved in mishaps when on December 28 1984 # *160740* was stuck in a crevasse on the Starshot Glacier 240nm from McMurdo. The Hercules was only taxiing to the landing site at the time but was still extensively damaged. A major recovery operation was mounted, and two weeks later the C-130R was flown out from the site. Two months later LC-130R # *160741,* while on a return flight to the United States was extensively damaged by fire on the tarmac at Naval Air Station Barber Point Hawaii after a turbine failure, and did not return to its base at Point Mugo until mid March.

Late in the evening of January 17 1988 two LC-130H's # *830492* and # *830493* of the NYNG 109th Airlift wing, were the first of the squadron's aircraft to touch down on the skiway at Williams Field after the two aircraft had been on a training flight and 12 supply missions to the South Pole, Siple and D-59, in preparation for the full takeover from VXE-6 in the next decade. The familiarisation flights were to be deployed throughout the next two seasons, and during *Deep Freeze 90*, the crews of both VXE-6 and the 109th would rotate flights after the first week of operations.

On November 1 1989 a USAF's C-141B undertook a special airdrop mission to the South Pole delivering 32,225 lbs of essential construction materials, while at the same time demonstrating the Air Forces ability to airdrop such large quantities of cargo to interior bases using cargo platforms. Named Low Velocity Airdrop [LVAD] systems, these enabled the dropping of three platforms of cargo sequentially in one pass over the drop zone before returning to McMurdo. The mission was such a success that it has been employed ever since.

On October 13 1992, the squadron suffered a fatal accident, involving a HH-1N # *158249,* when it crashed in the vicinity of Wohlschag Bay [near Cape Royds]. The helicopter was on a routine flight back to McMurdo from Cape Byrd, when the crew encountered deteriorating weather and crashed into the glacier, where it slid and rolled 100 feet then dropped and spun until it hit rocks below, so reported the field science manager Steve Dunbar, who had led the search and rescue team that responded to the accident.

One of the early impacts threw mechanic Ben Micou from the helicopter, in which two New Zealander support service workers were also travelling, and both Garth Varcoe and Terry Newport died from serious injuries after being tossed from the aircraft.

It took over five hours to find the wreckage and treat the injured, with conditions that day a whiteout with 20-30 feet visibility. *'Once in awhile the clouds opened up and we could get a glimpse of the wreckage'* said Dunbar and although the pilot Lt Cdr. Ed Crews and the co-pilot survived, immediately after the crash Ed Crews was injured to the point that he was unable to move but later crawled to reach an emergency radio in the back of the helo. Search and rescue were not within radio distance but fortuitously one of squadron's team rescue helicopters was close to the crash site and picked up the call.

Neither the stranded pilot nor the rescue party could see each other's helicopter through the storm, nor even when the rescue copter was directly overhead, but once Crews heard the helicopter's blades, he called a radio message to Dunbar and actually talked them to the location, *'You have to be bloody awfully close because I can hear you, mate.'*

Some of Micou's former VXE-6 crew who had worked with him, knew him as a very kind and gentle man with a cheerful disposition and a generous heart, and a man who was excited about Antarctica and the job he was doing for his country and VXE-6. *'He had this infectious enthusiasm about him and he was just one of those good guys,'* recalled Mike Hush, the air transportation service supervisor. *'He was just 35 years when he died, and was the kind of person who made the best of all situations, and never had foul words for anyone, even when there were some people he didn't like as he was able to put that behind him.'*

He had a wife Janice and an adopted son.

A wooden cross near the edge of McMurdo Sound in honour of the helicopter mechanic stood proud for eight years but was later relocated due to the concern of those who knew Micou, as the monument stood too close to a set of pipes that had been installed only two feet away. To VXE-6 boys the cross needed a more appropriate place, so was relocated near the helicopter hanger where he had worked. Micou is also being memorialised at NAS Fallon, Nevada, where he was stationed before joining VXE-6 and going to Antarctica, the First Class Petty Officer's Association in Fallon have named its new meeting building after Micou.

That disaster was the last in which a person working with USAP died in a helicopter crash.

During the Navy's last season on the Ice 1998/99 the squadron operated 5 C-130's *BuNo 148321-XD-03, #159130-XD-04, #1591291-XD-05 #48320 XD-06* and *#148319* XD-07 and 9 Sikorsky HH-1N Helicopters *BuNo 158283/XD-10, #158234/XD-11, #158235/XD12, #158288/XD-14, #158238/XD-15, # 158272/XD-16, #158249/XD-17* and *#158255/XD-18*

Words of Lt.Col.Richard Saburrro, New York Air National Guard, now commander of Operation Deep Freeze, Christchurch Detachment 13, in paying tribute to the role the US Navy has played in Antarctica.

'They blazed the trails, and they were the true pioneers of Antarctica opening up the continent to exploration to today's more routine logistic operations- if one could describe Antarctic flying as routine. They remind me of the American westward movement, covered wagons with trails turning into dirt roads to paved highways with gas stations and fast-food outlets.'

CHAPTER SEVENTEEN

THE NAVY ENTERS ITS LAST DECADE IN ANTARCTICA TO PROVE THAT 'GIRLS CAN DO ANYTHING.'

*The squadron enters a new decade in Antarctica when an all women
crew flies a Hercules to the South Pole to open the season,
proving that 'girls can do anything'.*

Modifications were made to the ice runway at McMurdo in preparation for the arrival of the USAF's Lockheed C-5A Galaxy transport, when the width of the runway was increased to 197 metres, the turnaround area to 152.5 metres and the taxiways to 122 metres. While the thickness of the ice was a little under 200 cm [78 inches] it was less than ideal to handle the giant C-5A Lockheed transport, even though engineers at McMurdo were more than confident the ice was capable of supporting it.

It was not the aircraft's first visit to Christchurch, as the large jet had touched down in the city in February 1989 when it was conducting a fuel containment and personnel mission to Punta Arenas, Chile, after the Argentine vessel *Bahia Paraiso* had run aground near the United States Palmer Station, on Anvers Island, and the subsequent fuel spillage had threatened to be a massive environmental disaster. The aircraft from the 60th MAW base at Travis AFB California, was used by the USAF as a long-range training and exploratory transport, and later was to become an integral part of the Antarctic operations specialising in oversized cargo.

The USAF landed the giant C-5B Galaxy [87 0042] on the blue ice runway on 4th October 1989, making it the first aircraft of its class to have landed in Antarctica, and the largest to land on the sea-ice runway, carrying some 76 tonnes [168,000 lb] of cargo, 72 personnel and two fully assembled UH-1B helicopters for VXE-6.

A second flight was made two days later, with the USAF providing these two flights at no cost to the Antarctic programme, as the Air Force combined the flights for training purposes too.

Weighing some 870,000 pounds, the C-5B became a regular transport to McMurdo, with an annual commitment to the movement of oversized cargo, together with the C-141, that took over from the US Coast Guards valuable four-piston engine Douglas C-124 Globemasters.

The high winged, long-range C-5A freighter had five times the capacity of the C-141A, and a payload in excess of 260,000 pounds, and combined with its straight through loading and unloading of vehicle and cargo, it made the aircraft ideal for Antarctic operations with the added ability to operate from semi-prepared ice runways.

However, the C-5A operation at McMurdo had not been without risk due to the aircraft's weight leaving heavy 'footprints' on the ice, necessitating the sea ice ramps to be constantly monitored for cracks and the aircraft to be repositioned during unloading. The C-5A utilized its extensive hydraulic systems to raise and lower the fore and aft cargo doors, ramps and the aircraft's kneeling landing function, which was often hampered by the temperatures at McMurdo.

With the official opening of the new International Antarctic Centre near the Christchurch International Airport, the United States Antarctic Programme moved from the site they had occupied since March 1959 at the airport site, to the architecturally designed modern buildings purpose built to include offices, passenger processing terminal, and cold weather clothing stores, while sharing the two-storied building with the New Zealand Antarctic Programme and the Italian Antarctic Programme. The United States Antarctic Programme including the NSF and the Naval Antarctic Support [NASU] along with a number of civilian contractors, moving into the centre from their central city premises.

The *Deep Freeze* and squadron personnel had previously been accommodated on the old WW11 ex RNZAF barracks block, which was now too expensive to upgrade to meet the contemporary civilian standards, even though the barracks had been refurbished over the years, and subsequently from *Deep Freeze –92* all personnel were accommodated in Christchurch hotels.

During *Deep Freeze 90,* a new helicopter was introduced to Antarctic operations, with the US Coast Guard's Aerospatiale HH 65A Dolphin. This twin engine Dolphin design was deployed from the icebreaker *Polar Star,* based at Alabama's Coast Guard Training Centre.

In the past, VX-6 and the Marine and Army helicopters in Antarctic operations had suffered extensive damage to the tail rotary blades resulting from the volcanic dust and small rocks, stirred up from ground takeoffs. In order to arrest this costly problem, the Task Force began operating their helicopters from two helo pads at McMurdo to reduce and minimize maintenance. Using a new material with a composite rotor head, fibreglass blades and a shrouded eleven-blade tail rotor, the operational problems were finally solved after it had frustrated the Antarctic Support Forces command for over 40 years. The HH-65's continued to operate in Antarctica each season from aboard the icebreakers and they were deployed offshore after Christmas to assist in support operations.

The same year, engineers from the US Army's Cold Regions Research and Engineering Laboratory travelled to Antarctic to evaluate the feasibility of constructing a new runway on McMurdo's permanent ice shelf. Annually, wheel aircraft operations had to be terminated after the sea ice runway broke up and floated into the Ross Sea, and it had always been the command's goal to develop air facilities that would enable the squadron and the supporting USAF to operate throughout the whole season.

The navy 'think tank' studied all the related historical material of records and photographs, that drew the group to consider an area some 7 miles south of McMurdo close to the abandoned C-121 Super Connie *Pegasus.* So this new landing strip was appropriately named after her, and the memories of those VXE-6 crews who flew this beautiful aircraft. Located on 'blue ice' that is about 30 metres thick, an automated weather station was established and maintained throughout 1988, to monitor the conditions before construction could begin the following year.

During the first three years of the 1990's, American engineers were developing a new concept of stripping the accumulated snow from the 3,000 by 300 feet area to expose the solid ice surfaces to test a series of takeoffs and landings prior to the scheduled first flight by VXE-6 Squadron's LC-130 carrying 34 passengers from Christchurch on February 8 1993, and to accommodate the larger C-141's and C-5A transport aircraft which were becoming the norm for resupplying the operations.

But the new Pegasus airfield was really tested on February 7 the following year, when a USAF C-141 *# 65.0238* giant transport landed, and while the C-141's used the ice strip operationally for the first time in 1996 for *WINFLY* operations, these mid winter flights were carried out by VXE-6's LC 130R's operating from Williams Field's skiway. On January 8 1997, the RNZAF used the new Pegasus runway when they delivered Sir Edmund Hillary and the New Zealand Prime Minister.

The old cliché *that 'girls can do anything'* was certainly proven on October 25 1991, when the stereotyping myth of Antarctic aviation as the sole domain of barnstorming male aviators was shattered. A milestone was reached in United States aviation history, when for the first time, a seven member all female crew of a VXE-6 C-130 Hercules flew a ski-equipped C-130 commanded by Lt Rhonda Buckner from McMurdo Station to Amundsen- Scott South Pole Station. This was her fourth and final flight on the ice when the mission opened up the US Navy Science Station for *Deep Freeze 92,* having sufficient girls at McMurdo who were all qualified in positions to fly the ski-equipped Herk as an all female crew.

Rhonda Buckner, who retired from the navy and was until recently flying twin-engine turbo-prop aircraft for Horizon Air in North West America, recalls the historic event:

'A couple of our enlisted crewmembers had the support of the Commander Officer Cdr. Wayne Reeves, when the 'skipper' scheduled the flight which would open up the South Pole Station for the season, a flight which was just a traditional flight with several National Science Foundation chiefs and a few medical people to evaluate the winter over personnel' recalled Rhonda, who was assigned to VXW-6 in December 1988, as aircraft commander, *'These types of flights were pretty common in the 1980's, when women were making tremendous gains and inroads in non traditional fields.'*

Rhonda's aviation career began after joining the navy right out of high school and was lucky enough to land a seat in a short lived and little known naval programme called Limited Duty Officer-Aviator Programme flight school. The navy selected between twenty and thirty enlisted personnel every year and sent them through officer candidate school.

Those who made it through the fourteen hard weeks were supervised by, in Rhonda's words *'VERY tall men and mean marine drill instructors'*. The navy selected between 20 and 30 enlisted personnel every year and sent them through Officer Candidate School and then the successful candidates were sent off to Corpus Christi NAS in Texas for multi engine flight training. Rhonda became a flight instructor for five years at Pensacola NAS in Florida.

Before leaving McMurdo on their historic flight to the polar plateau, the C-130R *' went down on its pre-checks with a wing isolation bleed valve, which usually stays open and is shut if there is a bleed air leak, which is a safety flight issue. The only other aircraft on the line was the skippers, and being a gentleman, Commander Reeves gave it to Rhonda and her all girl crew.*

This was a career first, as normally commanding officers do not give up their spot on a flight schedule or 'give' their aircraft to junior officers' recalled Lt. Buckner.

Now assigned to the Hercules XD 02 # *160740,* the all girl crew sat on the flight deck in true naval professionalism and with the traditions of the squadron, carried out their pre flight checks as a top team, with Buckner having flown with each of her crew before.

Lt. Rhonda Buckner, –[Pilot]-PH-2 Tammy Trefts, –[Utility crewman]- Lt. Patricia Turner, –[Co pilot] – AD-3 Nancy Kelson- [loadmaster] – Lt. Susan Wells,- [Navigator] – AE-2 Tami Tudor, [Flight Engineer]- AT-2 Jane Alstott, – [Loadmaster].

'The weather was fair, no cloud, with light to moderate winds, as we took off on our five hour flight to the Pole, the flight was uneventful, but flying over the trans-Antarctic mountains was wonderful' Cdr Buckner said. *'Antarctic has a constant reminder of how hazardous the operations are, and we could spot the wreckage of a twisted helicopter resting ungainly atop a rocky outcrop, at McMurdo, the twisted wreck of the C-122 –Connie 'Pegasus' which crashed on landing in October 1970, while the landmark at the South Pole is the anti-collision light and the only signs of a C-130 which lay buried there.'*

On the flight was Erick Chiang, Section Head of Polar Research Support Section Office of Polar Programmes for the National Science Foundation and Dr. Peter Wilkness. The weather at the polar plateau was as good as could be expected, as the giant ski-equipped plane touched down for the first time in the season after the wintering over party had toiled to present a beautifully prepared ski-runway for the landing.

After unloading the 1,150 lbs of cargo and the 39 passengers, it was time for socializing in real southern fashion, making the ladies welcome by opening several bottles of cooled champagne which spewed out and froze immediately as the spray hit the air.

It's not uncommon for the Hercules to contrail on the ground, and temperatures at the pole provide a similar climate for the fog from the exhaust. The contrail fog can be a problem if there is no wind to move it from the skiway, especially when crews are ready to takeoff as it can get so thick very little else can be seen.

During the time on the ground waiting for the returning passengers, *# 160740* sprung several hydraulic and fuel leaks which kept Tami Tudor the flight engineer busy, but once the passengers were ready to go back to McMurdo and civilization, the transport taxied out onto the ski-runway for take off when it developed a few problems.

'We had a couple of ski problems- no big deal, a very common problem. My flight engineer assured me that everything on the skis were fine – 'just flat' – a term for loss of air pressure. My co-pilot Patricia Turney was at the controls for the return flight, and on the take off slide the flight engineer noticed that number 3 and 4 engine oil temps were higher than normal so we aborted the take-off and discussed on the flight deck what the cause might be. We made another takeoff attempt and again number 3 and 4 engines began to overheat. Aborting the take off again we taxied back to the dome.'

Having experienced this problem on a couple of occasions before earlier in the Antarctic season, Lt. Buckner said normally it was just one engine but never two, let alone on the same side. The C-130 taxied back to the dome, and shut down the overheating engine, and while the flight engineer checked out the mechanical problems, the race was to get the engines restated as soon as possible as the weather was getting colder and the prospects of a stay over didn't really appeal to the crew.

'The theory behind the high oil temps at the pole is caused by the high altitude and thin air, as there is not enough air flow through the engine cooler while the plane is on the ground during the take-off slide to keep the oil temperatures within limits- but even Lockheed doesn't quite know for sure- it was just an idea, so we decided to go with the airflow theory.' Rhonda said.

A second C-130 arrived and with it, the contrail fog which became an additional problem, taking several minutes to clear from the two C-130's before they could see the ski-runway and before the new incoming passengers could be unloaded and the departing passengers loaded for their flight back to McMurdo. Lt. Buckner would attempt to fly home with only a minimum crew, just in case her theory was incorrect and she ended up flying on two engines on the same side, *'By the time I made a decision to go, a third Hercules was air bound for the pole, so I requested it delay its landing just in case I had to make an emergency landing back on the site fogged in by our own airplanes.*

We made another attempt at take-off and once again the oil temp began to climb on number 3 and 4 engines, but we agreed to continue the take-off even with the temperatures exceeding the limits, but the motors were running smooth and getting the 'old girl' airborne. Once we got to 1000 feet, the oil temps began to cool, eventually falling back to normal, however, the nose ski wouldn't come up even with the engineer working like a demon on the problem, but the rest of the trip to McMurdo was uneventful.

I'm always amazed at what our people can do here. Every flight is a team effort, it doesn't matter who you are, but whatever the situation wherever you are in Antarctica, you are always happy to be back at MacTown. This time McMurdo was a balmy minus 17 degrees.'

In all her twenty years in the Navy as an aviator, she said she has never seen anything anywhere with the degree of dedication, determination and talent that our crews, especially flight engineers and maintenance crews, displayed on a daily basis. When asked if she ever had any close calls in Antarctica, she replied that she had her share of in-flight challengers but those were mainly in bad weather. *'The key is always leaving yourself an out.'*

Maybe it is the circumspect woman's approach to flying because the one's who got themselves into trouble were the guys who took the gamble and didn't have an alternative plan; then again, those Antarctic pioneering aviators flying cold in R4-D's over unknown and uncharted terrain in primitive conditions maybe were barnstorming- but Rhonda agrees. *'They didn't have the luxurious aircraft and communications of those of us that followed.'*

Asked how the guys in the squadron treated their female counterpart aviators on the ice, Buckner was quick to respond. *'This has never been a problem during my time in the squadron, we were always treated as equals, but sometimes they were somewhat ambivalent about our flight, which is fine with me. I wanted my legacy to be just that I was a professional aviator and naval personnel. I considered I was good at what I did, not just being a woman that they let do it.'*

The problems encountered on this flight were not out of the ordinary and Rhonda Buckner would be the first to agree. *'At one point during out troubleshooting of engine problems, I remembered looking back behind me at the first engineer and hearing her say, 'what's next, something from the electrical system?'- I felt as if I had spent the entire day in a flight simulator dealing with various problems and trying to come up with the best and safest solution in getting my crew and Herk back home.'*

Touching down at the Pole, not only for the first time but also on every occasion, is far from being just a routine flight, as the mystique coupled with the sheer charm of its remote location never fails to impress. I have read no better description than that of Dr Nielson in her book *'Ice Bound'* which is a doctor's incredible battle for survival at the South Pole.

'It's not easy landing 65 tons of sheet metal on skis, as is the LC-130 cargo plane as it touches down on the icy landing strip with flaps pulled back, propellers in reverse and all four engines howling like angry animals. I was one of a dozen passengers strapped in the dark belly of this aircraft, confined to a windowless bench seat. I hoped to watch our descent over the Polar Plateau and catch a glimpse of the continent's most famous landmark, the geodesic dome at the centre of the Amundsen-Scott Pole Station. Still, I could picture the ice-bound world beneath us, as I visited my imagination so many times since I was a child.

We barrelled along the taxiway until the plane bounched to a stop near the Dome. Bundled again in my brand new ECW'S complete with big fur gloves and colossal white boots, I felt very much like the Michelin Man as I hauled my carryon luggage up to the passenger door. I stepped out of the blinding light into the whitest world under an impossible blue sky.

The naked sun seared me right through my polarized goggles, and the next thing that hit me was the cold so deep and complete, it was surreal as my breath touched my throat and chilled my lungs. It was cold from another dimension, from an ice planet in a distant galaxy and this was summer in the Southern Hemisphere!

After a few stabbing gulps of thin air I was quickly reminded that I had gained almost two miles in altitude during the three hour flight from McMurdo. While the plateau was flat as a griddle, it was also as high as the Austrian Alps. The South Pole Station rests on a 9,000 foot thick slab of ice soaring 9,300 feet above sea level. I immediately felt light headed, lead footed and slightly nauseated, but I still had to drag my bags to the Dome. I forced my body to move, even though it felt like I could not. Then I noticed two figures in bright red pakas walking up to the plane, waving and laughing- presumably at me as I struggled down the stairs.

The Pole is a great physical leveller. At first glance, everyone looks the same, dressed in 20 to 30 pounds of almost identical clothing with heads and faces completely covered. They were almost in front of me when I recognized one of the figures as Mike Masterman the winter over station manager, and with him was Will Silva, the doctor I had come to relieve. I couldn't hear them over the noise of the engines, but they were shouting and pointing skywards. I looked up and saw the sun was ringed with a brilliant halo of ice crystals and framed with an array of sundogs like blazing outriggers. Will slapped me on the back and smiled, and as we walked together towards the entrance of the Dome I felt like I was finally coming home.'

I was about to have the indulgence, no, the privilege of flying to the South Pole in 1984, however while waiting for such a flight that is one of the quintessential Antarctic experiences, the Polar weather said NO this day, just as the blizzards had said no to Scott and his men trapped in their tents. No you must wait, and alas I did, but my time ran out, for I received the call that our flight was heading back to Christchurch earlier than I had envisaged pending an expected whiteout, and with my work completed, I had to go dog tags and all and more than a little disappointed.

I now understood that every photograph I had ever seen of the continent before I arrived was so erroneous, as unlike the rest of the world Antarctica appears to have no edges, and no photographer no matter his skills can create an image which would illustrate its grandeur and mystique considering my first impression of the Antarctic's landscape were from the glossy pages of *National Geographic,* I realised that even they couldn't do justice to this breathtaking beauty. So writes the author of this book.

The Air National Guard established a working group in 1990 to study ideas that were for the ANG to convince the Air Staff in Washington to commit their long-term resources to an area of the world that had not been declared a war-fighting region. The ANG since the mid 1970's had supported military operations in Greenland and the Arctic [including classified Navy operations] with ski-equipped C-130's, and it had convinced headquarters at US Air Force that it was not in the nation's best interests to abandon the capability to achieve a quick and reliable air access to both polar regions.

So in March 1993, the US Navy hosted a two day workshop with personnel from the Air Guard and the NSF, along with representive from VXE-6 squadron and other interested parties to explore the logistics and support options for such an operation.

A draft concept had been prepared by the Air Directorate of the NGB earlier, and in February 1996 a commitment was made to transfer the mission that had been known as *Operation Deep Freeze* since 1955.

The US Coast Guard's suggestion of taking over the mission as an extension of its current C-130 operations was rejected after being considered briefly, and then passed up was the National Oceanic and Atmospheric administration's fleet of aircraft which were supporting their scientific missions.

The NSF encouraged a closer look at the Air National Guard as being a potential single point management for fixed wing ski equipped aircraft, so a process of transition began with ANG aircrews flying in support of VXE-6 in Antarctic operations and the 109th Air Wing providing air transport for the Arctic. The Antarctic operations in support of the National Science Foundation and the Space Administration [NASA] in the United States were requested, under the Air Combat Command directives, to provide tactical airlift and aero medical evacuation support for combat and humanitarian relief missions worldwide.

The Navy began to re-evaluate its Antarctic operations and planned to phase out their support mission, with this proposal receiving the seal of approval from the US Department of Defence in 1995. With the aircrews of the ANG's 109th Air Wing carrying out an increased participation with their C-130's, the US Navy began the first phase withdrawal of the VXE-6 helicopter wing component of the squadron. The helicopter's long association with Antarctic logistical support ended with the squadron's last flight made on February 3 1996, a sad day for VXE-6 Squadron, when Commander Stedman landed his HH-1N # *158 288* at McMurdo.

The two year contact with three one year options was awarded to an American helicopter company Petroleum Helicopters Inc by the NSF, and with the company's fleet of more than 300 helicopters, they operated in more than 40 countries.

Under the transition plan which had developed, the Air National Guard would continue to augment the navy during the October 1996 to March 1997 operating season, when it would assume command of the programme. During the third year of the transition, October 1998 to March 1999, the Navy would augment the ANG until the Guard took over the entire programme the following year.

The agreement signing was the last in a series of events which completed the airlift transition, with ceremonies held at McMurdo Station, Antarctica, Christchurch and Port Hueneme Calf, symbolically bringing closure to the United States Navy and VXE-6 logistic support on the Antarctic continent.

At first the company operated only four helicopters but then they took over the squadron's Antarctic role with one Bell 212- that is similar to VXE-6's HH-1N, and three Aerospatiale AS350-B2A Stars, which were transported to Antarctic from the United States by USAF Lockheed C-5A's, with seven PHI pilots and a machine team of five. This contract was renewed under similar conditions in 2000-01 season, when one of the A-Stars was replaced with an additional Bell 212 for the following season.

Outlining the US Navy's post World War 11 involvement in Antarctic beginning in 1947 with the largest expedition ever to explore the continent and its surrounding waters, nearly 12 years later world-wide interest in the Earth's environment led to the International Geophysical Year as part of this imitative, Robert Pirie said, that twelve other countries had established 65 research stations on Antarctica, with the US occupying seven of these including one at the South Pole.

However, in 1976, the National Security Division, memorandum number 318 directed that the US Antarctic Programme be fully managed by the National Science Foundation, who would budget for all science and logistic functions and reimburse other agencies supporting the programme. This followed a White House Memorandum 6646 of February 5 1982.

By 1996, the NSF had three permanent stations in Antarctica to support their research programme, and during the austral summer there were almost 2500 scientists and support personnel.

In March 1993, the navy hosted a two-day workshop with representatives from the NSF, the Coast Guard, the Air National Guard and the National Oceanic and Atmospheric Administration [ACAA] to begin exploring other logistic support alternatives with the group proposing a three-phase Navy withdrawal plan to:

[1] Commercialise base support functions.
[2] Commercialise Antarctic helicopter operations.
[3] Withdraw the Navy from LC-130 operations.

The Navy and NSF have been successfully implementing the first two recommendations, and most of the base support functions have now been contracted out by the NSF, thus reducing the Navy's manning levels by almost 300 billets. In the second week in July 1996, the NSF had awarded a contract for commercial helicopter operations, which would reduce the Navy's strength by almost 100 personnel. A detailed list of functions being contracted out, and their transition status, was outlined in the National Science and Technology Council's April 1996 report on the US Antarctic Programme.

With their robust and well-maintained LC-130 infrastructure, the mission was funded to train, maintain and fly ski-equipped LC-130's for Arctic missions and augment the Navy's support to the US Antarctic Programme by almost 500 hours annually. The transition provided substantial savings to the NSF, since operational requirements for each pole occur in opposite seasons, and both missions could be supported by the same aircraft, infrastructure and personnel, with only a small enhancement of current ANG levels, both complementing each other, and the greatest savings to the NSF was in terms of direct costs and reimbursable expenses to the DOF. The merging of Arctic and Antarctic activities onto a full year-round polar operation, reduced the number of fulltime personnel by over 50 per cent, and the transition also provided the opportunity to defer procurement of new aircraft within six years.

Deep Freeze–97 was the first season of a three-year transition under the command of Cdr Stedman, that the VXE-6 crews flew approximately two thirds of the flying hours, while the 109th made up the balance.

A bronze plaque honouring four participants in Operation High Jump was unveiled at a dedication ceremony outside the chalet, taking place exactly 50 years after one of the squadron's planes a PBM-5 Mariner crashed in West Antarctica. From aboard the *USS Pine Island*, a Navy seaplane tender, the aircraft, code named George One, had left the decks on December 30 1946 on a aerial reconnaissance mission over the Walker Mountains with nine crew aboard including the Commanding Officer of the *Pine Island*, Captain Henry Caldwell.

After encountering a heavy cloud cover, the plane's pilot decided to head back to the ship, and at this point the fully fuelled keel of George-One caught the edge of an unseen mountain and exploded. The crash proved fatal for three-crew members-ENS Maxell Albert Lopez, RM1 Wendell Keith Henderson and MM Frederick Warren Williams.

The *USS Pine Island* sent out another Mariner to locate them, and in the meantime the survivors had found shelter and food in the aircraft's wreckage and awaited their rescue which came after 13 days of delays due to heavy cloud cover, but fine weather prevailed on January 11 1947 and the six survivors were saved.

The entire Antarctic claimed four live's that summer season, and the plaque was dedicated to all these men, including Seaman First Class Vance Woodall who was fatally injured while operating a tractor on the continent. Speaking at the ceremony were McMurdo Station's Manager Al Martin, Commander Navy Support Force Antarctica, Capt Hugh Smith and Naval Chaplain Lt Mark Smith.

'The placement of the plaque in Antarctica will facilitate the long overdue recognition of the contribution made by Task Force 68', Al Martin said, reading from a letter from Don Leavitt the National Coordinator, of *Operation Highjump.*

On the accident of LC130-*# 20195*, Ginny Figar wrote an article with a contribution from Alexander Colhoun in the *Antarctic Sun* which was later placed on Bob Homes excellent web site, and while I had no trouble with the authenticity of the story, there was no reference to the part the staff of Air New Zealand's Christchurch engineering workshop played in the rescue mission, so I have to put the record straight, after the Air National Guard and the NSF sought their assistance and technical knowledge.

Like a medieval White Knight wandering in search of chivalrous adventures, Air New Zealand's engineers came to the assistance of the New York Air National Guard when one of their LC - 130 Hercules *# 20195*, during a routine flight to a route camp in the Antarctic interior in an area known as 'Upstream D' in Marie Byrd Land, became lodged in a snow covered crevasse on landing, causing major damage to the $100m aircraft owned by the US National Science Foundation. 'Upstream D' is located deep within a perpetually ice covered region known as West Antarctica.

A group of scientists from California University were carrying out studies of an ice sheet, which was understood to be moving at a rate of 2 inches an hour, and this, says the scientific world, backs their evidence of their global warning supposition.

It had just delivered supplies to the party and was taxiing when the right ski broke through a snow bridge which spanned a 35 metre deep crevasse. The crew immediately sensed serious damage as the Heculas right wing had dropped, causing the outer starboard propeller to strike the snow that was unseasonably soft on top.

As the aircraft came to an abrupt stop, its left ski had gone through the snow bridge, with the wing tip and outer port propeller imbedded in the snow. Speaking from Antarctica at the time to Associate Press, Simon Stephenson, of the National Science Foundation, said with tongue in cheek, *'It's pretty safe where it is, nobody's going to touch it, and it's not going to move.'*

Prior to any recovery plans, Engineers at the Cold Regions Research & Engineering Laboratories [CRREL] in Hanover, NH, and field safety experts from Antarctic Support Associates [ASA] Denver, Colo, surveyed the site and surrounding areas to insure it was safe for technicians from the Air Force Personnel and an Air New Zealand Engineering team from Christchurch.

This operation involved recently developed ground penetrating radar, along with Arial satellite imaging that was able to detect crevasses beneath the icy surface. Had this science been available to the early *Operation Deep Freeze* aviators, dozens of lives would have been saved.

Commenting on the procedure employed, Major Bob Bullock, the 109th Public Affairs Officer. *'The ASA team operating heavy equipment, including two bulldozers flown in from McMurdo, worked for days filling a board section of the deep ice fissure.'*

Up to 30 maintenance personnel from the 109th Airlift wing, together with the Combat Logistics Support Squadron from Robbins Air Force Base Ga., stabilized the area under the aircraft's main ski using plywood planking and 12 x 12-foot airbags, and by digging the snow from under the right main and nose skis, allowing the C-130 to be raised to a level position.

A mayday went out to the engineers from Air New Zealand's Engineering Maintenance workshops in Christchurch, New Zealand, by Chief Master Sergeant Arthur Bleich of the New York ANG, for technical skilled assistance and to assist in the assessment of the LC-130.

Soon a team lead by Dave Roche, with Aircraft Maintenance foreman Peter Thomson, and Design Engineer Graeme Howden were boarding a RNZAF C-130H enroute to McMurdo, arriving on the third attempt.

'We had the basic details, but didn't really know what to expect until we arrived on site.' says Dave Roche. *'John and I did the initial survey, and we were there for around 19 days, spending four hours surveying the aircraft. It was in much better shape than we thought it might be, so John came back to Christchurch a little early to work on the technical aspects.*

The AUSAF were responsible for procuring the parts, while our basic task was to provide technical advice, what they could do, and basically how to get the aircraft out of the crevasse; what needed to be done on site, and what could be done at McMurdo before flying the machine back to Christchurch-that kind of thing.' a very modest Dave Roche told me. The ANZES team then had to establish an inspection schedule before leaving Christchurch.

Returning to McMurdo and after preliminary meetings with the Guard, the crew made two attempts before arriving at Upstream D on the far side of the Ross Sea Ice Shelf. In the past, extensive damage had been caused in these recovery situations by inadequate technical knowledge, however, Dave Roche had a lot of experience with the C-130 skis, resulting in a different methodology and "Kiwi" applied science. John Thomson designed a new type of towing bridal after Dave had sketched out the initial requirement, while Bob Howden Engineering manufactured the sling after Graeme Howden spent some five weeks in Antarctica in sub zero temperatures. The other two entrepreneurial Air New Zealand engineers flew back earlier.

'The Herc's skis are very delicate and require special treatment to avoid serious and expensive damage' Dave Roche said *'Hence the meticulous engineering application which went into the final design, based on our knowledge of the C-130's and their ski structure.'*

Preparations for the recovery operation were finalized on Christmas Day, and the Herk was towed out of the crevasse by bulldozer to an area where repairs could be carried out.

On January 4th after temporary site repairs to the right aileron, and after various detailed structural checks in below zero conditions, the thirty year old -*# 159130 XD/04* LC-130 was flown to the United States Naval Facilities at McMurdo, then on to Air New Zealand's Engineering facilities in Christchurch on January 6, where maintenance staff undertook a number of checks, including a complete X-Ray analysis and the fitting of a new engine.

Coincidentally, the VXE-6 C-130 # *148321*, which crashed on December 1971 and was abandoned only to be retrieved from its frozen resting place in December 1986, repaired on the site and returned to Antarctic operations, had Dave Roche as the Foreman in charge of repairs while Graeme Howden was an apprentice.

Air New Zealand was appointed as an approved Hercules Service Centre by Lockheed Martin Aeronautical Systems early in 1997.The appointment recognizes the capabilities of ANZES to provide support for tactical military C-130 and the commercial Hercules L-100 aircraft. The company had had extensive experience in servicing Hercules for the RNZAF, the RAAF, and the LC-130's operated by the Air National Guard and previously the US Navy's VXE-6 Squadron for the National Science Foundation.

ANZES, a division of Air New Zealand, employs over 2,000 staff in its Auckland, Christchurch and Blenheim facilities where they are authorized by Lockheed Martin to provide repairs maintenance, overhauls and modification services on Hercules at their Christchurch facilities, while engine overhauls are handled in Auckland, and the Blenheim workshops overhaul propellers.

There has never been any love lost between the two military units providing air support and logistic service to *Operation Deep Freeze,* while the US Navy and the USAF do work in close relationship, the Air Force is a different story. To my knowledge there has never been a military organization that did not in some way, compete with one another even when on the same side. Peter Lund a network engineer for Antarctic Support Association wrote in 1998.

'They compete to see who is the best, the toughest, the meanest, the loudest, the quietest, the deadliest, the bravest, the smartest, the fastest and any other 'est' you can think of [get your mind out of the gutter.] In this spirit, the US Air Force and the US Navy have been competing with each other for some time, roughly since 1947, and more recently since the retirement of the Navy Support Force Antarctic [NSFA] and the downsizing of VXE-6.

The Navy has had a presence in Antarctica for 42 years with the official mission ending in 1999 when the NSFA left, but the need for military support did not vanish. It was still necessary to utilize military aircraft to provide logistical support for personnel and critical cargo, and it was at this point that the US Air Force and NYANG was brought into the picture.

When the Navy flew in at the WinFly station opening they flew their ski equipped LC-130, and there were times,' writes Lund, *'when the weather was rough enough to force the Navy to turn around and try again another day - weather similar to a hurricane. Down here we call that a Herbie. Regardless, the first flight always brought in freshies, but for some reason in the two years since the Air Force has been flying at WinFly, there has never been any plane except the first that brings in the freshies- although it's never planned that way, there is always some kind of excuse given.*

This year [1998] the Air Force continues it's mighty tradition of making the Navy look really good. When a little LC-130 can land in whiteout conditions it boggles the mind as to why it's so hard to land a big jet powered C-141 when the skies are clear, the wind is calm and the sun is high.

To date for this season, there have been eleven attempts to deliver passengers and cargo to McMurdo by USAF C-141. Of these eleven attempts, only four flights have actually successfully reached their destination, roughly a 36 percent success rate. That's amazing since they have us line the runway with tail wire wrapped poles so the runway outline would show up on radar. The NSF has planned 300 flights to the South Pole this year but at this rate they'll only break 100, so it's a good thing they're bringing back VXE-6 for one more season.

I must say I'd rather have a safe pilot than a daredevil. Arriving alive is a lot better than arriving with your bunny boots wrapped around your ears. However, when the guys in weather say clear and bright sunny skies, no crosswinds, and the pilot decides that means glare on the ice so it might be hard to see, turn around – you've gotta wonder. Especially since C-5 pilots who took off an hour behind the C-141, somehow managed to land despite the good weather. I'm told that the successful pilot gave quite a ribbing to the other.'

Peter Lund has praise for the NYANG aircrews just as he has for VXE-6, recalling early October 1998 *'with conditions at the runways, where one couldn't see ones hand in front of ones face, it had been two weeks since the last plane had landed, and while an attempt was made each day to depart Christchurch, the passengers there were subject to endless call ups then delays. The USAF had decided to give up their attempts at landing a C-141 or a C-5A on the ice as they had originally planned, and instead they decided to use an LC-130 flown by the 109th Air-Wing -New York National Guard. They figured that if all else fails this plane could land in a whiteout zone like their Navy counterparts.*

On it, their most important passengers are a very senior US Air Force weather observer, the kind of guy who is capable of revising the Air Force Visual Flight Rules [VFR] policies. Apparently the way that the policies are written there is absolutely no way for an Air Force plane to land unless there is some officer, senior to the pilot nearby, who can take the blame if something goes wrong. Once he's there, he'll look out the window and say, 'Things look nice- the pilot can land'.

This takes the onus off the pilot and places it on himself, so if the pilot crashes the plane, he can say, 'The weather guy made me do it', and the weather guy will say 'Conditions were acceptable, the pilot must have made an error'. Since the weather guy is senior, everyone will agree with him. The pilot will probably be ok, but he'll never make General, worse is he could fly for United Airlines and make it.

Of course, what will really happen is something much more tame. The USAF weather observer will determine that conditions for landing are acceptable, and flights of C-141 and C-5's will resume. Weather conditions will be the same as all other days that the planes turn around, only this time the planes will land. The Air Force will continue that it will be necessary to have a senior person on station prior to all Main Body flights since that's almost the only way that an Air Force plane can land anywhere.

At some point we might even get an Instrument Landing System [ILS] installed making this all moot. At the end of the day what does all this jabber mean? It means that for the last two weeks there have been people stuck here who don't want to be here anymore. The winter crew needs to rotate out and get some much deserved and needed rest and relaxation. The newcomers need to get their excited and rested butts down here and get to work. But this whole thing can be distilled even further in just one sentence. The Navy would have landed.' concludes Peter Lund.

CHAPTER EIGHTEEN.

COMMANDER JACKSON'S LAST RIDE.
AFTER 44 YEARS IN CHRISTCHURCH VXE-6 GO HOME.

An end of an era-the United States Navy hands over the command of
Operation Deep Freeze to the New York Air National Guards 109th Air Lift
wing and the squadron flies out of Antarctica and Christchurch
after 44 years of 'A Job Well Done.'

On February 17 1999, VX-E-6 Commander David W Jackson lifted the last aircraft, a Lockheed C-130 # *159130* appropriately name *The Spirit of Willy Field* from the McMurdo ice airstrip effectively ending 44 years service and a long tradition of the US Navy's involvement with the most remote part of the world and the close association with the City of Christchurch which had become the squadron's second home.

As he circled out over the Ross Sea Ice, passed over McMurdo, Scott Base, and took a last look at Willy Field and the Old Little America V for the last time, memories flooded back. Cdr Jackson, his eyes moist, remembered all those squadron members from Capt Hawkes and Lt Shinn to his own 178th squadron personnel with pride in the knowledge of a job well done.

Touching down at Christchurch International Airport, the Squadron's home since 1955, was an emotional one, but a number of the squadron's veterans now living in Christchurch felt more than a little anger and a complete sense of loss at VXE-6 being phased out, and the somewhat ungainly Hercules, the Ice Queen to some, being mothballed in the burning desert air of Arizona. This boneyard was lined with rows of military and commercial aircraft, unwanted and waiting for the grim reaper to visit their resting area.

During *Deep Freeze-99* the Squadron's LC-130 airlift schedule was the busiest on record flying almost 500 missions, and 320 of these to the South Pole alone. During this remarkable season, a contrast to the previous when the Antarctic was plagued by the worst weather in 24 years, *Deep Freeze* 99 saw uncharacteristically mild weather at McMurdo Station, while being extremely variable in the field. The squadron flew over 1200 hours delivering two and a half million pounds of cargo without mishaps or injuries. Following the closure of the South Pole Station summer operations in mid February, VXE-6 return to ANS Point Muga CA to be disestablished.

Then late in the afternoon as the sun was setting, a large gathering of Squadron members, media and friends, watched as the lone VXE-6 C-130 made its approach to Christchurch International Airport, its bright red tail so familiar in the city's sky for over 44 years, come into view. Lt Commander Dave Jackson made several low passes over the airfield before coming to rest outside the squadron's hanger off Orchard Road, signalling the end of the US Navy's VXE-6 squadron presence in Christchurch, to a sad conclusion.

While waiting for Lt Commander Jackson to taxi # *159130* to the hanger I [the author] had a chance to meet again with an old friend Frank Kazukaitis, the photographer with inspiration and enthusiasm, and one of the squadron's charismatic characters. 'Kaz' could well have come straight from the pages of Readers Digest's *The Most Unforgettable Character.*

Above the noise of the Hercules's turbo-prop engines, Frank told me a little about his naval photography career where during more than sixty years he had been taking photographs to document his experiences of places and events from where he had travelled throughout the world for the US Navy.

Born in St Louis, Missouri in 1927 to Lithuanian immigrant parents, Kaz soon developed an interest in photography, when at an early age, he aquired his first camera as a prize in a competition in the Bob Hope Show. He lived in Christchurch for a number of years, but following a stroke in 1999 Kaz became confined to a wheelchair, but his home is a reservoir of pictorial knowledge and a true visual history of America's military and civil combats. He joined the Navy in 1945 when a vacancy became available on the Navy News for a photo lithographer, which he felt was a position just right for him. At first his application wasn't taken seriously, but persistence and the same determination that he later applied to his photography won through, and he was subsequently appointed to the post.

His photography involved long hours, not only documenting naval activities on Guam, but also the aftermath of the war and the trials of Japanese war criminals. Later Kaz was to spend two years on roving photographic assignments in the Pacific, before joining the crew of USS *Burton Island* with *Operation Micro X* in the Arctic. During this mission he captured some remarkable photographic imagery of sea and ice, which was certainly advantageous to his later commissions with *Operation Deep Freeze* a decade later.

With the beginning of hostilities in Korea on June 25 1950, Kaz was posted to the UN Headquarters in Kaesong to cover the war, and for the next three years witnessed and photographed many aspects of the conflict, not only of the American Marine forces, but the civilian population too, in both the North and South Korea. He was the only photographer permitted by the North Koreans to be present at the signing of the armistice and he volunteered for Operation Deep Freeze in 1958 joining VX-6 squadron in Antarctica.

Kaz wintered over at McMurdo for the 1958-59 season, arriving in Christchurch in October 1958 before travelling south for the next seventeen months. In March 1960, he returned to Christchurch, but during 1961-62 and 63 went back to Antarctica to do summer work on the staff of Commander US Navy Support Force.

Returning to the States in 1963, he worked for a time at the US Navy's Photographic Centre in Washington DC, before taking up a posting as President Johnson's wife's [Ladybird Johnson] official photographer at the White House. Retiring from the Navy in 1968, Kaz returned to Christchurch to live, working for Television New Zealand, and it was during this time he was selected to go to the Antarctic to cover the tragic Flight 901.

In September 1995 Kaz held the first major exhibition of his work entitled '*Visions of the Ice*' as part of the US Navy's 40th anniversary celebrations of Operation Deep Freeze, and three years later he was at the closing ceremony unofficially taking many more photographs.

As Commander Jackson climbed down from his aircraft BuNo *#159130* he was warmly greeted by the remaining squadron members and received the Navy's traditional dousing of cold water. He told the media '*It's a sad day and it's very emotional, but a proud and sombre day for the men and women of VXE-6 and today I am proud to say that our mission is done*'.

As I stood on the apron amidst misty eyed squadron members, one could almost reach out and touch these gallant aviators, these OAE greats of yesteryear who departed for Antarctica and the unknown from RNZAF AFB, Wigram a few miles east of Christchurch International Airport on December 20 1955, just 44 years ago on that cold Christchurch morning, to following in the footsteps of other pioneering aviators.

Sadly many of these pioneers have passed away but they would have been settled in their celestial Mess enjoying a quiet drink while looking down on Cdr Jackson and his crew finishing a Job

Well Done, and satisfied in their own minds that under his command VXE-6 had continued in the true tradition of the squadron's motto- *'COURAGE-SACRIFICE- DEVOTION.'* As they raised their glasses on high to salute a whole generation of Antarctic aviators, they would be reminiscing about their early years in Antarctica, on the cold R4-D flights, living in tents at Hut Point until the ships brought in supplies and building materials, and the hardships which prevailed in sub zero conditions.

All those who followed at times could best be described as swashbuckling, but always unyielding in the tasks assigned them even if this meant going beyond the norm, but they were never foolhardy, as they respected the Antarctic and its treacherous terrain and its extreme quickness and unpredictable weather.

Cdr Jackson, who took over the Squadron's command from Cdr W Warlock III in early June 1998, was designated a Naval Flight Officer in 1982, completing his first fleet tour with the Patrol Squadron 43 [VP-47] at NAS Moffett Field, after which he qualified in the P-3c aircraft. In 1989, after a tour of duty as an instructor to the west coast P-3 Fleet Readiness Squadron, Cdr Jackson served as the P-3c Commander Sea Duty Component, Dallas Detachment as Special Officer.

After completing this tour of duty, he attended the Naval War College in Newport where he earned a Master of Arts Degree in National Security and Strategic Studies. Returning to the fleet in 1992, Cdr Jackson completed his department head tour with Patrol Squadron 40 at NAS Moffett Field, serving as the Safety Officer, Training Officer and Operations Officer, and in addition, he was O-I-C for detachments to Adak Alaska, and Acapulco Mexico, and completed a deployment to Misawa, Japan. Cdr David Jackson reported to VXE-6 in April 1997 as the Executive Officer, before assuming Command.

During his career right up to the end of VXE-6 Command, he had accumulated over 4200 flight hours, and was awarded the Defence Meritorious Service Medal, the Meritorious Service Medal, the Navy Commendation Medal with one star, the Navy Achievement Medal and various unit and service awards.

One of the last four C-130's to return from Antarctica was piloted Lt Nancy Hadeau, who also doubled as Public Affairs officer. When asked of the Hercules, she spoke affectionately of the aircraft. *'They, like the Douglas R4-D's, were the workhorses -one of these is 39 years old, even older than me, but we have certainly had good use of them. They have had to work in extremely harsh conditions like the day I flew to the South Pole, it was negative 51 degree Celsius and that's not including the wind-chill factor.'*

The day after his arrival, over a quiet and pleasant lunch with Major Bob Bullock the ANG's public affairs Officer, Cdr. Jackson said of the Navy, *'there has been a lot of tremendously meaningful moments this week, as the era of VXE-6 squadron in Christchurch came to an end with the last flight from the south Pole and the last from McMurdo and the culmination of the final arrival. It's all meant so much to the people of Christchurch; it's a monumental step really and is the end of a tremendous journey. The squadron members had built up strong ties with the city where many had met their wife's here.'*

Kaz loaded with his prize collection of cameras was one of the last to leave the squadron's hanger. He knew a few old faces but not too many, but whatever, the sight of the C-130 and its crew brought back a flood of memories to this now frail Old Antarctic Explorer. Since then I have indeed had the privilege of spending many hours in his quaint old English style Christchurch home with its walls lined with original black and white photographs of some of his prized works.

It's a microcosmic flash back of those pioneering days of Deep Freeze, with Kaz reliving his time on the ice. During the intervening 44 years, VXE-6 Squadron's aircraft transported more than 195,000 passengers, 240 million pounds of dry cargo and almost 19 million gallons of fuel to Antarctic sites.

A few days later, tears were the order of the day, as the US Navy said farewell to Christchurch, thus ending over four decades of close collaboration with the city, when the Squadron was disestablished in an emotional ceremony at the Christchurch Antarctic Centre at the city's International airport, thus handing over the Antarctic operation to the New York Air National Guard 109th airlift wing. The city said goodbye to the US Navy whilst welcoming the New York Air National Guard.

Speakers emphasised the close association between the US Forces and Christchurch. The United States Ambassador to New Zealand, Josiah H Beeman, was on hand on December 2 1996 at the dedication ceremony for the ANG's LC-130 *The City of Christchurch*.

'*It was fitting,*' the Ambassador told me, '*that the Air National Guard named their newest Lockheed after the city of Christchurch. Let this sincere gesture of respect and friendship serve as a reminder of the stability of the relationship we, the US have enjoyed with your community.*'

After years in the Navy, the outgoing Commanding Officer of *Operation Deep Freeze*, Commander John W Stotz, a native of Elizabethtown, Pennsylvania, had been the groups commander since 1996. He said the Navy's role in Antarctica had been in transition for the past 15 years, with services such as construction crews and food services at McMurdo being handed over to private contractors.

'*The Navy's Seabees carried out all the services and they built McMurdo and all other stations,*' John told me with a little nostalgia, tinged with a degree of sadness.

'*In those days conditions in the Antarctic were almost impossible to imagine by to day's aircrews, as to day MacTown is a small America with radio, television, four-star living conditions with air conditioning, bars, theatres and motel type accommodation.*'

Commander Stotz's next posting was a new position as bomber Ranger Management, Naval Strike and Warfare, Nevada.

With the change over from the US Navy to the USAF's Air National Guard, the command of Operation Deep Freeze was passed to Lt Col Richard M Saburro, himself a veteran of Antarctic and no stranger to polar flying.

He recalled in a forward to Tony Phillips's superb book '*Gateway to the Ice*' -*Christchurch International Airport- Antarctic Air Links from 1955* the trailblazing accomplishments of the US Navy's Antarctic Development Squadron-VXE-6 and the exploits of early USAF and Royal New Zealand Air Force.

'*Monday, 12 February 2001 was clear and sunny. We were descending from cruise altitude of 25,000 feet over the polar plateau and I was in the pilot's seat grabbing some 'stick time'. I was escorting the Air Mobility Command director of operations, Major General Roger Brady on a visit to the South Pole. At 30 miles out I had completed the descent and began flying the airborne radar approach to the skiway. I was now focused on my instruments and the task at hand, not giving immediate thought to the significance of this particular flight.*

This approach and ski landing would be my last of 22 years as a polar qualified LC-130 pilot. It would also be my final mission to the South Pole after countless Pole missions in my 11 years of Antarctic flying. The landing was smooth and uneventful – always a good way to end a day, as well as a career. As the aircraft slid along the skiway I gradually relaxed my concentration and began scanning the landscape searching in anticipation for my first glimpses of the new South Pole station, which had began taking shape just weeks before.

There it was! The shell of the first section was standing tall and proud, elevated on columns high above the snow, prominent against the polar landscape. In contrast, the famous dome now receded into the background.

This was a proud moment for me. The new structure vividly represented the hundreds of LC-130 flights and the efforts of hundreds of Deep Freeze contractor personnel since the South Pole moderation programme began many seasons ago.

Project engineer John Rand, gave General Brady and myself a tour of the new station and as we walked about the interior John pointed out the areas that would become the sleeping quarters, kitchen and dinning area, and I was struck by the spaciousness and comfortable warmth. Windows at the front allowing a bird's eye view of the famous 'ceremonial' barber pole and geographic pole markers outside. I didn't feel like I was at the South Pole. Previous to this the only window view I had had of the South Pole markers was from inside the cockpit of an LC-130.

My tour of the new station left me thinking back to how it used to be eleven years ago when I made my first flight and much further back to Gus Shinn's famous first landing in Que Sera Sera.

Christchurch International Airport has been the main staging location for Antarctic logistics operations for over 40 years, and Christchurch is ideal owing to its proximity to Ross Island, the southern most location permitting access to the sea and only 800 miles from the South Pole. But beyond the geographic imperative, Christchurch holds a special significance for all who are involved in the Antarctic programme. Through the years the people of Christchurch have embraced Antarctic exploration and the explorers, and we feel welcome and among friends here as the people of Christchurch have a profound understanding and appreciation for what we do. They are justifiably proud of their Antarctic heritage.

As I write this forward I am preparing to depart the city, soon completing my assignment as Operation Deep Freeze Commander. But, as with many before me, Christchurch will never leave my memory or my heart.'

Lt Colonel Richard Saburro had been flying Arctic mission support for the Distant Early Warning radar sites on the Greenland Ice-cap. He advanced through the 139th Airlift Squadron chain of command from flight commander to executive officer then chief pilot to Squadron Commander to *Operation Deep Freeze's* first Air Force command.

A bachelor of Science with a degree with Physics he began his USAF career in the late 1960's when he was assigned to the 6th MAS at McGuire AFB as a Lockheed C-141 pilot, where he flew airlift Channel missions, Presidential support, nuclear and combat support to Southeast Asia during the Vietnam conflict.

The then vice commander of the NYNG, Colonel Graham Pritchard, began his polar career with an assignment, after initial pilot training with the 17th Tactical Airlift Squadron of the Alaskan Air Command at Elmendorf AFB, Alaska, he has a long association with the C-130 to flying the C-130D, and told the large gathering at the disestablishment ceremony, that after flying LC-130's in the Arctic and Antarctica, *'You're always careful to watch the weather and you watch the condition of the aircraft because it's a very different flying environment. You can never take it for granted even when you're familiar with it.*

The New York Air National Guard has 24 ice trained crews each comprising five personnel and will be deploying five crews and aircraft from Christchurch. The guard is a mixture of permanent and reserve staff members, liable to be called up from their regular civilian jobs in New York for short stints.

Although I am experience in the Arctic, the vastness and distances of the Antarctic are so much greater. You get to the edge of the continent and then it's a further two hours until you finally reach McMurdo, so the vastness of the continent is quite impressive. How those guys from VX-6 did it in twin engine R4-D's and Neptune's I will never know.' he concluded.

American Ambassador to New Zealand Josiah Beeman praised the contributions the US Navy made in the peaceful pursuit of Antarctic exploration and science, as unparalleled.

'It was Byrd who piloted the first flight over the South Pole in 1929, a flight which sparked the imagination of people everywhere. It was Byrd who commanded the US Naval forces of the US Antarctic Service Expedition from 1939-40 when scientific investigation assumed a prominent role. It was Byrd who served as officer-in-charge in 1947 for the largest Antarctic expedition in history, the

US Navy Operation Highjump. It was Byrd who raised the US flag over the base camp at Little America in 1955-56 in preparation for US participation in the IGY IN 1977-58. It was Byrd under the direction of President Eisenhower who helped supervise preparations for Operation Deep Freeze.

The greatest tribute to the US Navy, and VXE-6 in particular, I believe, is the knowledge that its efforts will be the foundation upon which all future US endeavours in Antarctica are built in the 21st century and beyond. The US Navy's contributions will not and cannot be forgotten.

Although the US Navy's VXE-6 Squadron served one more year in an auxiliary role in LC-130 flight operations during 1998-99 scientific research season it will be the New York State Air National Guard that will step in as from today, assuming full responsibility for all Hercules flights in support to the ice beginning next year. Although there will be fewer uniformed military personnel on the ground in Christchurch, I have no doubt that in both their professional and civic life, the officers and air crews of the ANG will build their own legacy of excellence as the ASNG serves the United States Antarctic Programme. Already under the fine leadership of Lt Colonel Richard Saburro it began to build positive relationships with the wider Christchurch community.

We enthusiastically welcome the ANG to Christchurch. In addition some aspects of the Navy's work will be taken over by civilian contractors, which will create more opportunities for New Zealand companies, such as the recent maintenance contract awarded to Air New Zealand. Today we celebrate the bright future of the US Antarctic Programme as we honour the exceptional contribution of the US Navy we know that the character of the US Antarctic Programme has been forever influenced by those contributions.

While the international community has accomplished much in Antarctica through cooperation under the Treaty system, we acknowledge that there are countless questions concerning the continent still unanswered. We have just begun to tap into the scientific story of Antarctica.

The NAS with the support of the ANG and in cooperation with other treaty nations especially New Zealand, will continue to bring honour and success to future research and science endeavours on the ice.'

Ambassador Beeman then thanked the City of Christchurch for its continued support and concluded with a quote from President John F Kennedy which within its contents emphasized the contribution the US Navy and the men and women of VXE-6 Squadron made to Antarctic exploration. *' Science is the most powerful means we have for the unification of knowledge, and the main obligation of its future must be to deal with problems which cut across boundaries, whether boundaries between the sciences, boundaries between nations, or boundaries between man's scientific and his humane concerns. Scientific advances have not only made international cooperation desirable, but they have made it essential. The oceans, the atmosphere, outer space, belong not to one nation but to all mankind.'*

Other speakers at the Navy's Disestablishment and Antarctic Programme Transition Ceremony were the Assistance Secretary of the Navy, Robert Pirie Jr, the Commander Naval Base Pearl Harbour and Commander Naval Surface Group Middle Pacific, William Sutton, the Commander of the Naval Support Force Antarctica, Capt Hugh Smith, the Polar Research Support Section, NSF's Erick Chang and the USNR Chaplain Lt Cdr Manuel Mak.

The invocation by the squadron's Chaplain Lt Cdr Mark Smith USN told those gathered.

'Almighty God, Navy Victor Xray Echo Six is prepared to land. Grant us clear deck in the known world, for the Pirates have conducted their final raid on the icy continent and are bringing their treasures home. Treasures gained from 44 years of soaring skies above the terrain few others have seen. Treasures born of devoted and courageous aviators sharing a mission unlike any others, and the memories of what we did together for the benefit of humankind.

Though we as a squadron will not fly Antarctica again in planes, we will continue the flight in the stories we have to tell.

For like any aviators before us, we have loosed the surly bonds of earth and been blessed to reach out and touch your face. But we have also held your hidden handiwork in trust, and seen crystalline sparkles of what could almost be your frozen tears of joy from the day of creation. Some of our tears remain there also, for so do the spirits of our comrades who did not return with us. May memories be ever sacred in our hearts, as we remember their sacrifice, and as we pass this trust of our treasures on to those who will continue the adventures we must leave. Bless all who discover the wonders of your creation, and keep them safe wherever they must go in your name and mercy. Amen.'

The Navy left the City of Christchurch on February 22 1999, two days after the city of Christchurch held a farewell function in Air New Zealand's maintenance facility at Christchurch International Airport. The last VXE-6 aircraft to leave the city were # *148320* and # *148321* respectively, an hour apart, hence severing their 44 year link.

The NYANG's 109th Air Wing is based at Schenectady, near Albany, in upstate New York where their history began in 1948 as the then 139th Fighter Squadron commissioned to fly the P-47 Thunderbolts and reorganized as the 139th Fighter Interception Squadron converting to F-94A Starfires in 1956. The unit was again brought up to date with the issue of the F-86 B Sabre jet when it then became the 109th. In 1969 the airlift wing assumed the cargo carrying missions as a member of the Military Airlift Command [MAT], when the group acquired a Boeing C-97 Stratocruiser that was equipped to airlift for the direct support of US troops around the world.

In October 1961, the unit was activated in support of the Berlin Crisis, flying cargo and personnel primarily to Europe, where the men and women of the 109th completed this mission with distinction and since then the 109th has performed its assigned missions on virtually every continent.

In 1971 the 109th missions again changed with the acquisition of their Hercules C-130A's, when the group subsequently began providing airlift transport in support of ground operations under the direction of the Tactical Air Command [TAC].

Four years later the 109th was awarded the polar cap airlift mission in addition to its other responsibilities. Their C-130D's arrived straight from the production line of Lockheed, equipped with skis for the aircraft to land on the snow and ice of Greenland, and they received four new C-130's in 1984, and three more in 1996.

In 1975, the USAF directed the ice cap resupply of the Distant Early Warning [DEW] defence radar site in Greenland with fuel oil, personnel and large cargo. This mission was now transferred to the Air National Guard with the 109th thus ending the era of the 17th TAS, who had assumed the role on July 1 1964 becoming know as The Firebirds by taking its name from the Jet Assisted Take-Off bottles. The squadron's non-ski C-130D's were used to service the remote radar sites in Alaska, most of which had gravel runways, leaving their two ski-equipped Hercules who were unsuitable for the gravel landing strips, stationed at Sondrestrom.

On a weekly rotational basis it was flown from Sondrestrom to Elmendorf on the long flight over the high ice covered Arctic, where it relieved the other C-130, and the Firebirds continued these missions for ten years with only one serious accident when on June 5 1972 # *70495* stalled out on an attempted flight around at DYE 3 and crashed onto the ice. Although the crew suffered only minor injuries, the aircraft was a write off, so parts were salvaged as spare components, leaving the aircraft on the ice to eventually be buried by the snow.

The possibility of the Air National Guard taking over *Operation Deep Freeze* from the Navy's VXE-6 squadron emerged in 1988, with them inheriting the responsibility of the airlift support and logistics for the NSF in Antarctica. The ANG 109th airlift wing had been notified almost overnight that with the end of the cold war, one of the Distant Early Warning [DEW] Line radar sites that it supported in Greenland was going to shut down, and other Arctic sites would soon follow leaving the unit largely out of business.

While the wing had been keeping tabs of the Navy's LC-130's informally for a year or so, they noted that the Navy's Hercules were older than those being operated by the 109th with a number of them spending periods with the squadron's maintenance in both Christchurch and the US.

The US Navy had requested that the 109th provide a limited emergency search and rescue capability for two years, so the ANG accepted the chance of flying in the Antarctic where some of their aircraft had flown before, although not on a regular basis. Some within the 109th believed that it was muddle headed for its aircraft and experienced crews to be deployed just to wait to conduct backup in an emergency, so instead it asked the Navy if the unit could assist by carrying cargo to the South Pole.

At first this was rejected on the grounds that the Navy's procedures and cage configurations differed from those of the Guard's, however, the Navy relented, so that the main mission of VXE-6 and the LC-130's of the 109th was to airlift supplies and fuel to the National Science Foundation's station at the Pole for the personnel wintering there and isolated between February and October.

With the advancement of today's Antarctic aviation with its modern technology and aircraft design, the logistic missions handed over to the NYNG's 109th by VXE-6 was now a simpler one, or in the words of Colonel Saburro 'rather routine'. With frequent flights south by the USAF's C-141B Starlifters and Lockheed C-15B Galaxy's coming and going from Christchurch to Antarctica, it must seem routine to the casual observer.

On June 11 1999, a few months after the VXE-6's official disestablishment, a small cadre of Squadron personnel gathered in the detachment office to witness their last CO Cdr. J Dickinson present the 1998 Grampaw Pettibone Unit Award for safety to the squadron's Safety Officer Lt Cdr Evans.

In the official notification message R.Adm.Nathman sent his personal congratulations to the men and women of VXE-6, accumulating 44 years of Antarctic flying and a long history of safety article submissions, prior to decommissioning.

'The Ice Pirates of VXE-6 had demonstrated tremendous achievements in aviation safety. Over the previous ten years and in particular 1998, you submitted a stream of outstanding safety related articles to 'Approach' magazine. You had the unique opportunity to operate in the worst flying environment on earth and passed your lessons learned on to fellow aviators who have benefited tremendously by the publications and articles contributed significantly to your squadrons safety awareness, and reflected the strength of your command's safety programme. This award serves as a well deserved tribute and farewell to VXE-6.'

Commander Dickinson also praised Lt Cdr Evans for the prestigious award, saying that he was the driving force behind all the articles the squadron had submitted to 'Approach'. 'He beat the drum to convince squadron personnel to document their experiences in a user-friendly easy to read format. The chain of command above the Safety Officer did very little in the way of polishing the articles, as 'Approach' magazine is known for it's first hand stories. Aviators read the stories because they are written by other aviators, that empathy value alone keeps readers coming back, regardless of the type of aircraft we fly.

In the history of Naval Aviation, only a small handful of aviators and aircrews have operated ski-equipped aircraft in the middle of an Antarctic snowfield. Nonetheless, the majority of professional aviators have had to deal with icing conditions, cold temperatures, low visibility or high altitude, VXE-6 aircrews simply encountered these challenging conditions as a matter of routine for five months out of the year, for 44 consecutive years. Our stories did not need to be embellished to be entertaining, if anything, they had to be toned down to appear plausible.'

Following the March disestablishment, the majority of the Ice Pirates were transferred to a variety of duty stations as diverse and widespread as the Navy itself. 'If there is one single location that is the most convenient for the majority of us, it is probably San Diego' said Cdr Dickinson, 'I selected that location first, as a lot of our folk are either in San Diego or somewhere nearby in

Southern California. If we can spare the time, we will all find some way to get there. The other reason is a little more tactical, I needed someone to buy the cake and host Admiral Nathman.'

At the time of the presentation, Cdr.Dickinson was logistic Programmes Officer, Naval Weapons Test Squadron at Point Mugu. Also attending the function were the squadron's Commanding Officer Cdr. David Jackson and Captain Mawhinney.

During the 44 years *Operation Deep Freeze* was based in Christchurch, a large number of American Navy personnel married Christchurch girls, and an equal number of those marriages lasted only a season or two, but there were the exceptions, with a number of VX-6 squadron still living happily in Christchurch and other parts of New Zealand. Aviators such as David Weyer who owns the Ranfurly Hotel in Southland, David, whom I had the pleasure of spending a weekend with recently, was an aviation Machinist Mate 2nd Class who wintered over at the time when R4-D's were stored during the winter months and who's job it fell to dig them out for restoration in readiness for the summer season. David was an Otter Plane Captain and C-47 Flight Engineer.

One of the success stories, and there were many, is Dennis Brown who began his VX-6 duties in 1972/77 as an AT2 [E1] and during his second tour of duty [1981-94] was an ATCS- [Senior Chief]. During his first deployment, he met and married Denise Mehlhopt during *Deep Freeze 77*, a Timaru girl whos father Jack, in Dennis' words, was *'a retired social worker, a terrific man who eats and sleeps aviation and vintage cars. In fact he was involved with a group of aviation enthusiast who attempted to get Richard Pearse's plane 'The Flier' airborne early in 2003. Pearse's first flight on March 31 1904, when he made one powered take off, is considered by New Zealanders as the first man to fly- nine months before the Wright Brothers.'*

Married against the desire of the Officer in Charge in Christchurch, he received official Navy permission to marry by his commander Lt.Cdr Ken Gainer, who told Dennis that the odds of a lasting relationship were statistically against him, and that he was not speaking ill of Kiwi women.

When the Old Antarctic Explorers gather in Pensacola for the squadron's 50th anniversary, the memorabilia and memories of their days on the ice and their stay in the Garden City of Christchurch, will be told and retold as coloured nostalgic stories.

May I end this history of 44 years with a story told by Farrell Whitney, another OAE who married a Christchurch girl, in a nostalgic look at the early years of Deep Freeze during his time at Wigram, the RNZAF station near Christchurch. Here he remembers the recipes for chow that was served in the mess hall, whether they ate them or not.

'I can smell them still! You sat at the table with all the white linen and all properly laid out in the Sergeant's Mess and the waiter took your order. The toast was hand cut and thick as the back of your hand and stacked in a wire rack like sheets of plywood side by side, with the menu all hand written to perfection. What to order?

This day I will have the eggs over easy and bacon.

Tea! How many Yanks drink tea for breakfast? Bring me coffee, strong and black, and that is exactly how it arrived! New Zealand coffee was not made only of coffee, but had chicory added and was bitter. Thank God for the great milk of New Zealand with its thick cream on top of the bottle.

And now the bacon and eggs have arrived, and as the waiter places the plate in front of you the eggs magically slide back and forth on the plate between the bacon [and they are thick slices of what we call Canadian Bacon] before coming to 'parade rest!' Ah, this looks good. So you carve up a chunk of bacon and dip it into the yolk and to keep the yolk from dripping, you bend over the plate and it is at this time that the scent enters your nostrils. Your stomach churns and you swallow rapidly to retain the 'libation' you imbibed the night before, with your mind questioning.

What is that vile smell? How can anything look so good and smell so putrid? I call upon my good friend of the NZ Air Force, Phillip 'Hoss' Boyd to give me a tour of the galley. The galley is immaculate as are the chefs, but my main concern was how the eggs were cooked, then I observed this large vat of bubbling fluid into which the cooks would crack open and drop the eggs.

Once the egg was cooked it would float to the surface, where upon the cook would take a skimmer and retrieve the egg and deposit it on a plate where it would swim before drying, and what was this magical fluid?- mutton grease! Now you show me the Yank who had a strong enough stomach to take that lot! Our true savoir was the canteen, which opened for morning tea and you had best get in the line first. There were trays of fresh cut sandwiches covered with a damp tea towel to keep them fresh, only this time the bread had been cut so thin they must have used a razor. The ingredients were put into the sandwiches and then the crusts were removed and the bread was quartered into mini sandwiches. So at sixpence to nine pence a sandwich, the Kiwis made a fortune off the Yanks.

It didn't make any difference that the ingredients were not what we were accustomed to because we were hungry. The egg salads were the first to disappear and if you were near the end of the line, you had your choice of the following; Beans, spaghetti, cucumber or marmite [a yeast meat paste, tasting of pure salt].

For those of you who missed eating in the mess halls of Wigram, you missed a very memorable occasion.'

When he retired from the Navy in 1972, after 25 years, Petty Officer Whitney left the states to live in Christchurch, New Zealand with his Kiwi wife Jane, '*I had more e-mails sent to Whitney Farrell than Farrell Whitney, hence I just use F W Whitney - but most refer to me as Whit which I prefer.'*

When Whit first joined VX-6 in April 1958 as a first class Petty Officer, he spent his first summer season at McMurdo, being sent to the old Byrd Station to set up a re fuelling station. In 1960, he set up an emergency fuel station on The Barrier and became a loadmaster on C-130 *3148321 The Old Grey Mare.* Here he was in for a lot of 'firsts'. Rear Admiral Tyree made most of his flights with this crew. '*And that is when I meet my 'Waterloo', when Admiral Tyree asked me if I had ever wintered over and I related that I had tried but there was always no billet available. He told me I should put in my request for that year so I did and was selected to winter over, not in Antarctica, but at Harewood International Airport as Chief in Charge of the Detachment. I met my wife Janet in June 1962 and we were married in February the following year.'*

Janet Catherine Mary Anderson of Kaiapoi, near Christchurch, was the lucky girl, and after the couple married at St Patrick's Church in the Christchurch suburb of Papanui, they built a house in that area and remained there until 1978, when the couple returned to the US due to an illness in his family. Janet has two brothers Noel and Errol and two sisters who all live in the Kaiapoi area.

After being transferred to short duty at Norfolk Virginia, Whit volunteered to return to VXE-6 and spent the years 1964-67 as Chief Master at Arms and Terminal Chief, in the Garden City. Whit now lives in Southwick Massachusetts.

This book began with the new brand of naval adventurers setting out from the United States in Antarctica – the aviators of VX-6 flying into the unknown, so it is therefore fitting I conclude with one of these aviators Cdr James Edger Waldron, US Naval Reserve [Ret] with views of his first tour of duty wintering over on the white continent in 1956-57.

After his last operational mission on the ice, the commander departed Antarctica homeward bound aboard a squadron's R5-D Skytrain, but as they needed replacement parts from storage in Christchurch, made a round trip.

'I shall never forget while skirting the range of mountains I had flown along for the past 16 months prior, how it was still a beautiful site to see as we left the continent behind us and entered the night stretching out before us. I saw no need for looking out the window since there was nothing to see

for a thousand plus miles. I had brought along my sleeping bag so I climbed into it and slept the rest of the way to Christchurch.

When I woke I was told we were approaching the coastline of New Zealand's South Island, so I went forward to the cockpit for my first glimpse in a long time without ice and snow. It was late spring in New Zealand and my eyes were overwhelmed with the green that covered the earth from horizon to horizon. Remember, I hadn't seen green for many months and my eyes were dazzled and enchanted with so many colours before me and it took me days to adjust to the flood of colour that surrounded us every day. After landing in Christchurch I discovered that I would have to wait several days before any aircraft departed for the States, so I spent my waking hours visiting friends I had met just before departing for the Antarctic on October 16 1956. Everyone that I knew had followed our exploits on a daily basis and they were all happy to see my return.

I went to the ice to test myself in several ways. Could I face extraordinary cold and hazardous flying conditions of Antarctica? Could I handle almost total isolation from civilization, cramped quarters, extreme cold, all with little recreation? Could I live among men also facing isolation and survive in an acceptable manner? I believe I managed to do all this and as a result I came out a much better person. I saw a few who had not managed very well when faced with the terrors and isolation of life on the continent, so I feel fortunate that none of the trials that I faced either broke me or weakened me. All in all it was a wonderful adventure.'

I shall conclude with a quotation from one of the early 20th century Antarctic explorers Sir Douglas Mawson, who gave perhaps the most unimpeachable description of those winds and their effects on men. *'The actual experience is something else. Picture a snowdrift that blots out the world that is hurled, actually screaming with energy, through space in a 100mph wind when the temperature is below freezing. Then shroud these infuriated elements with polar night, and to plunge into such a black white, a writhing storm to stamp on the senses, an indelible, awful impression, seldom equalled in the whole gamut of natural experiences. The world becomes a void, fierce, grisly, appalling; a fearful gloom in which the merciless blast is an incubus of vengeance that stabbed, froze and buffeted intruders with this stinging drift that chokes and blinds.'*

APPENDIX –1.

VX-6 AND VXE-6 SQUADRON COMMANDERS
1955-99.

Cdr E M Ward [acting commander]	17 January 1955-02 April 1955
Cdr G L Ebbie	02 April 1955 to 16 January 1956
Capt D L Cordiner USN	16 January 1956 to 10 May 1957
Cdr V J Coley USN	10 May 1957 to 07 July 1958
Capt Slagle USN	07 July 1958 to 04 May 1959
Cdr J M Barlow USN	04 May 1959 to 21 July 1959
Capt W H Munson USN	21 July 1959 to 01 June 1961
Cdr M D Grennwell	1 June 1961 to 25 April 1962
Cdr W H Everett USN	25 April 1962 to 29 April 1963
Cdr G R Kelly USN	29 April 1963 to 06 May 1964
Cdr F S Gallup USN	06 May 1964 to 05 May 1965
Cdr M E Morris USN	05 May 1965 to 17 June 1966
Cdr D Balish USN	17 June 1966 to 26 April 1967
Cdr A F Schneider USN	26 April 1967 to 14 June 1968
Cdr E W Van Reeth USN	14 June 1968 to 10 July 1969
Cdr J R Pilon USN	10 July 1969 to 24 June 1970.
Cdr D B Eldridge USN	24 June 1970 to 01 July 1971
Cdr C H Nordhill USN	01 July 1971 to 30 June 1972
Cdr J B Dana USN	30 June 1972 to 27 June 1973
Cdr V W Peter USN	27 June 1973 to 18 July 1974.
Cdr F C Holt USN	18 July 1974 to 11 December 1976
Cdr D A Desko USN	11 December 1976 to 02 June 1977
Cdr J W Jeager USN	02 June 1977 to 31 May 1978
Cdr W A Morgan USN	31 May 1978 to 11 May 1979
Cdr D A Srite USN	11 May 1979 to 30 May 1980
Cdr V L Pesco USN	30 May 1980 to 22 May 1981
Cdr P R Dykeman USN	22 May 1981 to 28 May 1982.
Cdr M J Harris USN	28 May 1982 to 27 May 1983.
Cdr M J Radigan USN	27 May 1983 to 25 May 1984
Cdr D D Fisher USN	25 May 1984 to 24 May 1985
Cdr P J Derocher USN	24 May 1985 to 18 April 1986
Cdr J D Mazza USN	18 April 18 1986 to 22 May 1987
Cdr J B Rector USN	22 May 1987 to 27 May 1988.
Cdr J V.Smith USN	27 May 1988 to 26 May 1989.
Cdr K. S Armstrong USN	26 May 1989 to 25 May 1990.
Cdr S E Sebastian USN	25 May 1990 to 22 May 1991
Cdr W.R Reeves USN	22 May 1991 to 15 May 1992
Cdr J D Keho USN	15 May 1992 to 07 May 1993
Cdr M J Duvall USN	07 May 1993 to 19 May 1994
Cdr S G Gardner USN	19 May 1994 to 25 May 1995.
Cdr J P Morin USN	25 May 1995 to 24 May 1996
Cdr W B Stedman USN	24 May 1996 to 06 June 1997

Cdr W F Warlick 111 USN   06 June 1997 to 22 May 1998
Cdr D W Jackson USN   22 May 1998 to 31 March 1999

APPENDIX 2

LEST WE FORGET...
'COURAGE SACRIFIC DEVOTION'

Fifty Americans died in Antarctic during Operation Deep Freeze 1955-99.

By paying the ultimate price for the advance of science, twenty-six sailors, aviators and Marines gave their life while assigned to VX-6 and VXE-6, while in support of the Antarctic operations.

At the International Antarctic Centre, at Christchurch International Airport, a rock which came from the Bell Hill Gold Mine in the Greymouth River Valley on the West Coast of the South Island of New Zealand and believed to be an Alluvial Glacial Deposit, bears a memorial plaque honouring the names of these Americans. This rock is believed to be Greywacke, but with a higher concentration of iron than Greywacke would normally have, measuring approximately three cubic metres in volume and weighing eight tons.

This rock was chosen because its characteristics are similar to the geology of Antarctica, having been carved by glacier and water for tens of thousands of years giving it the look and aura of Antarctica and New Zealand's isolation.

During Operation High jump 1946-47

Ensign Maxwell A Lopez USN – USS Pine Island on December 30 1946

ARM1 Wendell K Henderson USN –USN USS Pine Island December 30 1946

ARM1 Frederick W Williams USN –USS Pine Island Decembe4 30 1946

PBM-5 "George 1" crashed on Pine Island was aboard and survived the crash. Williams died two hours after the crash.

SN Vance N Woodall USN -USS Yancey while unloading cargo in 1946 [*Polar Times* June 1947]

Lt. John P Moore USNR –USS Atka, January 22 1955 a helicopter pilot killed in a crash at Kainan Bay near Little America –pre Deep Freeze site survey [*Polar Times* June 1955]

During Operation Deep Freeze 1955-99

CD3 Richard T Williams USN on January 1 1956

Killed when his DC-8 Tractor broke through the ice at McMurdo, the Williams Field was later named in his honour.

CD3 'Max ' Fat Max' R Kiel USN, on March 5 1956, when his tractor fell into a crevasse en-route from Little America to establish Byrd Station. [*Polar Times* June 1956]

Lt. David W Carey USNR VX-6

Captain Rayburn A Hudman USMC. VX-6

AD 1 Marian O Marze USN. VX-6

AT1 Charles S Millar USN VX-6

When their P2-V Neptune crashed during a whiteout while landing at McMurdo on October 18 1956 during the fly in from New Zealand in *Deep Freeze 11*.

Theirs was the first aircraft to land in Antarctic

Cdr Ollie Bartley USN died when his Weasel crashed through the ice at Hut Point on January 14 1957.

AD2 Nelson R Cole, USN VX-6 died from burns when his helicopter crashed in the vicinity of McMurdo during the austral winter on July 12 1957.

SA Richard T Oppegaard USN killed on November 8 1957 in a shipboard accident.

SSGT Leonard M Pitkevitch USAF

TSGT Iman Fendley USAF

TSGT Nathaniel Wallis USAF

A1C Richard De Angelo USAF
A2C Robert L Burnette USAF
A2C Kelly Sloan USAF
Killed when they're C 124 Globemaster 'City of Christchurch' enroute from Christchurch crashed in the Admiralty Mountains on their way to make a cargo and mail drop to Hallett Station. Seven crew survived the accident. On October 16 1958.
Lt. Harvey E Gardner USN VX-6
Lt JG Lawrence J Farrell USN VX-6 Killed when their Otter crashed while making a take off at Marble Point on January 4 1959.
Lt. Tom Couzens, Armoured Corps New Zealand Army Killed in a crevasse accident on November 19 1959
BU Paul V O'Leary USNR ASA from accidental poisoning on November 28 1959.
SWI Orlan F John USN ASA Killed in an accidental explosion at McMurdo on November 2 1960.
Lt Cdr William D Counts USN VX-6
JTJG Ronauld P Compton USN VX-6
AMHI William W Chastain USN VX-6
Adr 2 James L Gray USN VX-6
Civilian Dr Edward C Thiel
Killed when their P2V Neptune crashed and burned on take-off from Wilkes Station, a range of mountains was named after Dr Thiel on 9 November 1961.
[All other VX-6 crew members killed have also had mountains named after them].
Civilian Carl R Disch-Ionospheric Phy USARP disappeared at Byrd Station on 8 May 1965
Lt.Cdr Ronald Rosenthal USN VX-6
Lt. Harold M Morris USN VX-6
Lt. William D Fordell USN VX-6
ATI Richard S Simmons USN VX-6
ARD2 Wayne M Shattuck USN VX-6
ADJ3 Charles C Kelly USN VX-6
Killed when their LC-47 crashed on the Ross Sea on 2 February 1966
SK1 Andrew B Miulder USN ASA Crushed between the Hercules ramp and cargo shed at the South Pole on February 13 1966.
Civilian Jeremy Sykes New Zealand film Director NZRP
Civilian Thomas E Berg Geologist USARP
Killed in a Helicopter crash near Mount McLennan on 19 November 1969.
ADC William D Decker USN VXE-6 died in his sleep at McMurdo's CPO Quarters. Decker was VXE-6 LCPO.
Civilian Wolf V Vishniac Microbiologist USARP Killed when he fell off mountains in Asgard on 11 December 1973.
Civilian Greg Nickell- Lab Manager USARP Killed in a truck wreck between McMurdo and Scott Base when his truck rolled over a 600foot cliff on 15 May 1974.
Civilian Jeffrey D Rude Oceanographer USARP, Drowned when his trucked vehicle broke through the ice in McMurdo Sound on 12 October 1975.
SN Gerald E Reily Jr USCG-. Electrocuted aboard ship while operating in the Amundsen Sea on 22 January 1976
Raymond C Porter USCG, Killed when the forklift he was operating, off loading cargo from USNS Bland, rolled over and crushed him on 8 February 1979.
Civilian Casey A Jones H&N USARP, a cook at the South Pole Station died, when a column of snow and ice fell on him while in the intake shaft, on 9 January 1980, he was cremated in New Zealand and his remains were scattered on the Beardmore Glacier.

BM1 Raymond USN knocked overboard while offloading *SS Southern Cross* on 8 February 1982, his hardhat was made into a memorial.

Civilian Matthew M Kaz ITT Employee USARP

Civilian John E Smith ITT Employee USARP

Died when they fell into a crevasse while walking two miles east of McMurdo on 23 November 1986.

Lt.Cdr Bruce Bailey USN VXE-6

AK1 Donald M Beatty USN VXE-6, Died while landing their C-130 at D-59

Lt.Cdr Joseph Dale Cerda.

Lt.Cdr Stephen Bernard Duffy

ADCS Kevin Michael Kimsey

ADAN Eric John Kugel.

Killed with their UHE-6 Helo crashed in southern California on July 28 1987 while on a training flight. The pilot was making an unauthorized manoeuvre when it crashed, believed to have been pilot error, on 9 December 1987

AMSI Benjamin Micou USN VXE-6

Civilian Garth Varcoe New Zealander attached to the DSIR TSO NZARP

Civilian Terry Newport New Zealander attached to the DSIP TS0 NZARP

Killed when their helicopter crashed near Cape Royds on 31 October 1992

AMS1 James D Sparks USN. Killed while off loading cargo near Castle Rock on 30 January 1995.

FCCM Charles Gallagher USN [RET] ASA. Died from an apparent heart attack during pneumonia and dehydration, Gallagher worked for a private contractor, but had been NSFA CMC.

APPENDIX 3

OPERATION DEEP FREEZE PERSONNEL AND THE ANTARCTIC LOCATIONS NAMED AFTER THEM

Lt JG F ALLEN	MOUNT ALLEN
Cdr D BALISH	BALISH GLACIER
Lt.Cdr R E BERGER	BERGER ROCKS
AD2 H E BLOUNT	BLOUNT NUTATAK
LT R I BOLT	MOUNT BOLT
LT J L BOLTON	MOUNT BOLTON
Lt.Cdr A BORCIK	MOUNT BORCIK
LT J M BOWER	BOWER PEAK
AD1 H J BRACKEN	BRACKEN PEAK
LDR J E BRANDAU	BRANDAU GLACIER
Lt.Cdr J CAPLEY	MOUNT CAPLEY
LT D W CARTER	CARTER ISLAND
AMI W W CHASTAIN	CHASTAIN PEAK
ADJI C C CHRISTY	CHRISTY GLACIER
AD2 N R COLE	MOUNT COLE
Cdr V J COLEY	MOUNT COLEY
LTJG R P COMPTON	COMPTON VALLEY
Capt D CORDINER	CORDINER PEAKS
Lt J W CORNWELL	MOUNT CORNWELL
Lacer W D COUNTS	COUNTS ICEFULL
ADJ2 A N COX	MOUNT COX.
Lt.Cdr A Y CRAVEN	MOUNT CRAVEN
Lt.Cdr R E CURTIS	CURTIS PEAKS
Maj.L L DARBYSHIRE	MOUNT DARBYSHIRE
ADR2 R DENAURO	MOUNT DENAURO
Lt.Cdr R DICKERSON	MOUNT DICKERSON
Lt D L DEITZ	MOUNT DEITZ.
Lt O T DOCKERY	MOUNT DOCKERY
Cdr E W DONNALLY	DONNALLY GLACIER
Cdr J M DRISCOLL	DRISCOLL GLACIER
Lt.Cdr E D DRYFOOSE	MOUNT DRYFOOSE
Cdr G K EBBE	EBBE GLACIER
ADRC J C EBLEN	EBLEN HILLS
Lt J R EDIXON	MOUNT EDIXON
PH2 J B H FARNELL	FARNELL VALLEY
LTJF L J FARRELL	MOUNT FARRELL
Lt.Cdr J FENDORF	FENDORF GLACIER
ADC J FERRARA	MOUNT FERRARA
Lt W D FORDELL	MOUNT FORDELL
Lt.Cdr W J FRANKE	MOUNT FRANKE
AE1 T A FUSCO	FUSCO NUNATAK
Cdr F S GALLUP	GALLUP GLACIER

Lt H E GARDNER	MOUNT GARDNER
ATC F GORECKI	MOUNT GORECKI
AD2 L F GRAY	GRAY SPUR
Cdr M D GREENWELL	GREENWELL GLACIER
Lt P GURNON	GURNON PENINSULA
ADR2 J PRINCE	MOUNT PRINCE.
ADR2 C E RATCLIFF	MOUNT RATCLIFF
Lt.Cdr R E HALL	MOUNT HALL
LTJG J B HANSEN	HANSEN GLACIER
HMC H D HARRIS	HARRIS POINT.
Capt W M HAWKES	MOUNT HAWKES
LTJG H S HEMPHILL	MOUNT HEMPHILL
Lt J A M HICKEY	CAPE HICKEY
PHC J O HILL	HILL NUNATAK
Capt R A HUDMAN	HUDMAN GLACIER.
ATC G HUNT	HUNT SPUR.
Lt G J JANULIS	JANULIS SPUR
Lt.Cdr H JARINE	JARINE NUNATAK
Lt.Cdr S W JONES	JONES BLUFF
Lt.Cdr H P JORDA	JORDA GLACIER
PHC F KAZUKAITIS	MOUNT KAZUKATIS
PH1 M B KEIM	KEIM PEAK
ADJ3 C C KELLEY	KELLEY PEAK
Cdr G R KELLY	KELLY PLATEAU
1ST Lt L S KENNEY	MOUNT KENNEY
LCdr B KOLOC JR	KOLOC POINT.
Lt Col H P KOLP	MOUNT KOLP
YN2 K KOOPMAN	KOOPMAN PEAK.
Cdr M KREBS	MOUNT KREBS
SSgt A L KRING	MOUNT KRING.
PH1 F P LEE	LEE PEAK.
AD2 L H LIPTAK	MOUNT LIPTAK
AT1 A L KISHNESS	KISHNESS PEAK
Lt O B LOVEJOY	LOVEJOY GLACIER
AT1 D V MALONE	MOUNT MALONE
Cdr R MARVEL	MOUNT MARVEL
AD1 M O MARZE	MARZE PEAKI
Lt R V MAYER	MAYER CRAGS
Lt.Cdr C J MC CARTHY	MC CARTHY INLET
AT2 C S MILLER	MILLER PEAK.
Lt R H MILLER	MILLER VALLEY
AD2 P G MILTON	MOUNT MILTON
Lt D M MOODY	MOUNT MOODY
Lt F M MOODY	MOODY NUNATAK
AN1 J L MOODY	MOODY PEAK
LCdr CC MORAN	MORAN BUTTRESS
Lt H M MORRIS	MORRIS GLACIER
Lt I J MORRISON	MORRISON HILLS.
Lt.Cdr J A MORTON	MORTON GLACIER

Capt W H MUNSON	MOUNT MUNSON
Cdr L E NEWCOMER	NEWCOMER GLACIER.
GYSGT W C NOXON	MOUNT NOXON.
PH2 M J PEREZ	MOUNT PEREZ.
LTJG R PEREZ	PEREZ GLACIER.
PHC F PRICE	PRICE PEAK
Lt.Cdr D L RECKLING	RECKLING PEAK.
PHC DD REIMER	MOUNT REIMER
LT D W ROE JR	MOUNT ROE
Lt.Cdr R ROSENTHAL	MOUNT ROSENTHAL
AT1 G M SAMPLE	SAMPLE NUNATAKS
Lt.Cdr T L SCHANZ	SCHANZ GLACIER.
AE1 W J SCHOBERT	SCHOBERT NUNATAK
CSC C W SEGERS	MOUNT SEGERS
ADR3 M SHATTUCK	MOUNT SHATTUCK.
JO2 J SHEETS	SHEETS PEAK.
SSgt J K SHIELDS	MOUNT SHIELD.
Lt.Cdr C S SHINN	MOUNT SHINN
SW02 D F SIGLIN	SIGLIN ROCKS.
AT1 S SIMMONS	MOUNT SIMMONS.
Lt B SIMPSON	MOUNT SIMPSON.
TSGT T E SOUTHWICK	MOUNT SOUTHWICK.
SSgt R SPANN	MOUNT SPANN
Lt H G SPEED	MOUNT SPEED
PH2 M J SPRINGER	SPRINGER PEAK.
SSgt F STREITENBERGER	STREITENBERGER CLIFF.
Cdr R C THOMPSON	THOMSON ESCARPMENT.
LT P TIDD	MOUNT TIDD
Lt.Cdr J E WALDRON	WALDRON SPUR.
Lt.Cdr J H TORBERT	TORBERT ESCARPMENT.
Lt J E WALDRON	MOUNT WALDRON.
Capt J G WALKER	WALKER SPUR.
JSGT C OC WARREN	MOUNT WARREN.
Lt.CDdr F WASKO	MOUNT WASKO.
PH2 H N WILLIAMS	WILLIAMS BLUFF
Lt W W WORKS	MOUNT WORKS.
Lt.Cdr C H ZILCH	ZILCH CLIFFS.

THE ANTARCTIC AIRCRAFT...
... AND THE MAGNIFICENT MEN WHO FLEW THEM.

'A few of our designs attained some degree of fame and one of them, the DC-3, has became almost legendary. It seems to go on forever for her commercial and military pilots, who have worked and lived with her in all corners of the world. To these men must go the largest measure of credit for the multiple exploits, the almost incredible adventures, and even more importantly, the solid years of dependable and workaday accomplishments that combine to perpetuate the DC-3 legend.'

Donald W Douglas Sr.
In the foreword to Lt Col Carroll Glines
& Lt Col Wendell Moseley's book
'Grand Old Lady"

One day in 1892, when Lincoln Ellsworth was 12 years old, he looked at his father's oversized atlas and became intrigued by the blank spaces marked 'Unexplored' that capped both ends of the earth and dotted several continents. 'Why don't people go there?" he wondered. 'What can there be in those white spaces?'

In the early years of the century and right up until the First World War, many brave aviators, Ellsworth among them, went in search of the answers, these early pioneers added in their quest by developing long range aircraft, enabling them to vault the barriers, which had held others back from the mystiques of polar aviation.

'Discoveries leap upon the aerial adventurers down there' wrote Richard Byrd, of his first flight across Antarctica in 1928. In 1929, the Australian explorer George Hubert Wilkins exulted *'we covered 1,200 miles in a straight line in the Arctic, that had never been seen by man last year. We added another 1200 miles to the map in Antarctica last December. This year we hope, by flying from the Ross Sea, south of New Zealand, to add another 2,000 miles of coastline to the Map.'*

Pilot Brent Balchen, who accompanied Byrd on the 1929 flight over the South Pole, felt that another motive might be involved. *'What driving force causes a man to leave the comfort and security and risk hunger and privation and even death in search of something he cannot keep even when he finds it?'*

The aviators and their aircrews were, without a doubt the true *Magnificent Men in Their Flying Machines* flying aircraft in the early pioneering days of Antarctic exploration.

Since 1955 a variety of cargo-transport aircraft have been utilized to support the US Antarctic Programme in Antarctica. The Antarctic Development Squadron Six or VXE-6 [the former VX-6]had pioneered air logistic support from the operation's staging area at Christchurch to the glacial covered Antarctic continent.

The Squadron has used a number of different aircraft over their 44 years, before handing the operations over to the New York Air National Guard in 1999, these included the R4-D Dakotas, C-5-D Skytrain, C-121 Super Constellations As well as the Lockheed PV-2 Neptune's, the C-54/c-57 Skymasters, the C-130 Hercules, the first ski equipped C-130 arrived in 1961.

On August 2 1932 thirty-eight year old Donald Douglas received letter from Jack Frye, the vice president in charge of operations for Transcontinental & Western Air [later Trans World Airlines – TWA] for the manufacture of an all-metal monoplane with a maximum gross weight of 14,200 pounds a fuel capacity for a cruising range of 1,080 miles at 145 MPH, with a capacity for carrying 12 passengers. Frye's letter concluded with a simple question. 'Approximately how long would it take to turn out the first plane for service tests flights?'

Little did Douglas's design and engineering team of Dutch Kindleberger, Arthur E Raymond, and Fred Herman. Lee Atwood, Ed Burton, Fred Strinewood and Harry E Wetzel, know that the DC-1, the first forerunner to the now amazing Gooney Bird known to US Naval aviators as the R4-D would be flying in the Antarctic twenty-three years after the first test flight on July 1 1933.

Arthur Raymond, whose aircraft design ushered in an era of global air travel and made the world a smaller place, died a few days before his 100th birthday in 1999. Raymond was largely responsible for the Gooney Birds design, the world's most popular for two decades. The DC-2 its predecessor, revolutionised the then fledging US aviation business in 1924, by becoming the first passenger plane able to turn a profit without subsides from the US Mail.

In 1935 his rugged, economical twin engine DC-3 was introduced and quickly became the worlds most popular aircraft. Over 11,000 of the 21 seats passenger planes rolled off the assembly lines and dominated the airline market until the advent of the Boeing 707 in the late 1950's. The DC-3 incorporated much of aviation's cutting edge technology, including semi-retraceable landing gear and wing flaps, and the plane was so aero-dynamically sound that pilots and VX-6 aviators said it almost flew itself.

A total of thirteen R4-Ds were written off by VX-6 during the years they were used in Antarctica. The Gooney's *BuNo 50832,* which was rebuilt from parts, cannibalised from other Gooney's, such as '*Charlene*'. After this fatal crash, the R4-Ds were mostly used for cargo flights and many of these shuttled to Hallett Station and back to McMurdo. During D.F.68 only one of the three remaining Gooney's were placed into operational service; this aircraft made over 25 flights flying some 86 hours, on December 2 1967 flew its last mission.

It was during D.F.68, that marked the end of their glorious service with VX-6, when # *99853 'Wilshie Duit'* while being back loaded aboard the *USNS Pvt John Towle*, had all hands cheering as they said good bye and perhaps 'good riddance', but instead of going back to the States, she found a watery grave at the bottom of the Ross Sea. While being loaded on the ship's deck, the Gooney was dropped and smashed, bringing tears to the eyes of those watching. Being a true OAE of long standing, # *99853* who had arrived on the ice on October 1 1957, didn't give up easily after being dropped from the sling. '*Wilshie Duit*' was pushed out on to the ice to drift away and sink into the icy waters of McMurdo, but was still plainly visible from MacTown a year later.

Of all the Gooney's remaining entombed in the Antarctic ice, only *#50832* cost any lives. This versatile aircraft was immortalized in Antarctica by having three geographic locations on the Antarctica map name after it. *Dakota Pass, R4D Nunatak* and *Skytrain Rise.*

LC-47H ## 17107 'Ahab Clyde' & 'Deep Freeze Express'

Douglas s/n 11938
Order by USAF as C-47A-1 serial number 42-108809
Delivered to USN as R4D in Sept 1943
Redesignated LC-47H
VX-6 in 1962.
Crashed in the Horlick Mountains on December 5 1965.
LC-47H # 12407 '*Us Know How*'
Douglas s/n 91179 – ordered by the USAF as C-47A-1-DL serial number 42-23317.
Delivered to USMC as R4-D-5 in March 1943
Assigned to VX-6 in Antarctica on October 20 1963;
Crashed on October 22 on Little Glacier. Antarctica.
R4D-8L # 17154; *Negatus Perspirus*

Douglas s/n 12427.

Ordered by USAF as C-47A-10-DK. USAF s/n 42-92608.

Delivered to USN as R4-D –5 on 6 February 1944.

Converted to R4-D-8L and assigned to VX-6 in 1958

On Christmas Eve 1959, an R4-D-8L crashed while trying to land during a whiteout condition at Byrd Station. Lt Garland, M Regenar was on the final approach when the aircraft stalled and the right wing dropped. Although Regenar applied power and used his rudder to compensate, the right wing hit the surface and broke. No one was injured but the plane was destroyed.

R4D-6L # 17274. 'Charlene' & 'Tawaiki'.

Douglas s/n 25777

Ordered by the USAF as C-47B – 1- DK –USAF s/n 43- 48516

Assigned to VX-6 Squadron in December 1955, flew to the Antarctic on October 17 1956.

Used as a taxi with the wings removed: removal date unknown.

Left on the ice flow in the Ross Sea in 1962 for disposal

Footnote:

Many stories have been told re *Charlene* a few are told elsewhere in this book, by James Waldron and Eddie Frankiewicz, the aircraft's commander. She was one of only two engine ice taxis in the world, it was the only R4-D with Teflon covered skis, which had a far lower coefficient of friction than the plastic coating used on the squadron's other R4-Ds. When Frankiewicz got to the ice in DF 11 in October 1956, he tried to have it scheduled to make the first South Pole landing, thinking that the lower coefficient of friction could spell the difference between a successful mission to the Pole and one which might be a failure.

His suggestion was ignored by the Admiral, as there was no proof it would have gone better, had his aircraft been selected instead of 'Que Sera Sera'.

Buz Dryfoose recalls the wings were removed at the joint outboard of the engines, along with its radio, instruments and everything else that could be removed. She ever ran on contaminated fuel. 'In the Cruise book for DF-60 in a section called 'more R4-D's there is a picture of 'Charlene' in all her glory. *I drove her on her maiden run with Capt Munson, our skipper, it took four to five minutes from Mac to Willy Field. 'We just got in and loaded it up with Paz and firewalled the go handles.*

When the tail came up and I had rudder control we were off and running, though slowing down and stopping was more trouble. We drove through the snow about twenty feet off the roadway from Mac to Willy, Lots of fun was had by all' recalled Dryfoose.

LC-117D # 17188 'Lou Bird 11' – *"Big Daddy" & The Loser'*

Douglas s/n 12847 ordered by the USAF as C-47A-20-DK –USAF s/n 42-92986.

Delivered to USMC as R4D-5 in April 1944;

Converted to R4D-8 in early 1950 with new Douglas s/n 43384, converted to R4D-8L; assigned to VX-6 Squadron in 1958, redesignated LC-117D in 1962.

Crashed on Sentinel Ridge on November 22 1962.

LC-47J # *50778 'Gotcha'*

Douglas s/n 26383 ordered by the USAF as a C-47B-10-DK USAF s/n 43 –49122.

Delivered to USN at NAS San Diego as R4D-6 in October 1944.

Converted to R4D-6L; assigned to VX-6 Squadron in October 1962; redesignated LC-47J in 1962.

Crashed on the Shackleton Glacier, Antarctica on January 11 1965

LC –117D # *99853   ' Wilshie Duit' and 'Divine Wind'*

JD-7 with Jack McKillop and JD-10 with Buz Dryfoose

Douglas s/n 33337 ordered by USAAF as TC-47B-35-DK, USAAF s/n 44 –77005.

Delivered to USN as R4D-7 in May 1945.

Converted to R4D-8L; assigned to VX-6 Squadron on October 1 1957; redesignated LC-117D in 1962.

Withdrawn from use in January 1967 at McMurdo Sound, Antarctica.

Damaged beyond repair in January 1968 during loading aboard a ship for the US, set out on the ice flow, drifted out into the Ross Sea.

Buz Dryfoose recalls that during DF-3 in a rough landing at A-5, the landing gear was damaged necessitating emergency repairs to get the plane home, it was then sent to Jacksonville and the entire mid-box section of the wing was rebuilt, using thee-times stronger material than originally called for. *'Witshie Duit'* flew with the same engines for two seasons in Antarctica, without an accident. In D.F. 60 it was the first plane into all the outlying Antarctic stations.

LC 117 D # *12441 'Simper Shafter' & 'City of Invercargill'*

Douglas s/n 9674 ordered by USAAF as C-47A-35-DL USAAF s/n 42-23812,

Delivered to USM as R4D-5 in June 1943

Converted to an R4-D-8 in the early 1950's and given a Douglas s/n 43389

Redesignated to LC-117D in 1966.

Assigned to VX-6 Squadron on December 15 1964.

Struck off the Navy's inventory- returned to the US and stored at Davis-Monthan AFB Arizona, sold with engines on October 30 1974.

LC –117D # *17092 'Would You Believe It'*

Douglas s/c 11788 ordered by USAAF as C-47A-DK, USAAF S

S/n 42-108792.

Delivered to USN as R4D-5 in May 1943.

Converted to R4D-8 and assigned a new Douglas s/n 43381.

Assigned to VX-6 Squadron as LC-117D in November 1966

Returned to the US in January 1968, and stored at Davis Monthan AFB –sold without engines on October 30 1974.

R4R-5L # *17163 'Takahe'*

Douglas s/n 12519- ordered by the USAAF as a C-47A-10-DK, the USAAF s/n 42 92690.

Delivered to USN at Mayfair CA on February 1944.

Assigned to VX-6 Squadron on October 17 1956

Crashed at Cape Hallett on 15 September 1959.

After touchdown on the ice at Cape Hallett Station the starboard landing gear collapsed. The plane was declared a strike because it was not economical to repair it, due to its age.

Writes James Waldron. *'The pilot, Harvey Speed, was one of the finest aviators I have ever known, he was a picture of 'cool' when things got tough and very accomplished in handling emergencies.'*

He once handled three engine failures in one day. He had made a forced landing on the Antarctic Plateau, when there was only one aircraft on the Antarctic continent that might have rescued him. He never complained about long hours or lack of recognition, he was a leader of men, and when there was physical work to be done, like digging out snow covered aircraft, Harvey was always first on hand'.

The aviator died of MS, long before the time it seems he should have gone to meet his maker, he was missed by all OAE's who knew him and flew with him.

LC –47H # *17239. 'Snafu' & ' Hallmark'*

Douglas s/n by USAAF as C-17A-30-DK. USAAF s/n 43-48163.

Delivered to NSN as R4D-5 at NAS San Diego in July 1944

Assigned to VX-6 Squadron on November 20 1961 and converted on November 20 1961 and converted to R4D-5L, Redesignated to LC-47H in 1962

Crashed at Williams Field. McMurdo on 6 October 1965

On October # *17239* crashed on the Ross Sea Shelf some three miles from the Williams airfield, while taking off to practice an open landing. The airplane received damage when an improperly rigged ski cable slipped and the front of one sky dug into the snow. Daniel Dompe the PC

on the flight writes of the accident. # *317239* crashed on a open field, Cdr Van Reeth was the pilot, Len Edleman was the radioman and he thinks Moe was the co pilot. *We hit a sastrugi, the port wing dropped, took the prop and nose off the engine, the prop came through the fuselage between Crd Van Reeth and me. It was my 3ʳᵈ flight on the ice and I was thinking; what the F... am I doing here'*
LC-117D # *17253*
Douglas s/n 25628 ordered by USAAF a C-47B-1-DK, USAAF s/n 43-48367.
Delivered to USN as R4D-6 at NAS Norfolk VA in August 1944.
Assigned to VX-6 unknown.
Redesignated lc-117D in 1962
Destination unknown, however, in December 1979, the aircraft was at MCAS, Iwakuni.Japan.
LC- 47J #*50777*
Douglas s/n 26378 – ordered by USAAF as C-47B-10-DK –USAAF s/n 43-49117
Delivered to USN as R4D-6 at San Diego NAS in October 1944.
Assigned to VX-6 Squadron in October 1962 as LC-47J.
Crashed ON Davis Glacier on 25 November 1962,
The LC-47H # 50777 was lost on November 25 1962, while making a jet assisted take off at Davis Glacier. A JATO canister was released accidentally before it stopped firing, hitting a propeller. The aircraft lost an engine and crashed.
LC-47J # *50832 'The Spirit of McMurdo".*
Douglas s/n 26983, ordered by USAAF as C-47B-20-DK. USAAF s/n 43-49722
Delivered to USN as a R4D-6 on January 2 1945.
Assigned to VX-6 on 6 November 1965.

Crashed on the Ross Ice Shelf on 2 February 1966.
It was the third Deep Freeze 66 aircraft involved in a crash. The LC-47J crashed while in a landing approach at mile 60 on the Army-Navy trail on February 2 1966. The plane stalled while about 200 feet above the surface. The rightwing dipped, the pilot corrected and the left wing dipped. # *50832* hit the snow surface while nearly inverted.

The wings broke off and the fuselage broke in two places, before the plane caught fire and the JATO canisters on board exploded.
All six men aboard the plane were killed. Lt Harold Morris -aircraft commander. Lt William D Fordell - co pilot, Lt Commander Rosenthal – navigator – AT1 Richard S Simmons- radioman – ADJ3 Charles C Kelley – plane captain – ADR3 Wayne M Shattuc'-plane captain [trainee]
JC-47H # *17221 'Kool Kiwi' 'Yankee Tiki A Te Hu' 'Mutha Goose' and 'The Emperor'*
Douglas s/n 13319, ordered by USAAF as C-47A-25-DK, USAAF s/n 42 93410

One of only two VX-6 Squadron's R4-D's which has been preserved is #17221 in the Ferrymead Aeronautical Historic Society Museum.

It was delivered to the US Navy at NAS at San Diego on 21 November 21 1944, and after seeing service with various Naval Squadrons, the aircraft was converted into a transport carrier and prepared for operational service with VX-6 Squadron on October 20 1963, for service in Antarctica, At first it carried a tail-code JD and named ' *Mutha Goose'* then '*Kool Kiwi'* and a tail number 14. It was later named '*Yankee Tiki A Te Hau'*.

Withdrawn from Antarctic operational service on April 28 1969, and then handed over to the New Zealand Government by the then American Ambassador Henning. The NZ Government then handed the airplane over to the City of Christchurch and onto the Ferrymead Aeronautical Society on what Paul Panehal recalls the crew of #17221 at the time of the hand over was Earl Rudder ASC, Chuck Ratliff, and Ray Berger, who had just been transferred, and himself.
He also recalls that they had just painted it before turning it over to New Zealand. The crews names were those who had died on 2 February 1965, it had Ray's little Kiwi bird and the inscription '*It ain't*

no big thing.' it and the number 14 were the only items left on the nose from the 1966 rework at NAC workshops.

Delivered Douglas s/n 9358 – Ordered by the USAAF as aC-47A-20-DL USAAF s/n 42-23496

Delivered to USN as R4D –5 on April 8 1943.

Assigned to VX-6 Squadron as R4D=8.

The first plane to land at the South Pole on October 31 1956.

Presented to the Smithsonian and now on display at the National Navy Museum in Pensacola FL.

LOCKHEED C-121 CONSTELLATION '

Connie'C-121 # *131624 'Phoenix'*

Lockheed model 1049B-55-75 Lockheed s/n 4125.

Delivered to the US Navy as an R7V-I on May 8 1953.

First assigned to Fleet Transport Squadron Seven at Hickman AFB and then to the same Squadron at NAS Moffett CA in 1957. Transferred to Command, Navy Air Force Atlantic Fleet [COMAIRLANT] at NAS Norfolk, VA in 1958 and then to VX-6 at NAS Quonset Point in September 1958 coded 'JD' and named 'Phoenix'.

Used on Operation Deep Freeze annually and stationed at the Royal New Zealand Air Force Station, Wigram each summer from approximately September to March.

First visited New Zealand on September 20 1958, and operationally used on Wigram/Christchurch-McMurdo Sound, Antarctica flights. Modified by November 1969 with a trap on the starboard side of the nose to catch on board plankton. Coded JD-6 from August 1962.

One penguin was painted on the side nose wheel door for each completed Deep Freeze mission.

Modified again to P7V-1P for the 1961-62 Operation Deep Freeze season, redesignated C-121J in 1962.

Left Christchurch on March 16 1971 after its final season of Antarctic operations and ferried via NAS Quonset Point to Davis, Monthan AFB for storage in March 1971. Removed from inventory of MASDC at Davis, Monthan on May 25 1971 with 15,609 hours on the airframe. *'Phoenix'* was put up for sale by DOD ON 23 March 1977, but there were no takers, she was scrapped.

C-121 # *131644 'Pegasus'*

Lockheed Model 1049B-55-75 Lockheed C/N 4145Delivered to USN as a P7V-1 on December 19 1953, then assigned to NAS Patuxent River MD in December 1953, coded RP-644 and named *'Taurus'*, Transferred to Airborne Early Warning Squadron at NAS Patuxent River MD in 1955. To Early Warning Maintenance Squadron –2 [AEWMATRON-2] NAS Barbers Point, TH by 1955, redesignated C-121J.

In 1962 and to Airborne Earning Barrier Squadron T Barbers Point in December 1962.Transferred to VX-6 Squadron NAS Quonset Point on September 1 1964. Coded JD-6 and named *'Pegasus'*, for operational use with Deep Freeze annually. One penguin painted on side of nose wheel door for each completed mission- Code JD-7 from March 1966.Modified with new antenna under tail unit for airborne ice-sounding in late 1967 and flight tested in December 1967.Damaged beyond repair landing at Williams Field, McMurdo Sound at 2010 hours local time on October 1970.

The aircraft with 80 on board was flying from Christchurch on the first flight of the 1970-71 season. After making six low level passes over the airfield, the C-121J attempted to land in zero visibility, winds gusting to 40 MPH in a snowstorm and 90-degree crosswinds.

The starboard wing was torn off completely and the tail unit broken- there were only slight injuries to five on board and the aircraft was subsequently broken up at McMurdo.

Billy Ace Penguin recalls the flight. 'About midnight a Navy stake truck driven by BMC Parker [ASA-CMAA] stopped at my house on Cranbrook Avenue, Christchurch and picked me and my seabag up and took me to Harewood with the rest of the brown-baggers. I was on *Phoenix 6*, which was the first aircraft leaving Harewood heading for the ice. Cdr.Dave Eldridge wanted all the squadron to go on opening day.

An hour later *Pegasus* took off followed by the Herks, all staggered at one-hour intervals. During the night the C-130's overtook and passed the Connies and in due course landed one by one.
DOUGLAS R5-D'S SKYMASTERS.
R5-D # *56528* The Admiral's Plane. *'Carole Jeune'*
Was originally ordered by the USAAF in 1942 as a C-54D-15-DC, the USAAF s/n 42-72749
It was transferred to the US Navy as a R4D-3 on August 1 1945. The aircraft was assigned to VX-6 Squadron in October 1945, it was the first aircraft to arrive at McMurdo during Deep Freeze 1 in December 1955, redesigned as C-54.
R5-D-3 #*56505* *'Have Gum Will Travel'* *'Marilyn'* *'Rosemary'*
Was originally ordered by the USAAF in 1942 As a C-54D-5-DC with a USAAF s/n 42-72560. The aircraft was transferred to the US Navy as a R4D-3 on April 13 1954, it was assigned to VX-6 Squadron in October 1958 in 1964 was sent to NAS Glenview IL, sold as surplus in February 1975 and sold to Central Air Services CA for aerial fire fighting assigned Air Tanker number 149, sold to Travis Air Museum in December 1989 and now on display at Travis AFB.
Lockheed P2V-2N – P2V-7 LP; Neptune's
P2V-2N # *122465* *'Boopsie'*
Crashed during landing at McMurdo, Antarctica on October 1956 in supporting Operation Deep Freeze, killing four crew Lt Cary, Capt Hudman, ATI Miller, and ADI Marze- see chapter 6 for detailed story.
P2V-7LP # *140434* *'George'*
Crashed while landing August 11 1958, prior to Operation Deep Freeze 1V, while landing at Ontario, CA after acceptance, the Neptune was destroyed, no one was injured. - The loss of the aircraft was never made up
P2V-7LP/ LP-2J # *140436* *'Candid Camera'*
Escaped the scrapper's torch and is located in the Walter Sollata collection.
P2V-7LP/LP-2J # *140437* *'City of Auckland'*
Scrapped at Davis-Monthan AFB
P2V-7LP # 140439
Crashed while taking off from Wilkes Station, Antarctica on November 9 1961, on the skiway; of the nine men aboard, only four survived. Killed were Dr Edward Thiel, Lt.Cdr William Courts. LTJG Romauld Compton, AMHI William Chastain and AD2R James Grey.
Buz Dryfoose recalls the crash.
'I flew the C-130 to Wilkes to review the crash and pick up the survivors; I walked the entire runway with Cdr Forshi, our maintenance officer at the time. We found parts that had fallen off the Neptune from the beginning of its take off slide. The landing had been so violently rough that it had broken loose the 400 gal internal tank in the bomb bay and the 4-inch filler pipe was spewing out raw fuel running from the bottom of the plane on takeoff.

At ignition of the JATO on the take off run, it was like a Roman candle, with the burning of the fibreglass tail cone, all the smoke was drawn right into the cockpit blinding the pilots. They tried to return to the field and just couldn't make it. The pilot managed to level the wings before they hit, that saved some of the guys. We took the body bags and survivors back to McMurdo, after Cdr. Forshi finished his examination and what was left of the aircraft.

All below the snow line was pretty much in tact and that above the snow line looked like a skeleton.'

During the 44 years in Antarctica VXE-6 Squadron two aircraft, the workhorses of Antarctic operations –these two iconic aviation machines stood out like the famous Antarctic atmosphere phenomena- the Aurora Australis over other aircraft- not since the Wright Bros first flew their heavier than air plane at Kitty Hawke in 1903, has no much been owed to these two aircraft and their engineers

These two aviation greats are, without any doubt, the Douglas R4-D Gooney Birds and the Lockheed C-130 Hercules. No book on Antarctic aviation could be written without paying a tribute to the two great engineers who designed these two aircraft- both of whom have passed away- but they did live long enough to witness their 'works of art' operate in, without any doubt, the harshest climate in the world.

Standing alongside Arthur Raymond is Wills M Hawkins, a Lockheed engineering legend who was the principal designer of the C-130- the cargo and military transport that has remained in continuous production for over 50 years- longer than any other aircraft in history- died on September 28 2004 of natural causes at his Los Angeles. He was 90.

During the last four decades, the Herk has continued the Antarctic 'Workhorse' role previously undertaken by Arthur Raymond's pride and joy- the 'Gooney Bird'. Since its first test flight at Burbank on August 23 1954, the Hercules has built for itself one of the most storied records in aviation history. In fact the plane still flies like it did 51 years ago and Lockheed Martin has a backlog of orders for the latest incarnation, the C-130J, which retains the ungainly appearance of the ordinal YC-130 [53 3397.

Mr Hawkins's team delivered a blueprint for the C130 that would not win any beauty contest. It was a bulky, low-slung workhorse with a cargo area as big as a standard American railroad boxcar.

When Clarence 'Kelly' Johnson, the visionary engineer behind Lockheed's famous 'Skunk Works' operations was asked his opinion of the model Hawkins provided, he said, 'If you send that damn thing in, you'll destroy Lockheed.

Lockheed won over bids from Douglas, Boeing and Fairchild aircraft companies and the rest is history.

Mr Hawkins's many honours are the Navy's Distinguished Pacific Service Award in 1961 for his work on the Polaris, the first missile launched from underwater using a submarine as a firing platform. He received the National Medal for Science in 1988.

Unlike Arthur Raymond, Wills Hawkins was not known by many pilots who flew his aircraft, but he will be best remembered for opening up the polar regions and the contributions they made to commercial and military aviation and above all polar aviation.

LOCKHEED C-130 HERCULES
LC-130R2 # *160740*
Lockheed production number 4725 Lockheed s/n 382C-65D
USAF s/n 76-0491 NSF s/n 76-3301 built in 1976 VX-6 side number XD 02
LC-130R2 # *160741 'Spirit of Oxnard'*
Lockheed production number 4731- Lockheed s/n 382C-65D. USAF s/n 76-0492, NSF s/n 76-0492
US Navy # 160741, Built in 1976 VX-6 side number XD-01-transferred to NYANG.
LC 130R1 # *159 129 'Crippled Pete'*
Lockheed production number 4508. Lockheed s/n 382C-26B, USAF s/n 73-0839, NSF s/n 73 3300.
Built in 1973, VXE-6 side number XD-05 transferred to NYANG.
LC –130R1 # *159131*
Lockheed production number 4522, Lockheed s/n 382C-26D, USAF s/n 73.0841
Built in 1973, VX-6 side number N/A, VXE-6 side number XD-04.
Crashed while attempting landing during the recovery of # *148321 'Phoenix'* – *'The Old Grey Mare'* and *'The Crown'*
LC-130 RI # *159130 'The Spirit of McMurdo',* and *'Chilly'*

Lockheed production number 4516, Lockheed s/n 382C-26D, USAF s/n 73 0840 built 1973, VX-6 side number N/A, VXE-6 side number XD-04. Storage at Davis-Monthan AFB 8 March 1999.

LC-130R # *148321 'Phoenix'. 'The Old Grey Mare' and 'The Crown'*

Lockheed Production number 3567,Lockheed s/n 282C-6B USAF s/n 59 5925 built in 1959, VX-6 side number, JD-18 VXE-6 side number XD-03 –the second C-

Recovered after being buried by snow for 17 years in Antarctica. After unloading a French traverse team on December 4 1971, the pilot made a JATO take off to return to McMurdo, some 750 nautical miles away, at an altitude of about 50 feet, two JATO bottles separated from the left hand side of the fuselage and struck the inboard engine and propeller.

With the gearbox and propeller torn off and the outboard engine damaged by flying debris, the aircraft was seriously damaged on impact. The ten men aboard were uninjured, but had to live in survival shelters for 80 hours until the weather improved enough to allow a rescue plane to land

LC-130F # *148320 'The Emperor', 'Ciudad De Punta Arenas'*

Lockheed production number 3565, Lockheed s/n 262C-6B, USAF s/n 59 5914, built 1959, VX-6 side number JD-20 VXE- side number XD-06,

In storage at Davis –Monthan AFB March 1999,

LC-130 F # *148318 'City of Christchurch' – 'The Adelie'*

Lockheed production number 3562 Lockheed s/n 282C-6B, USAF s/n 59-5922, built 1959, VX-6 side number JD-18

Crashed while attempting to take off from McMurdo Station on February 1971. The aircraft was in taxi-ing prior to takeoff in poor visibility at Williams Field, when its left main ski went over a 1.7 metre snow bank. The starboard wing hit the ground and separated between the two engines, the escaping fuel ignited and, fanned by high Antarctic winds, the C-130 was quickly engulfed in fire. The crew of nine and one passenger made a hasty exit from the burning aircraft, however, the crash crews were unable to control the fire because of the strong winds and the Hercules was subsequently destroyed.

LC-130F # *148319 'Penguin Express'*

Lockheed production number 3564 Lockheed s/n 282C-5B. USAF s/n 59-5923, built in 1959, VX-6 side number JD-19, VXE-6 side number XD –07,

Storage at Davis Monthan AFB on 10 March 1999.

LOCKHEED LC-130 # *3155917 'AO-TE-A-ROA*

Lockheed production number 4305

Lockheed s/n 382C-9D.

USAF s/n n/a

Built 1968

VX-6 side number JD-17

VXE-6 side number n/a

Crashed on landing at the South Pole Station on January 28 1973, the aircraft is still a quarter of a mile off the approach end of the South Pole runway, and used as a. guidance marker.

Recalls Bob Nyden who was on the ice 71/72, 72/73 and 73/74, '*the crash site pretty well covered the length of the skiway at the Pole and it was quite a mess for the rest of the year, after the accident, however, because of the C-130's loss, it placed the workload on the only other two Herks [#319 and #320], air operations were severely curtailed. For SAR purposes, both planes had to be mechanically up for either to fly, and by that time of year most of the flights were turnaround to Christchurch.*

By the time we got back in '73, there was no trace of the wreck. The winter- over crew had apparently dragged it all off and repaired the skiway.'

LOCKHEED TC-130Q

#159348 XD-00

This TC-130Q was the first generation, survivable, communications link with submarine forces, providing high frequency and very low frequency high-powered transmission coverage of the Atlantic and Pacific. TACAMO [take charge and move out].

At the end of its operational life as a TACAMO communications platform, #159348 was also used as a 'bounce bird' by TACAMO community after the communications gear was removed in 1989. It was operated during Desert Storm as a 'trash and cattle' hauler by VQ-4 until the TACAMO mission tempo for VQ-4 increased. #159348 was loaned to VR-22; they operated it as an additional asset during the end of Desert Storm. At the end of the war, the TC-130Q went to the boneyard and was resurrected by VXE-6 to be used as a 'bounce bird' and as a 'trash and cattle' hauler during Operation Deep Freeze from 1992- 95.

With its mission avionics removed for installation in a VQ-4 E-6A Mercury aircraft, as part of an agreement sponsored by Commander Naval Forces Pacific, the aircraft was transferred to VXE-6, the Navy's Antarctic Exploration Squadron. It flew three years between Christchurch and McMurdo bringing in supplies to support the NSAF and the Naval Support Forces Antarctica

When *#159348* came to the end of its required service life, no one wanted to pay for the rework, although the US Forest Service, the Drug Enforcement Agency and a couple of other 'Alphabet soup' named government agencies were interested, but having no takers, the workhorse was given an early retirement at Tinker AFB.

DE HAVILLAND AIRCRAFT UC-1/U-IB OTTERS.

The specific purpose of the Navy's Otter acquisition for their Antarctic operations was to support their exploration programme on a continent which had remained relatively unexplored, the Otters were to carry out aerial support work and compliment the R4-D's, Neptune's and helicopters.

In September 1956, a group of VX-6 Squadron pilots made their way to De Havilland's plant in Canada to pick up the first of the UC-1's, among them were Commander Ken Snyder and Lt Con Jabury- both later volunteers at the Naval Museum. Once at Quonset Point, the first four Otters, were to have been delivered in June, however, a strike at the DHC plant delayed the delivery date, the first #142424 was accepted by the Squadron on July 18 at Downeview, but delivery of the remaining four were postponed until the following March.

The Royal Canadian Air force kindly helped out, and three of their recently delivered Otters [numbers 60,62 and 66] were transferred to the US Navy and given s/n's #144269-# 144259 and # 144261

The Otters had to be disassembled and packed away in crates and transported to the Weddell Sea aboard the USS Wyandot [AKA –92]. Once ashore, after a rough journey ploughing its way through 1,600 miles of ice covered waters before finding a suitable site for their base on January 27 1957.

The ship had spent 42 days on the ice and penetrated 300 miles further into the Weddell Sea, than any other ship had done before.

Once in Antarctica, events moved very quickly, the squadron's personnel began the arduous task of unloading over 6,000 tons of cargo, assembling the aircraft and locating a suitable landing field. On December 22 1955, the Squadron's first Otter #142424 crashed on take off at McMurdo when it hit tail first,

 # 142424

Crashing on takeoff near Cape Byrd, Ross Island, Antarctica on December 22 1955, the aircraft commander reported that the flight controls didn't feel 'right' and could not be moved forward of the neutral position. About 50 feet after take-off the Otter's ski's brushed the snow and the aircraft hit, but flat. Both ski struts were forced into the fuselage to such an extent that the aircraft was a strike.

Spilling one crewmember completely out of the aircraft- the Otter was a total loss, having flown only eight hours, mostly on training flights. Salvageable parts were removed and the aircraft was left to float out on the sea ice and sink.

#142425.

After finishing its tour of duty with VXE-6 '425' went to the Naval Aerospace Recovery Centre at El Centro, California, it was also with the Parachute Test Range at the same centre. The facilities at the centre, had as its mission, the air development test and evaluation of parachutes, human escape methods and systems of rescue survival and personnel safety equipment. For this unit, the Otter was used as a 'jumper' – a platform from which parachutists jumped in testing equipment. The facilities remained at El Centro until March 1975.

From there it then sold and operated as N1037 by 40 Mile Air of Tok, Alaska, then purchased by a private party in Auburn, Washington and registered N129JN. During this time it was converted to a turbine Otter, with a PT-6 engine. It was later sold to North Star Air of Pickle Lake, Ontario, registered as C-GCOA.

 # 142426.

While parked at Little America V an 80 mph windstorm opened the tie down rings and the aircraft was blown away.

#142427.

Cracked its fuselage during taxiing on the Ross Sea, on October 22 1958. The aircraft was supporting a science party taking observation readings on the Ross Ice Shelf. During the ground taxi to take the science part to another observation site, the fuselage cracked. It could be flown back to McMurdo. The Otter was not repaired and was stuck in McMurdo.

#144259

When UC-1 3 144260 crashed into the mountains on Edward VII Peninsula on February 3 1956, *#144259* was placed on board the *USS Glacier* to transport it from McMurdo to Little America V to assist in the rescue of the downed aircraft on the mountainside. On February 10 1956, during the offloading process a hoist cable broke and the Otter plunged onto the ice shelf, landing on its right wing and landing gear. The fall damaged the wing extensively and fractured the fuselage. The Navy considered the Otter a strike.

#144260

Crashed into the mountain summit on Edward VII Peninsula. On February 3 1956, two hours after leaving Little America V while en-route to Mile 38 of the Army-Navy Trail, the Otter started picking up ice on the propeller and the aircraft flew into the summit of a snow covered mountain in the Edward VII Peninsula. The impact of the crash was slight and no one on board was injured.
The survivors walked 40 of the 110 miles back to Little America V before being rescued by a VX-6 Squadron's helicopter.

 # 144261

#144669

In 1965, the Comite Antarctique Belgo Neelandais [the Belgian- Dutch Antarctic Expedition was loaned # 144669 from the US Navy and it was transferred to them in February 1969, it was registered as OO-HAD. It crashed at the South African SANAE Station in the Antarctic on February 1970 and was a complete write off, as well as all the expensive scientific equipment on board, some parts were recovered and used in the restoration of its twin OO-SUD Otter in the Royal Army Museum in Brussels. Writes Guy Van de Merckt.

 # 144670

A US Naval Test Pilot School, is the last US Military Otter fling, the sole remaining active Otter is based at PAX River and is still active for Naval Test Pilot School.

#144671.

#144671 was accepted to the Naval Test Pilot School on 29 November 1974 and, without having been flown. It actually went to the Army National Guard's 162nd ATB of the Connecticut National Guard. In 1979, the aircraft went back to the Navy at the Naval Test Pilot School at PAX River, MD and was sold some months later on the civil market.

Writes Johan Pieters. *#144671* was the first Otter out of its packing case on the Squadron's Weddell Sea base in early February 1957, and with Lt.Cdr Snyder at the controls, it carried Capt Edwin McDonald, the Commander of the Weddell Sea Task Group to meet Sir Vivian Fuchs, commander of Shackleton Base, the nearby British Base.

The following day *#144672* took off for its first flight with Lt Jabury at the controls, logging a 2-hour flight over the Weddell Sea to Gould Bay.

After the Otter was sold it was trucked to Calgary, Alberta, intended to be rebuilt, but was destroyed in a hanger fire on 14 May 1983, reports Karl Hayes.
#144672

Entering service with VX-6 Squadron in October 1957, with Lt Jabury at the controls, who between October 3 1957 and January 8 1958, spent over 30 hours in the cockpit, transporting cargo and flying in support of scientific field parties operating from various points in Antarctica. The paths of *#144672* and its pilots diverged after their time together on the ice during the late 1950's, while Jabury and Snyder served in various capacities on their way to retirement as Captain and Commander respectively

Re-designated NU-1B, it is on display at the National Aviation, Pensacola, FL.
The Museum's Otter # *144672* had wintered at Antarctica during Deep Freeze 11 and 111, was returned to the Navy for an overhaul, designated and assigned to the Test Pilot Training School NATC PAX River, following that tour it was assigned to the Navy Air Training Command at Pensacola and thence to the Museum in a flyable condition.

Today, again fitted with skis and adorned with a brilliant orange and silver hue, she stands proudly alongside the Squadron's famous R4D-5L – '*Que Sera Sera*
#144673

On January 4 1959, *#144673* crashed while taking off from Marble Point's dirt runway. As the Otter departed the runway, it made a very steep left turn and the left wing hit a small knoll, the aircraft cart wheeled and crashed, killing the three aboard, the cause of the crash was never determined.
#144674

This Otter # 144674 was retired from VXE-6 IN September 1966 logging 741 hours. Like #144671, it also served with the Army National Guard's 142 nd TARS of Missouri, while the Guard retained its Navy's colour scheme of day-glow underside, wingtips and tail, with silver wings and upper fuselage, but adopted a hybrid serial number 0-4574, being the 0- used by the Army to indicate aircraft ten year old together with the last four of the Navy s/n .In June 1970, *#144674* was stricken from the Naval inventory. It joined the Civil Air Patrol [Southwest Region as N5348G and was registered to them in 1977.

Later the Otter was sold to Parsons Airways Northern of Fin Flon, Manitoba as G-GGSL, then to Selkirk Air of Selkirk, Manitoba, who still operates it; it has been re-engine with Polish PZL 1000 HP engines.
#147574

Otter *#147574* began operational service as XL 710 of the Royal Air Force. Acquired for use in the Antarctic during the 1958 IGY. After the RAF service, it was handed over to the US Navy, which explains why its Navy tail number is higher than the rest of the Squadron's Otter fleet, because it was acquired later.

On December 29 1957, after the British Expedition had departed South Ice Base en- route for the South Pole, their Otter *#147574* took off from the deserted base on its trans-Antarctic flight and encountered bad weather, apart from the navigational difficulties, one of the main proposes of the flight was to report on the state of the terrain for the benefit of the ground party. As this proved impossible, due to low cloud the Otter returned to base, here a somewhat demoralised RAF crew had to re-open the base, and then sit out the bad weather.

They took off again at 1148 pm on January 6 1958. This time the weather had improved, two hours later they passed over the expedition's ground party on its journey to the Pole, the crew sighted the South Pole Station at 1628, having picked up the Pole homing beacon 30 miles out, they then flew directly over the Station at 2000 feet, almost exactly eleven hours after take off and touched down at Scott Base at 2245, after a flight of 1430 statute miles. *XL 710 [#147574]* was escorted down the runway by two US Navy Otters who had flown out from McMurdo to meet them, before climbing away. An international recognition quickly followed this epic flight.

It was the first single engine aircraft to fly across the continent of Antarctica.

Footnote: In 1935, the American explorer Lincoln Ellsworth did fly across the continent in his single engine Northrop Gamma, but he made four intermediate landings before running out of fuel 16 miles short of his destination and was forced to walk home, so his achievement is not quite comparable to *#147574.*

When the Navy finished with it, it was then purchased by the New Zealand Air Force as NZ-6081 intended to be operated by the Kiwi's in Antarctica, but this never happened. Originally the Otter was stored in the Scott Base hanger for the winter, and then prepared for transport back to New Zealand. The US Navy dismantled the Otter at the New Zealander's Antarctic base, crated and towed on a sledge across the Ross Sea Ice Shelf for loading.

However, while in transit it was damaged in an accident with a Navy bulldozer. The Otter was shipped to Lyttelton were it was met by a party of RNZAF mechanics from their air base at Wigram, who uncrated the Otter and towed it over Christchurch's Port Hills on its main undercarriage. Later transported to Harewood airfield, then flown to Wellington by UDSAF C-124 Globemaster for repairs at De Havilland Aircraft Company at Rongotai [Wellington].

It was later sold in Canada in 1964 and registered CF-PNV to Georgian Bay Airways of Toronto. Later sold to La Ronge Aviation of La Ronge Saskatchewan and crashed at Lyan Lake, Manitoba in May 1976. The wreck was sold to Cox Air Resources. Ray Cox, a well know fellow in Otter circles was making the Otter Turbine conversion, Otter 421, as soon as this was certificated; he was going to rebuild 126 as a turbine.

Unfortunately his prototype turbine conversion crashed and he ran out of money. Otter 126 was then sold and is now registered N63535 to another Otter rebuild located just north of Seattle, it was never repaired after its May 1976 crash and finished up sitting in his yard.

The US Navy's VXE-6 Squadron's 14 Otters proved their worth in Antarctica and ideal for the task they had been acquired for- they flew more than 10,400 hours in Navy service. Performing an exemplary job of work in the difficult and hazardous support of the Antarctic research effort. The survivors of their number, demonstrated their versatility by serving a number of divergent roles with the Navy,

SIKORSKY HELICOPTERS
HUS-1 / LC-34D ' Seahorse'
144655
Sikorsky c/n 58 510
Struck from Navy inventory May 27 1969 –NARF Pensacola
#144657
Sikorsky C/N 58 545
Struck from Navy inventory 1969 NAPR Pensacola
Sold to Stinson Field Aircraft in San Antonio TX, Purchased from Stinson in April 1974 by Carson Services Inc Perkasia PA. From Jeff Hill Carson Helicopters 'this was a purchase of eleven aircraft that were incomplete. We brought them for their transmissions and rotor heads; there were no engines or blades. These aircraft were never assembled as aircraft and have been scrapped'.
#144658

Sikorsky C/N 58 546
Crashed, McMurdo 23 December 1962
          Larry Lister relayed a item re *#144658* 'this particular H-34 had a hydraulic servo throttle and an engine start, there was a 'run in' [normal throttle was a cable set-up manually controlled] The engine over speed, shedding fan blades from the big cooling fan mounted on the prop shaft, cutting fuel and hod lines in the clutch compartment, resulting in a fire. It couldn't be put out so a Seabee on his cat, pushed it over the hill, when I first got there in October '65, we were finding pieces of it just below the hill.
#144662
Sikorsky c/n 58 614
Unknown
#145717
Sikorsky C/N 58 804
'Gentle 1'
Transferred to Naval Air rework Facility, Quonset Point to Bradley Air Museum, struck from Naval inventory on October 19 1973 t.
#145710
Sikorsky C/N 58 806
Crashed at Wright Dry Valley 11 November 1962
#148112
Skorsky c/n 58 1240
'Gentle 119' Unknown
#148119
Sikorsky c/n 58 1263
Unknown. Kept at NAS Quonset Point for training – Larry Lister
' #148121
Sikorsky No 58 1265
'Gentle 3'. Struck from Navy inventory 1969 NARF Pensacola. Sold to Stinson Field in April 1974, by Carson Services INC Perkasie PA, From Jeff Hill, Carson Helicopters. 'This purchased of eleven that were incomplete- same as for *#144657*
#148122
Sikorsky c/n 58 1273
'Gentle 4' same as for *#144657.*
#150220
Sikorsky c/n 58 1560'
          'Gentle 5' Crashed and declared a loss in 1964, recovered by sailors from VX-6 and the *USS Staten Island*, repaired and returned to service. Crashed again on 19 November 1969 when engine failed. Lt.Cdr Brandau auto rotated the H-34 down and it struck the side of a slope, slid down and caught fire. Two men were killed-American Thomas and New Zealander Jeremy Sykes-The helicopter was destroyed.
          Larry Lister writes. 'Prior to 1962 when McNamara did his 'lets change designation of military airplanes to the Air Force way' the H-34 was known as HUS/hss-1. Deep Freeze H-34 was UH-34D's with some cold weather mods, making them LH-34D's.
The biggest mod was the installation of the Andover APU instead of the small Waukesha unit. The Andover was a V-2 air-cooled united with a started/Gen mounted on it that could supply total electrical power to the aircraft in the event of an electrical failure. It was also used as a boost to start the big motor, instead of having to use external power. The other mod was the installation of a 150 gal external fuel drop tank on the port side of the fuselage and a better heating system.

The rest of the aircraft was just a regular UH-34D. The difference in the landing gear the earlier Buno had what was called 'bent-leg gear'. This a single bent strut mounted in a sleeve bearing, allowing for smoother [?] landings. There was too much movement on the set down, as the fuselage moved forward a bit as the collective was lowered and the entire weight was settled.

The later aircraft had the 'V-leg' gear, which gave better stability on landing. I'm not sure the time the change took place, but I think it was around the 148 series. During my first tour in the Squadron [65-69] the Hello's were painted all orange, when # 150220 returned to us it was painted gloss grey and remained that way. It was actually easier to see against the ice and snow, but VERY hard to see in the Dry Valleys. The numbers and letters were black on the orange bird but white on #220.

The Sikorsky model S-58 was a very successful general duty helicopter. The radial engine was fitted in the nose as in the H-19, but the fuselage was more streamlined; the box-and boom design of the H-19 was replaced by a simple tapering structure, the aft end of which could be folded.

The type was known as HSS or HUS in the US Navy USMC services. The S-58 also pioneered airline helicopter operations. Some are still flying, often converted with turbine engine –2,261 were built.

BELL HECOPTERS.

UH-1D UN-1N/HH-1N 'Iroquois 'Huey'.

The first UH-1N arrived at Quonset Point in July 1971 –Lt.Cdr Blackwelder and Lt.Cdr Kinsey flew the first two there from Fort Worth, Texas,

#65-9739 Bell UH-1D

Transferred from the US Army to VXE-6 in 1970, converted to a UH-1H, was spotted with the Connecticut ARNG in December 1989, in 2002 it went to Jordan-Jeff Rankin-Lowe.

#65-9740 Bell UH-1D.

Transferred from US army to VXE-6 in 1970- unknown

#66 1012 Bell UH-1D.

Transferred from the US Army to VXE-6 in 1970- written off on January 9 1975.

#158234 Bell UH-1N/ HH-1N *'Gentle 11'*

Struck from Navy inventory 1996

#158235 Bell UH-IN/HH-1N

To AMACRC as *7H0246* on April 3 1996. In December 1973 the helicopter was blown on its side by an. estimated 90 mph wind, it was salvaged by a team that traversed the same hazardous path over which Garry-Gerard had gone in 1911 and which prompted his work 'The Worst Journey in the World'.

#158236 Bell UH-1N/HH-1N - '

Crashed, during a ferry flight from the factory, Forth Worth.

#158237 Bell UH-1N / HH-1N. Gentle 14

Crashed Flat Top Mountain, Antarctica 18 January 1986.

#158238 Bell UH-1N/HH-1N.

To AMARC as 7H02248 on January 20 1996

#158 239 Bell UH-1N/HH-1N.

Crashed, Darwin Glacier Antarctica 7 January 1979

#158240 Bell UH-1N/HH-1N

To AMARC as 7HO241 on April 17 1995

#158241 Bell UH-1N/HH-1N

Crashed, California 17 February 1970

#158249 Bell UH-1N/HH-1N

Crashed Wohlschlag Bay 13 October 1992.

#158272 Bell UH-1N/ HH-1N

Search and Rescue NAS Fallon NV.
#158283 Bell UH-1N/HH-1N
To AMARC as 7HO247 on April 3 1996
#158284 Bell UH-1N/HH-1N
Search and Rescue NAS China Lake CA.
#158288 Bell UH-1N/HH-1N
HMT-303 MCAS Camp Pendleton CA.

The US Army began support VX-6 in Antarctica with the H-1 aircraft in 1961. The Army transferred three UH-1D Huey's to VXE-6 in 1969.

The US Army [USAF s/n 62 12544] while landing near the summit of a 13,800 foot peak at the Admiralty Mountains of Victoria land on November 8 1964, about 39 n/miles from Hallett Station, there were no injuries but the plane was written off.

A US Army UH-1D [USAF s/n 9741], crashed during a white-out on November 5 1966 at Marie Byrd Land Camp No 1, no injuries.

During the 44 years the United States Navy's involvement in logistic support for Operation Deep Freeze, a number of other US military, government departments and other countries provided aircraft and aircrews either supporting the US Navy or their own country involvement in the IGY's Programme.

The National Aeronautics & Space Administration [NASA]
4 aircraft- Convair 880, Douglas DC-8 and Lockheed ER-2.
8 aircraft- LC-130R Hercules
United States Army.
11 aircraft- Bell HU-1B Iroquois helicopters and Bell HU-D Iroquois helicopters.
United States Air Force, including the 109th New York Air National Guard.
713 aircraft – Lockheed LC-130H Hercules. Boeing C-27A Globemasters – Boeing C-67 – Boeing C-135- Douglas SC-54D Rescuemasters- Douglas C-118 Liftmasters – Douglas C-124 Globemasters- Douglas C-133 Cargomasters – Lockheed C-5 Galaxy- Lockheed C-121 Supper Constellations – Lockheed WC –130A Hercules – Lockheed WC-130B Hercules -Lockheed C-130D Hercules- Lockheed C-130E Hercules- Lockheed C-130H Hercules - Lockheed C-141 Starlifters and McDonald Douglas KC-10a Extenders.

United States Navy Icebreaker Helicopters

56-Helicopters –Bell HTL-4/5 7 6- Bell HUL-1 – Kaman UH-2A & B's Seasprite –Sikorsky HO4S-3 & HRS-3.
United States Marine Corps.
30 aircraft- Douglas R5D [C-54 Skymasters] –Lockheed KC-130F Hercules-Lockheed KC-139R Hercules and Lockheed KC 130T Hercules.
United States Coast Guard.
55 aircraft- Aerospatiale HN-65A Dolphin- Lockheed HC-130h Hercules and Sikorsky HH-52A Sea` Guard.
Royal New Zealand Air Force.
22 aircraft- Auster MK 7C – Bell UH-1H Iroquois- De Havilland Canada DHC-2 Beaver- De Havilland Canada DHC-2 Beaver. - Lockheed C-130H Hercules and Lockheed P-3B/K Orion.
Royal New Zealand Navy.
1 aircraft – Kamand SH-2F Seasprite
Other Military Aircraft from other Nations.
144 Aircraft-
Helicopters [New Zealand] Limited

29 helicopters.

Other US Navy Aircraft.

33 aircraft-Douglas R5D-4R Skymasters-Douglas R6D-1- Lockheed C-130F Hercules- Lockheed C-13-T Hercules-Lockheed TC-130Q Hercules- Lockheed R7V-1 Supper Constellations- Lockheed WV-2 and Lockheed RP-3D Orion.

The nose artwork on all Deep Freeze aircraft were normally the prerogative of the crew and generally once the name and the creativeness was painted on the squadron's aircraft, it remained. However there were exceptions, one such case involved *BuNo 17221*, originally named '*Mutha Goose*' when it first arrived in Antarctica in 1965, [now one of only two R4-D's who survived along with the famous '*Que Sera Sera*' now in the National Museum Pensacola Fl.]

The story behind the imaginative art decoration of # *17221* began with a skinny goose with a long neck, painted on the nose in February 1966. Additional art at the exhaust port for the Auxiliary Power Unit [APU] aft of its cargo door pictured the back end of the skinny goose looking over her shoulder with the butt centred on the APU exhaust port.

In June 1966 after New Zealand National Airways [NAC] rework and paint, the aircraft was renamed '*Kool Kiwi*' showing a kiwi bird on skis.

Paul Panehal did the original sketches while staying at the White Heron hotel, situated close to Christchurch Airport that was the squadron's drinking hole. Paul's creativity began as a penguin on skis but it was difficult to come up with a unique name without copying '*Puckered Pete*'. '*After some more rum and Coke, the sketches changed from a penguin to a Kiwi and the name came before I finished my sketch*' Paul recalled to me several years ago. '*After we accepted the aircraft from NAC, the original crew names including Jim and I can be seen, the small kiwi was by Lt.Cdr Berger, which was accompanied by the words 'It ain't no big thing'.*

In October 1969, the old girl was renamed '*Yankee Tiki Te Hau*', with a green stone Tiki, with the squadron number changed back to # 4. Nose art work and crew names prior to the aircraft being decommissioned [removed from the US Navy's inventory] and given to New Zealand as a gift from the Americans in October 1969, as a memento for the early days of VX-6 and as a close bond between the squadron and the people of Christchurch.

A final word from Paul speaking for himself and thousands of other squadron members '*I received my orders to Glynco [Brunswick] Georgia and returned to the States, leaving behind my many good Kiwi friends, the drinking and darts mates at the Russley Hotel and other downtown pubs, fellow bowlers and many fond memories. Maybe someday, my wife and I will return for a visit and tour the islands. Of course it will never be the same.*'

A postscript: The R4-D and it association with the Americans Antarctic operations which spanned over 44 years, but both the Argentine Navy and Air Force flew the DC-3 on the continent. As early as 1954, the Argentine Air Force created an Antarctic Air Task Force that, among other aircraft, employed Dakotas to fly weather reconnaissance missions between its Rio Gallegos Air Base in Southern Patagonia and the Antarctic.

During the 1961-1962 season, the Navy flew two DC-3's to the South Pole by way of a temporary base camp on the Larsen Ice Shelf and Ellsworth Station. They arrived on January 7 1962 and after a two hour stay at Amundsen-Scott South Pole Station, began their return flight. Fuel and JATO bottles and maintenance support at the South Pole was provided by VX-6 Squadron and the US Navy.

The following season an Argentine Air Force DC-3 attempted to duplicate this feat but the aircraft caught fire on take off from Ellsworth Station and was a total loss, fortunately no crew were injured. However, the Air Force was successful in establishing regular cargo and personnel flights between Rio Gallegos and Teniente Matienzo Station also located on the Larsen Ice Shelf in the vicinity of Robertson Island.

The Air Force did not relinquish its ambition to reach the South Pole, putting the accident of 1962 behind them, and in October 1965 it launched another successful attempt to make the flight, using a DC-3 and two single engine Beavers. The DC-3 was especially modified for the mission; DC04 engines replaced its normal engines and a jet propulsion unit with a 600-kilogram thrust installed in its tail. The route followed was basically the same as that used by the Navy in 1962, from Rio Gallegos the plane flew to Teniente Matienzo then on to the General Belgrano Station on the Flichner Ice Shelf. In company with two Beavers, the DC-3 laid down an emergency cache at 83-degrees South Latitude, from which point they proceeded to the South Pole, arriving on November 3 1965, and a few days later the DC-3 continued on to McMurdo Station. Thus completing the crossing of the continent. After a period of maintenance at McMurdo, the DC-3 took off, and as it flew over the South Pole, the two Beavers joined in and headed for home-the journey was uneventful.

During 1967, the Air Force sent three DC-3's to Teniente Matienzo, while there, the aircraft carried out a number of activities resembling those performed by VX-6 Dakotas on the other side of Antarctica, flying photo reconnaissance missions, supplying shelters to other outlying stations and carrying fuel, passengers and supplies. One of these aircraft visited the Argentine Eperanza Station at Hope Bay.

The Soviets submitted to the SCAR Logistics Working Group, the specifications and performance data for their three twin engine aircraft that they had employed in Antarctica; -the IL-14, IL-12 and LI-2. Of these three, the LI-2 has the characteristics and performance quite similar to that of the LC-47/LC-117. In appearance, it resembled the LC-47 [the IL-14 and IL-12 appeared to be different versions of the same basic aircraft but were larger and more powerful than the LI-2 and had a tricycle landing rear.]

The Soviets also prepared a summary of their air operations in Antarctica for the SCAR. While this document contains discrepancies, some of which may have been the results of poor translation, it did provide a general informative review of Soviet employment of aircraft. Just as the United States had depended heavily on their C-47's [R4-D's] in the years from 1956 through to 1961, so did the Soviets rely on their LI-2. Unlike the United States and Argentina, the Soviet transported their aircraft to Antarctica by ship, rather than fly them in for their first expedition [1955-56] when they took two LI-2'S to Mirnyy Station, the following year they had six and by early 1958 had seven aircraft at the Station.

The manner in which the Soviets employed their aircraft was quite similar to that of the US Navy in using their LC-47 and LC-117's, on one of their first missions on reaching Mirnyy was to make a reconnaissance flight to the east, shortly, thereafter, they participated in establishing a scientific party at Bunger Hill. During 1956, the two LI-2's then at Mirnyy, along with an IL-12 and a single engine AN-2, delivered 14 men and 12 tons of cargo to Pionerskaya Station located on the polar plateau, the same aircraft transported the personnel and equipment to establish a scientific party in the Bunger Hills in August and September.

The LI-2s carried out seismic sounding of Drygalski Island and also landed scientists to make astrofixes at various points. Other Soviets aircraft appeared to have been specially equipped for various types of scientific investigations. One use for these aircraft had no counterpart in the VX-6 experience with fixed wing aircraft in the Antarctic, was the ferrying ashore both passengers and cargo from ships unable to penetrate the pack ice. For example, in 1966, approximately 32 tons of goods and 93 passengers were shuttled back and forth between Mirnyy and the expeditions ships.

The short summary of air operations does not indicate any conclusions that the Soviets may have drawn from the experience with LI-2's, nor does it indicate why they were fazed out of their programme. Presumably, it was because of the greater capabilities of their IL-12 and IL-14 aircraft, their mission, however, seems similar to those performed for *Operation Deep Freeze* by the Gooney Birds.

After leaving the ice in the late 1960's, the sight of an old DC-3 originally working for its keep in Antarctica in the 21st century was one you wouldn't expect to see. However, the DC-3 has survived many attempts to pension it off, but in January 2000 the latest of the old war birds of Antarctic once again proved it could fill a valuable aviation role when Adventure network International chartered a Basler BT-67 [a DC-3] *N200AN* aircraft from Basler Turbo Conversions. The Wisconsin company extended the fuselage of the Gooney Bird, whose airframe was built in 1944, lengthened the wingspan, replaced the cylinder engines with turboprops, installed 'state-of-the–art' navigational equipment, including two GPS systems and made extra room inside for a greater payload. Since its debut in the 1930's, the DC-3 has been modified and transformed into dozens of different incarnations. It has flown in all four continents and is still relied upon by operations ranging from the Bolivian military to the Royal Thai Air Force, to smoke jumpers in the State and all kinds of deep-field workers around the world.

In the Antarctic the Basler BT-67 aircraft was used to transport a number of field parties from Patriot Hills to various camps and on one occasion to the South Pole. This particular trip carried a party of NASA meteorite hunters, including American Astronauts Jim Lovell and Owen Garriott. The following November, the NSF decided to charter the same aircraft for a month to fill in a perceived logistics gap between the small twin aircraft and the larger ski-equipped Hercules operated by the NYANG, it was the first time the Foundation had chartered an ANI aircraft. This was perhaps also a response by NSF to the Air National Guard's current inability to provide sufficient flights to the South Pole.

'The beauty of the DC-3 has always been its rugged reliability' said Rom Weigt, president of Basler Turbo conversions, *'Overall it is unmatched by anything in the market today.'* This would be endorsed by all those OAE's who flew the 'old girl' in the Antarctic.

'It was a magnificent airplane, it could carry a great load of ice on its wings and with a great big barn door for a rudder, it made for easy cross wind landing' Eddie Frankiewicz said.

'For open snow landings at the reduced weight of the R4-D, they could land where there were possible snow bridges over crevasses that could not be seen' Buz Dryfoose said when explaining the reasons its as good as any mid weight aircraft in Antarctica.

Cdr Jim Waldron remembers the aircraft fondly *'It was a very reliable aircraft, we put it through a lot of terrible weather and cold, but it was always stable and had few failures, it was terrific for what it could do.'*

When built in the 30's the aircraft could have been purchased off the Douglas production line for $US138.000- today that cost is in excess of $US.5 million.

It was the first DC-3 to be seen in the skies over McMurdo since the Navy's VX-6 last employed them two decades previously. The United States Navy withdrew its last 'Gooney Bird' from service in the mid 1970's

POLAR AIRCRAF TURNING BACK FOR TAIERI BASE

The Press

U.S. HELICOPTER WRECKED

Crash Into Inner Harbour

SERIOUS LOSS TO EXPEDITION

Taieri-based Aircraft To Fly Today

-way Switch Ma By A rosses

Two Nava In Antarctic 'Plane Crash

Rescue by Helicopter After Days on Ice

UNITE

U.S. FLIGHT TO ANTARCTIC

EARLY ANTARCTIC AVIATION

Top and left :Wilkins –Hearst Antarctic Expedition 1928-30 Lockheed #X3903
Below:
Wilkins inspects his plane prior to the 1928 expedition.

Above:
Members of the first Wilkins-Ellsworth Antarctic exploration.

Admiral Richard Byrd's 'The William Horlick', a long range Curtis-Wright Condor, equipped with skis and floats –powered by two Supercharged Wright Cyclone engines -each capable of 725 hp.

Above: Admiral Byrd on the Barkley-Glow, a twin engine seaplane on the 1939-40 Antarctic expedition carried to Antarctic aboard the USS Bear. Ellsworth's crippled Polar Star # 12289 during the 1933-34 Antarctic expedition

Byrd's wrecked plane during his 1928-30 Antarctic expedition.

Byrd's Fokker Super Universal 'The Virginian' on the surface of Lake Aquamarine, Rockefeller Mountains-this photo was taken on December 1998. Photo Max Wenden

Above: Herbert Hollock-Kenyon meets Lincoln Ellsworth on November 27 1935 during the 1935-36 Antarctic expedition

*Right: Admiral Byrd's plane
the 'Virginian' at the Rockefeller
Mountains at the time it was wrecked
by a severe storm. Photo by Brent
Balchen from 'Come North with Me.'*

*Right: One of Lincoln Ellsworth's
Dornier Flying Boats in the Arctic
during his 1935 polar expedition.
Photo taken at Kings Bay,
Spritzbergen on May 21 1925.*

*Above: Byrd's 55 feet long by 20 feet wide motorized 'monster' designed to carry an aircraft- but never used
after it was taken to Antarctic for his 1939-41 expedition. Right Brent Balchen.*

Above: Lincoln Ellsworth.
Right: Sir Herbert Wilkins, with his pilot
Carl Ben Eielson and their Lockheed Vega.
Photo Australian Antarctic Division.

Ellsworth's 'Polar Star' buried in the snow at Little America for three days while the crew waited to fly to the Bay of Whales on November 27 1935

Top: Two penguins look on with interest as Sir Herbert Wilkins and his crew prepare their Lockheed Vega on their 1911 Antarctic expedition.

Above: Wilkins was the first person to fly a plane in Antarctic. Unable to find runways long enough, he was beaten in the race to be the first to fly to the South Pole. Photo Ohio State University.

Top: Captain Robert Scott became the first Antarctic aeronaut on February 4 1902, when he went up in a balloon. Photo Christchurch Star Collection
Right: Captain Robert Falcon Scott.

The SS 'Terra Nova' at Lyttelton in 1904, the Terra Nova was the expedition's relief ship with the Sir Robert Scott's 1901-04 British Antarctic Expedition. The Paddy tug 'Lyttelton' is assisting Scott's vessel. Photo Christchurch Star Collection.

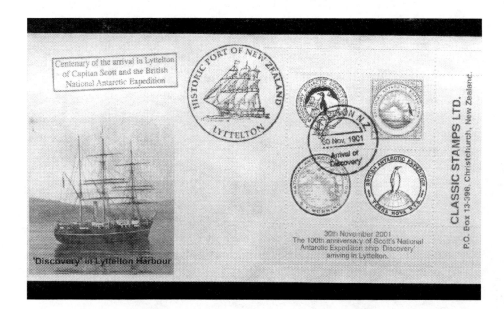

*Above: A cover to mark the 100th
Year of Captain Robert Scott's
British Expedition to arrive at
Lyttelton Harbour on November
9th 1901
Photo Classic Stamps Christchurch.*

*Right: Captain Scott's ship
the Discovery berthed along side Scott's
Hutt. McMurdo. This was the first
Location of Deep Freeze air
facilities, with McMurdo Station
sited beyond and the left of the
Hut today.*

364

*Above:.The US Coast Guard icebreaker 'Northwind' at Wellington in March 1947, after Operation Highjump.
Note the Grumman J2-6 Duck amphibian and the Nikolsky HNS-1 helicopter #39043 on board. The helicopter
was the first to fly in New Zealand.. Photo. The Christchurch Press Collection.*

*The Royal Australian Air Force Catalina at Wigram airfield in August 1948. The Australian amphibian
had just completed the first flight from Macquarie to Christchurch; note the JATO bottles behind the wheel bay.
Photo RNZAF Museum.*

Wilkins was the first person to fly airplane in Antarctica, unable to locate runways long enough, he was beaten in the race to be the first to fly to the South Pole. Photo Ohio State University.

In 1938 Wilkins returned to Antarctica with Lincoln Ellsworth, to assist in the discovery of new land. This photograph shows his Catalina Flying Boat during the search for Russian aviators in 1937. Photo Ohio State University.

**OPERATION
HIGHJUMP
1946-47**

*Top: A Douglas R4-D at Little
America during Operation Highjump
in 1946-47.*
*Right: Rear Admiral Richard Byrd
checking his position over the
South Pole with his sun-compass
on February 16 1947.*
Photos US Navy

*Aviation Machinist Mate
Fred Williams holding a cable while
being filmed in Antarctica during
Operation Highjump.
Photo US Navy*

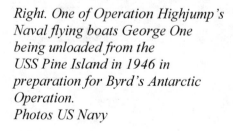

*Right. One of Operation Highjump's
Naval flying boats George One
being unloaded from the
USS Pine Island in 1946 in
preparation for Byrd's Antarctic
Operation.
Photos US Navy*

Right: Five of the six survivors of George One which crashed on December 29 1946.
Left to right. William Warr, James Robbins, Capt H Caldwell, the commander of the USS Pine Island, LTJG William Kearns
the co-pilot Owen McCarty.
missing from the photograph is Wendell Hendersin, the radio man.
Photo US Navy.

Rear Admiral Richard E Byrd with a penguin and guest during Operation Highjump.
Photo US Navy.

Top: The crew assigned to George 2-left to right. Robert Jones, Navigator and 2nd co-pilot, Bob Geoff co-pilot and Lt James Ball, the planes commander [unfortunately the rest of the crew have not been identified] although the crew also comprised John Shafer, Murray Schmidt, Milton Blake Jr, Jeremere Riley and James Payne [photographer]Above: The crew assigned to George 1 from left to right Richard Simpson, First pilot Dale Mincer, John Howl, Martin Lutz, Second pilot and navigator, Vermont Hogback, bottom row from left to right William Smith, George Marck. Phillip Wexford and the Second Engineer William Mills...Photos US Navy

Top: The assigned crew of George 3. Back from left to right, Owen McCarty, William Kearns [co pilot] Ralph Le Blanc [plane Commander]. Maxwell Lopez [navigator] and W Henderson [radioman].
Bottom row from left to right; J D Dicken [Plane Captain] Bill Ware [Flight Engineer] James Robbins [radioman]

The crash site of George One.
Photos US Navy.

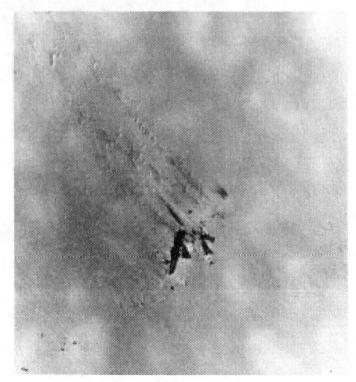

Top left: Admiral Richard Byrd reading.
Top right: The USS Carrier Philippine
Sea with the squadrons R4-D's on her deck.
Above: the crash site of George One, with
a 'rescue us' sign painted on the wing.
Right: The rescue plane George Two
setting out in search for the missing
Marine Flying Boat.
Photos US Navy

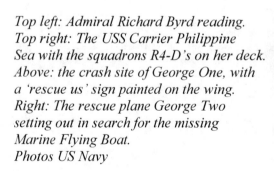

372

Above: Two photographs taken on January 29 1947, shows Lt 'Gus' Shinn with Rear Admiral Richard Byrd aboard takes his R4-D Gooney Bird off from the deck of the USS aircraft carrier 'Philippine Sea' [CVA-47] to make aviation history.
Right: One of the R4-D's takes off from Little America, while three others are on the ice runway. Photos US Navy

77

Right: a Gooney Bird takes off from Little America with the assistance of Jet Assisted Take-off [JATO] in January 1947, during Operation Highjump.

Right A Sikorsky Helicopter lands aboard one of the Task Force Naval ships of Operation Highjump in 1947.

Right: Preheating and refuelling a Squadron's R4-D during Operation Highjump in Antarctica.
Photos . US Navy

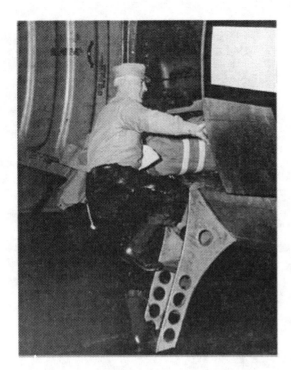

Above: The Grandfather of United States Navy's Antarctic exploration Admiral Richard Byrd.
Right: The Commander of the U.S.N. Task Force 43 D.F. George Dufek.

Above: Commander Edward Ward, the Squadron's First CO. Right: Marine Lt Colonel H R [Hal] Kolp the Squadron's first executive officer. Photos US Navy

George Eastman filming Admiral Byrd with his Cine-Kodak movie camera in 1927 after the Admiral had visited the Eastman's residence to solicit funds for upcoming Antarctic exploration. The photo is an original image bearing Associated Press markings and tongue in cheek [for the 1920's]- a caption on a typewritten slip attached to reverse side-'Eastman shoots Admiral Byrd.' Photo Associated Press

Dr Paul Siple, senior representative of the US War Department [left] with Admiral Richard Byrd at Little America during Operation Highjump in 1947. Photo US Navy.

Admiral George Dufek [third from left] arrives at the New Zealand Air Force Station, Wigram on December 12 1955 with him left to right. Commander V Pendergraff [staff officer] Capt C W Thomas [expedition logistics, Dufek and Commander Donald Kent [Dufek's Chief of Staff] Photo Christchurch Star Collection

Capt George Dufek receives his Rear Admiral's rank insignia from Admiral R B Carney USN in 1955, looking on is the famous American Antarctic explorer Rear Admiral Richard Byrd. Photo US Navy

Above: The Flagship ,USS Arneb
entering Lyttleton harbour,
Christchurch at the end of
Operation Deep Freeze 1.
Top: The mangled remains of
a VX-6 H04S-3 Sikorsky
Helicopter # 138519 at Lyttelton
Harbor in December 1955
Right: Command planning:
Cdr Gordon Edde and Lt Col
Kolp, discussing the Antarctic
before departing in 1955.
Bottom: Deep Freeze II
Rear Admiral George Dufek
with Capt Douglas
Cordiner- VX-6 CO
exchange pleasantries
before departing for the
Antarctic aboard the
Admiral's plane from
Wigram on October
17 1956, with the pair is
Dufek's Chief of Staff
Cdr Kent.
Photos US Navy

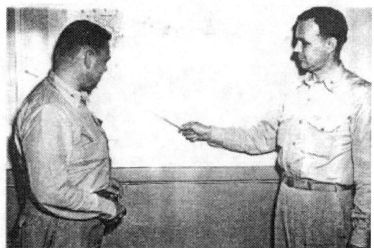

Full dress rehearsal for squadron members at Wigram AFB, Christchurch before departing for the Antarctic, involving mounting JATO bottles on the aircraft. Photo US Navy

Capt Willam Hawkes, Lt D J Shinwinski and Lt Commander Jack Torbert at a weather briefing at Wigram AFB, Christchurch, prior to departing for Antarctica in December 1955.Photo US Navy

Aircraft commanders of the first aircraft to fly from Christchurch to Antarctica at their New Zealand base at Wigram Station on December 20 1955.
Left to right: Lt Commander Bob Graham, Lt Commander Jack Entrikin, Lt Commander Hal Kolp, Lt Commander Harold Hanson, Lt Commander Henry Jorda and Lt Commander Jack Tolbert. Photo US Navy

Captain Gerald Ketchum photographed with the commander of the Admiral's Flagship USS 'Arneb' Capt Robert Kinchley at Lyttelton in December 1955.Photo Christchurch Star Collection.

VX-6 Commanders study weather maps at Wigram station Chrustchurch before departing for Antarctica on 17 October 1956 for Deep Freeze II. From left to right: Commander Henry Jorda, navigator Dick Swadener [standing behind] Capt Cordiner and the Task Force 43 aerologist Commander John Mirabito. Photo Christchurch Star.

The first aircraft to depart from Christchurch for Antarctica to commence Operation Deep Freeze the Lockheed P2V-2N Neptune # 122465 blasts off with assistance of JATO in December 1955. This aircraft was the first to reach Antarctica, sadly this ill fated converted bomber was first to arrived the following year, but crashed on landing, killing four of its eight crew and passengers. Photo Christchurch Press

About to set out on another airlift mission to Antarctica on November 12 1956 as the first of three USAF C-124 Globemasters the 'State of New Jersey' taxies out on the runway at Christchurch Airport. The crew from left to right: Capt Ronald Chandler [RNZSC] Capt Oscar Cassity Ist Aerial Port Squadron] Col Horace Crosswell [Commander USAF Task Force] and Capt Jesse Jumper, the Globemaster's Captain. Photo Christchurch Star Collection'

Hut Point Antarctica in 1955 after the first personnel arrived, note Cpt.Scott's Hut to the left. Photo US Navy

The crew of one of the squadron's Gooney Birds at Little America in 1956 Photo US Navy

United States Navy's icebreaker USS Glacier at McMudo in 1955. Photo US Navy

A Squadron member makes friends with a young local Christchurch lad at Wigram Station, before departing for Antarctica. His Neptune is being serviced in the background. Photo US Navy.

A crew of a Neptune chats before another Antarctic mission. Photo US Navy

A Squadron's Lockheed P2V-2N on the 'deck' at McMurdo with a helicopter in the background. Photo US Navy

A Squadron's R-4D 'Gooney Bird' lands on the ice runway at Little America after another Antarctic mission during Deep Freeze II. Photo US Navy

A Cold day at McMurdo as Squadron personnel leave the station aboard the most suitable transport after a heavy snowstorm, with the Chapel of the Snows nestled under Mt Discovery. Photo US Navy

Working on a R4-D at Little America in 1956. Photo US Navy

Above: A Gooney Bird in its winter storage at Little America awaiting the approaching summer season. Below: Being towed out in preparation for the Squadron personnel to arrive from New Zealand Photos US Navy

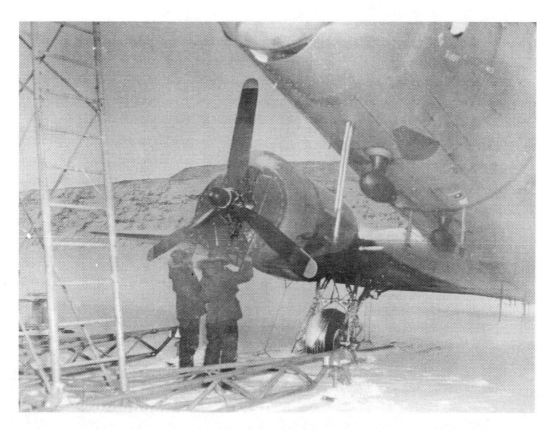

VX-6 ground crews work on the engine of one of the Squadron's Gooney Birds. Photo US Navy

The chosen seven to make the historic polar landing at the South Pole on December 31 1956. Photo US Navy

Above: The historic landing at the South Pole on December 31 1956, when Lt Commander 'Gus' Shinn landed his R4-D [appropriately named 'Que Sera Sera'] on the polar ice cap, was photographed from a circling USAF C-124 Globemaster. Below: the only photograph taken of #12418 on the South Pole, This photo was taken by the plane's navigator Lt John Swadener and it appeared in the December issue of Time Magazine under the simple captain 'Dufek's party at the Pole, from eleven bottles, a wrench and a stagger' Photo US Navy

'Charlene' # 17274, the aircraft flown to Antarctic in 1956 by Lt Commanders Eddie Frankiewicz and his co-pilot James Waldron. Eddie named the plane photographed here at Beardmore Station after a little Michigan girl Charlene Hall, who was dying of an incurable disease. Photo James Waldron Collection

390

Lt Commander James Waldron, who wintered over in 1956 as the Squadron's executive Officer. Photo James Waldron Collection

A Squadron's Otter in the field in Antarctica. Photo US Navy

*Above: Que Sera Sera being loaded aboard the Cargo
Ship USNS Wyandot on her way back to the US.
Right: The lone figure of Joe Arno stands beside.the
historic Gooney Bird, he had been selected to accompany
the R4-D backs home. Note the preservative to protect the
aircraft's skin from salt water and air.
Top: Que Sera Sera having her wings removed in readiness
for her shipment back to the United States to be placed
on display at the Naval Aviation Museum at
Pensacola. Photos US Navy*

Top: The First USAF C-124 Globemaster to arrive in Christchurch in preparation for Deep Freeze II In October 1956 flies over the city.
Photo USAF.
Below: The ill-fated C-124 Globemaster the 'City of Christchurch' on display at the RNZAF Station Whenuapai in December 1956. This Globemaster crashed at Hallett Station on October 15 1958.
Photo RNZAF Museum.

*Top: The crew and passengers of a US Navy
VX-6 Neptune, bow their heads while the
Naval chaplain blesses the flight from McMurdo
to the South Pole Station on October 30 1957.
Photo US Navy.
Right: Colonel Horace A Cresswell commander
of the USAF 63rd Troop Carrier Squadron
operating out of Christchurch with Operation
Deep Freeze.
Photo USAF*

394

Top: Lt.Cdr. Gus Shinn and 'Que Sera Sera' in the field to assist a Kiwi party-

While there were no fatalities, one passenger-Cdr George Oliver suffered a broken leg. The Pilot of the Otter was Capt William Hawkes. Right: VX-6 personnel unload the injured from their Helicopter to the medical facilities at McMurdo after the squadron's Otter #142424 had crashed on take off near Cape Bird, Ross Island on December 22 1955.
Photos. US Navy.

Lt Commander Eddie Frankiewicz arrives back home at the end of Deep Freeze I on January 31 1956- he didn't make the Antarctic that year, as his and the other R4-D had to return to New Zealand and never made it back again that season. This photograph from The 'Tester' the NAS Patuxent River Md. shows Frankie being assisted down from 'Charlene' by his plane captain Jack Crisp and radioman Jack Covalt.
Photo 'The Tester'.

The US Navy's Icebreaker USS 'Glacier' with a cargo ship in McMurdo Sound 1955.
Photo US Navy

Top: VX-6's #17163 on a supply drop to an inland field between Little America and Byrd Station during Deep Freeze II.

Rear Admiral George Dufek the Commander of Task Force 43, congratulates Lt Commander 'Gus' Shinn after his historic landing on the South Pole on December 31 1956.Photos US Navy

A Squadron's Gooney Bird undergoing its maintenance checks under cover at Little America in 1956
Photo US Navy.

One of 'Que Sera Sera' crews in Antarctica.   Photo US Nav

398

*All in the days for ground crews digging out a R4-D from her winter quarters.
Photo US Navy.*

399

A Squadron's Neptune blasts off from Christchurch Airport on its way south to Antarctica in 1957. Photo US Navy

The ill fated Neptune that crashed in the jungle en route to Antarctica from the United States via South America in 1956- the plane was totally destroyed but no one aboard was killed.
Photo US Navy

Three photographs of the ill fated Neptune #122465 'Boopsie' first out of the blocks and first to arrive in Antarctic in 1955, crashed killing four of the eight crew and passengers aboard on October 18 1956. Photos US Navy except for the the bottom photo, which is from the Hudman Collection.

Above: Rear Admiral George Dufek makes a dedication speech at McMurdo Station on January 23 1957 to mark the commissioning of the South Pole Station.
Below: 'Oh what a day"- another vehicle falls into a crevasse at Little America.
Photos US Navy.

Top: The aftermath of 'Frankie's' Gooney Bird # 99853 at Little America on November 9 1957. Among the crew and passengers awaiting rescue were the Operation's Commander Admiral Dufek, the Squadron's CO Cdr Coley, four other Commanders and two pressmen, Rennie Taylor, Associate Press and Bill Becker New York Times.

Below:. Frankie's Gooney Bird 'Charlene' with her wings removed is converted into a taxi. Photos US Navy

Top: *A Squadron Otter at the 'Marble Point Oil Station'.*

Bottom: *USAF C-124 Globemasters on the ice runway at Hallett Station during Deep Freeze III. Photos US Navy.*

404

Lt Commander Eddie Frankiewicz and his
crew with their Gooney Bird #99853
before departing for New Zealand on September
4 1957 for another Antarctic deployment.
Left to right: Lt Frank Wasko, Commander
Eddie Frankiewicz, Lt Robert Epperly, Chief
[ADC] Ackman, Radio. Radarman ATI
Al Lishness and Sgt Tom Southwick the planes
Navigator. Photo Frankiewicz Collection.

Below: Refuelling USAF C-124 Globemasters at
Hallett Station in 1957
.US Navy Photo from
Bob Epperly Collection.

Top: PHI [AC] John Reimer a photographer with VX-6 checking the Trimetrogon aerial mapping camera system in the after station of a P2V-7 Neptune # 140437 in Antarctica.

Below:A squadron photographer at work over the continent. Photos US Navy.

Lt Commander Don Miller walks away from his R4-D Gooney Bird which crashed on take off some 145 miles from McMurdo Station on November 25 1962.

#17239 crashed on October 6 1965, while carrying out open field take-offs and landings three miles from Williams Field. McMurdo. Photos US Navy

"OUR LADY OF THE SNOW"
McMurdo 1957

*Above: Driver Third Class Richard Williams
the first American killed during Operation
Deep Freeze, when his D-8 tractor weighing over
30 tons crashed into a huge crevasse on
Friday January 1956.
Photo US Navy.
Right: The memorial to Richard Williams-
'The Lady of the Snow' looks over and guards
McMurdo Station like a Guardian Angel.
Photo, US Navy.
Right top: Lt Commander Robert Epperly
shortly after he stepped from his Gooney
Bird at Hallett Station after a long flight from
Invercargill, NZ on October 11 1958.
Standing in front of his 'Negatus Perspirus'
'The clothing was new and I had put it on
over what I was wearing when leaving
New Zealand.
I believe it was unpacked and donned before
disembarking from the aircraft after landing.
I remember being a little miffed because I
couldn't find a belt.'.
Photo from Robert Epperly's collection.*

Lt John Jaminet shows his novelty licence plates which he designed and had manufactured by a Christchurch advertising firm.
Photo US Navy.

Billy-Ace Baker RM1 Supervisor Section Two, with his
Assistant Supervisor William McKay discussing message.
Baker's dragon cinch may be seen on his collar.

A USAF C-124 Globemaster at McMurdo after the long flight in from Christchurch. Photo US Navy.

C-124 unloading an Otter at McMurdo. Photo US Navy.

Rear Admiral James R Reedy took up his Antarctic assignment as Commander of Task Force 43 from Rear Admiral David Tyree, at the age of fifty-two. Admiral Reedy, known to all who worked under him as 'Sunshine Jim' had already logged an impressive amount of naval experience- both in war and peace. Below: One of the squadron's Gooney Birds on the ice. Later #17188 crashed on Sentinel Ridge November 22 1965.
Photos US Navy

Above: Utz –Lt Commander 'Buz' Dryfoose's dog.
Utz came from Garmisch/Partinkerschin Germany
and was trained for border patrol by Gernat Reeidel, the
noted German trainer. He was trained for obedience and
fighting; a small dog at only 125 pounds he rode
next to the navigator's station in Lt Commander 'Buz'
Dryfoose's [right] Gooney Bird .
Photos from 'Buz' Dryfoose Collection.

*'Buz' Dryfoose and his R4-D 'Wilshie Duit' in the field- note the JATO bottles on the
sled. at right.*
Photo. US Navy

Above: Lt Commander Robert Epperly [centre] receives an award from Rear Admiral Dufek while his commanding Officer Capt Slagle looks on.
Photo Robert Epperly Collection.

Right:. The Crew of 'Buz' Dryfoose C-130 crew. Front row left to right:.
Ens Bob Brow, navigator,
Lt Tom Hale-Co-pilot.
Lt Commander Dryfoose. Pilot.
AMI Bob Weyrauch, Metalsmith.
Back row left to right:.
ADJI Jack Biser Fight Engineer.
AE Bob Richard Radioman.
ABI Don Guy Loadmaster.
AD2 DC Friend flight engineer.
The back hats worn by Don Guy DC Friend and Buz were all purchased when they made a flight to Australia.
Photo US Navy from Buz Dryfoose Collection

Above when Lt Commander Epperly required a new cylinder on his Gooney Bird's 'Negatus Perspirus' engine at the isolated Byrd station in 1958, the squadron flew a replacement in from McMurdo aboard #17246 'Little Horrible' [which was struck from Navy record in May 1961] Here with Lt Commander Epperly is Lt Douglas and the crew of #17246.
Photo US Navy from Robert Epperly Collection.

The Neptune that didn't make it to Christchurch, let alone Antarctica. 'George' #140434, crashes on its acceptance check flight at Ontario, on August 11 1958. Photo US Navy.

414

Top: The official opening of the United States Naval Support Force, Antarctica, Advanced Headquarters building at Christchurch International Airport on March 31 1959.
Photo Christchurch Press.

Above: Eight USAF C-124 Globemasters lined up on the Squadron's tarmac at Christchurch in October 1947-note a small VX-6 R4-D-8 at the top right of the photograph. Photo V.C Browne & Son.

*Two of the early VX-6 Gooney Bird pilots- Lt Commander Bob
Anderson and Lt Commander Harvey Speed, whose deeds in Antarctic
aviation are legendary.
Photo from James Waldron Collection.*

*Refuelling a helicopter from a bladder at Marble Point.
Photo US Navy.*

One of the saddest days for the squadron in Antarctica -. February 2 1966, a R4-D #50832 crashed while in a landing approach at Mile 60 on the Army-Navy trail on the Ross Ice Shelf. The Gooney Bird stalled while 200 feet above the ice surface, the right wing dropped, so the pilot Lt Harold Morris corrected and the left wing dropped. The plane hit the snow surface while almost inverted, the wings broke off and the fuselage broke in two. places before the plane caught fire and the JATO canisters on board exploded. All six men on board were killed. Photos US Navy

Top: An historic day for the Squadron and Operation Deep Freeze with the arrival of the first ever commercial aircraft, and the female Stewardesses to set foot on the surface of the continent. On October 10 1957 a giant Pan American Boeing 377 Stratocruiser landed at Williams Field, McMurdo Sound, carrying among its passengers 36 Navy Seabees.
Photo Christchurch Press.

Below: A painting commissioned by Pan American to mark the occasion.
Painting Pan American World Airways.

418

Top: Three USAF Globemasters on the flight lines at Williams Field.
Photo US Navy.

Above: The USAF 'brainwave' that gave a laugh to the Navy personnel at McMurdo- the Air Force 'powers that be' transported a number of pine trees to Antarctica and planted them in the ice to act as markers on the runway.   Photo E Egnot.

The Squadron's WinFly
Mission to Antarctica on June
4 1967.Top: The crew on the
historic mission photographed
before departing from Christchurch.
Right: the 'City of Christchurch' just
after she landed at McMurdo.
Below:. Sorting WinFly mail,
is winter Postmaster at McMurdo A.C Webb in white shirt. Others are unidentified.
Photos US Navy

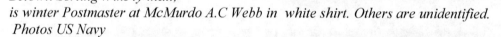

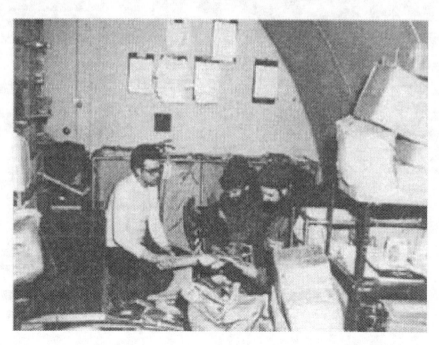

Right: The US Navy Seabees erecting the prefabricated hanger in Orchard Road, at the Christchurch International Airport in September 1959.
Photo Christchurch Star.

The first Neptune to land in Antarctica on December 20 1955 from left to right; Lt Cdr JW Entrkin, Lt E D Ellena, R M Lynch, E H Gann and P Rosenberg. Photo US Navy

Top: The twisted remains of the USAF C-124 Globemaster, the 'City of Christchurch' which crashed into the surrounding icy mountains near Cape Hallett on a plateau surrounded by crevasses and steep cliffs, on October 15 1958, killing six of those of those on board.

Top: photographs the Christchurch Press. Bottom. US Navy.

Top: # 48319 had her skis buried in four feet of snow which had accumulation over night after a heavy storm on February 2 1961.
Below: Prior to her next mission,.Emmett Cracken a crewman of #148319 shovels snow from the fuselage.
Photos. US Navy

Top: *A squadron helicopter on a re supply mission flying over the three USS Icebreakers entering McMurdo Sounds. Photo US Navy*

The one who didn't make it to Antarctica –this US Coast Guard version of the Albatross was brought to Christchurch as part of the Squadron's Deep Freeze fleet, but after being forced to turn back to New Zealand in 1955- returned to the US and never returned.
Photo US Coast Guard.

424

Lt.Cdr.Eddie Frankiewicz.
Top: Welcoming his crew aboard his
Gooney Bird #17274 'Charlene' at
Dunedin before departing for
Antarctica in December 1955.
Above: With a young friend who came to
give the crews a real Southern send off.
Right:. Eddie as an Antarctic tourist-
with camera around his neck outside
Scott Hut at Hut Point.
Photographs from Eddie Frankiewicz
Collection

Top: The end of the line for 'Charlene' brought to Antarctic in 1955 by Lt Cdr. Eddie Frankiewicz and his Co pilot Lt Cdr. James Waldron, became the MacTown Taxi travelling between Little America and McMurdo, shown being pushed out into the icy waters of the Ross Sea to her frozen grave and Last Resting Place.

Above:Two of the Squadron's R4-D's have an evening bath during the winter months- Photos US Navy.

426

Crew of the R7V: Standing: Lt Edward W. Oehlbeck; MSgt Billy M. Baker, USMC, Ltjg John W. Hilt, Robert Davis, AD2; Harry J. Matthews, AT2; George E. McFatridge, AD1; Willie L. Cole, ADC, and Lcdr Darold L. Reckling. Front: Jack B. Mitts, AE2; GySgt Charles P. Jewell, USMC; Earl D. Rudder, AD2; Jack H. Tankersley, AM1; Glenn Stevens, ADC, and James W. Garwood, AM1.

A Connie Crew.
Photo US Navy.

One of the squadron's C-130's being preheated before an Antarctic mission.
Photo US Navy.

Operation Deep Freeze Task Forces ship 'Mills' at Lyttelton Harbour. Christchurch Photo US Navy.

One of the Squadron's Neptunes 'on the deck' at McMurdo. Photo US Navy

428

Top: Postmaster Byrd Station 1960.
Bottom: Buz Dryfoose's #99853 1959/60 crew left to right 'Buz' Dryfoose, George Janulis, Art De Bolt, Larry Sharp and Billy Jones.
Photos US Navy.

Top: 'See ya! A lone Gooney Bird sits on the ice surface at an interior Antarctic field camp.
Above: A lone Gooney Bird sits on the ice 'runway' at Beardmore Glacier Station. Photos US Navy.

McMurdo Station—Helo Fire 22 December 1962.

Helo being retrograded from Ellsworth at end of Deep Freeze IV
summer season when station was turned over to Argentina.
Note: JD squadron letters on tail. From USS *Edisto* DF-IV cruise
book. The caption identified this as an Otter.

VX-6 ground maintenance crew engaging in outdoor checks on one of the squadron's helicopters. Photo US Navy

The crash of one of the Squadron's helicopters on November 28 1963. A CH19-E #144255 attached to the USS Atka. The helicopter crashed four miles from McMurdo Station.
Photo US Navy

Top:The first helicopters to land at the South Pole were three Army UHI-B Turbo- engine machines attached to the US Army Transportation Board being used in Topo East West Traverse landing on 4 February 1963.
Bottom: Pilots and crews of the Iroquois helicopters. Photos US Navy.

Annually the squadron in conjunction with Operation Deep Freeze put on an Antarctic display at Christchurch International Airport to 'say thanks' to Christchurch for being their home away from home. This photograph taken on September 27 1965, when not everyone were as lucky as these youngsters to get so close to the 'action' Flight Engineer Bob Owler and Lt Paul Gurnon have a friendly chat with Cheryl and Susan Pate, Neil Reid and Michael Pate during the Open Day. Photo Christchurch Star

434

Operation Deep Freeze Base Commander Cdr Frank Kimberling with the United
States Air Attaché Commander Lloyd Chester at Christchurch Antarctic Headquarters
on August 3 1060.
Photo Christchurch Star.

An engine change to one of
The Squadron's C-121 Lockheed
Super Constellations at Williams
Field, McMurdo.
Photo US Navy.

The frosted beard of Equipment Operator Third Class James C Peterson moments after he disembarked from the Squadron's C-121 Super Constellation after he arrived at McMurdo along with the Task Force's Commander Rear Admiral David Tyree in October 1960. The freezing minus 39 degree F, which greeted the Navyman, whitened and froze his beard. This Prize photograph was taken by the late PHC Frank 'Kaz' Kazukaitis who had flown south with the Admiral and exited the aircraft first to captured this photo. Photo US Navy.

A US Army HU-1B Iroquois helicopter rests atop Mt Discovery, near the Naval Air facilities to await an engine change. The Iroquois had shut down on the 9,900 ft peak during a series of progressively higher altitude landings for cold engine start tests. When the turbine powered engines failed, it necessitated an engine change in temperatures of minus 20 degrees F on the peak. Photo US Navy

Two VX-6 R4-D's prepare to take a New Zealand party with dog team to a remote Antarctic field site. Photo US Navy.

Top: The first ever C-130 Hercules to land at the South Pole. USAF C-130 # 488 just after it landed at McMurdo at 1755 on January 1 1960. The aircraft was from the 61st Troop Carrier Squadron from Stewart AFB, Tennessee that brought seven ski equipped aircraft to Antarctica, and between January 25 and February 5 that season carried out 38 missions to the South Pole.

Middle: Lt Clarence Dumais, the Navy's Military leader at the South Pole meets with Rear Admiral David Tyree, who made the historic flight.

Bottom: Aviation gasoline being unloaded from the Hercules at the Pole.

Photos US Navy.

Late evening on February 2 1961 fire destroyed two Quonset Huts at McMurdo causing $20,000 damage. Fire fighters were hampered in their efforts to control the fire by 25-35 knot winds. When the fire was first discovered at 10pm, it was feared that Richard Spaulding, Parachute Rigger Second Class was in his bunk in the parachute loft, however, he was one of the first to arrive on the scene when the alarm was sounded. Photo US Navy

The crew of the squadrons first winter medical evacuation mission to Antarctic in April 1961, photographed at McMurdo soon after they arrived in Antarctica.
Photo US Navy.

Another view of the #321 at McMurdo with the crew making pre flight checks before heading onto Byrd Station, preparations were made by the light of the moon and vehicle headlamps. Photo US Navy.

440

Top: While the ill Russian scientist Mr Kuperov was being loaded aboard the C-130 at Byrd Station, the crew were off loading freshies. Above: The C-130 commander Cdr Lloyd Newcomer with the Russian aboard, attempts a take off from the specially prepared ice strip at McMurdo and head back to Christchurch.. Photos US Navy.

Top: Rear Admiral David Tyree shakes hands with Capt William Munson, the commanding officer of VX-6 while the aircraft commander Cdr Lloyd Newcomer looks on, soon after the C-130 landed in Christchurch after the Antarctic mission.

Above: RADM Tyree greets the Russian scientist on his arrival back in Christchurch.
Photo US Navy.

Above: Two photographs of the C-121 Super Constellation which crashed on landing at Williams Field, McMurdo on October 31 1965. The plane, a Lockheed XV-2 Warning Star #126513 was part of the Navy's 'Project Magnet'.
Photos US Navy.

*The crash scene of one of the
Squadron's Otters #144673, which
crashed after taking off from the dirt
runway at Marble Point on October
22 1959, killing its two crew-pilot
Lt Harvey Gardener and Lt [jg]
Lawrence Farrell, the co-pilot.
They were making a steep takeoff
towards a glacier, when the left wing
hit a small knoll and the aircraft
cart-wheeled and crashed.
Photos US Navy.*

El Paisano crashed in bad weather on landing at McMurdo on 31 October 1960. The Connie was part of the Project Magnet program in the Southern hemisphere.

Photo US Navy.

A squadron's Neptune flies over the countryside outside Christchurch.
Photo US Navy.

The interior of a VX-6 Otter.
Photo US Navy.

446

Top: X-6 C-130 and a Neptune sit on the runway at Williams Field.

Above: the USS Oil Tanker USS Nespelen..
Photos US Navy

Old meets new- crews of a R4-D and a C-130 Hercules gather for a quite cup of coffee, catch up with the news and exchange stories. Photo US Navy

Three Gooney Birds sitting on the 'docks' at McMurdo awaiting shipment back to the United States. Photo US Navy

Kneeling (l to r) Gy/Sgt Spangler, Ltjg Bennett, LCdr Sherrod, LCdr Morrison, Lt Kiindig, ADR1 Roessler.
Standing (l to r) ATR2 Clark, PH1 Peterson, PH3 Black, ADR1 Wellman, AMS2 Eaton, AE3 McGuire, ATN2 Burkett, ADRC Newlen.

SUPER CONNIES'

Kneeling (l to r) ADJ1 Garrett, AT1 Sexton, AT1 Grimes, AE2 Clark, AMH2 Hayworth, AE1 Frazer.
Standing (l to r) ADR1 Barrett, Ltjg Fuller, Lt missildine, LCdr Stallings, LCdr Sloan, Lt Hart, ADR2 Moorehead, AMH1 King.

Two 'Connie' crews. Photo US Navy

Bringing relief; the first plane to land at the South Pole Station on October 28 1961, carrying the commander of Operation Deep Freeze Rear Admiral David Tyree, delivering mail and much needed supplies to the men who had wintered over at the station. Photo US Navy

Unloading a Helicopter from the USS Atka at Little America. Photo US Navy

450

The first VX-6 C-130BL to arrive at McMurdo was # 321 on 29 October 1960 and commenced cargo flights the following day with an initial flight to the South Pole. Was terminated in February 1961 with a final flight to Byrd. Photo US Navy

'Hi Guys Welcome to Antarctica, we've been year for centuries' Photo US Navy

Top: Crew of the two C-130's which flew the historic Mission from South Africa to Antarctica in October 1962 .

Below: The VX-6 Connie 'Phoenix' # 131624 unloading at McMurdo behind the Kiwi dog team.
Photos US Navy

452

On February 8 1967, a United States Navy's VXE-6 C-130 # 321 caused alarm at Christchurch Airport. coming in on a belly landing. The Hercules broken port-landing ski was dangling at a 30-degree angle arousing fears that the 46-ton aircraft would overturn when the ski dug in. On landing the C-130 slewed and then came to a halt with flames and smoke rising from its buckled undercarriage-this fire was quickly dealt with and no one was injured. The Top photo shows the aircraft about to touch down and the bottom as the aircraft was approaching the airfield.. Photos Christchurch Star

Top: 'Goodbye and God bless you', Rear Admiral Bakutis Task Force 42 Commander bids farewell to Lt Jimmy Gowan the first CO of the Plateau Station.

Right: NSFA Chief of Staff Captain D Byrsik congratulates Cdr 'Moe' Morris who had just landed a plane were no other plane had ever landed before.

Photos US Navy

On December 1 1960, a C-130 # 319 landed on the ice plateau at Eights Coast to re supply a scientific party camped there, after completing the 1290 miles from McMurdo- it was the first time an aircraft had landed there. Cargo was off loaded by slowly moving the aircraft forward as this allows the shortest time on the surface conserving critical fuel for the return trip.
Photo US Navy

Commander 'Moe' Morris- the first pilot to land an aircraft at the Polar Plateau, was appointed VXE-6 Squadron Commander. Well liked, 'Moe' was the quintessential US Naval aviator.
Photo US Navy

A New Zealand Maori welcoming party joins the Squadron in full dress uniform to say 'Hi' to the new Commanding Officer of Operation Deep Freeze Task Force 43, Rear Admiral David Tyree as he steps from his Super Constellation # 131624 at Christchurch International Airport. Photo US Navy

McMurdo Station by the light of the moon in 1962. Photo US Navy

Top: Unloading a C-130 in the field. Below: Loading a Gooney Bird #99853 on the Eight Coast in January 1961. From Left to Right Henry Brown, M/Sgt, USMC loads JATO's while AT2 Robert Martin Lt Robert Farrington and Lt George Janulis load general gear. Photos US Navy

Top: A forward view if a squadron's R4-D-8 #17188 'Takahe' showing the accumulation of drifted snow while the Gooney Bird was in winter storage in 1961. Above: the same aircraft. Note the wire fixing the aircraft to the surface. Photos US Navy.

458

Top: A USAF C-130 Hercules at the South Pole.
Below: A VXE-6 C-130 unloading in an 'open field.'
Photos US Navy

459

Top: Ground Control crews direct a C-121 Super Constellation to take off on a trip back to Christchurch.

Above: Moving aviation fuel.
Photos US Navy

One of the two Squadron Super Constellations –C-121's 'Phoenix' #131624. Landing and taking off from McMurdo Photos US Navy

October 8 1970, one of the Squadron's C-121 Lockheed Constellations # 131 1644 'Pegasus'- the flying horse' crashed near the runway at McMurdo after a mishap. Top: This photograph show the crash site in detail. Above: A photo taken from the front. Photos US Navy.

462

The crash of the' flying horse' at McMurdo.
Photos US Navy

'Pegasus' in 1999 shows NSF's Erik Barnes walking atop the crashed aircraft.
Photos NSF Josh Landis.

December 4 1971 one of the Squadron's LC-130's
piloted by Lt Commander Ed Gabriel was damaged on
from a remote East Antarctic site named D59, some
850 miles from McMurdo. At an altitude of only 50
feet two of the JATO bottles broke off -one
went up the tailpipe of #2 engine, the other
struck the # 2 propeller. The top two photos where taken
moments after the plane landed.
 Right: The mounts on the left side of the aircraft, with burn
marks from the bottles that broke free. #321 remained
at Dome 59 for fifteen years before being recovered and
returned to Antarctic service. Photos US Navy

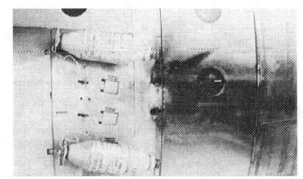

On January 28 1973, the second of the Squadron's LC-130 suffered a mishap when it crashed while approaching the South Pole Station in poor weather, and the plane caught fire. Photos US Navy.

317 –Broken, twisted and
burning at the South Pole Station
after crashing on January 28
1973. Photos US Navy

Moving the wreck off the runway days after the crash-Photo US Navy

A stark reminder of antarctic aviation- the burnt out wreck of # 155917 contasting against the snow and dull Polar skyline. Photo US Navy

During take off from Dome Charlie on January 15 1975 another of the Squadron's LC-130 Hercules # 148319 crashed. It was dispatched to the site to pick up a glaciological team of American and French scientists who had been in the area since late December. During take off from the site a JATO bottle exploded and caught fire. Photos US Navy.

Sad and lonely – but # 319 would be repaired, recovered and returned to antarctic service. Photo US Navy

#319 being towed to the repair site. Photo US Navy.

Scaffolding erected over the Hercules , so work can proceed on the repairs. Photo US Navy

Taking a break at the Dome Charlie repair camp. The sign reads as follows:

We've been doing so much for so long with so little
that now we can do anything with nothing forever!

Photo US Navy

Installing new engine on 319.

New prop for 319

Photos US Navy

Worker bees at Dome Charlie LC-130 salvage camp.

Not sure about this one. They are either removing burned sections or constructing a lift stand.

Photo US Navy

Pilot and crew before initial test flight of 319.

319 being towed to camp for more repair work.

Photos
US Navy

CDR Desko CO VXE-6 (left) and CAPT Lefty Nordhill
Task Force commander (right) toast completion of
319 salvage work at Dome Charlie.

474

Top: Another VXE-6 LC-130 mishap. In January 1975 # 159129 was on a mission near McMurdo when the crew responded to the accident of #319 at Dome Charlie. After reaching the site and taking the passengers on board from the disabled LC-130 it was on takeoff run without JATO's and during its take off the nose ski landing gear assembly collapsed..
A third Hercules was then dispatched to Dome Charlie to evacuate the crews and passengers from both disabled Hercules.
Photo US Navy
Right: The new nose panels are obvious in this view of # 129 at Christchurch in January 1976. The aircraft was nicknamed 'Crippled Pete' after its accident at Dome Charlie in January the previous year and returned to New Zealand for further repairs at the Squadron's New Zealand base engineering workshops of Air New Zealand. Photo. Christchurch Star.

Ciudad De Punta Arenas #320 unloading building materials at the South Pole Station. Photo US Navy
 # 320 unloading building materials at the South Pole Station.
Photo US Navy.

Two VXE-6-LC-130's at Amundsend-Scott South Pole Station in January 1972, the aircraft just lifting off the snow surface #917 was lost in a landing mishap a year later; the other Hercules is #320.
Photo US Navy

476

November 29 1979 was the most tragic
day in Antarctic aviation- the day
Air New Zealand Flight 901 - a
DC-10 ZK-NZP crashed into the slopes of
Mt Erebus, killing all 257 crew and
passengers aboard.
Top: The ill-fated jet on approach to
Christchurch Airport in October 1976.
Photo D Bates.
Centre: The view from the flight deck of
Air New Zealand DC-10 [ZK-NZR]
over Antarctica on the airline's inaugural
tourist flight in October 1977.
Photo Christchurch Star.
Right. The fin and casting of the tail
mounted engine of Flight 901 lies
amongst the wreckage on the lower
slopes of Mt Erebus.
Photo. Antarctic New Zealand

A tent city set up on the lower slopes of Mt Erebus by VX-6 Squadron and the New Zealand Police after the crash of Flight 901. Note a Squadron helicopter to the top left of the photo. Photo Brian Vorderstrasse Collection

Top: Loading the remains of those killed, on to an RNZAF C-130 at McMurdo to be flown back to Auckland, N.Z.
Right: Personal efforts being bagged up at the crash site.
Photos New Zealand Police

The grim task at the crash site, with VX-6 Squadron members playing a major role in the body recovery operations.
Photo New Zealand Police

A Royal New Zealand Air Force C-130 on the 'deck' at McMurdo. Photo RNZAF.

October 31 1979, a USAF Starlifter who's undercarriage gave problems on the way back to Christchurch from McMurdo, crash landed at Christchurch International Airport, causing damage to the airport's recent runway extentions. Photo Christchurch Star.

The USAF C-141 Starlifter which had followed Air New Zealand's ill fated Flight 901 to Antarctica and the last to make voice contact with the crew of the DC-10 .After landing at McMurdo on a routine flight, it then back tracked to Christchurch, following the flight path of the Air New Zealand aircraft, here photographed being serviced at Christchurch after its fruitless search for the missing DC 10.
Photo Christchurch Star

480

The Crew of the Hercules rescue aircraft photographed at Christchurch Airport before heading to the Antarctic to pick up an injured US Navy Seabee Bethael Lee McMullen from the continent. Photo US Navy from the Christchurch Star collection

Loading a C-130 at Christchurch before heading south. Photo. US Navy.

A Squadron's LC-130 on the ice runway at Williams Field, McMurdo.

A wintering over party at McMurdo in 1961. Photo US Navy

'Mr Antarctic' Lt Commander John [Jack] Paulus in front of his LC-130 at Christchurch Airport on February 18 1981, before heading down to Antarctica on his last mission. This veteran VXE-6 Squadron pilot completed nine seasons on the ice and made a record 285 polar landings at the South Pole. The skiway at the Amundsen-Scott Station was named after him- the 'Jack Paulus Skiway'. Photo Christchurch Star.

Above
The 1998 VXE-6 'Ice Pirates' award cake-Photo
US Navy

Right
'Have you a warmer job for us?'
Unloading cargo from #321 somewhere in
Antarctica.
Photo US Navy

Left to right: LTJG John F. Townsend, LT Lee E. Goewey, LT Robert V. Mayer, Robert H. Kline, ADJ1, Robert S. Sames, ABH1, Alfred L. Lozier, Jr., ADR1, and Ronald J. Smith, AE3.

Left to right: LT John J. Hanley, Jr., Jack H. Tankersley, AMH1, LT Richard W. Hendel, LT Samuel C. Lindsay, James A. Fitch, ADRCA, William G. Clegg, AMS1, and Robert L. Crain, Jr., ATCA.

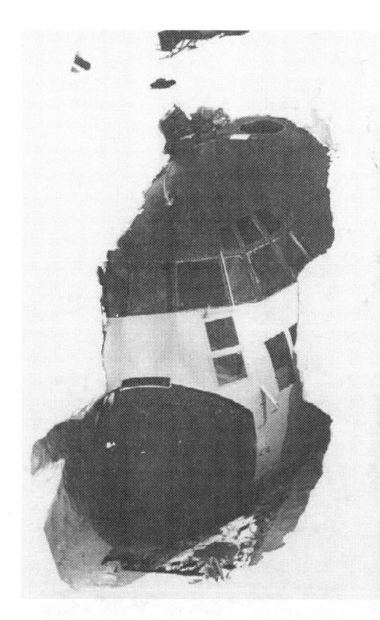

Above: after a few weeks of digging out #321 at D 59, shows the nose and flight deck. Photo US Navy

Right: So accustomed to wearing a bowler hat he was still wearing one when he stepped down from a Squadron's C-121 Constellation when he arrived back from the Antarctic. His friends have dubbed Capt Maurice Le Bas president of the Polar Bowler Hat. Photo Christchurch Star.

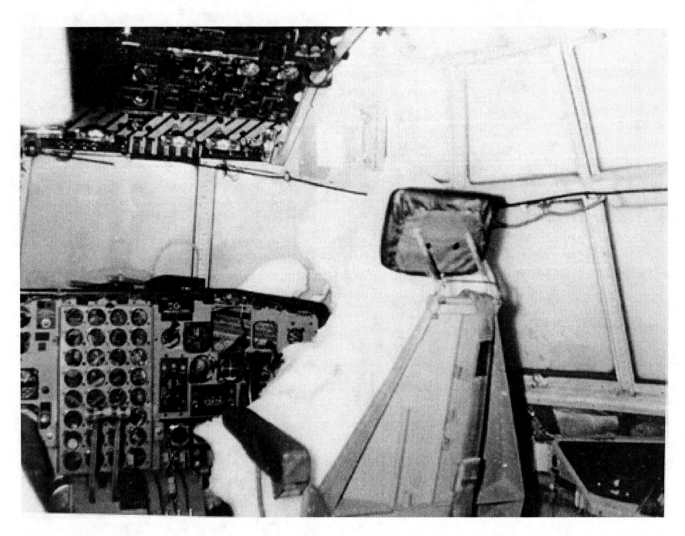

Inside the flight deck of #321 when the recovery team were able to take a look inside.
Photo US Navy

Top:
Nearing the end of the excavation of #321
Right:. The excavation team has removed dense concrete like snow around the plane's fuselage

These photographs taken in the early days of the excavation project, the lower one shows another C-130 in the background. Photos US Navy.

Above: The overall height of the C-130 Hercules is 38 feet 3 inches or 11.66 metres- to give readers an idea of how much of this aircraft is under snow.

Below: Expedition Polaries Francaises personnel pass '#321' in January 1976 during their annual traverse. Only five years after the crash, drifting snow has already substantially buried the Hercules. Photos US Navy

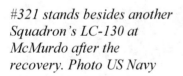

#321 stands besides another Squadron's LC-130 at McMurdo after the recovery. Photo US Navy

490

Top: #321 prepared to take off from the East Antarctic site- known as D-59- where she had been buried in the snow for sixteen years, in the background is the escort Hercules beginning its ascent.
Above: United States military greets #321 pilot Cdr Jack Rector, the Squadron's CO and the flight crew as they leave the aircraft at Williams Field.
Right:. Under low cloud on January 10 1986 the ski equipped Hercules piloted by Cdr Jack Rector lifts off the snow
at D-59 and begins its five hour flight to McMurdo.
Photos US Navy

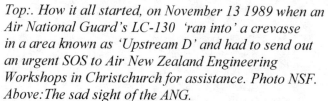

Top:. How it all started, on November 13 1989 when an
Air National Guard's LC-130 'ran into' a crevasse
in a area known as 'Upstream D' and had to send out
an urgent SOS to Air New Zealand Engineering
Workshops in Christchurch for assistance. Photo NSF.
Above:The sad sight of the ANG.
Right: The LC-130 seated over the crevasse.
Photos Dave Roche Air New Zealand

VXE-6's # 740 in trouble. Photos US Navy

The crew of Crew 4 'Humping to Please'-the aircraft modes number 00 or 'double nuts' The Twin humps on the camel represent the OO's. Humping comes from humping and passengers from New Zealand to Antarctica and back-the camel is there because Lt Commander Romine said so... From back to front, left to right. LCDR Ron Romine PTAC, Lt Milk Golding PTAC, Lt David Kahlow PNAV, Lt Wayne Slocum 2P, AMSC Mike Kennedy PLE, AD2 Kevin Hardt PLMM, AMS2 Bryant Granthem PEE and AMS2 Joe Hawkins PLM.

Below: ' Unknown' 'Double Nuts' crew on the runway, at McMurdo Station Antarctic. Photos US Navy

Top: The USS Buchanan the ship, which caused all the fuss.after New Zealand's nuclear free policy .

Right: The new Generation US Navy Icebreakers for Deep Freeze the USS Polar Sea. Photos US Navy

Right. The two left wing labour Politicians that many including this writer consider to be responsible for the US Navy's Operation Deep Freeze taking their two state of the art Diesel-electric powered icebreakers to Tasmania, hence costing Lyttelton, Christchurch, and New Zealand as a whole, millions of dollars in loss of trade with the United States due to the anti nuclear policies.

Bottom: left the late Hon David Lange and the Hon Helen Clark[right]

Right. Air New Zealand's engineers at Christchurch make repairs to # 321 in August 1988, following the aircraft's recovery from Dome 59.
Photo Christchurch Star

Above and right:. After sixteen years buried in the frozen snow of Antarctica, # 321 receives final repairs and painting in the US before being retuned to Antarctic Operations. Photos US Navy

496

The Last VXE-6 Departure from Williams Field , Antartica

February 17, 1999

Top: VXE-6 'Ice Pirates' base at Christchurch International Airport.
Above: The last flight to leave the South Pole Station on February 17 1999.
leaving McMurdo after the squadrons 44 years on the continent. Photos US Navy

497

The last flight out of the South Pole Station leaves a vapour trail behind as it heads for McMurdo. Photo US Navy

Above: The last drink in Antarctica for the last Commanding Officer of VXE-6 Cdr David Jackson in the Officers Mess at McMurdo.
Right: Commander Jackson.
Photos US Navy

Right Top:
The Memorial plaque honouring the
Americans who lost their lives in
Antarctica placed outside the Antarctic centre
near Christchurch International Airport.
The rock came from the
Bell Hill Gold Mine in the Greymouth
River Valley on the West Coast of the South
Island of New Zealand and is considered to be
an Alluvial Glacial Deposit, believed to be
Greywacke that has similar characteristics as
the Geology of Antarctica.
The rock weighs eight ton and is approximately
three cubic metres in volume.
Photo Noel Gillespie.

Right Bottom. The plaque remembering the six
Squadron members who lost their lives in the
1965 tragic R4-D crashes on the Ross Sea Ice
Shelf.

FOUNDED 1999

COURAGE • SACRIFICE • DEVOTION

500

Top: 'Gone Fishing' Squadron members try their luck at a little fishing at Williams Field. Photo US Navy
Below: The South Pole Station as it is today- a far cry from 1956. Photo National Science Foundation

Top One of the last Squadron's C-130 crews of 1999-drink a toast at McMurdo before heading back Home to end 44 years in antarctica –Photo US Navy

Above: Towed clear to begin repairs, by the Kiwi's. Photo Dave Roche.-Air New Zealand.

502

Commander David Jackson greets squadron members at Christchruch Airport after he touched his C-130 down on VXE-6's last flight from Antarctica . Photo. Christchurch Press.

Colonel Richard Saburro, the first United Air Force's commander of Operation Deep Freeze, after the departure of the Navy in 1999. Photo Noel Gillespie.

**THE NEW ZEALAND
BASE ON THE ROSS SEA
- THE AMERICA
NAVY'S NEIGHBOURS
FOR 44 YEARS.,**

This photograph was taken from the stern of the US Navy's Icebreaker USS 'Glacier' as she led the HMNZS 'Endeavour' through the thick pack ice near the entrance to McMurdo Sound in January 1957. A Bell HTL-5 helicopter can be seen on the 'Glacier's' flight deck. :Photo US Navy.

Above: Scott's Base on the Ross Sea Ice Antarctica with Mt Erebus standing like a Guardian Angel in the background.

504

Sign Posts at the New Zealander's Antarctic 'Home' at Scott Hut on the Ross Sea.

*Top: the first building
At Scott Hut, Antarctica.*

*Right:. The present day camp
Photos Seth White.*

506

*The 'Orange Roughy'
-the Bell UH-1H
[NZ 3808] is unloaded
from an RNZAF C-130
at McMurdo in October
1985.
Photo Christchurch Star*

*Top: One of the RNZAF's C-130 # NZ.700 taxies to the ramp at McMurdo during
Deep Freeze '70.
Photo Antarctic New Zealand Pictorial Collection*

Sergeant L Tarr fits the skis to a RNZAF Antarctic Flight Auster # NZ1707 at Wigram in August 1956. Looking on from left to right are Flying Officer W J Cranfield and Squadron Leader J R Claydon. Photo Christchurch Press

Top: Helicopters [NZ] Ltd pilot Grant White with one of the Aerospatiale #.AS350 Squirrels chartered by the Italian Antarctic Programme at Christchurch in October 1989, in the background is an Italian Air Force C-130 # MM619995 which was also supporting the Antarctic programme. Photo Christchurch Star.

Top: Squadron Leader Allan King, RNZAF, and the first New Zealander to pilot an LC-130 at the South Pole. At the time of this landing in November 1980, he was a No 40 Squadron pilot, serving in the Antarctic on a VXE-6 exchange programme.
Photo Christchurch Star.

Right: The RNZAF Chief of Air Staff, Air Vice Marshal David Crooks, greets Murray Ball's popular cartoon character 'Dog' at Scott Base in December 1985. The Cartoon was painted on the front door of NZ3808. Photo Christchurch Press

The New Zealand cargo loaders at McMurdo with their 50th load for the construction of the new Pole Station. Photo US Navy

KIWI CARGO 1998/99
SGT Murray Green   LCPL Conan McKinstry
SGT Tom Kelly   BDR Sam Mill   LMT Chris Fleck   LSEA John Burridge   W/O Monty Campbell   LAC Troy Patchett   LCPL Shane Pretty
AC Aaron Wright   CPL Rachel Bean   LCPL Jared Drake   AMEM Glenn Malcolm   FLTLT Tim Scott

Photo US Navy

510

Sir Edmund Hillary in 1958 after the Trans-Antarctic expedition.

Above: Scott Base on the Ross Sea Ice Shelf.
Photo US Navy.

*Right: The New Zealand Navy's
Antarctic ship HMNZS 'Endeavour'.
Photo NZ Navy*

*The set of stamps issued by
New Zealand Post in 1984
to mark the New Zealand
Antarctic Research
Programme as a tribute to
the expert team at Scott
Base.
Stamps and miniature
set designed
by R M Conly.*

512

Top: A Royal Air Force C-130 XV 306 at Christchurch Airport in December 1972, this was one of two British Hercules which flew Antarctic mission during Deep Freeze 73, assisting both the New Zealanders and Americans. Photo D Bates.

Above: A royal Australian C-130 at McMurdo in December 1978. Photo. Christchurch Star.

Top: Penguins painted on the side of this RAF C-130 XV 193 at Christchurch Airport in December 1992. Each little black and white fella, represents the number of turnaround Antarctic missions.
Right: The RAF crew on the flight deck of the first Australian C-130 A 97-005 to fly to the Antarctic. From left to right, Warrant Officer Bob Heffernman [loadmaster] Squadron Leader Stuart Dalgleish [pilot] Sergeant Bill de Boer [flight engineer] back to camera and Pilot Officer Ian Morris [co pilot].
Photos Christchurch Star.

Hallett Station, that the New Zealanders shared Operation with the US Navy.